TREATY ENFORCEMENT AND INTERNATIONAL COOPERATION IN CRIMINAL MATTERS

ORGANISATION FOR THE PROHIBITION OF CHEMICAL WEAPONS

TREATY ENFORCEMENT AND INTERNATIONAL COOPERATION IN CRIMINAL MATTERS

WITH SPECIAL REFERENCE TO THE CHEMICAL WEAPONS CONVENTION

edited by

Rodrigo Yepes-Enríquez
former Legal Adviser, OPCW

Lisa Tabassi
Legal Officer, OPCW

with a Foreword by
M. Cherif Bassiouni

T·M·C·ASSER PRESS

Published by T.M.C. Asser Press
P.O. Box 16163, 2500 BD The Hague, The Netherlands

ISBN 90-6704-150-5

Produced under the auspices of the
Organisation for the Prohibition of Chemical Weapons
Johan de Wittlaan 32
2517 JR The Hague
The Netherlands
Tel.: + 31 70 416 3300
Fax: + 31 70 306 3535
Website: www.opcw.org

FOREWORD

The humanisation of international armed conflict has its origin in many civilisations sharing the values of humanism. Though these civilisations have manifested and applied these values in different ways, the international community, as of the late 1800's, has come together to express its agreement on establishing certain international protections in the course of armed conflict, including the elimination of certain weapons which cause "unnecessary pain and suffering." The first of these weapons conventions was the 1868 St. Petersburg Declaration, which prohibited the use of explosive projectiles, followed by the 1899 Hague Declaration concerning the Prohibition of Use of Projectiles Diffusing Asphyxiating Gases. This was reiterated in the 1907 Hague Regulations and then specifically embodied, after the tragic experiences of World War I, in the 1925 Geneva Protocol for the Prohibition of the Use in War of Asphyxiating, Poisonous or other Gases and of Bacteriological Methods of Warfare.

In 1922, the Treaty in Relation to the Use of Submarines and Noxious Gases in Warfare stated in Article V:

> "The use in war of asphyxiating, poisonous or other gases, and all analogous liquids, materials or devices, having been justly condemned by the general opinion of the civilized world and a prohibition of such use having been declared in treaties to which a majority of the civilized Powers are parties,
> The Signatory Powers, to the end that this prohibition shall be universally accepted as a part of international law binding alike the conscience and practice of nations, declare their assent to such prohibition, agree to be bound thereby as between themselves and invite all other civilized nations to adhere thereto."

Few treaty provisions so eloquently state the prohibition of chemical weapons and its universality.

The prohibition of chemical weapons (CW) is part of customary international law, in addition to its conventional international law prohibition under the 1925 Geneva Protocol and the 1993 Chemical Weapons Convention.

In 1972, another convention was developed to prohibit biological weapons but, even though the reasons for prohibiting both chemical and biological are the same, the 1972 Biological Weapons Convention contained weaker normative provisions than those contained in the 1925 Geneva Protocol.

Chemical, as well as biological weapons, have no other purpose than to cause indiscriminate harm to human beings leading to severe injury, disfigurement and death. In addition, they cause serious damage to the environment. The harmful effects of these weapons speak for themselves and they are all too well-known, yet, surprisingly, the international community, driven by difficult-to-understand political considerations, has allowed these types of weapons to be developed, stockpiled and, on occasion, even used.

R. Yepes-Enríquez and L. Tabassi. (eds.), Treaty Enforcement and International Cooperation in Criminal Matters

The terrible consequences of the use of chemical weapons in World War I have unfortunately been forgotten all too soon, as Mussolini ordered his troops to use chemical weapons in Italy's invasion of Abyssinia, Eritrea and Somalia in 1935-36. Regrettably, nothing was done about that at the time, just as nothing was done about the use of chemical weapons by Iraq against Iran in 1983, and against the Kurds in Halabjah in March 1988.

After World War II, governments developed extensive chemical and biological weapons programs, even though the 1925 Convention prohibited such weapons. Ostensibly, the argument advanced was that if such weapon-systems are available to others, it justifies their development as a precautionary self-defence. The rationale of mutual deterrence prevailed during the "Cold War," and even survived it, only to be confronted with the reality that the weaponisation or the use of chemical and biological substances against civilian populations by non-State-actors places the problem in a different context. In that new context, mutual deterrence and mutual political interests in which governments believe in, no longer apply.

As the threat of using chemical and biological agents increased at the potential hands of organised criminal groups seeking to either terrorise or extract concessions or benefits from a given society, the international community was forced to reconsider its position on the total ban of such weapons. Surprisingly however, a distinction was still being made between chemical and biological weapons. Understandably, the administrative control scheme for these two types of weapons would be different, nevertheless, the enforcement scheme would be the same for both. Thus, the separation between chemical and biological weapons is essentially the product of politics as evidenced by the fact that even though the Chemical Weapons Convention was adopted in 1993, the 1972 Biological Weapons Convention was not updated, even though for the last two decades the United Nations Conference on Disarmament has been trying to develop a Protocol to that Convention similar in approach to the Chemical Weapons Convention. To date, and essentially because of the Bush Administration's opposition (over concerns for the private sector), the international community's efforts to prohibit biological weapons in the same way as it has prohibited chemical weapons, has been dangerously forestalled – terrorism threats notwithstanding.

The Chemical Weapons Convention is a comprehensive ban on chemical weapons. The entire category of this weapon of mass destruction is prohibited. The Convention has an extensive control inspection and enforcement mechanism. As of this writing, the Convention has 145 State Parties with the expectation that another 29 Signatory States will ratify. Considering the number of States Parties and the historical antecedents mentioned above, it can be concluded that the prohibition of chemical weapons is prohibited by customary, as well as conventional, international law. Yet, this has not prevented the use of chemical weapons in the context of an international armed conflict when Iraq used such weapons against Iran, in an internal armed conflict when Iraq used such a weapons in Halabja against its Kurdish civilian population and in an act of domestic terrorism when the Aum Shinrikyo used chemical weapons in a Tokyo subway. Subsequent to the events of 11 September 2001 in the United States, anthrax was used in different parts of the northeastern United States but it was never ascertained by who, or for what purpose, anthrax was used.

While most governments seem convinced that chemical weapons should not be used in any type of conflict, there are still a number who either maintain a chemical weapons programme or a stockpile of these weapons. Some governments have expressed their willingness to eliminate such a stockpile but argue that they cannot do so because of financial hardship and the lack of capabilities to do so. Thus, even in light of the express prohibitions contained in the Chemical Weapons Convention, and what can be said to be part of customary international law, the elimination of chemical weapons stockpiles is still far from being achieved, as is the total ban on such weapons.

Since the Gulf War in 1991, the United Nations Security Council has focused its attention on Iraq's development and stockpiling of chemical weapons, as well as biological weapons, and also possibly nuclear capabilities. The absence of an inspection regime in that country makes verification impossible, though interestingly, the Security Council's concerns with Iraq have not been matched with similar concerns about chemical weapons, as well as biological weapons, in other countries.

The 9/11 events, as well as the subsequent use of anthrax which, as stated above, remains unknown to date as to its perpetrators and intended purposes, have heightened the concerns of peoples all over the world with the potential use of weapons of mass destruction by non-State-actors, whether they be terrorist groups, organised crime groups or individuals. Nevertheless, these real dangers have not been reflected in governmental actions to enforce existing norms, such as those contained in the Chemical Weapons Convention, strengthen institutions, such as the OPCW and develop new norms such as the Protocol to the 1972 Biological Weapons Convention. Furthermore, very little has been done to advance a comprehensive ban on the use of nuclear weapons, let alone on the elimination of such weapons *in toto*. These failures can only be attributed to the political perceptions of a number of governments, some of which are among the world's major powers and others representing smaller countries. Notwithstanding the diversity that exists between such countries, they share a narrow perception of what their national security requires, irrespective of the broader perspective of what international security requires. It is certain that they do not see their national security as being achieved in the context of an international security regime which comprehensively and totally bans the use of weapons of mass destruction with an effective and verifiable inspection and sanctions regime. Admittedly, this is not an easy task, but it is one worth trying to undertake.

The elimination of weapons of mass destruction as evidenced by the comprehensive nature of the Chemical Weapons Convention requires essentially three components. The first is the existence of an effective set of prevention and control mechanisms to ensure against the use of chemical agents in weapons or as a means to inflict harm on other people. The second is the establishment of an international implementation structure such as the OPCW. The third is an effective enforcement scheme which relies on the modalities of international cooperation in criminal matters. This book is dedicated to this third component which is the enforcement basis of the Chemical Weapons Convention.

International criminal law enforcement in the practice of States relies on six modalities of inter-State cooperation in criminal matters. These modalities are: extradition, legal assistance, transfer of sentenced persons, transfer of penal proceedings, seizure and forfeiture of illicit proceeds of crime, and recognition of foreign penal judgments. These modalities, though independent of one another, are nonetheless interrelated and are found in specialised multilateral and bilateral treaties as well as in multilateral treaties whose subject-matter concerns one of the 28 categories of international crimes. A seventh modality which is central to the effectiveness of prevention is intelligence and police cooperation and information-sharing. The latter, which is commonly resorted to by law enforcement and intelligence agencies all over the world, though in a haphazard manner, is done on an informal bilateral basis. This practice, notwithstanding its potential for error and abuse, as well as its potential for violations of privacy rights, is nonetheless unregulated and mostly beyond judicial scrutiny. There are no multilateral or bilateral treaties regulating these unofficial practices, other than the institutionalised inter-police relations through Interpol and Europol.

International cooperation in criminal matters relies on these same six modalities to enforce international, transnational and domestic crimes. Thus, irrespective of the nature of the crime, States, as well as international organisations, rely on these same modalities and do so in the same ways. Thus, international judicial bodies such as the International Criminal Tribunal for the Former Yugoslavia (ICTY), the International Criminal Tribunal for Rwanda (ICTR) and the International Criminal Court (ICC) rely on these same six modalities in their statutes and rules; and, with respect to the ICTY and ICTR, in their practices.

International organisations, as well as international judicial bodies and national legal systems, rely on the national legal systems of the requested States to carry out the execution of these six modalities in accordance with the latter's domestic laws and procedures. While international judicial institutions may have certain preferred channels, either by virtue of the treaty establishing them, such as the ICC, or as a result of the authority which established them, such as the Security Council with respect to the ICTY and ICTR, they nonetheless depend on the national legal systems of the requested States through whose procedural channels they have to go through. Thus, the ability of such bodies to enforce the penal provisions contained in their statutes depends on the effectiveness and voluntary cooperation of States. Consequently, the less effective States bring down to their level the most effective States participating in the enforcement scheme.

Many States, however, do not have adequate legislation to regulate the practice of these modalities of international cooperation in criminal matters, and also lack sufficient expert personnel. All of this renders the worldwide practice of inter-State cooperation in criminal matters with respect to the Chemical Weapons Convention somewhat aleatory. This is essentially the weakness of what I call the "indirect enforcement system" of international criminal law.

The States Parties can rely on the Chemical Weapons Convention, on conventional and customary international law, as well as on bilateral treaties to engage with other States in the processes of international cooperation in criminal matters, including police and intelligence cooperation and information-sharing to prevent, control and suppress chemical weapons violations. How effective these efforts are likely to be will depend on the effectiveness of national legal systems and their commitment to enforce the Chemical Weapons Convention. Such efforts, however, must go beyond international cooperation in criminal matters, and that is not yet evident.

It is the great merit of this publication to examine all the aspects of international cooperation in criminal matters and jurisdiction with respect to the enforcement of the Chemical Weapons Convention. The contributions of leading experts contained in the chapters that follow, as well as in the discussions of the important symposium that the

OPCW held on this subject in 2001, are the first effort made in the direction of enhancing enforcement of the Convention.

Ambassador Yepes-Enríquez and Ms. Lisa Tabassi are to be congratulated on this important initiative and for this book, which is a credit to the OPCW.

M. Cherif Bassiouni

Professor of Law, DePaul University College of Law; President, International Human Rights Law Institute, DePaul University College of Law; President, International Association of Penal Law.

SUMMARY TABLE OF CONTENTS

PART II. JURISDICTIONAL ISSUES

SECTION II.1. Case Studies: Concurrent Jurisdiction

SECTION II.2. Case Studies: Cooperation with or between International Organisations

SECTION II.3. Intrusive International Control Regimes and Breaches of Confidentiality: Aspects of the Exercise of National Jurisdiction

PART III. MODALITIES

SECTION III.1. Case Studies: Extradition and Special Challenges to Administrations in Transition

SECTION III.4. Customs Enforcement and Initiatives to Strengthen Regimes

SECTION III.5. Addressing Transboundary Criminal Activity through National Criminal Law Systems

PART IV. CHALLENGES

Section IV.1. International Cooperation in Protection against Terrorism

Section IV.2. Prosecution of Individual Violators of the Chemical Weapons Convention: Possible Legal Framework for Compliance with Article VII(2)

SECTION IV.3. Overcoming Obstacles in Achieving Wide Adherence to Multilateral Legal Assistance Instruments

SECTION IV.4. Protection of National Security or Confidential Business Information in Judicial Proceedings

ANNEXES

INDICES

PREFACE

In February 2001, the Organisation for the Prohibition of Chemical Weapons organised and hosted a major international symposium at its headquarters in The Hague, the Netherlands. The symposium, attended by more than 200 leading jurists and representatives of many major international organisations, addressed an issue of concern to the membership of the OPCW in the implementation of the Chemical Weapons Convention — the unequivocal, but unelaborated, requirement for all Member States to cooperate and provide legal assistance in appropriate forms, as set out in paragraph 2 of Article VII of the Convention.

Of course, in attracting such an audience at that time, it became clear that the issue had, and has, much wider ramifications.

- The Issue: cooperation and legal assistance for international agreement enforcement.
- The Challenge: effective implementation.

The events of 11 September 2001 brought both the issue and the challenge into sharp focus in relation to the threats posed by international terrorist activities and networks. This book is no longer, therefore, a collection published to reproduce the proceedings of February 2001. In light of subsequent developments, many of the authors in this volume have revised their papers to reflect current realities, and new authors have been added.

International cooperation and assistance have many faces. Particularly in their legal and multi-jurisdictional aspects, they are essential, and often complex, elements in the implementation equation.

The OPCW and its Member States are responsible for the implementation of the Chemical Weapons Convention, which emphasises verification and compliance measures. Signed in 1993, and entering into force in 1997, it is the first convention of its type to provide for the elimination of an entire category of weapons of mass destruction, while at the same time being non-discriminatory in its application, and establishing a verifiable regime for its implementation.

The OPCW Secretariat received a mandate from the Conference of the States Parties to the Convention — the principal organ of the OPCW — to search out pathways to cooperation, and to develop a more detailed approach to avenues of legal assistance, through the convening of the symposium. Given its importance, T.M.C. Asser Institute, the Institute for International Law of Peace and Armed Conflict of the University of Bochum, the University of Leiden Faculty of Law, and the Harvard Sussex Program on CBW Armament and Arms Limitation joined as co-organisers. A number of sponsors came forward from relevant branches of governments, international organisations, and from universities and specialist research institutes. Our gratitude is expressed in the Acknowledgements.

It bears repeating: cooperation and assistance have many faces, and operate at many levels — between governments, industry, academics and other practitioners, as well as international organisations, bodies and networks.

One thing appears certain — the scope and the resources for cooperating in the prevention, prosecution and enforcement of legal norms and obligations are unlikely to be

R. Yepes-Enríquez and L. Tabassi. (eds.), Treaty Enforcement and International Cooperation in Criminal Matters

available on a scale which could effectively be addressed on a single subject matter basis in all, or even most, countries and regions. Moreover, when it comes to jurisdictional issues, or the modalities of international cooperation, and in particular when confronting the challenges to the development of such cooperation, we must recognise that there is unlikely to be precise replication from State to State or region to region.

Of course, there may well be significant overlaps between the locations of cooperating agencies, but these may be imperfect and sometimes confusing in their degree of matching. To take the National Authorities under the Chemical Weapons Convention as just one example, it may be seen that, in well over half of the cases, these are located in Ministries of Foreign Affairs or the equivalent. However, in a significant number of countries the relevant authorities are found in the areas of trade, industry, economy, defence, export control, science and technology, justice, health, or the environment, or as a separate institute, interministerial or high-level advisory body.

Authorities at the national and sub-national level traditionally deal with investigatorial, judicial and jurisdictional issues relating to many serious crimes with international features. They will often, but not always, have similar roles, responsibilities, and methods of organisation and operation, whether the subject matter consists of major weapons offences or other transboundary activities, such as money-laundering, narcotics, endangered species, cultural property, transport of hazardous materials and other environmental matters, or international terrorism.

A coordinated and well-understood framework for cooperation will be essential, to ensure that resources are used efficiently, and that the various subject matters — which are dealt with by a vast array of international agreements and arrangements — are addressed and implemented effectively.

This publication goes to the heart of both the preventive and prosecutorial aspects of legal enforcement, and raises issues entailing cooperation between many different agencies of national governments. It includes contributions from leading international experts and practitioners in their fields. Whether your particular interests lie in the area of jurisdictional issues, or whether you are concerned with the modalities of international cooperation or the challenges to the development of such cooperation, I am confident that the chapters of this book hold a wealth of information and insight. The special legal issues raised by the stringent confidentiality regime of the Chemical Weapons Convention, and the implications at the national level and for other international regimes, are also featured.

I would like to express my gratitude to Professor Cherif Bassiouni for his support in providing the foreword to this volume, and to all of the contributors published here. I would also like to acknowledge, in particular, the very small group of staff in the Secretariat of the OPCW without whose dedication and untiring efforts the results presented to you through this important publication would not have been possible.

It is my hope that this contribution to the cause of international cooperation and legal assistance will be a spur to encourage further work in this field in the years ahead — and to uphold and strengthen commitments to effective implementation of international agreements.

John Gee

Acting Director-General, OPCW
July 2002

ACKNOWLEDGEMENTS

The OPCW gratefully acknowledges the generous support it received from its co-organisers for the OPCW International Symposium on "Cooperation and Legal Assistance for the Effective Implemention of International Agreements," held 7-9 February 2001 in The Hague:

T.M.C. Asser Instituut

Institute for International Law of Peace and Armed Conflict, University of Bochum

University of Leiden, Faculty of Law

and to the organisational and institutional sponsors of the OPCW Symposium:

Commonwealth Secretariat
Council of Europe
European Commission
Europol
Harvard Sussex Program on CBW Armament and Arms Limitation
International Human Rights Law Institute, DePaul University College of Law
Interpol
Institute for International Law of Peace and Armed Conflict, University of Bochum
Kluwer Law International
Municipality of The Hague
Science Applications International Corporation (SAIC)
T.M.C. Asser Instituut
University of Leiden, Faculty of Law
Utrecht University, Faculty of Law
Wladimiroff Waling Schreuders
World Customs Organisation

and to the sponsors of the subsequent publication of this volume:

Harvard Sussex Program on CBW Armament and Arms Limitation
T.M.C. Asser Press

The OPCW is also very grateful to all the chairpersons, panelists and rapporteurs who participated in the OPCW Symposium, and to the authors, listed *verso*, who contributed to this book. In addition, the Editors would like to express their appreciation and gratitude for the advice and assistance of **Horst Fischer**, **Samir Mechken** and **Gabriela Murino** in the organisation of the OPCW Symposium, and of **Pamela Mills**, **Caroline Harnois**, **Robert Delonis**, **Pablo Kapusta**, **Tarso Calixto** and **Marjolijn Bastiaans** in the preparation of the manuscript of this book.

Sincere thanks and appreciation are extended to the authors who contributed to this book:

Hans-Jürgen Bartsch
M. Cherif Bassiouni
David Bazerashvili
Eduardo A. Bertoni
Willy Bruggeman
Richard H. Burgess
William W. Burke-White
Robert Delonis
Ihor Drizhchany
John Dugard
Treasa Dunworth
Maria Teresa Dutli
Brigitta Exterkate
Daniel Feakes
Harald Felgenhauer
Horst Fischer
Stephen E. Flynn
John Gee
John A. Gilbert
Fabricio Guariglia
Caroline Harnois
Cecil Hunt
Nina Jørgensen
Pablo Kapusta
Stephen R. Karangizi
Barry Kellman
Victor Philip LaCorbiniere
Hafida Lahiouel
Stephen Lustig
Roberto Maroto
Mónica Martínez
Maria-Luisa Martinod-Jacome
Clemence Masango
Avril McDonald
Samir Mechken
Matthew Meselson
Chiseche Mibenge
Pamela G. Mills
Daryl A. Mundis
Eric P.J. Myjer
Mtshana M. Ncube
Jaroslava Novotná
The OPCW Technical Secretariat
Mohamed Othman
Faiza Patel King
Nancy L. Paterson
John C. Ploeg
Kimberly Prost
Robert Reid
Julian Perry Robinson
Laura Rockwood
Jörn Sack
Ercan Saka
Camilo Sanhueza Bezanilla
Alex P. Schmid
Yasuo Seto
Daphna Shraga
Göran Sluiter
Harriet Solloway
Bert Swart
Paul C. Szasz
Lisa Tabassi
Fiona Tregonning
Keith Wilson
Michail Wladimiroff
Rodrigo Yepes-Enríquez

LIST OF ABBREVIATIONS

AFRC	Sierra Leone Armed Forces Revolutionary Council
AJIL	American Journal of International Law
AND	Aggregate national data
APC	Sierra Leone All People's Congress
ASF	Interpol automated search facility
ASYCUDA	Automated System for Customs Data and Management
AVEGA	Association for Genocide Widows in Rwanda
BSC	Bosnian, Serbian and Croatian
BWC	1972 Biological Weapons Convention
CA	Confidentiality Annex to the 1993 Chemical Weapons Convention
CAB	Interpol Crime Analysis Branch
CARICOM	Caribbean Community
CBI	Confidential business information
CBW	Chemical and biological weapons
CC	OPCW Confidentiality Commission
CCP EC	Common commercial policy
CEN	WCO Customs Enforcement Network
CET	Common External Tariff
CFSP	EU common foreign and security policy
CIS	Commonwealth of Independent States
COMESA	Common Market for Eastern and Southern Africa
CP	OPCW Policy on Confidentiality
CSP	OPCW Conference of the States Parties
CTBT	Comprehensive Nuclear Test-Ban Treaty
CTBTO	Comprehensive Nuclear Test-Ban Treaty Organization
CTN	Common Tariff Nomenclature
CW	Chemical weapons
CWC	1993 Chemical Weapons Convention
CWCIA	United States Chemical Weapons Convention Implementation Act of 1998
CWCR	United States Chemical Weapons Convention Regulations
CWPF	Chemical weapons production facility
DG	Director-General
DOC	Discrete organic chemical
DoD	United States Department of Defense
DPRK	Democratic People's Republic of Korea
EC	European Community
EC	OPCW Executive Council
ECD	Belastingdienst FIOD-ECD (Netherlands Economics Investigations Agency)
EI	Electron Impact Ionisation
EIF	Entry into force
ELB	Interpol European Liaison Bureau
ELOs	Europol Liaison Officers

EU	European Union
Europol	European Police Office
FADO	European Image Archiving System of the European Union
FBI	United States Federal Bureau of Investigation
FOIA	United States Freedom of Information Act
FSL	Nagano Forensic Science Laboratory
FTA	Free Trade Area
GC/MS	Gas chromatography/mass spectrometry
GRULAC	Latin America and the Caribbean regional group
HS	Harmonised System
IAEA	International Atomic Energy Agency
IBUKA	Association of Genocide Survivors in Rwanda
IC	Isobutane chemical ionisation
ICC	International Criminal Court
ICCPR	International Covenant on Civil and Political Rights
ICID	OAS Inter-American Council for Integral Development
ICPC	International Criminal Police Congress
ICPO	International Criminal Police Organisation (Interpol)
ICRC	International Committee of the Red Cross
ICTR	International Criminal Tribunal for Rwanda
ICTY	International Criminal Tribunal for the former Yugoslavia
IFOR	NATO Implementation Force
IGO	International, intergovernmental organisation
IHL	International Humanitarian Law
ILANUD	United Nations Latin American Institute for the Prevention of Crime and the Treatment of Offenders
ILEA	International Law Enforcement Academy
ILM	International Legal Materials
ILOAT	Administrative Tribunal of the International Labour Organisation
IMU	Islamic Movement of Uzbekistan
INCB	International Narcotics Control Board
INTERPOL	International Criminal Police Organisation
IOM	International Organization for Migration
IRA	Irish Republican Army
IWETS	International Weapons and Explosives Tracking System
JHA	EU justice and home affairs (third pillar)
KDOM	Kosovo Diplomatic Observer Mission
KLA	Kosovo Liberation Army
KVM	Kosovo Verification Mission
LAC	New Zealand Legislation Advisory Committee
LJ	Law journal
LJIL	Leiden Journal of International Law
LNTS	League of Nations Treaty Series
MOU	Memorandum of Understanding
MPD	Tokyo Metropolitan Police Department

NATO	North Atlantic Treaty Organization
NBC	Nuclear, biological, chemical
NCBs	Interpol National Central Bureaux
NGO	Non-governmental organisation
NPT	Treaty on the Non-Proliferation of Nuclear Weapons
NRIPS	National Research Institute of Police Science, Tokyo
NTB	Non-tariff barriers
OAS	Organization of American States
OAU	Organisation of African Unity, succeeded by the African Union (AU) on 8 July 2002.
OECD	Organisation for Economic Cooperation and Development
OECS	Organisation of Eastern Caribbean States
OHCHR	Office of the United Nations High Commissioner for Human Rights
OJ	Official Journal of the European Communities
OLAF	European Union Anti-Fraud Office
OPBW	Organisation for the Prohibition of Bacteriological (Biological) and Toxin Weapons
OPCW	Organisation for the Prohibition of Chemical Weapons
OSCE	Organization for Security and Co-operation in Europe
OTP	ICTY/ICTR Office of the Prosecutor
PCIJ	Permanent Court of Arbitration
PIC	Prior Informed Consent Procedure for Certain Hazardous Chemicals and Pesticides in International Trade
POLRI	Indonesian Police Force
POPs	Persistent Organic Pollutants
PrepCom	Preparatory Commission
PTA	Preferential Trade Area for Eastern and Southern Africa
RILO	(WCO) Global Regional Intelligence Liaison Offices
RUF	Sierra Leone Revolutionary United Front
SADC	Southern African Development Community
SAIC	Science Applications International Corporation
SFOR	NATO Stabilisation Force
SIS	Schengen Information System
TEC	Treaty on the European Community
TEU	Treaty on the European Union
TNI	Indonesian Armed Forces
TOC	Transnational Organised Crime Group
UKTS	United Kingdom Treaty Series
UN	United Nations
UN TOC	United Nations Convention Against Transnational Organised Crime
UNAMET	United Nations Mission in East Timor
UNAMIR	United Nations Mission in Rwanda
UNAT	United Nations Administrative Tribunal
UNCATOC	United Nations Convention Against Transnational Organised Crime
UNDCP	United Nations Drug Control Program

UNGA	United Nations General Assembly
UNHCR	Office of the United Nations High Commissioner for Refugees
UNJSPF	United Nations Joint Staff Pension Fund
UNMIK	United Nations Interim Administration in Kosovo
UNPROFOR	United Nations Protection Force
UNSC	United Nations Security Council
UNTAET	United Nations Transitional Administration in East Timor
VA	Verification Annex to the Chemical Weapons Convention
VRS	Bosnian Serb Army
VRU	Victims Participation and Reparation Unit
VWU	Victims and Witnesses Unit
WCO	World Customs Organisation
WHO	World Health Organization
WMD	Weapons of mass destruction
WTO	World Trade Organisation

INTRODUCTION:

ENFORCEMENT OF THE PROHIBITION OF CHEMICAL WEAPONS IN ITS WIDER PERSPECTIVE

Rodrigo Yepes-Enríquez*

1. INTRODUCTION

The Chemical Weapons Convention[1] is intended to be a verifiable comprehensive ban on chemical weapons as an entire category of weapons of mass destruction. Today there are 145 parties to the Convention. A further 29 States have signed it and they are, in accordance with Article 18 of the 1969 Vienna Convention on the Law of Treaties, under the interim obligation to refrain from any acts which would defeat the object and purpose of the treaty. Thus the conventional comprehensive ban on chemical weapons under any circumstances has nearly become a universal norm.

The key question remains, however: Is the ban enforceable? Could or would persons violating the ban anywhere, anytime be apprehended and punished? The ability to enforce a ban gives it its true meaning. Absent effective enforcement, universality remains a hollow accomplishment.

There are a number of factors in the equation for effective enforcement: national implementing legislation, the modalities of international cooperation and assistance, overcoming problems that can arise politically or constitutionally in trying to put the modalities into practice, as well as actual situations that are faced in the field in trying to prosecute offenders in an international context.

When specifically considering the enforcement of the ban on chemical weapons, one underlying thread should be kept clearly in mind: which norm is being enforced? The conventional norm has gone through several evolutions, each one formulating a stricter norm and each one gaining a greater number of parties. The number of parties to the Chemical Weapons Convention poses a good question for legal scholars to consider now: in the year 2002, what is the content of the customary norm?

* Former Legal Adviser to the Organisation for the Prohibition of Chemical Weapons (OPCW). The views expressed are the author's own and are not attributable to the OPCW. The author would like to express his appreciation to Lisa Tabassi for the assistance provided in researching the subject of this chapter.

[1] 1993 Convention on the Prohibition of the Development, Production, Stockpiling and Use of Chemical Weapons and on Their Destruction, entered into force on 29 April 1997. Text, as corrected and changed, available at http://www.opcw.org.

R. Yepes-Enríquez and L. Tabassi. (eds.), Treaty Enforcement and International Cooperation in Criminal Matters

2. The 1993 Chemical Weapons Convention

The Chemical Weapons Convention represents a total ban. The definition is very complete: all toxic chemicals are considered to be a chemical weapon unless they are intended for a purpose not prohibited.[2] Even the empty munitions, devices and equipment, if specifically designed for use in dispersal of toxic chemicals for harm to humans or animals, are banned.[3] Besides its disarmament purpose, the Convention establishes a regime for non-proliferation as well: through the device of trade restrictions, States Parties are under the obligation to control, in varying degrees, the toxic chemicals and their precursors. Transfers of such chemicals to States not Party to the Convention is banned (for the chemicals of most serious concern) or is only possible under strict conditions. In its Article I,[4] The Chemical Weapons Convention, provides:

1. Each State Party to this Convention undertakes never under any circumstances:
   (a) To develop, produce, otherwise acquire, stockpile or retain chemical weapons, or transfer, directly or indirectly, chemical weapons to anyone;
   (b) To use chemical weapons;
   (c) To engage in any military preparations to use chemical weapons;
   (d) To assist, encourage or induce, in any way, anyone to engage in any activity prohibited to a State Party under this Convention.

The words "never under any circumstances" mean that the Convention applies during peace and during armed conflict, be that international or internal. No reservations are permitted to the Articles of the Convention.[5]

---

[2] Article II(1) of the Convention.

[3] Article II(1)(b) and (c) of the Convention

[4] The Chemical Weapons Convention, Article I (General Obligations) provides:

1. Each State Party to this Convention undertakes never under any circumstances:
   (a) To develop, produce, otherwise acquire, stockpile or retain chemical weapons, or transfer, directly or indirectly, chemical weapons to anyone;
   (b) To use chemical weapons;
   (c) To engage in any military preparations to use chemical weapons;
   (d) To assist, encourage or induce, in any way, anyone to engage in any activity prohibited to a State Party under this Convention.
2. Each State Party undertakes to destroy chemical weapons it owns or possesses, or that are located in any place under its jurisdiction or control, in accordance with the provisions of this Convention.
3. Each State Party undertakes to destroy all chemical weapons it abandoned on the territory of another State Party, in accordance with the provisions of this Convention.
4. Each State Party undertakes to destroy any chemical weapons production facilities it owns or possesses, or that are located in any place under its jurisdiction or control, in accordance with the provisions of this Convention.
5. Each State Party undertakes not to use riot control agents as a method of warfare.

[5] Article XXII of the Convention.

3. The Preceding Instruments

For the few States not Party to the Convention (19 States never signed and an additional 29 States have signed but not ratified), the preceding instruments are binding upon them since those instruments are now recognised as forming part of customary international law. The preceding instruments are the 1899 Hague Declaration[6] and Hague Regulations,[7] the 1907 Hague Regulations[8] and the 1925 Geneva Protocol.[9] The Geneva Protocol is the widest in scope. Expanding upon the preceding instruments, the parties to the Geneva Protocol agreed to accept the prohibition on the "use in war of asphyxiating, poisonous or other gases, and of all analogous liquids, materials or devices" but also to extend the prohibition "to the use of bacteriological methods of warfare." As of 2002, there are 132 parties to the Geneva Protocol. The instrument has a number of weaknesses, however. First, it only applies during war. Second, reservations are permitted, and the effectiveness of the prohibition has been reduced by the fact that over 40 parties to it made their adherence subject to a reservation. In essence, the reservation specified that the Protocol would only be binding in respect of the other parties and would cease to be binding in regard to any State whose forces or whose allies failed to respect the prohibition.[10] Thus the Geneva Protocol in effect constituted only a prohibition against *first use* in war. The Parties' need to continue to be prepared to retaliate justifies the continued development, production and stockpiling of chemical weapons.

4. The Customary Norm

In the North Sea Continental Shelf cases (1969 ICJ Reports 3) the International Court of Justice first recognised the co-existence of identical rules in treaty law and customary law. As it later stated in the Case Concerning Military and Paramilitary Activities in and against Nicaragua, "To a large extent [the North Sea Continental Shelf cases] turned on the question whether a rule enshrined in a treaty also existed as a customary rule, either because the treaty had merely codified the custom, or caused it to 'crystallise', or because it had influenced its subsequent adoption." (1986 ICJ Reports 14, at para 177). Examining treaty and customary law again in the Nicaragua case, the Court rejected the argument that customary principles are subsumed or supervened by treaty law and went on to recognise that parallel treaty and customary obligations could be identical or different.

Since States are separately bound by the rule under customary international law, the question then arises: What is the content of the customary norm today? There is no doubt that the prohibition of *use* of chemical weapons exists as a principle of customary law. The

[6] Declaration II Concerning Asphyxiating Gases, annexed to the 1899 Hague Convention, 26 Martens (2nd) 998; UKTS 32 (1907); IAJIL Supp. 157.

[7] Convention II with Respect to the Laws and Customs of War on Land and annex, Regulations Respecting the Laws and Customs of War on Land, 26 Martens (2nd) at 949; UKTS 11 (1901); I AJIL Supp. at 134.

[8] Regulations Concerning the Laws and Customs of Land Warfare, annexed to the 1907 Hague Convention regarding the laws and customs of land warfare (Hague IV).

[9] Protocol for the Prohibition of the Use in War of Asphyxiating, Poisonous or Other Gases, and of Bateriological Methods of Warfare, XCIV LNTS (1929) no. 2138.

[10] Following conclusion of the Chemical Weapons Convention, a number of States have in recent years withdrawn their reservations

value of identifying the rule, distinct from the treaty obligation, is twofold. First, it is applicable to all States, even those which have not become party to the treaty. Second, parties to the treaty may not opt out of adhering to the rule by withdrawing from the treaty or by exercising their right to terminate or suspend the operation of the treaty on the ground of the violation by another party of a "provision essential to the accomplishment of the object or purpose of the treaty."

Identifying the scope and content of the customary rule thus warrants significant attention. This is not a simple task since, as seen above, the rule evolved and expanded over time as it was interwoven through successive treaties that crystallised it and developed it further. "Custom" has been described as "an authentic expression of the needs and values of the community at any given time.... It reflects the consensus approach to decision-making with the ability of the majority to create new law binding upon all...."[11] The two elements of international custom, as reflected in Article 38(b) of the Statute of the International Court of Justice ("general practice accepted as law") are state practice and *opinio juris*. *Opinio juris* constitutes the psychological element by which States, in carrying out their practice, do so not out of courtesy or morality but because they believe such practice is consistent with law. As indicated in the 1925 Geneva Protocol, the use in war of asphyxiating, poisonous or other gases, and all analogous liquids, materials or devices, has been justly condemned by the general opinion of the civilised world. The Geneva Protocol has long been considered to be declarative of customary international law.[12] The language of the Geneva Protocol was confirmed in the most recent multilateral statement of the content of customary international law in respect of the prohibition of chemical weapons, i.e. the Statute of the ICC,[13] adopted by the United Nations Diplomatic Conference of Plenipotentiaries (with delegations from 160 States participating).[14] Article 8, paragraph 2(b), provides as follows:

> 2. For the purpose of this Statute, "war crimes" means: ...
>   (b) Other serious violations of the laws and customs applicable in *international armed conflict*, within the established framework of international law, namely, any of the following acts:
>   (xvii) Employing poison or poisoned weapons;
>   (xviii) Employing asphyxiating, poisonous or other gases, and all analogous liquids, materials or devices; [Emphasis added]

---

[11] M. Shaw, International Law 57-58 (1997).

[12] In 1969 a majority of the UN General Assembly adopted the Resolution 2603 A (XXIV) expressing the view that the Protocol embodied the generally recognised rules of international law prohibiting the use in international armed conflicts of all biological and chemical methods of warfare, regardless of any technical developments. In particular, the resolution declared as contrary to the rules of international law the use in international armed conflicts of: (a) any chemical agents of warfare — chemical substances, whether gaseous, liquid or solid — which might be employed because of their direct toxic effects on man animals or plants. See: J. Goldblat, Arms Control: A Guide to Negotiations and Agreements 91 (1994).

[13] 1998 Rome Statute of the International Criminal Court, entered into force 1 July 2002; UN doc. A/CONF.183/9*, as corrected by the procès-verbaux of 10 November 1998 and 12 July 1999. Corrected text available at http://www.un.org/law/icc.

[14] UN press release L/ROM/22, dated 17 July 1998, available at http://www.un.org.

The definition of the crime as set forth in the ICC Statute contains the limitation that it is applicable only in *international* armed conflict. Article 120 provides that no reservations may be made to the Statute, which expands the prohibition beyond first use to *any use at all in international armed conflict.* Is the content of the customary rule limited to the prohibition in international armed conflict? It could be argued that it is not. The ICC Statute is reflective of the consensus that could be reached by States in respect of *crimes for which they were willing to confer jurisdiction upon a permanent international criminal court.* In their own national jurisdiction, or before an ad hoc tribunal, States may be willing to view the crime more widely.

What is the content of the customary rule in respect of internal armed conflict? State practice consists not only of "external conduct" in respect of other states, but also the state's internal conduct, including its national legislation, judicial decisions, diplomatic communications, government memoranda, and unilateral declarations (e.g., ministerial statements in Parliaments and elsewhere).[15] In 1995, the International Tribunal for the former Yugoslavia ("ICTY"), in an *obiter dictum*, examined state practice and *opinio juris* and determined that the customary rule prohibits the use of chemical weapons by a State on its own population. Using the most recent, publicised allegation of chemical weapons use (the 1988 alleged chemical attack by Iraq on the Iraqi village of Halabja), it examined the reaction of the Security Council and the international community to that attack and concluded:

> It is therefore clear that, whether or not Iraq really used chemical weapons against its own Kurdish nationals — a matter on which this Chamber obviously cannot and does not express any opinion — there undisputedly emerged a general consensus in the international community on the principle that the use of those weapons is also prohibited in internal armed conflicts.[16]

Where does the Chemical Weapons Convention fit into this? In its most recent codification, the prohibition of chemical weapons constitutes the object and purpose of the most innovative and complex international verification regime ever, encompassing reporting obligations, intrusive international inspections, and trade restrictions. However, the Chemical Weapons Convention is a novelty in the field of international disarmament and arms control law. At this point in time, what is the content of the codified and crystallised rule and what is developing under the Convention as emergent customary law? As adherence to the Convention becomes ever wider, over time its impact on custom will become markedly significant.

Some of the 1993 Chemical Weapons Convention is clearly codification of existing customary international law. The Convention sets forth the prohibition in terms of "never under any circumstances" (Article I), comprising peacetime, armed conflict (international or internal), acts of State and acts of individuals (thus covering terrorist acts). The reactions of the international community to the incidents of alleged use, whether international armed conflict (Iran-Iraq war), internal armed conflict (Halabja), or peacetime terrorism (Tokyo subway incident) have all been negative. It is clear that *opinio juris* does not condone use in

---

[15] R. Jennings and A. Watts (eds.), I Oppenheim's International Law 26 (1992).

[16] *Prosecutor v. Tadic*, Case no. IT-94-1-AR72, Appeals Chamber Decision on the Defence Motion for Interlocutory Appeal on Jurisdiction, (2 October 1995), para. 124.

any circumstances and any incidents of state and individual practices have been seen as shocking, unlawful acts.

However, the Chemical Weapons Convention sets forth much more than the prohibition of use. It also prohibits development and stockpiling and requires destruction of existing stockpiles (all of which are a logical consequence of a total ban on use). It prohibits the use of riot control agents as a method of warfare (to close a near loophole). Its non-proliferation element (the Article I obligation not to "assist, encourage or induce, in any way, anyone" and Article VI obligations concerning dual-use chemicals) prescribes trade restrictions against States not Party (implying export/import controls). Its extensive verification regime involves intrusion into State sovereignty by eliminating the right of States to refuse entry to international inspectors. Article XXII permits no reservations to the Articles of the Convention, thus making these non-derogable norms.

To what extent are those additional treaty obligations developing the content of customary international law? Much will depend on the extent to which the Chemical Weapons Convention is considered to be a law-making treaty.[17] The process for the development of custom under a treaty has been stated by the International Court of Justice in the North Sea Continental Shelf cases[18] in the following terms:

> "... a rule has come into being since the Convention, partly because of its own impact, partly on the basis of subsequent State practice, and ... this rule, being now a rule of customary international law binding on all States ..." (para. 70).

> "... involves treating that Article as a norm-creating provision which has constituted the foundation of, or has generated a rule which, while only conventional or contractual in its origin, has since passed into the general *corpus* of international law, and is now accepted as such by the *opinio juris*, so as to have become binding even for countries which have never, and do not, become parties to the Convention. There is no doubt that this process is a perfectly possible one and does from time to time occur: it constitutes indeed one of the recognised methods by which new rules of customary international law may be formed. At the same time this result is not lightly to be regarded as having been attained" (para. 71).

The Court indicated criteria for state practice forming a rule of customary international law to be (a) the amount of time the rule has been adhered to; (b) the number and type of states adhering to the rule (especially states having an interest affected by the rule); and (c) uniform state practice. In this respect it stated:

> "...Although the passage of only a short period of time is not necessarily, or of itself, a bar to the formation of a new rule of customary international law on the basis of what was originally a purely conventional rule, an indispensable requirement would be that within the period in question, short though it might be, State practice, including that of States whose interests are specially affected, should have been both extensive

[17] I. Brownlie, Principles of Public International Law 11-13 (1998).

[18] *North Sea Continental Shelf cases* (Germany v Denmark; Germany v the Netherlands), 1969 ICJ Reports 3.

and virtually uniform in the sense of the provision invoked — and should moreover have occurred in such a way as to show a general recognition that a rule of law or legal obligation is involved" (para. 74).

Practice under the Chemical Weapons Convention has undoubtedly been short (since 1997), however, the number of States is large and includes all declared chemical weapons possessor States and nearly all States having chemical industry relevant to the Convention. As consensus-building and interpretation continues, the decisions of the organs of the treaty-implementing body (the OPCW), are drawing state practice into greater uniformity.[19] Over time this aspect may become the most significant feature.

An interesting topic for further research would be an examination of state practice and *opinio juris* in respect of: (a) export/import controls; and (b) intrusive inspections. Principally under the Chemical Weapons Convention (due to the wide adherence to this innovative instrument), but also supported elsewhere, both are emerging as customary norms. The other existing regimes banning weapons of mass destruction (e.g., the 1972 Biological Weapons Convention[20] and the rolling text of its proposed Protocol), the 1999 Landmines Convention[21] and arms control regimes (the 1970 Nuclear Non-Proliferation Treaty,[22] the voluntary Missile Technology Control Regime) imply export controls. There is also, for example, an informal voluntary arrangement, dating back to 1984, among States, to implement strict export controls on a list of dual use substances and equipment. Under modern treaty law, bans or restrictions on weapons of mass destruction are linked with a non-proliferation element in order to make the ban effective. Reactions by the international community to use of chemical weapons, or threat of use, have also prompted strict export controls. For example, the Security Council resolutions during the Iran-Iraq war called upon all States to continue to apply, to establish, or to strengthen strict control of the export of chemical products serving for the production of chemical weapons, in particular to parties to a conflict, when it is established or there is substantial reason to believe that they have used chemical weapons in violation of international obligations.[23] Also, the Chapter VII ceasefire resolution in the 1991 Gulf War set forth an absolute prohibition on exports to Iraq of all components, means of production, technology or know-how related to weapons of mass destruction and created the binding obligation upon all States to maintain national controls and procedures to ensure compliance with that prohibition.[24] Given this practice and the wide adherence to the Chemical Weapons Convention, under emergent customary international law, will a State's failure to prevent the export of chemical weapons constitute a breach, leading to State responsibility[25] and individual criminal

[19] See: L. Tabassi (ed.), OPCW: The Legal Texts, 117-206 (1999).

[20] Convention on the Prohibition of Development, Production, and Stockpiling of Bacteriological (Biological) and Toxin Weapons and on Their Destruction.

[21] Convention on the Prohibtion of the Use, Stockpiling, Production and Transport of Anti-Personnel Mines and on Their Destruction.

[22] Treaty on the Non-Proliferation of Nuclear Weapons, entered into force 5 March 1970.

[23] United Nations Security Council resolutions 612 (1988) and 620 (1988).

[24] Paragraphs 24 and 27 of United Nations Security Council resolution 687 (2 April 1991).

[25] P. Rubenstein, *State Responsibility for Failure to Control the Export of Weapons of Mass Destruction*, 23 Calif. West. Int'l. L J, 319-372 (1993).

responsibility for the perpetrators? At first glance, one would think not. But today, the ICTY is prosecuting individuals for violations of customary norms. Time will tell.

The second aspect is the elimination of the right of a State, under the Chemical Weapons Convention, to refuse intrusive international inspections. Is this simply a treaty obligation or is there state practice to support this rule outside the treaty regime? Two recent examples are the United Nations missions sent to investigate the alleged use of chemical weapons in Iran and Iraq during their war 1980-88 and UNSCOM, created under the 1991 Security Council ceasefire resolution to uncover and destroy Iraq's weapons of mass destruction capability, including its chemical weapons capability. It seems the international community views independent international verification to be warranted in such cases.

Two additional aspects meriting further discussion and research would be (a) the practical effect of a State's right to withdraw from the Chemical Weapons Convention, and (b) the reasons why the small remainder of States have not adhered to the Convention (are they opposed to the ban or are there other reasons unrelated to the ban?).

On the first point, it could be argued that the right of withdrawal, termination or suspension of the treaty would only absolve the State from its obligations to contribute to the budget of the treaty's implementing body (the OPCW), its obligations to report on its relevant chemical activities to the OPCW, and its obligation to accept OPCW inspections. Article XVI(3) specifically provides that "The withdrawal of a State Party from this Convention shall not in any way affect the duty of States to continue fulfilling the obligations assumed under any relevant rules of international law, particularly the Geneva Protocol of 1925." And the States not Party to the Convention? The majority of them have not adhered to the Convention for two reasons: (a) they are non-possessor States with little or no relevant chemical industry whose governments attribute little political priority to adhering to the Convention; or (b) they are States which on principle refuse to adhere to an inequitable treaty that requires renunciation of chemical arsenals but leaves nuclear arsenals untouched, particularly since Israel is not yet a State Party.[26] It is perhaps only the smallest minority which actually believe that they should retain the right to use chemical weapons. It is significant that 14 of the States which have neither signed nor ratified the Chemical Weapons Convention participated in the Conference of States Parties to the Geneva Protocol and Other Interested States, held in Paris in 1989, and did not block consensus on the Final Declaration calling for a comprehensive ban on chemical weapons.

War crimes are considered to form part of *jus cogens*, and a few authors have even gone so far as to propose that the prohibition of use of chemical weapons explicitly forms part of *jus cogens*. Two elements must be present for a crime to be *jus cogens*: (1) the crime must threaten the peace and security of humankind; and (2) the crime must shock the conscience of humanity.[27] The advantage of recognising the norm as a norm of *jus cogens* is that it is non-derogable by all States under any circumstances (peace or war); the duty to prosecute or

---

[26] See: P. Herby, The Chemical Weapons Convention and Arms Control in the Middle East (1992); J. Goldblat, Arms Control: A Guide to Negotiations and Agreements 101-102 (1994); E. Kwakwa, The International Law of Armed Conflict: Personal and Material Fields of Application 15 (1992); F. Harbour, *Islamic Principles and the Chemical Weapons Convention of 1993*, 1973 Journal of Religious Ethics 69, 77-79 and 81-86.

[27] M.C. Bassiouni, *The Sources and Theory of International Criminal Law: A Theoretical Framework* in M.C. Bassiouni, I International Criminal Law 3, 42 (1999).

extradite (*aut dedere aut judicare*) becomes applicable; any statute of limitations become inapplicable; the theory of universal jurisdiction applies; and States have the obligation *erga omnes* not to grant impunity to the violators.[28] While it is clear that the prohibition against chemical weapons is non-derogable, it could be argued that clearer determination on the part of States to prosecute the perpetrators of the use of chemical weapons is necessary before it can be considered to be a *jus cogens* crime. Historically, such determination is not evident, as will be seen further below. "The gap between legal expectations and legal reality," as Professor M. Cherif Bassiouni puts it,[29] is omnipresent in cases of chemical weapons use. Perhaps the inclusion of the crime (albeit narrow in scope) in the Statute of the ICC is the first step towards its establishment as a *jus cogens* crime.

5. Horizontal (Indirect) Enforcement

The 1899 Hague Declaration and Regulations, the 1907 Hague Regulations and the 1925 Geneva Protocol are all silent on the manner in which they are to be enforced. As they are applicable in "war", they form part of international humanitarian law which States normally must make provision for in their military penal codes. It is uncertain to what extent States have done so. In contrast, the Chemical Weapons Convention makes specific provision under Article VII that States must "adopt the measures necessary" to: prohibit (including penal legislation), "not permit" (i.e., enforce), and extend such penal legislation to prohibited acts undertaken anywhere by natural persons possessing its nationality. States Parties are thus under the obligation to prosecute and punish in their national jurisdictions. This is the indirect way of enforcing international law and is termed "horizontal enforcement".

Mueller and Besharov have succinctly summarised horizontal enforcement and the problems inherent in it:

> The advantage of enforcing [international criminal law (ICL)] on the national level is obvious: the entire machinery of municipal criminal law can be used for enforcement purposes. The courts' edicts can be easily enforced. Sentences can be readily executed.
>
> But politics do play their role under such a scheme as well. Depending on political exigencies, there may never be an indictment in the first place, apart from the fact that the locally applicable penal code or code of criminal procedure may not envisage such a jurisdiction. The world simply cannot force national legislatures to include the totality of ICL — and jurisdiction — within the ambit of municipal law.[30]

The two main obstacles to horizontal enforcement can thus be said to be the following: (1) possible political unwillingness to prosecute; and (2) the necessary criminalisation of the act in order to permit prosecution.

Enforcing prohibitions against diversions of chemical agents can only be possible if the export controls are in place to begin with. The greatest barrier of all to enforcement may be the slow pace, or the failure, of States to enact the requisite implementing legislation.

[28] *Id.*, at 39.
[29] *Id.*, at 40.
[30] G. Mueller and D. Besharov, *Evolution and Enforcement of International Criminal Law* in M.C. Bassiouni, I International Criminal Law, 257, 267 (1999).

The OPCW Conference of the States Parties has noted that only 38% of States Parties have complied with their obligation to notify the measures they have taken under Article VII.[31] If the remaining 62% of the States Parties all enjoy a monist legal system, one could argue that the Convention is enforceable in their jurisdictions. Research into the legal systems of those 90 States is beyond the scope of this chapter, but it could safely be assumed that there are at least a number of dualist systems among them. Failure to enact implementing legislation does not absolve the State of its treaty obligation but it will impair its ability to prosecute individuals.

To rule out the possibility that criminals might evade the Chemical Weapons Convention regime by moving their activities to the territory of a State not Party, Article VII(1)(c) requires States Parties to extend their penal legislation covering the prohibitions to "any activity prohibited to a State Party under this Convention undertaken anywhere by natural persons, possessing its nationality, in conformity with international law." However, less than 15% of States Parties have notified the OPCW that they have done this.[32] This obligation may be problematic for many States Parties which do not recognise the principle of extraterritorial jurisdiction.[33] Even if the penal legislation is extended extraterritorially, it will only be done so in respect of natural persons, leaving open the problem of transnational corporations which have manufacturing operations in another (State not Party) country.[34] During the negotiations of the Chemical Weapons Convention, the United States representative reported that any corporation incorporated under United States law wherever its activities took place would be prohibited from aiding a State not Party in chemical weapons production.[35] In the United States Chemical Weapons Convention Implementation Act of 1998, Section 229 provides:

> 229. Prohibited activities ...
>
> (c) Jurisdiction. Conduct prohibited by subsection (a) is within the jurisdiction of the United States if the prohibited conduct:
>
> (1) takes place in the United States;
>
> (2) takes place outside of the United States and is committed by a national of the United States;
>
> (3) is committed against a national of the United States while the national is outside the United States; or,

[31] See Report of the Sixth Session of the Conference of the States Parties, OPCW document C-VI/6, dated 19 May 2001, subparagraph 10.3, available at http://www.opcw.org.

[32] See: OPCW Secretariat, Survey of National Implementing Legislation, document S/259/2001 (16 May 2001).

[33] See: M. Gestri, *Control by States Parties over private extraterritorial activities: issues of jurisdiction and international responsibility* in M. Bothe et al., The New Chemical Weapons Convention — Implementation and Prospects 463-486 (1998).

[34] See: W. Krutzsch and R. Trapp, Commentary on the Chemical Weapons Convention 113-115 (1994).

[35] Conference on Disarmament document CD.PV.42.

(4) is committed against any property that is owned, leased, or used by the United States or by any department or agency of the United States, whether the property is within or outside the United States.[36]

From section 229 of the United States implementing legislation, it is clear that the United States intends to exercise criminal jurisdiction over alleged offenders based on: (a) the territoriality principle (the offence was committed within its territory); (b) the nationality principle (the accused is a United States national); and (c) the passive personality principle (the injured is a United States national).

The implementing legislation of another State Party, Sweden, made the offence a crime of universal jurisdiction, for Sweden. Chapter 2, Section 3 of the Swedish Criminal Code (as amended) provides that:

> Chapter 2, Section 3. A crime against the Convention will be sentenced by Swedish law and at a Swedish court even if the crime is committed abroad and irrespective of the perpetrator's nationality.[37]

6. Vertical (direct) Enforcement

An international tribunal directly enforcing an international norm is vertical enforcement. There is, as yet, no instance of proceedings instituted before an international tribunal for chemical weapons related offences. This is not surprising since, despite the number of allegations of chemical weapons use (one database shows official and unofficial reports of 47 countries having used some form of toxic warfare since World War I),[38] the only possible fora so far where some of those allegations of use could have been prosecuted directly have been three: (1) the tribunal(s) provided for under the 1919 Treaty of Versailles (which in the end resulted in national prosecutions in Leipzig); (2) the International Military Tribunal for the Far East (the Tokyo trials) at the end of World War II; and (3) the International Criminal Tribunal for the Former Yugoslavia (ICTY) in The Hague.

Jurisdiction over chemical weapons related offences are explicitly provided for in Article 3 of the Statute for the International Criminal Tribunal for the Former Yugoslavia (ICTY):

> Article 3. Violations of the laws or customs of war. The International Tribunal shall have the power to prosecute persons violating the laws or customs of war. Such violations shall include, but not be limited to: (a) employment of poisonous weapons or other weapons calculated to cause unnecessary suffering; ...

No one has yet been indicted by the ICTY for the use of chemical weapons.

---

[36] Reprinted in the OPCW Survey of National Implementing Legislation, document S/259/2001 (16 May 2001), Annex, 86-87.

[37] Reprinted in the OPCW Survey of National Implementing Legislation, document S/259/2001 (16 May 2001), Annex, 85.

[38] See: Table 1 annexed to J. Perry Robinson, *The negotiations on the Chemical Weapons Convention; a historical overview* in M. Bothe et al., The New Chemical Weapons Convention — Implementation and Prospects 17 at 33-35 (1998).

The Rome Statute of the International Criminal Court[39] also gives rise to some questions. Under it, jurisdiction over chemical weapons offences is defined very narrowly:

Article 8. War Crimes

2. For the purpose of this Statute, "war crimes" means: ...
   (b) Other serious violations of the laws and customs applicable in international armed conflict, within the established framework of international law, namely, any of the following acts: ...
   (xvii) Employing poison or poisoned weapons;
   (xviii) Employing asphyxiating, poisonous or other gases, and all analogous liquids, materials or devices; ....

Under that definition, the International Criminal Court (ICC) only has jurisdiction over the *use* of chemical weapons in international armed conflict, and based on the principle of complementarity, the crimes under the Chemical Weapons Convention would go unpunished, e.g., developing, producing, otherwise acquiring, stockpiling, retaining or transferring chemical weapons, engaging in any military preparations to use chemical weapons, or assisting, encouraging or inducing in any way anyone to engage in any activity prohibited to a State Party under the Convention. Even the use of chemical weapons would go unpunished by the ICC if it occurred in internal armed conflict (which most conflicts in the world today are) or if it were a terrorist act, no matter how serious.

However, Article 21 of the ICC Statute goes on to provide:

Article 21. Applicable law

1. The Court shall apply:
   (a) In the first place, this Statute, Elements of Crimes and its Rules of Procedure and Evidence;
   (b) In the second place, where appropriate, applicable treaties and the principles and rules of international law, including the established principles of the international law of armed conflict; and,
   (c) Failing that, general principles of law derived by the Court from national laws of legal systems of the world including, as appropriate, the national laws of States that would normally exercise jurisdiction over the crime, provided that those principles are not inconsistent with this Statute and with international law and internationally recognised norms and standards.

There is an apparent contradiction here but it is probably solved by the hierarchy. The ICC has jurisdiction over the crime of use of chemical weapons in international armed conflict. Secondarily it could apply the Chemical Weapons Convention directly. In the third place it could apply general principles of law derived from the body of national implementing legislation for the Chemical Weapons Convention. While the hierarchy is clear, how it will

[39] Entered into force 1 July 2002. Text available at www.un.org.

work in practice is less clear. Article 22(2) of the ICC Statute seems to indicate that the crime would remain very narrow:

> Article 22. *Nullum crimen sine lege* ...
>
> 2. The definition of a crime shall be strictly construed and shall not be extended by analogy. In case of ambiguity, the definition shall be interpreted in favour of the person being investigated, prosecuted or convicted.

The other gaps discussed above in relation to direct enforcement of the Chemical Weapons Convention would not exist under the ICC Statute: Article 9 provides that the Elements of Crimes shall be adopted by the Assembly of States Parties, which thus will fill the void left by the lack of an international criminal code. The necessary specificity, a basic constituent of the principles of legality, will be satisfied.

7. The Principles of Legality

Underlying any discussion of enforcement are the principles of legality which give enforcement its legitimacy. There are three principles of legality and they are universally present in all national legal systems,[40] international human rights instruments[41] and the ICC Statute:[42]

(1) *nullum crimen sine lege* — no crime without a law;
(2) *nulla poena sine lege* — no punishment without a law; and,
(3) *non-retroactivity ratione personae* — no *ex post facto* application of law.

The first two principles have been discussed in the international jurisprudence[43] and existing doctrine on this subject. Professor Bassiouni added the third principle. The underlying rationale for these principles serves justice. As Bassiouni puts it:

> To satisfy the principles of legality, a crime must be defined sufficiently to put people on notice that a particular conduct has been characterised as criminal ... These principles are deemed part of fundamental justice because they protect against potential judicial abuse and arbitrary application of the law.[44]

---

[40] M.C. Bassiouni, *Sources and Theory of International Criminal Law* in Bassiouni (ed.), I International Criminal Law, 3, 33 (1999).

[41] Article 11(2) of the Universal Declaration of Human Rights, Article 15(1) of the International Covenant on Civil and Political Rights; Article 7(1) of the European Convention for the Protection of Human Rights and Fundamental Freedoms, Article 9 of the American Convention on Human Rights; Article 6 of the African Charter on Human and Peoples' Rights.

[42] Articles 22, 23 and 24 of the ICC Statute.

[43] Permanent Court of International Justice, *Advisory Opinion on the consistency of Certain Danzig Legislative Decrees with the Constitution of the Free City* (4 December 1935), 1935 PCIJ 3 (Series A/B) no. 65 at 514, cited in M.C. Bassiouni, The Law of the International Criminal Tribunal for the Former Yugoslavia 283 (1996).

[44] M.C. Bassiouni, *Sources and Theory of International Criminal Law: A Theoretical Framework* in M.C. Bassiouni (ed.), I International Criminal Law, 3, 33 (1999).

Professor Bassiouni has pointed out that the problem of enforcing customary norms is that they are dynamic. Custom can be created and custom can be abandoned, giving rise to problems in spatial and temporal application.[45] The judges of the ICTY, when faced with a *lacuna* not covered by the Statute, have resorted to national analogies. In any event, in almost all cases international crimes will be prosecuted at the national level, horizontally. Penal legislation which is consistent with respect to prohibited activities provides a more solid basis for the purposeful interaction of States Parties in the prosecution of such activities. Otherwise, the principles *nullum crimen sine lege* and *nulla poena sine lege* could stand in the way of legal assistance. The same could be the case if the penalties foreseen in the law of one State Party fall outside the range of the penalties in the law of the other States Parties involved. In most cases the necessary instrument(s) must also be in place for international cooperation in criminal matters to take place.

That brings us to the subject of this book: treaty enforcement and international penal cooperation, the facets and practicalities of which are examined in the following chapters.

[45] *Id.*, at 35-36.

PART I

"COOPERATION AND MUTUAL LEGAL ASSISTANCE": LEGAL BASIS

PART I
"COOPERATION AND MUTUAL LEGAL ASSISTANCE": LEGAL BASIS

INTRODUCTION AND SUMMARY

Multilateral normative treaties will typically confront legal practitioners with provisions related to international cooperation in criminal matters. While the following provision has been taken from the Chemical Weapons Convention (Article VII, paragraphs 1 and 2), it is representative of that type of cooperation provision, and should not, therefore, be seen as limited to the subject matter of any particular treaty:

General obligations

1. Each State Party shall, in accordance with its constitutional processes, adopt the necessary measures to implement its obligations under this Convention. In particular, it shall:
   (a) Prohibit natural and legal persons anywhere on its territory or in any other place under its jurisdiction as recognised by international law from undertaking any activity prohibited to a State Party under this Convention, including enacting penal legislation with respect to such activity;
   (b) Not permit in any place under its control any activity prohibited to a State Party under this Convention; and
   (c) Extend its penal legislation enacted under subparagraph (a) to any activity prohibited to a State Party under this Convention undertaken anywhere by natural persons, possessing its nationality, in conformity with international law.

R. Yepes-Enríquez and L. Tabassi. (eds.), Treaty Enforcement and International Cooperation in Criminal Matters

2. Each State Party shall cooperate with other States Parties and afford the appropriate form of legal assistance to facilitate the implementation of the obligations under paragraph 1.

In implementing that normative treaty nationally, what are the practical implications of those provisions?

- legislate to criminalise the prohibited activities;
- extend that legislation extraterritorially;
- enforce the prohibitions, i.e., monitor to prevent those crimes and prosecute any violations;
- engage in inter-State cooperation to prevent or detect those crimes and assist with prosecutions, upon request; and,
- establish the legal basis to permit, with all other States Parties to the treaty, all modalities; of inter-State cooperation in criminal matters.

What are the modalities of cooperation in criminal matters that a State may be requested to provide?

To prevent crime:
- police and customs cooperation, intelligence and information-sharing; and

To detect and prosecute the crime once it has been committed:
- legal assistance by officers of the judiciary and/or police (*inter alia*, taking evidence or testimony, assisting with investigations, serving judicial documents, executing searches and seizures, providing documents and records, tracing proceeds);
- extradition;
- transfer of proceedings;
- seizure and forfeiture of illicit proceeds of crime;
- transfer of sentenced persons; and,
- recognition of foreign penal judgments.

What legal basis is needed to permit cooperation in those modalities? This will vary from jurisdiction to jurisdiction. Political considerations in a specific case can either facilitate or frustrate the process. In some cases, especially between similar legal systems, cooperation may be based on reciprocity, or even on international comity. Bearing those special considerations in mind, one can say that to prosecute crimes, the following would generally be the case:

For cooperation by a State with another State:
- generally, the act must be defined as a crime in both jurisdictions, and must be penalised by at least one year imprisonment;

- a bilateral or multilateral treaty in force, to which both States are party, covering that specific modality of cooperation; or,

For cooperation by a State with an international court:

- legal obligation of the State under the court's statute to cooperate, which may be derived from a treaty or a United Nations Security Council Chapter VII resolution.

In all cases,

- domestic legislation will be needed to regulate the internal procedure to make or respond to requests for cooperation;
- an administrative structure and trained personnel will be needed to make or respond to the requests.

Inter-State cooperation to prevent crime is a different modality altogether. It depends more on political willingness than legal considerations. Customs administrations may be cooperating in accordance with guidelines agreed within the forum of the World Customs Organisation. The police may be voluntarily cooperating through Interpol and/or, if applicable, Europol. Any sharing of information or intelligence will be based on a high degree of trust, and possibly reciprocity.

It is quite apparent that there is no easy answer here. With no universal multilateral regime in force covering all modalities of cooperation, is there no shortcut readily available now? One author in the following section has suggested the following in the short-term: the United Nations Convention Against Transnational Organised Crime, opened for signature in December 2000. Crimes of a magnitude to warrant being covered by treaty would often involve transnational activity and involve a structured group of three or more persons. Those criteria met, the crime could fall within the ambit of that Convention which doubles as an instrument covering the full scope of modalities of inter-State cooperation in criminal matters. At the time of writing, the Convention is not in force. Forty parties are needed for it to enter into force and it already has 16, with another 125 signatory States presumably actively pursuing ratification. It is a promising suggestion.

In the meantime, and for cases falling outside that regime, the key word in the treaty provision is *shall*. In "Each State Party *shall* cooperate with other States Parties and afford the appropriate form of legal assistance." This is a positive obligation for each State Party which cannot be refused. In the view of one author, that alone could imply the *aut dedere aut judicare* obligation for each State Party – extradite or prosecute – as the bottom line, with the Convention creating its own standards of cooperation. If States Parties can find the political willingness to embrace that teleological interpretation, need we say more? The prospects for implementation of the cooperation and legal assistance provision, together with the flexibility that may be needed to interface with the current progressive development of international criminal law, may be quite bright after all.

Lisa Tabassi

Rapporteur for the plenary of the 2001 OPCW International Symposium; Legal Officer, OPCW Technical Secretariat, Office of the Legal Adviser. The views expressed are not attributable to the OPCW.

THE CHEMICAL WEAPONS CONVENTION AND INTERNATIONAL COOPERATION IN CRIMINAL MATTERS

Bert Swart*

1. The Duty to Cooperate in the Convention

Article VII, paragraph 2, of the Chemical Weapons Convention[1] imposes a duty on States Parties to cooperate with other States Parties and to "afford the appropriate form of legal assistance" to facilitate the repression of activities that they all are under an obligation to penalise in their national laws. Pursuant to paragraph 1 of the same Article, the obligation to enact penal legislation refers to the activities summed up in Article I, paragraph 1, of the Convention. Some of these activities are international crimes independent of the Chemical Weapons Convention. This is, in particular, the case for the use of chemical weapons in international armed conflicts and, it must now be assumed, also for their use in internal armed conflicts.[2] The character of these activities as international crimes derives from treaties[3] as well as from customary international law. Other activities, in particular the development, production, acquisition, stockpiling, retention and transfer of chemical weapons, are international crimes only by virtue of the Chemical Weapons Convention.

Article VII, paragraph 2, is a very short and rather enigmatic provision. It simply states that each State Party shall cooperate with other States Parties in the repression of the crimes under the Convention, and it adds that they shall afford each other the "appropriate form of legal assistance" in this respect. What could be meant by a duty to cooperate and afford the appropriate form of legal assistance? I have been unable to find any material in the *travaux préparatoires* to the Convention shedding some light on the question. All one can say is that the provision was introduced in the Draft Convention in 1991 and remained unchanged in substance afterwards.[4] In the absence of any useful material, different interpretations offer themselves.

One interpretation would be to assume that a State Party to the Convention is under an obligation to afford another State Party every form of assistance the other State Party may need in order to be able to successfully repress crimes related to the production and the use of chemical weapons. In this interpretation, the word "appropriate" is understood to refer

* Professor of International Criminal Law at the University of Amsterdam and Judge on the Amsterdam Court of Appeal.

[1] 1993 Convention on the Prohibition of the Development, Production, Stockpiling and Use of Chemical Weapons and on Their Destruction, entered into force on 29 April 1997. Text, as corrected and changed, available at http://www.opcw.org.

[2] Cf. *Prosecutor v. Duško Tadić*, Appeals Chamber of the ICTY 2 October 1995, para. 124. (Case IT-94-1-AR72).

[3] Article 23(a) of the Hague Regulations and the 1925 Geneva Protocol.

[4] See the Report of the Ad Hoc Committee on Chemical Weapons to the Conference on Disarmement on work during the period 8-18 January 1991, Conference on Disarmament doc. CD/1046, 29, 170-171.

R. Yepes-Enríquez and L. Tabassi. (eds.), Treaty Enforcement and International Cooperation in Criminal Matters

to the object and purpose of the Convention itself, which is to eliminate any risk that chemical weapons might ever be used. The consequences of that interpretation would be considerable, since it would imply that the Convention aims to create a system of cooperation that is both self-contained and all-embracing. States Parties would, for instance, not be able to refuse assistance in situations in which they normally refuse to do so, or would at least be obligated to prosecute an alleged offender themselves if they are unwilling to extradite him to another State Party. It is true that, in recent decades, quite a number of multilateral treaties have been adopted which aim at creating such a system with regard to specific international crimes. But, in them, the various obligations of the Parties to cooperate are carefully formulated and detailed. One must assume that if it had been the intention of the framers of the Chemical Weapons Convention to create a similar system, it would be apparent from the drafting history of the Convention and would have led to the inclusion of provisions that leave no doubt about that intention.

The second interpretation is to assume that Article VII, paragraph 2, merely requires States Parties to the Chemical Weapons Convention to cooperate with one another in criminal matters in conformity with international conventions on interstate cooperation in criminal matters to which they are party or, for that matter, with customary international law, as well as with their national laws in the matter, for the purpose of repressing crimes under the Convention. One could call this the minimalist position, as opposed to the maximalist position discussed above. In this interpretation, Article VII, paragraph 2, does not add much in terms of obligations to the obligations already deriving for the States Parties from other sources of international law. Basically, it confirms them where crimes under the Chemical Weapons Convention are concerned. The most important aspect of paragraph 2 would then be that it would probably obligate the competent authorities of States Parties to render assistance to one another in situations in which other conventions or domestic legislation leave them discretion as to whether or not to do so. This interpretation seems to prevail in state practice with regard to the implementation of the Convention. A good example is The Netherlands. In its Explanatory Memorandum to the bill submitting the Convention for approval to Parliament, the Dutch government paid scant attention to paragraph 2 of Article VII. They limited their discussion of that provision to the remark that existing legislation offered sufficient possibilities for international cooperation.[5] Consequently, the 1995 Act on the Implementation of the Chemical Weapons Convention does contain a number of penal provisions and one on jurisdiction but is silent where legal cooperation is concerned.[6] This approach seems to be shared by other States Parties. From a survey of national implementing legislation conducted by the Secretariat of the Organisation for the Prohibition of Chemical Weapons in 1998, it appears that no State having become a State Party to the Convention at that time had bothered to introduce special legislation with regard to the duty to afford legal assistance, with the only exception being Switzerland.[7] In its introduction to the survey,[8] the Secretariat itself made the following remark: "The Convention does not elaborate the cooperation and legal

[5] Explanatory Memorandum, Bijl. Hand II 1994-1995, 23910 (R 1515), nr. 3, at 35.

[6] Act of 8 June 1995, Staatsblad 1995, 338.

[7] Survey of National Implementing Legislation, OPCW Secretariat, OPCW doc. S/259/2001 (16 May 2001), Annex at 87-88. Swiss legislation has regard mainly to the provision of data to the competent authorities of other States.

[8] *Id.*, subparagraphs 2 and 3.

assistance which may be required of States Parties under Article VII, paragraph 2. As it stands now, States Parties will draw on existing international agreements on legal assistance and related domestic legislation as well as ad hoc arrangements to be reached between States Parties concerned." This suggests that the Secretariat basically shares the opinion of the States Parties concerned. The same seems to be true for the (sparse) literature on the matter.[9]

It is obvious that the "minimalist" interpretation of Article VII, paragraph 2, leads to a rather disappointing outcome. It implies that the Convention does not create its own standards of cooperation in criminal matters but falls back on what is available in international and domestic law. In order to assess what the obligations of the States Parties to the Convention to cooperate with one another are, we must look to other sources. In discussing the matter I will first focus on global and regional frameworks for cooperation in criminal matters and then turn to the various forms of cooperation as well as to the most common legal obstacles to rendering assistance. Two general remarks are in order here. First, in discussing international cooperation one should make a distinction between the use of chemical weapons on the one hand and other crimes under the Convention on the other. The use of chemical weapons, being a war crime, is a crime under general international law. This entails that different, more stringent, rules apply to the rendering of legal assistance with regard to this crime than to the rendering of assistance with regard to the other crimes. Moreover, there is now also a developing system of adjudication of war crimes and other crimes under general international law by international tribunals, and of concomitant obligations for States to render assistance to these bodies in the repression of these crimes. Secondly, interstate cooperation in criminal matters is a particularly dynamic area of international law. It is in constant evolution. As a consequence, the duties of States to cooperate in criminal matters are, at this moment, considerably broader and more varied than they were at the time the Chemical Weapons Convention was adopted, and one may expect this process to continue in the next decades. Cooperation on the basis of the Convention may profit from these developments.

2. Frameworks of Cooperation

It is an important aspect of developments after 1945 that interstate cooperation in criminal matters is, to an ever increasing extent, based on multilateral conventions rather than bilateral ones. These multilateral conventions have been developed by international organisations such as the United Nations, the Council of Europe, the European Union and the Organization of American States.

Until recently, the United Nations did not engage in the drafting and adoption of general conventions with regard to international cooperation in criminal matters. Instead, it concentrated on the development of conventions with regard to particular classes of transnational crimes and cooperation between States in repressing these crimes, the best known convention probably being the 1988 United Nations Convention against Illicit

[9] Cf. Barry Kellmann and Edward A. Tanzman, Manual for National Implementation of the Chemical Weapons Convention (1998), 60, stating i.a. that "States Parties may be obligated to do what they can to fulfill a request for assistance"; Krutzsch and Trapp, A Commentary on the Chemical Weapons Convention (1994), 118-119 (according to whom paragraph 2 "alludes to the international practice already existing").

Traffic in Narcotic Drugs and Psychotropic Substances and the most recent one being the 1999 International Convention for the Suppression of the Financing of Terrorism. This has now changed. In December 2000, work was finally completed on the United Nations Convention against Transnational Organised Crime, which does not limit itself to particular classes of crimes but covers all crimes provided that they have been committed on an organised basis and carry a maximum punishment of at least four years' imprisonment.[10] Since it is hardly conceivable that the crimes under the Chemical Weapons Convention would be committed by isolated individuals, the new United Nations Convention promises to be of eminent significance for the application of Article VII, paragraph 2, of the Chemical Weapons Convention, provided of course that the new Convention is widely ratified. The fact that the Convention only applies to offences of a transnational nature reduces that significance perhaps somewhat, but probably not seriously given the international nature of the production of, and the trade in, chemical substances. An important aspect of the new Convention is also that it systematically deals with a variety of forms of cooperation, from police cooperation to cooperation in confiscating the proceeds of crime.

The most important other international organisations to be mentioned here are the Council of Europe, the European Union and the Organization of American States. The work of the Council of Europe in the field of cooperation in criminal matters is well known and hardly invites comment. Since the beginning of the 1950's, the Council of Europe has been engaged in systematically developing various forms of interstate cooperation in criminal matters (with the exception of police cooperation) and it is still pursuing this path. As a result, cooperation between the Member States in the repression of crimes under the Chemical Weapons Convention will normally not present special difficulties. The practical importance of the Council of Europe's network of conventions increased considerably when the countries of Eastern Europe became members of the organisation in the 1990's. As far as the European Union is concerned, since its foundation in 1993 it has shown an exceptional determination in further developing cooperation in criminal matters between its members on the basis laid by the Council of Europe. Its most recent and most ambitious project is to develop a general system for mutually recognising judicial decisions in criminal matters which, if adopted, might well result in a system of cooperation that is not too different from that between the component parts of federal states. Finally, there is the Organization of American States, with its own multilateral conventions on extradition, on mutual assistance in criminal matters and on serving criminal sentences abroad.

What this very cursory survey indicates is that cooperation in criminal matters with regard to the crimes of the Chemical Weapons Convention outside the limited framework of Europe and the Americas is still largely a matter of using bilateral treaties and national statutes. This raises the question of whether Asian and African countries in particular are sufficiently able to provide assistance to one another and to countries in other parts of the world where the Chemical Weapons Convention is concerned. I am unable to answer that question. But if they have problems in this respect, the quickest way to overcome them might perhaps be for these States to ratify the United Nations Convention against Transnational Organised Crime.

[10] United Nations doc. GA A/55/383, Annex I, article 2(b).

Finally a few words on the use of chemical weapons as a crime under general international law. The fact that the use of chemical weapons is such a crime has a number of consequences for international cooperation. The first one is that States may have to cooperate with international judicial bodies in its repression. Both the Statute of the ICTY and that of the ICTR mention the employment of poisonous weapons as a crime over which these ad hoc international tribunals have jurisdiction. The same is true for Article 8 of the Rome Statute of the International Criminal Court, although the jurisdiction of the Court is limited to the use of chemical weapons in international armed conflicts. As a consequence, Member States of the United Nations, in the case of the ad hoc tribunals, and States Parties to the Rome Statute, in the case of the International Criminal Court, are under a general obligation to assist these judicial bodies in a variety of ways, notably by surrendering suspects or accused on request, but also by providing other forms of assistance. These systems of cooperation supplement existing systems of interstate cooperation and impose obligations on States that are, in many respects, more strict and far-reaching.

It is also important to note here that many States wanting to become a party to the Rome Statute have decided to revise and modernise their domestic legislation in the field of crimes under general international law in order to be better able to repress these crimes themselves. It is not impossible that these revisions will also extend to domestic legislation with regard to interstate cooperation. This could have an important spin-off effect for cooperation on the basis of Article VII of the Chemical Weapons Convention.

Finally, there is the question of whether or not customary international law imposes a duty on States either to extradite a person accused of having committed an international crime or to try that person itself. It is still a matter of some controversy whether such a rule of customary law does indeed exist already.[11] An affirmative answer has recently been given by the Appeals Chamber of the ICTY in an *obiter dictum* in its decision in *Prosecutor v. Tihomir Blaškic* where grave breaches of international humanitarian law are concerned.[12] Be that as it may, one of the important aspects of recent developments in state practice stimulated by the Rome Statute of the International Criminal Court is that an increasing number of States are now prepared to apply the universality principle as a basis for national jurisdiction over international crimes, including the use of chemical weapons. In Article VII of the Chemical Weapons Convention, the obligation for States Parties to establish criminal jurisdiction over crimes is limited to those committed on their territory or other places under their control and those committed by their nationals.

3. Forms of Cooperation

International cooperation in criminal matters may take many different forms. Some of them have a long tradition, others are of recent origin. Some of them are relatively complicated and only granted when many different conditions have been met; others are more easily obtained. Some of them involve police authorities only; others require the intervention of public prosecutors and courts. The United Nations Convention against Transnational Organised Crime gives a good impression of current international practices,

[11] For discussions see M.C. Bassiouni and E.M. Wise, Aut Dedere aut Judicare; The Duty to Extradite or Prosecute in International Law, (1995); M.C. Bassiouni, Crimes Against Humanity, 217-221 (1999).
[12] Appeals Chamber 29 October 1997, Case No IT-95-14-AR 108 *bis*, para. 29.

although within regional frameworks developments have gone further in a number of respects, in particular where police cooperation is concerned.

Roughly speaking there are four different forms of international cooperation in criminal matters: extradition, mutual assistance in the investigation and prosecution of criminal offences, transfer of criminal proceedings, and transfer of the enforcement of criminal judgements (consisting, for instance, of transfer of sentenced persons, or of the enforcement of foreign judgments with regard to the confiscation of proceeds of crime). All of these forms may be relevant where cooperation on the basis of the Chemical Weapons Convention is concerned. However, it is not likely that they will all be used by States Parties to the Convention with the same frequency and the same ease. Extradition and transfer of enforcement of criminal judgments in particular are, from a legal perspective, relatively complex forms of international cooperation. Moreover, in actual practice they presuppose a considerable degree of mutual trust between the parties in the proceedings and some degree of familiarity with each other's legal system. The fact that the Chemical Weapons Convention is not itself a treaty on cooperation in criminal matters may play an important role here. One may, therefore, expect that these forms of cooperation will mainly be practised between those States Parties to the Convention that have already developed considerable experience with extraditing persons to one another and with enforcing each other's criminal judgements. As far as transfer of criminal proceedings is concerned, this really is a rather obscure form of cooperation in criminal matters, rarely resorted to even among the Member States of the Council of Europe, where it was first systematically developed. It is, moreover, a form of cooperation that is rather alien to the spirit of the common law. This leaves us with mutual assistance in the investigation and prosecution of criminal offences as probably being the form of cooperation that is most likely to be successful.

Within the span of a few pages it is hardly possible to give a fair impression of the enormous diversity of the forms mutual cooperation in criminal matters may take. Article 18(3) of the United Nations Convention Against Transnational Organised Crime contains a non-exhaustive list of eight different forms, but that list could easily be made much longer. Moreover, practices in the field of mutual assistance tend to follow developments in national systems of criminal justice, as well as technical developments, with some delay. As a result, new forms and techniques of cooperation are constantly emerging on the international scene, for example the case for the hearing of witnesses by means of transnational video- or audioconferences or the interception of telecommunications by satellite. Finally, the phenomenon of transnational crime provokes its own transnational responses, like the formation of joint investigation teams, transnational controlled deliveries, or transnational undercover operations. All this easily makes mutual assistance the most dynamic and lively part of international cooperation in criminal matters. There is perhaps also no form of international cooperation where there is so much variation in the extent and degree to which States are able to render assistance to other States.

Often, especially in civil law jurisdictions, a distinction is made between police cooperation on the one hand and so-called judicial assistance on the other. Given the fact that the delimitation of competences between police and prosecutorial authorities may vary from country to country, this distinction is not always very helpful. It is perhaps more useful to distinguish between assistance that can be given without the intervention of national courts of the requested State on the one hand, and assistance that makes their intervention necessary on the other. Intervention of national courts is usually necessary where assistance cannot be given without some degree of interference with basic individual rights. This is, for instance, the case with the seizure of objects, the search of premises, the freezing of assets, or the interception of telecommunications. Interference with basic individual rights makes it necessary that the person whose rights might have to be, or have already been, infringed upon is able to contest these measures. Systems of review or appeal may, therefore, make the rendering of assistance a rather time consuming process in these cases.

A second important category of cases usually involving some activity of a national court of the requested State is the interviewing of persons, especially where their depositions are intended to be used as evidence in a court of law of the requesting State. It is a positive development of recent years that many States have become much more willing than they were in the past to permit the parties to the proceedings in the requesting State to do the questioning themselves and to permit procedural rules of the requesting State to be applied during the process. Another welcome development is the emergence of transnational video- or audioconferences as an effective means of questioning witnesses who are not willing to travel to a court of law in the requesting State.[13]

4. Conditions and Obstacles

Finally, a few remarks should be made on the most common conditions for and obstacles to international cooperation in criminal matters.

A number of States traditionally make the rendering of certain forms of assistance conditional on the existence of a treaty. The treaty requirement is especially common where extradition and transfer of enforcement of criminal judgements are concerned. These States will probably not consider Article VII of the Chemical Weapons Convention to provide a sufficient basis for rendering these forms of assistance. In quite a few multilateral treaties regarding specific transnational crimes, provisions can be found declaring that a State Party may, at its option, consider the treaty itself as a legal basis for cooperation. Article 16 of the United Nations Convention Against Transnational Organised Crime follows these examples where extradition is concerned, and this might have consequences for the application of the Chemical Weapons Convention.

An even more common, indeed probably universal, condition for rendering assistance is that the acts in question constitute criminal offences in the laws of both the requesting and requested State. Exceptions to this requirement are usually only made in the rendering of mutual assistance not involving the application of coercive measures. This requirement of dual criminality should present no particular problems where the Chemical Weapons Convention is concerned. If the States Parties to the Convention have implemented the Convention properly, they will have legislation in place making the activities summed up in Article I criminal offences. Moreover, from the 1998 survey of national implementing legislation conducted by the Secretariat of the Organisation for the Prohibition of Chemical Weapons, one gets the general impression that States Parties have made these activities

[13] See, for instance, the very detailed rules on the matter in the recent Convention on Mutual Assistance in Criminal Matters between the Member States of the European Union, Brussels, 29 May 2000, Official Journal of the European Community 2000 C 397/7.

offences punishable by the maximum deprivation of liberty that would enable them to extradite the person requested.

May the traditional exception for political offences also be invoked where crimes under the Chemical Weapons Convention are concerned? In my view, it may not. This is particularly true in the criminalization of the use of chemical weapons under general international law -- a crime which all States have a common interest in repressing as guardians of the international legal order. I believe that, in the past few decades, many important developments have taken place warranting the conclusion that a rule of customary international law has emerged forbidding States to invoke the political offence exception as a justification for refusing to cooperate with other States in repressing crimes under general international law. Recently, the Appeals Chamber of the ICTY confirmed the existence of such a rule in an *obiter dictum* in its decision in *Prosecutor v. Anto Furundzija.*[14] If that is the situation in international law regarding the use of chemical weapons, what could be valid reasons to refuse to cooperate with other States where the other crimes of Article I of the Chemical Weapons Convention are involved, even if it is true that they constitute international crimes only by virtue of the Convention? As far as the protection of individual persons against unfair and partisan justice in the requesting State is concerned, one of the traditional rationales for the political offence exception, that aim can and should be pursued by other means.

This brings me to the protection of individual human rights as a necessary, un-transgressable limit to international cooperation. Recent decades have seen the gradual emergence of a general principle that interstate cooperation in criminal matters should be refused if granting cooperation would result in a violation of a person's internationally protected basic rights by the requesting State, or is likely to have that effect. International bodies, such as the European Court of Human Rights and the United Nations Human Rights Committee, have played an important part in developing that principle. This principle is explicitly recognised in a rapidly growing number of international instruments regarding cooperation in criminal matters. In my view, the UN Convention against Transnational Organised Crime could have paid more attention to these developments.

Finally, it is common practice in the field of mutual assistance in the investigation and prosecution of criminal offences to refuse cooperation if granting it is likely to prejudice the sovereignty, security, *ordre public* or other essential interests of the requested State. This exception is, for instance, included in Article 18(21) of the UN Convention against Transnational Organised Crime. Given the extremely sensitive nature of the matter dealt with by the Chemical Weapons Convention, this is probably the exception that will create the most frequent obstacles to Convention-based cooperation. States may have valid reasons for invoking the exception in specific cases, but it may also happen that they make use of it as a pretext for not rendering assistance. Since I am not at all familiar with the law on chemical weapons, I am unable to suggest solutions. All I can say is that States Parties should carefully watch practices that may have developed on the basis of the Convention and try to find remedies if there appears to be a need for them.

[14] Appeals Chamber ICTY 10 December 1998, Case No. IT-95-17/1-T, para. 157.

LEGAL ASSISTANCE: THE CHEMICAL WEAPONS CONVENTION AND COMPLEMENTARY AGREEMENTS

Cecil Hunt*

1. Introduction

Cooperation amongst States Parties to facilitate implementation of their treaty obligations may involve more than law enforcement activities directed at violators of treaty related laws, but it is this law enforcement context that is addressed in this chapter, as it is, more broadly, in this volume. More specifically, my focus is on the potential impact of the Chemical Weapons Convention[1] (hereinafter, "Convention") on State action against non-State actors that violate the prohibitions and rules that States Parties maintain pursuant to their Convention obligations. I refer in this chapter to "terrorists" engaged in "terrorist activity." This usage is, in part, for brevity and convenience. Use of the terms also reflects an expectation that the instances in which the mechanisms for Convention-related legal assistance will be most needed will be those that relate in some way to what may properly be characterised as terrorism.

2. Legal Assistance under the Chemical Weapons Convention

I believe that it is right to state at the outset my view that, from the perspective of international law enforcement, the legal assistance language in the Convention leaves much to be desired.

Paragraph 2 of Article VII of the Convention reads:

> Each State Party shall cooperate with other States Parties and afford the appropriate form of legal assistance to facilitate the implementation of the obligations under paragraph 1.[2]

The use of the word "shall" establishes the obligatory character of this provision, but, beyond this, the scope and effect of the obligation are unspecified.

* Harris, Wiltshire & Grannis LLP, Washington, DC. This chapter was written while the author was serving as Deputy Chief Counsel for Export Administration, United States Department of Commerce. This chapter represents the personal views of the author, and it is not an official statement or interpretation of legal provisions nor of government policy.

[1] 1993 Convention on the Prohibition of the Development, Production, Stockpiling and Use of Chemical Weapons and on Their Destruction, entered into force on 29 April 1997. Text, as corrected and changed, available at http://www.opcw.org.

[2] Convention, *supra* note 1, art. VII. 2.

R. Yepes-Enríquez and L. Tabassi. (eds.), Treaty Enforcement and International Cooperation in Criminal Matters

The "obligations" under paragraph 1 of Article VII are the national implementation measures that each State Party is to adopt. Essentially, these are the necessary legislative measures, including enactment of penal legislation, to prohibit persons within the described jurisdictional reach from undertaking activity prohibited to a State Party. Commentators have observed that cooperation with respect to such preparatory activity might take the form of the harmonisation of projected legislation or the development of model legislation and regulations.[3]

Can we conclude that the obligation under the Convention to cooperate and afford legal assistance extends beyond such preparatory work and into the area of operational law enforcement activity? I have found nothing in the Convention negotiating history that sheds light on this question.

Textual analysis of paragraphs 1 and 2 of Article VII suggests to me, however, that "the appropriate form of legal assistance" does involve such legal assistance as that relating to the obtaining of evidence for criminal prosecution and the apprehension of alleged offenders. I must acknowledge, however, that the textual support for this conclusion is not perfectly clear.

First, I would note that, although the measures that are specified in paragraph 1 appear to be confined to legislative and regulatory action, the use of the term "in particular" implies that such specification is not intended to *confine* the scope of the phrase "necessary measures to implement ... obligations under this Convention" to legislative and regulatory action.

Further, I believe that the use in paragraph 2 of both the term "cooperate" and the phrase "afford the appropriate form of legal assistance" is significant. The term "cooperate" would have sufficed to refer to the efforts involved in preparing and harmonising legal texts. Elsewhere in the Convention the terms "cooperate" and "cooperation" are used without reference to "legal assistance."[4] I think that the addition of the term "legal assistance" in paragraph 2 indicates intent to connote the normal sense of international legal assistance. In specific cases, such assistance could relate to various types of action, such as investigation, detention of suspects, and prosecution.

3. Other Agreements

This sole Convention provision on legal assistance appears to be disappointingly modest and imprecise when contrasted with provisions in some treaties directed at terrorist activity.[5] A useful indicator of what *might* have been included in the Convention in support of law enforcement can be found in the 1998 International Convention for the Suppression of Terrorist Bombings (hereinafter the "Terrorist Bombings Convention").[6] This convention

[3] Walter Krutzsch and Ralf Trapp, A Commentary on the Chemical Weapons Convention, 117-118 (1994).

[4] See, e.g., Article VII para. 3, Article I, Article IX, para. 1.

[5] A sense of the extent of the adherence to these instruments can be gained from the table entitled "Comparison of Parties to the Instruments Used in Compiling the Draft Optional Protocol relating to Article VII, paragraph 2, of the Chemical Weapons Convention" contained in Annex VI to this volume.

[6] United Nations International Convention for the Suppression of Terrorist Bombings, opened for signature at New York, 12 January 1998; entered into force 21 May 2001, 37 ILM 249.

and others are emerging in response to United Nations General Assembly resolution 51/210 of 17 December 1996 that initiated steps to establish a comprehensive legal framework of conventions dealing with international terrorism.

Let me note in abbreviated form the pertinent elements contained in the Terrorist Bombings Convention:

- The defined offences must be *criminalised* under domestic law, irrespective of the motivation of the perpetrator, and be made punishable by penalties appropriate to the grave nature of the offences;
- Each State Party must take such measures as may be necessary to establish its basic jurisdiction over these offences and may extend its jurisdiction to a specifically stated and expansive extent that includes the "passive personality" principle;
- Upon receipt of information that an alleged offender is within its territory, a State Party shall investigate the facts and, if warranted, ensure, as appropriate, that person's presence for prosecution or extradition; and,
- States Parties shall afford one another "the greatest measure" of assistance in criminal investigations, prosecutions, and extraditions, including assistance in obtaining evidence.

The Terrorist Bombings Convention has various provisions for facilitating extradition, bars refusal of extradition on political offence grounds, and imposes an "extradite or prosecute" requirement. It also provides for prisoner transfer to assist in investigation or prosecution of covered offences.

In due time, when the Terrorist Bombings Convention has gained broad participation, it could serve to overcome, to a great extent, the absence of specific legal assistance obligations in the Chemical Weapons Convention. It is noteworthy that this more recent convention defines offences that cover conduct that is also outlawed pursuant to the Chemical Weapons Convention. The Terrorist Bombings Convention applies to the delivery, placement, discharge, or detonation of an explosive "or other lethal device". The definition includes a weapon or device that has the capability to cause death, injury, or substantial material damage through, *inter alia*, the release of toxic chemicals. The offences covered by this convention include attempts and conspiracy. It seems possible, therefore, that, when States that are parties to both conventions are dealing with one another regarding conduct that both have outlawed in accordance with the two conventions, the more specific legal assistance provisions of the Terrorist Bombings Convention would be available and would be invoked.

The modest Chemical Weapons Convention provisions on legal assistance should also be viewed in light of the political significance of the Convention and against the background of other legal assistance agreements to which States Parties to the Convention are party. Consider, for example, how the Convention may interact with the 1976 European Convention on the Suppression of Terrorism. That convention requires that Contracting States afford one another "the widest measure" of mutual assistance in criminal matters involving covered offences. Assistance may not be refused on the sole ground that it concerns a "political offence", but the requested State may refuse assistance if it has substantial grounds for believing that the race, religion, nationality or political opinion of the accused prompts the charges or may prejudice the position of the accused in the proceeding.[7]

The very existence of the Chemical Weapons Convention, however, makes it less likely that legal assistance would be refused according to this "out" in the European Terrorism Convention in a case involving chemical weapons related activity prohibited by the Chemical Weapons Convention. Every State Party has undertaken to outlaw, within its jurisdiction, the acquisition, retention, transfer, or use of toxic chemicals and their precursors except for purposes not prohibited under the Convention. This mutual outlawing of defined conduct should serve to give chemical weapons-related requests for legal assistance a presumption of legitimacy. This shared condemnation of chemical weapons should serve also to place a heavy burden on a requested State Party that might consider challenging the request as being one that has been prompted or prejudiced by discriminatory considerations.

4. Extradition and the Political Offence Exception

Although the Chemical Weapons Convention contains no reference to extradition, the existence of the Convention could help in providing for extradition. First, by fulfilling their obligation under the Convention to extend their penal legislation to prohibited activity, the States Parties may satisfy, regarding extradition requests between them, any "dual criminality" requirement contained in national legislation or applicable international agreement. I say that a dual criminality requirement "may" be satisfied. This is because the use of the term "penal" legislation in paragraph 1(a) of Article VII of the Convention has been said to have been understood by the negotiators to encompass criminal, civil and/or administrative legislation, so long as penalties are involved.[8] The United States implementing legislation provides for both criminal and civil penalties.[9]

Another important consideration is the impact of the Chemical Weapons Convention on the "political offence" basis for refusing an extradition request. Whether the political offence exception is being defined by reference to the criminal actor's political motivation or by reference to the nexus of the criminal conduct to a political disturbance, it can reasonably be asserted that the exception should not apply when the crime involves activity prohibited pursuant to the Convention. When the requesting and requested States are parties to the Convention, they have agreed to exercise their jurisdiction to outlaw chemical weapons related activity. These are offences that can be objectively defined. Given this, it is hard to conceive of a requested State finding that it is in its own interest to give weight to the motive or context of a person's attempt to acquire weapons which that State Party has itself given up.

---

[7] See European Convention on the Suppression of Terrorism, 15 I.L.M. 1272 (1976), signed by 17 member states of the Council of Europe, Strasbourg. 27 January 1977, 16 I.L.M. 233 (1997), art. 8.

[8] See United States Senate Treaty Doc. 103-21, Article-by-Article Analysis, p. 40, accompanying the 20 November 1993 Letter of Submittal from the Acting Secretary State to the President, accompanying the 23 November 1993 transmittal of the Convention by the President to the Senate for its advice and consent to ratification).

[9] See Chemical Weapons Convention Implementation Act of 1998, Pub. L. 105-277, Div. I, Title II, Subtitle A, section 201(a) adding section 229 A to Title 18 United States Code.

5. Universal Jurisdiction

Notwithstanding the broad participation in the Convention, there remains the possibility that a government will need to take enforcement action against a non-state actor that is neither a national of nor operating within the territory of a State Party. Consider this scenario: a terrorist group operating in an Asian country that is not a party to the Convention obtains precursor chemicals in that country and produces a chemical weapon. Authorities in the United States obtain evidence of this activity and they alert the government of a European party to the Convention. The European government then apprehends a participant in the weapons project as the person is travelling through that European country. What effect, if any, does the Convention have on the ability of either that European government or of government of the United States to punish that participant in chemical weapons activity? The answer may depend upon the applicability of the concept of universal jurisdiction.

The preamble to the Convention includes the declaration that the States Parties are, "Determined for the sake of all mankind, to exclude completely the possibility of the use of chemical weapons...".[10] The Convention goes on to bar not only the use of chemical weapons, but also the development or possession of such weapons. Can the broad adherence to the Convention be said to establish the development and possession of chemical weapons as "offences recognised by the community of nations as of universal concern"?[11] This is language used to describe "universal crimes",[12] as to which a State has jurisdiction to define and adjudicate with respect to conduct that has no special jurisdictional links to that State. The Restatement of Foreign Relations Law of the United States says that "perhaps [certain acts of] terrorism" are recognised as universal offences. The comment to section 404 of the Restatement says that there has been wide condemnation of terrorism, but it notes that inability to agree on a definition of the offence has been an obstacle to international agreements to punish terrorism.[13] However, this definitional difficulty should not be an obstacle to characterising as a universal offence any chemical weapons-related conduct that is outlawed under the Convention. Again, this is because the Convention deals with conduct that is objectively defined without regard to motivation or circumstances.

Whatever the ability of the European State in the scenario to prosecute the accused offender under its laws, the United States would not be able to do so if that person were apprehended in or brought to the United States. Although international law is law of the United States, an international offence must be defined under and the punishment established by United States statutory law before it can be prosecuted in US courts.[14] In implementing the Convention, the US Congress extended penal jurisdiction no further than the Convention required, reaching conduct in the United States, conduct by or against a US national, wherever occurring, and conduct committed against property, wherever located, that is owned, leased, or used by the United States.[15] Jurisdiction without such links — that

---

[10] Convention, *supra* note 1, at Preamble.

[11] Restatement (third) Foreign Relations Law of the United States section 404 (1987). See Theodor Meron, International Criminalization of Internal Atrocities, 89 AJIL 554, 568-574 (1995).

[12] Restatement, *supra* note 10, section 423.

[13] *Id.*, section 404 cmt. A.

[14] See *U.S. v. Hudson and Goodwin*, 11 U.S. (7 Cranch) 32, 34 (1812).

[15] See Act, *supra*, note 8, section 201(a), article 229(c).

is, universal jurisdiction — has been provided by U.S. legislation for the universal offences of aircraft piracy and hostage taking.[16]

6. Conclusion

The intensity of the abhorrence of chemical weapons is such that it seems likely that there would be political support in the legislatures of States Parties to go beyond the requirements of the Convention and to enact strong provisions with respect to jurisdiction, extradition, and legal assistance.

One possible explanation for the absence of strong and specific Convention provisions in support of law enforcement assistance is that the primary focus of the Convention is on prohibitions and requirements directed at the conduct of States Parties. The Article VII obligation on each State Party to take implementation measures to reach natural and legal persons could have been seen as important, but ancillary. In contrast, conventions such as those on air piracy, hostage taking, and terrorism had their focus on the conduct not of States but of individuals, so it could be expected that these conventions would place greater emphasis on how individual violators could be brought to justice.

The following observations are offered in closing. The generality of Article VII, paragraph 2, should not lead us to conclude that the Chemical Weapons Convention is not significant with respect to the prospects for international legal assistance in dealing with individual conduct that is outlawed under the Convention. The establishment of these offences in the domestic law of States Parties will support the use of extradition and legal assistance tools that are already provided for in national law or international agreement or practice. Viewing the Convention as having confirmed that the use or attempted use of a chemical weapon is a universal offence, States Parties should be prepared to exercise their jurisdiction over an alleged perpetrator found within their territory even if other jurisdictional bases are absent. Finally, a State Party should view participation in the Convention as precluding a "political offence" refusal of extradition in a chemical weapons case.

Hopefully these observations will point to how the Convention can work in combination with other legal bases to support international legal assistance for enforcement. I hope, further, that there will be a greater effort in future negotiations to integrate appropriately specific legal assistance obligations into existing and new treaties that seek to protect humanity against outrageous weapons and conduct.

[16] See 49 U.S.C. section 46502 (b)(2).

NATIONAL LEGISLATION TO IMPLEMENT LEGAL ASSISTANCE AND COOPERATION

Barry Kellman*

1. Introduction

It could not be more timely and important that an international weapons control organisation is raising the subject of legal assistance and cooperation. Our task is to consider the briefly stated obligation contained in the Chemical Weapons Convention[1] ("Convention") Article VII, paragraph 2 to "cooperate with other States Parties and afford the appropriate form of legal assistance..." This oblique requirement, containing terms that are well-known to international lawyers, implicates as-yet unfulfilled capabilities for international efforts to preclude use of weapons of mass destruction. Yet, international lawyers should focus not only on the abstract significance of these treaty terms; it is incumbent to consider the disappointment of their actual implementation.

The purpose of a legal assistance and cooperation obligation arises from the risk of clandestine or criminal weapons programs. Illegal syndicates might split production of lethal agents among numerous facilities in various nations, complicating detection. In this event, OPCW inspectors would only detect discrete, seemingly innocuous operations in each State but might overlook the overall scheme. The problem is worsened by the dynamic international trade in chemicals; many participants engage in transnational activities either by operating affiliates or by extensive contractual arrangements with other firms in foreign jurisdictions.

We need only remember Aum Shinrikyo's chemical weapons attack in the Tokyo subway system on 10 March 1995.[2] The group punctured bags of sarin nerve gas on subway trains, killing 12 people and injuring more than 5,000. Subsequent investigations revealed sophisticated facilities, plans, and materials to produce and disseminate both chemical and biological agents. This attack should serve as a clarion call to anyone concerned for public safety and international security. Precursor chemicals are easy to get, and fashioning them into a crude terrorist device is within the competence of many groups. Using chemical weapons offers significant advantages to terrorists — a point further developed in the chapters on terrorism in this book.

Significantly, the legal assistance and cooperation obligation was included in the Convention because the negotiators realised that national chemical weapons programs are not the only problem needing to be addressed. Indeed, all of Article VII is designed to

* Co-Director, International Criminal Justice and Weapons Control Center, DePaul University College of Law, Chicago.

[1] 1993 Convention on the Prohibition of the Development, Production, Stockpiling and Use of Chemical Weapons and on Their Destruction, entered into force on 29 April 1997. Text, as corrected and changed, available at http://www.opcw.org.

[2] See *infra*, Y. Seto, Forensic Investigation of the Sarin Gas Attacks in Japan.

R. Yepes-Enríquez and L. Tabassi. (eds.), Treaty Enforcement and International Cooperation in Criminal Matters

expand the treaty's prohibitions to reach the conduct of private persons and subnational groups. Each State Party must enact penal legislation to prohibit anyone within its jurisdiction from undertaking activities that would violate the treaty if undertaken by the State. But the importance of extending the treaty's reach to private conduct was corralled by a second realisation: the Chemical Weapons Convention is a disarmament and non-proliferation treaty, not an international criminal law enforcement pact, much less an elaborately developed counterterrorism initiative. The negotiators, therefore, included an obligation for States Parties to assist and cooperate in law enforcement, but endowed that obligation with virtually no elaboration or definition.

It should also be noted that among other multilateral weapons control treaties, a legal assistance and cooperation obligation is contained only in the Convention on the Physical Protection of Nuclear Material, a treaty which overtly deals with threats of theft and other criminal activity. Thus, the weapons control community, in contrast to those who combat the international narcotics trade or international crime generally, has scant frame of reference for this obligation.

It is in this context that we must consider not only the unprecedented legal potential of the Article VII obligation but also the unimpressive condition of its implementation. Starkly put: over 75 percent of the world's nations have joined the Chemical Weapons Convention; less than half of those have drafted implementing legislation. Of these nations, the overwhelming majority are not States Parties to multilateral weapons control treaties except perhaps the Treaty on the Non-Proliferation of Nuclear Weapons or the Biological Weapons Convention, neither of which contain legal assistance and cooperation obligations. Moreover, the overwhelming majority of States Parties to the Chemical Weapons Convention are not parties to the various highly-developed legal cooperation agreements that require many of the nations of Europe and North America to establish formal modalities for such cooperation. Thus, for many if not most States Parties to the Convention, the Article VII legal assistance and cooperation obligation is novel both for their executive bodies that focus on weapons control and non-proliferation as well as their executive bodies that focus on international criminality. Most important of all, States Parties have, with barely a few exceptions (to my knowledge, only one), wholly ignored this obligation, leaving its practical implications in serious doubt.

To understand the current confused condition of legal cooperation, two questions deserve analysis. First, how is "illegal activity" defined so as to trigger the performance of legal assistance and cooperation obligations under the Convention? Second, once it is determined that relevant obligations have been triggered, how are they to be performed and by whom?

2. Illegal Activities that Trigger Legal Assistance and Cooperation

For a State Party to the Convention to provide legal assistance and cooperation to another State Party with respect to alleged illegal activity, the conduct in question must be illegal under the national laws of both States. Satisfaction of this basic requirement — double criminality — in connection with the Convention, however, is not as simple as it sounds.

Initially, it should be noted that Article VII requires each State Party to enact legislation to prohibit "any activity prohibited" under the Convention, but the term "any activity prohibited" is otherwise undefined in the Convention. There should be little question that the term includes conduct that contravenes the requirements of Article I; and virtually every State Party that has enacted implementing legislation under the Convention includes a provision that prohibits development, production, or use of chemical weapons or engagement in preparations for use, or assisting other States Parties in such conduct.[3] Thus, if a group is found to directly engage in chemical weapons activities and if legal assistance and cooperation is necessary for apprehension or prosecution, there should be little difficulty in establishing double criminality.

But more problems arise if the conduct in question is not so overtly associated with chemical weapons. For example, consider the Convention limitation, contained in Part VI of the Verification Annex, on production, acquisition, retention, or use of Schedule 1 chemicals. Assume that a commercial entity produces a Schedule 1 chemical in excess of those limitations but is otherwise not engaged in any activity that could be construed as involving an Article I violation. Clearly, the State Party having jurisdiction over that entity would be in violation of this limitation, yet only a few States Parties have enacted domestic legal provisions to criminalise overproduction of Schedule 1 chemicals. If the host State Party has not made such activities illegal and if another State Party is investigating a multinational chemical weapons plot for which it requests legal assistance, the absence of double criminality could be a barrier to pursuing that investigation effectively.

This problem is compounded by the fact that few States Parties have enacted domestic legal provisions to criminalise exports of scheduled chemicals which are not in compliance with relevant Convention restrictions. For example, Schedule 1 chemicals "shall not be retransferred to a third State."[4] It is likely that a private entity engaged in a multinational conspiracy would violate this restriction, yet the fact that only a handful of States Parties have criminalised such conduct would complicate the efficacy of legal assistance.

A somewhat different problem is raised by violation of verification obligations. Consider the possibility that a private entity provides false information or tampers with OPCW monitoring equipment. Suppose further that another State Party suspects that entity's involvement in a broad conspiracy but does not want to make use of the Convention provisions for a challenge inspection lest its investigation be exposed. While all States Parties with implementing legislation recognise their obligation to comply with verification modalities, not all have not enacted penal provisions that would render the private entity's conduct illegal. Once again, the efficient use of legal assistance capabilities could fall victim to the fact that, under relevant domestic law, private interference with verification obligations is not illegal in both States.

A potential answer to these concerns are domestic penal provisions that address "organised crime" or "terrorism" or "criminal conspiracy" generally. If a State Party's penal laws are sufficiently broad to obviate the need for additional prohibitions in its implementing legislation under the Convention and specifically provide for legal assistance and cooperation modalities, then the problems heretofore mentioned may be resolvable. But not all States Parties criminalise participation in an international plot to develop weapons of mass destruction. In the absence of such criminal provisions, of course, the Convention's legal

[3] See OPCW Survey of National Implementing Legislation, OPCW doc. S/259/2001 (16 May 2001).
[4] Verification Annex to the Convention, Part VI, para.4.

assistance and cooperation obligations cannot be fulfilled in connection with other international law enforcement activities.

A similar point can be made with respect to nations which, by ratification of the Convention, automatically adopt it as part of their domestic legal framework. For such States Parties, it might be argued that specific legislation to implement the legal assistance and cooperation obligation would be redundant: its inclusion in the treaty and the treaty's adoption into domestic law suffice to give the obligation full force and effect in domestic law. There is no need to take issue with this abstract legal proposition here, except to ask whether such automatic adoption brings with it devotion of sufficient capabilities to actually carry out relevant obligations should that be necessary — a point to be elaborated momentarily.

Another problem is that of the "political offence exception." The essential concern is that "terrorist" groups propound an agenda that might find a sympathetic ear in some nations; such groups will usually seek refuge or hide in such a sympathetic State. If legal assistance and cooperation is thwarted by invocation of the political offence exception, it will be impossible for the requesting State to proceed against such individuals without violating some aspect of international law, in particular Article 2(4) of the Charter of the United Nations and the prohibition against aggression. In order to avoid jurisprudential confusion and inconsistencies, legislative criteria should be set forth determining what the political offence exception is, excluding therefrom international crimes.

3. Performance of Legal Assistance and Cooperation Obligations

The actual carrying out of legal assistance and cooperation obligations is complex under the best of circumstances — a condition that will be addressed in detail elsewhere in this book. Essentially, the requesting State, by asking another State to undertake some law enforcement activity, is seeking to intrude on the requested State's sovereignty over law enforcement within its jurisdiction by availing itself of the services of a typically overburdened administrative capability. Even where such capabilities are abundant, differences among legal systems — such as between civil and common law systems — render the performance of legal assistance and cooperation obligations highly problematic.

In order to make such performance more effective, bilateral or regional arrangements have been negotiated which specify relative rights and obligations; where such arrangements exist, the complexity of this process has at least been addressed in advance of the actual request, and procedures to carry out obligations have been stipulated. To repeat a point made earlier, to the extent that the Convention's legal assistance and cooperation obligation can be folded within existing elaborations of legal assistance generally, cooperation as to chemical weapons activities should be more effective.

In the absence of such an arrangement, however, requests for legal assistance must be transmitted through the diplomatic channels. The judicial authority conducting the criminal proceeding for which the cooperation of the foreign state is required refers the request to its foreign ministry through the official channel prescribed by local rules. The request is then communicated via the embassy of the State in which the request for judicial assistance is sought to be executed, to the foreign ministry of the requested State and from there dispatched to the authority or court considered competent to execute it. It is at this point that the unique aspects of legal assistance in connection with the Chemical Weapons Convention arise.

Consider again the potential scenario: authorities in one State suspect that non-state actors are engaged in a conspiracy to develop chemical weapons, and that conspiracy extends to other States' jurisdictions. For either political reasons or because of concerns for divulging the nascent investigation, the suspicious authorities choose not to make use of the Convention's procedures that apply to such situations and instead seek the assistance of another State's authorities. Initially, a crucial question is whether such authorities include only traditional law enforcement officials. More likely, because of the need to link information about production, acquisition, and consumption of sophisticated chemicals with evidence of a criminal conspiracy, it is advisable if not inevitable that the investigation will include the respective national authorities established under the Convention.

While every State Party must establish a national authority, the treaty itself says little about their structure and composition. Moreover, while every State Party has extensive obligations to fulfil, it is not mandatory that its national authority be the entity to fulfil them. The Convention requires that the national authority serve as liaison, but virtually all other obligations may be carried out by any administrative agency. Furthermore, the national authority may be a newly-established agency, an already existing agency, or a working group made up of representatives of other agencies or offices. Moreover, there is considerable variation as to the power of the national authority, ranging from mere ministerial responsibilities to supreme oversight of treaty compliance. In sum, national authorities vary among nations depending on the dictates of national law; indeed, the range of options is quite dramatic.

Most national authorities are located within ministries of foreign relations or of international trade. In no instance is a national authority located within a law enforcement agency, and in only a remarkably few instances do representatives of a nation's law enforcement services have any formal connection to the national authority whatsoever. It seems likely therefore, that a request for legal assistance and cooperation on matters pertaining to chemical weapons will face a bureaucratic hurdle, in addition to the hurdles that already apply to assistance requests generally, as national law enforcement agencies strive to gain relevant information from their own national authority in order to respond to the request.

Another problem here concerns access to and use of highly confidential information gathered pursuant to the Convention's extensive verification obligations. Indeed, no weapons control convention demands information of comparable quality and sensitivity from private enterprises. This phenomenon has been extensively analysed by the OPCW and discussed in academic and trade journals. At its essence, the potential problem can be put as follows: in order that private entities willingly cooperate with Convention verification measures and that domestic legal challenges do not impede State compliance, domestic implementing legislation should narrowly confine both access to and use of Convention-relevant information. That is, information that is declared pursuant to Convention requirements or discovered during inspections should be seen only by those officials who have a Convention-related reason for looking at that information and should only be used for the purpose of complying with treaty obligations.

If Convention-relevant information is disseminated more broadly or used for additional purposes, then enterprises will resist providing that information and will initiate legal challenges to compliance efforts. For this reason, many State Parties have, in connection with their national implementing legislation under the Convention, included provisions that strictly regulate who receives information and the purposes that the information may serve. Manifestly, the use of information declared pursuant to a Convention obligation for conducting penal investigations would undermine this complex system for protecting the information's confidentiality. Consider the reaction of a private chemical enterprise upon learning that its extremely valuable and sensitive proprietary information, which has been reported pursuant to Convention compliance obligations, may be handed over to another State Party upon a request for legal assistance and cooperation.

The point here is that even in the best situation — where the investigated activities are manifestly criminal under the domestic laws of both States and where both States have capabilities to fulfil relevant obligations — the execution of a request for mutual legal assistance and cooperation in regard to chemical weapons will focus, centrally if not exclusively, on dissimilar national authorities that are disconnected to law enforcement officials within the same government and will implicate specific information that, in many States, law enforcement officials would be denied access to but which is available only for the remarkably unique purpose of verifying compliance with the Convention. And these complications will often take place in the many States Parties that substantially lack established and effective capabilities for meeting even the most basic legal assistance and cooperation obligations. And, finally and most important, for virtually all States Parties, relevant legislation provides not a word of guidance or support.

4. Conclusion

By including a legal assistance and cooperation obligation in the Convention, the negotiators took a bold step toward joining weapons control to counterterrorism, and by drawing attention to this subject, the OPCW recognises the importance of that step. That said, the negotiators left to each State Party the task of making that obligation meaningful and effective.

Perhaps the concerns raised here are all much ado about nothing. Of the 145 States Parties, it is unlikely that more than a small percentage, perhaps 5%, will either request or receive a request for legal assistance. Because the triggering condition of a request would be suspicions of criminal chemical weapons activities, we certainly share the profound hope that legal assistance is never needed. And even in the rare circumstance that legal assistance regarding chemical activities is sought, many States Parties have in place bilateral arrangements or are parties to a regional treaty that establishes relevant procedures and which has already compelled member States to develop modalities for responding to such requests. For the many States Parties who are not already members of such arrangements and do not have established procedures for making or processing legal assistance requests, setting up such capabilities may not be worth the bureaucratic costs to deal with a potentiality that is unlikely to occur, at least in the near term.

Thus, each State Party to the Convention faces a cost/benefit choice of whether implementing Article VII's obligation to provide appropriate legal assistance and cooperation is worth the effort and expense. In view of the fact that only one State Party's implementing legislation refers to this obligation, the cost/benefit choice of most States Parties is clear.

Yet, it must be noted that if an individual or group or enterprise engages in illegal chemical weapons activities for which international legal assistance could be valuable to uncover and prevent, it will be far too late at that moment to develop the requisite capabilities. Phrased somewhat differently, States Parties, to fulfil their Article VII obligation, need to enact requisite legal authorisations and expend current resources now to have sufficient capabilities when and if they are needed. In this respect, a failure to plan could spell an inability to prevent catastrophe.

PARALLELS: AN OVERVIEW OF COOPERATION AND ENFORCEMENT INITIATIVES UNDER THE 1988 NARCOTICS CONVENTION

John C. Ploeg and Robert Delonis*

1. Introduction

International cooperation is an essential component of the prevention or prosecution of many types of crime. Several forms of mutual legal assistance centre around the exchange of information as their main means of preventing crime, whether that be in monitoring, international police cooperation or customs enforcement. In considering the practical aspects of implementation of cooperation and legal assistance under Article VII, paragraph 2, of the 1993 Chemical Weapons Convention (CWC),[1] it is useful to examine the experience gained under precursor legislation to implement and enforce the 1988 Narcotics Convention.[2]

The non-proliferation pillar of the Chemical Weapons Convention is based upon, and requires States Parties to, regulate and monitor the flow of the toxic chemicals and precursors that could be used to produce chemical weapons. Prevention of illicit traffic in narcotics also involves regulating and monitoring the flow of chemicals and precursors that could be used to manufacture narcotics illegally. Many States Parties have already enacted legislation, and channels are operating both nationally and internationally, to monitor and control the flow of the chemicals and precursors covered under the chemical weapons and, even more so, narcotics control regimes.

This chapter examines the system in place to implement the 1988 Narcotics Convention, both internationally and in the Netherlands specifically. It also considers whether some of that system can be adapted or used as a model to implement similar aspects of the Chemical Weapons Convention.

* John C. Ploeg is a Policy Advisor in the Chemicals Unit, Economic Investigations Agency of the Netherlands Ministry of Finance. Robert Delonis is a student at New York University School of Law and an Intern in the OPCW Technical Secretariat Office of the Legal Adviser, and the Media and Public Affairs Branch of the External Relations Division. The authors gratefully acknowledge the assistance of Catherine Volz, Chief, Treaty, Legal Affairs and Commission, Secretariat Branch, United Nations Office for Drug Control and Crime Prevention; Els Brands, Department of International and Legal Policy Affairs, Netherlands Ministry of Defence; and Lisa Tabassi, OPCW Technical Secretariat Office of the Legal Adviser, for their assistance and input in the preparation of this chapter. The views expressed are the authors' own and are not attributable to the Netherlands Ministry of Finance, New York University or the OPCW.

[1] 1993 Convention on the Prohibition of the Development, Production, Stockpiling and Use of Chemical Weapons and on Their Destruction, entered into force on 29 April 1997. Text, as corrected and changed, available at http://www.opcw.org.

[2] United Nations Convention against Illicit Traffic in Narcotic Drugs and Psychotropic Substances, Vienna, 20 December 1988, entered into force 11 November 1990. Text available at http://www.incb.org.

R. Yepes-Enríquez and L. Tabassi. (eds.), Treaty Enforcement and International Cooperation in Criminal Matters

2. THE 1988 NARCOTICS CONVENTION: OBLIGATIONS AND HISTORY

The cooperation obligations imposed by the 1988 Narcotics Convention and the Chemical Weapons Convention share much in common.[3] The major difference between them lies in the degree of detail. Article VII, paragraph 2 of the Chemical Weapons Convention states, "[e]ach State Party shall cooperate with other States Parties and afford the appropriate form of legal assistance to facilitate the implementation of the obligations [to enact penal legislation prohibiting activities prohibited by the Convention and extend it extraterritorially to their nationals; and to enforce the Convention]."

In contrast to this single sentence, the Narcotics Convention spells out its Parties' obligations in nine different Articles comprised of over fifty paragraphs, covering everything from evidence taking, service of judicial documents, searches and seizures to enforcement in free trade zones, at sea, and in the mail system.[4] But while these obligations are spelled out in greater detail than those in the CWC, the types of monitoring and specific practices they address would be identical to those implicitly required of CWC States Parties to meet their Article VI enforcement responsibilities[5] regarding the general purpose criterion.[6]

There is not yet an established practice in international cooperation and legal assistance in criminal matters under the Chemical Weapons Convention. A "National Authority" is being established in each State Party, and bilateral dialogues between the Technical Secretariat of the OPCW, the CWC implementing body, and between the National Authorities themselves, is beginning, but is still underdeveloped at present.

---

[3] See G.S. Pearson, *Further Chemical Control Regimes: Narcotic Drugs and Psychotropic Substances*, 51 The CBW Conventions Bulletin, Quarterly Journal of the Harvard Sussex Program on CBW Armament and Arms Limitation, 2 (March 2001).

[4] Article 6, Extradition; Article 7, Mutual legal assistance (see the subparagraphs to paragraph 2 for detailed obligations); Article 8, Transfer of proceedings; Article 9, Other forms of co-operation and training; Article 10, International co-operation and assistance for transit states; Article 15, Commercial Carriers; Article 17, Illicit traffic by sea; Article 18, Free trade zones and free ports; and Article 19, The use of the mails.

[5] Chemical Weapons Convention, Article VI, paragraph 2.

[6] Article II, paragraph 1(a) of the Chemical Weapons Convention includes, in the definition of "chemical weapons," "toxic chemicals and their precursors, except where intended for purposes not prohibited under [the] Convention, as long as types and quantities are consistent with such purposes." Thus the definition of chemical weapons is purpose-driven rather than based on a list of banned substances. The implication is that States Parties must monitor the uses to which *all* toxic chemicals and precursors are being put in their jurisdiction or territory under their control. See also, *infra* in this volume, D. Feakes, Challenges in the Implementation of Export Controls under the Chemical Weapons Convention, and G.S. Pearson, *The CWC General Purpose Criterion: How to Implement?*, 49 The CBW Conventions Bulletin, Quarterly Journal of the Harvard Sussex Program on CBW Armament and Arms Limitation, 1 (September 2000).

Established practices and mechanisms do exist, however, in the field of narcotics precursors to exchange information and enforce the Convention.[7] This greater development, compared to the chemical weapons control system, is a function of the conventions' histories. Prior to the 1997 entry into force of the Chemical Weapons Convention, controls for those relevant chemicals and precursors were primarily implemented by the Australia Group members since 1984,[8] and to a certain extent, by the States participating in the Wassenaar Arrangement since 1996[9] and its predecessor, COCOM.[10] As a result, there were no embryonic global chemical weapons institutions or general mechanisms to build upon.

In contrast, several multilateral instruments preceded the 1988 Narcotics Convention, including the 1961 Single Convention on Narcotic Drugs, as amended by the 1972 Protocol, and the 1971 Convention on Psychotropic Substances.[11] Controls and arrangements developed over time, including, as detailed below, the International Narcotics Control Board (INCB). By studying the products of this growth and development, the CWC regime can benefit from the narcotics control regime's past experiences.

3. Implementing the Narcotics Convention: Provisions, Institutions and Experiences

3.1 Convention Provisions

Article 12, paragraph 1, of the Narcotics Convention states that "[t]he Parties shall take measures they deem appropriate to prevent diversion of substances...used for the purpose of illicit manufacture of narcotic drugs or psychotropic substances, and shall co-operate with one another to this end." The means of fulfilling this general cooperative mandate are

[7] The scope of this chapter is precursor monitoring, but there are a number of other well developed areas of cooperation under the Narcotics Convention carried out through complementary agreements. For example, the Narcotics Convention prompted a new series of bilateral and regional legal assistance agreements covering, *inter alia*, mutual legal assistance, illicit trafficking at sea and seizure of assets. There are also a host of informal memoranda of understanding addressing law enforcement cooperation in narcotics control. Some of these agreements, such as those developed in the Council of Europe, particularly after the Narcotics Convention entered into force, are actually not narcotics specific and cover general cooperation in criminal matters. On this point see further, *infra*, H.-J. Bartsch, Overcoming Obstacles in Achieving Wide Adherence to Multilateral Instruments: Some Comments from the European Perspective. The most recent initiative is being developed by France, the Netherlands, the United Kingdom, the United States and a number of countries in the Caribbean concerning a possible regional treaty for the Caribbean to repress illicit narcotics traffic by sea. The proposed treaty would regulate maritime cooperation between Coast Guard, customs, police and other administrative officials.

[8] The Australia Group is an informal group of States which agreed to establish a set of export controls following reports of chemical weapons use in the Iran-Iraq war in 1984. See P. Rubenstein, *State Responsibility for Failure to Control the Export of Weapons of Mass Destruction*, 23 Cal. W. Int'l L.J. 319, 340 (1993); and R.J. Matthews, *A Comparison of the Australia Group List of Chemical Weapons Precursors and the CWC Schedules of Chemicals*, 21 The CBW Conventions Bulletin, Quarterly Journal of the Harvard Sussex Program on CBW Armament and Arms Limitation, 1 (September 1993).

[9] The Wassenaar Arrangement on Export Controls for Conventional Arms and Dual-Use Goods and Technologies, agreed in The Hague 29-30 March 1994 and established 11-12 July 1996. See http://www.wassenaar.org.

[10] Co-ordinating Committee for East-West Trade Policy, a Cold War regime and embargo which was dissolved on 31 March 1994. See SIPR Yearbook, 619-623 (1995).

[11] The texts are available online at http://www.incb.org.

later specified in Article 12, paragraph 9, to include the establishment of cooperative trade monitoring systems, substance seizure procedures, proper labelling and documentation procedures and, most relevant to this discussion, the notification of other States' national authorities of suspicious transfers, including the information that led to that suspicion.

Specific cooperation details are also discussed in Article 7, which addresses mutual legal assistance. Paragraph 1 is based upon the European Convention on Mutual Assistance in Criminal Matters and mandates assistance in "investigations, prosecutions and judicial proceedings in relation to criminal offences...."[12] The subsequent paragraphs spell out detailed obligations involved in this assistance, including, *inter alia*, taking evidence or statements, effecting service of process, executing searches and seizures, providing information, and providing documents, including bank documents and records.

Narcotics Convention Parties' implementation of their obligations under Articles 12 and 7 has opened many communication channels, both formal and informal, between States. While the Chemical Weapons Convention regime currently lacks any similar specific guidelines regarding the requirements of its cooperation channels, an Optional Protocol that addresses many of these matters has been proposed.[13]

3.2 AUTHORITIES, LEGISLATION AND AGREEMENTS

Cooperation in narcotics precursor matters occurs between States' national authorities and, in the Netherlands, is based on the Narcotics Convention, European Union legislation, regional and bilateral agreements, and national law. The National Authorities' actions cover a wide spectrum of governmental sectors, including customs, law enforcement and financial agencies (the latter involved in addressing economic crimes, for example, the laundering of the proceeds from drug sales). In the Netherlands, the Belastingdienst FIOD-ECD (Economic Investigations Agency, ECD), a division of the Ministry of Finance, employs investigators to monitor the flow of all the precursors listed in the Chemical Weapons Convention, *and* all those listed in the Narcotics Convention.[14] Trade in precursor chemicals is prohibited in the Netherlands unless a licence has been granted by the responsible Minister, and the ECD monitors by means of a "one inspection" system, during which all precursors are investigated simultaneously. The firms involved appreciate the system's efficiency and the simplicity of a single point of government contact.

The Netherlands' national legislation on narcotics chemical precursors, the Law for Prevention of Improper Use of Chemicals, is based on the 1988 Narcotics Convention. This system of national laws modelling a governing multilateral convention was followed

[12] Commentary on the United Nations Convention against Illicit Traffic in Narcotic Drugs and Psychotropic Substances, 177 (United Nations 1988).

[13] See, *infra* in this volume, L. Tabassi, Legal Assistance under the Chemical Weapons Convention: an Optional Protocol to the Convention?

[14] See the Chemical Weapons Convention, Annex on Chemicals, and the 1988 Drugs Convention, Tables I and II. See also, Precursors and chemicals frequently used in the illicit manufacture of narcotic drugs and psychotropic substances, Report of the International Narcotics Control Board for 2000 on the Implementation of Article 12 of the United Nations Convention against Illicit Traffic in Narcotic Drugs and Psychotropic Substances (United Nations, 2001).

by the Netherlands in its legislation to implement the Chemical Weapons Convention.[15] The statute includes stiff penalties for its violation: a prison sentence of up to 6 years or a fine up to 1 million guilders (approximately euros 454,000).

Internationally, the European Union ("Union," EU) is responsible for international trade with third countries and prevents internal rivalry between Union members. The EU is a Contracting Party to the Drugs Convention, has enacted legislation regarding chemical precursors,[16] and manages the exchange of information regarding precursors.[17] The EU has created bilateral agreements on precursor control with several countries, including the United States, and the agreements include provisions providing for the protection of sensitive information. The background instruments of general international criminal law also provide additional mechanisms of cooperation.

It is important to note that these cooperative agreements are characterised by informality and a high degree of trust. Direct communication between agencies is the most effective means of preventing or stopping illicit precursor chemical flows, but that communication is precluded when excessive bureaucracy prohibits timely investigation, or when the communicating parties do not trust each other enough to share all their relevant information. The practices of the Netherlands provide an example of how to avoid these pitfalls.

3.3 THE MONITORING PRACTICES OF THE NETHERLANDS

After the 1995 implementation of their national legislation, the first priority of the Netherlands Government was to register all the chemical companies and ensure that they manufacture and trade legally. Investigators were dispatched to explain the new law to all companies involved with chemical precursors. Careful monitoring then began, and the ECD developed its body of data so it now "knows" all the players in its chemical trade markets: the buyers, sellers, producers, and brokers, as well as what they do, import, export or produce. This data is used to perform detailed checks on firm behaviour, including monitoring the origin and destination of chemicals, the process line, the base of calculation, and even a firm's bookkeeping. Observation is needed on all these levels to make it extremely difficult to divert legitimate chemicals for illicit purposes.

ECD investigators carry this database of information with them on laptop computers and use it for on-the-spot verification. This database includes information on all the chemicals involved in the control regime, along with details such as their danger level, colour, and the law they fall under. Also provided is information on prior and ongoing criminal investigations, gathered from exchanges with the police, customs, Interpol, INCB, the European Union Anti-Fraud Office (OLAF), Europol, and the Licence Department. The authority for these transfers of information is provided in international treaties and agreements, especially Article 12 of the Narcotics Convention.

---

[15] For a more in-depth discussion of National Authorities, see *infra* in this volume, M. Ncube, Divergent National Implementing Legislation and Non-Uniform Implementation: Threat to the Object and Purpose of the Chemical Weapons Convention?. See also, National Authorities Advisor materials, available at http://www.opcw.org.

[16] See EU Council Directive 92/109/EEC (OJ no. 370, 19/12/92).

[17] See generally, Communication from the Commission to the Council and the European Parliament on a European Union Action Plan to Combat Drugs, COM(1999) 239 final (26/05/99), at 21-32.

The ECD is also in frequent contact with other parties, including OLAF, the INCB and authorities of the countries involved, when its investigators need clarification on an issue or a case. These inquiries are only slightly formalised; they are usually accomplished by sending the export license and relevant information (occasionally through special forms) to these other organisations by fax machine, telephone or email. Reference is frequently made to the 1988 Convention and, if possible, to a special agreement. The ECD has been generally pleased with the effectiveness of this system, and considers it a success since it has no indications that criminals are using factories or persons operating with a Netherlands license.

In addition to information transfers with authorities, the ECD communicates with organisations such as the Commission on Narcotic Drugs, the INCB, the United Nations International Drug Control Programme and the World Health Organization. These exchanges occur through many channels, including seminars, common reports, international operations and training. They are most effective when done directly between agencies, and, while the issue is usually handled by other law enforcement agencies, ECD's experience is that the most efficient system for executing constraint measures, like search and seizure requests, is a letter rogatory.[18]

The INCB plays a particularly leading role in both these exchanges and the broader international narcotics regime; as such, it merits a brief discussion here since could provide a model for reference in any future discussions in the OPCW on improving or devising cooperation mechanisms under the Chemical Weapons Convention.

4. The International Narcotics Control Board and its Operations

The INCB, created in 1968 by the Single Convention on Narcotic Drugs of 1961,[19] is the independent treaty body that implements the United Nations' drug control treaties. Its membership is composed of all Parties to the various UN narcotics and drug conventions. It therefore shares a great degree of kinship, in both international function and membership, with the OPCW.[20] The organisation works closely with branches of the UN and OLAF, and is active in monitoring and assisting governments in the design and implementation of their chemical control systems, assessing which chemicals should be controlled, acts as a centralised point of information exchange between various national authorities, and helps coordinate international operations.[21]

The INCB's monitoring regime is based upon estimates of legitimate international drug flows generated from voluntary data submission from its Parties, and utilises shipment tracking techniques in an attempt to detect and prevent illicit flows and diversions.[22] The

[18] "The medium whereby one country, speaking through its courts, requests another country, acting through its own courts and by methods of court procedure peculiar thereto and entirely within the latter's control, to assist the administration of justice in the former country." Black's Law Dictionary 905 (6th ed. 1990).

[19] Role of the INCB, available at http://www.incb.org.

[20] The Narcotics Convention has 167 parties, the CWC 145. Almost all CWC parties are party to the Narcotics Convention. See Annex VI, *infra* in this volume, for the comparison of States Party membership.

[21] See *supra* note 12.

[22] See Precursors and chemicals frequently used in the illicit manufacture of narcotic drugs and psychotropic substances, *supra* note 13.

number of precursors it monitors is smaller than the OPCW's,[23] and in 2000 and 2001 it focused upon monitoring programs for two chemicals of particular concern to illicit narcotics manufacture: Operation Topaz, covering acetic anhydride, a heroin precursor, and Operation Purple, covering potassium permanganate, a cocaine precursor.[24]

Operations Topaz and Purple were designed to help develop the INCB's monitoring efforts regarding both of these chemicals. The Operations called for increased and immediate communication between Central National Authorities (CNAs) regarding the flows in these chemicals. Emphasis was placed upon developing a single point of contact approach; encouraging the rapid and broad dissemination of chemical transfer notifications through the use of standardised forms, as well as the distribution of information on smuggling interceptions, stopped shipments and laboratory seizures; and the incorporation of background and random spot checks to verify the validity of transfers.[25] Manufacturers were also encouraged to contribute to the effort through the use of more clearly labelled, and sometimes repackaged, chemical shipments.

Both Operations required a great deal of coordination in their promotion and featured centralised information flows. The INCB acted as a clearinghouse for all information gathered through the Operations, and coordinated exchanges between CNAs, OLAF, the World Customs Organisation, and international law enforcement agencies like Europol and Interpol. A multitude of transmission channels were used, especially faxes and (sometimes encrypted) email. Both operations were successes: interdictions increased, diversions appeared to be deterred, and more information was gained for future monitoring efforts.[26]

5. Conclusions

There are many parallels between the demands of the international narcotics control regime's precursor monitoring efforts and the non-proliferation role of the OPCW, especially after all declared chemical weapons stockpiles have been destroyed. At the moment, however, many of the legal tools available to the drug control community are lacking in weapons control. Little or no comparable legislation has been enacted on the topic; action plans, if any, are only in rudimentary stages; few joint operations have been planned;[27] and no special bilateral cooperation agreements have been created. These tools need to be developed.

It is also clear that the field of cooperation on chemical transfers is a complex one, with multiple individual, corporate, national, regional and international actors. The web of controls, actors and agreements that make up the narcotics control regime has developed

[23] The 1988 Narcotics Convention Tables detail 22 precursors that the INCB monitors; by comparison, the Chemical Weapons Convention Schedules of Chemicals list 53 specific toxic chemicals and precursors, as well as 12 broader families of chemicals with multiple members. The total number of chemicals which require monitoring, then, is in fact much higher than 53. See also D. Feakes, *supra* note 6.

[24] Precursors and chemicals frequently used in the illicit manufacture of narcotic drugs and psychotropic substances, Report of the International Narcotics Control Board for 2000 on the Implementation of Article 12 of the United Nations Convention against Illicit Traffic in Narcotic Drugs and Psychotropic Substances (United Nations, 2002), at x.

[25] *Id.* at 8-13.

[26] *Id.* at x.

[27] For further discussions of the joint customs work done regarding the CWC, see, *infra* in this volume, Section III.4., Customs Enforcement and Initiatives to Strengthen Regimes.

over many years, and a tremendous degree of trust is needed for their proper functioning. The important efficiency gains accomplished with a single point of State contact also require the thorough development of effective National Authorities.

The OPCW is facing these coordination and development challenges, and the narcotics control regime can act as a model for either new OPCW bodies, a modified mandate for the OPCW Secretariat, or even partners for OPCW cooperation and integration. In choosing between these options, the experiences of the Netherlands ECD suggest that integrating the controls of the Chemical Weapons Convention into the currently existing chemical monitoring regime would be the most efficient and successful route. The single point of contact is better for industry, and the elimination of task and mandate duplication between organisations would save money at the national level.

There are two principal obstacles to this approach. First, the Chemical Weapons Convention covers a much broader swath of chemicals, so the international drug control monitoring regime would likely need expansion and additional resources to successfully integrate CWC activities into its *dossier*. Second, the international community, and particularly the drug control regime's primary financial sponsors, would need to summon the political will to modify, expand and adapt their chemical control regime to meet its new demands. The post-11 September realisation of the threats posed by non-State, terrorist actors may alter the political calculus underlying such decisions, and one can only hope that such a change is not motivated in response to a major chemical weapons incident. But whatever the source, the will is still needed, for the future of a chemical weapons-free world hinges upon the success of effective non-proliferation techniques. The OPCW would do well to look to the international narcotics control regime for inspiration, or even partnership, as it considers its approach to the decades ahead.

PART II
JURISDICTIONAL ISSUES

SECTION II.1

CASE STUDIES: CONCURRENT JURISDICTION

Introduction and Summary

Over the past decade, issues of competing national jurisdictions (or what may be termed horizontal jurisdictions) in criminal matters have become steadily more prominent and complex. The traditional bases for jurisdiction are the territorial or extended territorial principle; the nationality principle; the protective principle; the passive personality principle; and universal jurisdiction. Increasingly, however, jurisdictional issues have arisen, and will continue to arise, not simply in respect of competing jurisdictions between States, but also in respect of concurrent or complementary jurisdiction between national and international courts over the same crimes.

This is, in part, a reflection of the relatively recent proliferation of international fora in which the enforcement of prohibitions against serious crimes can take place. It can also be attributed to a growing consciousness of the international nature of some crimes and the corresponding need for domestic tribunals to be able to play their part in the suppression of such crimes. Accordingly, cooperation and interaction between national and international legal organs is integral to meeting the primary objective of these organs: to ensure that no one is beyond the reach of justice.

The relevance of this to the Chemical Weapons Convention ("the Convention") will be immediately apparent. The jurisdiction of States Parties and international courts to prosecute violations of the Convention goes directly to the heart of the enforcement, and ultimate effectiveness, of the prohibitions contained in the Convention. Article VII is the primary provision in the Convention dealing with jurisdiction. In brief, it provides that States

Parties shall: (a) enact penal legislation with respect to matters prohibited by the Convention; (b) not permit prohibited activities in any place under their control; and (c) establish extraterritorial jurisdiction in respect of activities prohibited under the Convention over natural persons holding the nationality of the State Party. Further, States Parties are required to "cooperate with other States Parties" and provide appropriate legal assistance to facilitate the implementation of the Article VII requirements. The extraterritorial nature of the penal legislation required under the Convention may increase the likelihood of concurrent jurisdiction arising. As examples of vertical jurisdiction, the statutes of concurrent jurisdiction provisions contained in the International Criminal Tribunal for the former Yugoslavia (ICTY) and the International Criminal Tribunal for Rwanda (ICTR) explicitly spell out the existence of concurrent jurisdiction for both the relevant international tribunal and national courts in respect of serious violations of international humanitarian law. The statutes go on to specify that the international tribunals have primacy (though not exclusivity) over the national courts of all States, and provide for the obligation of States to cooperate with the Tribunal in more detail than appears in the Convention. While the ICTY and ICTR cannot be supposed to be examples directly and in entirety applicable to the Convention, the need for a clear legal framework detailing the procedures for cooperation between States and the relevant international fora is evident from the experiences of the ICTY and the ICTR.

With specific reference to the Convention, and now that the Statute of the International Criminal Court (ICC) has entered into force, one can envisage situations where more than one State, or more than one international court, if one counts the ad hoc fora, conceivably would have jurisdiction to prosecute a violation of the Convention. In that situation, while the availability of a number of fora for prosecution would assist in preventing violators of the Convention from slipping through the cracks of the legal system, it could also create conflict and confusion. It is for that reason that detailed rules specifying both how legal cooperation under the Convention should be carried out, and how disputes as to jurisdiction should be resolved, would be of considerable benefit.

What, then, would be examples of situations where there could be a variety of available legal fora and/or disputes over who would have jurisdiction to prosecute under the Convention? First, under the statutes for the ICTY and ICTR, if chemical weapons had been used in the conflicts in the former Yugoslavia or Rwanda, or if a new ad hoc tribunal were established along similar lines to the ICTY and ICTR, the tribunal in question would have jurisdiction on the basis that the use of chemical weapons is a serious violation of international humanitarian law. In fact, the Statute of the ICTY specifically confers jurisdiction on the Tribunal in respect of the use of chemical weapons as a violation of the laws or customs of war.

The ICC is a second possible forum which could claim jurisdiction. In the event of a use of chemical weapons that constituted a war crime or crime against humanity in the context of international armed conflict, the ICC might, if the criteria of the Statute of the ICC were met, be able to prosecute. It must not be forgotten, however, that key to the system established by the ICC is the concept of complementarity, namely, the idea that States have first option to exercise their own national jurisdiction to prosecute a contravention of international humanitarian law. The ICC will only admit cases which the State having jurisdiction is unwilling or unable to prosecute, and which also fall within the narrow jurisdiction of the ICC.

Apart from international judicial organs, one should not overlook the availability of domestic fora as well. As is made clear in this section, depending on the circumstances, the domestic court, or a foreign court, or an internationalised domestic court such as that established in Sierra Leone, may be well suited to prosecute the offence. For example, it is integral to the Convention that any State Party to the Convention which has the required national legislation in force can prosecute its nationals (natural persons) for the development, production, stockpiling or use of chemical weapons, wherever that national may have carried out the prohibited activity. It should be noted that this is considerably wider than the more "international" options outlined above; that is, States Parties can domestically prosecute the development, production and stockpiling of chemical weapons, as well as their use alone. For example, the threat of use of chemical weapons as a terrorist act would not, in most cases, be in the context of an *international* armed conflict and thus the jurisdiction of the ICC would be precluded.

A fourth possibility is universal jurisdiction over the crime of the use of chemical weapons. It would appear that there is acceptance that such a crime is of international concern and that it forms part of customary international law. However, while the argument for universal jurisdiction in relation to the use of chemical weapons is strong, it has not yet been put beyond doubt by an actual case. Thus, while it may afford another layer of jurisdiction to States, at the present date this cannot be affirmed with absolute certainty.

For all of these options, there are both advantages and disadvantages from a policy perspective. Domestic courts and military tribunals are all too susceptible to charges of political bias, while international tribunals on occasions duplicate existing (and well functioning) domestic court systems at considerable expense. Moreover, in the context of States undergoing transition and reform after internal conflict, the disparity between judicial standards, procedures and even sentences in international tribunals and domestic courts can be socially divisive and detrimental to the national healing process: here one need only point to the situation in Rwanda.

What this short survey indicates is that more thought, and more detail, is needed to ensure that otherwise well founded judicial organs do not become mired in the problems associated with an international legal system which is increasingly characterised by a multiplicity of horizontal jurisdictional possibilities. This is not an issue which relates purely to chemical weapons or solely affects the Convention; rather, it is a problem which hinders the efficient administration of justice at a global level. A resolution of the current jurisdictional complexities and a model for international cooperation in criminal matters, while perhaps unlikely to come soon, would be of benefit to all those working in the emerging arena of international criminal law.

Fiona Tregonning

Précis-writer for Section II.1; Harvard Sussex Program Researcher at the OPCW Technical Secretariat, Government Relations and Political Affairs Branch. The views expressed are not attributable to the Harvard Sussex Program on CBW Armament and Arms Limitation or the OPCW.

CONCURRENT JURISDICTION: DEVELOPMENTS AND ISSUES

Horst Fischer*

1. Basics

In older textbooks of international law one can hardly find the term 'concurrent jurisdiction.' The reason for that lies in the meaning of the term, which signifies a situation in which two or more States have jurisdiction over a certain event. Traditionally such a situation was hardly foreseeable. The famous *Lotus* case,[1] decided by the Permanent Court of International Justice (PCIJ) is an example of the traditionalist view that jurisdiction is a matter of one State since jurisdiction was usually based on territory: every State claims jurisdiction over acts committed in its territory, even by foreigners. In the *Lotus* case, the PCIJ followed the territorial principle to solve the jurisdictional dispute between France and Turkey. However, ships, aircraft, and troops on foreign soil are not the only situations that have shown that the exclusive jurisdiction of a State is not always appropriate to deal effectively with acts by an individual or organs of another State. Today it is commonly accepted that there are five bases of jurisdiction: (1) the territorial or extended territorial principle; (2) the nationality principle; (3) the protective principle; (4) the passive personality principle; and (5) universal jurisdiction.

Obviously, the traditional bases for jurisdiction, if not exercised in a particular case, give rise to instances in which prohibited activities would go unpunished due to unwillingness of the State which has jurisdiction to prosecute, while other States that would be willing to prosecute have no jurisdiction. The first four types of jurisdiction are based on the origin of the crime or the nationals or the interest.

The fifth type — universal jurisdiction — is gaining increased importance and recognition because it is not based on the traditional criteria. Universal jurisdiction is very special. It denotes the possibility for States to invoke jurisdiction over crimes committed independently of the criteria for the traditional bases for jurisdiction. Universal jurisdiction has its origin

* Professor of Public International Law and Red Cross Chair of International Humanitarian Law, Institute for International Law of Peace and Armed Conflict, University of Bochum, Germany and Leiden University Faculty of Law, the Netherlands.

[1] *The Case of the S.S. Lotus*, (France vs. Turkey), Judgement of 7 September 1927, PCIJ Reports, Series A, No. 10, p. 4.

R. Yepes-Enríquez and L. Tabassi. (eds.), Treaty Enforcement and International Cooperation in Criminal Matters

in the grave breaches provision of the Geneva Conventions[2] and the acceptance by States that, for certain other crimes, this basis for jurisdiction also exists. Today it is debatable whether universal jurisdiction can be based on treaty law. And in this respect, would it exist only for the States Parties to the treaty, or also for States not party? Could it only be based on customary law? What is generally accepted is that universal jurisdiction encompasses the *aut dedere aut judicare* principle. If the State does not investigate and, if appropriate, prosecute an individual, then it has the duty to extradite the individual to the State that has requested extradition. This principle is valid for, *inter alia,* piracy, sabotage, hostage-taking, and terrorism.

Independently of where one finds the legal basis for the universal jurisdiction, one has to accept that this type of jurisdiction is the most comprehensive method to deal effectively on a universal level with certain crimes.

I have not yet mentioned the term 'concurrent jurisdiction.' In contrast to universal jurisdiction, the term 'concurrent jurisdiction' means that jurisdiction may be invoked by one or more States and/or an international organ, such as a tribunal established by the international community for certain actions without necessarily accepting that such jurisdiction is universal. Concurrent jurisdiction can be based on one of the traditional bases for jurisdiction.

The Statute of the International Criminal Tribunal for the former Yugoslavia (ICTY)[3] is a good example to demonstrate clearly what concurrent jurisdiction actually means. Article 9 of the ICTY Statute uses the term concurrent jurisdiction to describe its own jurisdiction and the possibility for national courts to exercise jurisdiction over crimes committed in the former Yugoslavia (if such jurisdiction in the specific case exists). At the same time it states the rule of primacy of the ICTY's jurisdiction over that of the national courts. Moreover, it sets rules for the implementation of the primacy rule with regard to the obligation of States to cooperate with the ICTY,[4] a topic which has been covered elsewhere in this volume.[5] What is important to appreciate is the combination of parallel jurisdiction being complemented by a system of obligations and procedural rules on how to implement such a parallel system.

[2] Convention (I) for the Amelioration of the Condition of the Wounded and Sick in Armed Forces in the Field, Geneva, 12 August 1949, 75 UNTS 31; Convention (II) for the Amelioration of the Condition of the Wounded, Sick and shipwrecked Members of Armed Forces at Sea, Geneva, 12 August 1949, 75 UNTS 85; Convention (III) relative to the Treatment of Prisoners of War, Geneva, 12 August 1949, 75 UNTS 135; Convention (IV) relative to the Protection of Civilian Persons in Time of War, Geneva, 12 August 1949, 75 UNTS 287; Protocol Additional to the Geneva Conventions of 1949 and relating to the Protection of Victims of International Armed Conflicts (Protocol I), 8 June 1977, 1125 UNTS, no. 17512; Protocol Additional to the Geneva Conventions of 1949 relating to the Protection of Victims of Non-International Armed Conflicts (Protocol II), 8 June 1977, 1125 UNTS, no. 17513. Texts available on-line in the IHL database of the ICRC at http://www.icrc.org/ihl.

[3] Originally published as Annex to the Report of the Secretary-General pursuant to paragraph 2 of Security Council resolution 808 (UN doc. S/25704) (1993).

[4] Article 29 of the ICTY Statute.

[5] See *infra* in this volume F. Guariglia, Interaction between International and National Criminal Courts in the ICTY; D.A. Mundis, State Cooperation with the ICTY; R. Reid, Practical Aspects of Gathering Evidence in an International Environment; and N. Paterson, Protecting National Security and other Confidential Information.

Concurrent jurisdiction in this respect is more than a simple acceptance of parallel jurisdiction. It is the combination of the elements of different aspects of traditional types of jurisdiction, universal jurisdiction, and procedural elements which give it a specific meaning.

Thanks to the Statute of the International Criminal Court,[6] we may also speak of 'complementary jurisdiction.' Let me only say at this point that this term denotes the jurisdiction of the International Criminal Court (ICC), which is dependent, on the one hand, upon the substance of the crimes committed and the (lack of) exercise of jurisdiction of the States concerned. On the other hand, it is dependent upon the action of the United Nations Security Council. Particularly if one takes into account the global application of the ICC's jurisdiction, this type of jurisdiction is not comparable to universal jurisdiction, and is also not comparable to concurrent jurisdiction.

2. Concurrent Jurisdiction and Treaty Implementation

Why is it now important to examine the foundations and recent developments in systems of jurisdiction?

First of all, we should remind ourselves that the effective implementation of the obligations of a treaty with a global aim is dependent upon the jurisdiction States Parties and States not party will have over violations of the treaty, and how they can make use of their jurisdiction to enforce it. Specifically, we can look at how the Chemical Weapons Convention[7] incorporates one or more bases for jurisdiction over the effective implementation of the treaty rules. If one looks at the treaty text, the term 'jurisdiction' is used more frequently than in most of the other important multilateral treaties.

In the Chemical Weapons Convention (Convention), jurisdiction is not only mentioned in Article VII on National Implementation Measures, but it also is referred to in Articles I, II, III, IV, V, VI, as well as in several paragraphs and subparagraphs of the Annexes. Taking a closer look, most of the references are identical and appear in the phrase, "located in any place under [the State Party's] jurisdiction or control." This phrase is an essential part of the Convention's definitions as well as the operative paragraph for verification and it describes the range of the application of the Convention.

It, nevertheless, does not entail the typical jurisdiction clauses. The most important provision in the Convention in respect of jurisdiction and effective implementation is Article VII:

> ARTICLE VII. NATIONAL IMPLEMENTATION MEASURES
>
> General undertakings
>
> 1. Each State Party shall, in accordance with its constitutional processes, adopt the necessary measures to implement its obligations under this Convention. In particular, it shall:

[6] 1998 Rome Statute of the International Criminal Court, entered into force 1 July 2002; UN doc. A/CONF.183/9*, as corrected by the procès-verbaux of 10 November 1998 and 12 July 1999. Corrected text available at http://www.un.org/law/icc.

[7] 1993 Convention on the Prohibition of the Development, Production, Stockpiling and Use of Chemical Weapons and on Their Destruction, entered into force on 29 April 1997. Text, as corrected and changed, available at http://www.opcw.org.

(a) Prohibit natural and legal persons anywhere on its territory or in any other place under its jurisdiction as recognised by international law from undertaking any activity prohibited to a State Party under this Convention, including enacting penal legislation with respect to such activity;

(b) Not permit in any place under its control any activity prohibited to a State Party under this Convention; and,

(c) Extend its penal legislation enacted under subparagraph(a) to any activity prohibited to a State Party under this Convention undertaken anywhere by natural persons, possessing its nationality, in conformity with international law.

2. Each State Party shall cooperate with other States Parties and afford the appropriate form of legal assistance to facilitate the implementation of the obligations under paragraph 1.

3. Each State Party, during the implementation of its obligations under this Convention, shall assign the highest priority to ensuring the safety of people and to protecting the environment, and shall cooperate as appropriate with other States Parties in this regard.

The structure of the Article is important to appreciate. In the first paragraph it deals with the obligation to establish national laws for the implementation of the Convention. The second paragraph deals with the cooperation and mutual legal assistance obligation of States Parties, while the third paragraph is limited to safety of people and the protection of the environment.

Obviously, the text does not contain explicit reference to concurrent jurisdiction. To find out whether the Convention is implicitly providing concurrent jurisdiction, or under what circumstances one can identify concurrent jurisdiction, we need to have a closer look at the text and look at some examples.

In the first paragraph, subparagraph (a) obliges each State Party to enact penal legislation in respect of activities prohibited under the treaty. Subparagraph (b) obliges the State Party not to permit prohibited activities in territory under its control, which is generally understood as a clause dealing with occupied territory. Only subparagraph (c) deals explicitly with jurisdiction by requiring each State Party to establish extraterritorial jurisdiction based on the nationality of the offender.

Only the latter is an obvious case for concurrent jurisdiction in the meaning defined above. Nonetheless, compared to the prototype of a concurrent jurisdiction system (i.e., that of the ICTY), Article VII does not provide for specific rules on cooperation, which would be essential for implementation. It only refers very generally to the cooperation clauses under international law.

3. Additional Concurrent Jurisdiction Issues: Hypothetical Cases

In analysing the Convention's text, a comparison of potential violations of the treaty is useful to identify additional concurrent jurisdiction issues. The main features in the Convention for international humanitarian law are the provisions on the use of weapons.

Here indeed we already have a certain overlap of jurisdiction, despite the rather limited approach of the Convention.

3.1 USE OF CHEMICAL WEAPONS IN TERRITORY OF A STATE PARTY BY NATIONALS OF ANOTHER STATE PARTY, AND INVOLVING THE ICTY

Starting with an easy case, let's imagine for a minute that chemical weapons were used by Yugoslav nationals in Bosnia and Herzegovina after the Convention entered into force for both States. Under the Convention, jurisdiction could be invoked by the State of Bosnia and Herzegovina and the State of which the perpetrators held nationality, i.e., Yugoslavia. At the same time, under the ICTY Statute, the ICTY would have jurisdiction over the case and could exercise its primacy.

Cooperation and legal assistance between Bosnia and Herzegovina and Yugoslavia with the investigation and prosecution of the case would be governed by Article VII, paragraph 2, of the Convention (if no other bilateral agreement were available), while the more detailed rules of Article 29 of the ICTY Statute would govern the two States' cooperation with regard to the jurisdiction of the ICTY.[8] No other States would have jurisdiction under Article VII of the Convention unless their nationals were involved.

The interesting question is whether, at the same time, other States would also have jurisdiction under the principle of universal jurisdiction, and if so, how would cooperation and requests for legal assistance be dealt with? Could Germany argue that Bosnia and Herzegovina has to follow the principle of *aut dedere aut judicare*? What would govern the extradition procedure? For Germany to use such an argument would be almost impossible today, as the implementation law of the Convention limits the application of its penal provisions to German territory or German nationals. Sweden, on the other hand, has provided in its implementing legislation that, "A crime against the Convention will be sentenced by Swedish law and at a Swedish court even if the crime is committed abroad and irrespective of the perpetrator's nationality."[9]

3.2 USE OF RIOT CONTROL AGENTS IN AN INTERNATIONAL ARMED CONFLICT, AND INVOLVING THE ICC

Developing another hypothetical case, we now assume that members of a United Nations Security Council-authorised multinational security force use riot control agents to intervene in military combat between groups in an international armed conflict. If we also assume that the Chemical Weapons Convention, as well as the ICC Statute, are in force for all States involved, interesting questions regarding jurisdiction land on the table. First of all, the relationship between the definition of 'chemical weapons' under the Convention and the reference in the ICC Statute to the 1925 Geneva Protocol is important. If it is interpreted that the ICC reference indicates a more limited definition of 'chemical weapons' than the

[8] Note that Article 29 of the ICTY Statute is not necessarily self-executing. In the case of *Dusko Tadic*, the accused was in custody in Germany and Germany found it necessary to obtain parliamentary approval before the accused could be surrendered to the ICTY.

[9] Chapter 2, Section 3, of the Swedish Criminal Code, *Survey of National Implementing Legislation*, OPCW doc. S/259/2001 (16 May 2001) at 85.

Convention does, which I would doubt, then already, for some States, there might be a contradiction between their obligations under the Convention, and the penal legislation they have enacted pursuant to it, and the question of jurisdiction under the implementing legislation they have enacted for the ICC Statute. Depending on their legal system, for some States this question must be answered. If there are discrepancies in the definition of 'chemical weapons,' jurisdiction over the above hypothetical case may be existent or not. At least a situation of concurrent jurisdiction is hardly imaginable.

If the definition of 'chemical weapons' in Article II of the Chemical Weapons Convention and Article 8(2)(b) of the ICC Statute are to be interpreted as identical, then the format of the ICC national implementing legislation is decisive for the jurisdiction issue. Automatic and identical incorporation of the ICC Statute into national law will lead to a situation of concurrent jurisdiction only with regard to the territorial State and the State of which the accused hold nationality. Third states would have no jurisdiction. The ICC would only have jurisdiction if the criteria of the Statute are fulfilled — international or non-international armed conflict, etc. — and if the affected States do not perform well in the prosecution of the case, or if the case is transferred to the ICC by the United Nations Security Council. In the latter case the system of jurisdiction under the Chemical Weapons Convention is somewhat broadened, but only with regard to the use of chemical weapons, and only with regard to a small group of actors.

Regarding the universal jurisdiction question and the ICC Statute, the fact that the Chemical Weapons Convention is reaching the point of universal acceptance by States could be a strong argument to accept universal jurisdiction over the crime of the use of chemical weapons. Let me add that such conviction should not be limited to international armed conflict as embodied in the ICC Statute, which is one of the major flaws of that instrument.

3.3 USE OF CHEMICAL WEAPONS IN AN INTERNAL ARMED CONFLICT IN THE TERRITORY OF A STATE NOT PARTY

A third hypothetical example could be one dealing with a war in the Congo in which Congo is using on its territory chemical weapons in combat against armed opposition groups. Congo is not a State Party to the Chemical Weapons Convention; it has only signed it. Under the Chemical Weapons Convention there is no provision which would grant jurisdiction over violations of the Convention in the territory of a State not party (leaving aside for a moment discussion of the interim obligations of signatory States under Article 18 of the Vienna Convention on the Law of Treaties) if the chemical weapons were produced domestically or obtained from a State not party. Not even the ICC would have jurisdiction over such a case. Only if we accept the principle of universal jurisdiction would other States have jurisdiction.

3.4 COMPARISON OF THE RESULTS

Comparing the above three hypothetical cases leaves us with a certain uneasiness:

- Concurrent jurisdiction is provided for by the Chemical Weapons Convention only for a case in which States Parties can invoke jurisdiction based on the nationality principle (Article VII(1)(c)) or on the territorial principle (Article VII(1)(a)). Only with regard to specific established international tribunals is the situation different;
- The cooperation system compared to other systems as such is rather underdeveloped;
- For specific relevant cases there is almost no possibility of providing a basis of jurisdiction to States Parties *vis-à-vis* States not party;
- States should be more outspoken on the acceptance of universal jurisdiction for the use of chemical weapons.

3.5 OTHER CASES INVOLVING VIOLATIONS OTHER THAN 'USE' OF CHEMICAL WEAPONS

So far we have only addressed the use of chemical weapons and questions of concurrent jurisdiction. Let us now turn to other areas of interest with regard to other prohibited activities under the Convention, such as illegal trade or production of chemical weapons on foreign soil. If, in such a case, the perpetrator is a national of the State Party claiming jurisdiction, the above-mentioned rules would apply by giving additional (concurrent) jurisdiction only to the territorial State Party. As both the ICTY Statute and the ICC Statute confer jurisdiction only on the *use* of chemical weapons, neither tribunal could invoke jurisdiction over the case.

It would be interesting to debate the question of universal jurisdiction over the illegal trade, production, etc., of chemical weapons. As the Convention contains no provision in this regard, could we say today that customary international law permits the exercise of universal jurisdiction not only in cases of use of chemical weapons, but also in cases of illegal trade and production? If so, would we also accept that such universal jurisdiction would cover nationals of States not party? The results of the Rome conference, which drafted the ICC Statute, are not helpful in this respect. Nevertheless, the growing number of States Parties to the Chemical Weapons Convention, coupled with the urgent need to prevent proliferation of weapons of mass destruction and the growing danger of terrorist attacks, might lead to a new perspective or interpretation acceptable to the international community.

3.6 MULTINATIONAL COMPANIES AND SUBSIDIARIES

The Chemical Weapons Convention only provides for extraterritorial jurisdiction over natural persons holding the nationality of a State Party. Going further with these questions, the debate could also necessarily include the question of multinational companies, the actions of subsidiaries in foreign territory, and the punishment of the personnel working for those subsidiaries.

Let us review the focus of that debate in the past. There has been intensive debate in the literature about jurisdiction for prohibited activities performed by companies in foreign countries, in particular if the executive branch of the company had an independent status under the laws of the countries concerned. Obviously in the past States preferred to look at such activities from the perspective of separate personality of the parent and subsidiary company in order to assert jurisdiction over the whole transnational group. Some States had argued that the separate legal personality of the subsidiary is a bar to any control by the home State of the parent, which would exclude jurisdiction over prohibited activities by the subsidiary (Barcelona Traction judgement).[10] The focus of that debate had been on control and the administrative and legal measures to prevent such activities.

By looking at multinational corporations from the perspective of universal jurisdiction penal sanctions, the debate could gain new momentum and direction. The ICC Statute provides for the responsibility of military commanders for crimes within the jurisdiction of the Court. But it also includes in Article 28 the responsibility of other superiors (civil):

Article 28. Responsibility of commanders and other superiors

In addition to other grounds of criminal responsibility under this Statute for crimes within the jurisdiction of the Court:

...

(b) With respect to superior and subordinate relationships not described in paragraph (a) [military commanders], a superior shall be criminally responsible for crimes within the jurisdiction of the Court committed by subordinates under his or her effective authority and control, as a result of his or her failure to exercise control properly over such subordinates, where:

(i) The superior either knew, or consciously disregarded information that clearly indicated, that the subordinates were committing or about to commit such crimes;

(ii) The crimes concerned activities that were within the effective responsibility and control of the superior; and,

(iii) The superior failed to take all necessary and reasonable measures within his or her power to prevent or repress their commission or to submit the matter to the competent authorities for investigation and prosecution.

That specific rule is based on the conviction of civilian superiors having been responsible for serious crimes during the Second World War.

[10] International Court of Justice, *Case Concerning the Barcelona Traction, Light and Power Company, Limited* (Second Phase), (Belgium v. Spain), Judgement of 5 February 1970, 1970 ICJ Reports, 3.

4. Main Deficiencies of the System of Concurrent Jurisdiction

The following summarises what I consider to be the main issues under the heading of (concurrent) jurisdiction:

- The Chemical Weapons Convention does not provide for a comprehensive system with regard to jurisdiction which leaves open the possibility that serious violations of the Convention will not be prosecuted, unless States Parties are able to invoke, for example, protective jurisdiction or the passive personality principle.
- Since the adoption of the Chemical Weapons Convention, international criminal law has developed in a way which requires a closer and more critical look at its implementation clauses. The existing international tribunals provide for an improved system of concurrent jurisdiction, but they are limited to crimes involving the use of chemical weapons. These, however, at least provide the option to prosecute crimes involving violations of the Convention independent of its own jurisdiction clauses.
- The most important step would be to develop the universal jurisdiction concept with regard to the serious violations of the Chemical Weapons Convention. Only then would the Convention and its implementation system be equal to other systems of comparable importance for the international community, in particular for its security and stability.

CONCURRENT JURISDICTION: LEGAL AND POLICY CONSIDERATIONS

Mohamed Othman*

1. Introduction

This chapter examines legal and policy considerations in the exercise of concurrent jurisdiction, by States and the United Nations, in the investigation and prosecution of serious violations of international humanitarian and human rights law. It analyses the application of concurrent jurisdiction by the International Criminal Tribunal for Rwanda (ICTR),[1] the United Nations Transitional Administration in East Timor (UNTAET)[2] and States, with a view to discussing emerging practices and lessons learned.

2. Concurrent Jurisdiction: Rwanda Tribunal

Before appraising the application of concurrent jurisdiction by the Rwanda Tribunal and States, it is important by way of introduction to recapitulate the jurisdictional parameter of that Tribunal. The Rwanda Tribunal's temporal jurisdiction is limited to acts committed between 1 January 1994 and 31 December 1994. Its subject-matter jurisdiction is for the crime of genocide, crimes against humanity and serious violations of Article 3 common to the four Geneva Conventions of 12 August 1949 on the Protection of Victims of War, and of the 8 July 1977 Additional Protocol II thereof.[3] Personal jurisdiction extends to

* Former General Prosecutor for East Timor, United Nations Transitional Administration in East Timor (UNTAET); formerly Chief of Prosecutions, International Criminal Tribunal for Rwanda (ICTR) (1998-2000). The views expressed are those of the author and do not represent those of the United Nations.

[1] ICTR, established pursuant to Chapter VII of the UN Charter by UNSC Res. 955, UN SCOR, 3453d. Meeting, UN doc. S/RES/955 (1994), 8 November 1994. The Statute is annexed to the Resolution. The International Criminal Tribunal for the Prosecution of Persons Responsible for Serious Violations of International Humanitarian Law committed in the Territory of the Former Yugoslavia since 1991 (ICTY) was established by UNSC Res. 827, UNSC OR, 48th Session, 3217th meeting, UN doc. S/RES/827 (1993), 25 May 1993. Both Statutes were amended by UN Security Council resolution 1411 (2002) on 17 May 2002.

[2] Established by UNSC Res. 1272 (1999), 25 Oct. 1999.

[3] Convention (I) for the Amelioration of the Condition of the Wounded and Sick in Armed Forces in the Field, Geneva, 12 August 1949, 75 UNTS 31; Convention (II) for the Amelioration of the Condition of the Wounded, Sick and shipwrecked Members of Armed Forces at Sea, Geneva, 12 August 1949, 75 UNTS 85; Convention (III) relative to the Treatment of Prisoners of War, Geneva, 12 August 1949, 75 UNTS 135; Convention (IV) relative to the Protection of Civilian Persons in Time of War, Geneva, 12 August 1949, 75 UNTS 287; Protocol Additional to the Geneva Conventions of 1949 and relating to the Protection of Victims of International Armed Conflicts (Protocol I), 8 June 1977, 1125 UNTS, no. 17512; Protocol Additional to the Geneva Conventions of 1949 relating to the Protection of Victims of Non-International Armed Conflicts (Protocol II), 8 June 1977, 1125 UNTS, no. 17513. Texts available on-line in the IHL database of the ICRC at http://www.icrc.org/ihl.

R. Yepes-Enríquez and L. Tabassi. (eds.), Treaty Enforcement and International Cooperation in Criminal Matters

both Rwandan nationals and non-nationals for crimes committed in the territory of Rwanda, and only to Rwandan citizens for acts committed in the territory of neighbouring States, during the above mentioned period.[4]

In particular, with regard to concurrent jurisdiction, the ICTR Statute[5] provides:

Article 8. Concurrent jurisdiction

1. The International Tribunal for Rwanda and national courts shall have *concurrent jurisdiction* to prosecute persons for serious violations of international humanitarian law committed in the territory of Rwanda and Rwandan citizens for such violations committed in the territory of neighbouring States, between 1 January 1994 and 31 December 1994.
2. The International Tribunal for Rwanda shall have *primacy* over the national courts of all States. At any stage of the procedure, the International Tribunal for Rwanda may formally request national courts to defer to its competence in accordance with the present Statute and Rules of Procedure and Evidence of the International Tribunal for Rwanda. [Emphasis added]

The regime of concurrent jurisdiction as outlined in Article 8(1) of the ICTR Statute is based on the recognition of dual competence by the Tribunal and the national courts of all States.[6] Independent UN inquiries, as well as prosecutions before ICTR, confirm that in the case of the Rwandan genocide[7] one is dealing with a situation in which the majority of suspects or accused are Rwandan nationals.[8] It follows from the sum total of jurisdictional principles that Rwanda has the prime interest in exercising concurrent jurisdiction to investigate and prosecute perpetrators. The territorial (the crimes took place in Rwanda), active nationality (the nationality of nearly all accused is Rwandan), passive nationality (the majority of direct victims were Rwandan), protective (vital State interests have been affected), and universal principle of jurisdiction support Rwanda's active exercise of concurrent jurisdiction. The rationale for universal jurisdiction, in general or with regard to specific Statutes, is that there exist certain offences which, due to their very nature, affect the interests

[4] ICTR Statute, Articles 1, 2, 3, 4, 7 & 8.

[5] The Rwandan Government objected to the Tribunal's temporal jurisdiction, which they wished to be extended to 1990 to encompass the planning phases of the genocide and other massacres committed before 1994; it also objected to the non-incorporation of the death penalty in the Statute. Although it formally requested the setting up of the Tribunal, it voted against UNSC Res. 955. It assured the UNSC of its intention to support and cooperate with the Tribunal.

[6] See also, *infra* in this volume, C. Mibenge, The Concurrent Application of International, National and African Laws in Rwanda.

[7] In *Prosecutor v. Clement Kayishema and Obed Ruzindana*, the Trial Chamber was of the view that a plan of genocide existed and perpetrators executed the plan in Rwanda between April and June 1994, Case No. ICTR-95-1-T, 21 May 1999, para. 291; "It is common ground in this Appeal that the acts of violence were in the order of genocide and of crimes against humanity, with Tutsis and moderate Hutus as victims," *Prosecutor v. Omar Serushago*, Appeals Chamber, Reasons for Judgement, ICTR-98-39-A, 6 April 2000; see also, Report of the International Panel of Eminent Personalities to Investigate the 1994 Genocide in Rwanda and the Surrounding Events, established by the Organization of African Unity, www.oau-oua.org, 2000.

[8] Of the forty-four accused persons currently detained by ICTR, only one accused, i.e. Georges Ruggiu, is non-Rwandan. He has dual nationality (Belgian/Italian), *Prosecutor v. Georges Ruggiu*, Case No ICTR-97-32-I, Judgement and Sentence, 1 June 2000.

of all States, even when committed in another State or against another State, victim, or interest.[9] It assumes that each State has an interest in exercising jurisdiction to combat offences that all nations have condemned.[10] Rwanda, like many States, has incorporated the prosecution of these crimes within its domestic legislation. To date, it remains the front runner of national courts in exercising concurrent jurisdiction in relation to crimes committed in Rwanda in 1994.

The legislative basis for the prosecution of genocide and crimes against humanity in Rwanda is the Organic Law on the Organisation of Prosecutions for Offences Constituting the Crime of Genocide or Crimes Against Humanity Committed Since 1 October 1990.[11] This law groups suspects or accused persons into four categories:

Category 1

(a) Persons whose criminal acts or those whose acts place them amongst planners, organisers, supervisors, and leaders of the crime of genocide or of a crime against humanity;

(b) Persons who acted in positions of authority at the national, prefectural, communal, sector, or cell level, or in a political party, the army, religious organizations, or militia and who perpetrated or fostered such crimes;

(c) Notorious murderers who by virtue of the zeal or excessive malice with which they committed atrocities, distinguish themselves in their areas of residence or where they went;

(d) Persons who committed acts of sexual violence.

Category 2

Persons whose criminal acts or whose acts of criminal participation place them amongst perpetrators, conspirators, or accomplices of intentional homicide or of serious assault against the persons causing death.

Category 3

Persons whose criminal acts or whose acts of criminal participation make them guilty of other serious assaults against the person.

Category 4

Persons who committed offences against property.

---

[9] M.C. Bassiouni, Crimes against Humanity in International Criminal Law, (1992), p. 512-513. "The universality principle is pre-eminently the jurisdictional principle that expresses international solidarity," M.J.Gerritsen, *Jurisdiction*, in B. Swart & A. Klip, (eds.), International Criminal Law in the Netherlands (1977), p. 62.

[10] *Id.*, p. 512-513.

[11] Organic law No. 08/96, 30 April 1996, Official Journal of the Republic of Rwanda, 1 September 1996, and 35th year, No. 17, (Genocide Law). See further, *infra* in this volume, C. Mibenge, Concurrent Application of International, National and African Laws in Rwanda.

As of December 2000, some 120,000 persons were suspected or accused of having committed offences under this law.[12]

The exercise of concurrent jurisdiction by the Rwanda Tribunal and national courts of States, as provided for in Article 8 (1) of the ICTR Statute, is subject to a unique rule of primacy of jurisdiction by the Tribunal. The special circumstances behind its creation — the Security Council's authoritative action under Chapter VII of the UN Charter — enabled Article 8(2) to give the Tribunal primacy of jurisdiction over the national courts of all States.

Where it appears to the Prosecutor that crimes which are the subject of investigations or criminal proceedings instituted in the courts of any state; are the subject of an investigation by the Prosecutor, or should be the subject of an investigation by the Prosecutor because of the seriousness of the offences, the status of the accused at the time of the alleged offences and the general importance of the legal questions involved in the case; or are the subject of an indictment in the Tribunal, the Prosecutor may apply to the Trial Chamber that a formal request be made that such court defer to the competence of the Tribunal.[13] Formal requests for deferral are addressed to States, who are required to comply without undue delay in accordance with Article 28 of the Statute (Cooperation and judicial assistance).[14] Non-respect of a Trial Chamber's request for deferral may lead to a complaint by the President of the Tribunal to the Security Council.[15] The rule obliges States to accede to, and accept requests for deferral on the ground of suspension of their sovereign rights to try the accused themselves, and compels States to accept the fact that certain domestic crimes are really international in character, endanger peace, and should be tried by an international tribunal.[16] It cuts national borders to bring to justice persons guilty of serious international crimes.[17]

---

[12] See, *Justice pour Tous au Rwanda*, Avocats sans Frontieres, Rapport Annuel, 1999, Bruxelles, p. 45. The Rwanda Government intends to put in place a community/participatory justice system, "Gacaca Jurisdictions", for dealing with Category 2 to 4 suspects in order to respond to the particular requirements of the delivery of justice for this case load of detainees. "Full trial of 90,000 defendants — more than one percent of the national population — would be infeasible in even the wealthiest nation and is emphatically not an option in Rwanda", M. Morris, The Trials of Concurrent Jurisdiction: The Case of Rwanda, American Diplomacy, www.unc/edu/depts/diplomat/AD_Issues/amdipl_6/morris.html, p. 7.

[13] ICTR Rule 9, 'Prosecutor's Application for Deferral', (adopted at Forth Plenary Session, Arusha, 2-6 June 1997). The corresponding ICTY Rule 9 is slightly different, and among the motivating reasons is that it is intended to shield the accused from international criminal responsibility if there is lack of independence or impartiality in the proceedings in the national court. Deferral requests by a Trial Chamber have been made in a number of instances by ICTR and ICTY, e.g. Decision on the Formal Request for Deferral presented by the Prosecutor in the Radio Television Libre des Mille Collines SARL Case, ICTR-96-6-D, 12 March 1996; Decision on the Proposal of the Prosecutor for a Request to the Federal Republic of Yugoslavia (Serbia and Montenegro) to Defer the Pending Investigation and Criminal Proceedings to the Tribunal, *Prosecutor v. Mile Mrksic, et al*, ICTY, IT-95-14-R61, 10 Dec. 1998.

[14] Rule 10 (C), ICTR.

[15] ICTR, Rule 11, 'Non Compliance with a Formal request for Deferral'; ICTY, Rule 11;. c.f. "unlike extradition transfer is not discretionary, and States have a Charter-based obligation to surrender suspects to the Tribunal", O'Shea, S. *Interaction Between International Criminal Tribunals and National Legal Systems*, in T.M. Franck & H.P. Gregory, International Law Decisions in National Courts, (1996), p. 292.

[16] Separate Opinion, Judge Sidhwa, *Prosecutor v. Dusko Tadic*, Defense Motion for Interlocutory Appeal on Jurisdiction, ICTY Case No. IT-94-1-AR72, 2 October 1995, para 83.

[17] *Id.*, para. 83.

The Tribunal's primacy of jurisdiction is an entitlement and not an obligation. It is to be exercised at the discretion of the Tribunal whose decisions, should deferral be ordered, are binding on States. The grant of primacy of jurisdiction to the Tribunal is an explicit feature of that institution, given the secure mandate given to it by the Security Council under Chapter VII of the Charter. Primacy of jurisdiction does not imply exclusivity of jurisdiction. It was never intended that the Rwanda Tribunal would be the only judicial authority empowered to prosecute.[18] Indeed, in *Ntuyahaga*, the Trial Chamber emphasised that, in line with the UN General Assembly and the Security Council, it encourages all States, in application of the principles of universal jurisdiction, to prosecute and judge those responsible for serious crimes such as genocide, crimes against humanity and other grave violations of international humanitarian law.[19]

Concurrent jurisdiction for the prosecution of criminal acts committed during the events in Rwanda is not only being exercised by the Rwanda Tribunal and Rwanda, but also by other States. Switzerland exercised concurrent jurisdiction in relation to the former Bourgmaster of Mutshubati commune who was tried and sentenced by the Swiss Military Tribunal for violating the laws of war, recognised as offences under the Military Penal Code. Belgium has begun proceedings against a number of Rwandans under the Belgium Law of 16 June 1993 relating to the suppression of breaches of the four Geneva Conventions of 1949 and Additional Protocols (1977). France has also instituted legal proceedings against a priest suspected of committing similar crimes in Rwanda in 1994. The exercise of concurrent jurisdiction by these States has its motivation not only in the mere presence of such persons within the territory of these States, but in the taking of effective measures to combat flagrant violations of international humanitarian law to ensure that suspects do not receive judicial shelter. The demand for justice by resident victims who had constituted themselves as civil litigants also added to the motivation to investigate and prosecute.

2.1 COMPETING CLAIMS OR SHARED INTERESTS

The exercise of concurrent jurisdiction should not always be viewed as that of competing claims in such vital matters as the prosecutions of persons responsible for serious international humanitarian and human rights law violations. It is a recognised form of jurisdictional outreach that inflates the scope of criminal accountability and penal sanctions. There is shared interest in the recognition and application of this mode of the exercise of jurisdiction. Cooperative judicial arrangements that are aimed at facilitating and ensuring that no person suspected of such serious offences escapes justice are what is required. Impunity, the very cause of repeated atrocities, can only be effectively redressed by multiplicity of jurisdictional competence.

[18] "It is our understanding that the International Tribunal for Rwanda is designed not to replace, but to complement the sovereignty of Rwanda. The international and impartial character of the Tribunal, will, in our view, enhance prospects for national reconciliation in Rwanda, Justice and fairness....", Statement of the Delegate of Nigeria; "We do not believe that the new Tribunal on its own will be able to take on the whole burden of prosecuting those responsible for these dreadful crimes", Statement of United Kingdom Delegate; Provisional Verbatim Record of the Security Council, Forty-Ninth Year, 3453[Rd] Meeting, UN doc. S/PV.3453, 8 Nov.1994.

[19] *Prosecutor v. Bernard Ntuyahaga*, Decision on the Prosecutor's Motion to Withdraw the Indictment, Case No. ICTR-98-40-T, 18 March 1999, p.5.

The early years of the Rwanda Tribunal demonstrates that the application of concurrent jurisdiction can be the subject of contest and controversy.[20] One of the issues faced by the ICTR and Rwanda was that of apportioning or repartitioning accused persons, especially those who held superior or command positions and who were considered as the architects and planners of the genocide.[21] The initial ICTR caseload was that which the Government of Rwanda had been pursuing, and for which it had already approached other States for cooperation in the arrest and extradition of suspects to Rwanda.[22] This is best exemplified by the separate initiatives made first by Rwanda and Belgium on 15 April 1996, and immediately thereafter on 17 April 1996 by the Rwanda Tribunal, to the Government of Cameroon seeking the arrest, transfer, or extradition of a group of key Rwandan suspects.[23] In this particular case, the Cameroon Court of Appeal rejected Rwanda's extradition request and pronounced itself in favour of transfer to the Tribunal, due to the latter's exercise of primacy of jurisdiction, the lack of relevant domestic laws or treaties permitting extradition to Rwanda, and those related to respect of fundamental human rights.[24] From the standpoint of the ICTR, the major objectives of the Security Council are in large part not fulfilled if only low-level figures, rather than the civilian, military and paramilitary leaders who were allegedly responsible for the atrocities, are brought before the Tribunal for justice.[25] The international community's requirement for full accountability from those who committed or authorised the commission of serious international humanitarian law violations requires prioritisation in the exercise of personal jurisdiction over "persons who bear the greatest responsibility".[26] The determination of the meaning of this term in any case falls initially to the Prosecutor, and ultimately to the Court itself.[27] Persons in such a

[20] For an account of some of the tensions, See, M. Morris, *supra* at note 12, at. p. 7.

[21] The international community's interest in demanding that those responsible be brought to justice definitely encompasses the prosecution of those most responsible for the preparation and planning of serious and massive violations of international humanitarian and human rights law.

[22] Instances include that of Jean Paul Akayesu, C. Kayishema, and George Rutaganda, arrested by Zambia; Col. Alphonse Ntenzilyayo, arrested by Burkina Faso; and Andre Rwamakuba, arrested by Namibia.

[23] For procedural history, See, Decision, *Jean-Bosco Barayagwiza v. The Prosecutor*, ICTR, In the Appeals Chamber, 30 November 1999.

[24] Decision of 21 February 1977, Court of Appeal of Yaounde.

[25] Report of the Expert Group to conduct a review of the effective operation and functioning of the International Criminal Tribunal for the Former Yugoslavia and the International Criminal Tribunal for Rwanda, UN doc. A/54/634, 22 Nov. 1999. ICTR's accused (tried, in trial or awaiting trial) include one Prime Minister, ten former Cabinet Ministers, six senior politicians, four senior military officers, three provincial governors, and five Mayors, See Report of Expert Group, *supra*, para. 95.

[26] UNSC Res. 1315 (2000), 14 August 2000, UN Doc. S/RES/1315 (1999) para. 3; Report of the Secretary General on the establishment of a Special Court for Sierra Leone, UN Doc. S/2000/915, 4 October 1999, para. 29; Letter dated 22 December 2000 from the President of the Security Council addressed to the Secretary General, UNSC Doc. S/2000/1234, 22 Dec 2000, para. 1; c.f. Cambodia, Art. 1, "The purpose of this law is to bring to trial senior leaders of the Democratic Kampuchea and those who were responsible for the crimes and serious violations of Cambodian penal law, international humanitarian law and custom, and international conventions recognized by Cambodia, that were committed during the period from 17 April 1975 to 6 January 1979," Law on the Establishment of Extra Ordinary Chambers in the Courts of Cambodia for The Prosecution of Crimes Committed During the Period of the Democratic Kampuchea, adopted by the National Assembly 2 January 2001.

[27] See, Letter dated 12 January 2001 from the Secretary-General addressed to the President of the Security Council, SC Doc. S/2001/40, 12 Jan. 2001, para. 2. "Most responsible" therefore, denotes both a leadership or authority position of the accused, and a sense of the gravity, seriousness or massive scale of the crimes, Report of the Secretary-General, *supra*, paras. 30 & 31.

position include not only those in a leadership, authority or command positions, but also lower level perpetrators, depending on the gravity, seriousness or massive scale of the crimes.[28]

Compared to the early years of the Rwanda Tribunal, considerable headway has been made in the cooperation between Rwanda, the Tribunal and other States. This has been more marked in investigation than in prosecutions.[29]

2.2 REFERRAL

The duality of jurisdiction in the system of the UN Ad Hoc Tribunals, which extends prosecution to both the Tribunal and national courts, is enhanced by a novel injection into the Tribunal's Rules of procedure and evidence of what may be termed "referral". Rule 11 *bis* (ICTY Statute)[30] allows a Trial Chamber to order the suspension of an indictment pending proceedings before national courts in cases where the authorities of a State in which an accused was arrested are prepared to prosecute the accused in their own courts and it is appropriate in the circumstances for the courts of that State to exercise jurisdiction over the accused. Where such an order is made and the accused is in the custody of the Tribunal, the person has to be transferred to the State authorities concerned.[31]

In practice, the application of this rule remains embryonic. Although well intended and meant to facilitate the exercise of concurrent jurisdiction, it falls short of bridging the jurisdictional pitfall in national and international prosecutions. In *Ntuyahaga*,[32] the Prosecutor, pursuant to Rule 51 of the Rules of Procedure and Evidence, sought to withdraw the indictment against the accused, a former senior officer of the Rwandan Armed Forces, on the basis that the prosecution of a single count relating to the murder of Agathe Uwilingiyimana, the former Prime Minister of Rwanda, and 10 UNAMIR (United Nations Mission in Rwanda) Belgian soldiers in Kigali on 7 April 1994 would not serve her objective of exposing the totality of the crimes committed in Rwanda in 1994; that the decision of the Judge who confirmed the Indictment had limited her capacity to prosecute the accused; and that withdrawal would facilitate prosecution by national courts. She requested the Trial Chamber to order the handover of the accused to the authorities of the United Republic of Tanzania, the Host Country, to which extradition requests by both Rwanda and Belgium have been lodged. Belgium also argued, as *amicus curiae* before the Trial Chamber, that the Tribunal had the power to transfer the accused to Belgium to be tried before its national courts and that the indictment should be withdrawn. The Trial Chamber granted the withdrawal of the indictment and ordered the immediate and unconditional release of the accused from the Tribunal's detention facility. It categorically stated that it was not within the powers of the Tribunal, as defined in the Statute and the

[28] C.f. The Rwanda Genocide Law includes in Category I those who acted in position of authority at the cell (nyumba kumi) (ten houses) level, as well as notorious murders who by virtue of the zeal or excessive malice committed atrocities.

[29] 'Rwanda Genocide Court seeks suspects in Zambia', *The Guardian*, Dar es Salaam, 29 Dec. 2000.

[30] No such corresponding rule has been incorporated into the ICTR Rules of Procedure and Evidence.

[31] Rule 11*bis* (B), ICTY.

[32] *Prosecutor v. Bernard Ntuyahaga*, ICTR-98-40-T, Decision on the Prosecutor's Motion to Withdraw the Indictment, 18 March 1999. On his release from the ICTR Detention Facility, Tanzanian Authorities immediately arrested Ntuyahaga. He is currently facing extradition proceedings before Tanzanian Courts, based on Rwanda's extradition request to the Government of Tanzania.

Rules, to order that a released person be handed over to the authorities of any State, including the Host Country of the Tribunal.[33] This decision highlights one of the problems in the effective exercise of concurrent jurisdiction that exists when there is no statutory or legal connecting tissue between international and domestic judicial systems. The jurisdictional infirmity represented in *Ntuyahaga* can only find cure in prior and agreed judicial cooperation arrangements in criminal matters.

3. Concurrent Jurisdiction: East Timor

The investigation and prosecution of serious international humanitarian and human rights law violations committed in East Timor in 1999 represents another model in the exercise of concurrent jurisdiction between the United Nations and States, in particular Indonesia. It is an amalgam of international and national legal and policy options. As we shall illustrate, the UN, Indonesia, or other States can adjudicate crimes against humanity committed in 1999 in East Timor.

Following the results of the popular consultation, organised under the auspices of the UNAMET[34] (United Nations Mission in East Timor), declared on 4 September 1999, and in which 78.5 per cent of East Timorese voted against the proposed special autonomy under the Unitary State of the Republic of Indonesia, an orchestrated campaign of violence by pro-autonomy militia escalated throughout East Timor.[35] These widespread and systematic attacks on the civilian population were committed with the active involvement of large elements of the Indonesian Armed Forces (TNI) and the Indonesian Police Force (POLRI).[36] Intimidation, terror and acts violating the basic rights to life were allowed to be carried out by the authorities with impunity.[37]

On 10 September 1999, the UN Secretary General called upon Indonesia to seek help from the international community in fulfilling its responsibility to bring order and security to East Timor, and warned that if it refused to do so, it could not escape responsibility of what could amount to crimes against humanity.[38] On 15 September 1999, the Security Council expressed concern at reports indicating that systematic, widespread and flagrant violations of international humanitarian law had been committed, condemned the acts of violence, and demanded that those responsible be brought to justice.[39] It considered the situation a threat to peace and security and, acting under Chapter VII of the Charter, authorised a multinational force under a unified command structure, pursuant to Indonesia's

---

[33] "The Chamber is of the opinion that primacy recognized by the Statute is clear in as much as the Tribunal may request any national jurisdiction to defer investigations or ongoing proceedings, whereas the reverse, namely deferral of investigations and proceedings by the Tribunal to any national jurisdiction, is not provided for," *Prosecutor v. Bernard Ntuyahaga, supra*, note 31, 18 March 1999.

[34] Established by UNSC Res. 1246 (1999), 11 June 1999; UNSC Res. 1257 (1999), 3 August 1999.

[35] See Report of International Commission of Inquiry on East Timor, UN. Doc. A/54/726, S/2000/59, 31 January 2000; Report of the High Commissioner for Human Rights on the situation in East Timor, Doc. E/CN.4/S-4/CRP.1, 17 September 1999.

[36] *Id.*, Report of the International Commission, paras. 93, 123, 142, 138-140.

[37] Report of the Security Council Mission to Jakarta and Dili, UNSC Doc.S/1999/976, 14 September 1999, para. 14

[38] Secretary-General's Press Conference, 10 September 1999, in The United Nations and East Timor, Self-determination through popular consultation, DPA, UN , N.Y., 2000, para 75.

[39] UNSC Res. 1264 (1999), UN doc. S/RES/1264, 15 September 1999

request to restore peace and security in East Timor, and authorised it to take all necessary measures to fulfil its mandate.[40]

While actively seized of the matter, the Security Council acted on 25 October 1999 under Chapter VII and established, by Resolution 1272 (1999), the United Nations Transitional Administration in East Timor (UNTAET), endowing it with the overall responsibility for the administration in East Timor and empowering it to exercise all legislative and executive authority, including the administration of justice.[41] The Council further condemned all acts of violence, and those in support of it, and demanded once again that those responsible for such violence be brought to justice.[42]

3.1 CRIMINAL ACCOUNTABILITY

Well-documented reports by the Special Rapporteurs of the UN Human Rights Commission indicate that the Indonesian Armed Forces (TNI) were sufficiently involved in the operational activities of the militia, which for the most part were the direct perpetrators of the crimes, to incur the responsibility of the Government of Indonesia.[43] The report of the International Commission of Inquiry on human rights violations in East Timor also highlights the direct involvement of the TNI and the POLRI,[44] a finding corroborated by the Indonesian Commission on Human Rights.[45] In discussing the East Timor events, the UN Special Rapporteurs did not envision an ad hoc international criminal tribunal, and the nearest they went was to put such a possibility in abeyance conditional to steps by the Government of Indonesia to investigate TNI involvement, "both in the way of credible clarification of the facts and the bringing to justice of the perpetrators — both direct and by virtue of command responsibility, however the level of responsibility."[46] The International Commission of Inquiry, on the other hand, recommended the establishment of an international human rights tribunal, to be composed of judges appointed by the UN, Indonesia and East Timor, that would sit in Indonesia or East Timor to adjudicate the crimes committed.[47]

3.2 CONCURRENT JURISDICTION: LEGAL FRAMEWORK

The regulatory scheme governing the United Nations exercise of jurisdiction to investigate and prosecute serious international humanitarian and human rights violations in East Timor is UNTAET Regulations 1999/1, "On the Authority of the Transitional

[40] *Id.*, UNSC res. 1264, para. 3.
[41] UNSC Res.1272, UN doc. S/RES/1272, 25 October 1999.
[42] *Id.*, para. 16
[43] See Report of the Special Rapporteur on extrajudicial, summary or arbitrary executions, the Special Rapporteur on the question of torture, and the Special Rapporteur on violence against women, "Situation of Human Rights in East Timor," Note by the Secretary-General, UNGA, 54th session, Agenda Item 116(c), 8 December 1999.
[44] UN Doc, A/54/726, 5/2000/59, 31 January 2000; see also Question of East Timor, Progress Report of the Secretary-General, UN doc. A/54/654, 13 December 1999, UNGA, 54th Session, Agenda item 96: Question of East Timor, para 32.
[45] Indonesian Commission for Human Rights Violations in East Timor (KPP-HAM), Executive Summary, 31 January 2000.
[46] Report of Special Rapporteurs, *id.*, para. 74(6).
[47] Report of the International Commission of Inquiry, *id.*, para. 153.

Administration in East Timor," Regulations 2000/11 "On the Organization of Courts," and 2000/15, "On the Establishment of Panels with Exclusive Jurisdiction over Serious Criminal Offences," which establish "Panels" for Serious Crimes at the Dili District Court.[48] These have exclusive jurisdiction to try serious criminal offences, defined to include genocide and crimes against humanity, as well as murder and sexual violence prosecutable under the Penal Code of Indonesia, if committed between 1 January 1999 and 25 October 1999.[49] Regulation 2000/15 mirrors the Statute of the International Criminal Court.[50] The Panels for Serious Crimes have universal jurisdiction with regard to the crime of genocide and crimes against humanity, and jurisdiction extends irrespective whether the offence occurred within the territory of East Timor, was committed by an East Timorese Citizen, or the victim was an East Timorese national.

Two periods of temporal jurisdiction are envisaged: for crimes in which the Panels for Serious Crimes have universal jurisdiction, no time period is prescribed; for serious crimes under the Penal Code of Indonesia, the requirement is that crimes should have been committed between 1 January and 25 October 1999, insofar as the law applicable does not conflict with the standards reflected, in particular, in the universal human rights instruments, are not discriminatory on the grounds recognised under international law (race, ethnic origin, religion, political opinion, social origin, language, sex, etc.) or with the fulfilment of UNTAET's transitional mandate or any other regulation issued by UNTAET.[51] The Panels for Serious Crimes are each composed of one East Timorese judge and two international judges at both the Trial and Appeal Chambers. In cases of special importance or gravity, the Appeal Chamber is to be constituted by a panel of five judges comprised of three international and two East Timorese judges.[52] As of 31 December 2000, twenty-four persons had been charged in twelve indictments alleging serious crimes under the Penal Code of Indonesia and one indictment containing crimes against humanity charges. Article 10.4 of Regulation 2000/11 provides that the establishment of the Panels for Serious Crimes with exclusive jurisdiction over serious offences shall not preclude the jurisdiction of an international tribunal for East Timor over these offences, once such a Tribunal is established. As stated by the UN Secretary-General on 18 February 2000, the setting up of an international court would be dependent on action taken by Indonesia to prosecute those responsible for the violence.[53]

[48] Reg. 1999/1, UNTAET/REG/1999/1, 27 Nov. 1999, Sec. 1, 3, 4, & 8; Reg. 2000/11, UNTAET/REG/2000/11, 6 March 2000, amended by UNTAET Reg. 2000/14, 14 May 2000; Reg.2000/15, UNTAET/REG/2000/15, 6 June 2000.

[49] Sec. 10, UNTAET Reg. 2000/11 on the 'Organization of the Courts in East Timor' 6 March 2000; and Sec. 1, UNTAET Reg. 2000/ 15 of 6 June 2000, UNTAET/REG/2000/15.

[50] 1998 Rome Statute of the International Criminal Court, entered into force 1 July 2002; UN doc. A/CONF.183/9*, as corrected by the procès-verbaux of 10 November 1998 and 12 July 1999. Corrected text available at http://www.un.org/law/icc. See especially sections 2, 4 to 7, and 11 to 21, Regulation 2000/15.

[51] Sec. 2.4, UNTAET Reg. 2000/15; Sec. 2 & 3, UNTAET Reg.1999/1, 27 November 1999, UNTAET/REG/1999/1.

[52] Part IV, Sec. 22, UNTAET Regulation 2000/15.

[53] Statement of the Secretary-General, 18 February 2000, cited in "The United Nations and East Timor, Self-determination through popular consultation," DPI, UN, N.Y. 2000, para. 92, "International Tribunal likely as TNI refuses UN Quiz," Indonesian Observer, 13 December 2000; "Refusal to be Investigated by UNTAET, An International Tribunal can be Enforced," Kompass, Jakarta, 11 Dec 2000; "East Timor leader warns of war crimes tribunal," Reuters, 24 January 2001.

Indonesia exercises concurrent jurisdiction in relation to the 1999 events in East Timor by virtue of its authority and responsibility over East Timor, personal jurisdiction over its nationals, and the express demands made to it by the international community to bring to justice those responsible for the violence. The jurisdictional principles we have noted earlier, such as the active nationality and universal principles, also support this exercise of concurrent jurisdiction. This notwithstanding, Security Council resolutions 1272 (1999) and 1319 (2000) have expressly demanded that those responsible be brought to justice in East Timor or Indonesia. Indonesia has reaffirmed its commitment to pursuing investigations and prosecutions.[54] The Indonesia House of Representatives has adopted the necessary legislation for the establishment of a Human Rights Court to deal with the crimes of genocide and crimes against humanity.[55]

This legislation fills in the legal void that existed in Indonesia for the prosecution of serious violations of international humanitarian and human rights law committed in East Timor.[56] The Human Rights Court is a special court within the courts of general jurisdiction (Article 2) with special authority to hear and rule on cases of gross violations of human rights perpetrated by an Indonesian citizen outside the territorial boundaries of the Republic of Indonesia (Article 5). The Court is required to apply the provisions of the criminal procedure code (Article 10) and lays down prescribed time limits for the judicial process. The Attorney General of Indonesia has been designated as the Investigator and Prosecutor of gross human rights violations (Article 12). The legislation authorises inquiries into cases of gross human rights violations to be undertaken by the National Commission of Human Rights, whose findings are to be submitted to the Attorney General, should it consider that there is sufficient preliminary evidence that a gross human rights violation has taken place (Articles 18 to 20).

Nineteen suspects were officially named on 7 January 2000 by Indonesia's Attorney General. They included Militia commanders, District Military Commanders (Dandim), District Administrators (Bupati), Regional Military commanders (Danrem), the Chief of Police (Kapolda), the Military Area Commander (Pangdam) and the ex Governor of East Timor.[57]

The twin track exercise of concurrent jurisdiction by UNTAET and Indonesia prompted the formalisation of cooperation through a Memorandum of Understanding (MOU) on

---

[54] Report of the Security Council Mission to Dili and Jakarta, 9-17 November 2000, UN doc. S/2000/1105, 20 November 2000; "The Government of Indonesia is duty-bound to respect the independence of all these legal processes, including the ongoing investigations into human rights violations in East Timor", Letter dated 27 November 2000 from the *Chargé d'affaires* a.i. of the Permanent Mission of Indonesia to the United Nations, addressed to the President of the Security Council, UNSC doc. S/2000/1125, 27 Nov. 2000, para. 17; "The issue of (law and human rights) violations in East Timor must be immediately solved or else the international community will question our consistency in upholding the law", Statement of Attorney General of Indonesia, in "Chief Prosecutor says UN Timor probe has no political motives," AFP, 11 Dec. 2000; "Human Rights Abusers in East Timor to be tried in Indonesia: Official," Xinhua News Agency, 14 Dec. 2000.

[55] Republic of Indonesia, Act No 26/2000 Concerning Human Rights Court, House of Representatives of the Republic of Indonesia. The Act was assented to by the President of Indonesia on 23 Nov. 2000.

[56] Investigations were commissioned by the Attorney General of Indonesia on the basis of the KPP-Ham Report (1999) before the passing of the Human Rights Court law.

[57] Additional persons have since been named making a total of 22 persons as of 31 Dec. 2000. However, as yet no formal charges have been instituted.

"Cooperation in Legal, Judicial and Human Rights Related Matters."[58] The MOU reaffirms the parties' mutual commitment to hold accountable the perpetrators of the serious violations of international humanitarian and human rights law in East Timor. It draws inspiration from the UN General Assembly Model Treaty on Mutual Assistance in Criminal Matters[59]and the Model Treaty on Extradition.[60] Modalities and procedures for mutual assistance in investigations, exhumations and forensic examinations, arrest, access to information, questioning of witnesses, transfer of suspects or accused, witness protection and court proceedings have been spelled out in the MOU.[61]

4. Conclusion

Concurrent jurisdiction provides the safety net for ensuring the effective investigation and prosecution of serious international and human rights law violations. This duality of competence, if exercised, hikes the propensity for criminal accountability. It remains a viable form of complementary judicial action in the international and domestic fields. The exercise of concurrent jurisdiction works well where the legal framework is well established. The enactment of appropriate domestic penal legislation remains a prime requirement. In the case of UN bodies, such as the UN Ad Hoc Tribunals (ICTY and ICTR) and UNTAET, an overarching Security Council mandate under Chapter VII of the UN Charter has broadened the pathway and accelerated the investigation and prosecution of international crimes bv these institutions.

The incorporation of a system of referral by the ICTY is a well-thought out measure intended to extend the scope of concurrent jurisdiction between it and the national courts of all States. This possibility, however, remains untested. In situations of serious international humanitarian and human rights law violations, the up-front articulation of appropriate cooperation arrangements on judicial and legal assistance enhances the prospects for the effective exercise of concurrent jurisdiction. It helps avoid feuding in the apportioning of suspects or accused. To ensure that concurrent jurisdiction does not lead to competing claims, but mutual partnership in the repression and prevention of serious crimes, there still remains a need to further intertwine international and domestic penal procedures.

[58] Signed 6 April 2000. For full text, see Official Gazette of East Timor, UNTAET/GAZ/2000/Add.2, Vol.1, No. 3, 22 May 2000, p. 93–96.

[59] Annex to UNGA Res. 45/117, UNGA doc. A/RES/45/117, 14 Dec.1990.

[60] Annex to UNGA Res. 45/116, UNGA doc. A/RES/45/116, 14 Dec.1990.

[61] Recently, the MOU has been challenged by a legal team representing TNI (TNI Officers Human Rights Advocacy Team), on the grounds that it was entered into illegally and in violation of Act. No. 24/2000, of 23 October 2000, concerning ratification of International Agreements; See also, Report of the Secretary-General on the United Nations Transitional Administration in East Timor (for the period 27 July 2000 to 16 January 2001), S.C. Doc. S/2001/42, 16 Jan. 2001 para. 25; "Indonesia Army Chief backs lawyers refusing UN probe over Timor," AFP, 12 Dec 2000.

WHAT IF: PROSECUTING CRIMES OF CHEMICAL TERROR

William W. Burke-White*

1. INTRODUCTION

Amidst the horror of 11 September, one terrible fear thankfully was not realised. The planes which struck the World Trade Centers and the Pentagon did not release a cloud of chemical weapons over their target cities, exponentially increasing the death toll of an already gruesome tragedy. As the anthrax attacks reminded us all, however, the possibility of mass use of biological or chemical weapons is all too real.

What if, however, the events of 11 September had included an attack with chemical agents? This chapter poses the hypothetical that the attacks of 11 September did, in fact, use chemical weapons. How could the perpetrators of such acts be brought to justice? What mechanisms exist to prosecute individual terrorists who use chemical weapons against civilian populations?

Significant developments in international criminal law over the past decade have expanded the prosecution options available to States, and to the international community, for such crimes. First, the ad hoc International Criminal Tribunals for Yugoslavia and Rwanda have developed a *corpus* of international criminal law. Further, United States President Bush's creation of military tribunals in the wake of 11 September indicate the potential for military justice. The Pinochet case, in which the former Chilean leader was brought before British courts, reflects the growing use of universal jurisdiction to prosecute domestically crimes that occur extraterritorially. Finally, the Rome Statute of the International Criminal Court[1] entered into force on 1 July, 2002, adding a significant new means for international prosecutions.

2. POSSIBLE FORA

By posing the hypothetical "what if" 11 September included a chemical attack, this chapter will systematically address the options for prosecution of individual perpetrators of a chemical weapons attack and will consider the potential fora for prosecution of chemical terror. The pros and cons of these fora are weighed and the potential charges that could be brought are considered.

The vocal debate as to the preferred means of prosecuting Al Qaeda suspects and the increasing options for prosecuting chemical crimes have led to some public confusion.

---

* Special Assistant to the Dean, Woodrow Wilson School, Princeton University.

[1] 1998 Rome Statute of the International Criminal Court, entered into force 1 July 2002; UN doc. A/CONF.183/9*, as corrected by the procès-verbaux of 10 November 1998 and 12 July 1999. Corrected text available at http://www.un.org/law/icc.

R. Yepes-Enríquez and L. Tabassi. (eds.), Treaty Enforcement and International Cooperation in Criminal Matters

Broadly speaking, five different types of fora exist in which perpetrators of a chemical weapons attack could be tried: (1) the domestic courts of the State in which the crime occurred (in our 11 September hypothetical, the United States); (2) the domestic courts of another State (perhaps where the alleged perpetrators were apprehended or where they held citizenship); (3) a military tribunal; (4) an international court; or (5) an internationalised domestic court.

2.1 LOCAL DOMESTIC COURTS

Local courts have long been, and will continue to be, the backbone of any system of global justice. The local courts of the State where the chemical attack occurred (again, in our hypothetical, the United States) have jurisdiction over events perpetrated on their territory and are therefore empowered to prosecute such crimes. Likewise, courts in the State of the perpetrators' nationality have jurisdiction to prosecute their own nationals and would likewise be considered a local domestic court with jurisdiction over the accused.

Most local courts apply domestic law pursuant to the country's penal code. The perpetrators of a chemical attack would, therefore, have to be charged with domestic crimes under that penal code. In the United States, criminal charges for a chemical attack could be brought under both state and federal law. Under state law, they would likely include murder and/or attempted murder. Under federal law they could include conspiracy and terrorism, among others. Two recent cases are illustrative of these possible charges under domestic federal and state law. First, Richard Reid, the alleged "shoe-bomber" who, in December, 2001, attempted to bring down an American Airlines' flight from Paris to Miami, has been indicted on nine counts in United States Federal Court, including: planting an explosive device on an aircraft, willfully attempting to set fire to and destroy an aircraft, and attempted wrecking of a mass trasportation vehicle.[2] Second, Zacarias Moussaoui, accused of conspiring with Al Qaeda as the twentieth hijacker of 11 September, has been indicted on six counts in the Federal District Court for the Eastern District of Virginia: conspiracy to commit acts of terrorism, conspiracy to commit aircraft piracy, conspiracy to kill United States employees, conspiracy to destroy aircraft, conspiracy to use weapons of mass destruction, and conspiracy to destroy property.[3] Under federal law in the United States, most of these charges could carry the death penalty.

In our hypothetical case adding a chemical weapons component to the 11 September terror, the accused could also be charged specifically with the use of chemical weapons. The Chemical Weapons Convention requires each State Party to "Prohibit natural and legal persons anywhere on its territory or in any other place under its jurisdiction as recognised by international law from undertaking any activity prohibited to a State Party under this Convention, including enacting penal legislation with respect to such activity."[4] Thus, States are obligated to enact requisite enabling legislation to criminalise chemical attacks and to allow prosecution thereof. This provision has been codified in United States law as 18 U.S.C.A. § 229, which makes it "unlawful for any person knowingly ... to develop, produce,

[2] United States of America v. Richard Colvin Reid, Indictment No. 02-10013-WGY, 16 Jan. 2002.

[3] United States of America v. Zacarias Moussaoui, Indictment, Dec. 2001.

[4] 1993 Convention on the Prohibition of the Development, Production, Stockpiling and Use of Chemical Weapons and on Their Destruction, entered into force on 29 April 1997, at Article VII, 1(a). Text, as corrected and changed, available at http://www.opcw.org.

otherwise acquire, transfer directly or indirectly, receive, stockpile, retain, own, possess, or use, or threaten to use, any chemical weapon."[5] United States Courts are given jurisdiction over such offences when the crime occurs in the United States, is committed by a United States national, or is committed against a United States national or United States property.[6] Only nation States which have enacted such specific legislation criminalising the use of chemical weapons would be able to charge the accused directly with a chemical weapons crime.[7] States which have not adopted such specific legislation would be able to prosecute a chemical weapons attack by charging the underlying constituent elements of the crime such as murder or attempted murder.

Each country's domestic courts follow a different set of procedures and rules, determined either at the federal or state level. In a gross over-simplification of the procedures in the United States, prosecution would begin with an investigation by local and/or federal authorities. Then, a district attorney, presumably at the federal level, would draft an indictment that would be presented to a grand jury. The grand jury, in turn, would formally indict the accused. The accused would have a right to counsel, provided by the State if necessary. After suitable (often significant) time for preparation of the case, the accused would be entitled to an adversarial trial by jury, during which he could both present and confront witnesses. If convicted, he would have a right to appeal questions of law to a federal court of appeals and would have the right to a discretionary appeal to the United States Supreme Court. The accused would be entitled to all federal and state constitutional guarantees, including the right to *habeas corpus* to petition against detention in violation of the federal Constitution. Such rights would include procedural guarantees at trial, the admission of evidence, as well as conditions of detention and punishment. Procedure in most common law countries is comparable, though many would prohibit the death penalty.

In the emerging regime of international criminal law, local courts are and should be the legal front-line for the prosecution of all crimes, supplemented when necessary. First, local courts are ubiquitous. Nearly every State has courts of justice, though these differ in form, structure and procedure. Second, local courts are more likely close to the acts in question. Given physical proximity, local courts may have the best access to information about the events in question. Third, local courts are most likely to serve restorative as well as retributive justice. As these courts usually sit in or near the affected communities, they may be more likely to play a role in the local healing process after acts of reprehensible violence.

There are, however, significant dangers in the local prosecution of international crimes. First, local courts are more likely to be biased. After all, the very proximity to the crime, the local press coverage, and the searing pain of knowing victims and survivors, may undermine the fairness of the procedure. Second, the quality of justice in local courts varies drastically. Third, in an international prosecution there is often a need to convince a global polity of the fairness of the criminal procedure. Local courts are least likely to be viewed as fair and unbiased by outside observers. Nonetheless, local courts do have an important role to play

[5] 18 U.S.C.A. § 229.

[6] *Id.*

[7] Russia, for example, has adopted such legislation and could charge chemical attacks directly. See, e.g., Penal Code of the Russian Federation, Ministry of Justice of the Russian Federation (1996) at Article 355 *et. seq*; see also Marc Weller & William Burke-White, No Place to Hide: New Developments in the Exercise of International Criminal Justice (forthcoming 2002) at ch. 2 (providing pertinent portions of various State national codes).

in the prosecution of international crimes. There may be times and circumstances when such local courts need to be strengthened, supplemented or have their credibility reinforced by other mechanisms of justice.

2.2 FOREIGN DOMESTIC COURTS

The case of Augusto Pinochet, in which a Spanish judge brought charges against the former Chilean general and sought his extradition from England, is illustrative of the principle of universal jurisdiction.[8] The universality principle allows any State which apprehends the perpetrator of the most serious crimes to prosecute him, even if the State is not otherwise connected to the crime itself. Only the most serious international crimes such as genocide, crimes against humanity, torture, and war crimes can be prosecuted under this principle.[9]

For the perpetrators of a chemical attack to be prosecuted through the use of universal jurisdiction, they must be charged, not simply with domestic crimes such as murder, but with particular international crimes. While a chemical attack alone has not yet been deemed an international crime giving rise to universal jurisdiction, the background circumstances of the attack are likely sufficient to constitute a war crime or a crime against humanity. War crimes, as defined in the Geneva Conventions, must occur as part of an armed conflict. If a chemical attack was part of such an armed conflict, it may constitute a grave breach of the Geneva Conventions, subject to universal jurisdiction. Crimes against humanity consist of a number of acts, such as murder or rape, conducted as part of a systematic attack on a civilian population.[10] Where a chemical attack caused deaths as part of an organised campaign targeted against civilians, the attack could be considered a crime against humanity. The accused could be charged therewith and prosecuted under the universality principle.

Even if the requisite elements of a war crime or crime against humanity were not met in the case of a particular chemical attack, it is at least possible that the use of chemical weapons itself could give rise to universal jurisdiction. If this were the case, the perpetrator could be charged and tried directly for the use of chemical weapons, rather than for the commission of a war crime or a crime against humanity. Given that chemical weapons attacks are intended to take civilian life indiscriminately, such attacks share with war crimes and crimes against humanity the characteristic of being directed against all civilised peoples and all countries. Perpetrators of such attacks could be considered *hostis humane generis* — enemies of all human kind who have forfeited the protection of any State and can be prosecuted by any State. While the Chemical Weapons Convention does not specifically authorise universal prosecution of chemical attacks, it does not prohibit such jurisdiction. The Convention does call for broad jurisdiction, requiring States to be able to prosecute their own nationals for chemical attacks "undertaken anywhere." Given the grave nature of a chemical attack, the extension of prosecution of chemical attacks to any person "undertaken anywhere" would be a logical progression.

---

[8] See, e.g., Marc Weller, *On the Hazards of Foreign Travel for Dictators and other International Criminals*, Volume 75, no. 3 International Affairs 599-617 (July 1999).

[9] Princeton University Program in Law and Public Affairs, The Princeton Principles on Universal Jurisdiction 28 (2001).

[10] See, e.g., Guenael Mettreaux, *Crimes Against Humanity*, 43 Harvard International Law Journal 237 (2002).

Many States have enacted domestic legislation to enable prosecutions of war crimes, genocide, and crimes against humanity under the universality principle. Where the requisite background elements of these crimes were met, such States would be able to prosecute the perpetrator of a chemical attack not otherwise connected to the State. Such States include, to mention just a few, Belgium,[11] Brazil,[12] Canada,[13] Chile,[14] Denmark,[15] El Salvador,[16] Ethiopia,[17] Finland,[18] Germany,[19] Honduras,[20] Israel,[21] Norway,[22] Portugal,[23] Romania,[24] Spain,[25] Sweden,[26] Switzerland,[27] Uruguay,[28] and Yugoslavia.[29] While universal prosecutions remain rare, there are a growing number of examples beyond the much-cited Pinochet case. Belgium has convicted numerous individuals of war crimes against civilian populations in Rwanda.[30] Likewise, Germany has prosecuted war crimes against civilians in Bosnia.[31] Cases brought under the universality principle would follow the criminal procedure of the court in which the case is brought, though customary international law guarantees a free and fair trial with appropriate procedural safeguards.[32]

The principal benefit of the use of universal jurisdiction is the provision of an alternate means of bringing to justice serious criminals when the State where the crimes occurred is unable or unwilling to prosecute. In the Pinochet case, for example, Chile was neither able

---

[11] *Loi du 3.12.1998* and *Code d'instruction criminelle, Article 10.* Also, *Loi relative à la répression des violations graves du droit international humanitaire*, Article 7 (10 February 1999).

[12] *Codigo Penal Militar de Brazil*, Article 208.

[13] The Crimes against Humanity and War Crimes Act of 2000.

[14] Penal Code article 150 and *Código de procemiento penal*, Articles 6 and 8.

[15] See Bukh, Marianne, *Prosecution Before Danish Courts of Foreigners Suspected of Violations of Human Rights or Humanitarian Law*, 6 European Review of Public Law 339 (1994). Also, Article 8(6) of the Danish Penal Code.

[16] *Código Penal de El Salvador*, Article 361.

[17] Penal Code of Ethiopia, Articles 17(1) and 281.

[18] Penal Code of Finland (1975).

[19] German Penal Code, Article 220a and Article 6(1).

[20] *Código Penal de Honduras*, Articles 5(5) and 319.

[21] Israeli Criminal Code, Section 169.

[22] Norwegian Penal Code, Articles 12, 223, 224, and 225.

[23] Art. 5(1)(b) and 239 of the *Código Penal Português* (Portuguese Penal Code).

[24] Penal Code of Romania, Article 358. The act must also be criminal in the place of commission for Romania to be able to exercise jurisdiction. Article 357 defines genocide as a crime.

[25] *Ley Orgánica del Poder Judicial. Boletín Oficial del Estado*, No. 157, Art. 23.4 of the 1985 Organic Law of the Judicial Branch; Penal Code Article 607.

[26] Penal Law on Genocide of Sweden, (1964) Article 169.

[27] Swiss Military Penal Code, Article 109. Switzerland can only exercise universal jurisdiction when the crime is committed as part of an armed conflict.

[28] Penal Code of Uruguay, Article 10(7) and draft Law XLIII, Articles 7 and 8.

[29] *La Loi Pénale de la République Socialiste Federative de Yougoslavie*, 28 September 1976.

[30] The Belgian, *Loi relative à la répression des violations graves de droit international humanitaire* (10 Feb. 1999), published in the Moniteur Belge (23 Mar. 1999), Article 7, allows prosecution under the universality principle. Cases have included the trials of two Catholic nuns, Consolata Mukangango and Julienne Mukabutera, who were sentenced to over 10 years imprisonment. See World News Connection (10 October 2001), 2001 WL28793236.

[31] See, e.g., *Prosecutor v. Novislav Djajic*, 92 American Journal of International Law 528 (1998) (prosecution under the universality principle for killing unarmed Muslim civilians); see also *Prosecution v. Nicolai Jorgic*, Oberlandesgericht Dusseldorf, 26 September 1997.

[32] See, e.g., International Covenant on Civil and Political Rights codifying many of the customary international rules relating to rights to a fair trial.

nor willing to prosecute its ex-president. Universal jurisdiction offered an alternative recourse to ensure that Pinochet did not escape justice. Among the drawbacks of prosecutions under universal jurisdiction are that the prosecuting court may be far removed from the locus of the crime, making investigation and community engagement with the proceedings more difficult and the potential reconciling effects of justice more elusive. Second, some individuals and groups may not recognise the right of the prosecuting State to exercise universal jurisdiction, impeding the perceived legitimacy of the process. Third, many States have not enacted the requisite domestic legislation to prosecute crimes universally, making prosecution impossible in some cases. Finally, as the Pinochet case indicates, such prosecutions are easily politicised and may cause conflict between a State's judicial and foreign affairs functions. Nonetheless, in many cases, prosecution under the universality principle is the best or the only way to avoid impunity for serious international criminals.

To return to our hypothetical, had the attacks of 11 September used chemical weapons and the perpetrators were apprehended in Belgium, for example, they could have been prosecuted under the universality principle. Belgium has enacted the requisite domestic legislation and, assuming the accused were apprehended in, or extradited to, Belgium, it would be in a position to prosecute. Belgium would then try the accused in its own national courts following its domestic procedures. In order to establish jurisdiction under the universality principle, charges would have to include war crimes or crimes against humanity.

2.3 MILITARY COURTS

United States President Bush's decision to create military tribunals for the trial of Al Qaeda suspects and 'detainees' raises the possibility of military trials for certain classes of international criminals. Had the perpetrators of the attacks of 11 September used chemical weapons, they too would have become subject to Bush's military order of 13 November 2001. That order requires the United States Secretary of Defense to set regulations for and establish military courts to try any non-United States citizen who "has engaged in, aided or abetted, or conspired to commit, acts of international terrorism."[33] While military courts are extremely rare, there are some precedents. With varying degrees of constitutional legitimacy, the United States used military courts after the Civil War and World War II;[34] Great Britain convened the Diplock Courts to deal with crimes in Northern Ireland; and Israel has relied on military justice in relation to the first Intifada.

The exact structure and the procedures of military courts vary dramatically. President Bush's original order was drafted with extreme breadth, allowing for secret tribunals without guarantees of the core minimum rights to free and fair trial. A vigorous debate has apparently affected some policy shifts within the United States administration. Indications are now that military courts will only be used for some suspects and that the operative regulations, when issued, will provide significantly more procedural protections, including rights to public trial, the right to confront witnesses and the right to counsel.[35] Notably, these military trials will not allow for any appeal to US Federal courts, nor will they provide for the

---

[33] George W. Bush, Military Order, 13 November 2001.
[34] See e.g., *Ex Parte Quirin*, 317 US 1, 31 July 1942.
[35] See e.g., Charles Lane, *Terrorism Tribunal Rights are Expanded,* The Washington Post (28 Dec. 2001) A1.

writ of *habeas corpus*. Both the British Diplock Courts and the Israeli military courts have included many of these protections for the accused.

Like the structure and procedure of military courts, the applicable law is likely to vary widely. The law applied by such courts depends upon the statute or military order authorising such tribunals. The law applied could include the code of military justice of the prosecuting State as well as crimes under customary international law. Charges brought before military courts therefore may include both violations of the relevant code of military justice as well as internationally defined war crimes. In our hypothetical, adding a chemical component to the events of 11 September, and a subsequent United States prosecution by military tribunal, such charges could include murder as a violation of the Uniform Code of Military Justice as well as grave breaches of the Geneva Conventions of 1949.

While military tribunals may offer the promise of short run expediency, such tribunals are not a preferred option for the prosecution of the perpetrators of our hypothetical chemical attack. President Bush and Defense Secretary Rumsfeld have argued that military tribunals are necessary to allow swift trials which do not jeopardise witnesses, judges, and the public at large.[36] However, the successful trials of the first World Trade Center bombers in federal court suggest that ordinary courts can try high-level terror suspects safely and efficiently. The most significant argument against military courts is that any victory in the so-called war on terrorism depends on convincing world opinion that United States actions in Afghanistan and elsewhere were/are justified and that the apprehended individuals are, in fact, proven guilty of terrorist acts. Military courts, which, through the military chain of command, are directly accountable to the President, are widely viewed, both inside and outside the United States, as biased and susceptible to executive pressure. In the case of a terrorist or chemical weapons attack, such perceived bias could undermine the crucial effort to convince the global community that legal proceedings are free and fair. Perceived bias would be compounded by the possibilities for procedural short-cuts, which may exist (or be perceived to exist) when defendants are not guaranteed fundamental rights to trial and have no recourse to an independent appeals court to enforce those rights. In situations where global opinion matters, the need for transparency, procedural regularity, and conformity with international obligations outweighs any expediency military tribunals may offer and militates against the use of such tribunals.

2.4 AN INTERNATIONAL TRIBUNAL

The 1990s witnessed the growth of international tribunals as a viable means of international justice. Though the first such tribunal was convened at Nuremberg in the wake of World War II, it was not until the mid-1990s, with the establishment of the International Criminal Tribunal for the Former Yugoslavia (ICTY) and the International Criminal Tribunal for Rwanda (ICTR), that international courts truly came of age. These two ad hoc tribunals were created by the United Nations Security Council acting under Chapter VII and have very narrow jurisdictional mandates: they are only able to prosecute crimes committed on the territory of the former Yugoslavia after 1 January 1991,[37] and in Rwanda during the period

[36] See, e.g., Mike Allen, *Bush Defends Order for Military Tribunals*, The Washington Post (19 November 2001) A14.

[37] Article 8 of the ICTY Statute, Basic Documents of the ICTY, 1998.

1 January through 31 December 1994,[38] respectively. Since our hypothetical chemical attack happens on United States territory, neither the ICTY nor the ICTR would have jurisdiction, but the tribunals for the former Yugoslavia and Rwanda provide both a useful model for the structure of international tribunals and a growing body of jurisprudence.

The establishment of the International Criminal Court (ICC) in July, 2002 provides a second, though highly limited, option for international prosecution. The ICC lacks retrospective jurisdiction and therefore cannot prosecute crimes that occurred before entry into force.[39] Thus, a past case, such as our hypothetical, would be excluded from its jurisdiction.

Assuming that a chemical attack occurred *after* the ICC Statute entered into force, in limited circumstances the ICC might be available to afford justice. Since the jurisdiction of the ICC is limited to cases of war crimes, crimes against humanity, genocide, and aggression, a chemical attack could only be prosecuted were it to be deemed a war crime or a crime against humanity. Even if the ICC could assert subject matter jurisdiction over the chemical crime, any assertion of personal jurisdiction over the accused would require either that the State of which the accused is a national or the State on whose territory the crime occurred to be party to the Statute or to consent to prosecution. In addition, if any State court with jurisdiction over the crime were undertaking or had undertaken a good faith investigation or prosecution thereof, the ICC could not pre-empt or proceed with its own prosecution. If all of these prerequisites to jurisdiction were met, an ICC case would begin with an investigation by the international prosecutor, who would then present the case to the pre-trial chamber for authorisation of a full investigation. Thereafter, a trial would be heard by a panel of elected international judges following a set of procedural rules still to be established and subject to a right of appeal.[40]

For our hypothetical 11 September chemical attack, however, the ICC Statute was not yet in force. International prosecution would still be possible through a special United Nations-created international court along the lines of the ICTY and the ICTR, or through a Security Council referral of the matter to the ICC pursuant to the ICC Statute. In point of fact, such an ad hoc international court, which would presumably have been created pursuant to a Chapter VII Security Council resolution, was proposed after the 11 September attacks.[41]

In our hypothetical, such a court would have had the specific mandate of prosecuting the perpetrators of the chemical attack and would consist of distinguished international jurists from the victim States of the attack or from a larger pool of qualified international judges. The statute of this international court would specify the procedures to be followed, the applicable law, the rules of evidence, and the nature of appellate review.

The principal difficulty of the international court model is that, until the ICC Statute entered into force, international justice remained an ad hoc enterprise requiring a United Nations Security Council resolution. For political reasons, in many cases such a resolution was difficult or impossible to attain. In addition international courts are extremely expensive. In 2001, the ICTY and ICTR together consumed nearly 10% of the United Nations'

[38] Article 7 of the ICTR Statute, adopted by the United Nations Security Council on 8 November 1994 in resolution SC 955 (1994).

[39] See Rome Statute of the International Criminal Court, 17 July 1998, at Article 11.

[40] See generally, Rome Statute of the International Criminal Court, 17 July 1998.

[41] Anne-Marie Slaughter, *Terrorism and Justice*, The Financial Times (12 October 2001).

assessed budget; the ICTY budget alone was almost US $100M.[42] Where, however, there have been serious international crimes, the benefits of an international court may justify these costs. International courts by their nature involve the global community in the pursuit of justice. In so doing, they imbue the proceedings with the legitimacy which is often essential to meaningful resolution and eventual reconciliations. International courts are also most likely to comply with the basic minimum procedural safeguards contained in the Universal Declaration of Human Rights, the International Covenant on Civil and Political Rights and the Geneva Conventions, to name a few. Finally, international courts may be best able to serve a global deterrent effect, highlighting the consensus and will of the international community to see that the perpetrators of chemical crimes are brought to justice.

2.5 INTERNATIONALISED DOMESTIC COURT

The most recent developments in international justice are internationalised domestic courts. These courts are part of the domestic justice systems of their host countries but include a mix of local and international judges who can apply both international and domestic law. Such courts are currently in operation in East Timor[43] and Kosovo[44] and are soon to come into operation in Sierra Leone[45] The internationalised court in East Timor provides a useful example. The Dili District Court includes a Serious Crimes Special Panel, which can hear cases of crimes including murder, genocide, and crimes against humanity. This panel consists of one East Timorese judge and two international judges. Decisions can be appealed to a similarly structured court of appeals. In the proposed Cambodian example,[46] which at a late stage was abandoned, the Extraordinary Chamber was empowered to prosecute high level crimes committed by the Khmer Rouge regime. It would have consisted of three Cambodian judges and two international judges, but would have required a supermajority of four judges to reach a verdict.[47] Procedurally, these courts follow the basic codes of the respective country's domestic courts with some modifications to accommodate an international bench.

---

[42] Patricia M. Wald, To "Establish Incredible Events by Credible Evidence": The Use of Affidavit Testimony in Yugoslavia War Crimes Tribunal Proceedings, 42 Harvard International Law Journal 535, 536 (2001).

[43] See UNTAET Regulation 2000/11 and *supra* in this volume, M. Othman, Concurrent Jurisdiction: Legal and Policy Considerations.

[44] See UNMIK Regulation 2000/64.

[45] Statute of the Special Court for Sierra Leone (2001), established by agreement between the UN and the Government of Sierra Leone pursuant to the UNSC resolution 1315(2000) of 14 August 2000; see also *infra* in this volume, D. Shraga, *id.*

[46] Law on the Establishment of Extraordinary Chambers in the Courts of Cambodia for the Prosecution of Crimes Committed During the Period of Democratic Kampuchea, as adopted by National Assembly on 2 January 2001; see also *infra* in this volume, Daphna Shraga, Implementing International Criminal Legislation in Mixed Tribunals for Cambodia and Sierra Leone.

[47] His Excellency Sok An, Senior Minister and President of the Task Force for Cooperation with Foreign Legal Experts and Preparation of the Proceedings for the Trial of Senior Khmer Rouge Leaders, "Presentation and Comments on the Draft Law on the Establishment of Extraordinary Chambers in the Courts of Cambodia for the Prosecution of Crimes Committed During the Period of Democratic Kampuchea", 29 December 2000.

In our hypothetical case, the internationalised court model would involve creating a special mixed bench of United States and international judges in the federal justice system. While in the United States this would unquestionably raise significant constitutional challenges given the requirements of Article III of the United States Constitution, it is possible that, pursuant to Article III, the United States Congress could authorise the creation of such a special court or could internationalise the military tribunals, which the Bush administration claims are largely exempt from constitutional protections. This could be accomplished through an act of Congress and/or through the specific rules and regulations for the operation of military tribunals to be issued by the Secretary of Defense. The charges to be heard by such international courts would, of course, depend on the jurisdiction granted in the specific enabling legislation creating the courts. Based on the East Timorese model, the courts could hear international crimes, including crimes against humanity, war crimes, and the use of chemical weapons, as well as the lesser included domestic law offences such as murder.

Internationalised domestic courts — as contrasted with international tribunals or ordinary domestic courts — offer a unique combination of the benefits of many of the models discussed above. First, they can provide some of the legitimacy of an international tribunal, as foreign judges are more likely to be impartial and viewed as such by the larger global community. Likewise, internationalised domestic courts can demonstrate the general global consensus that chemical attacks will not be tolerated. Domestic internationalised courts are also far easier to establish and more inexpensive to operate than their fully internationalised counterparts.[48] They do not require a Security Council resolution and, as they are part of a State's pre-existing domestic judiciary, they can draw on resources already in place without the need to create and fund an entirely new judicial entity. Like pure domestic courts, internationalised domestic courts are proximate to the events in question, have the best access to relevant evidence, and may be able to play a positive role in the local reconciliation and healing processes. Internationalised domestic courts, specially established to deal with the hypothesised chemical crime and properly implemented, might then offer a powerful new mechanism for the enforcement of international criminal law.

3. Conclusion

In the past ten years the options available for the prosecution of serious international crimes such as a chemical weapons attack have expanded greatly. This proliferation of fora for prosecution has provided new mechanisms to ensure that the most serious international criminals do not escape justice. However, unlike domestic criminal justice systems, there are no clear lines and procedures to determine which courts will hear which cases, nor is there a hierarchy of courts as provided by the domestic appeals process. Instead, the emerging system of international criminal law consists of a horizontal network of courts with potentially concurrent and competing claims to jurisdiction. The challenge which lies ahead

[48] Of course, the quality of justice rendered will be directly proportional to the funding provided to the internationalised court. Savings may be available in terms of infrastructure as the court may draw on the pre-existent domestic legal system. However, a clear lesson from East Timor is that where funding is limited or non-existent, the court may not be able to function and certainly will not be able to meet the standards of well funded, fully internationalised courts.

is to devise and institutionalise a set of rules and procedures to navigate this network of courts to maximise its legitimacy, efficiency, and effectiveness.

In determining the appropriate forum to hear our hypothetical case, a few key considerations emerge. First, the basic operating presumption should be that the local domestic court will have jurisdiction to prosecute the crime. Where, however, that State is unable or unwilling to prosecute, or where such a domestic prosecution would not satisfy international demands for a free and fair trial, alternate mechanisms of justice would need to be considered. Where the international community is able to bear the political and economic costs of a fully internationalised tribunal to try the highest level offenders, such as the perpetrators of our hypothetical attack, such a tribunal would likely be the best option. Where the international community cannot bear such costs but the domestic local justice system is willing and able to cooperate, a hybrid internationalised court within the local system may be the preferred option. Where the international community is unwilling to bear significant costs and where the local government is unwilling to cooperate by internationalising its domestic judiciary, prosecution would probably occur in a third State under the principle of universal jurisdiction. In our hypothetical case, international demands for justice militate against the use of purely domestic courts. The decision as to which of the other aforementioned models should be deployed would, of course, depend on the specific context of the case, a context which the deterrent effect of the emergent system of international justice might help prevent ever being realised.

INTERACTION BETWEEN INTERNATIONAL AND NATIONAL CRIMINAL COURTS IN THE ICTY

Fabricio Guariglia*

1. Introduction

This chapter will discuss some of the issues stemming from the regime of concurrent jurisdiction as enshrined in Article 9 of the Statute of the International Criminal Tribunal for the former Yugoslavia (ICTY Statute)[1] and some of the practical experiences the Tribunal has had. It will finish by presenting some interesting examples of what can be called "interactive jurisdiction" or "interactive concurrent jurisdiction" between an international tribunal and domestic authorities.

2. Article 9: Concurrent Jurisdiction and Primacy

Article 9 of the ICTY Statute establishes two principles. The first one, contained in paragraph 1 of Article 9, is the principle of concurrent jurisdiction, clearly indicating that the Tribunal has concurrent jurisdiction with national courts. In paragraph 2 of the same provision, however, it is clearly stated that the Tribunal has primacy over national courts and therefore, in the case of an ongoing national prosecution, the Tribunal is vested with the authority to request the national court to defer to the competence of the Tribunal. In other words, it may step in at any stage of the procedure and basically claim for itself the prosecution of the case, exercising its jurisdiction, which is a natural consequence of the Tribunal's primary mandate for prosecuting serious violations of international criminal law in the territory of the former Yugoslavia.

As far as this principle of primacy is concerned, the Appeals Chamber stated in the *Tadic* decision on jurisdiction[2] that the primacy of the Tribunal over national courts is not inconsistent with the principle of the sovereignty of States under international law. The crimes within the jurisdiction of the Tribunal are universal in nature, transcending the interest of any State. The sovereign right of States cannot take precedent over the right of the international community to act appropriately. In this line of reasoning, primacy appears

* Appeals Counsel, International Criminal Tribunal for the former Yugoslavia (ICTY). The views expressed herein are solely the author's and do not express those of the ICTY or of the United Nations.

[1] Statute of the International Tribunal, adopted 25 May 1993 by UN Security Council resolution S/RES/827 (1993), as amended by UN Security Council resolutions S/RES/1166 (1998), S/RES/1329 (2000) and S/RES/1411 (2002). Amended text available at http://www.un.org/icty.

[2] *Prosecutor v. Tadic*, Case no. IT-94-1-AR72, Appeals Chamber Decision on the Defence Motion for Interlocutory Appeal on Jurisdiction (2 October 1995).

R. Yepes-Enríquez and L. Tabassi. (eds.), Treaty Enforcement and International Cooperation in Criminal Matters

to be an essential element for a successful accomplishment of the very goals of the international tribunal.

Conversely, a very relevant issue is how an international criminal tribunal can constructively coexist with the exercise of jurisdiction by domestic courts over identical crimes on the principle of territoriality, active or passive nationality, or the principle of universal jurisdiction. The latter, as we know, is becoming increasingly relevant for what today has been characterised as an emergent system of international criminal law. In this sense, prosecution by States for serious violations of international humanitarian law is actually a tool to ensure accountability instead of impunity. To a large extent, due to the unavoidable practical limitations of international criminal tribunals, as already highlighted in this volume,[3] it is inconceivable that a structure such as the ICTY would be capable of prosecuting the multiplicity of potential perpetrators of serious violations of international humanitarian law during the Yugoslav conflict. So in this sense, concurrent jurisdiction, as opposed to exclusive jurisdiction, is clearly more effective as a tool against impunity. This, in my view, highlights the importance in this emerging system of international criminal justice of the horizontal enforcement of international humanitarian law, as described in the introduction to this volume.[4] This notion of horizontal enforcement is, at the end of the day, the cornerstone of the Statute of the International Criminal Court (ICC) and its complementarity principle: the assumption that States will exercise jurisdiction nationally vis-à-vis serious violations of international humanitarian law. And it is also important to note that both the ICTY and the International Criminal Tribunal for Rwanda (ICTR) have encouraged all States to prosecute and try those persons responsible for international crimes committed in the former Yugoslavia and in Rwanda without prejudice to the option that both Tribunals eventually may have to assert their own primary jurisdiction.

3. Scope of the Principle of Primacy

Having said this, let's focus for a moment on the scope of the principle of primacy in the ICTY and its consequences. Again, in the *Tadic* jurisdiction decision, the Appeals Chamber stated that, "when an international tribunal such as the present one is created, it must be endowed with primacy over national courts. Otherwise, human nature being what it is, there would be a perennial danger of international crimes being characterised as 'ordinary crimes'..., or proceedings being 'designed to shield the accused,' or cases not being diligently prosecuted.... If not effectively countered by the principle of primacy, any one of those stratagems might be used to defeat the very purpose of the creation of an international criminal jurisdiction, to the benefit of the very people whom it has been designed to prosecute."[5] We may wish to keep that statement in mind when considering the similarity between the arguments supporting the principle of primacy of the tribunal and the very similar arguments that have been offered in support of the ICC, this one vested not with primary jurisdiction or concurrent jurisdiction, but with complementary jurisdiction.

[3] See *supra* in this volume, M. Othman, Concurrent Jurisdiction: Legal and Policy Considerations.

[4] See *supra* in this volume, R. Yepes-Enríquez, Introduction: Enforcement of the Prohibition of Chemical Weapons in its Wider Perspective.

[5] *Prosecutor v. Tadic, supra* note 2, at para. 58.

4. CONSEQUENCES OF THE PRINCIPLE OF PRIMACY

Let's highlight now the consequences of the principle of primacy as defined by the ICTY Appeals Chamber. The immediate consequences are formulation of the *non bis in idem* principle in such a way that on the one hand, it allows an examination by the Tribunal of national prosecutions and a subsequent prosecution before the International Tribunal — not only where national proceedings are sham proceedings or proceedings have been tailored in such a way that the main objective is to shield the accused from international prosecution, but also where the crime has been characterised as an ordinary crime. It is interesting to note here that this, to a certain extent, resembles what is found at times in federal jurisdictions. In that scenario, the supremacy of federal law allows a second prosecution at the federal level for exactly the same factual transaction but under a new *nomen iuris* (legal characterisation) which reflects that a different body of law has been affected by the crime, that second body of law being federal law. Following that reasoning, in the case of the ICTY this flexible principle of *non bis in idem* allows the ICTY to conduct a second prosecution at the international level to defend the values protected by international law that have been violated by the conduct. At the same time, the flexible formulation of the principle of *non bis in idem* in Article 10 of the ICTY Statute ensures the finality of decisions by the International Tribunal by precluding subsequent prosecutions at the national level once a person has been tried by the international tribunal.

The second, and perhaps more important, immediate consequence of the principle of primacy is the authority of the ICTY, especially the Prosecutor of the ICTY, to obtain information on national prosecutions or to make a request to national States for cooperation and judicial assistance in respect of any investigation or prosecution that the State may be conducting on crimes that fall within the jurisdiction of the International Tribunal. Such a request by the Prosecutor triggers the duty of each State to respond promptly under Article 29 of the ICTY Statute and Rule 8 of the ICTY Rules of Procedure and Evidence.[6] The Prosecutor also has the authority to make a formal request for deferral under Rules 9 and 10 of the ICTY Rules of Procedure and Evidence on the basis of the same exceptions that apply to the *non bis in idem* principle, i.e., in the case of the characterisation of the crime as an ordinary crime in the national proceedings, or in the case of sham proceedings or proceedings designed to protect the accused. Rule 9 goes even further, however, highlighting the broad powers with which the Tribunal is vested, and provides authority to the Prosecutor to make a formal request for deferral when the importance of the factual or legal questions involved in the case so justify. So basically the bottom line is that the Tribunal has a broad authority to step in and request deferral of jurisdiction, such request being binding on any State. States must then comply with the request for deferral coming from the International Tribunal.

Interestingly, and also in my view an indicator of the importance of balancing the principle of primacy with concurrent jurisdiction, Rule 11 *bis* gives an ICTY trial chamber

6 ICTY doc. IT/32/REV.22, dated 13 December 2001, as amended on 23 April 2002. Text available at http://www.un.org/icty.

the authority to suspend an indictment that has already been issued by the ICTY, either upon application by the prosecution or *propio motu*, if the trial chamber is satisfied that: (1) the national authorities of the State in which the accused was arrested are prepared to prosecute the accused in their own courts, and (2) that it is appropriate in the circumstances for the courts of the State to exercise jurisdiction. So the Tribunal can also, when it deems it appropriate, refer a case to the national authorities, even after an indictment has already been issued, an arrest warrant has been executed and the person is already in the custody of the Tribunal. If such a decision is taken, its immediate consequences are the transfer of the accused, if the accused is in the custody of the Tribunal, to the State that initially arrested him or her. The Prosecutor may then transmit information to the national authorities and this may reflect the fact that cooperation for the exchange of information between the Office of the Prosecutor and national authorities is governed by a discretionary authority of the Office of the Prosecutor, balancing its duties *vis-à-vis* confidentiality of information and protection of victims and witnesses. The Prosecutor may also direct trial observers to monitor how the national proceedings are evolving. Finally, the order that refers the case to the national authority may be rescinded at any time by the Tribunal and a new request for deferral or a first request for deferral may be issued. That means that if the Tribunal is not satisfied by the pace of national proceedings, or if the Tribunal considers that national proceedings are not being conducted in an appropriate fashion, the Tribunal still retains the authority to get the case back through a renewed use of Rules 9 and 10. Here again, it is interesting to compare this system of deferral of cases with a regime of challenges to the admissibility of a case before the ICC, as enshrined in Articles 18 and 19 of the ICC Statute,[7] and to compare how the principles of primacy and complementarity, in a somewhat inverted angle, visualise the same situation.

The last consequence which I consider particularly important is the implication that the exercise of primary jurisdiction under the principle of primacy entails particular duties. The failure to properly comply with these duties may even lead to the consequence of the Tribunal being ousted of jurisdiction. In the ICTR decision on *Jean-Bosco Barayagwiza v. The Prosecutor*,[8] the Appeals Chamber considered that the failure by the Prosecutor to obtain the prompt transfer of a person being held in detention in Cameroon amounted, in the circumstances of the case, to a repeated violation of that person's rights which ousted the Tribunal of jurisdiction. In that first decision the Appeals Chamber decided to terminate proceedings with prejudice to the Prosecutor, meaning the Prosecutor could no longer bring charges against that person before the ICTR. The decision was subsequently reconsidered by the Appeals Chamber in the light of new evidence and ultimately modified, but what is interesting to note is that the exercise of primary jurisdiction by the Tribunal has a chilling effect: once a request for transfer of an accused or deferral of a case has been made, the national proceedings are frozen. From that point forward only the Tribunal can exercise jurisdiction. This fact entails duties and that means, in the reasoning of the ICTR Appeals Chamber, that the trial chamber needs to act promptly to ensure that the accused

[7] 1998 Rome Statute of the International Criminal Court, entered into force 1 July 2002; UN doc. A/CONF.183/9*, as corrected by the procès-verbaux of 10 November 1998 and 12 July 1999. Corrected text available at http://www.un.org/law/icc.

[8] Decision, *Jean-Bosco Barayagwiza v. The Prosecutor*, ICTR-97-19, In the Appeals Chamber, November 1999. See also *supra* in this volume, M. Othman, *supra* note 3.

is not held in limbo while the prosecution languishes. The individual must be promptly transferred to the seat of the Tribunal and criminal proceedings promptly initiated.

5. Interactive Concurrent Jurisdiction: the "Rules of the Road"

As a last point, I would like to discuss an example of what can be called "interactive concurrent jurisdiction": the "Rules of the Road" project. This project is a particular feature of the ICTY and has given rise to particular developments within the Tribunal that I consider to be of particular importance for the subject addressed in this volume.

On 6 February 1996, two generals from the Republika Srpska were in transit through Sarajevo. They apparently lost their way and found themselves in the centre of Sarajevo where they encountered a Bosnian military police patrol who promptly arrested them on suspicion of having committed war crimes. This initial arrest had an immediate ripple effect and triggered a series of totally arbitrary and politically motivated detentions and arrests undertaken by the different opposing forces in the former Yugoslavia. These developments endangered significant aspects of the Dayton Agreement[9] and especially the rights guaranteed under Annexes 6 and 7, particularly the right of free transit throughout the territory of Bosnia and Herzegovina as enshrined in the Dayton Agreement as well as, later, the suspension of all programmes for prisoner exchanges. Thus at that point in time this was seen as a noble threat to peace and security in the region. On 18 February 1996, the parties to the Dayton Agreement convened in Rome to address these issues. As a result of those negotiations the so-called "Rome Agreement"[10] was adopted, informally referred to as the "Rules of the Road" intended precisely to cover the circumstances that had led to the detention of the two generals in Bosnia-Herzegovina.

The significant aspects of the Rome Agreement are twofold. On the one hand, it confirms the obligation of all States in the former Yugoslavia to actively cooperate in any investigation or prosecution of serious violations of international humanitarian law. On the other hand, it establishes in its Article 5 a totally novel institution, actively involving the ICTY in an indirect way in national prosecutions for violations of international humanitarian law. Article 5 of the Rome Agreement reads as follows:

> Persons, other than those already indicted by the International Tribunal, may be arrested and detained for serious violations of international humanitarian law only pursuant to a previously issued order, warrant or indictment that has been reviewed and deemed consistent with international legal standards by the International Tribunal. Procedures will be developed for expeditious decision by the Tribunal and will be effective immediately upon such action.

The Rome Agreement's assignment of the role of reviewing authority to the Office of the Prosecutor is interesting because it is not a statutory duty for the Office of the Prosecutor

[9] The General Framework Agreement for Peace in Bosnia and Herzegovina, Paris, 14 December 1995, UN doc. A/50/79C and S/1995/999, reprinted at 35 ILM 223 (1996). Text available at http://www.nato.int/ifor.

[10] Agreed Measures reflecting the work of the Joint Civilian Commission Sarajevo Compliance Conference, Rome, 18 February 1996. Text available at http://www.nato.int/ifor.

under the ICTY Statute. The Statute is totally silent in this respect. The Office of the Prosecutor voluntarily accepted this duty and decided to act as a reviewing authority for national indictments, with a view to preventing arbitrary and unfounded indictments, and arbitrary arrests and detentions. The acceptance of this duty caused the Office of the Prosecutor to establish a unit within the Office of the Prosecutor, dealing only with the mandate to review these cases. At the same time it is also interesting that this automatically created an interaction between national courts and the Office of the Prosecutor whereby national courts submit to the Office of the Prosecutor files and the Office of the Prosecutor then applies international legal standards and determines, inter alia, whether the facts as described in that draft indictment amount to violations of any rule of international humanitarian law. The Office of the Prosecutor also determines whether the evidence as described in the file submitted by the national prosecuting authorities appears to constitute a sufficient basis or *prima facie* case for issuing an indictment. Once the determination has been made, the Office of the Prosecutor marks the files with different standards, either: (1) approved for indictment; (2) more investigation required; or (3) requests for deferral.

The Rules of the Road project provides the Office of the Prosecutor with an ancillary benefit: the ability to have access to information that may enable the Office of the Prosecutor to discover a case in which the Office has a concrete interest. On the basis of that review, the Office may then identify a case as one in which it wishes to exercise jurisdiction and will make a request for deferral. As mentioned above, the national authorities must then comply with the request submitted. Conversely, one could also argue that the Prosecutor perhaps assumes another new duty in this role — not just the duty to review material provided by national authorities but also the duty to review the material for the purpose of detecting whether there is any exculpatory information that needs to be disclosed to any of the accused that are held before the International Tribunal.

The Rules of the Road project is in principle binding for all States parties to the Dayton Agreement. Regretfully, only the Federation of Bosnia and Herzegovina has actively complied with its duties under the Rome Agreement. The Republika Srpska initially refused to co-operate, but has submitted a number of files this year in what may constitute a drastic change of attitude *vis-à-vis* the Agreement. The Republic of Croatia does not seem to consider itself bound by the Agreement, and has yet to deliver its first file to the Office of the Prosecutor for the purposes of a determination under Article 5 of the Rome Agreement. The other problem that arises is that there is no system in place for verification of the manner in which the national proceedings are being conducted. Thus it is not too hard to imagine that a case that should actually be characterised as a war crimes case, and therefore submitted for review under Article 5 of the Rome Agreement, is characterised as an ordinary murder case and the Tribunal never, or only exceptionally, hears of it under the "Rules of the Road" duty.

Nevertheless, what I consider of significant importance in the Rules of the Road project and the way it has developed is this component of interaction between an international tribunal and national jurisdictions. In the case of the Rules of the Road, this emerged from a crisis situation that led to an international agreement that involved a pre-existing international body of criminal adjudication, the ICTY. However, it is not hard to imagine that in the future, similar agreements may be undertaken by the Office of the Prosecutor of the ICC or the Presidency of the ICC, especially if one bears in mind that the ICC will necessarily be extremely selective. The territorial jurisdiction of the ICC is, potentially, the world. It is not confined to the former Yugoslavia or Rwanda. That means that the Prosecutor of the ICC will have to, within the broad universe of a situation referred to the court, make very precise selections of those cases that he or she would prosecute, leaving to national authorities all the rest. It is conceivable that in a number of situations national authorities will not know how to efficiently conduct investigations and prosecutions for these types of cases. So this kind of agreement, or this kind of exchange between an international body and national courts, may be crucial in order to effectively avoid impunity.

The transition in international criminal law from concurrent jurisdiction to complementary jurisdiction will be full of challenges and this requires, in my view, a particularly creative approach to the way in which national jurisdictions and international bodies would interact. I think the Rules of the Road provide one solution, but clearly the ICC will have to develop further solutions in order fully to be able to comply with its mandate.

6. Conclusion

I have only highlighted some of the various issues raised by the co-existence of domestic and international jurisdictions related to the same universe of crimes. The entry into force of the Rome Statute and the establishment of the ICC will further stress the complexities arising from this coexistence. These complexities will require the ICC to adopt a professional and prudent approach to the exercise of jurisdiction by national courts on the one hand, but, on the other, they will demand an innovative, creative and constructive approach by national jurisdictions to the required interaction with the Court. The success of the emerging system of international justice will, to a large extent, depend upon how fruitful this process of interaction is.

CONCURRENT APPLICATION OF INTERNATIONAL, NATIONAL AND AFRICAN LAWS IN RWANDA

Chiseche Mibenge*

1. Introduction

The Republic of Rwanda accepted concurrent jurisdiction for the prosecution of alleged perpetrators of the crime of genocide, crimes against humanity and war crimes. Since the mid-nineties, two tribunals have administered criminal justice concurrently for the prosecution of international crimes. The International Criminal Tribunal for Rwanda (ICTR) applies, and when necessary creates, a body of international criminal law jurisprudence while Rwanda's national courts administer criminal justice in the civil law tradition that is a legacy of Belgian colonial rule.

Article 14(1) of the International Covenant of Civil and Political Rights (ICCPR) provides for equality of all persons before tribunals: everyone shall be entitled to a fair and public hearing by a competent, independent and impartial tribunal established by law.[1] This Article also provides for minimum guarantees for a fair trial in "full equality."

The question raised in this chapter is whether concurrent jurisdiction has facilitated a process whereby the national courts and the ICTR can both administer the minimum guarantees for a fair trial in full equality in the spirit of the ICCPR. In other words, are rights enshrined in Article 14, such as the right to counsel or to be tried without undue delay, guaranteed to accused persons in both tribunals? Or is there a discrepancy in the standard of justice emanating from this instance of concurrent jurisdiction?

Concurrent jurisdiction occurs when a particular set of facts gives rise to the jurisdiction of two or more courts. Most instances of concurrent jurisdiction in international law occur when two or more States have jurisdiction. In Rwanda's case, concurrent jurisdiction has arisen between an ad hoc international tribunal and the Rwandan national courts. Strictly speaking, legally, "concurrent jurisdiction" in this instance only mandates the primacy of the ICTR over the national courts in respect of any particular offender. Nevertheless, ideally, one would hope that concurrent jurisdiction should indicate cooperation,with a common point and harmonisation of efforts. In this instance, the perceived disparity in the fair trial standards between the international tribunal and the national courts has harmed and even impeded the process of transitional justice at both the international and domestic level.

The case studies in the following pages, taken from both the national and international tribunals, will illustrate the several ways that concurrent jurisdiction can compromise the principle of equality before the law as enshrined in Article 14 of the ICCPR and numerous

* Researcher, SIM, The Netherlands Institute of Human Rights, Utrecht.

[1] United Nations General Assembly resolution 2200A (XXI), 21 U.N. GAOR Supp. (No. 16) at 52, UN doc. A/6316 (1966), 999 U.N.T.S. 171, entered into force Mar. 23, 1976.

R. Yepes-Enríquez and L. Tabassi. (eds.), Treaty Enforcement and International Cooperation in Criminal Matters

other international covenants, including the Universal Declaration of Human Rights. This article will also utilise comparative analysis of the Statute of the ICTR and Rwanda's Organic Law for the prosecution of genocide and crimes against humanity to illustrate inequalities in justice experienced by accused persons.

2. Creation of Concurrent Jurisdiction

On 14 April 1994, Rwandan President Juvenal Habyarimana and his Burundian counterpart were killed in a plane crash over the capital city of Kigali. The death of Habyarimana was the catalyst for violence on an unprecedented scale that stunned the international community. The genocidal massacre that followed prompted the United Nations Security Council to pass Resolution 955, establishing the International Criminal Tribunal for Rwanda, in 1996, and Rwanda's Transitional National Assembly in 1996 to enact the Organic Law on the Organisation of Prosecutions for Offences Constituting the Crime of Genocide or Crimes Against Humanity Committed Since 1 October 1990.

On 18 January 2001, Rwanda's Constitutional Court declared the creation of a third jurisdiction, known as *gacaca* jurisdictions, for the prosecution of international crimes. Since their inauguration in June 2002, these courts have employed the procedure and principles of criminal justice as embodied in national and international penal law whilst incorporating those principles of participatory justice which are a cornerstone of Rwanda's traditional justice. For the purposes of this article, the descriptive examination of the gacaca tribunals provided below will suffice, and the term 'concurrent jurisdiction' will apply exclusively to the relationship between the ICTR and the Specialised Chambers created and mandated by the Organic Law. Nevertheless, Table A herein illustrates the relationship of concurrent jurisdiction as it exists today. Therefore, the Specialised Chambers created under the Organic Law do not appear, as their mandate was discontinued in 1990 and transferred to the ordinary national courts and the *gacaca* jurisdictions.

2.1 The International Criminal Tribunal for Rwanda

Sixteen months after the establishment of the International Criminal Tribunal for Yugoslavia, the interim government of Rwanda requested that the United Nations establish an International Criminal Tribunal for Rwanda for the prosecution of the crimes of genocide, crimes against humanity and war crimes committed in that country. The drafting of the Statute was, however, contentious — so much so that Rwanda, who held a seat on the UN Security Council at the time, cast the sole vote opposing adoption of the Resolution. The government of Rwanda's objections were a reaction to various provisions of the Statute of the ICTR regarding temporal jurisdiction, severity of penalties and the location of the seat of the Tribunal in Arusha. Article 8(1) of the ICTR Statute provides that the ICTR and national courts shall have concurrent jurisdiction to prosecute persons for serious violations of international humanitarian law, and Article 8(2) emphasises that ICTR shall have the primacy over the national courts of all States. Further, the ICTR may formally request national courts to defer to its competence.

2.2 THE ORGANIC LAW OF 1996[2]

In 1994 Rwanda was a signatory to the Convention on the Prevention and Punishment of the Crime of Genocide of 1948, the Fourth Geneva Convention relative to the Protection of Civilian Persons in Time of War of 1949 and its additional protocols, as well as the Convention on the Non-Applicability of Statutory Limitations to War Crimes and Crimes Against Humanity of 1968. Therefore, the Organic Law was enacted specifically to adopt provisions to prosecute and adjudicate the perpetrators and accomplices of the crimes of genocide and crimes against humanity. Article 19 of the Organic Law established, within the courts of first instance and the military courts, Specialised Chambers with exclusive jurisdiction over genocide and crimes against humanity.

The Organic Law covered offences committed between 1990 and 1994 in order to address massacres that occurred during the civil war, well before the death of President Habyarimana. Suspects were classified under four categories according to their degree of culpability in the Rwandan genocide. The first category included leaders and organisers of the genocide and perpetrators of particularly heinous murders or sexual torture. All others who committed homicides fell under category two. Category three offenders included perpetrators of grave assaults against a victim not resulting in death. Those who committed property crimes in the context of the genocide fell into category four.[3]

The legislation introduced unique improvisations to Rwanda's traditionally inquisitorial judicial system, such as the system of plea agreements, which is an adversarial system concept introduced to expedite the specialised criminal justice process contained in the legislation. All perpetrators, apart from category one offenders (who are subject to the death penalty), were entitled to receive a reduced sentence as part of a guilty-plea agreement requiring an accurate and complete confession, a plea of guilty to the crimes committed, and an apology to the victims by the accused.[4] The effect of the guilty plea agreement on sentence reduction is illustrated on Table A – it applies to the ordinary courts as it applied to the Specialised Chambers.

The Specialised Chambers created under this Organic Law had prosecuted approximately 5,000 people by 2000, and a remainder of approximately 120,000 accused awaited trial before the national courts. In 1990, the Specialised Chambers transferred their jurisdiction over category two, three and four offenders to the *gacaca* tribunals, and jurisdiction over class one offenders to the ordinary penal courts existing prior to the 1994 conflict. For this reason, Table A below does not include the specialised chambers.

2.3 ORGANIC LAW SETTING UP *GACACA* JURISDICTIONS (*GACACA* LAW)

Historically, the *gacaca* is a traditional community-based mechanism of dispute resolution, and a literal translation into English is "lawn" or "yard," referring to the fact that parties to a dispute and members of the *gacaca* sit on the grass whilst resolving the dispute. However, it is not the intention of the government of Rwanda to duplicate the traditional *gacaca*

---

[2] Loi Organique du 30 aout 1996 sur l'organisation des poursuites des infractions constitutives du crime de génocide ou des crimes contre l'humanité commises à partir du 1er octobre 1990.

[3] *Id.*, at Article 2.

[4] *Id.*, at Article 6.

courts for the prosecution of perpetrators of genocide and crimes against humanity. The "new *gacaca*" will be a unique process with similarities to the traditional dispute settlement mechanisms but also incorporating a contemporary legislative framework.

Local *gacaca* tribunals have been set up throughout the country, from Rwanda's lowest political and administrative level of the cell, to that of the sector, district and province. Each *gacaca* jurisdiction includes a general assembly, a seat, and a coordinating committee.[5] The National Electoral Commission of Rwanda reported that over 90% of the Rwandan electorate attended the *gacaca* elections in October 2001.[6] And the six-week training of the 254,152 judges elected by their peers began in April 2002. 781 trainers were trained between 4 February and 14 March 2002. The trainers are all magistrates or final year law students.[7]

As mentioned earlier, the preliminary stage of the *gacaca* system precludes any scientific analysis of this jurisdictions impact on the scheme of concurrent jurisdiction within this chapter.

3. Issues Raised by Concurrent Jurisdiction

3.1 TEMPORAL JURISDICTION — THE *KABUGA* CASE

Article 7 of the Statute of the ICTR provides that the temporal jurisdiction of the ICTR extends from a period beginning on 1 January 1994 and ending on 31 December 1994. The Organic Law, on the other hand, gave the Specialised Chambers jurisdiction over offences committed between 1990 and 1994. The Government of Rwanda protested the issue of temporal jurisdiction before the Security Council on the ground that the leaders and planners of genocide who were to be prosecuted by the ICTR would not be punished for the international crimes they committed since the early 1990's. The government argued that without the "pilot massacres" of the early nineties, the genocidal massacre of 1994 would never have been so successfully implemented

The effect created by this inconsistency in the statutes of the respective tribunals regarding temporal jurisdiction directly impacts the equality of all persons before a tribunal as enshrined in Article 14 of the ICCPR. The leaders of the genocide are, in effect, more narrowly accountable than the low level offenders detained in Rwanda's prisons, particularly with regard to crimes such as conspiracy to commit genocide. The doctrine of conspiracy is one under which it is a criminal offence to conspire or to take part in an allegiance to achieve an unlawful object or to achieve a lawful object by unlawful means.[8] It is unlikely that the genocidal massacres occurred spontaneously with the downing of a presidential plane on 14 April 1994.

However, the mandate of the ICTR only permits it to prosecute crimes committed within the prescribed twelve-month span. The culpability for genocide, therefore, can be established at the international level only in the context of the civil war. Therefore, one group of persons, i.e., those appearing before the international tribunal, are exempt from accountability for earlier crimes.

---

[5] *Id.*, at Article 5.
[6] www.rwanda1.com/government.
[7] 8 April 2002, Hirondelle news agency (Lausanne) at fr.allafrica.com/stories
[8] United Nations War Crimes Commission (1948), p. 196.

For example, consider Felicien Kabuga,[9] who was allegedly the chief financier of the 1994 conflict and was said to have established a fund for the defence of the nation to assist the interim government in its genocidal campaign. The funds were allegedly used to buy arms, vehicles and uniforms for militia and the army.[10] However, the temporal jurisdiction of the ICTR precludes investigations into the responsibility borne by Kabuga for acts committed before January 1994.

It can be argued that the *non bis in idem* rule would not preclude the courts of Rwanda from prosecuting individuals convicted by the ICTR subsequently for crimes committed before January 1994. [11] However, the likelihood of the national courts having the capacity to prosecute the current case load and the ICTR's convicted suspects for crimes falling outside of the ICTR's temporal jurisdiction is unlikely.

It cannot be said that there is equality before the law when there is such a wide divergence in the temporal jurisdiction of the ICTR and national courts.

3.2 INDEPENDENCE AND IMPARTIALITY — THE *BARAYAGWIZA* CASE

The *Barayagwiza* case[12] illustrated the way in which concurrent jurisdiction can be perceived to compromise the independence and impartiality of both the ICTR and the national prosecutions. Barayagwiza was arrested in Cameroon on 15 April 1996 at the request of the Rwandan government. He was a founding member of the *Coalition pour la défense de la République* (CDR), a Hutu political party which held and expressed extremist views in the period leading up to the genocide in Rwanda. Supporters of the CDR participated actively in the massacres of 1994. Barayagwiza served as CDR president in the Gisenyi prefecture, and he was a policy director in the government's Ministry of Foreign Affairs during the genocide and a founding member of the *Radio Télévision Libre des Milles Collines*, which made broadcasts before and during the genocide inciting Hutus to eliminate their Tutsi neighbours.

On 17 November 1998, Trial Chamber II of the ICTR dismissed Barayagwiza's motion for orders to review and nullify his arrest and provisional detention due to unreasonable delays by the prosecution in bringing him before the competent Trial Chamber after his arrival at the seat of the Tribunal. He lodged an appeal with the Appeals Chamber, in accordance with Rule 72 of the Rules of Evidence and Procedure. The Appeal Chamber allowed the Appeal on 3 November 1999. It found that the fundamental rights of the Appellant had been repeatedly violated and the Prosecutor's failure to prosecute the case was tantamount to negligence. Consequently, it dismissed the indictment against Barayagwiza and ordered his immediate release.

Rwanda's government immediately severed cooperation and relations between the national courts and the ICTR. In an attempt at reconciliation, the head prosecutor of the ICTR announced her intention to visit Rwanda to try and resolve the impasse, but the

---

[9] ICTR-98-44-T. Kabuga remains at large, www.ictr.org.

[10] Internews, United States Offers Reward for Genocide Financier, June 11 2002 at allafrica.com/stories.

[11] Article 9 of the Statute of the ICTR provides that 'No person shall be tried before a national court for acts constituting serious violations of international humanitarian law under the present Statute, for which he or she has already been tried by the International Tribunal for Rwanda'.

[12] *Jean-Bosco Barayagwiza v. The Prosecutor*, Case No. ICTR-97-19-AR72 (12 September 2000), www.ictr.org.

Rwandan government emphatically stated that she would not be allowed to visit Rwanda until the Tribunal took action to allow the trial of Barayagwiza to proceed. Rwanda's General Prosecutor, Gerald Gahima, argued that the payment of damages would be sufficient to remedy the violation of Barayagwiza's rights. Rwandan civilians also reacted with anger to the decision of the Appeals Chamber, and about 5000 people demonstrated in Kigali in protest and called on the Tribunal to arrest Barayagwiza or send him to Rwanda for a real trial.[13]

The prosecutor had, in the meantime, submitted a motion for review in accordance with Rule 120 of the Rules, and this motion was successful. On 31 March 2000, the Appeals Chamber reviewed its earlier decision of 3 November 1999, apparently in the light of new facts presented by the prosecutor. It arrived at the conclusion proposed by Gahima, that although the rights of the accused had been violated, these violations did not justify dismissal of the indictment. It therefore rejected Barayagwiza's application for release and decided that he was instead entitled to other remedies. Although the reversal of the first decision is meticulously clothed in legal procedure, the Tribunal was accused by defence counsel and ICTR detainees of having succumbed to external pressure from the Rwandan government.

The ICCPR states that a tribunal must be independent and impartial in order to administer a fair trial. Therefore, in the case of the ICTR it must, while operating in the framework of concurrent jurisdiction, be seen as independent of interference from the government of Rwanda. The *Barayagwiza* case illustrated the dangers of administering justice in strict conformity with fair trial standards that would demand the strict protection of the rights of the accused. However, the ICTR does not operate within a vacuum, and unlike a national criminal court created to administer penal justice, the ICTR, in the framework of concurrent jurisdiction and transitional justice, has a more ambitious mandate. Its mandate resonates with lofty aspirations: restoration of peace and national reconciliation.[14] Further, as a UN organ, the ICTR administers its mandate in a highly politicised environment. The ICTR has two demanding audiences to play to: the international community and the Rwandan government.

It is impossible to overlook the implications of the ICTR's dependence on the goodwill of the Rwandan government for efficient prosecutions. This does impact its independence and impartiality, as was seen when the Appeal Chamber decision provoked a reaction from the government of Rwanda that, in short, stated that if the ICTR would pass decisions that would threaten Rwanda's peace and reconciliation process, the government of Rwanda would paralyse the jurisdiction of the ICTR. Witnesses would not be permitted to travel from Rwanda to Arusha, ICTR investigators would not be granted access to information within Rwanda and so on.

This is certainly not a desirable result of concurrent jurisdiction, however, it is questionable whether the situation of the ICTR Seat in Kigali would have exacerbated this situation or else allowed the Prosecutor more independence with regard to carrying out investigations and summoning witnesses.

---

[13] BBC Net News, November 15, 1999, at news.bbc.co.uk/hi/english/world/africa.

[14] Resolution 955 indicates that the establishment of the Tribunal was to prosecute and punish the perpetrators of atrocities in Rwanda in such a way as to put an end to impunity and thereby promote national reconciliation and the restoration of peace.

3.3 SENTENCING PRACTICES — THE *AKAYESU*, *BIZIMANA* AND *GATANAZA* CASES

During the drafting of the Statute of the ICTR, the government of Rwanda took umbrage at the refusal of the Security Council to prescribe the death penalty for those convicted of committing genocide, crimes against humanity and war crimes. Capital punishment is applied in Rwanda, and in 1998 Rwanda's Specialised Chambers ordered the public execution of 22 people convicted of genocide and crimes against humanity. In an interview in 1997, General Prosecutor Gahima objected to the ringleaders of the genocide, including Akayesu, 'escaping' capital punishment before the ICTR; he concluded that: 'It would be better for the ICTR to disband completely and the money used for rehabilitation schemes such as helping widows and orphans in our country.'[15]

Once again concurrent jurisdiction created an inequality before the law for the accused detained in the Arusha detention facility and those in Rwanda's prisons. Those class one offenders detained in Rwanda may receive the death penalty whilst class one offenders before the ICTR are exempt from this form of punishment.

Jean Paul Akayesu was the *bourgmestre* of Taba commune. He was individually charged with genocide, complicity in genocide, direct and public incitement to commit genocide, extermination, murder, rape, torture, cruel treatment, other inhumane acts and outrages upon personal dignity, all of which he allegedly committed in Taba commune.

The first to be sentenced in Rwanda to the death penalty by the national courts were Deo Bizimana and Egide Gatanaza. Bizimana and Gatanaza pled not guilty to all eleven charges against them, including organising massacres and raping and pillaging their Tutsi neighbours. The two men were found guilty by Rwanda's domestic courts in Kibungo, in south-eastern Rwanda, of planning genocide, genocide, crimes against humanity and rape following a trial that lasted four hours. Throughout the trial the gallery booed the defendants and cheered prosecutors.[16] The haste of the trial and the hostile sentiment of the gallery raised strong concerns about the impartiality and independence of this trial, particularly in light of the severity of the penalty.

The *bourgmestre* of a commune is a Presidential appointee, and in Rwanda he is the most powerful figure in the commune. His *de facto* authority in the area is significantly greater than that which is conferred upon him *de jure*.[17] In contrast to Akayesu, Deo Bizimana was a hospital aide, and Egide Gatanaza was a local administrator, but not of Akayesu's standing. Like Akayesu, they were categorised as category one offenders. They did not have legal representation,[18] and both alleged that their confessions were the product of mistreatment during interrogations. The chief trial judge asked each to prove that their confessions were not made freely, which, given the lack of prison medical records, failure to

---

[15] The Rwandan Genocide Trials: Building Peace through Justice 19 February 1997, www.africapolicy.org/docs97/rwan9703.1.htm.

[16] Armando Franco, Rwanda Sentences 2 to Death, Boston Globe, January 4 1997, p. 1.

[17] *The Prosecutor v. Jean Paul Akayesu*, ICTR-96-4-I Amended Indictment (6 June 1997), available at www.ictr.org.

[18] Impunity-Info, First Convictions of Genocide Participant by Rwandan Courts, Volume 1, number 5, at page 1 (February 1997). Available online at www.ichrdd.ca/111/english/commdoc_publications/impunity/News0297.html#TITLE1.

subpoena the person(s) alleged to have caused the mistreatment, significant passage of time since the alleged incident and lack of defence counsel, proved impossible.[19]

Clearly, when it comes to penalties and due process in this system of concurrent jurisdiction, there is greater protection from the law before the ICTR than the national prosecutions. This is unacceptable, particularly when it is the inherent right to life that is violated. This failure to resolve the death penalty stalemate at the drafting stage between the two tribunals has greatly and perhaps irreparably undermined the principles of equality that are the cornerstone of a fair trial. The issue was resolved in favour of excluding the death penalty from the ICTR, which is a United Nations institution. The Rwandan government chose to follow the death penalty in its own laws. The practice in the Rwandan instance thus shows that "concurrent jurisdiction" need not mean the same treatment.

4. Conclusion

The jurisprudence of the ICTR has greatly contributed to international criminal law and the evolution of international humanitarian law. Indeed, the ICTR, with the ICTY, are regarded by many as prototypes for the International Criminal Court (ICC). The trials and errors encountered by the ad hoc tribunals can be anticipated and avoided by the ICC. And conversely, the ad hoc tribunals' jurisprudence will be a primary source of judicial precedent for the ICC. Further, the ICTR is known as the first international tribunal to prosecute a Prime Minister for the crime of genocide.[20] And the Akayesu case is renowned for adjudging rape explicitly for the first time as a crime against humanity. In addition to this, the court decided that sexual violence is an integral part of destruction in relation to genocide.[21] International humanitarian law has been greatly invigorated, and with regard to the protection and enforcement of women's rights by international humanitarian law, I would say that the ad hoc tribunals effected a revolution.

But the jurisprudence of the ICTR is of little significance to the national penal process in Rwanda. This is because the tribunals exist concurrently and separately. From a human rights standpoint, this is a most unfortunate way of exercising concurrent jurisdiction. Concurrent jurisdiction is not inherently liable to compromise the independence of tribunals or take away the equality of accused persons appearing before the various tribunals in existence. Indeed, it is highly doubtful whether Rwandans could have witnessed the prosecution of their most powerful officials without the establishment of the ICTR. For one, the establishment of the Tribunal by Security Council resolution immediately created an obligation on the entire international community to cooperate with the ICTR. This alone ensured that those indicted were extradited to Arusha from as far afield as Canada, Switzerland, Cameroon, Namibia and the United States.

The major discrepancy occurred at the drafting stage of the Statute of the ICTR. In the end, the United Nations chose a different approach from that of the Rwandan government. As a result, whilst Rwanda requested the creation of the ICTR, it was perceived in Rwanda that insufficient regard was given to the objections to the ICTR's jurisdiction and of the

[19] H. Carla J. Feistman, African Journal of International and Comparative Law 9 (9) 1997, Domestic Trials for Genocide and Crimes against Humanity, p. 870–871.
[20] Judgment and Sentence, *The Prosecutor v. Jean Kambanda*, ICTR-97-23-S (4 September 1998), www.ictr.org.
[21] *The Prosecutor v. Jean Paul Akayesu*, ICTR-96-4-T (9 February 1998), www.ictr.org.

Rwandan people's expectations of international justice. The ensuing years have only heightened the tensions existing in the concurrent relationship created between the international tribunal and national prosecutions. As I stated earlier, ideally concurrent jurisdiction should denote a spirit of cooperation and adopt a unified approach to the administration of justice. This spirit was seen between Belgium and Rwanda when Belgium prosecuted and convicted four Rwandans, including two Benedictine nuns charged with taking part in the 1994 massacre of 800,000 people in Rwanda. The suspects were among the first to be charged under the Belgian Law that allows individuals, including non-Belgians, to be tried in Belgium for war crimes committed elsewhere. The four accused were living in Belgium at the time of their arrest. Rwanda made no objection to this exercise of jurisdiction by Belgium and commended the prosecution process.

It has, however, been the practice of the national courts and the ICTR to request that third States extradite, and, it is therefore difficult to suggest with any conviction that if concurrent jurisdiction had been exercised more frequently by extraditing States such as Kenya, Zambia, Uganda, the United Kingdom and Switzerland, greater cooperation would have been possible. This form of concurrent jurisdiction, arising from universal jurisdiction over high crimes such as genocide, would, of course, also not guarantee that minimum fair trial standards were upheld.

While concluding with few recommendations for the enhancement of concurrent jurisdiction, I will reiterate my conviction that, if established with deeper foresight, concurrent jurisdiction has the potential to enrich the judicial process of all prosecuting tribunals. In particular, concurrent jurisdiction is an essential mechanism for the process of transitional justice where a country is faced with the task of reconstructing a judiciary before commencing with the prosecution of widespread human rights violations. Unfortunately, due to the pressing demand for justice in the wake of Rwanda's genocide, the creation of the ICTR had to be expedient, and lengthy negotiations over issues of temporal jurisdiction could simply not be entertained.

However, transitional justice is a dynamic process. This is especially clear in the case of Rwanda, where in less than a decade the ICTR administering international law will be expected to operate concurrently with national courts administering civil law and *gacaca* tribunals administering a medley of African, civil and even international law. With the advent of *gacaca* tribunals, it is my belief that the trials or teething problems of concurrent jurisdiction experienced between the ICTR and Specialised Chambers will serve as lessons for the new concurrent jurisdiction evolving. The *gacaca* proposes a prosecution style that is, at first glance, anathema to international fair trial standards (for example, accused and victims are not allowed legal representation). Despite this, the international community has largely intimated that they support this creative approach to the unprecedented judicial crisis faced by Rwanda's new judiciary. The Special Representative of the Commission on Human Rights has reported, "In an effort to ease overcrowding in jails, promote reconciliation at the community level and, importantly, ensure that justice is seen to be done, the Government plans to revive a system of traditional justice, known as *Gacaca*...there is no doubt that

Gacaca does seem the only viable alternative and the Special Representative therefore supports this approach."[22]

Shifting attitudes toward concurrent jurisdiction can also be observed within the ordinary courts with regard to sentencing practices. The Organic Law did not allow the Specialised Chambers any discretion with regard to the mandatory death penalty for convicted leaders of the genocide and notorious killers. However, it is evidence of a burgeoning human rights culture within Rwanda's judiciary that class one offenders may now apply to the confession and guilty plea procedure in exchange for a significantly reduced penalty (see Appendix A). Further, the ordinary courts may exercise discretion in determining factors that would mitigate the death penalty. This can be attributed in part to the influence of the ICTR and its observance of fair trial standards, particularly with regard to sentencing. It is also likely that the passage of time has mellowed the overriding demand by survivors for revenge by public execution in the first few years following the genocidal massacres. Survivors would not have legitimised prosecutions before Specialised Chambers that did not issue the death penalty in the wake of the genocide. It seems that, with regard to sentencing practices, the national courts are now prepared to move further away from the death penalty and closer to the sentencing practices of the ICTR. This could be interpreted as a significant affirmation by the national courts of the jurisdiction of the ICTR and concurrent jurisdiction.

This receptivity to the *gacaca* jurisdictions by the international community hopefully signals a new phase in the relationship of concurrent jurisdiction. It may be that, after the initial ambivalence, the government of Rwanda and the international ad hoc tribunal are realising that concurrent jurisdiction does not always have to be a contentious exercise, and can allow for legal co-existence coupled with political cooperation.

[22] Situation of human rights in Rwanda, prepared by the Special Representative of the Commission on Human Rights pursuant to Economic and Social Council decision 1999 288 of 30 July 1999, submitted 17 September 1999.

TABLE A: Concurrent Jurisdiction for the Prosecution of Genocide, Crimes against Humanity and War Crimes in and for Rwanda.

		Class of Offenders	Principal Organs	Function	Sentencing / Penalties		
					Max	Confession Before	Confession After
Gacaca Formal and Traditional Jurisdiction	Cell	IV	General Assembly Seat Coordinating Committee	Property Crimes	Damages	No Effect	No Effect
	Sector	III		Assault Crimes	5 to 7 years	1 to 3 years	3 to 5 years
	District	II		Killing / Accomplice Killing	25 years to life	7 to 12 years	12 to 15 years
	Province	Appeal		Appellate			
Formal Justice System	National Court	I	High Court OTP Subordinate Supreme Court	Genocide and Sexual Violence (leaders and notorious killers)	Death	7 to 12 years	12 to 15 years
	International Criminal Tribunal for Rwanda	I	OTP Registry Chambers	Genocide and Other International Crimes (leaders and planners)	Life	NA[23]	

[23] Guilty plea agreement: Not applicable as in national and *gacaca* courts. The Chambers exercise great discretion with regard to plea agreements. Prime Minister Jean Kambanda's life sentence was not mitigated by his immediate guilty plea and cooperation with prosecutors (*The Prosecutor v. Jean Kambanda*, ICTR-97-23-S 09 (09 April 1998)), whereas George Ruggiu's plea agreement with the prosecutor's and his full confession were considered by the Tribunal as mitigating factors – he was sentenced to 12 years for the crime of direct and public incitement to commit genocide and of crime against humanity (persecution) (*The Prosecutor v. George Ruggiu*, ICTR-97-32-I (1 June 2000)).

SECTION II.2

CASE STUDIES: COOPERATION WITH OR BETWEEN INTERNATIONAL ORGANISATIONS

INTRODUCTION AND SUMMARY

International criminal law has come into the forefront during the final decade of the millennium. Faced with situations of great magnitude, the international community took major steps to ensure that certain crimes should not be met with impunity. It established courts to prosecute those crimes, and mandated that States should cooperate with those courts. The courts took the form of subsidiary organs of the United Nations Security Council (the International Criminal Tribunals for the former Yugoslavia and for Rwanda (ICTY and ICTR)), a treaty-based organisation (the International Criminal Court (ICC)), and a new hybrid (the mixed tribunal model of Cambodia or Sierra Leone). The extreme political circumstances in which the ICTY and ICTR began their work brought into focus the fact that officers working on a case pending in an international court may encounter the personnel of a multitude of other organisations which are pursuing different mandates in the same territory. For example, if chemical weapons were used, it is conceivable that the OPCW, under its own flag or the United Nations', would be found at the scene carrying out an alleged use investigation under the Chemical Weapons Convention. Would the samples taken and findings of the OPCW's investigation later be requested as evidence in international criminal proceedings? Could OPCW inspectors be compelled to testify or would arguments similar to those of the ICRC in *Prosecutor v. Simic* (ICTY decision of 7 June 2000) be raised? These are matters which have not yet been considered.

The recent international and regional crises which gave rise to the establishment of the new courts emphasised the need for cooperation with and between intergovernmental and

R. Yepes-Enríquez and L. Tabassi. (eds.), Treaty Enforcement and International Cooperation in Criminal Matters

non-governmental organisations and actors. Solutions had to be found in order to respond to the multiple challenges generated by a crisis situation and the achievement of a range of international objectives. International organisations responded to these challenges in three ways: cooperation, synchronisation and integration.

First, following the genocide in Rwanda the Office of the Prosecutor (OTP) of the ICTR received assistance and cooperation from different actors. For example, the OTP benefited from assistance by Office of the United Nations High Commissioner for Human Rights monitors who were familiar with the region, had knowledge of the local infrastructure and rapport with the inhabitants, in order to more efficiently search for information and gather evidence. NGOs and journalists also played a helpful role in the OTP investigation by contacting, for example, witnesses who might have been difficult to locate or of whom investigators might not have been aware. Secondly, the Organisation for Security and Cooperation in Europe (OSCE) undertook in 1999 the Kosovo Verification Mission (KVM). However, the continual violation of the cease-fire rendered the KVM task and mandate of monitoring human rights abuses impossible in the circumstances. The KVM was then metamorphosed into the Task Force for Kosovo. Different actors and organisations deployed their forces to deal with this new perspective of the conflict, including the OSCE, UNHCR, the International Organisation for Migration (IOM), the Kosovo Diplomatic Mission (KDOM), the OTP of the ICTR and different NGOs and journalists. All these actors had to synchronise their efforts and work to avoid trauma to victims and facilitate the efficient collection of evidence. Finally, the most recent form of cooperation is integration. An example would be the United Nations Interim Administration in Kosovo (UNMIK) which co-existed with different organisations integrated into one command structure. In future, variations on these models will have to be developed to meet the objectives of international cooperative action.

The effectiveness of an ad hoc tribunal such as the International Criminal Tribunal for the Former Yugoslavia (ICTY) is directly related to cooperation with the relevant States since it is the States that will arrest individuals indicted by the Tribunal, provide access to official documents, facilitate or assist in gathering evidence, and accept to incarcerate convicted and sentenced persons. The obligation of States to cooperate with the ICTY is derived from different sources. First, the ICTY was created by the Security Council as a Chapter VII enforcement measure and, as such, all States are under the obligation under the UN Charter to respond to the tribunal's orders and requests for assistance. Second, the obligation to cooperate is specifically stipulated in the ICTY Statute. Finally, the obligation to cooperate flows from the General Framework Agreement for Peace in Bosnia and Herzegovina (the "Dayton Agreement"), and from the agreements between the ICTY and States for the enforcement of sentences. When a State refuses or fails to meet its international obligations to the ICTY, the president may or must, depending of the gravity of the violations, report the non-compliance of the State to the United Nations Security Council. The Security Council then has the discretion to take measures against the recalcitrant State. The most common response of the Security Council has been to make reference to the non-compliance in a resolution or Presidential statement.

The mixed tribunal model for Cambodia (now abandoned) and for Sierra Leone constitutes another type of cooperation between a State and an international organisation. Unlike the ICTY and ICTR, the mixed tribunals were to be established by agreement between the United Nations and the concerned State. The modalities of cooperation, the operation and the basic legal framework for the tribunals were being established on a consensual basis. The subject-matter jurisdiction of the mixed tribunals was, with a few exceptions, close to the one of the international tribunals because of the similarities of the crimes committed and the nature of the conflict. However, some unique aspects of the respective conflicts in Cambodia and in Sierra Leone influenced the scope of personal jurisdiction. In the case of Cambodia the personal jurisdiction was to be extended to "senior leaders and those most responsible for the crimes committed in Democratic Kampuchea." In the case of Sierra Leone, in addition to those who bear the "greatest responsibility," two unusual categories of persons were included in the personal jurisdiction of the Mixed Tribunal: children between 15 and 18 years of age, and peacekeepers of United Nations peacekeeping or other United Nations authorised operations. Unlike the international tribunals, the Mixed Tribunals for Cambodia and Sierra Leone foresaw a mixed composition of national and international judges, prosecutors and administrative staff members. Mixed tribunals, created to bring justice in part of the world where victims and perpetrators still co-exist, are another model which is likely to continue to play a role in the implementation of international criminal law in specific national crises.

The year 2002 was marked by the entry into force of the Rome Statute and the establishment of the International Criminal Court (ICC). This permanent institution, with jurisdiction over some of the most serious international crimes, could never function effectively without the cooperation and assistance of the States for the arrest and surrender of accused persons, the collection of evidence and the enforcement of sentences imposed by the ICC. The principal legal basis for the obligation to cooperate is, obviously, the ICC Statute that binds the States Parties. The legal assistance regime has three important characteristics that distinguish it from other cooperation regimes. First, the ICC Statute contains a number of grounds for refusal that are different from, or at least applicable in a different degree than, that in inter-State regimes. Another characteristic is the lack of reciprocity: States must provide legal assistance to the ICC but, on the other hand, the ICC may, but has no corresponding duty, to assist States. Finally, the ICC Statute regulates the settlement of disputes by providing that disputes concerning the judicial functions of the court, including the issues concerning cooperation and legal assistance, shall be settled by decision of the ICC itself. Even if the content of the obligation to cooperate is not explicitly delimited in the Statute, it is clearly expressed that the States are obliged to "cooperate fully". Its cooperation regime has not been created by the judges but is, rather, a compromise between different State interests for this permanent institution with no geographically limited jurisdiction. As such, the creation of the ICC constitutes, without a doubt, a great achievement for international cooperation in criminal matters.

Caroline Harnois

Précis-writer for Section II.2; Senior Administrator, Hague Conference on Private International Law. The views expressed cannot be attributed to the Hague Conference on Private International Law or the OPCW.

COOPERATION WITH AND BETWEEN INTERNATIONAL ORGANISATIONS: NAVIGATING THROUGH THE OBSTACLE COURSE

Harriet Solloway*

1. INTRODUCTION

The need for cooperation with and between international and regional organisations has been brought to the fore with recent initiatives in compliance monitoring and enforcement. Contemporary innovations in rapid response to crises of international and regional character have left many questions relating to cooperation and coordination to be resolved by secretariats and those responsible for field operations, rather than by policy-making organs. This ad hoc approach has met with varied success. This chapter shares some concerns that are likely to continue to arise, particularly in light of the trend of splitting, between organisations and agencies created for specific purposes, the responsibility for monitoring and enforcing compliance with internationally and regionally adopted standards of State and individual conduct. While the composition of membership may vary from one intergovernmental organisation (IGO) to another, widespread recognition of the legitimacy of the respective interests of each organisation and agency, as well as those of many non-governmental organisations (NGO's), governments, and journalists, cannot be disputed. Coordination and cooperation can enhance the ability to accomplish mission objectives in the interest of the international community, while any failure to coordinate may compromise the effective implementation of international agreements. Challenges must be identified and addressed.

2. CHALLENGES

2.1 OVERLAP

While most intergovernmental organisations have separate and distinct objectives, there may be territorial, functional, and operational overlap.

(a) Territorial overlap

It is not unusual to have several agencies responding simultaneously to a crisis situation that falls within each of their separate respective mandates. Rapid deployment into a territory places a strain on local resources that are often limited due to the realities that have led to

* Former Senior Legal Adviser to the Organization for Security and Co-operation in Europe (OSCE) Mission in Kosovo; Former Legal Adviser for Sex Crimes at the International Criminal Tribunal for Rwanda. The opinions expressed are those of the author, and are not to be imputed to the OSCE.

R. Yepes-Enríquez and L. Tabassi. (eds.), Treaty Enforcement and International Cooperation in Criminal Matters

international intervention. The race for space for both mission-related and residential purposes can lead to snap decisions and the willingness to pay top international dollar/euro. Not only does this ensure that funding is not rationally expended, but may also result in *de facto* space allocation that is less than optimally efficient. The competitive scramble to obtain supplies of limited availability and to hire qualified local personnel also contributes to an over-expenditure of international funding. Not to be neglected is resulting inflation with which the local population cannot keep pace, exacerbating many of the humanitarian concerns that gave rise to international intervention in the first place.

(b) Functional overlap

Functional overlap may occur when a crisis generates both regional and international concern, or when two or more organisations have opposing objectives.

In the first case, response to a particular facet of a given crisis may fall squarely within the mandates of more than one intergovernmental organisation. As each organisation struggles to gain the confidence of the local population and government as the one in which international trust has been vested, confusion and inefficiency result, thereby undermining the credibility of the efforts of all concerned. Unhealthy competition for the limelight in the quest for validation of the very legitimacy of an organisation, or a component of an organisation, is detrimental to achieving desired results.

In the second case, and particularly regarding investigations relating to compliance-monitoring or enforcement, or the enforcement of international criminal law, different protagonists may operate at cross-purposes, seeking to inculpate or exculpate specific governments or individuals. This could lead to intentional or inadvertent manipulation of crime scenes or locations in which there is an alleged use of a prohibited weapon of mass destruction or other violations of international humanitarian law.

(c) Operational overlap

Even when the respective objectives of organisations or agencies remain separate and distinct, operations required to meet objectives may overlap. Whether investigation is required for fact-finding, verification, or prosecution, or to determine whether or not there has been use of prohibited chemical or biological weapons or land mines, or whether it is to monitor or document alleged human rights abuses, investigators from different agencies and organisations may require information from the same witnesses, locations, and evidence. Without a systematic approach, crime scenes may be inadvertently contaminated, chain of custody may be broken, and witnesses interviewed by so many investigators that they become confused, risking self-contradiction or worse — becoming so disabused and resentful of having to give repetitive accounts of the most traumatic events of their lives that they become unwilling to participate in further investigation or legal process. Moreover, the same documentary evidence may be essential to the investigations of more than one organisation.

2.2 NON-GOVERNMENTAL ORGANISATIONS

It is usual for NGOs to be active in the same areas at the same time as intergovernmental missions. Much of the overlap operating between IGOs also operates between IGOs and NGOs. Respected NGOs play a vital role in the international response to crisis and many are vital partners with IGOs in the implementation of programmes. There does, however, exist within the NGO community varying degrees of experience, legitimacy and competence, and they are not subject to any centralised coordinating authority. The potential therefore exists for less experienced NGOs to hinder more than help in the achievement of the range of objectives of international initiatives, not the least of which is the risk of interfering with the collection of evidence.

2.3 JOURNALISTS

Journalists are often among the first members of the international community to arrive in a crisis zone. Their work is invaluable, often serving to attract attention and raise international consciousness regarding circumstances that call for international intervention. Further, their early presence places them in a prime position to witness and visually document realities that may rapidly disappear from view. There is, however, the risk that in efforts to achieve their goals of providing newsworthy information to the public, crime scenes and other evidence may be contaminated, diminishing the weight that such evidence may eventually have in Court. Worse still, evidence may not be recognised as such, and may be inadvertently destroyed.

3. RESPONSES

International organisations and others have recently responded to the challenges outlined above through cooperation, synchronisation and integration.

3.1 COOPERATION

In post-genocide Rwanda, for example, Human Rights monitors mandated by the Office of the United Nations High Commissioner for Human Rights (OHCHR) provided much needed assistance to the Office of the Prosecutor of the International Criminal Tribunal for Rwanda (ICTR), particularly in the build-up phase of investigations. The OHCHR had a network of monitors in the field with coverage of the entire territory of Rwanda. ICTR investigators were much fewer in number and were based in Kigali, the nation's capital. The familiarity gained by the OHCHR monitors with factors particular to each region, including historical and geographical knowledge, contacts with local authorities and leaders, knowledge of local infrastructure, and perhaps most important, an established rapport with local inhabitants, were of great assistance to Tribunal investigators in the earlier moments of their search for information and evidence regarding the tragic events of the Rwanda genocide.

At the same time, many of the challenges outlined above were non-existent, as the mandates of the two Organisations were temporally disjointed (with the ICTR investigating events occurring in 1994 and the OHCHR monitoring current activities) and mutually exclusive. Overlap was therefore confined to territory. Competition for residential accommodation and other necessities of life did give rise to considerable inflation with which the local population could not keep pace, except perhaps for the few fortunate owners of internationally desireable residences.

NGOs and journalists also played a role in the investigations conducted by the Office of the Prosecutor. Published reports of human rights violations that constituted offences under the Statute of the ICTR provided, to some extent, leads in the investigation of certain aspects of the Rwanda tragedy. Reports issued by conscientious NGOs were often very helpful. Moreover, certain NGOs assisted in contacting witnesses who might otherwise have been difficult to locate, and provided sociological and other expertise that proved essential in understanding the context in which the heinous crimes had come to be committed.

Conversely, some reports were revealed to be inaccurate and even erroneous, leading investigators down paths that ended nowhere. Misrepresenting facts and distorting the content of testimonials given by alleged witnesses and victims of crimes can only undermine the eventual investigation and prosecution of those crimes. As NGOs increase in their importance as actors in the international arena, so does the level of responsibility that they assume. The NGO community might do well to consider some form of self-regulation or accreditation, to assure to the extent possible that international efforts of all kinds are not jeopardised.

Journalists were among the first members of the international community to arrive in Rwanda after the genocide. The photographic images that appeared in publications and were broadcast throughout the world were an important catalyst in awakening the world to the horrors of 1994. Later, the cooperation of many print, photo, and broadcast journalists with Tribunal investigators was beyond reproach, assisting in piecing together elements of the puzzle that could only be elucidated by those who were present at devastatingly key places and times. Journalists were also able to provide leads to witnesses of whom investigators might not otherwise have been aware.

3.2 SYNCHRONISATION

In 1999 the Organization for Security and Co-operation in Europe (OSCE) undertook the Kosovo Verification Mission (KVM), planning to deploy some 2,000 unarmed verifiers from OSCE participating States into Kosovo for the purpose of verifying the Federal Republic of Yugoslavia's compliance with United Nations Security Council Resolutions 1160 and 1199. The international mandate conferred upon this regional organisation included verifying the cease-fire, monitoring movement of forces, providing assistance in the return of refugees and displaced persons, supervising elections and promoting human rights. Reports were to be provided to the OSCE Permanent Council and the United Nations Security Council, and other organisations.

The mission never made it past the build-up phase. The constant violation of the terms of cease-fire rendered the tasks of the unarmed verifiers, who had grown to a force of 1,400, almost impossible. This was underscored by the discovery of the massacre at Racak. Eventually, the failure of the parties to reach agreement in Rambouillet led to the now familiar events of the spring of 1999: the NATO air campaign over the Federal

Republic of Yugoslavia and the mass influx of Kosovar refugees into Albanian and Macedonian territories.

Prior to the withdrawal of the KVM from Kosovo, notwithstanding the broad mandate of the mission, it is fair to say that efforts had been concentrated on the verification and promotion of a cease-fire. While the mission had been preparing to deal with other elements of its mandate, such as supervising elections and development of institutions, no real progress could possibly be made in those areas without achieving basic stability. Following the withdrawal of the KVM from Federal Republic of Yugoslavia territory on 20 March 1999, and given the uncertainty of the timing or the outcome of the conflict, the mission was significantly reduced in number. The question of whether to completely disband the mission or maintain readiness to return was a constant preoccupation. Questioning was short-lived, however, in view of the numbers of refugees flooding the Albanian and Macedonian borders. It became clear that the KVM mandate to monitor human rights abuses could be accomplished through debriefings with Kosovars who had fled to the neighbouring territories. Moreover, the OSCE was the only international organisation in place with sufficient resources, both human and material, to respond during the early moments of the humanitarian crisis. The operational metamorphosis was astounding. The KVM was ended and the Task Force for Kosovo was born.

The international community soon realised that the military conflict in and over Yugoslavia might last longer than originally expected. International organisations responded. The Office of the United Nations High Commissioner for Refugees (UNHCR) and the International Organization for Migration (IOM) appropriately assumed the lead in dealing with the refugee crisis with the OSCE continuing to provide support, although many refugee camps were, in fact, run by military contingents from several different countries. The Kosovo Diplomatic Observer Mission (KDOM), in particular the United States component of that mission, deployed observers to the area for the debriefing of refugees. The OHCHR in Skopje was also present, as was a seemingly infinite number of NGOs striving to fulfil their respective mandates, and journalists, who were bringing the crisis into the living rooms of the world. Of course, the Office of the Prosecutor of the ICTY increased its presence in the region, with a view to investigating possible violations of international law subject to prosecution. The initial result was that refugees were interviewed and reinterviewed by journalists, NGOs, KDOM, OSCE Human Rights, OHCHR, and the ICTY. Victims and witnesses to crimes no longer understood to whom they were talking or the purpose of the interviews. Personnel of each organisation blamed the others for the general pandemonium and the negative effect this was having on the already traumatised population.

The IGOs did agree, however, that the work of the Office of the Prosecutor of the ICTY should not be hindered and, to the extent possible, should be supported. Finally, those operating on the ground agreed to cooperate to avoid further trauma to victims and to facilitate the efficient collection of data. A standard interview form was developed and interviewees were systematically asked whether or not they would be willing to have the confidential information forwarded to the ICTY. Interviews conducted by the OSCE and KDOM were then used as a screening tool to assist Tribunal investigators in identifying potentially important witnesses. Although some competition remained, a workable solution was found. Still, there was no mechanism for the control of NGOs.

It should be noted that during this crisis very few organisations, including NGOs, possessed the capacity for the rapid deployment of large numbers of experienced, qualified investigators. Notwithstanding all the noble intentions in the world, every organisation has the duty to limit its activities to those that its agents are able to professionally perform. It is inappropriate, for example, to assign the responsibility of investigating sexual assault to someone with little or no relevant experience. Limitations should be recognised and issues referred to those investigators within and outside the organisations capable of effectively executing required tasks.

Responsible journalists played an important role in the Rwanda crisis, and will undoubtably play a prominent role in future crises. Notwithstanding the journalistic requirement to seek out and report information, journalists must respect commitments made by international investigators and organisations to maintain the privacy of victims, and the confidentiality of their statements, as well as the need to protect the integrity of investigations. Organisations may not always be in a position to provide journalists with the information they require. Further, while most journalists respect the fragility of persons who have suffered trauma, there are journalists for whom the story is more important. Although few in number, they bring their profession into disrepute and may aggravate the damage already done by the perpetrators of criminal acts.

3.3 INTEGRATION

The newest form of cooperation between international organisations is integration. The first large-scale experiment of this kind is the United Nations Interim Administration in Kosovo (UNMIK) established by the United Nations Secretary-General pursuant to Security Council Resolution 1244. UNMIK was originally comprised of four pillars led by missions established by different organisations, all of which reported to the Special Representative of the Secretary-General who, in turn, reports to the Secretary-General of the United Nations. The organisations were the United Nations, UNHCR, the European Union (EU) and the OSCE. The Heads of each mission were appointed as United Nations Deputy Special Representatives of the Secretary-General, while other mission staff were appointed and administered in accordance with the rules of each respective organisation. With the refugee crisis in hand, UNHCR has left the UNMIK structure.

The goal, which was achieved, was to ensure that all activities of the international community in Kosovo, flowing from the Security Council mandate, were carried out in an integrated manner with a clear chain of command.

As the first effort of its kind, UNMIK has been quite successful in its objective of integrating different organisations into one command structure. It has enabled the international community to maximise the strengths of different organisations working for a common purpose. There have been some bumps along the way, regarding the harmonisation of regimes of privileges and immunities; competition for infrastructure; and competition for the limelight. Some problems remain, but all in all the mission has found its way, maximising available international resources in a way that might not have been possible only a short while ago. Continuing to move in this direction can only be to the advantage of the members and participants of all international and regional organisations which have a vested interest in the preservation and promotion of peace and security.

4. The Future

Other contributors to this book have referred to the vagueness of a number of provisions in international agreements. Ambiguity and vagueness often facilitate accession to treaties, enabling each State Party to presume an interpretation favourable to its own respective position. The consequence is that the interpretation of such provisions in the implementation of the mandates conferred upon an international organisation will be determined by the Secretariat or even by those participating in field missions. Rapid deployment and the need for urgent action does not allow for consultation of States Parties prior to taking action. People in the field, one way or another, will find a way to get the job done.

Technological advances in modern warfare have given rise to a number of international treaties and organisations. While one does not easily entertain the notion that allegations of the use of chemical, biological, and nuclear weapons, and land mines, and allegations of war crimes, crimes against humanity and other human rights violations may relate to the same territory at the same time, it is difficult to exclude such a possibility. Six or seven international organisations may be called upon to investigate alleged use and alleged violations at the same time, not to mention NGOs, journalists, individuals, and States that may have an interest in gathering information. If the objectives of each treaty and organisation are to be achieved, if the credibility of international cooperative action is to be maintained, and if the members of each international organisation are to have their funds expended to the best advantage of the international community, variations on the models of cooperation, synchronisation, and integration will have to be developed. It is unrealistic to expect to be prepared for any eventuality. Still, given the speed with which organisations are called upon to act in a crisis, some thought must be given to some level of advance joint consultation so that inspectors, verifiers, and investigators are not impeded in their efforts to collect evidence and to avoid, to the extent possible, organisational conflicts on the ground. Most importantly, communication between organisations, particularly regarding the alleged use of weapons of mass destruction and other hazardous materials, is essential for the protection of investigators who might otherwise unwittingly expose themselves to risks of contamination. While this may seem obvious, it is sometimes the obvious that is overlooked, leading to disastrous consequences.

STATE COOPERATION WITH THE ICTY

Daryl A. Mundis*

1. INTRODUCTION

The last decade of the twentieth century witnessed a virtual revolution in the development of institutions to enforce international criminal law. With the creation of the International Criminal Tribunal for the former Yugoslavia (ICTY or "Tribunal") in 1993, the United Nations Security Council took the first step in the establishment of this international criminal justice system.[1] Following the genocide that occurred in Rwanda the following year, the Security Council created a second ad hoc Tribunal to prosecute those most responsible for the crimes that were committed in that State.[2] In 1998, 120 States signed the Rome Statute of the International Criminal Court ("ICC Statute"), and a permanent International Criminal Court (ICC) was established when the Statute entered into force in 2002.[3] Because the ICC has prospective jurisdiction only,[4] however, there were efforts underway to establish additional *ad hoc* tribunals to prosecute those responsible for committing violations of international humanitarian law in Sierra Leone[5] and in Cambodia

* Legal Officer (International Law), Legal Advisory Section, Office of the Prosecutor, International Criminal Tribunal for the former Yugoslavia. The views expressed here are solely those of the author and are not to be imputed to the United Nations, the ICTY or the Office of the Prosecutor.

[1] The ICTY was established by the Security Council pursuant to Resolution 827 on 25 May 1993 (UN doc. S/RES/827, 1993), following consideration of the Report of the Secretary-General pursuant to paragraph 2 of Security Council Resolution 808 (3 May 1993, UN doc. S/25704, "Secretary-General's Report"). The ICTY has competence to prosecute persons responsible for serious violations of international humanitarian law committed in the territory of the former Yugoslavia since 1991 (ICTY Statute, Article 1).

[2] The International Criminal Tribunal for Rwanda (ICTR) was established by the Security Council on 8 November 1994 pursuant to Resolution 955 (UN doc. S/RES/955 (1994)).

[3] 1998 Rome Statute of the International Criminal Court, entered into force 1 July 2002; UN doc. A/CONF.183/9*, as corrected by the procès-verbaux of 10 November 1998 and 12 July 1999. Corrected text available at http://www.un.org/law/icc.

[4] ICC Statute Article 11(1).

[5] See UN docs. S/2000/786 (10 August 2000); S/RES/1315 (14 August 2000); S/2000/915 (4 October 2000); S/2000/1234 (22 December 2000); and S/2001/40 (12 January 2001). See also *infra* in this volume, D. Shraga, *Implementing International Criminal Legislation in the Mixed Tribunals for Cambodia and Sierra Leone.*

R. Yepes-Enríquez and L. Tabassi. (eds.), Treaty Enforcement and International Cooperation in Criminal Matters

(during the Khmer Rouge reign of terror).[6] Simultaneously, international prosecutors working under the auspices of the United Nations Mission in Kosovo and the United Nations Transitional Administration in East Timor[7] were prosecuting offenders in local courts for violations that occurred in those regions.

The eventual success of these judicial institutions and mechanisms, however, may well depend upon the level of cooperation they receive from States. All States depend on effective means of compliance in order to enforce judicial orders, decisions and judgments. National systems ultimately rely upon police forces to implement the decisions, and orders of courts. The evolving international criminal justice system lacks such enforcement mechanisms. It should be noted, however, that the lack of effective enforcement mechanisms is not unique to the international *criminal* legal system. International law generally lacks effective enforcement and compliance mechanisms, which leads some critics to conclude that international law fails to meet the traditional definition of a legal system.

The practice of the ICTY demonstrates the need for a high degree of cooperation with — and reliance upon — the international community. The ICTY must rely on States and other international organisations to be effective. For example, it is States that: (1) arrest individuals indicted by the Tribunal; (2) provide access to official archives; (3) undertake searches for evidence; and (4) agree to incarcerate individuals convicted and sentenced by the Tribunal. In the event that States fail to comply with judicial orders and decisions of the Tribunal, the ICTY possesses no independent police or military force to ensure compliance. Rather, as a subsidiary organ of the Security Council, the Tribunal must look to that body to enforce its orders in the event of non-compliance by States.

Other international actors, such as international peacekeeping forces, other UN agencies, and non-governmental organisations (NGOs) also play an important role. The primary focus of the present work, however, is on the obligations of States to cooperate with the ICTY.[8] This chapter will set forth analyses of both the sources of the obligation of States to cooperate with the ICTY and the procedures employed by the ICTY in the event a State fails to comply with its obligations to the Tribunal.

2. Sources of the Obligation to Cooperate

There are several sources of the international obligation of States to cooperate with the ICTY. These sources include the Charter of the United Nations, the Statute and Rules of the Tribunal, treaty obligations, and agreements between States and the Tribunal for the enforcement of sentences. Each of these sources will be briefly described.

---

[6] On 2 January 2001, the Cambodian National Assembly approved a law designed to create a tribunal with international assistance to prosecute former Khmer Rouge leaders. See, Seth Mydans, *Cambodian Deputies Back War Crimes Tribunal to Try Khmer Rouge*, New York Times (3 January 2001). The Cambodian law was based on an agreement between Cambodia and the United Nations. See further *infra* in this volume, D. Shraga, Implementing International Criminal Legislation in the Mixed Tribunals for Cambodia and Sierra Leone.

[7] See further *supra* in this volume, M. Othman, Concurrent Jurisdiction: Legal and Policy Considerations.

[8] Although the ICTY is the subject of this chapter, States owe similar obligations to the ICTR. Moreover, the problems encountered by the two ad hoc Tribunals are generally similar, although the ICTR has a better track record with respect to the arrest and detention of those most responsible for the genocide that occurred in Rwanda.

2.1 THE CHARTER OF THE UNITED NATIONS

The ICTY was created by the Security Council in accordance with Chapter VII of the UN Charter based on a determination that the situation in the former Yugoslavia constituted a continuing threat to international peace and security.[9] Such a finding is necessary for the Security Council to act pursuant to Chapter VII. Once the Security Council takes Chapter VII action, however, such measures are binding with respect to the parties to the conflict and third States.[10] It is of no legal consequence that the resolution in question makes no reference either to Chapter VII or to the specific article of Chapter VII under which such measures are adopted.[11]

Since Chapter VII enforcement measures are binding on all States, it follows that requests for assistance and orders of the Tribunal, which is a Chapter VII Security Council subsidiary organ, are binding on States as a matter of general international law. This fact was emphasised in the Secretary General's Report,[12] which was appended to Security Council Resolution 827, establishing the Tribunal. This Report is unambiguous with respect to the binding nature of judicial orders of the ICTY Trial Chambers: "[A]n order by a Trial Chamber for the surrender or transfer of persons to the custody of the International Tribunal shall be considered to be the application of an enforcement measure under Chapter VII of the Charter of the United Nations."[13] Moreover, in the same report, the Secretary-General stated that the Security Council's decision to establish the Tribunal created a "binding obligation on all States to take whatever steps are required to implement this decision."[14]

2.2 ICTY STATUTORY PROVISIONS

Notwithstanding the general binding nature of ICTY requests for assistance and orders, the drafters of the ICTY Statute[15] took the additional step of including several specific provisions in the Statute regarding the obligation to cooperate with the Tribunal. There are three primary provisions of the ICTY Statute concerning the obligation of States to assist the Tribunal in carrying out its mandate that merit attention.[16] First, Article 29 of the ICTY Statute sets forth the general obligations of States to comply with requests for assistance or

[9] UN doc. S/RES/827 (1993).

[10] See Jochen Abr. Frowein, *Chapter VII Action with Respect to Threats to the Peace, Breaches of the Peace and Acts of Aggression*, in Bruno Simma (ed.), The Charter of the United Nations: A Commentary, at 613.

[11] *Id.*

[12] Secretary-General's Report (see *supra* note 1).

[13] *Id.*, at para. 126.

[14] *Id.*, at para. 125.

[15] Statute of the International Tribunal, adopted 25 May 1993 by UN Security Council resolution S/RES/827 (1993), as amended by UN Security Council resolutions S/RES/1166 (1998), S/RES/1329 (2000) and S/RES/1411 (2002). Amended text available at http://www.un.org/icty.

[16] There are two other provisions of the Statute that address areas of cooperation between the ICTY and States in the context of imprisonment of convicted persons and procedures for the pardoning or commutation of sentences. Article 27 provides that sentences imposed by the ICTY are to be served in States willing to accept such convicted persons, while Article 28 requires the State imprisoning convicted persons to consult with the President of the Tribunal prior to pardoning or commuting the sentence of an individual convicted by the Tribunal.

orders issued by the Trial Chambers of the Tribunal. This article, titled "Cooperation and judicial assistance," provides:

1. States shall cooperate with the International Tribunal in the investigation and prosecution of persons accused of committing serious violations of international humanitarian law.
2. States shall comply without undue delay with any request for assistance or an order issued by a Trial Chamber, including, but not limited to:
   (1) the identification and location of persons;
   (2) the taking of testimony and the production of evidence;
   (3) the service of documents;
   (4) the arrest or detention of persons;
   (5) the surrender or the transfer of the accused to the International Tribunal.

The ICTY Appeals Chamber has indicated that Article 29 sets forth an obligation *erga omnes*.[17] In the *Barcelona Traction, Power and Light Company* case, the International Court of Justice discussed the obligations of States "towards the international community as a whole" and defined them as obligations *erga omnes*.[18] Because these obligations are owed to the international community as a whole, all States have an interest in the observance of such obligations. As the Appeals Chamber noted in the *Blaskic Subpoena Judgement*, "every Member State of the United Nations has a legal interest in the fulfilment of the obligation laid down in Article 29."[19]

Second, Article 18 of the ICTY Statute, which governs investigations and the preparation of indictments, envisions that States will provide information to the Prosecutor so that investigations may be conducted.[20]

Pursuant to paragraph 2 of Article 18, the Prosecutor may seek the assistance of States in conducting on-site investigations and the collection of evidence:

> Para. 2. The Prosecutor shall have the power to question suspects, victims and witnesses, to collect evidence and to conduct on-site investigations. In carrying out these tasks, the Prosecutor may, as appropriate, seek the assistance of the State authorities concerned.

Finally, States may not disregard their obligations to the ICTY by asserting the primacy

---

[17] *Prosecutor v. Tihomir Blaskic*, Judgement on the Request of the Republic of Croatia for Review of the Decision of Trial Chamber II of 18 July 1997, Case No. IT-95-14-AR108 *bis*, ICTY A. Ch., 29 Oct. 1997 ("*Blaskic Subpoena Judgement*"). "Article 29 imposes an obligation on Member States towards all other Members or, in other words, an 'obligation *erga omnes partes*'." *Id.* at para. 26.

[18] 1970 ICJ Reports, para. 33.

[19] *Blaskic Subpoena Judgement*, para. 26.

[20] ICTY Statute Article 18(1) provides:

> 1. The Prosecutor shall initiate investigations *ex-officio* or on the basis of information obtained from any source, particularly from Governments, United Nations organs, intergovernmental and non-governmental organizations. The Prosecutor shall assess the information received or obtained and decide whether there is sufficient basis to proceed.

of their national judicial systems over the Tribunal's jurisdiction. Pursuant to Article 9(2) of the ICTY Statute, the Tribunal has primacy over national courts, notwithstanding the fact that concurrent jurisdiction exists between the Tribunal and national courts. Article 9 is entitled "Concurrent jurisdiction" and provides:

> 1. The International Tribunal and national courts shall have concurrent jurisdiction to prosecute persons for serious violations of international humanitarian law committed in the territory of the former Yugoslavia since 1 January 1991.
>
> 2. The International Tribunal shall have primacy over national courts. At any stage of the procedure, the International Tribunal may formally request national courts to defer to the competence of the International Tribunal in accordance with the present Statute and the Rules of Procedure and Evidence of the International Tribunal.

Thus, States may not avoid their obligations to the Tribunal on the basis of pending judicial activity by their domestic judiciary system.

2.3 ICTY RULES

In order to give effect to these statutory provisions, there are several rules that set forth obligations with which States must comply. These rules appear in various sections of the ICTY Rules of Procedure and Evidence.[21] For example, in Part Two of the Rules, governing the primacy of the Tribunal, Rules 8 to 13 are relevant for the present discussion. Pursuant to Rule 8, which governs requests for information, once the Prosecutor determines that a crime within the jurisdiction of the Tribunal has been committed (or is the subject of an investigation or criminal proceeding in the courts of any State), the Prosecutor may request that State to forward all relevant information regarding that investigation or proceeding. The State is required to transmit such information in accordance with Article 29. Rules 9 and 10 govern the procedures whereby the Tribunal may request a State to defer its investigation or prosecution of a case for which the Tribunal has jurisdiction.

In the context of investigations, several Rules set forth the obligations that States owe the Tribunal. For example, Rule 39, which sets forth the procedures for the conduct of investigations, permits the Prosecutor to, *inter alia,* summon and question suspects, collect evidence, seek the assistance of any State or international organisation, and request such orders as may be necessary from a Trial Chamber or Judge. Rule 40, entitled "Provisional Measures," authorises the Prosecutor, in the event of urgency, to request any State to provisionally arrest a suspect or accused, to seize physical evidence, and to take all necessary measures to prevent the escape of the suspect or accused, injury to or intimidation of a victim or witness, or the destruction of evidence. Pursuant to the terms of that Rule, States must comply with such requests in accordance with Article 29.

There are several relevant rules pertaining to judicial orders for the production of documents and arrest warrants. Rule 54 and Rule 54*bis* provide a procedure whereby a party may request a State to produce documents or information relevant to any matter in issue

[21] ICTY doc. IT/32/REV.22, dated 13 December 2001, as amended on 23 April 2002. Text available at http://www.un.org/icty.

before a Judge or Trial Chamber.[22] In the context of arrest warrants, which are governed by Rule 55, Rule 56 provides that:

> The State to which a warrant of arrest or a transfer order for a witness is transmitted shall act promptly and with all due diligence to ensure proper and effective execution thereof, in accordance with Article 29 of the Statute.

Moreover, Rule 58 prevents a State from citing to its own national extradition provisions as an impediment to the transfer or arrest of one of its nationals.

2.4 TREATY OBLIGATIONS

The General Framework Agreement for Peace in Bosnia and Herzegovina ("the Dayton Agreement"),[23] signed on 14 December 1995, contains several obligations upon the Parties to cooperate with the Tribunal, thereby supplementing both the ICTY Statute and the Rules. For example, the Dayton Agreement requires the Federal Republic of Yugoslavia, Croatia, and Bosnia and Herzegovina, as States Parties to the Dayton Agreement and as those States most affected by the conflict in the former Yugoslavia, to:

- cooperate fully with all entities involved in the peace process, specifically including cooperation in the investigation and prosecution of war crimes and other violations of international humanitarian law;[24]
- cooperate with the Tribunal in relation to the arrest or detention of, and surrender to, the Tribunal of prisoners of war indicted by the Tribunal;[25]
- provide the Tribunal with unrestricted access to areas over which the Parties exercise control;[26] and
- allow all international organisations full and unrestricted access to all refugees and displaced persons on the territory of the States Parties.[27]

Moreover, the Constitution of Bosnia and Herzegovina, which formed Annex 4 to the Dayton Agreement, prohibits persons indicted by the Tribunal, but who have refused to comply with orders to appear before it, from holding public office in Bosnia and Herzegovina.[28]

---

[22] For a discussion of issues relating to States and disclosure of national security and confidential information in the context of ICTY trials, see *infra* in this volume, Nancy Paterson, Protecting National Security and Other Confidential Information.
[23] UN doc. A/50/79C and S/1995/999, reprinted at 35 ILM 223 (1996).
[24] Article IX of the Dayton Agreement.
[25] Article X of Annex 1-A (Agreement on Military Aspects of the Peace Settlement) to the Dayton Agreement.
[26] Article XIII(4), Annex 6 (Agreement on Human Rights) to the Dayton Agreement.
[27] Article III(2), Annex 7 (Agreement on Refugees and Displaced Persons) to the Dayton Agreement.
[28] Article IX(1), Annex 4 (Constitution of Bosnia and Herzegovina) to the Dayton Agreement.

2.5 AGREEMENTS BETWEEN STATES AND THE TRIBUNAL FOR THE ENFORCEMENT OF SENTENCES

Finally, as noted above, Article 27 of the ICTY Statute envisions that individuals convicted by the Tribunal will serve their sentences in States that have expressed their willingness to incarcerate such persons. Thus, unlike most of the other types of assistance which States provide to the Tribunal, agreements between the Tribunal and individual States, rather than the UN Charter, Statute, Rules or treaties, govern the enforcement of sentences.[29] There are currently seven such agreements in force.[30]

In order to give effect to Article 27, the ICTY Registry and the United Nations Office of Legal Affairs coordinated efforts in drafting a "model agreement" to serve as the basis for concluding agreements between States and the ICTY for the enforcement of sentences:[31]

The model agreement provides that the Registrar of the Tribunal will first contact the State and request that State to enforce the Tribunal's sentence, providing relevant information regarding the convicted person and his/her sentence; the State will then promptly make a decision on that request in accordance with its national law. Thus, it is clear that each request will be treated on a case by case basis, so that the State is not bound to agree to any particular request. Thereafter, the convicted person will be transferred to the appropriate authorities in the receiving State; the costs of transfer of the convicted person are to be borne by the Tribunal, but all other costs associated with the transfer are the responsibility of the State.[32]

Notwithstanding the entirely voluntary nature of enforcement of sentence agreements, States that undertake this obligation typically must amend their national legislation in order to enter into such agreements.[33] They must also subject themselves to the Tribunal's supervision vis-à-vis the incarceration of individuals convicted by the Tribunal.[34] For example, the Tribunal has the right to ensure that individuals convicted by its Trial Chambers are actually being imprisoned and that the State is maintaining minimum human rights standards with respect to the conditions of imprisonment.[35]

3. REPORTS OF NON-COMPLIANCE

In the event that States fail to meet their international obligations to the Tribunal, the ICTY Rules either permit or require, depending on the nature and severity of the alleged non-compliance, the President to report such States to the Security Council for non-compliance. For example, Rule 11 authorises the President to report the failure of a State to comply with a request for deferral to the Tribunal's competence pursuant to Rule 9 and Rule

---

[29] David Tolbert, *The International Criminal Tribunal for the former Yugoslavia and the Enforcement of Sentences*, 11 Leiden J. of Int'l Law 655, 658 (1998).

[30] See UN doc. A/55/273-S/2000/777 (seventh annual report of the ICTY), para. 249. In addition, there is one ad hoc agreement between the Federal Republic of Germany and the Tribunal for the imprisonment of Duško Tadic. ICTY Press Release JL/P.I.S./538e, 31 October 2000, available on the ICTY website: http://www.un.org/icty.

[31] See Yearbook of the International Criminal Tribunal for the former Yugoslavia 1996, at 227. For an in depth analysis of issues raised by enforcement of sentence agreements, see Tolbert, note 29 *supra*, 655-669.

[32] Tolbert, note 29 *supra*, at 664.

[33] *Id.*, at 663.

[34] *Id.*, at 659.

[35] *Id.*

10. Rule 13 permits the President to report a State's failure to permanently discontinue its proceedings against an individual already tried by the Tribunal in accordance with the principle of *non bis in idem*. Pursuant to Rule 59, the President may report a State's failure to execute a warrant of arrest or order for transfer. In accordance with Rule 61, the President (after consulting with the Presiding Judges of the Chambers) must report non-compliance in the event that a Trial Chamber certifies that a State has failed or refused to arrest an individual indicted by the Tribunal.

In addition, Rule 7*bis*[36] sets forth a mandatory scheme for reporting non-compliance to the Security Council if certain "triggering" events occur. Rule 7*bis*(A) establishes a residual reporting requirement for any matter falling outside the scope of Rule 11, Rule 13, Rule 59 or Rule 61, whenever a Judge or Trial Chamber is satisfied that a State is in non-compliance with its obligations and so advises the President. Pursuant to Rule 7*bis*(B), the Prosecutor may request the President to make a finding of State non-compliance with Article 29, and if the President makes such a finding, the Security Council *must* be notified.

The President of the Tribunal has made eleven written reports to the Security Council concerning the failure by a State or an entity[37] to comply with its international obligations under Article 29.[38] These reports have been made at the request of a Trial Chamber, *proprio motu*, or at the request of the Prosecutor pursuant to Rule 7*bis*(B).[39] There have also been instances where the President, in orally addressing the Security Council, has raised instances of non-compliance that were also the subject of the written requests.[40] The ICTY annual reports, submitted in accordance with Article 34 of the Statute, also set forth examples of

---

[36] Rule 7*bis*, entitled "Non-compliance with Obligations," states:

(A) In addition to cases to which Rule 11, Rule 13, Rule 59 or Rule 61 applies, where a Trial Chamber or a permanent Judge is satisfied that a State has failed to comply with an obligation under Article 29 of the Statute which relates to any proceedings before that Chamber or Judge, the Chamber or Judge may advise the President, who shall report the matter to the Security Council.

(B) If the Prosecutor satisfies the President that a State has failed to comply with an obligation under Article 29 of the Statute in respect of a request by the Prosecutor under Rule 8, Rule 39 or Rule 40, the President shall notify the Security Council thereof.

Rule 7*bis* was adopted at the 13th Plenary of the ICTY Judges on 25 July 1997, one week after ICTY Trial Chamber II delivered its Decision on the issuance of *subpoenas*. This Decision became the disputed issue in the *Blaškic Subpoena Judgement*, in which the Appeals Chamber stated that "the adoption of Rule 7*bis* is clearly to be regarded as falling within the authority of the International Tribunal."

[37] As used by the Tribunal, the term "entity" typically refers to Republika Srpska.

[38] Immediately prior to her retirement from the ICTY, President Gabrielle Kirk McDonald submitted a list to the Security Council outlining all outstanding matters of State non-compliance. See UN doc. S/1999/1117 (2 November 1999).

[39] For a detailed analysis of Rule 7*bis*, including descriptions of all reports of non-compliance made pursuant to this Rule, see Daryl A. Mundis, *Reporting Non-Compliance: Rule 7bis*, in May, Tolbert, Hocking, Roberts, Jia, Mundis and Oosthuizen (eds.), Essays on ICTY Procedure and Evidence In Honour of Gabrielle Kirk McDonald, 421-438 (2001).

[40] For example, on 2 October 1998, President McDonald addressed the Security Council concerning non-compliance by the Federal Republic of Yugoslavia. See ICTY Press Release CC/PIU/349-E, 2 October 1998, available on the ICTY website: http://www.un.org/icty.

non-compliance.[41] Finally, the Prosecutor has also raised issues of non-compliance with the Security Council.[42]

With respect to Rule 7*bis*, there have been three instances when the President has invoked this Rule, on the basis of requests from the Prosecutor, to report non-compliance to the Security Council. The first instance concerned the failure of the Federal Republic of Yugoslavia to issue visas to Tribunal investigators to enter Kosovo and search for evidence relating to alleged crimes committed there. Without specifically citing Rule 7*bis*, President Gabrielle Kirk McDonald reported this non-compliance to the Security Council on 6 November 1998.[43] The second such report occurred on 16 March 1999 and also concerned the continuing non-cooperation of the Federal Republic of Yugoslavia vis-à-vis the investigation in Kosovo.[44] The third Rule 7*bis* request was with respect to Croatia and its failure to provide evidence regarding "Operation Flash" and "Operation Storm" and its failure to transfer Mladen Naletilic.[45]

In addition, several reports of non-compliance cover the same repeated failure to comply and were made pursuant to Rule 61. For example, the failure of the Federal Republic of Yugoslavia to arrest and transfer to the custody of the Tribunal three individuals indicted for crimes allegedly committed in Vukovar (known as the "Vukovar Three") was initially reported to the Security Council on 24 April 1996[46] and subsequently reported on at least four other occasions.[47]

Upon receipt of the ICTY President's report of non-compliance, the Security Council has discretion with respect to what action — if any — to take in order to attempt to bring the recalcitrant State into compliance with its obligations. As should be clear from the repeated reports of non-compliance concerning the same circumstances, the Security Council has largely failed to effectively respond to ICTY reports regarding non-compliance by States. The typical Security Council response is a brief reference to the non-compliance in a

[41] See, for example, paras. 155-167 of the seventh annual report of the International Tribunal for the Prosecution of Persons Responsible for Serious Violations of International Humanitarian Law Commited in the Territory of the Former Yugoslavia since 1991 (UN doc. A/55/273-S/2000/777 (7 August 2000)) and paras. 90-106 of the sixth annual report (UN doc. A/54/187-S/1999/846, 25 August 1999).

[42] See, for example, UN doc. S/1998/1124 (27 November 1998) in which the Prosecutor, in a letter to the President of the Security Council, complained of the failure of the Federal Republic of Yugoslavia to provide her investigators with visas to enter Kosovo to investigate allegations of crimes committed there in 1998.

[43] UN doc. S/1998/1040 (6 November 1998).

[44] UN doc. S/1999/383 (16 March 1999).

[45] UN doc. S/1999/912 (25 August 1999). Naletili was subsequently transferred to the Tribunal on 21 March 2000.

[46] UN doc. S/1996/319 (24 April 1996).

[47] See UN docs. S/1996/556 (11 July 1996); S/1998/839 (8 September 1998); President McDonald's Address to the Security Council, ICTY Press Release CC/PIU/349-E, 2 October 1998 (available on the ICTY website at: http://www.un.org/icty); UN doc. S/1998/990 (22 October 1998); and Address of President McDonald to the Security Council, ICTY Press Release JL/PIU/371-E, 8 December 1998 (available on the ICTY website at: http://www.un.org/icty). This failure to comply was also mentioned in several annual reports of the ICTY. See UN docs. A/51/292-S/1996/665 (16 August 1996), Annex II; A/52/375-S/1997/729 (18 September 1997), para. 188; and A/54/187-S/1999/846 (25 August 1999) at paras. 92-94.

subsequent resolution[48] or the issuance of a Presidential Statement.[49] Perhaps the strongest Security Council response was contained in Resolution 1207, in which the Council deplored the continuing failure of the Federal Republic of Yugoslavia to cooperate.[50]

4. Conclusion

Without the active assistance of States, the ICTY would not be able to function effectively. A variety of sources establish obligations upon States to cooperate with the Tribunal. Such assistance is necessary for the Tribunal to perform its mandate. For example, the Tribunal relies upon the assistance of States in order to carry out investigations, to arrest individuals indicted for crimes and to imprison persons convicted by the Tribunal.

In the event a State fails to comply with its obligations, however, the Tribunal possesses no recourse except to report such failures to the Security Council. As demonstrated above, there have been numerous reports to the Security Council of such non-compliance, including several instances where the same failure to comply has been repeatedly reported. Yet, the Security Council seems unwilling — or unable — to effectively coerce such recalcitrant States to comply with their international obligations. The proliferation of judicial institutions to prosecute those most responsible for the most serious crimes known to humanity provides ample evidence that the international community has accepted the notion that criminal prosecutions play an important role in maintaining international peace and security. Nevertheless, the fact that some States still do not live up to their obligations, while the international community seems oblivious to such non-compliance, does not bode well for the future of the international criminal justice system.

---

[48] See, for example, Resolution 940, in which the Security Council demanded all States, and in particular those from the former Yugoslavia, to comply with requests for assistance or orders of a Trial Chamber under Article 29 of the Statute. (UN doc. S/1995/940 (9 November 1995)).

[49] For an example of a Security Council Presidential Statement concerning the failure of the authorities in the Republika Srpska and the Federal Republic of Yugoslavia to arrest Radovan Karadžic and Ratko Mladic, see Presidential Statement, 8 August 1996, UN doc. S/PRST/1996/34. See also Presidential Statement, 8 May 1996, UN doc. S/PRST/1996/23 regarding the failure of the Federal Republic of Yugoslavia to arrest and transfer the Vukovar Three.

[50] After making an explicit reference to Chapter VII of the UN Charter, the Security Council, *inter alia*, stated that it:

1. *Reiterates* its decision that all States shall cooperate fully with the Tribunal and its organs in accordance with Resolution 827 (1993) and the Statute of the Tribunal, including the obligation of States to comply with requests for assistance or orders issued by a Trial Chamber under Article 29 of the Statute, to execute arrest warrants transmitted to them by the Tribunal and to comply with its requests for information and investigations;

2. *Calls again upon* the Federal Republic of Yugoslavia, and all other States which have not done so, to take any measures necessary under their domestic law to implement the provisions of Resolution 827 (1993) and the Statute of the Tribunal, and *affirms* that a State may not invoke provisions of its domestic law as justification for its failure to perform binding obligations under international law;

3. *Condemns* the failure to date of the Federal Republic of Yugoslavia to execute the arrest warrants issued by the Tribunal against the three individuals referred to in the letter of 8 September 1998, and *demands* the immediate and unconditional execution of those arrest warrants, including the transfer to the custody of the Tribunal of those individuals.

UN doc. S/RES/1207 (17 November 1998) (emphasis in the original).

STATE COOPERATION WITH THE ICC

Göran Sluiter*

1. Introduction

After years of difficult negotiations, agreement was reached on an international criminal court and the Statute was adopted at a diplomatic conference in Rome in July 1998.[1] Upon entry into force of the Statute in 2002, the International Criminal Court (ICC) was established as a permanent institution with jurisdiction over the most serious international crimes. At the outset, it was clear to the drafters that the ICC, like the ad hoc Tribunals for the former Yugoslavia and Rwanda ("the ad hoc Tribunals"), could never function effectively without the required assistance from States. Like the ad hoc Tribunals, the ICC has no team of law enforcement officials at its disposal who are empowered to undertake various (coercive) actions on the territories of sovereign States. The cooperation of States is furthermore not only indispensable in the form of "legal assistance," but also in more practical matters, in particular the financing of the ICC.

This chapter is only concerned with the legal aspects of cooperation. These "legal aspects," or legal assistance, can be divided in three main areas of cooperation: assistance in the arrest and surrender of accused persons; assistance in the collection of evidence; and assistance in the enforcement of sentences imposed by the ICC. All these forms of assistance are of vital importance to the ICC.

It by far exceeds the scope of this chapter to explore all the matters pertaining to each of these aspects of legal assistance with the ICC. I will therefore confine myself to some general observations on the ICC cooperation regime. These observations are aimed at providing a better understanding of the key elements of the ICC cooperation regime. Before focusing on these key elements, it is first necessary to determine which legal basis, or bases, underlie the duty to provide legal assistance (section 2 below). In the third section, I will then turn to what can be considered to be the central features of the ICC cooperation regime. These central features can best be understood by comparing the ICC cooperation model with the traditional inter-State cooperation model. Section 4 builds on section 3 and takes a more detailed look at the content of the duty of States to cooperate. Section 5 deals with the important question of how the duty to provide assistance can be enforced.

* Lecturer in International Law, Utrecht University, the Netherlands. This contribution borrows significantly from his book entitled International Criminal Adjudication and the Collection of Evidence: Obligations of States, Intersentia, Antwerpen (2002).

[1] 1998 Rome Statute of the International Criminal Court, entered into force 1 July 2002; UN doc. A/CONF.183/9*, as corrected by the procès-verbaux of 10 November 1998 and 12 July 1999. Corrected text available at http://www.un.org/law/icc.

R. Yepes-Enríquez and L. Tabassi. (eds.), Treaty Enforcement and International Cooperation in Criminal Matters

2. Legal Bases for the Duty to Cooperate

The first and obvious legal basis for the duty to cooperate is the treaty, the ICC Statute. It is a general principle of the law of treaties, known as the principle of *pacta sunt servanda*, that States Parties to a treaty are bound to perform treaties in good faith.[2] This implies that upon entry into force the contracting parties are, on the basis of the ICC Statute, under a duty to cooperate in good faith with the ICC in the manner and under the conditions set out in the Statute.

The question arises as to whether a possible legal basis for the duty to cooperate for States not Party may be identified. Compared to the ad hoc Tribunals, the ICC will be confronted with a substantially larger number of States not party, which are not bound under the Statute to cooperate with the ICC. Nonetheless, the assistance of States not party may, in certain investigations and prosecutions, be crucial to the effective functioning of the ICC. We have to bear in mind the general principle of treaty law of *pacta tertiis nec nocent nec prosunt*.[3] The drafters of the ICC Statute were aware of this rule and they tried to come up with devices regulating the cooperation of a State not Party.

First of all, a State not Party may, pursuant to Article 12(3) of the Statute, accept the ICC's jurisdiction on an ad hoc basis. This entails the duty to cooperate with respect to a particular case, in accordance with Part 9 of the ICC Statute. As a result, with respect to a particular case, the State has accepted the same duties as a State Party.

As far as States are concerned that are not (yet) parties and that have not accepted the ICC's jurisdiction on an ad hoc basis, Article 87(5) of the Statute enables the ICC to conclude ad hoc cooperation agreements with States not Party. The existence and extent of a duty to cooperate on the basis of an ad hoc arrangement depend entirely on the content of the arrangement or agreement. It could vary from assistance at the discretion of the State not Party with respect to a particular case, or even a particular act of assistance, to full cooperation by a State in accordance with the Statute.[4] One has to bear in mind that a State not Party is, in this respect, in a rather strong negotiating position and can easily impose its terms and conditions for the provision of assistance.

When we consider the legal basis of the duty to cooperate with the ICC, it is imperative to take into account the special role of the United Nations Security Council. According to Article 13 of the ICC Statute, the Security Council, when acting under Chapter VII of the UN Charter, may "trigger" the jurisdiction of the ICC by referring to the Prosecutor a situation in which one or more of the crimes mentioned in Article 5 appear to have been

[2] See Article 26 of the Vienna Convention on the Law of Treaties (1969) which provides as follows: 'Every treaty in force is binding upon the parties to it and must be performed by them in good faith'.
[3] These principles find expression in Article 34 of the Vienna Convention on the Law of Treaties (1969).
[4] The latter could arise, for example, in the case of a signatory State which is expected to ratify the Statute soon, but the cooperation of which is required urgently.

committed.[5] The Statute is silent on the question as to what this means for the duty of States to cooperate.

A Security Council resolution submitting a matter to the ICC may provide for States an additional, or for some States even an exclusive, basis for the duty to cooperate. In case the Council will decide to trigger the ICC's jurisdiction in the future, it is possible to distinguish *grosso modo* three alternative modes of submitting a matter.

First of all, the Security Council may refer a situation, which it may describe in more detail, in a resolution, without any further comments or details. In this scenario the matter will be dealt with in accordance with the Statute and the duty to cooperate will be exclusively based on the Statute, meaning, for example, that States not party are generally under no obligation to assist the ICC.[6] Such a "blank submission," with no reference to assistance to the ICC by all UN members, appears an unlikely option given the nature of referral. The Council can only refer a matter when acting under Chapter VII. In other words, it must consider investigation and prosecution by the ICC necessary to restore or maintain international peace and security, which, one may argue, requires cooperation by all UN members, including States that are not party to the Statute.

A second, more likely, scenario therefore is that a Chapter VII resolution submitting a matter to the ICC will decide that all States — or rather all UN members — shall cooperate with the ICC in accordance with its Statute. The resolution, and ultimately the UN Charter, would then constitute the legal basis for the duty of all UN members to cooperate. The duty to cooperate would, for States that are members of the United Nations but not party to the Statute, be confined to the investigation submitted to the ICC by the Council. The scope of the duty to cooperate would not differ from that incumbent on States Parties in the case of an investigation triggered by a State or initiated by the Prosecutor. As a result, the grounds of refusal set out in the Statute are applicable to, and can be invoked by, the States not party.

The third and final option is that the Security Council, with a view to restoring international peace and security, will decide that all UN members should be under the obligation to cooperate fully with the ICC. To be more specific, the Council could decide that (certain of) the grounds for refusal in the ICC Statute are not applicable to UN members. This is, again, an unlikely situation because it would require the Council to shape a new cooperation regime, which may be difficult to reconcile with the legal framework in which the ICC has to operate.

In addition to the above-mentioned legal bases for a "general" duty to provide legal assistance, mention should also be made of future agreements that will regulate specific aspects of the functioning of the ICC, and which may as such serve as the legal basis for particular obligations. In this respect, one can envisage the Agreement on the Privileges and

[5] The possibility of the Security Council referring "cases" to the Court had already been recognised in the 1994 ILC Draft (see Article 23(1) of UN doc. A/49/10 at 84). However, within the compilation of proposals forming the basis for the negotiations in Rome, the possibility of the Security Council submitting cases to the Court was only mentioned as an option in square brackets (see UN doc. A/CONF.183/2/Add.1, at 34). On the relationship between the Court and the Security Council, see L. Yee, *The International Criminal Court and The Security Council: Articles 13(b) and 16*, in R.S. Lee, The International Criminal Court: the Making of the Rome Statute: Issues, Negotiations, Results (1999) at 143-152.

[6] Of course, States not party may be obliged to cooperate on the basis of an ad hoc arrangement or agreement.

Immunities of the ICC, the Headquarters Agreement with the Netherlands, and agreements regulating the enforcement of sentences imposed by the ICC.

It follows from the above that there are a number of possible legal bases underlying the duty to cooperate. The exact extent of the duty to provide assistance obviously depends on the relevant and applicable legal basis. For practical reasons, I will concentrate in sections 3 and 4 on the cooperation regime as contained in the ICC Statute.

3. Nature of the ICC Legal Assistance Regime

The distinctive features of the ICC cooperation regime can best be described by comparing it with cooperation regimes with which States are already familiar, namely, inter-State legal assistance. Although one has to be careful with generalisations, there are a number of features common to the inter-State, or horizontal, legal assistance regimes. It has been assumed that the ad hoc Tribunals do, and the ICC will, operate in a hierarchical relationship above States, which has resulted in qualifying these cooperation models as "vertical" or "supranational".[7] But what does this "verticalism" really mean? In my view there are three important distinctive characteristics of the ICC cooperation regime, and that of the ad hoc Tribunals, which will be discussed further below.

3.1 GROUNDS FOR REFUSAL

The traditional treaties regulating cooperation in criminal matters between States generally contain a variety of grounds on the basis of which the requested State may — or sometimes even must — refuse the requested assistance. As a result, the extent of the obligation to provide assistance to another State is quite limited.

In a cooperation relationship of a more vertical nature, meaning assistance to a supranational criminal tribunal, the grounds for refusal set out in the inter-State legal assistance treaties are not applicable, or at least not to the same degree. It will be demonstrated below in section 4 that the ICC Statute contains a number of grounds for refusal. Although they are not as many and as extensive as those contained in inter-State extradition and mutual legal assistance treaties, the extent of the duty to assist the ICC is not as far-reaching as the duties *vis-à-vis* the ad hoc Tribunals. The Statutes of the latter do not contain any grounds at all on the basis of which States could refuse assistance. On this point, one should therefore position the ICC cooperation regime between the traditional inter-State cooperation regime and that of the ad hoc Tribunals.

[7] The concepts of horizontal and vertical legal assistance relationships were introduced by the ICTY Appeals Chamber in the *Blaškic subpoena* case, with a view to indicating the hierarchy between the jurisdiction of the ad hoc Tribunals and in order to indicate the consequences thereof for the provision of legal assistance by States. See Judgement on the Request of the Republic of Croatia for Review of the Decision of Trial Chamber II of 18 July 1997, *Prosecutor v. Blaškic*, Case No. IT-95-14-AR108 *bis*, A. Ch., 29 October 1997, para. 47.

3.2 RECIPROCITY

States are generally only prepared to provide legal assistance to another State under the expectation of reciprocity.[8] The principle of reciprocity is laid down in, or follows from, the various legal assistance treaties. International criminal tribunals have been created to prosecute a limited number of crimes only. Assistance is, therefore, in principle meant to be given exclusively by States to the tribunals. This is not to say that in certain situations assistance from international criminal tribunals to States may not be welcome. Here we have to bear in mind that a situation of concurrent jurisdiction implies that these institutions cannot prosecute all perpetrators.

The drafters of the ICC Statute have acknowledged that assistance by the ICC to a State may advance the prosecution of war criminals in general and have provided within the Statute for the *possibility* of offering assistance to States. Article 93(10) of the ICC Statute authorises the ICC to cooperate with, and to provide assistance to, a State Party, in respect to crimes within the ICC's jurisdiction or a serious crime under the national law of the requesting State. It imposes no duty upon the ICC to provide any assistance,[9] and this makes it difficult to speak of a reciprocal and equal cooperation relationship. This lack of reciprocity is another distinctive feature of the ICC cooperation model.

3.3 DISPUTE SETTLEMENT

If, in the horizontal legal assistance relationship, a dispute occurs regarding the extent of the duty to cooperate, dispute settlement — if States wish to settle the dispute — is put in the hands of an impartial third party. It is unthinkable in the horizontal cooperation relationship that either the requesting or requested side will decide disputes regarding the duty to provide legal assistance.

In a vertical cooperation relationship, involving the assistance to a hierarchically superior international criminal tribunal, a *compulsory* dispute settlement mechanism exists in the form of the requesting international criminal tribunal. The attribution of the task of settling disputes to the requesting party is undoubtedly the most fundamental deviation from the horizontal legal assistance model and most indicative for a legal assistance relationship based on hierarchy. Contrary to the Statutes of the ad hoc Tribunals, the ICC Statute explicitly regulates the settlement of disputes between States and the ICC. Article 119(1) of the ICC Statute provides as follows: "Any dispute concerning the judicial functions of the Court shall be settled by the decision of the Court."

Questions concerning cooperation with, and legal assistance to, the ICC may be considered part of the "judicial functions of the Court".[10] Therefore, by ratifying the ICC Statute, and in particular by accepting Article 119 of the ICC Statute, States Parties have

---

[8] This is not to say that "lack of reciprocity" is always a material ground for refusing the requested assistance. See H. Grützner, *International Judicial Assistance and Cooperation in Criminal Matters*, in M.C. Bassiouni and V.P. Nanda, A Treatise on International Criminal Law, Volume II, Jurisdiction and Cooperation (1973) at 230.

[9] See K. Prost and A. Schlunck, *Articles 93, 94, 95, 96, 97, 98, 99 and 100*, in O. Triffterer, Commentary on the Rome Statute of the International Criminal Court, (1999) at 1117.

[10] In this sense, see R. Clark, *Article 119*, in O. Triffterer, Commentary on the Rome Statute of the International Criminal Court (1999) at 1245.

conceded the ultimate interpretation of the extent of the duty to cooperate to the requesting side — the ICC.

4. Content of the Duty to Cooperate

In the previous paragraph reference has already been made to the far-reaching duties imposed on States to assist the ICC in its work. It should be noted that the imposition of far-reaching duties upon States Parties was by no means an obvious matter for a number of delegations, which preferred modelling the ICC cooperation regime on the traditional inter-State experience.[11] One can therefore find a number of compromises in the ICC Statute which reduce a State's obligations compared to its obligations to provide assistance to the ad hoc Tribunals. Yet one will also notice that grounds for refusal which are characteristic of inter-State cooperation, such as the refusal to extradite nationals, the political offence exception and the double criminality requirement, are not applicable.

I will confine myself in this chapter to some general observations as to the extent of a State Party's duty to provide assistance under the ICC Statute. A distinction will be made between a State's procedural duties and its material duties with respect to the provision of legal assistance.

The procedural aspect of the duty to cooperate concerns the question as to what States should do when confronted with problems in the implementation of requests and how a dispute over the implementation of a request is settled.

Under the ICC Statute, States have an explicit obligation to consult with the ICC when they identify problems which may impede the execution of the request. The duty to consult, aiming at resolving "obstacles" in the provision of legal assistance, occupies a prominent place throughout Part 9 of the ICC Statute.[12] It is used several times with respect to specific obligations to cooperate and there is one general provision, Article 97, imposing upon States a duty to consult with respect to every request for assistance issued under Part 9 of the ICC Statute. From the perspective of effective legal assistance, the importance of the existence of a duty to consult should not be underestimated. It allows for misunderstandings to be eliminated and alternative modes of cooperation to be considered.[13]

The ICC Statute is also very clear as to how disputes over the extent of the duty to cooperate should be settled. It has already been mentioned that Article 119 attributes to the requesting side, being the ICC, the task as arbiter, which is unique for the cooperation relationship between States and international criminal tribunals.

It should be noted that the procedural mechanisms to solve differences of opinions regarding the extent of the duty to cooperate — consultations followed by dispute settlement — say nothing about the content of the duty to cooperate itself. However, the existence of these mechanisms imply, in my view, that States are not *a priori* prevented from submitting grounds for refusal to the ICC for evaluation, even if these grounds are not explicitly

---

[11] On the negotiations, see P. Mochochoko, *International Cooperation and Judicial Assistance*, in R.S. Lee, The International Criminal Court: the Making of the Rome Statute: Issues, Negotiation, Results (1999) at 305-317.

[12] See also B. Swart and G. Sluiter, *The International Criminal Court and International Criminal Cooperation*, in H.A.M. von Hebel, J. Lammers and J.G. Schukking, Reflections on the International Criminal Court (1999) at 103.

[13] *Id.*, at 104.

recognised by the Statute. They differ from grounds for refusal explicitly set out in the Statute in that the latter are absolute and must be honoured by the ICC, whereas grounds outside the Statute may be balanced, as interests of States, against other, possibly stronger, interests, such as the accused's right to a fair and expeditious trial.

Turning to the substance of the obligations, it follows from the second paragraph that the primary legal basis for the duty to cooperate with the ICC is the ICC Statute. Under this complex instrument, States have a variety of obligations. These obligations are not confined to the provision of legal assistance in a strict sense. For example, on the basis of different provisions in Part 2 of the Statute, States must accept the exercise of jurisdiction by the ICC in accordance with these provisions. Pursuant to Article 55 of the ICC Statute, part of Part 5 of the Statute, States can be said to have undertaken the duty to protect the different rights of persons during an investigation.

Be this as it may, the essential provisions on cooperation can be found in Part 9 of the Statute, entitled "international cooperation and judicial assistance".[14] Part 9 of the ICC Statute contains three categories of provisions: general provisions related to every request for assistance; provisions related to requests for surrender; and provisions related to other forms of cooperation.[15] Its basic structure is, in a way, similar to that of Article 29 of the ICTY Statute and Article 28 of the ICTR Statute. It contains a general provision imposing a generic duty to cooperate (Article 86), just as the first paragraph of Article 29 of the ICTY Statute and Article 28 of the ICTR Statute, and provisions imposing duties to cooperate in relation to specific forms of assistance, just as the second paragraph of the ICTY and ICTR provisions do. The major difference with the Statutes of the ad hoc Tribunals is that the provisions within Part 9 of the ICC Statute are more elaborate and therefore also more complex, having the objective to spell out in detail the content of the duty to cooperate, including possible grounds for refusal.

Article 86 of the ICC Statute is entitled "general obligation to cooperate", and provides as follows:[16]

> States Parties shall, in accordance with the provisions of this Statute, cooperate fully with the Court in its investigation and prosecution of crimes within the jurisdiction of the Court.

The more specific duty to comply with a specific request for assistance can be found in other provisions in the Statute. Article 89(1) of the ICC Statute obliges States Parties to "comply with" requests for arrest and surrender, and Article 93(1) imposes upon States Parties the duty to "comply with requests by the Court" to provide certain types of assistance.

The wordings of these provisions all indicate the imposition of unequivocal legal obligations upon States. One should mention that Article 86 of the ICC Statute contains

---

[14] It should be noted, however, that assistance with respect to the enforcement of sentences is the object of Part 10 of the Statute. It is of less relevance because assistance in this field is in principle provided on a voluntary basis.

[15] See C. Kress, A. Schlunck, K. Prost and P. Wilkitzki, *Preliminary Remarks*, in O. Triffterer, Commentary on the Rome Statute of the International Criminal Court (1999) at 1049-1050.

[16] The document constituting the basis for the negotiations in Rome contained very similar language (see Article 85 of A/CONF.183/2/Add. 1); only the last sentence of this provision, "States Parties shall so cooperate without [undue] delay", has been deleted.

even stronger language than Article 29 of the ICTY Statute and Article 28 of the ICTR Statute, obliging States to cooperate *fully*.[17]

The complexity of determining the content of the duty to cooperate under the ICC Statute lies in the presence of a number of grounds in the Statute on the basis of which States Parties may refuse or postpone assistance. The insertion of certain grounds for refusal and postponement of legal assistance in the ICC Statute is the result of protracted and sometimes painful negotiations between proponents of, and opponents to, far-reaching obligations of States towards the ICC.[18] Since the insertion of grounds for refusal and postponement of assistance is the result of long and complex negotiations, one may argue that, in addition to these grounds in the Statute, no other grounds may be advanced by States to refuse or postpone assistance. However, I believe this view is not in conformity with a systematic interpretation of the Statute. The duty to consult, as set out in Article 97 of the ICC Statute, is not necessarily confined to problems regarding the implementation of the request related to one of the grounds for refusal set out in the Statute. It is then, of course, for the ICC to decide whether grounds for refusal not mentioned in the Statute carry sufficient weight to justify refusal of the request.

The grounds for refusal in the Statute are the result of a compromise. Some of them are understandable or even inevitable, taking account of the fact that the ICC is a new international organisation established by sovereign States. In this respect I mention the refusal of assistance in case of prejudice to a State's national security (Articles 93(4) and 72 of the ICC Statute) and the refusal to provide assistance in case of a conflicting request for assistance (Article 90 of the Statute). Other grounds for refusal in the Statute can be regarded as less fortunate in the framework of an international criminal court with jurisdiction over the most serious crimes and to which States adhere voluntarily. As an example I mention Article 93(3) of the ICC Statute which allows States to refuse assistance "on the basis of an existing fundamental legal principle of general application." The Statute of the ICC, in particular the priority accorded to human rights pursuant to Article 21(3), offers, in my view, sufficient safeguards to make such a ground for refusal unnecessary.

The question arises whether the presence of a number of grounds for refusal in the ICC Statute may prevent it from fulfilling its mandate. It is undeniable that the ICC faces greater difficulties in the field of legal assistance than the ad hoc Tribunals. The latter not only benefited from more extensive obligations for States, but also could rely, at least on paper, on the assistance of practically every State in the world.

That being said, it is in my view that the presence of certain grounds for refusal in the Statute does not constitute the greatest threat to the functioning of the ICC. It is rather the defective regulation of certain important forms of assistance that raise most concerns. I will give two examples. The experiences of the ad hoc Tribunals illustrate the importance of live testimony in the courtroom and the conduct of on-site investigations. One would expect the ICC Statute to contain strong obligations for States to provide these forms of assistance. Surprisingly, this is not the case. Under the ICC Statute witnesses cannot be compelled to

---

[17] According to Kress, inserting "fully" alludes to the duty to cooperate in good faith; see C. Kress, *Article 86*, in O. Triffterer, Commentary on the Rome Statute of the International Criminal Court (1999) at 1053.

[18] For an account of the drafting history in this respect, see P. Mochochoko, *International Cooperation and Judicial Assistance*, in R.S. Lee, The International Criminal Court: the making of the Rome Statute: issues, negociations, results (1999) at 310-314.

testify.[19] This implies that witnesses may frequently have to be heard outside the courtroom, which will undoubtedly have an impact on the reliability and probative value of the testimony. As to the conduct of on-site investigations, there was in Rome strong opposition from certain delegations that felt that investigations on their territory amounted to too great an intrusion of their sovereignty. The final compromise is an only very limited duty for States Parties to allow on-site investigations on their territory, and only in respect of those of the Prosecutor.[20] One may indeed seriously wonder how investigations and prosecutions can be completed successfully if all involved in the proceedings — prosecutor, defendant and the Judges — cannot, or can only with great difficulty, familiarise themselves with the scene of the crime and conduct certain investigations there.

5. Enforcing the Duty to Cooperate

Undeniably, the actual provision of assistance to the ICC will depend on the availability and effectiveness of ways to enforce the duty to cooperate. Elsewhere in this book it has already been described how the duty to cooperate with the ad hoc Tribunals can be enforced.[21] In the case of the ICC, the mechanisms of enforcement differ depending on the legal basis underlying the duty to provide assistance.

I will concentrate first on the enforcement of duties of the contracting parties under the ICC Statute. Pursuant to Article 87(7) of the ICC Statute, there is a clear chronological order in the steps to be taken to induce compliance with a request for assistance. First of all, the ICC may make a judicial finding of non-compliance where a State Party fails to comply with a request to cooperate by the ICC contrary to the provisions of the Statute. A judicial finding of non-cooperation has a dual character. First, it is in itself already an enforcement measure. The impact of the fact that an impartial international judicial body has established that a State has breached its obligations under an international treaty should not be underestimated. It may convince the non-cooperating State of the illegality of its actions and induce compliance. Secondly, the judicial finding of non-compliance is a vital prerequisite for submitting the matter to the designated enforcing bodies by the Statute.

After a *judicial* finding of non-compliance, the ICC may refer the matter to the Assembly of States Parties ("the Assembly"). This excludes, in my view, the possibility for the Prosecutor to directly submit a situation of non-compliance to the Assembly. Although this body has been established by the "ICC Statute", it is difficult to consider it as part of "the Court". According to Article 1 of the ICC Statute, the international criminal court is established and, according to Article 112 (1) of the ICC Statute, an Assembly of States Parties is established. Their separate character is confirmed by Article 34 of the Statute, which does not include the Assembly of States Parties as an organ of the ICC. The Assembly has, pursuant to Article 112, a number of tasks, including to "consider pursuant to article 87, paragraphs 5 and 7, any question relating to non-cooperation" (Article 112(2)(f) of the ICC Statute). The fact that the Statute is silent on measures to be adopted *vis-à-vis* a State in breach of its obligation to cooperate is surprising and makes one wonder as to how

[19] Article 93(1)(e) and 93(7)

[20] Article 99(4)

[21] See *supra* in this volume, D. Mundis, State Cooperation with the International Criminal Tribunal for the ICTY.

effective responses by the Assembly to violations of the duty to cooperate will be. There is also some inconsistency in relation to a State's other duties under the Statute. If a State Party fails to meet its obligations regarding the financing of the ICC, the Statute provides for a specific sanction: the State shall, depending on the extent of the breach, have no vote in the Assembly and in the Bureau.[22] Similar measures could, probably, also be taken in reaction to a State that is in breach of its duty to provide legal assistance to the ICC.

Article 87(5)(b) of the Statute provides for the possibility of submitting to the Assembly a violation of the duty to cooperate on the basis of an ad hoc agreement concluded between the ICC and a State not party. This, then, implies that the State not party has agreed to such a submission. It should be borne in mind that a State not party whose cooperation is required is in a strong negotiating position and may wish only to provide ad hoc assistance subject to a number of conditions, which may exclude involvement of the Assembly. Even if a State not party accepts the role of the Assembly in enforcing the duty to cooperate, one may seriously question the effectiveness of the Assembly in this respect. What actions could it possibly take that might convince a State not party to comply with the terms of the ad hoc cooperation agreement? There is, for example, no vote in the Assembly to take away and no financial contribution to increase.

Finally, one has to consider the situation in which the ICC exercises jurisdiction following the referral of a case to it by the Security Council. When a State Party fails to cooperate under the Statute with respect to an investigation or prosecution triggered by a Security Council deferral, Article 87(7) of the ICC Statute is equally applicable. This means that, just as in the situation when the prosecution would have been triggered by a State Party or by the Prosecutor, the ICC may make a judicial finding of non-cooperation. However, the next step is different. Instead of referring the finding of non-compliance to the Assembly of States Parties, this finding will be submitted to the Security Council. This difference can be explained in part by the fact that the Council, in referring the case to the Prosecutor, has acted under Chapter VII of the UN Charter. This means that effective prosecution is required in the interests of international peace and security. Should effective prosecution be impossible, the same interests of international peace and security require that the Council be informed thereof. The Council is apparently considered by the drafters of the Statute to be a more effective enforcement mechanism than the Assembly. This explains that Article 87(7) of the Statute does not attribute at all an enforcement role to the Assembly in case of a prosecution triggered by the Security Council. This trust in the Security Council is, in my view, not entirely justified. For various reasons, the Council may not wish to respond, or is not in a legal position to respond, to breaches of the duty to provide assistance under the Statute.[23] Should this occur, it is desirable that the Assembly remain in a position to deal with violations by contracting parties of the duty to cooperate.

---

[22] See Article 112(8) of the ICC Statute.

[23] As to the legal incapacity of the UN Security Council to respond, it is my view that the Council can only enforce obligations of UN members under the Charter. As a result, when a UN non-member party to the ICC violates its duty to assist the Court, there is not much the Council can do about it.

6. Concluding Remarks

Since "the proof of the pudding is in the eating," it is probably too soon to judge the ICC cooperation model. Before any practical results can be considered, one can look at the model in two different ways.

It is fair to say that in general the ICC legal assistance regime is weaker than that of the ad hoc Tribunals. The difference in method of establishment is of course the major reason as to why this is the case. The ad hoc Tribunals have been established with a limited mandate. Their swift creation had, as a positive consequence, from the perspective of effective assistance, led to the situation that a great deal of the law had to be created by the Tribunals, i.e. by the Tribunal judges themselves. It comes as no surprise that the judges opted for what is, in their eyes, the most effective cooperation regime. On the other hand, the establishment by treaty of the ICC, a permanent institution with no geographically limited jurisdiction, triggered protracted rounds of negotiations which soon revealed that participating States were not prepared to have the institution shape its own law in any way. Since the shaping of the legal assistance regime was left to all the participating States, it is no surprise that a compromise ensued which is significantly weaker on a number of points.[24]

Thus, looking at it from the perspective of the ad hoc Tribunals, one may be disappointed by the ICC cooperation model, in terms of its effectiveness. However, if one looks at it from the perspective of inter-State cooperation in criminal matters, one can only be satisfied. Bearing in mind the widespread participation in the negotiations, including several States that probably have no interest in a strong Court, it is a significant achievement that the ICC cooperation regime is still of predominantly hierarchical, vertical nature. This is in my view best demonstrated by the fact that the ICC itself, and only the ICC, determines the precise content of the duty to cooperate.

[24] One could also look at the ICC cooperation regime from a different perspective than that of the ad hoc Tribunals. Compared to the recently created or proposed "internationalised tribunals" of Sierra Leone, Kosovo, East Timor and Cambodia which were alluded to in the introduction, the ICC is still a potentially powerful institution. These "internationalised tribunals" do not in any way enjoy the benefit of a vertical cooperation relationship and can only count on existing and applicable mechanisms of inter-State legal assistance. As a result, a considerable amount of evidence — and a considerable number of suspects — could be beyond their reach. On the other hand, the "internationalised tribunals", with the exception of the Sierra Leone Court, have the advantage of being integrated into a domestic legal order, enabling them to exercise enforcement powers over a certain territory.

THE MIXED TRIBUNALS FOR CAMBODIA AND SIERRA LEONE

Daphna Shraga *

1. INTRODUCTION

The establishment of the two ad hoc international tribunals for the former Yugoslavia and Rwanda triggered a proliferation of criminal jurisdictions. A precursor to the International Criminal Court — an international, truly universal criminal jurisdiction — they were also the model upon which the second-generation, country-specific mixed tribunals were conceived. In the decade that followed the establishment of the two ad hoc international criminal tribunals, countries emerging from bloody civil wars in which genocide, crimes against humanity or war crimes were committed on a massive scale called upon the United Nations to establish similar jurisdictions in their own territories. With their administration of justice devastated, biased or otherwise lacking the necessary judicial and administrative capacity, they sought the technical and financial assistance of the United Nations in the conduct of complex prosecution which they alone were unable or politically unwilling to undertake.

As the parent organ of both ad hoc tribunals, the United Nations Security Council was reluctant to replicate the experience and establish additional subsidiary judicial organs whose administrative structure, lengthy and costly proceedings would further increase the heavy financial burden on the Member States of the Organisation.[1] In face of the Council's inaction, the focus of expectation shifted to the United Nations Secretariat to develop a model similar in form, substance and international legitimacy to the two UN-based tribunals, but one which respects a nation's vision of justice, its choice of means of bringing it about, and its ownership, in part at least, of the judicial process. For the first time, therefore, a model of a "mixed tribunal" as a national court of mixed jurisdiction and composition was developed in Cambodia, followed by a *sui generis*, treaty-based court of similar jurisdiction and composition, for Sierra Leone. Different though they may have been in their legal basis, nature, and composition from the international tribunals for the former

---

* Senior Legal Officer, Office of the Legal Counsel, Office of Legal Affairs, United Nations. The views expressed in this paper are exclusively those of the author and do not necessarily reflect the opinion of the Office of Legal Affairs or of the United Nations.

[1] The establishment of the mixed tribunals by means other than a UN Security Council resolution was intended also to ensure that they do not operate as UN subsidiary organs financed through assessed contributions. The financial mechanism established for the Special Court for Sierra Leone, and the one envisaged for the Extraordinary Chambers for Cambodia, are based on voluntary contributions channeled into a Trust Fund administered by the United Nations.

R. Yepes-Enríquez and L. Tabassi. (eds.), Treaty Enforcement and International Cooperation in Criminal Matters

Yugoslavia and Rwanda, the mixed tribunals for Cambodia and Sierra Leone were in law, procedure, and organisational structure the replica of their antecedents.

2. The Legislative Process and the Legal Basis for the Establishment of the Mixed Tribunals

Conceived as a measure to restore and maintain international peace and security, the two international tribunals for the former Yugoslavia and Rwanda were established by a Security Council resolution adopted under Chapter VII of the United Nations Charter. In 1993, for the first time, a judicial measure was considered, along with the economic, political and military, an enforcement measure, and an international tribunal was endowed with Chapter VII powers to issue orders and requests binding and enforceable upon all States. Unlike the Chapter VII resolution-based tribunals, however, the mixed tribunals are established on a consensual basis. Their legal framework consists of an agreement between the United Nations and the State concerned stipulating the modalities of cooperation in the establishment and operation of the mixed tribunal, and an instrument containing the "law of the tribunal" — either in the form of a Statute annexed to the Agreement, as in the case of the Special Court for Sierra Leone,[2] or a national law adopted alongside the Agreement, as in the case of the Cambodian law on the Establishment of the Extraordinary Chambers.[3]

The legislative process that established the mixed tribunals was a negotiating process in which the principles and practicalities of the criminal jurisdiction envisaged had to be agreed upon between the United Nations and the government concerned. It was in the nature of the negotiating process, therefore, that political constraints dictated compromises on issues, such as personal and subject-matter jurisdiction, composition, and the organisational structure of the mixed tribunal.

3. Subject-Matter Jurisdiction

The similarities in the nature of the conflicts and of the crimes committed in the former Yugoslavia, Rwanda, Sierra Leone, and Cambodia warranted a similar choice of the applicable law in all jurisdictions whether national, international, or *sui generis* in character. With a few exceptions, therefore, they included the crime of genocide, crimes against humanity and, depending on the nature of the conflict, war crimes and other serious violations of

[2] Report of the Secretary-General on the Establishment of a Special Court for Sierra Leone (UN doc. S/2000/915 (4 October 2000), Annex and Enclosure). In subsequent communications exchanged between the President of the Security Council and the Secretary-General, further revisions were introduced into the draft Agreement and Statute (Letter dated 22 December 2000 from the President of the Security Council addressed to the Secretary-General (UN doc. S/2000/1234 (22 December 2000)), Letter dated 12 January 2001 from the Secretary-General addressed to the President of the Security Council (UN doc. S/2001/40 (12 January 2001)), and Letter dated 31 January 2001 from the President of the Security Council addressed to the Secretary-General (UN doc. S/2001/95 (31 January 2001)). The Agreement between the United Nations and the government of Sierra Leone on the establishment of a Special Court for Sierra Leone was concluded on 16 January 2002 (UN doc. S/2002/246 (8 March 2002) Appendix II and Attachment).

[3] Law on the Establishment of Extraordinary Chambers in the Courts of Cambodia for the Prosecution of Crimes Committed During the Period of Democratic Kampuchea. The version of the Law as adopted by the National Assembly on 2 January 2001 can be found in <http://www.phnompenhdaily.com/06-01-01.htm>. The Law was promulgated on 10 August 2001.

international humanitarian law.

In adapting the international criminal legislation to the specificities of Cambodia, the restrictive definition of the crime of genocide presented legal and conceptual difficulties. More perhaps than other similar mass killings in the second half of the twentieth century, the massive scale and systematic character of the killing by execution, starvation, malnutrition and disease of an estimated 2 million Cambodians during the Khmer Rouge reign resembled the crime of genocide. Perpetrated mostly, however, on political or social grounds by members of the same national, ethnic, religious or racial group, they did not technically amount to "genocide" within the meaning of Article 2 of the Genocide Convention.[4] The crime of genocide was nevertheless retained in the Cambodian law to cover the killing of members of minority groups, such as Muslim "Sham" and ethnic Vietnamese targeted on religious and ethnic grounds.

The decade-long internal conflict in Sierra Leone began in 1991 with the overthrow of the one-party military rule of the All People's Congress (APC) by forces of the Revolutionary United Front (RUF). While large scale violations of international humanitarian law (abduction, mass rape, forced recruitment of children and summary execution) were committed throughout the conflict, it was the period following the joint invasion of Freetown by the RUF and the Armed Forces Revolutionary Council (AFRC) on 6 January 1999 which marked the most intensified, systematic and widespread violations of human rights and international humanitarian law against the population of the capital. During its retreat from Freetown, the RUF abducted hundreds of young people, particularly young women, who were used as forced labourers, fighting forces, human shields, and sexual slaves.

The killings and mass executions committed during the internal conflict in Sierra Leone were not committed on ethnic, religious or racial grounds or with an intent to annihilate a group distinguished on any of these grounds as such. While the crime of genocide was thus omitted from the Statute of the Special Court, two international crimes were added to address the specificity of that conflict. These were: (1) attacks against peacekeepers involved in a humanitarian assistance or peacekeeping mission as long as they were entitled to the protection given to civilians under the international law of armed conflict,[5] a reference to the hostage-taking of 500 peacekeepers in May 2000 by the RUF; and (2) conscripting or enlisting children under the age of 15 years into armed forces or other groups, or using them to participate actively in hostilities — a practice prevalent among all armed groups involved in the conflict.[6]

[4] The crime of genocide is defined in Article 2 of the 1948 Convention on the Prevention and Punishment of the Crime of Genocide to mean any of the following: killing members of the group, causing bodily or mental harm, inflicting conditions of life likely to bring about the physical destruction of the group, imposing measures to prevent birth, or transferring children of the group to another group, when "committed with intent to destroy, in whole or in part, a national, ethnical, racial or religious group as such". Fifty years later, the conventional definition of genocide was incorporated without change in the Statute of the International Tribunal for the former Yugoslavia (Report of the Secretary-General Pursuant to Paragraph 2 of Security Council Resolution 808 (1993)) UN doc. S/25704 (3 May 1993), Annex, Article 4), the Statute of the International Tribunal for Rwanda (Security Council resolution 955 (1994), Annex, Article 2), and in the Statute of the International Criminal Court, adopted at Rome on 17 July 1998, Article 6 (UN doc. A/CONF.183/9, see also 37 ILM 1002 (1998) at 1004).

[5] Article 4(b) of the Statute.

[6] Article 4(c) of the Statute.

Judged complementary to the international crimes and of specific relevance in the particular conflict, both the Cambodian law on the Establishment of the Extraordinary Chambers and the Statute of the Special Court for Sierra Leone include crimes under their respective national laws.

4. Personal Jurisdiction

Personal jurisdiction of a limited scope was another distinctive feature common to both international and mixed tribunals. In defining the personal jurisdiction in each of these tribunals, the inclusion of the political and military leadership was imperative, as it is almost inherent in the nature of any international criminal jurisdiction. Limitation to the political and military leaders alone, however, would not have satisfied the sense of justice and the principle of accountability or contribute in any meaningful sense to breaking the cycle of impunity. However restrictively defined, the personal jurisdiction of all international or mixed tribunals was interpreted to include the top military and political leadership as well as others down the chain of command whose crimes were singled out for their magnitude, brutality, or heinous nature.

A restrictive definition of the personal jurisdiction of the Special Court in the cases of Cambodia and Sierra Leone was also a politically imposed necessity. In both cases it would have been the Government's political choice to spare from prosecution those among the most responsible who had defected to the Government's ranks, participated in a coalition government, or were otherwise amnestied. A selective choice of the accused, however, presented for the United Nations a dilemma of reconciling peace and justice, and applying uncompromising international standards of justice in circumstances of fragile peace.

In the case of Cambodia, the personal jurisdiction of the "Extraordinary Chambers" were to extend to "senior leaders and those most responsible for the crimes committed in Democratic Kampuchea," a definition which at present includes the only two persons arrested in connection with the Khmer Rouge period: Ta Mok, the undisputed military leader, and "Duch", the Director of the notorious Tuol Sleng prison.

In Sierra Leone, while the definition of the personal jurisdiction of the Court refers to "those who bear the greatest responsibility", two categories of persons never before prosecuted in an international criminal tribunal were included within its jurisdiction: persons between 15 and 18 years of age — "children" within the definition of the 1989 Convention on the Rights of the Child — and peacekeepers of United Nations peacekeeping or other United Nations authorised operations.

4.1 Prosecution of "Juveniles" between 15 and 18 years of age

The acts of brutality and savagery committed by children on a large scale in the last phase of the conflict in Freetown in January of 1999 demanded that this unique feature of the Sierra Leone civil war be addressed in all its horrific aspects. Mindful of the moral dilemma of prosecuting child-victims who were transformed into perpetrators through abduction, drugs, physical and psychological abuse, and slavery of all kinds, the drafters of the Statute provided for a process of judicial accountability affording all necessary guarantees of juvenile justice. Accordingly, under Article 7(1) of the Statute, juveniles before the Special Court shall be treated "with dignity and a sense of worth, taking into account his or her young age and the desirability of promoting his or her rehabilitation, reintegration into and assumption of a constructive role in society, and in accordance with international human rights standards, in particular the rights of the child". A fair balance was thus struck between the sense of justice to victims, accountability of perpetrators, the risks that a large scale prosecution of juveniles could entail for the rehabilitation and child-care programmes, and, above all, the educational value that a judicial process of accountability might have for future generations of children in Sierra Leone and in the region.

4.2 UNITED NATIONS PEACEKEEPERS

While in a number of peacekeeping operations peacekeepers have been known to have committed violations of international humanitarian law, no member of a United Nations operation has ever been prosecuted before an international criminal jurisdiction. In introducing, by analogy, the principle of "complementarity", the Statute of the Special Court provides that peacekeepers who "transgressed" — a code word for the commission of violations of international humanitarian law — would in the first instance be subject to the jurisdiction of their sending State, and may be subject to the jurisdiction of the Special Court only if the sending State is unwilling or unable to investigate or prosecute, and upon the authorisation of the Security Council.[7]

5. THE ORGANISATIONAL STRUCTURE OF THE MIXED TRIBUNALS

Like the subject-matter and personal jurisdiction of the mixed tribunals, their organisational structure was patterned along that of the ad hoc international tribunals. With the Chambers, Prosecutor's Office and the Registry forming part of one and the same structure, they too were conceived as self-contained entities. The mixed tribunals differ, however, from the two international tribunals in their mixed composition of national and international judges, prosecutors and administrative support staff.

The mixed composition of national and international components raised the immediate and most obvious question of who will control the majority vote in the Chambers, and the key positions in the Prosecutor's Office and the Registry. In the case of the Extraordinary Chambers in Cambodia, the debate over the composition of the Chambers was a debate over the control, or perceived control, of the legal process and the most crucial decision of who will be brought before the Chambers. In the negotiating process for the establishment of the mixed tribunals for Cambodia and Sierra Leone, it was the United Nations' position that for the tribunal to be and be seen to be free from political interference, to command credibility and to persuade the international donor community to partake in the operation, the international component must be substantial, with a majority vote and control positions in the respective organs of the tribunal.

[7]Article 1, paragraphs 2 and 3 of the Statute.

6. The Operation of the Mixed Tribunals in the Context of the National Legal System of the State of the Seat

The operation of a mixed tribunal in the territory of the State of the seat demanded a definition of the relationship between the law of the tribunal and the national legal system of the State within which it operates. Such a determination was necessary for both jurisdictions. For the UN-assisted court, it was necessary in order to give effect to the court's orders and requests, penalties imposed and rehabilitation measures ordered, as well as to guarantee the inviolability of the court's premises, archives and documents, the privileges and immunities of the judges, the Prosecutor, the Registrar, and national and international personnel. For the national legal system, it was necessary in order to resolve potential conflicts of laws between the law of the tribunal and the existing legislation.[8] In Cambodia and Sierra Leone, the single most notable example of conflict of jurisdictions was the validity of the amnesty granted for crimes falling within the jurisdiction of the mixed tribunal.

While in Cambodia amnesty was formally granted to only one person, Ieng Sary, by Royal Decree for his conviction in the 1979 trial for genocide, in the case of Sierra Leone a sweeping amnesty was granted under the 1999 Lomé Peace Agreement to Foday Sankoh in person and the collectivity of members of the RUF/AFDC armed groups for "any acts performed by them in the course of the conflict". When incorporated in the Lomé Agreement Act of 2000, the amnesty it contained became part of the law of the land.

The validity of the amnesty granted was determined in each of these cases according to the nature of the mixed tribunal as a national or treaty-based entity. In the case of the Extraordinary Chambers for Cambodia, which were to form part of the Cambodian court system, the law establishing the Chambers provided for a future oriented undertaking by the Government not to grant any more amnesties in respect of crimes committed during the Khmer Rouge regime. It thus implicitly condoned the existing one and deferred the decision on its applicability in any one case to the Chambers. In the case of Sierra Leone, where the Special Court is a treaty-based organ, the Agreement establishing the Court expressly invalidated any amnesty granted for genocide, crimes against humanity and war crimes for persons falling within the jurisdiction of the Court and provided that any amnesty granted shall not be a bar to prosecution. The validity of the amnesty in the national legal system, has otherwise remained unaffected.

7. Conclusion

Born of the need to bring justice to conflict-stricken areas, the mixed tribunals are established in the countries where the crimes were committed and where victims and perpetrators still coexist. In establishing a mixed jurisdiction in partnership with the national administration of justice, however meagre its resources may be, the United Nations' attempts to implement international criminal legislation in the specificities of each situation bring the message of accountability to places where it had never been known before, and, more importantly

[8] In March 2002, the Parliament of Sierra Leone adopted the Special Court Agreement, 2002 (Ratification) Act, 2002, as an implementing legislation to give effect to the powers and competencies of the Special Court in the national legal system of Sierra Leone.

perhaps, leave behind a legacy of enhanced administration of justice and a generation of judges, prosecutors and defence counsel trained in international standards of criminal jurisdiction.

In the practice of the Organization, however, the Special Court for Sierra Leone has been the only case, so far, of a UN-assisted court successfully established. Mandated by the Security Council, its legal framework was negotiated under the vetting eye of the Council, in broad consultation with civil society, both local and international NGOs, and in full co-operation with the Government of Sierra Leone. As such, it conforms fully to the UN vision of a mixed tribunal with a substantial international component; majority of international judges; an international Prosecutor and Registrar; guarantees of international standards of justice; a streamlined, functional structure of the Court; and an efficient, cost-effective administration. The absence of most, if not all these conditions was the reason for the failure to agree on a similar mixed jurisdiction for Cambodia.

Considering that the Extraordinary Chambers, as envisaged under the Cambodian Law, do not measure up to international standards of justice or otherwise afford the necessary guarantees for objectivity, impartiality and independence, the United Nations Secretariat decided in early February 2002 to withdraw from the negotiations. Disagreements on the governing instrument or the primacy of the Agreement over the Cambodian law, the lack of an appropriate mandate from any of the UN governing bodies, and the convoluted structure of the proposed Extraordinary Chambers, compared to the skeletal structure of the Special Court for Sierra Leone, were additional heavy-weight considerations in the decision to withdraw from the negotiations.[9]

Ultimately, the success of any UN-assisted court, whether established by law or international agreement between the United Nations and the Government concerned, depends on the willingness of third States and non-parties to the agreement to contribute in funds and personnel. However, for the international community of donors to be willing to contribute to the success of the tribunal, it must be convinced that the mixed tribunal, in both substance and form, affords guarantees of fairness, objectivity and impartiality of the legal process, or otherwise promises to uphold international standards of justice. If so perceived, mixed tribunals will continue to play a complementary role in conjunction with the universal or ad hoc international criminal jurisdictions as a tool for implementing international criminal legislation in specific national contexts.

[9] Statement by the Legal Counsel of the United Nations at a press briefing at UN headquarters in New York, 8 February 2002 (http://www.un.org/News/dh/infocus/cambodia/corell-brief.htm).

SECTION II.3

INTRUSIVE INTERNATIONAL CONTROL REGIMES AND BREACHES OF CONFIDENTIALITY: ASPECTS OF THE EXERCISE OF NATIONAL JURISDICTION

INTRODUCTION AND SUMMARY

The cornerstone of any multilateral treaty establishing an international control regime is transparency: all States Parties must openly demonstrate compliance in order for a State to be willing to submit itself to the regime. Treaties that encompass confidence-building measures – whereby compliance can be measured and assessed – necessarily mean giving access to information that might otherwise never be widely shared with other States. International inspections are intrusive. Declarations containing national information, submitted by States Parties to an international body which will process and analyse it and share the analysis with other States Parties, expose that information to unauthorised disclosure. The treaty will necessarily embody measures to protect that information. All players involved must be committed to that protection: the national civil servants who gather and process the national information into declarations, the inspectors and other international civil servants who receive and analyse the national declarations, and officials of other States Parties who receive classified information on other States Parties' compliance. In other words, there is a need to have an effective confidentiality regime to coexist with and complement the intrusive verification system — to balance transparency and confidentiality.

R. Yepes-Enríquez and L. Tabassi. (eds.), Treaty Enforcement and International Cooperation in Criminal Matters

What happens in the event of a breach of the confidentiality obligation by any of those players? Especially when the breach damages national security or economic interests? Where and how will that breach and the damages be addressed? This section discusses procedures and practice in the IAEA and the OPCW and illustrates different aspects of those questions.

The IAEA's confidentiality regime is balanced between the need for transparency in nuclear issues, the assurance of compliance by States with their non-proliferation obligations and their legitimate interest in the protection of sensitive information. The IAEA "comprehensive safeguards agreement" is based on on-site inspections. Serious concerns of Member States were raised about the sensitivity of the information to which the Agency would have access. In practice the industry and Member States have become accustomed to the system and confident in the way that confidential information is handled. In over 40 years of operation, the IAEA has had only one case of serious intentional breach of confidentiality. In 1997, the safeguards system was strengthened by a model Additional Protocol. It included provisions requiring that both the Agency and States Parties protect confidential information. What action may be taken in the event of unauthorised release of "safeguards confidential" information? The Director General will initiate an investigation, review the results, formulate conclusions and transmit them to the State concerned. If a dispute arises which is submitted to arbitration, the IAEA can be held responsible for damages resulting from the breach and the Agency would be legally required to pay such damages. The Secretariat would make all possible efforts to recover the amounts from the responsible staff member under the Staff Regulations and Rules. The Director General may also initiate internal disciplinary action and that action is appealable to the Administrative Tribunal of the International Labour Organisation (ILOAT).

The OPCW's regime for the protection of confidential information is one of the pillars of the Convention. The Convention establishes the protection of confidential information as a general principle to be followed by the OPCW in the course of verifying compliance, and, equally, by States Parties in preserving the confidentiality of information received from the OPCW. The Confidentiality Annex to the Convention establishes the procedural principles relating to the protection of confidential information and provides for procedures in case of breaches of confidentiality Although it is clearly indicated who is responsible for conducting investigations and imposing sanctions, the system needs legally binding instruments, at both the national and international levels, to execute the sanctions for breaches of confidential information.

At the State Party level, New Zealand's Chemical Weapons Act 1996 serves as one example of how the Convention's confidentiality regime has been incorporated into national procedures by a State Party in its jurisdiction. The Convention requires States Parties to keep information received *from* the OPCW confidential. However, it is silent concerning confidentiality of national information gathered by national authorities *within* the State Party's territory for subsequent reporting to the OPCW. It is of course up to the State Party to decide how to assure its own chemical industry that the confidential business information reported to the National Authority will be protected by it. In New Zealand this raised the issue of how to reconcile the confidentiality culture of the Convention with the culture of government transparency contained in the 1982 Official Information Act of New Zealand. This was resolved by including specific confidentiality provisions in the national implementing legislation and it leans more towards confidentiality than transparency. This approach is contrasted with the mechanisms in the United Kingdom and Australian legislation to address that concern, which employ a degree of parliamentary oversight by means of an annual report on Convention implementation to parliament.

In what scenario would civil or criminal proceedings be instituted in a national jurisdiction for a breach of confidentiality? That question is one of the unresolved issues remaining from the OPCW preparatory phase. A two-stage process can be envisaged: (1) an internal investigation in the OPCW which could lead to punitive and disciplinary measures; and, in case of a serious breach, (2) the staff member's immunity may be waived by the Director-General and proceedings brought in a court having jurisdiction. The possibility has been raised on several occasions that the Netherlands, as host country to the OPCW, would be the appropriate forum to take action against OPCW staff for serious breaches of confidentiality. The reasoning is that the OPCW's headquarters are located there, its information is stored there, OPCW staff generally reside there, and at least some of the acts relating to the breach would probably have occurred there. Under Netherlands law, civil proceedings may be brought if the defendant is resident in the European Union. Criminal proceedings may be brought if the offence was committed in the Netherlands or, if the offence occurred abroad, if the accused holds Netherlands nationality. How would the applicable regulations and rules of the OPCW be interpreted together with provisions of Netherlands law governing a serious breach of confidentiality? A preliminary review of Netherlands law shows that a serious breach of confidentiality in the OPCW could give rise to a cause of action in civil proceedings and/or an offence under the penal code. Thus, as it stands now, it is possible, but not certain, that proceedings could be instituted in the Netherlands in every case.

If there were sufficient interest by the international community to criminalise violations of the confidentiality rules that bind the staff of international organisations like the OPCW, IAEA, and any future OPBW, as well as the United Nations, an international convention on breaches of confidentiality in general could be concluded as one way to ensure action by States in this matter. The UN General Assembly or some similar body could draft such a treaty that would apply to all regimes that carry out intrusive activities in the territory of the States party to it. There would be provision to add new treaties as they are established. The treaty text should include an obligation for States to make such violations of confidentiality a crime under their national laws and it would also necessarily serve as an extradition treaty. At this point in time breaches of confidentiality would not constitute a crime over which the International Criminal Court would have jurisdiction; however, the first Review Conference in seven years time has the mandate to consider adding crimes to ICC jurisdiction.

Samir Mechken

Rapporteur for Panel A.4 in the 2001 OPCW International Symposium; Legal Assistant, OPCW Technical Secretariat, Office of the Legal Adviser. The views expressed are not attributable to the OPCW.

CONFIDENTIALITY: THE IAEA'S EXPERIENCE

Laura Rockwood*

1. Origins of the IAEA's Comprehensive Safeguards System

"Comprehensive safeguards agreements" require a State Party to place under safeguards of the International Atomic Energy Agency (IAEA or "Agency") all nuclear material in all peaceful nuclear activities of the State, and not to divert such material to nuclear weapons or other nuclear explosive devices.[1] These agreements are based on a document which was negotiated by an open-ended committee of the Board of Governors of the IAEA for use in connection with non-nuclear-weapon States' obligations under the Treaty on the Non-Proliferation of Nuclear Weapons (NPT), INFCIRC/153 (Corr.) and approved by the Board in 1971.[2]

IAEA comprehensive safeguards were the first global system of country-wide inspections. The safeguards system was also the first to require declarations by the State of all of its nuclear activities. Although a degree of transparency was necessary for the effective implementation of safeguards, the novelty and intrusiveness of the new system gave rise to serious concerns by a number of Member States who participated in the negotiation of INFCIRC/153 about the sensitivity of the information to which the Agency would have access, either through nuclear material accountancy or by virtue of physical access to nuclear facilities and other locations where nuclear material is located, and the potential for its negligent or intentional release and/or its misuse for other purposes. While States were already familiar with item-specific safeguards, they had, by and large, not experienced "full scope" or "comprehensive" safeguards. And they wanted some safeguards for themselves.

Thus, the *quid pro quo* for comprehensive safeguards became something akin to "negotiated access", the precursor of what is now referred to as "managed access". In terms of IAEA safeguards, this translated into the following provisions:

First, the Agency was permitted to request information concerning nuclear material subject to safeguards, and the features of facilities relevant to the safeguarding of such material. However, under INFCIRC/153 agreements, the Agency is entitled to require "only the minimum amount of information and data consistent with carrying out its responsibilities under the Agreement." In particular, information pertaining to facilities is limited to "the minimum necessary for safeguarding nuclear material subject to safeguards under the Agreement" (para. 8, INFCIRC/153). The Agency can also be requested by the State to examine facility design information which

* Senior Legal Officer, International Atomic Energy Agency (IAEA). Any views expressed are solely those of the author and are not attributable to the IAEA.

[1] Comprehensive safeguards agreements are distinguished from those concluded by the five nuclear-weapon States (China, France, Russia, the United Kingdom and the United States), which are referred to as "Voluntary Offer Agreements", and from those item-specific agreements based on INFCIRC/66/Rev. 2 concluded with a number of other States (Cuba, India, Israel and Pakistan).

[2] INFCIRC/153 has been used as the basis for comprehensive safeguards agreements concluded with other States as well (e.g., the Agreement between Argentina, Brazil, ABACC and the IAEA (INFCIRC/435)).

R. Yepes-Enríquez and L. Tabassi. (eds.), Treaty Enforcement and International Cooperation in Criminal Matters

the State considers to be particularly sensitive on the premises of the State; such information need not be physically transmitted to the Agency, provided it remains available for further examination by the Agency. This provision has been invoked in certain circumstances to require the Agency to leave on the premises certain surveillance films or tapes which the facility operator considers to be particularly sensitive.

Second, in terms of physical access, *routine* inspections are limited to strategic points agreed to with the State and incorporated in Facility Attachments, which are negotiated with the State on the basis of standard models developed by the Secretariat of the IAEA. These Facility Attachments correspond roughly to the OPCW's Facility Agreements and contain detailed information on the design of facilities and the relevant inspection activities. However, unlike the Facility Agreements, neither the standard models nor the specific Facility Attachments involve approval by the Board of Governors. Moreover, Facility Attachments concluded with a State are treated as "safeguards confidential" and are not published or distributed except to the State concerned.

Confidentiality has turned out to be less problematic than originally feared, partly because of the nature of the system and partly because the industry and States have become accustomed to it: practice has given rise to familiarity with the system and confidence in the IAEA's ability to exercise appropriate discretion in the protection of the legitimate interests of the States. In its over 40 year history, the IAEA has had only one instance of a serious intentional breach of confidentiality. It involved a safeguards inspector who, after having provided safeguards confidential information to the legislative branch of his country's government, was summarily dismissed by the Director General (and as a consequence, denied his repatriation grant of $5000). No further action against the staff member was found to be feasible.

2. Iraq, DPRK and South Africa: Shifting the Balance Towards Transparency

Under comprehensive safeguards agreements, the Agency has the right and the obligation to ensure that all source or special fissionable material in all peaceful nuclear activities of the State is subject to safeguards, and that safeguards are in fact applied to such material. The Agency's obligation is not limited to nuclear material and facilities actually declared by a State; it also extends to that which is required to be declared. Likewise, the Agency's right to information and its right of access to facilities and other locations are not limited to information, facilities, locations or material declared by the State. However, as mentioned above, the Agency's right to carry out *routine* inspections is limited to those locations within a nuclear facility, or other locations containing nuclear material (LOF),[3] through which nuclear material is expected to flow (strategic points).

Access to "undeclared" sites or to locations suspected of containing "undeclared" nuclear material has always been possible under the standard INFCIRC/153 provisions for *special* inspections. However, prior to 1990, there existed considerable political reservations among many States about the exercise of such a right by the IAEA. Not even these provisions were interpreted as permitting the IAEA to carry out activities on a regular basis to verify the absence of undeclared material or activities at locations which had not been declared by the State. Nor has

[3] LOF: location outside facility where nuclear material is customarily used in amounts of 1 effective kilogram or less.

the IAEA ever had available to it sufficiently specific information suggesting that such an action was called for.

It was not until 1990-1991 that sufficient political consensus had developed to support the full exercise of the IAEA's authority with a view to its providing improved assurances as to the absence, in a State with a comprehensive safeguards agreement, of undeclared nuclear material and activities.

By the end of the Cold War, States' perceptions of security concerns were changing. The international community was pressing for more active measures, with the goal of eliminating the risk posed by weapons of mass destruction. At the August 1990 NPT Review Conference, the States Parties agreed on language welcoming a study by the Agency of the possible scope, application and procedures for special inspections in NPT-safeguarded States where uncertainty existed about whether a State had conformed to the purpose of the NPT and, in particular, whether the State had declared to the Agency all nuclear material required to be subject to safeguards. Much of the momentum in this regard was attributable to growing concerns about compliance by Iraq and the Democratic People's Republic of Korea (DPRK) with their obligations under the NPT.

It was the discovery in early 1991 of Iraq's clandestine nuclear weapons programme which confirmed the need for IAEA assurances not only of the non-diversion of declared nuclear material, but also of the absence of undeclared nuclear activities in States with comprehensive safeguards agreements. This was reaffirmed by the Member States of the Agency later that year in their collective demand for assurances concerning the completeness of South Africa's initial nuclear material inventory declaration required in accordance with its NPT safeguards agreement.[4] The IAEA's experience in South Africa was positive, not only in terms of the cooperation and transparency of the South African government, which was voluntarily provided, but in terms of further assisting the Agency in developing new techniques for providing broader assurances. Using tools within the Agency's existing legal authority, and drawing upon its experiences in Iraq and in South Africa, the IAEA was later able to bring to the world's attention its concerns about the possibility of the existence in the DPRK of undeclared nuclear material and activities.[5]

It became clear to the Member States of the IAEA that, for the IAEA to provide increased assurance of the absence of undeclared nuclear material, it was imperative to update and strengthen the safeguards system by integrating into it measures that would give the Agency an improved capability of detecting clandestine nuclear activities.

The IAEA's efforts to do so were formalised into a programme established within the IAEA Secretariat: "Programme 93 + 2". The premise of this programme was that, to provide

[4] South Africa became a party to the NPT in July 1991. The safeguards agreement concluded by South Africa pursuant to the NPT was signed and entered into force on 16 September 1991 (IAEA document INFCIRC/394). In March 1993 South Africa announced that it had had six completed nuclear weapons, which it had dismantled prior to becoming party to the NPT. It voluntarily offered the IAEA extensive access to locations, information and materials with a view to assisting the inspectors in verifying the absence of undeclared nuclear materials and activities outside of IAEA safeguards.

[5] The agreement was approved by the Board of Governors on 12 September 1991, and was signed by both parties on 30 January 1992. However, the agreement did not enter into force until 10 April 1992. In attempting to verify the completeness and correctness of the DPRK's initial declaration of its nuclear material, the IAEA detected anomalies indicating the existence in the DPRK of an undetermined amount of undeclared separated Plutonium. The IAEA's request to carry out a special inspection in connection with these anomalies continues to be rejected by the DPRK.

a higher degree of assurance, the Agency needed more information on States' nuclear programmes, and greater access to locations in States, without having to resort to special inspections.

The first step in the strengthening of safeguards was to develop a "Physical Model", which identified and described every known process for carrying out each step necessary for the production of weapons-usable material and characterised each process in terms of the indicators of the existence of that process (such as specialised or dual-use equipment, nuclear and non-nuclear material, environmental signatures, and requirements for specific technical skills). With additional information and broader physical access to verify such information, the IAEA would be able to more effectively evaluate the correctness and completeness of the information provided by the State by comparing it with the Physical Model. This "comparison" is, in actuality, a detailed technical evaluation, first, of the internal consistency of the State's declaration and, second, of a point-by-point comparison of indications of activities from all information available to the Agency (e.g., State declarations, environmental sampling, open sources) and what the States says it is doing or plans to do.

Using the Physical Model and State evaluations as the conceptual bases, the Secretariat identified the technical measures which it believed would strengthen the IAEA's comprehensive safeguards system. The measures proposed by the Secretariat, and ultimately endorsed by the Board of Governors, included a number which were already possible under existing legal authority, such as the provision of additional information on facilities, the expanded use of unannounced inspections, the collection of environmental samples at locations where inspectors had access under existing agreements and the use of advanced technology to monitor remotely the movements of nuclear material.

The measures proposed by the Secretariat also included new ones which would require additional legal authority. These included, among others:

- greatly expanded information about all aspects of States' nuclear fuel cycle, including nuclear fuel cycle-related research and development; information on all buildings on the sites of nuclear facilities; and information on the manufacture and export of sensitive nuclear-related technologies and inspector access at manufacturing and import locations;
- broader access to such locations, along with short notice inspections on the sites of nuclear facilities;
- the collection of environmental samples at locations other than those declared by the State when deemed necessary by the IAEA; and,
- administrative arrangements that improve the process of designating inspectors, the issuance of multi-entry visas (necessary for unannounced inspections) and IAEA access to modern means of communication (e.g., satellite communications systems).

Having identified the new measures requiring additional legal authority, the Secretariat proposed their incorporation into a new legal instrument intended to complement existing safeguards agreements: the Model Protocol Additional to the Agreement(s) between State(s) and the IAEA for the Application of Safeguards (INFCIRC/540 (Corr.)).

3. Confidentiality Revisited

With proposals being made to broaden Agency access to information and to locations beyond nuclear material and facilities, States' concerns about confidentiality, particularly with respect to commercial, technical and industrial secrets, once again arose. However, the concerns were not just with respect to commercial sensitivity: there were political concerns (especially as regards the possibility of misuse of environmental sampling by conducting non-safeguards-related analyses, or by the release of information which might suggest environmental issues to non-scientific parties); concerns about physical protection (e.g., dissemination of information which could be useful to terrorist organisations), and proliferation sensitivities (by disseminating information related to nuclear technologies which are of particular sensitivity).

As a consequence, the Model Additional Protocol, which was negotiated by an open-ended committee of the Board of Governors, and approved by the Board in a special session in May 1997, ultimately included the following provisions:

- Article 7 of the Model requires the Agency, upon request by the State, to make arrangements for managed access under the Protocol in order to prevent dissemination of proliferation sensitive information, to meet safety or physical protection requirements, or to protect proprietary or commercially sensitive information. However, Article 7 also provides that "such arrangements shall not preclude the Agency from conducting activities necessary to provide credible assurance of the absence of undeclared nuclear material, including the resolution of a question relating to the correctness and completeness of the information declared by the State or of an inconsistency relating to that information."
- Article 15 of the Model Additional Protocol requires the Agency to "maintain a stringent regime to ensure effective protection against disclosure of commercial, technological and industrial secrets and other confidential information coming to its knowledge, including such information coming to the Agency's knowledge in the implementation of this Protocol." Article 15 also provides for an ongoing function of the Board of Governors, insofar as the Board is to approve and periodically review the Agency's regime. A description of that regime, as approved by the Board of Governors, is set out below.

Had the issue of confidentiality not been resolved to the satisfaction of Member States, we could still be negotiating a model protocol. The advantages of its resolution in the Model Additional Protocol are that: (1) it addressed the States' interest in protecting confidential information, while ensuring that that interest not serve to defeat the purpose of the document by hobbling the Agency's ability to fulfil its obligations under the strengthened safeguards system; and (2) while providing for a more active role of the Board of Governors in the review of the confidentiality regime, it avoided concretisation in Additional Protocols of detailed requirements for such a regime.

Prior to the conclusion of the negotiation of the Model Additional Protocol (and as an implied *sine qua non* for many States' agreement thereto), the Board of Governors undertook its initial consideration of the IAEA's confidentiality regime, as reflected in IAEA document GOV/2897 (13 February 1997). On December 1997, the Board of Governors approved that regime, as supplemented in GOV/2959 (14 November 1997).

4. The IAEA's Confidentiality Regime

This section is intended to highlight significant aspects of the regime as they relate to the subject of this book, focusing on what actions may be taken in the event of unauthorised release of "safeguards confidential" information. Much of the text is drawn from that of the Board documents referred to above.

4.1 Investigations

In the event of the loss or theft of safeguards confidential information (for example, through theft of an inspector's briefcase), the Safeguards Department Division of Operations concerned reports the loss or theft to the relevant police authorities and notifies the State concerned. Should the Director General receive a complaint from a Member State, on its behalf or on behalf of a private company, alleging that a current or former staff member is responsible for the intentional unauthorised disclosure of safeguards confidential information, the Director General would promptly initiate an investigation to determine whether such an unauthorised disclosure had occurred, and whether it was likely that the individual concerned had indeed violated the Agency's confidentiality regime.

The Director General may request assistance and information from Member States in the course of his or her investigation and may avail himself or herself of existing or ad hoc mechanisms within the Secretariat to assist in the investigation. The Director General, having reviewed the results of the investigation, will formulate his or her conclusions and transmit them to the State or States concerned.

4.2 Actions against the Agency

Pursuant to paragraph 17 of INFCIRC/153 (Corr.), all comprehensive safeguards agreements, as well as the voluntary offer agreements of the nuclear-weapon States, provide that any claim by one party thereto against the other in respect of any damage, other than damage arising out of a nuclear incident, resulting from the implementation of safeguards under the agreement, shall be settled in accordance with international law. As provided for in paragraph 22 of INFCIRC/153 (Corr.), any dispute arising out of the interpretation or application of such an agreement, except a dispute with regard to a finding under paragraph 19 of the agreement or an action taken by the Board pursuant to such a finding, which is not settled by negotiation or another procedure agreed to by the parties should, on the request of either party, be submitted to an arbitral tribunal. The arbitral procedure is to be fixed by the tribunal and the decision of the tribunal would be binding on both parties.[6]

In the event that a State believed that an unauthorised disclosure of safeguards confidential information relating to that State had occurred, the State should communicate its position to the Director General of the IAEA, with a view to immediately instituting an investigation, as indicated above. Ultimately, should the State disagree with the findings of the investigation, it

[6] The few item-specific INFCIRC/66/Rev. 2-type safeguards agreements currently implemented by the IAEA contain a similar disputes resolution clause, but do not, in general, contain a clause corresponding to paragraph 17 of INFCIRC/153 (Corr.).

could conclude that a dispute existed within the meaning of the provision in its safeguards agreement corresponding to paragraph 22 of INFCIRC/153 (Corr.) and initiate the process of setting up an arbitral tribunal.

Should the IAEA be held responsible by an arbitral tribunal for damages resulting from the breach of confidentiality, either by the organisation or by a current or former staff member, the Agency would be legally required to pay such damages. In the event such a case ever arose, the Secretariat would make all possible efforts to recover such amounts from the present or former staff member whom it considered responsible for the unauthorised disclosure through the institution of appropriate actions against that person as indicated below.

4.3 ACTIONS AGAINST PRESENT OR FORMER STAFF MEMBERS

(a) Internal administrative procedures and sanctions

The Director General may decide, on the basis of an investigation conducted in accordance with the procedures described above, to initiate a disciplinary action under Staff Rule 11.01.1 against the staff member concerned. As a consequence of a disciplinary action, the staff member may be censured, suspended without pay, demoted or dismissed for misconduct or summarily dismissed. In the event of summary dismissal, the staff member would forfeit his/her repatriation grant or end-of-service allowance and any termination indemnity to which the staff member might otherwise have been entitled.

Existing Staff Rule 13.03.4 permits recovery by the Agency from a staff member in reimbursement to the Agency "either partially or in full for any financial loss suffered by the Agency as a result of his/her negligence or of his/her having violated any regulation, rule or administrative instruction". Staff Rule 5.01.11 permits recovery of such indebtedness to the Agency through deductions from the staff member's salary. Staff Rule 5.01.11 also permits deductions from the staff member's salary for indebtedness to third parties, when a deduction for this is authorised by the Director General. Under existing Staff Regulations and Rules, the Agency may not deduct punitive damages, nor may it recover for damage suffered by a third party unless the IAEA were responsible for such damages.

Any action taken by the Director General may be appealed by the staff member to the Administrative Tribunal of the International Labour Organisation (ILOAT). The decisions of the ILOAT are final and unappealable, except that the executive board of the organisation concerned may submit the ILOAT's decision to the International Court of Justice for an advisory opinion if the Executive Board "challenges a decision of the Tribunal confirming its jurisdiction, or considers that the decision of the Tribunal is vitiated by a fundamental fault in the procedure followed" (Article XII.1 of the Statute of the ILOAT).

In the course of the Board's consideration of the confidentiality regime, a few States proposed as a deterrent measure that the Staff Rules relevant to disciplinary measures be amended to provide for a fixed monetary penalty in the event of an unauthorised release of information by a staff member (e.g., $200,000). In the view of the Secretariat, however, the deterrent value of fixed punitive damages was questionable, except possibly to deter unintentional or negligent release of such information. If an individual were revealing confidential information for financial gain, any fixed penalty would be unlikely to have much effect as those interested in obtaining the information would simply offer a staff member a financial incentive greater than the penalty. If an individual were motivated by political reasons, he or she is unlikely to be deterred by reason of such a penalty (especially if the information is being provided to a government which might be expected not only to decline to prosecute, but rather to reward, the individual concerned). Finally, in order for the penalty to have significant deterrent effect, it would have to be high. Imposing a penalty is only effective, however, if it is recoverable. The less likely the enforceability of such a provision, correspondingly, the less likely it is to have a significant deterrent effect.[7] Ultimately, the Board agreed with the Secretariat's assessment that the incorporation of a fixed penalty in the event of unauthorised release of confidential information would not be practical or useful as a deterrence to such breaches.

The question was also posed whether entitlements to pension payments from the United Nations Joint Staff Pension Fund (UNJSPF) may not be attached for purposes of recovery for financial losses suffered by the Agency or others by virtue of an unauthorised disclosure of safeguards confidential information. In accordance with Article 45 of the UNJSPF Regulations, adopted by the General Assembly of the United Nations, neither a participant nor a beneficiary may assign his/her rights under the UNJSPF Regulations. Thus, pension payments may not, under existing regulations, be attached for such claims. Under Rule B.4 of the Administrative Rules of the UNJSPF, not even information provided by, or in respect of, a participant (staff member or former staff member) may be released without his/her written consent or authorisation. Recently, a very limited exception was adopted by the Standing Committee of the UNJSPF Board which would permit information to be given to a judicial or civil authority in the context of divorce or family maintenance obligations. However, the benefits in such cases are still not attachable. This decision is in line with the position that a pension is a social security, not a fund from which penalties may be deducted, a position apparently reflected in various countries in which garnishment of pension benefits is allowed, if at all, only in exceptional and clearly defined circumstances. In order to modify this proscription, an amendment to the UNJSPF Regulations would have to be adopted by the General Assembly of the United Nations, after consultation with the UNJSPF Board. It was concluded that such a course of action would not be particularly viable or likely to succeed. Moreover, it was noted that not all staff members are participants in the UNJSPF.

(b) Criminal prosecution (domestic)

Criminal jurisdiction requires State legislation making particular conduct a criminal offence. In order for a domestic court to exercise criminal jurisdiction for unauthorised release of safeguards confidential information, the State would have to have in force legislation providing for such

[7] Moreover, in common law States, while it is possible for parties to a contract to agree on a certain sum to be paid upon breach of contract, such an amount may generally only be recovered in a civil action for breach of contract if it was really fixed upon as liquidated damages for non-performance (or mis-performance). However, if it was intended in the nature of a penalty excess of any loss likely to be sustainedwould be recoverable, recovery will be limited to the loss actually sustained by the complaining party. On the other hand, where a matter is of uncertain value, the sum may be treated as liquidated damages unless the sum is so greatly in excess of the probable damage as to show that the parties could not have fixed upon it otherwise than as a penalty. If the actual or presumed intention was to secure performance by imposing a penalty in excess of the actual loss, the amount will not be treated as liquidated damages, and recovery limited to restitution for actual damages. The higher the amount, and the clearer the intention of the deterrent and punitive nature of the penalty, the less likely such a provision would be enforceable in common law jurisdictions in connection with a cause of action based on breach of contract.

jurisdiction. In criminal cases, the State itself would normally prosecute; the current or former staff member concerned would be the named defendant (the IAEA, being immune pursuant to Article III.3 of the Agreement on the Privileges and Immunities of the IAEA from every form of legal process in its Member States, could not be a defendant).

In a case involving an Agency staff member employed at Headquarters, the legislation of Austria as the Agency's host country is of particular interest. Action against such a staff member would be consistent with Article III.7.(c) of the Headquarters Agreement between the IAEA and Austria, which provides that, "except as otherwise provided in this Agreement, the courts or other appropriate organs of the Republic of Austria shall have jurisdiction, as provided in applicable laws, over acts done and transactions taking place in the headquarters seat." Austrian law does provide for criminal prosecution, on request of the victim, of anyone who has secured unauthorised access to a commercial or enterprise-related secret with the intention either to utilise it, to pass it on to others for utilisation or to release it to the public. Thus, it might be possible that, under certain circumstances, insofar as at least part of the activity of securing unauthorised access to the secret has taken place in Austria, a criminal action could lie in Austria against a current or former staff member for the unauthorised release of confidential information. It does not appear, however, that, this law would cover the situation in which a staff member passed on information to which he had gained access in the fulfilment of his or her normal functions.

In the case of a current or former staff member not present in Austria, States which could claim jurisdiction over the action could be the State of nationality of the staff member, the State in which the damage or breach occurred, or any other State in which the staff member was physically present. However, it must be stressed again that only domestic legislation can provide a basis for jurisdiction, whether for personal jurisdiction over the staff member or for subject matter jurisdiction over the conduct and facts involved.

National legislation may vary greatly with regard to what constitutes a punishable breach of confidentiality, as well as to appropriate penalties therefor. If it were considered necessary to ensure consistency among Member States in the interpretation and application of the Agency's regime of confidentiality, the most effective means of doing so would be the drawing up of a multilateral treaty setting out the agreed upon elements of the crime in question, agreed upon penalties, commitments to incorporate the foregoing into domestic law and commitments to honour and enforce foreign judgments handed down pursuant to the treaty.[8] Another option would be for the Board to call upon all Member States of the Agency to cooperate and support

[8] For example, paragraph 1 of Article 194 of the Treaty establishing the European Atomic Energy Community provides as follows:

> The members of the institutions of the Community, the members of committees, the officials and other servants of the Community and any other persons who by reason of their duties or their public or private relations with the institutions or installations of the Community or with Joint Undertakings are called upon to acquire or obtain cognisance of any facts, information, knowledge, documents or objects which are subject to a security system in accordance with provisions laid down by a Member State or by an institution of the Community, shall be required, even after such duties or relations have ceased, to keep them secret from any unauthorised person and from the general public.
>
> Each Member State shall treat any infringement of this obligation as an act prejudicial to its rules on secrecy and as one falling, both as to merits and jurisdiction, within the scope of its laws relating to acts prejudicial to the security of the State or to disclosure of professionals secrets. Such Member State shall, at the request of any Member State concerned or of the Commission, prosecute anyone within its jurisdiction who commits such an infringement.

the Director General, to the extent possible, in investigating any breach or alleged breach of confidentiality and in taking appropriate action in case a breach has been established.

Pursuant to Article VI of the Agreement on the Privileges and Immunities of the IAEA, officials of the Agency are entitled to immunity from legal process in respect of words spoken or written and all acts performed by them in their official capacity. As this immunity is based upon functions performed while in the employ of the Agency, it continues to apply with regard to such functions after employment ceases.

In addition, pursuant to the Host Country Agreement, staff members at the P-5 level and above are entitled to personal immunity in Austria from legal process, including arrest and detention. Pursuant to Article VI of the Agreement on the Privileges and Immunities of the IAEA, the Director General, Deputy Directors General and officials of equivalent rank are accorded diplomatic status and are immune from legal process, including arrest and detention, in the territory of the parties to such Agreement. Pursuant to Article VII of the Agreement, Agency inspectors on mission are also entitled to immunity from arrest and detention. This immunity is personal and linked to a particular level while serving for the Agency. As opposed to functional immunity, personal immunity does not continue once employment ceases.

In Article VI, Section 21 and Article VII, Section 25 of the Agreement on the Privileges and Immunities of the IAEA, it is provided that such privileges and immunities are granted in the interests of the Agency and are not for the personal benefit of the individuals themselves. The Director General has the right and the duty to waive the immunity where, in his or her opinion, the immunity would impede the course of justice and can be waived without prejudice to the interests of the Agency.

It may be assumed that, if a staff member has intentionally disclosed safeguards confidential information in violation of the confidentiality regime, this conduct could be understood as falling outside the scope of his or her official duties and functions. Thus, the issue of waiving immunity would not arise unless the staff member were at a P-5 level or above. In either case, it would be for the Director General, in the first instance, to determine whether immunity existed and, if so, whether immunity should be waived pursuant to the terms of the Agreement on the Privileges and Immunities of the IAEA.

While attention has been focused on waiver of immunity of the accused staff member, the potentially more serious matter is waiver of the immunity of the Agency itself. If the Agency were the complainant in any criminal prosecution against any current or former staff member, or if its determination that a breach had occurred were critical for successful prosecution, both the prosecutor and the defence could be expected to request the court to order testimony by Agency officials. Subpoenas might also be issued by the court for the production of relevant internal Agency documents, ranging from personnel archives to possibly even safeguards confidential information. Agency safeguards procedures could be subjected to the scrutiny and review of a domestic court if the immunity of the Agency is deemed to have been waived. Thus, while the Agency will no doubt wish to cooperate in the prosecution of an individual whom it believes has intentionally or by gross negligence disclosed safeguards confidential information without the appropriate authority, the Agency must nonetheless reserve its position with regard to any blanket waiver of its own immunity or that of its officials (other than the accused's). Limited appearances in court or partial waivers may thus be more appropriate. However, such attempts to limit the waivers may not be accepted by the court concerned. In any event, the Director General would have to examine each situation on a case by case basis, determining what is in the best interests of the Agency and of justice.

(c) Civil litigation (domestic)

If a staff member's salary and emoluments did not satisfy amounts due to the Agency, if a third party claimed damages, or if the individual were no longer a staff member, the recovery of damages could be pursued in a civil action against the current or former staff member in a domestic court of a State with jurisdiction.

In some jurisdictions, an action in tort can be instituted based on the negligent or intentional breach of an individual's obligation to take reasonable care with protected information, and on the damage suffered as a result. Depending on the relevant domestic legislation, the plaintiff in such an action could be an injured State, a State on behalf of an injured private party, an injured private party and/or the IAEA itself. However, the Agency would only initiate action as a plaintiff in exceptional cases, since the institution of such an action could require a comprehensive waiver of the Agency's own immunity as well as that of its officials.

In some jurisdictions, an action for breach of contract may be brought against an employee of a company for violation of the employment contract. In such a case, the IAEA itself would necessarily be the plaintiff. In principle, the IAEA could waive its immunity and bring an action for breach of contract against a staff member for unauthorised release of confidential information. However, as in criminal cases and actions based in tort, the institution by the Agency of such an action could necessitate a comprehensive waiver of its own immunity and that of its officials. The Director General would only do so in the most exceptional of cases.[9]

A corollary issue with respect to civil litigation is the jurisdiction in which an action based on tort or breach of contract could be brought. Depending on the tort or contract law of the State in which jurisdiction is exercised, a suit might be brought: in the State where the tort occurred or the site of the contract; the State where personal jurisdiction of the staff member could be established (the State where the defendant is physically served with process); and the State of the staff member's nationality. Assuming the possibility of establishing personal jurisdiction over the staff member, or some "minimum contacts" jurisdiction over the property of the staff member, a suit might also be permitted in the State of the injured party.

The question of what constitutes reparable damages may vary from jurisdiction to jurisdiction, and depends on the legislation of the State in which the court exercising jurisdiction is located. Some jurisdictions limit recovery to financial damages, some for more esoteric damages, such as damages to reputation. If the action were brought by the IAEA, damages might include damages to reputation, financial damages, and/or damages for which the IAEA has been held

[9] It should be noted, however, that, as regards jurisdiction of domestic courts for claims based on breach of contractual obligations, courts in some European continental legal systems might not accept competence, as civil servants having the status of staff members are deemed to be governed solely by the statutory provisions of the legal system to which the employee (staff member) became subject by entering into an employment relation with the organisation, and, thus, the organisation may not appear as a plaintiff in a civil action against a current staff member unless the dispute involves a tortious act committed by the staff member. It is possible that such a position may be applied in such jurisdictions, by analogy, to the IAEA, precluding a cause of action for breach of contract.

responsible, by virtue of an arbitral tribunal award, or for which it has voluntarily assumed responsibility.

(d) Criminal prosecution (international)

At present, there is no customary international law which provides for the prosecution and punishment of individuals for a crime involving the intentional unauthorised release of confidential information. In order to establish such a cause of action, a treaty would be required specifying what conduct constituted an international crime, and containing provisions for extradition or prosecution for those accused of having committed such a crime. It may be noted that the Statute establishing the International Criminal Court does not include among the international crimes over which it has jurisdiction the unauthorised disclosure of confidential information or of trade, industrial or commercial secrets.

5. Summary

Since the IAEA's inception, the dissemination of information relating to the peaceful uses of nuclear energy has been one of its fundamental activities. The statutory objective of the IAEA to accelerate and enlarge the contribution of atomic energy to peace, health and prosperity throughout the world, and its statutory functions associated with fostering the exchange of scientific and technical information, have been the basis for the IAEA's policy of dissemination of information and transparency in its activities. However, in recognition of the legitimate interest of Member States in protecting certain information for safety or proprietary reasons, limitations on the dissemination of information and transparency can and do apply in connection with certain aspects of the IAEA's activities, including in particular safeguards.

Safeguards have always required concerted actions by the IAEA inspectorate, State authorities and nuclear facility operators. The strengthened safeguards system places an even greater emphasis on cooperation. That cooperation must be reflected in a proper balance between confidentiality and transparency, for:

- without confidentiality, there will be resistance by States to adherence to the regime; and,
- without transparency, States may see no benefit in assuming the additional obligations; transparency contributes to public confidence that the State is complying with its non-proliferation obligations. Failing such confidence, the public is unlikely to support growth in the industry.

There is no absolute security in any system of information protection: if an individual with access to sensitive information chooses intentionally to release it, it is not possible to prevent it. In light of the limited avenues of recourse for the breach of obligations to protect sensitive information, the most effective course of action for international organisations is to instil in their staff a culture of responsibility which encourages proper handling of information through appropriate training of the staff and the institution of procedures which would reduce the likelihood of inadvertent or negligent releases. In doing so, the organisation should strike a balance such that the procedures instituted to protect information are practical and not so burdensome as to result in hampering the work of the organisation.

THE CHEMICAL WEAPONS CONVENTION CONFIDENTIALITY REGIME

Camilo Sanhueza Bezanilla*

1. INTRODUCTION

The following will offer a broad panorama of the regime for the protection of confidential information contained, mainly, in the provisions of the Chemical Weapons Convention,[1] with special reference to the mechanisms for its implementation. I do not claim to provide solutions, merely a descriptive overview of the machinery available and its shortcomings. The historical background will first be examined, followed by an analysis of the main elements involving confidentiality and a review of the procedures and resulting protection.

Confidentiality, together with verification, destruction and international cooperation, are the pillars of the regime for the prohibition of chemical weapons. Duly incorporated into the Convention, these four aspects constitute a delicate but stable balance between the different interests represented.

In ensuring that confidential information is appropriately handled, both from the standpoint of national security and from that of the chemical industry, the confidentiality regime, together with the intrusive verification mechanisms designed to create a climate of trust, seeks to embody the compromise reached by the negotiators of the Convention. Indeed, the maintenance of this climate of trust is fundamental to the effective functioning of both the verification regime and the regime for the protection of confidential information. Far from being mutually incompatible, the two mechanisms must be combined to ensure the best possible application of the Convention. Thus, if properly applied, confidentiality will contribute to better verification.[2]

2. BACKGROUND

In 1992, after a decade of wide-ranging and difficult negotiations at the United Nations Conference on Disarmament in Geneva, Switzerland, the negotiators adopted the Chemical Weapons Convention. Later, the United Nations General Assembly adopted, without a vote, the corresponding resolution requesting the Secretary-General of the United Nations,

* Chair of the Confidentiality Commission of the OPCW, Member of the Chilean delegation to the Conference on Disarmament during the negotiations of the Chemical Weapons Convention, Diplomat at the Mission of Chile to the European Union, in charge of NATO and European Policy on Security and Defence, Ph.D. in Political Science. Any views expressed are those of the author and are not attributable to the OPCW or the government of Chile.

[1] 1993 Convention on the Prohibition of the Development, Production, Stockpiling and Use of Chemical Weapons and on Their Destruction, entered into force on 29 April 1997. Text, as corrected and changed, available at http://www.opcw.org.

[2] These guiding principles are set out in the Conference on Disarmament document CD/901 (16 March 1989).

R. Yepes-Enríquez and L. Tabassi. (eds.), Treaty Enforcement and International Cooperation in Criminal Matters

in his capacity of depositary, to open the Convention for signature on 13 January 1993, while accepting the invitation of the French President to make Paris the venue for this ceremony.[3] Thus, the adoption of the Convention was an event of historical importance for the multilateral effort to achieve disarmament and arms control. Although the Convention did not meet every concern, it took into consideration the security interests of States and led to the first big advance in the collective task of eradicating weapons of mass destruction and, more specifically, chemical weapons.

One of the most notable aspects of the negotiations was the verification regime, a mechanism without parallel in instruments of this kind. The particular intrusiveness of the system, especially designed to generate the indispensable trust in the implementation of the Convention, made it necessary for States to protect sensitive information. The search for a way out of this dilemma gave rise to a mechanism for the protection of confidential information which began to emerge towards the end of 1986 and the beginning of 1987.

In 1989 a framework for a comprehensive and intrusive verification system was reached. This contained guidelines on the development of a regime for the handling and protection of confidential information, as well as a classification system for this type of information,[4] which were evolutionary in nature. The situation was evolving because, step by step, the mechanisms of verification and protection of confidential information were gradually taking material form through procedures. The problem was solved by establishing guidelines for an international inspectorate[5] which contained, among other things, provisions on the protection of confidential information. In these guidelines the safeguards regime of the International Atomic Energy Agency (IAEA)[6] and the results of the bilateral negotiation of the Treaty between the United States and the Soviet Union on the Elimination of their Intermediate-Range and Shorter-Range Missiles[7] were especially taken into account. This concluded the search for a formula that would enable a balance to be struck between effective monitoring of compliance with the provisions of the Treaty and the need for States Parties to protect confidential military, commercial and industrial information.

Below, we shall see how the regime in question finally took shape and how it works in practice by considering its main elements and the rules it lays down concerning infringements and sanctions, cooperation, liability and compensation, and, finally, by examining the Confidentiality Commission.

---

[3] For details on the historical background of the discussion and negotiations on the issue of chemical weapons, at both the multilateral and the bilateral levels, see editions of The United Nations Disarmament Yearbook, in particular 1991, chapter XII.

[4] See the Report of the Ad Hoc Committee on Chemical Weapons to the Conference on Disarmament concerning the work done during the period from 17 January to 3 February 1989, Conference on Disarmament doc. CD/881 (3 February 1989).

[5] Conference on Disarmament doc. CD/795 (2 February 1988).

[6] See, *inter alia*, Article VII of the Statute of the International Atomic Energy Agency and the structure and content of the Agreements between the IAEA and the States Parties (IAEA doc. INFCIRC/153). See further, *supra* in this volume, L. Rockwood, Confidentiality: The IAEA's Experience.

[7] Treaty between the United States of America and the Union of Soviet Socialist Republics on the elimination of their intermediate-range and shorter-range missiles; commonly referred to as the Intermediate-Range Nuclear Forces Treaty or INF Treaty.

3. Main Elements

The Convention regime for the protection of confidential information takes a comprehensive approach to: (a) defining, with precision, the information required; (b) stipulating the appropriate conduct for inspectors and other members of staff having access to or handling confidential information; and (c) establishing a mechanism for administering the handling of confidential information, within the OPCW Secretariat.

4. Rules

The rules of the regime for the protection of confidential information are contained in three main provisions of the Convention: Article VIII, paragraph 5; Article VII, paragraph 6; and the Annex on the Protection of Confidential Information (CA).

Article VIII, paragraph 5,[8] establishes the protection of confidential information as a general principle for the entire OPCW. The idea that all the Organisation's activities should be carried out in accordance with this objective is, as we have already pointed out, a clear response to the broad scope and unprecedented intrusiveness of the Convention's verification measures.

Article VII, paragraph 6,[9] which requires States Parties to preserve the confidentiality of information received from the Organisation and further states that this information should be used exclusively for the purposes for which it was provided, should be understood as supplementing the previously mentioned Article VIII(5).

Finally, the Confidentiality Annex (CA) establishes the procedural principles relating to the protection of confidential information in general and, in particular, lays down the procedures for the implementation of the regime. Specifically, it is a question of guidelines containing the elements necessary to develop new procedures that allow the regime to function properly and facilitate its management by the OPCW Secretariat.

These guidelines enabled, first, the OPCW Preparatory Commission and then the OPCW itself to develop, *inter alia*, the OPCW Policy on Confidentiality (CP);[10] the OPCW Policy on Media and Public Affairs;[11] and the OPCW Manual of Confidentiality Procedure. Ultimately, these two policies and the procedures in the Manual, all derived from the CA, together with Article VII(6) and Article VIII(5), make up what has come to be known as the OPCW's regime for the protection of confidential information.

5. The Confidentiality Annex

The importance of the CA is that it makes Article VIII, paragraph 5, operative by establishing a system of authority and responsibility for its implementation. To this end, it stipulates, *inter alia*, that the OPCW Director-General is responsible for ensuring the protection of confidential information handled by the Secretariat and instructs him to establish a special regime for that purpose.

---

[8] Article VIII(A) entitled the Organization, General Provisions.

[9] Article VII entitled National Implementation Measures, General Undertakings.

[10] OPCW doc. C-I/DEC.13 (16 May 1997) and Corr.1.

[11] OPCW doc. C-I/DEC.55 (16 May 1997).

The guidelines contained in the CA may be grouped as follows: (a) handling of confidential information by the Secretariat; (b) employment and conduct of personnel; (c) protection of confidentiality during inspections; and (d) procedures in cases of breaches of confidentiality.

6. Breaches of Confidentiality

In order not to stray from the subject of the present section, only the aspect relating to the violation of confidentiality, in so far as it concerns the procedures to be followed in the event of breaches or alleged breaches of the confidentiality of information, will be considered below.[12]

With reference to breaches of confidentiality, it should be borne in mind that there is a possibility of non-material as well as material damage. The damage caused to the OPCW as a whole also includes the need to re-establish confidence in the implementation of the Convention, which may not be easy. The potential seriousness of the outcome emphasises the importance of the procedures to be followed in case of breaches of confidentiality. These procedures relate, in particular, to: (a) sanctions and disciplinary measures; (b) cooperation between States Parties in the relevant investigations; and (c) the role of the Confidentiality Commission.

7. Sanctions and Disciplinary Measures

According to paragraph 18 of Section D of the CA, the Director-General must establish necessary *procedures* to be followed in case of breaches of confidentiality, taking into account the recommendations of the OPCW Conference of States Parties.

These measures are spelled out in detail in Part IX.1 of the Policy on Confidentiality relating to breach investigation procedures.[13] This lays down a four-step procedure for investigating breaches and alleged breaches of confidentiality and violations of related obligations to protect confidential information, namely: Step 1, investigation by the Director-General; Step 2, interim action; Step 3, report of investigations; and Step 4, action in response to an investigation report.

Under paragraph 19 of the CA, the *investigation* mechanism is activated by: (a) the Director-General, if there is sufficient indication that obligations concerning the protection of confidential information have been violated; or (b) the State Party, if it makes an allegation concerning a breach of confidentiality. Under the CP, the investigation is conducted not by an existing body in the Secretariat, but under the direct responsibility of the Director-General, who is authorised to appoint a member of the staff for that purpose. The results of the investigation must be incorporated in a report that contains proposals for reforming and enhancing the OPCW's confidentiality regime. In addition to members of OPCW staff, the OPCW itself, an individual or entity outside the Secretariat or a State Party may be investigated.

---

[12] Confidentiality Annex, Section D: Procedures in case of breaches or alleged breaches of confidentiality.

[13] Part IX entitled "Breach Procedures" consists of three sections: Breach investigation procedures; Rules governing the Commission for the Settlement of Disputes Related to Confidentiality ("Confidentiality Commission"); and the Role of States Parties in relation to breach procedures.

The investigation and establishment of the facts must also be confidential and conducted on the basis of objectivity and due process. This means the rights to be notified of any allegations; to be assisted with one's defence; to rebut the charges; and to appeal the decision of the Director-General.

It is the responsibility of the Director-General to assess the *severity of the penalty*. For this purpose the Director-General must take into consideration such factors as whether or not the breach was deliberate; whether it involved a violation of the CP; the provisions of the relevant Secrecy agreements;[14] the degree of actual or potential damage; and the degree of any advantage gained through the breach.[15]

An impediment to the precise determination of sanctions is the fact that although the CP defines the term "breach of confidentiality",[16] it does not define the term "serious breach of confidentiality". A violation of this latter nature would certainly justify the withdrawal of immunity from jurisdiction and ultimately might lead to legal — criminal or civil — proceedings under an applicable national jurisdiction, such as that within which the breach was committed; within which the breach was suffered; and of the person by or against whom the breach was committed.

In its second sentence relating to the waiving of immunity from jurisdiction in cases of serious breaches, paragraph 20 of Part D could indicate the need for States Parties to have, at least for these cases, a *single criminal jurisdiction*.[17] However, the possible transnational nature of breaches of confidentiality might nevertheless create problems with respect to jurisdictional authority; non-uniform penalties; and lack of extradition facilities.

8. Cooperation Among States Parties in the Relevant Investigations

Paragraph 21 of the CA requires States Parties, *to the extent possible*, to cooperate and support the Director-General in investigating any breach or alleged breach of confidentiality and in taking appropriate action in case a breach has been established. A general obligation to cooperate can be found in Article VII(7)of the Convention, according to which "each State Party undertakes to cooperate with the Organization in the exercise of all its functions and in particular to provide assistance to the Technical Secretariat".

As we have said, a State Party may also be the subject of an investigation, and in this respect the obligation in question is of fundamental importance. Cooperation may take the form, for example, of supplying details of the handling of confidential information received from the OPCW or providing assistance in obtaining evidence.[18]

Despite the importance of this provision, its effect is weakened by the insertion of the words "to the extent possible". Although this wording reflects the tendency of national legal systems to impose certain limitations, it runs the risk of being used as a pretext for preventing the implementation of the Convention.

---

[14] CA(9) provides that the staff shall enter into individual secrecy agreements with the Secretariat covering their period of employment and a period of five years after it is terminated.

[15] CP, Part IX.1, paras. 3.5 and 5.3.

[16] CP, Part IX.1, para. 2.

[17] See F. Patel-King, Possible Action in the Courts of the Netherlands for Serious Breaches of the OPCW's Confidentiality Regime, in the present volume.

[18] With respect to the obligation on States Parties in relation to confidential OPCW information, see Convention Article VII(6) and paragraph 4 of the Confidentiality Annex.

9. Liability and Indemnification

Paragraph 22 of the CA is the only provision of the Convention to deal with the liability of the OPCW, and it does so in negative terms. The paragraph states that the OPCW shall not be held liable for any breach of confidentiality committed by members of the Secretariat. The intention of those who drafted the Convention was to protect the Organisation, and ultimately the States Parties, from claims that might amount to millions of dollars.

As a result of the impossibility of seeking redress from the OPCW, a State Party that has suffered significant damage as a result of a breach of confidentiality has almost no chance of receiving compensation. Even if the immunity of a member of the Secretariat staff were waived, which would allow him or her to be criminally prosecuted or sued in civil proceedings, it is highly unlikely that he or she would have the means necessary to pay the total damages.

As the OPCW's own activities, particularly inspections, involve the risk of causing damage, and as restrictions cannot be imposed on its work to remove that risk since that would only defeat its purpose, solutions must be sought that allow for indemnification, for example, the creation of a fund or taking out insurance, and ultimately the provision of sufficient resources for the OPCW to operate on this basis.

10. The Confidentiality Commission

The Confidentiality Commission (CC), established under paragraph 23 of the CA, is a body specially set up to settle disputes related to breaches of confidentiality. Although it is a subsidiary organ of the OPCW Conference of States Parties, it enjoys considerable independence in the performance of its quasi-judicial functions. Its jurisdiction in the field of dispute settlement covers the following situations: disputes between two or more States Parties; and disputes between one or more States Parties and the Organisation.

The rules governing its composition and operating procedures are contained in the above-mentioned CP. In accordance with that Policy, the Conference appoints 20 members for a two-year term; four members from each of the five regional groups under the Convention are appointed from a list of experts proposed by the States Parties.

The CC carries out its work in accordance with its Operating Procedures.[19] These Procedures are arranged in nine chapters comprising 50 rules and an annex. For the purposes of the present study, only those chapters that specifically relate to dispute settlement will be focused on.

Requests for the examination of a dispute by the CC may be made by:

(a) the Director-General, on behalf of the OPCW, or one or more States Parties, to the Chair of the CC through the Registry (Rule 12 of the CC Procedures);

(b) the OPCW Conference of the States Parties, to the Chair of the CC, (Rule 13 of the CC Procedures); and,

(c) the States Parties to the dispute, if they opt for the CC, to the Chair of the Commission through the Registry (Rule 14 of the CC Procedures).

[19] Operating Procedures of the Confidentiality Commission, OPCW doc. C-III/DEC.10 (20 November 1998) and Corr.1.

With a view to protecting and ensuring confidentiality, Rule 19 of the CC Procedures provides that:

(a) the deliberations of the Commission shall be confidential, and the documents considered at such meetings shall, when deemed necessary, be assigned the appropriate classification level in accordance with the CP; and,

(b) no information submitted by a member of the Commission, a party to the dispute, an interested third party or any other person shall be disclosed by any person present at the deliberations of the Confidentiality Commission.

Clearly, the intention of this provision is to discourage the presence of persons other than Secretariat personnel, and to limit the access of the latter in accordance with a "need-to-know" principle. The provision is therefore linked with Parts I and II of the CP. This does not preclude a party to the dispute from disclosing statements of its own position in a manner which fully takes into account the provisions of the CA, the CP, and the OPCW Media and Public Affairs Policy.

The same rule goes on to stipulate that:

(a) members of the Commission shall be bound by the provisions of the CA and of the CP and, when using confidential documents, must apply the OPCW Manual of Confidentiality Procedure, *mutatis mutandis*;

(b) the Director-General shall ensure that meetings of the CC at which confidential information is considered receive support only from those staff members of the Secretariat who have been specifically cleared by the Director-General after being proposed to and accepted by the parties to the dispute; and,

(c) the Chair of the Commission shall ensure that its meetings are attended only by persons whose functions require their presence and that those persons will have access to relevant confidential information only on the basis of a "need-to-know" principle.

Finally, the article in question requires members of the CC to enter into individual secrecy agreements with the OPCW Conference of the States Parties, in which they undertake to abide by the letter and the spirit of the CP of the OPCW. The format is similar to that for officials of the Secretariat.[20]

Meanwhile, Rule 21 relates to the establishment of a Registry for holding the information used by the Commission. In view of the possibility of a dispute between a Contracting Party and the OPCW, it was decided that the Registry should be established outside the Organisation. To this end, an agreement was concluded between the OPCW and the International Bureau of the Permanent Court of Arbitration in The Hague, the Netherlands, appointing the latter to act in that capacity.[21]

---

[20] Text of the Secrecy Agreement is found in the Annex to the Operating Procedures of the Confidentiality Commission, OPCW doc. C-III/DEC.10 and Corr.1 (20 November 1998).

[21] Registry Agreement between the Organisation for the Prohibition of Chemical Weapons and the Permanent Court of Arbitration, text available in the Annex to OPCW doc. EC-XII/DEC.6.

Under the chapter on Rules for Proceedings, in requesting the initiation of proceedings the initiator must submit a statement of claim which must be a concise statement of the facts supporting the request and which must include, *inter alia*, the following particulars: (a) a description of the infringement; (b) the circumstances under which the alleged infringement occurred; (c) an assessment of the nature and amount of actual or potential damage; and (d) the relief or remedy sought.

It is specified that the modes of dispute settlement applied (Rule 24) shall be in accordance with the relevant provisions of the Convention[22] and with the first paragraph of Article 33 of the Charter of the United Nations.[23] The reference to Article 33 is intended to leave the choice entirely to the discretion of the parties. The idea is that the panel established should be acceptable to the parties to the dispute.

The settlement procedures endorsed by the Procedures are: "mediation" (Section A, Rules 26 to 29); "fact-finding" (Section B, Rules 30 to 32); "conciliation" (Section C, Rules 33 to 35); and "arbitration" (Section E, Rules 38 to 40). The latter makes the decision binding on the parties.

It should be noted that the Commission must issue a final report on its findings and recommendations which, with respect to the fact-finding and conciliation mechanisms, must include, in accordance with CP Rule 3.5:

(a) a description of facts relating to the dispute;

(b) the findings and conclusions with respect to the dispute, as reflected in the panel report if confirmed, including:
   (i) whether a breach of confidentiality has occurred;
   (ii) the responsibility for that breach;
   (iii) the nature and amount of the damage caused by the breach;
   (iv) observations on reasons and circumstances which led to the occurrence of the breach; and,

(c) recommendations concerning the remedy for the situation and the prevention of the occurrence of similar events, as well as time limits within which each party must inform the Commission of its decision concerning the recommendations made.

11. Conclusion

This study demonstrates the need to preserve the fine balance struck by the negotiators of the CWC between the monitoring of compliance with the provisions, on the one hand, and the necessary protection of confidential information, on the other. The two components of the verification-confidentiality pair are equally indispensable, since one can only function properly if the other does too.

As no human institution is infallible, both regimes, verification and confidentiality, are susceptible to evasion and error. If confidentiality is the mechanism infringed, the first thing to do is to establish who committed the infringement and who is responsible for

[22] Article XIV of the Convention.

[23] Article 33 of the Charter of the United Nations (Chapter VI on the peaceful settlement of disputes).

carrying out the investigation. It follows from what has already been said that there are four possible infringers and three possible investigators. Thus, if the breach occurs:

- within a State Party, then the latter will be responsible for the investigation;
- within the Secretariat, then the Director-General will be responsible for the investigation;
- if the infringer is a State Party, then the CC, as the competent OPCW body, will be responsible for the investigation; and,
- if the infringer is the Organisation as a whole or the Director-General himself, then the CC will likewise be responsible for the investigation.

This analysis, although it shows who is responsible for conducting investigations and imposing sanctions, does not tell us much about the implementation of the decisions. Admittedly, a gap exists but, at the same time, experience teaches us that until we have a legally binding instrument to bridge it, it is practical and appropriate to improve and continue relying upon the traditional diplomatic mechanisms.

This does not mean that we should abandon our efforts to find a better solution. Events such as the holding of the OPCW Symposium on cooperation and legal assistance and the present publication are helpful in this respect and extend beyond the scope of the Chemical Weapons Convention. The opportunity for reflection, from so many different points of view, makes this a truly forward-looking initiative which, we are certain, will constitute a turning point in the progress of international regimes in particular, and multilateralism in general.

NATIONAL IMPLEMENTATION OF CONFIDENTIALITY OBLIGATIONS UNDER THE CHEMICAL WEAPONS CONVENTION: THE NEW ZEALAND EXPERIENCE

Treasa Dunworth*

1. INTRODUCTION

The need to protect confidential information is a key element in successful and effective implementation of the Chemical Weapons Convention.[1] Reflecting this, discussions on the confidentiality regime have developed hand in hand with negotiations on the verification system itself, because such an intrusive system of verification could never have been contemplated without the guarantees that a confidentiality system would bring. Thus, the proposed confidentiality regime was an important issue during the negotiations in Geneva,[2] during the preparatory phase in The Hague,[3] and has continued to be an important facet of the present implementation phase.[4] Over time, the discussions have varied in their focus, depending upon the particular context or concern, for example, security concerns with chemical weapons, the intellectual property concerns of civilian industry, and the need to protect the investment environment of multinational chemical corporations. What has remained constant, however, is agreement on the need to have an effective confidentiality regime to co-exist with and complement the intrusive verification system.

For all the attention that the issue has received at the level of international implementation, it has received relatively little in the context of national implementation. This is surprising given that the confidentiality regime can only be as effective as its weakest link, and if provisions at a national level are not altogether satisfactory, then the overall verification system will be adversely affected. A possible explanation for the relative neglect may lie in the emphasis which was placed on various unresolved issues pertaining to

* Lecturer in Public International Law, University of Auckland.

[1] 1993 Convention on the Prohibition of the Development, Production, Stockpiling and Use of Chemical Weapons and on Their Destruction, entered into force on 29 April 1997. Text, as corrected and changed, available at http://www.opcw.org.

[2] See for example the discussion in Krutzsch & Trapp, A Commentary on the Chemical Weapons Convention (1994) at 510-511.

[3] The Preparatory Commission for the Organisation for the Prohibition of Chemical Weapons (OPCW) was established by participating States as the Convention opened for signature. The Preparatory Commission was tasked with preparing for entry into force of the Convention and to that end, it established a number of Expert Groups. Its Expert Group on Confidentiality was responsible for further developing the Convention's provisions on confidentiality. For a detailed report on its work, see periodic reports in *Building the Organization for the Prohibition of Chemical Weapons*, The CBW Conventions Bulletin Issue No. 23 (March 1994) up to and including Issue No. 36 (June 1997) (available on http://www.sussex.ac.uk/spru/hsp/).

[4] See for example, Report of Pugwash Meeting No. 234, *CWC Implementation: Balancing Confidentiality and Transparency* (15-17 May 1998), Pugwash Newsletter, Vol. 35, No. 2 (November 1998).

R. Yepes-Enríquez and L. Tabassi. (eds.), Treaty Enforcement and International Cooperation in Criminal Matters

confidentiality and the growing concerns in the first years of implementation on the lack of compliance with the declaration obligations. These factors may have combined to overshadow the need to examine progress with national implementation of confidentiality obligations, such as ensuring that procedures are in place to cover the handling, transmission and storage of confidential information at the national level, and to develop mechanisms to deal with any breach of confidentiality within the State Party.[5]

This chapter examines the obligations of States Parties (as opposed to the obligations of the OPCW or of the Director-General and his staff) regarding confidentiality, and how these might be taken into account in the national implementation project. The New Zealand experience is considered as an example. Section 2 of the chapter provides an overview and discussion of the confidentiality provisions of the Convention with particular emphasis on those provisions which pertain to States Parties' obligations. In doing so, I identify a gap in the system as it is currently being operated, and two proposals are put forward which would help to close that gap. Section 3 turns to implementation at a national level and examines New Zealand's implementation of the Convention as it relates to confidentiality. The chapter explains the debate which took place in New Zealand about the confidentiality provisions in the course of enacting the implementing legislation. At the heart of the debate lay the tension which is so familiar from the international level — the need to reconcile confidentiality and transparency. Concluding that while the legislation is quite satisfactory in how it deals with protecting confidentiality, I argue that it could have gone further in promoting transparency at the national level. In particular, the accountability mechanisms introduced in the United Kingdom and Australia might serve as useful models in achieving greater transparency while holding fast to the fundamental principle of confidentiality.

2. Overview of the Convention's Provisions vis-à-vis Confidentiality

Taken as a whole, the provisions in the Convention dealing with confidentiality strive to achieve a balance between two competing interests: the need to engender confidence in the verification regime, while at the same time ensuring that confidential information (whether that be commercial information or chemical weapons related information) is protected. In other words, the provisions address the need to balance transparency and confidentiality. These twin elements permeate the general confidentiality provisions. For example, Article VI, paragraph 10,[6] provides that:

> In conducting verification activities, the Technical Secretariat shall avoid undue intrusion into the State Party's chemical activities for purposes not prohibited under this Convention and, in particular, abide by the provisions set forth in the Annex on the Protection of Confidential Information.

[5] For a brief overview of the various responsibilities arising from the Convention, see Gualtieri, Kellman & Tanzman, *Disarmament and Disclosure — How Arms Control Verification Can Proceed Without Threatening Confidential Business Information* 36 Harvard Int'l LJ 71 (1995) 95-101.

[6] Article VI, entitled "Activities not Prohibited under this Convention," deals with verification of non-military uses of chemicals.

In Article VIII, paragraph 5,[7] a similar obligation is imposed on the Organisation:

> The Organization shall conduct its verification activities provided for under this Convention in the least intrusive manner possible consistent with the timely and efficient accomplishment of their objectives. It shall request only the information and data necessary to fulfil its responsibilities under this Convention. It shall take every precaution to protect the confidentiality of information on civil and military activities and facilities coming to its knowledge in the implementation of this Convention and, in particular, shall abide by the provisions set forth in the Confidentiality Annex.

Even in the realm of challenge inspections,[8] confidentiality is protected with Article IX, subparagraph 11(c), conferring on the State Party being inspected the right "to take measures to protect sensitive installations, and to prevent disclosure of confidential information and data, not related to this Convention."

Perhaps the most relevant in the context of this discussion, however, is Article VII, paragraph 6,[9] which imposes an obligation on the *State Party*, as opposed to the Organisation or Secretariat, to protect confidential information. The paragraph provides:

> Each State Party shall treat as confidential and afford special handling to information and data that it receives in confidence from the Organization in connection with the implementation of this Convention. It shall treat such information and data exclusively in connection with its rights and obligations under this Convention and in accordance with the provisions set forth in the Confidentiality Annex.

This provision is essential in the light of the fact that each State Party has a right to receive information from the Organisation about other States Parties on their compliance record. Paragraph 2(b) of the Confidentiality Annex[10] provides:

> Data required by States Parties to be assured of the continued compliance with this Convention by other States Parties *shall* be routinely provided to them. (emphasis added)

Reinforcing the more general obligation to protect confidential information of Article VII, paragraph 6 of the Convention, paragraph 4 of the Confidentiality Annex provides:

> Each State Party shall treat information which it receives from the Organization in accordance with the level of confidentiality established for that information. Upon request, a State Party shall provide details on the handling of information provided to it by the Organization.

---

[7] Article VIII, entitled "The Organization," essentially contains the institutional and constitutional provisions of the Convention.

[8] In addition to allowing for routine inspections to verify the accuracy of declarations from States Parties, the Convention provides for challenge inspections to clarify and resolve any questions concerning possible non-compliance. The inspections are short notice and there is no provision for refusal. See Article IX (8-25).

[9] Article VII is entitled "National Implementation Measures".

[10] Article XVII of the Convention provides that the Annexes form an "integral part" of the Convention.

Supplementing these Convention provisions, subparagraph 1.2 of Part VI of the OPCW Policy on Confidentiality[11] provides that:

> States Parties which receive confidential information from the Organisation are required to protect it in accordance with obligations under paragraph 6 of Article VII and paragraph 4 of the Confidentiality Annex. States Parties should therefore establish or adopt suitable means of handling and protection for OPCW confidential information in a manner consistent with these principles.

And later, subparagraph 2.11:

> The method of provision of confidential information to a State Party by the Organisation shall be based on the need for continuity of protection, at a level linked to the sensitivity of the information. The receiving State Party is obliged in turn to afford such confidential information the special handling appropriate to its level of sensitivity, and *shall provide*, upon request, details on the handling of information provided to it by the Organisation. (emphasis added)

A literal reading of subparagraph 2(b) means that a State Party has the right to receive data on other States' declarations even if it has not provided information itself on how the information will be handled. This literal reading has so far prevailed in The Hague in that States Parties are being provided with information pursuant to subparagraph 2(b) of the Annex even when they have not honoured their obligation under paragraph 4. At the Fifth Session of the Conference of the States Parties, the Director-General reported that, as of 31 December 1999, only 42 of 128 States Parties had provided the requisite information to the Organisation.[12] Thus, a chasm has opened up in the confidentiality regime.

Such a literal reading is by no means inevitable. On traditional rules of treaty interpretation, the right to the information ought to be interpreted in a manner consistent with the other provisions of the Annex and in particular, with the Convention itself. Thus, the right to the information provided under subparagraph 2(b) of the Annex is limited by the obligation under paragraph 4 of the Annex to protect that information and upon request, to provide details on the handling of information. Further, the right should be read in conjunction with the provisions in the Convention itself. Reading Article VII, paragraphs 5[13] and 6 together, States are obliged not only to put in place procedures for confidential handling but to notify the Organisation of those measures as well. Adopting this interpretation,

[11] The OPCW Policy on Confidentiality elaborates the more general provisions in the Annex and taken together, they form the basis of the OPCW's system for managing confidential information. The Policy was adopted by the First Session of the Conference of the States Parties on 16 May 1997 (OPCW doc. C-I/DEC.13 (16 May 1997)) and is reprinted in L. Tabassi (ed.), OPCW: The Legal Texts (1999) at 209-254. Also available at the Organisation's website (www.opcw.org).

[12] Report by the Director General on Implementation of the Regime Governing the Handling of Confidential Information by the Secretariat in 1999, OPCW doc. C-V/DG.5 (8 May 2000) at para. 3. The report does not provide any information on how many States Parties have been provided with information pursuant to paragraph 2(b).

[13] Article VII(5) provides that "Each State Party shall inform the Organization of the legislative and administrative measures taken to implement this Convention."

whereby the right is conditional on the obligation being honoured, would be consistent with the supplementary requirements in the Confidentiality Policy.

To adopt this alternative interpretation, the Director-General could issue a Note to States Parties notifying them that, as the officer with primary responsibility for ensuring that confidential information is protected,[14] this is the interpretation which will be henceforth adopted. While such a course of action would seem to be within the Director-General's legal powers, it is unlikely to be politically acceptable. Therefore, an alternative course of action could be for the States Parties themselves to adopt a resolution calling on all States to observe their obligations pursuant to Article VII and the Confidentiality Policy prior to exercising their rights to information pursuant to the Annex. Such a resolution would be squarely within the spirit of the treaty and is entirely consistent with the actual terms of the treaty. It would serve to strengthen the confidentiality regime as a whole, both in terms of its political impact, stressing the importance of effective protection of confidential information at the national level, and its practical effect, in that States would have an immediate incentive to ensure that national protections are in place and that the Organisation is notified of those protections.

3. New Zealand and the Chemical Weapons Convention

Whatever difficulties may exist as regards the linkages between the right to information and the confidentiality obligations, there is no confusion at all as regards the obligations on States to protect confidential information. The remainder of this chapter considers the New Zealand experience as it pertains to its national implementation programme relating to confidentiality. I argue that while the legislation is satisfactory in terms of how New Zealand protects the confidential information it receives from the Organisation, it is less satisfactory in how it deals with the other side of the confidentiality equation — promoting transparency to the extent possible.

New Zealand was one of the original States Parties to the Convention, having deposited its instrument of ratification on 15 July 1996. Its implementing legislation, the Chemical Weapons (Prohibition) Act 1996, was enacted prior to ratification.[15]

Section 27 of the Act deals with the confidentiality aspects of the Convention and provides:

> (1) Every person must keep confidential any information that is given pursuant to this Act or the Convention concerning the affairs of another person.
>
> (2) Such information may be disclosed only with the consent of the person to whose affairs it relates or for the purpose of
>
> a) enabling New Zealand to fulfil its obligations under the Convention; or
>
> b) the enforcement of this Act; or,
>
> c) dealing with an emergency involving public safety.

[14] Paragraph 2 of the Annex on Confidentiality provides that the "Director-General shall have the primary responsibility for ensuring the protection of confidential information."

[15] The legislation is available electronically from http://rangi.knowledge-basket.co.nz/gpacts/.

(3) Every person who contravenes this section commits an offence, and is liable on summary conviction to imprisonment for a term not exceeding one year or a fine not exceeding $100,000.[16]

The intention of this provision was explained in the Explanatory Memorandum attached to the Bill, that is, to protect "the confidentiality of information obtained in the course of the administration of the Act, subject to specified exceptions." The Memorandum continued "The provisions of the Bill in this respect are intended to ensure full compliance with the Convention and its Confidentiality Annex."[17] It would seem to be closely modelled on the Canadian legislation[18] and the Australian Act.[19]

It was evident from the Bill's introduction to Parliament that the confidentiality clause (then Clause 28) would attract considerable debate. Speaking to the House on introducing the Bill for its First Reading, the then Minister of Foreign Affairs and Trade, Don MacKinnon, acknowledged the difficulties it might face but noted that the clause had been included in the Bill in order to engender confidence within New Zealand industry, as well as to ensure that New Zealand would be able to honour its obligations under the Convention.[20] In the debate that followed, confidentiality was indeed a key concern, being raised by almost every Member who rose to speak.[21] The confidentiality clause was also the subject of keen debate in the course of the select committee process. The Bill was referred to the Foreign Affairs and Defence Select Committee for examination, in the course of which it received detailed submissions from the Legislation Advisory Committee (LAC) on a number of issues, including the confidentiality clause.

One of the key concerns raised by the LAC was that while the Convention explicitly requires New Zealand to keep confidential information received *from* the Organisation, it is entirely silent about any confidentiality requirement regarding information received *within* New Zealand for subsequent transmission to the OPCW by way of declaration. Thus, the LAC argued that the legislation, by covering both categories of information, was drawn more broadly than required by the Convention.[22]

The LAC is perfectly correct in its observation that the clause (and now legislation) protects information from the OPCW and from New Zealand industry. However, it is entirely appropriate that the legislation is drafted in this way because, while the Convention does not explicitly impose any obligation of confidentiality in relation to information received from sources within the State Party itself, it can be argued that there is an implicit obligation to protect such information. Article VII, paragraph 1, provides that:

---

16 At the time of writing, worth approximately US$42,000.00.

17 Explanatory Memorandum to Bill No.139-1 (1995) at iii.

18 Section 17, An Act to implement the Convention on the Prohibition of the Development, Production, Stockpiling and Use of Chemical Weapons and on Their Destruction (also called: Chemical Weapons Convention Implementing Act).

19 Section 102 Chemical Weapons (Prohibition) Act 1994 (as amended).

20 *New Zealand Parliamentary Debates*, vol. 552, 10569 (12 December 1995).

21 See, for example, the statements of Joy McLauchlan, *New Zealand Parliamentary Debates*, vol 552, 10572 (12 December 1995), Geoff Braybrooke, *id.* at 10573 and Pete Hodgson, *id.* at 10576.

22 Legislation Advisory Committee, *Submission to the Foreign Affairs and Defence Select Committee on the Chemical Weapons (Prohibition) Bill*, 21 February 1996 at para. 7. On file with the author. See also *Report of the Ministry of Foreign Affairs*, note 18 at 5-6. On file with the author.

> Each State Party shall, in accordance with its constitutional processes adopt *the necessary measures* to implement its obligations under this Convention. (emphasis added)

New Zealand will only be able to comply with its obligations under the Convention if it has the full support and cooperation of industry. This will only be possible if industry continues to be confident that its intellectual property investment will be safeguarded against possible abuse. This has long been accepted at the international level, reflected in the ongoing involvement of industry representatives in the negotiations in Geneva, the preparatory period in The Hague and now, in the implementation phase. Just as the need for industry's cooperation is ongoing with implementation, the need to maintain confidence is ongoing. An assurance that first, the information will be treated as confidential, and second, that there are clear provisions in place to deal with any breaches, is essential. Thus, while the Convention does not explicitly require that domestic implementing legislation covers internally obtained information from industry, one can argue that the overall requirement to adopt whatever measures are necessary to ensure the effective implementation of the Convention comprises an implicit requirement that the legislation cover this information.[23]

At a more fundamental level, the LAC's submission is based on a concern about how to reconcile two radically different cultures — the culture of confidentiality emanating from the Chemical Weapons Convention, and the principle of availability enshrined in New Zealand's Official Information Act 1982.[24] Section 5 of that Act creates the principle of availability, that is, that official information is to be made available on request unless there is good reason for withholding it. This principle reversed the presumption of secrecy which had previously prevailed and it epitomises the trend in recent decades towards more open and transparent government.[25]

The LAC was of the view that the Official Information Act provided sufficient protection to satisfy the confidentiality requirements in the Chemical Weapons Convention. Although the principle of availability is widely drawn, there are a number of exceptions in the legislation which would seem to cover the information received pursuant to the Chemical Weapons Convention (whether from the OPCW or from national industry). Section 6(a) provides that information can be withheld if making it available would be likely to prejudice the security, defence or international relations of New Zealand. Section 6(b) allows information to be withheld if making it available would prejudice the entrusting of information to New Zealand by an international organisation and Section 9 allows information to be withheld to protect a trade secret or to prevent prejudice to a commercial position.

The advantage of relying on these exceptions to protect confidential information is that the general scheme of the Official Information Act and its culture of transparency would be preserved. Or, to put it another way, it was felt that by allowing the Chemical Weapons Bill to deal separately with the issue of confidentiality, the coherence of the existing system would be undermined. A detailed analysis of this debate is outside the scope of this

[23] See also Fox & Mathews, *The Future Chemical Weapons Convention and its National Implementation*, in Poole & Guthrie (eds), Verification Report 1992, 173-187 at 181.

[24] The legislation is available electronically from http://rangi.knowledge-basket.co.nz/gpacts/.

[25] See generally, New Zealand Law Commission, *Review of the Official Information Act 1982*, Report No. 40 (1997). For a recent discussion by the New Zealand Court of Appeal of this trend in the context of a public interest immunity case, see *Choudry v Attorney-General* (1999) 3 NZLR 399.

chapter, encompassing as it does a whole range of issues. However, in the specific context of the Chemical Weapons legislation, a number of points can usefully be made. First, given the critical importance of confidentiality in the Convention's implementation, it is politically valuable to address the issue in the implementing legislation. Second, it is preferable to rely on a more recent specific provision should there be any question about the status of information received under the Convention, rather than relying on legislation enacted more than 15 years before the Convention entered into force and with no specific connection to its operation. Third, in the event that there is a dispute about the precise meaning of section 27, the courts would be guided by the purpose of the legislation, that is, to implement the Chemical Weapons Convention. For these reasons, it seems appropriate to deal with the confidentiality issue outside of the Official Information Act, and the legislation as it stands in this respect is to be recommended.

4. The Need for Accountability

The very fact that section 27 as it stands leans more towards confidentiality than transparency raises the question of how else transparency might be promoted while continuing to protect the confidentiality provisions. This is particularly relevant where, as in this case, the Executive has been given increased powers in the form of being able to require the provision of certain information and allowing access to the OPCW for on-site inspections.[26] In my view, the New Zealand legislation has not achieved an appropriate balance between confidentiality and transparency, being weighted in favour of the former.

One possible means of redressing that imbalance can be found within the implementing legislation of the United Kingdom, as well as in the Australian legislation. In the United Kingdom, provision was made in the implementing legislation whereby the Secretary of State is required to report annually to Parliament on the operation of the Act.[27] An Advisory Committee was also established, which acts as a consultative structure facilitating contact between the industrial, scientific and academic communities affected by the Convention.[28] The Advisory Committee has the opportunity to consider, in its draft form, each report prepared by the Secretary of State, and it can communicate any concerns about the operation of the Act directly to the Secretary of State. The reporting mechanism and the role of the Advisory Committee mean that the activities of the Executive in implementing the

[26] See Sections 12-18, Chemical Weapons (Prohibition) Act 1996.

[27] Section 33, Chemical Weapons Act 1996 (UK). The transparency/confidentiality tension was discussed in great detail as the UK legislation was being drafted. See in particular J. Perry Robinson, *'Dual use', transparency, and the Chemical Weapons Convention: Approaches used in the UK implementing legislation*, paper presented to the Sixth Workshop of the Pugwash Study Group on the Implementation of the Chemical and Biological Weapons Convention, 11-13 October 1996, Noordwijk, The Netherlands; J. Perry Robinson, *The Chemical Weapons Bill Background Briefing*, paper prepared for the Royal Society of Chemistry for Members of Parliament, 20 November 1995; J. Perry Robinson, *A Commentary on the Legislation Needed to Implement the Chemical Weapons Convention in the United Kingdom*, discussion paper presented to the Harvard Sussex Program London CBW Seminar, King's College London, 27 September 1995, and N. Sims & J. Perry Robinson, *Aspects of the Chemical Weapons Bill*, International Security Information Service Briefing No. 48 (28 November 1995). All papers on file with the author.

[28] The Committee is not established by statute. See J. Perry Robinson, *'Dual use', transparency, and the Chemical Weapons Convention: Approaches used in the UK implementing legislation*, *id.* at 14-16.

Convention come under the scrutiny of Parliament, but not the world at large. In this way, greater transparency is achieved without sacrificing confidential information.

Similarly, in Australia the Director of the Chemical Weapons Convention Office must give to the Minister of Foreign Affairs and Trade an annual report of the operation of the Chemical Weapons (Prohibition) Act 1994 (as amended).[29] The Minister, in turn, is required to lay the report before Parliament within 15 sitting days.[30] In fact, it was these provisions which formed the basis for the United Kingdom legislation.

5. Conclusions

Effective national implementation of the confidentiality obligations in the Convention is critical to the well-being of the regime as a whole. There is no doubt that the confidentiality regime could be strengthened by linking the confidentiality obligations explicitly to the right to obtain data, and this chapter has proposed at least two means by which this could be achieved. The lesson from the New Zealand experience is that many countries may have to find a way to reconcile a clash of cultures — the now familiar confidentiality/transparency clash — and while it is commendable that New Zealand has not relied on more general legislation to deal with the issue of confidentiality, further steps could be taken to address the transparency concerns, such as those outlined for the United Kingdom or Australia.

[29] Section 96(1).

[30] Section 96(2).

POSSIBLE ACTION IN THE COURTS OF THE NETHERLANDS FOR SERIOUS BREACHES OF THE OPCW'S CONFIDENTIALITY REGIME

Faiza Patel King*

1. Introduction

Commentators on the Convention on the Prohibition of the Development, Production, Stockpiling and Use of Chemical Weapons and on their Destruction ("Convention") frequently remark on the extraordinary intrusiveness of the verification regime that the treaty establishes. The Convention requires States Parties to provide declarations not only on any chemical weapons and related capabilities, but also on a wide range of toxic chemicals that are used throughout the world for peaceful purposes. In addition to chemical weapons facilities, industrial, medical, research and pharmaceutical facilities are routinely inspected. Moreover, the Convention allows for the possibility of challenge inspections which can take place "any time, anywhere" on the territory of a State Party.

The high level of transparency required by the Convention has its corollary in the stringent confidentiality rules governing the handling of information provided by States Parties to the Secretariat of the Organisation for the Prohibition of Chemical Weapons ("OPCW" or "Organisation") as part of the verification effort.[1]

Within the OPCW, a great deal of attention has been paid to the procedures by which such information should be handled. It is also well-established that, normally, any breaches of confidentiality by members of the Secretariat would be handled by the internal disciplinary mechanisms of the OPCW.[2] In cases of serious breaches of confidentiality, however, the

* Senior Policy Officer, OPCW Secretariat. Any views expressed are those of the author and are not attributable to the OPCW..

[1] The OPCW confidentiality regime extends to the protection of information pertaining to the verification of civil and military activities and facilities. *See* Convention on the Prohibition of the Development, Production, Stockpiling and Use of Chemical Weapons and on their Destruction, Confidentiality Annex (hereinafter "CA") Part A, paragraph 1. The regime does not cover other types of sensitive information, such as personnel or financial information relating to the OPCW.

[2] It should be noted that the confidentiality of information provided to the Secretariat could also be compromised by persons outside the Secretariat. The Secretariat is required, under the Convention, to provide certain information (which may be classified) to States Parties upon request. For example, the Verification Annex (hereinafter "VA") provides that a list of plant sites declared under Part VII thereof, and specified information relating to such plant sites, shall be transmitted by the Secretariat to States Parties upon request; VA Part VII, paragraph 11. The VA contains similar requirements with respect to Schedule 3 plant sites and facilities producing unscheduled discrete organic chemicals; VA Part VIII, paragraph 11; Part IX, paragraph 8. In addition, the Secretariat provides classified information to States Parties in the form of its periodic verification implementation reports. Thus, the potential for breaches of confidentiality exists both in the Secretariat and in those institutions of Member States that handle OPCW information.

R. Yepes-Enríquez and L. Tabassi. (eds.), Treaty Enforcement and International Cooperation in Criminal Matters

Director-General may waive the immunity of the staff member concerned and such persons would then be susceptible to national jurisdiction.

The issue of how such serious breaches of confidentiality would be handled by national jurisdictions was considered by the Preparatory Commission for the OPCW. During the discussions of the Expert Group on Confidentiality of the Preparatory Commission, the possibility was raised on several occasions that the Host Country — i.e., the Netherlands — would be the appropriate forum for actions against OPCW staff for breaches of confidentiality. Indeed, specific proposals were made in this regard by the Chair of the Expert Group and the Netherlands delegation.

Although these proposals did not mature into a decision, the Netherlands would certainly be a logical place to take action against an OPCW employee for a serious breach of confidentiality.[3] The considerations leading to such a conclusion include the following: the Organisation's headquarters is located in the Netherlands; its information is stored there; OPCW staff members generally reside in the Netherlands; and it is highly probable that at least some of the acts relating to a breach will have occurred in the Netherlands. However, in the absence of an agreement with the Host Country on its exercise of jurisdiction in such cases, the matter would be settled in accordance with normal Dutch law. This paper will therefore consider the contours of the applicable law — of the OPCW and of the Netherlands — to indicate how the Dutch courts would treat actions based on serious breaches of confidentiality by an OPCW employee.

2. Confidentiality Obligations of OPCW Employees

The basic confidentiality obligations of OPCW staff are set out in the Confidentiality Annex to the Convention.[4] The Director-General has primary responsibility for ensuring the protection of confidential information and is obliged to establish a stringent regime governing the handling of confidential information by the Secretariat in accordance with certain guidelines.[5] The section of the Confidentiality Annex that is devoted to the "Employment and Conduct of Personnel in the Technical Secretariat" contains rules limiting staff members' access to confidential information, procedures for notifying States Parties of the names of staff members who will have access to confidential information, and training requirements. This section also specifically enumerates the duties of staff members with regard to the use and disclosure of confidential information. It provides as follows:

> The Director-General, the inspectors and the other members of the staff shall not disclose even after termination of their functions to any unauthorized persons any confidential information coming to their knowledge in the performance of their official duties. They shall not communicate to any State, organization or person outside the

[3] Such an action could, of course, also be brought in another country (e.g., the home country of the employee or the home country of the entity damaged by the breach). The availability of such actions would obviously depend on the municipal law of the country concerned.

[4] The basic framework of the Confidentiality Annex (hereinafter "CA") has been elaborated on by a number of documents, including the OPCW Policy on Confidentiality and the OPCW Manual of Confidentiality Procedure.

[5] CA Part A, paragraph 2.

> Technical Secretariat any information to which they have access in connection with their activities in relation to any State Party. . . .
> The staff shall enter into individual secrecy agreements with the Technical Secretariat covering their period of employment and a period of five years after it is terminated.[6]

These obligations are reiterated and further elaborated in the Staff Regulations[7] and Rules[8] of the OPCW. The Staff Regulations contain the usual provisions relating to the status of OPCW employees as international civil servants who owe their loyalty solely to the Organisation.[9] In addition, the obligation of confidentiality is specifically imposed as follows:

> Staff Members of the Secretariat shall not disclose even after termination of their functions to any unauthorised person, organisation or other entity any confidential information coming to their knowledge in the performance of their official duties. They shall also not communicate to any State, organisation or person outside the Secretariat any information, to which they have access in connection with their activities, in relation to any State Party.[10]

Furthermore, in accordance with the Confidentiality Annex, the OPCW Staff Rules provide that, "in evaluating job performance, specific attention shall . . . be given to the staff member's record regarding the protection of confidential information"[11] and require staff members to enter into individual secrecy agreements with the Secretariat.[12]

In sum, the Convention and the OPCW Staff Regulations and Rules make clear the obligation of OPCW employees not to reveal confidential information that they acquire in the course of their duties. As an indicator of the stringency of this obligation, each staff member is required to enter into a secrecy agreement with the Organisation and evaluation of a staff member's respect for confidentiality rules is made a mandatory part of performance appraisal.

3. OPCW Procedure in Case of a Breach of Confidentiality

In case of a breach of confidentiality, the Convention and the OPCW Staff Regulations and Rules envisage a process that has two stages, one internal and one external. In the first (internal) stage, the Director-General is obliged to investigate cases where: (a) in his judgement there is sufficient indication that obligations concerning the protection of confidential information have been violated; or (b) a State Party makes an allegation concerning a breach of confidentiality.[13] If the investigation reveals that a staff member has violated his or her

---

[6] CA Part B, paragraphs 7 & 9.
[7] OPCW Staff Regulations, OPCW-TS/DGB/3, 15 September 1999.
[8] OPCW Interim Staff Rules, OPCW-TS/DGB/4, 15 November 1999. These rules are being provisionally applied until their approval by the OPCW Executive Council.
[9] *See e.g.*, OPCW Staff Regulations 1.1, 1.4, 1.5 & 1.10.
[10] OPCW Staff Regulation 1.6(b)
[11] OPCW Interim Staff Rule 1.6.01(c).
[12] OPCW Interim Staff Rule 1.6.02.
[13] CA Part D, paragraph 19.

obligation to protect confidential information, "[t]he Director-General shall impose appropriate punitive and disciplinary measures."[14] Possible disciplinary measures and the procedures by which the Director-General may impose them are set out in the Staff Regulations and Rules.

The second (external) stage is normally reached only in cases involving a serious breach of confidentiality. "In cases of serious breaches, the immunity from jurisdiction [of a staff member] may be waived by the Director-General."[15] Neither the Convention nor the OPCW Staff Regulations and Rules contain guidance on what would constitute a "serious" breach of confidentiality. Presumably, the seriousness of a breach of confidentiality would be measured by factors similar to those used to measure the seriousness of other types of employee misconduct. Thus, the Director-General would primarily have to evaluate: the intent of the employee (e.g., was the breach intentional or accidental? was it motivated by personal gain? was it undertaken at the behest of an outside entity?) and the extent of damage caused by the breach.

Another avenue by which a staff member could find himself or herself vulnerable to legal action for breach of confidentiality is if the staff member occupies a position at a level below that at which full diplomatic immunity attaches (P 5). OPCW officials below this level enjoy only functional immunity: their immunity from criminal jurisdiction and their personal inviolability does "not extend to acts performed outside the course of their official duties."[16] Who decides whether a particular act was performed outside the course of a staff member's official duties? In light of a recent advisory opinion issued by the International Court of Justice, it seems fairly certain that this decision is within the discretion of the Director-General.[17]

In both of the scenarios discussed above, the Director-General would be the ultimate arbiter (either by waiving immunity or by finding that particular conduct was outside a staff member's official duties) of whether a staff member could be prosecuted in national courts. Where the Director-General lifts the protection afforded to the staff member, such staff member would be subject to the possibility of criminal and civil action for the breach. The imposition of liability would depend on whether there was jurisdiction in the court where the action was brought and on whether there was a substantive cause of action or crime for which the employee could be pursued. These issues are considered below in the context of Dutch law.

---

[14] CA Part D, paragraph 20.

[15] CA Part D, paragraph 20.

[16] OPCW Headquarters Agreement, Article 18(d), annexed to C-I/DEC.59 dated 14 May 1997.

[17] *Difference Relating to Immunity from Legal Process of a Special Rapporteur of the Commission of Human Rights*, ICJ Advisory Opinion of 29 April 1999, paragraphs 47-56.

4. Civil Action in the Netherlands

4.1 Jurisdiction

The courts of the Netherlands normally exercise jurisdiction in civil matters if the defendant is resident in the Netherlands.[18] Thus, the Dutch courts would clearly be able to exercise jurisdiction in cases where the OPCW employee is resident in the Netherlands at the time of the initiation of an action against him or her.

In addition, under the 1968 EC Convention on Jurisdiction and the Enforcement of Judgments in Civil and Commercial Matters ("Brussels Convention"), the Dutch courts have jurisdiction over persons domiciled in the parties to that treaty (i.e., the European Union countries) with respect to certain categories of matters, which are listed below:

(1) In matters relating to a contract, in the courts for the place of performance of the obligation in question; in matters relating to individual contracts of employment, this place is that where the employee habitually carries out his work, or if the employee does not habitually carry out his work in any one country, the employer may also be sued in the courts for the place where the business which engaged the employee was or is situated....

(2) In matters relating to tort, delict or quasi-delict, in the courts for the place where the harmful event occurred.[19]

Thus, for OPCW employees domiciled anywhere in the European Union, the Brussels Convention would allow the Dutch courts to have jurisdiction in matters relating to their employment contracts and in any tort action for breach of confidentiality committed in the Netherlands.

Even with the availability of Brussels Convention-based civil jurisdiction, there would undoubtedly be situations where the Dutch courts will not have jurisdiction for the full range of actions that could be brought in cases of breaches of confidentiality. In particular, certain types of tort claims could not be brought. For example, an inspector (who is a citizen of State X) goes on an inspection in State Y. The inspector comes across certain confidential information which is revealed to a third party outside the Netherlands. The information causes damage to a company located in State Y. By the time this breach is discovered, the inspector has returned to State X (which is outside the European Union) and is no longer resident in the Netherlands. The Dutch courts probably would not have any jurisdiction in a tort claim brought by either the injured party or by the OPCW: the

[18] Dutch Code of Civil Procedure, Article 126. These provisions of the code were extended to international cases by the Dutch Supreme Court in *Goes v. Schönstedt*, Nederlandse Jurisprudentie 1941, No. 312 (5 December 1940). It should be noted that Dutch courts have also sometimes exercised jurisdiction in cases where the action is brought by a claimant that has its residence in the Netherlands. However, courts outside the Netherlands have tended to refuse to enforce judgments grounded on this basis of jurisdiction and the new Dutch Code of Civil Procedure that will enter into force on 1 January 2002 will severely curtail such jurisdiction.

[19] Brussels Convention, Article 5. These jurisdictional grounds would also allow the bringing of suit in the courts of the other Contracting Parties to the Brussels Convention.

defendant is not resident in the Netherlands, the presumable plaintiff[20] from State Y is not resident in the Netherlands, and the key events did not occur in the Netherlands. In such a case, the injured party would have to attempt to bring suit in State X or, depending on the applicable municipal law, bring suit in State Y and attempt to enforce it in State X.

In an effort to ensure the jurisdiction of the Dutch courts, it was suggested during the discussions of the OPCW Preparatory Commission that the secrecy agreement which all staff members are required to sign include a provision acknowledging the jurisdiction of the Dutch courts for breaches thereof. This would not, however, be a satisfactory solution. Although the Brussels Convention provides for the possibility of choosing a forum for the settlement of disputes, it contains an exception for "matters relating to individual contracts of employment". If the secrecy agreement were considered a matter relating to the employment contract (which seems likely), the conferring of jurisdiction by the agreement would not be enforced on that basis. Moreover, the secrecy agreement could not create rights for third parties to bring actions against OPCW employees because such parties probably would not be considered to have the requisite "legal relationship."

4.2 CAUSE OF ACTION

The issue of jurisdiction is obviously linked to the question of what cause of action could be brought against the OPCW employee. As touched on above, the secrecy agreement signed by OPCW staff members, on its face, creates contractual obligations on the part of the employee vis-à-vis the employer. The Staff Regulations and Rules of the OPCW similarly set out the obligations of staff members vis-à-vis the Organisation. Thus the OPCW would certainly have a cause of action against its former employee for breach of contract.

Third parties would not, however, have a cause of action for breach of contract and would have to rely on a tort action. Article 162 of the Dutch Civil Code sets out the requirements for bringing such an action:

> (1) A person who commits an unlawful act toward another which can be imputed to him must repair the damage which the other person suffers as a consequence thereof.
> (2) Except where there is a ground of justification, the following acts are deemed to be unlawful: the violation of a right, an act or omission violating a statutory duty or a rule of unwritten law pertaining to proper social conduct.
> (3) An unlawful act can be imputed to its author if it results from his fault or from a cause for which he is answerable according to law or common opinion.

It seems likely that a serious breach of confidentiality would be considered an unlawful act under subparagraph (2) above. Such a breach could be characterised as the violation of the right of the OPCW to expect confidentiality from its staff or the violation of the statutory duty that requires an employee to respect the confidential information of its employer.[21] It is unclear, however, whether a breach of confidentiality would constitute a

[20] *See supra* note 18.
[21] Such a duty would be implied from the provisions of the Dutch penal code discussed *infra, section 5.2.*

violation of a "rule of unwritten law pertaining to proper social conduct," the ground on which a tort claim is most often based. Normally third parties would not have a right to expect confidentiality from OPCW employees. However, the situation could be different in light of the well-known obligations of such employees as set forth in the Chemical Weapons Convention and in various official OPCW documents.[22]

5. Criminal Action in the Netherlands

5.1 Jurisdiction

Under Article 2 of the Dutch Penal Code, barring special circumstances, "[t]he criminal law of the Netherlands is applicable to any person who commits a criminal offence within the Netherlands."[23] Accordingly, an OPCW staff member who committed a serious breach of confidentiality could be liable to prosecution in the Netherlands if the relevant facts occurred in the Netherlands. However, with respect to breaches occurring outside the Netherlands (such as in the example described earlier), the criminal law of the Netherlands could be applicable only if the offender was a Dutch citizen. The Dutch Penal Code states that the Netherlands' criminal law applies to any Dutch citizen who commits an offence that is considered a "serious offence" under the criminal law of the Netherlands and is also a criminal offence under the laws of the country where it was committed.[24] The serious offences defined by the Dutch Penal Code include violations of secrecy and theft, and it is almost certain that these two offences (or at least theft) would also be offences under the municipal laws of all other States Parties. In sum, an OPCW staff member who commits a serious breach of confidentiality in the Netherlands or who commits such a breach outside the Netherlands and is a Dutch citizen, could likely be prosecuted in Dutch courts for one of these offences.

5.2 Offences

There are at least two offences under the Dutch Penal Code — violation of secrecy and theft — that could potentially be alleged in case of a serious breach of confidentiality.

The "serious offence" of Violation of Secrecy is defined as follows:

> Article 272
>
> (1) A person by whom any secret which he either knows or should reasonably suspect that he is bound to keep by reason of his office, profession or a legal requirement, or his former office or profession, is intentionally violated is liable to a term of imprisonment of not more than one year or a fine of the fourth category. . . .

[22] *See supra*, section 2.

[23] Title 1, Article 2 of the Dutch Penal Code, The American Series of Foreign Penal Codes Volume 30 (1997). Under Article 3 of the Dutch Penal Code, special circumstances in which the Dutch criminal law would apply even to offences committed outside the Netherlands include situations where the offence constitutes a serious offence against the security of the state or royal dignity, where the offence occurred on board a Dutch vessel or aircraft, or where the offence relates to coins, notes, bonds or certificates issued by the Netherlands.

[24] *Id.*, Article 5(1).

Article 273

(1) A person who intentionally:

(1) discloses specific information related to a commercial, industrial or service organisation in which he is or has been employed, which he was bound to keep secret; or

(2) discloses, or uses for motives of pecuniary gain, data that have been obtained by means of a criminal offence from a computerised device or system of a commercial, industrial or service organisation and that are related to such oganisation, where the data, at the time of disclosure or use, were not generally known and where any disadvantage may ensue from such disclosure or use, is able to a term of imprisonment of not more than six months or a fine of the fourth category. . . .

On the face of it, it appears that a serious breach of confidentiality would constitute disclosure of a secret that an OPCW employee was bound to keep by a legal requirement (such as the OPCW Staff Regulations and Rules and the individual secrecy agreements that staff members sign) that could be prosecuted under Article 272. However, this article is generally construed by Dutch courts as applying only to professional privileges (e.g., the attorney-client privilege) and may not cover the broader employer-employee relationship.

It is unlikely that the OPCW would be considered a "commercial, industrial or service organisation" so as to allow prosecution under Article 272(1). The commentary on this provision of the Dutch Penal Code indicates that it is intended to cover only commercial enterprises. Article 273(2), however, certainly provides an avenue for prosecution if the breach of confidentiality also involved theft of data from a computer. In such cases, however, the prosecution would only take place upon complaint by the organisation's management.[25]

Another possibility would be to prosecute a serious breach of confidentiality as theft. The Dutch Penal Code provides that "[a] person who removes any property belonging in whole or in part to another, with the object of unlawfully appropriating it, is guilty of theft and liable to a term of imprisonment of not more than four years or a fine of the fourth category."[26] A breach of confidentiality — particularly when the breach is deliberate and for personal gain — could be regarded as a theft of information from either the OPCW or the State Party concerned.

6. Conclusion

In sum, the current situation with regard to bringing either a civil action or a criminal prosecution for a serious breach of confidentiality in the courts of the Netherlands is not wholly satisfactory. Utilisation of the courts of the Host Country would certainly work in cases where the employee has not left the Netherlands or where the breach of confidentiality occurred in the Netherlands, but could otherwise be difficult.

The evident difficulties in using the Dutch system for breaches of confidentiality suggests that some or all of these limitations probably exist in municipal laws of other States

[25] Dutch Penal Code Article 273(3).

[26] *Id.*, Article 310.

Parties. This makes it is necessary to consider the establishment of specific mechanisms for pursuing serious breaches of confidentiality in national courts. If the States Parties of the OPCW wish to pursue the matter further, the mechanism that was considered during the Preparatory Commission — i.e., for the OPCW to enter into an arrangement with the Netherlands so that its courts would have concurrent jurisdiction in such cases and other States Parties would assist in the exercise of jurisdiction (e.g., by extraditing defendants or providing evidence) — should be reconsidered.

DISCIPLINING INTERNATIONAL OFFICIALS

Paul C. Szasz*†

1. INTRODUCTION

The supervision of the implementation by States of certain important international treaties through on-site inspections and other control measures carried out by an international, intergovernmental organisation (IGO) by use of its own staff is, in historic terms, still a relatively recent phenomenon, and also a rather rare one. The only organisations that actually operate such control programmes are the International Atomic Energy Agency (IAEA) and the Organisation for the Prohibition of Chemical Weapons (OPCW), and there are only two other likely prospects in the arms control field: the nascent Comprehensive Nuclear-Test-Ban Treaty Organization (CTBTO) and the proposed Organisation for the Prohibition of Bacteriological (Biological) and Toxin Weapons (OPBW).

An important reason why such intrusive control systems are so rare — aside from the reluctance of States to permit such apparent intrusions on their sovereignty — is the real or pretended fear by States that allowing international personnel to examine reports concerning sensitive national activities, and to actually inspect them, could lead to the disclosure and dissemination of commercially valuable or security sensitive information. Consequently, it has been an important preoccupation in constructing such control systems to ensure, as far as possible, that no such unauthorised disclosures and dissemination take place. This, in turn, requires that the international officials who are to receive access to such confidential information be, in the first place, properly trained in the recognition and treatment of such data and, secondly, that they be intensely motivated to preserve such confidentiality by avoiding both careless and intentional disclosures.

The first organisation to face this problem was the IAEA, whose safeguards system was initially established in the early 1960s, but only attained prominence with the application of that system to police compliance with the Nuclear Non-Proliferation Treaty (NPT). Although care was taken from the beginning to ensure the preservation of confidential

* Professor Paul C. Szasz, 1930-2002, was a distinguished scholar and expert on international law. He began his career in practice in 1958 as a Legal Officer at the International Atomic Energy Agency, where he helped design the agency's safeguards system. He then moved to the World Bank, where he created the rules governing the arbitration and reconciliation procedures for the International Center for Settlement of Investment Disputes. In 1971, Prof. Szasz joined the legal department of the United Nations, where helped to establish the International Fund for Agricultural Development and the UN Industrial Development Organization. After his 1989 UN retirement, he helped draft the constitutions of the new States of Namibia and Bosnia and Herzegovina while also teaching at New York University School of Law. The Editors extend their sincere condolences to Prof. Szasz's family, friends and colleagues. His contributions to the field of international law remain as his legacy, and his extensive writtings continue to serve as valuable guidance to practitioners in the field.

R. Yepes-Enríquez and L. Tabassi. (eds.), Treaty Enforcement and International Cooperation in Criminal Matters

data,[1] the problem was not a serious one as long as nuclear reactors were the only subject of controls, and there were severe constraints in place to limit the activities of the inspectors. However, when inspections were extended to chemical reprocessing facilities, and especially when the former constraints on inspections were relaxed in the mid-1990s as a result of the disclosures of secret nuclear activities in Iraq, new concerns about confidentiality arose and more stringent procedures were introduced. These were in part inspired by those that had been included in the 1993 Chemical Weapons Convention[2] ("Convention") establishing the OPCW. In negotiating the Convention, account had naturally been taken of the experience that the IAEA had had up to then in administering its safeguards, as well as of the greater likelihood that valuable information might be obtained in controlling chemical rather than nuclear facilities; consequently, elaborate provisions are included in the treaty itself,[3] and a much more detailed "OPCW Policy on Confidentiality" was adopted by the OPCW Conference of the States Parties at its First Session.[4] The almost complete absence of relevant provisions in the Comprehensive Nuclear-Test-Ban Treaty (CTBT) presumably reflects the fact that the type of inspections foreseen therein are most unlikely to reveal commercially sensitive information.[5] Finally, the preliminary drafts of a Protocol to the Biological Weapons Convention (BWC) to establish an OPBW contained confidentiality provisions clearly based on the elaborate ones of the Chemical Weapons Convention.[6]

All these confidentiality provisions require the respective organisations to take certain measures to identify and to protect confidential information, and to induce those officials who deal with such information to observe these provisions scrupulously. The question to be explored in this chapter is how officials who have been properly trained in this respect can be induced to comply so as not to disclose sensitive data either through carelessness or intentionally.

2. Disciplinary Powers of International Organisations

By the nature of the problem of inducing officials to observe a high degree of sensitivity in protecting information defined as confidential, it is unlikely that positive inducements can be of much utility. It is not a question of rewarding officials who are particularly effective in protecting such information, since all affected staff must show a high degree of compliance if confidentiality is to be preserved, but of punishing the few who carelessly or intentionally do not observe the required standards. Thus it becomes necessary to consider

[1] A brief requirement to that effect is included in Article VII.F of the IAEA Statute.

[2] 1993 Convention on the Prohibition of the Development, Production, Stockpiling and Use of Chemical Weapons and on Their Destruction, entered into force on 29 April 1997. Text, as corrected and changed, available at http://www.opcw.org.

[3] In particular, the elaborate Annex on the Protection of Confidential Information ("Confidentiality Annex") to the Chemical Weapons Convention.

[4] OPCW doc. C-I/DEC.13 (16 May 1997), as amended by C-II/DEC.14 (5 December 1997) and C-II/DEC.14/Corr.1 (19 December 1997).

[5] See Article IV(8) of the CTBT, as well as Part II, paras. 89 and 102 of the Protocol to the Treaty. The Preparatory Commission for the CTBTO was given the task, in the Appendix to the resolution establishing the Commission, of developing "confidentiality procedures", though these appear to relate more to the conduct of States that acquire confidential information about others through the CTBTO.

[6] See the "Confidentiality Provisions" in Annex E to the proposed Protocol to the BWC set out in Annex I to the 1999 Report of the Ad Hoc Group of States Parties to the BWC (BWC/AD HOC GROUP/45 (Part I)).

what the disciplinary powers of international organisations are.

International organisations are not States, which can impose civil or criminal sanctions on their employees. In this respect, IGOs are more like private employers, whose direct disciplinary powers are limited to the employment relationship. Indeed, IGOs are in an even weaker position, for private employers can ultimately resort to their State's legal system to hold an employee accountable for serious transgressions, while IGOs have (as will be discussed later) only limited such possibilities.

Thus the disciplinary measures that IGOs can take, and that are usually provided for in their staff regulations and rules, are basically limited to employment and career-related ones: fines, suspension without pay, demotion and, ultimately, dismissal. In the latter instance, the dismissal may result in the loss of almost all benefits, except perhaps back pay and accumulated pension rights. Organisations, like the IAEA, that participate in the United Nations Joint Staff Pension Fund (UNJSPF) probably do not have the possibility of depriving an official of any pension benefits, no matter what claims they might have against him;[7] the OPCW does foresee the possibility of depriving an official of pension rights.[8] Although never listed as a disciplinary measure, blacklisting of errant officials is likely for those dismissed for serious cause. While the threat of such punishments should generally suffice to prevent an official from handling confidential information carelessly, it obviously will not deter an official who wishes to disclose such data for financial gain (which is likely to far exceed any losses the IGO can impose) or out of ideological motivations.

It should be noted that, in practice, disciplinary measures can hardly be taken against ex-officials, since it is unlikely that the employing IGO will have any effective financial hold on them and obviously no more career-related steps would be relevant.[9]

It should also be considered that, to the extent that the officials concerned, principally inspectors, are not employed on a career basis and particularly if they are employed for relatively short periods, the hold of the employing organisation on them will be correspondingly weakened. This is due in part to the lessened financial involvement that short-term staff have with the IGO, and also because psychologically non-career staff are

---

7 As originally formulated, the Regulations of the UNJSPF did provide for depriving participants who were dismissed on a disciplinary basis of their pension benefits, but that provision was eliminated by the United Nations General Assembly in the 1960s. The United Nations Administrative Tribunal (UNAT) has held that even in the case of a staff member who had been summarily dismissed because he had embezzled large sums from the employing organization, the latter could not require him to reimburse it from his pension benefits by refusing to certify his termination to the Pension Fund until he had agreed to such an arrangement (UNAT Judgement No. 358, *Sherif*, 7 November 1985). The UN Secretary-General's report, cited *infra* note 12, reports on a revision of Administrative Instructions to meet the Tribunal's objections, but admits that the new procedure has yet to be judicially tested (UN doc. A/48/572, paras. 7-8); that report also points out that an attempt to attach pension benefits directly would meet the objection that such benefits are often considered to be a social benefit and, in any event, would require complex arrangements with uncertain consequences (*id.*, paras 9-10).

8 Part IX.1(8) of the OPCW Policy on Confidentiality.

9 The OPCW Policy on Confidentiality does foresee the possibility of disciplining a former staff member (*id.*), but whether the measures proposed would be effective is questionable. It is interesting to note that while OPCW Staff Regulation 1.6(b) prohibits staff members from disclosing information even after the termination of their functions, para. 9 of the Confidentiality Annex to the Chemical Weapons Convention provides that staff are to enter into individual secrecy agreements covering their period of employment and a period of only five years after it is terminated.

likely to maintain their primary loyalty to an outside employer and to their national State.

Would it be possible to strengthen the disciplinary hold IGOs have on members of their staffs? Aside from the measures discussed below (suits against officials; waivers of immunity) that depend for execution on States, there does not seem to be any more that IGOs could do, even theoretically. During the past decade international criminal tribunals operated by IGOs, such as the former Yugoslavia and Rwanda Tribunals established by the United Nations Security Council, and the International Criminal Court established by its own treaty, have been given the power to arrange for convicted persons to be imprisoned by States that volunteer to do so. However, the extension of this possibility to persons "convicted" by an IGO of violating its confidentiality provisions is an unlikely development for the foreseeable future.

3. Suits by International Organisations Against Officials

IGOs have traditionally been reluctant to sue officials in national courts — though generally their legal status explicitly gives IGOs the right to bring legal process[10] — in part because they were reluctant to ventilate their internal affairs in such fora. However, in recent years, as occasional large-scale frauds or embezzlements have come to light, the United Nations has occasionally sought recovery in national courts.

Such suits could only be brought in national courts that have jurisdiction over an official or former official; usually that would imply residence, or at least sufficient presence that effective process can be served. The questions then become: is the applicable legal system such that it permits suits for violation of an IGO's confidentiality rules (on the basis of contract, or the local equivalent of a tort); is recovery possible for damages suffered by someone else than the IGO;[11] is the national legal system likely to be sympathetic to the IGO or to the official, who may have revealed the information in question to the national authorities or national enterprises; and does the official have assets in the jurisdiction that could be seized to satisfy a claim, or can a national judgment be executed in some other State in which such assets are located? Obviously, an intelligent "fugitive" official will avoid States where he or she can easily be reached by the former employer in a civil suit, and is indeed apt to settle in a country with a favourable legal system and perhaps the one he or she has benefited through the indiscretion.

A relatively recent report by the United Nations Secretary-General to the General Assembly on "Recovery of misappropriated funds from staff members and former staff members" discusses at some length the difficulties in pursuing civil actions for fraud against the organisation in national courts.[12] It also proposes a possible solution, consisting of empowering the United Nations Administrative Tribunal (UNAT) to judge cases of fraud brought against a staff member (thus avoiding the need to expose the internal rules and transactions of the organisation to scrutiny by national courts) and then seeking to

---

[10] For OPCW see Article VIII(48) of the Convention. For the IAEA, a more explicit provision is included in its Agreement on Privileges and Immunities ("IAEA P&I Agreement") (INFCIRC/9/Rev.2), Section 2(c).

[11] Under para. 22 of the Confidentiality Annex to the Convention, the OPCW itself cannot be held liable for damage incurred due to an inspector's breach of confidentiality rules.

[12] UN doc. A/48/572 (9 November 1993), paras. 12-18.

enforce the Tribunal's judgement through national courts. Such enforcement could best be done through a multilateral treaty or a series of bilateral treaties obliging States to provide for such enforcement, but might also be accomplished by a General Assembly resolution calling on States to do so voluntarily.[13]

Suits brought by an IGO will ordinarily be limited to civil ones, allowing at best monetary damages. In most legal systems, a private party cannot bring a criminal proceeding, though it may be able to file a complaint that might lead the national authorities to bring such an action — provided that the action complained of is criminal under national law.[14] Though the Chemical Weapons Convention requires States Parties to criminalise certain types of conduct,[15] it is not clear that this obligation extends to criminalising violations of the OPCW's confidentiality rules.[16]

4. Waiver of Immunity

Both the IAEA and the OPCW systems explicitly foresee the waiver of an official's, or ex-official's, immunity in case of a violation of confidentiality rules.[17] Indeed, staff members are explicitly informed of this possibility.[18] Such a waiver is not considered to be a disciplinary or punitive measure — actually, it is required under the very provisions that establish the immunity, which always provide that the organisation has the right and duty to waive the immunity of an official, where in *its* opinion the immunity would impede the course of justice and can be waived without prejudice to the interest of the organisation.[19] Part IX.1, subparagraph 9.1, of the OPCW Policy on Confidentiality requires that waiver of immunity be considered "only in the event of a serious breach, when individual responsibility has been established and damage has been suffered as a result thereof" and sets some other procedural requirements. Presumably if an organisation unreasonably refused to waive immunity, a State concerned could require that it submit to an available disputes settlement procedure to resolve this issue.

It should be noted that, in respect of the most serious violations of confidentiality provisions, i.e., a deliberate disclosure of restricted data either for ideological or pecuniary reasons, a waiver of immunity would be neither necessary nor appropriate. Most international officials enjoy immunity only for words spoken or acts performed "in their official capacity".[20] Since a deliberate improper disclosure cannot be said to have been performed in an official capacity, no immunity attaches, and none needs to be waived. Of course, before a State or its courts assume that there is no immunity, they should consult with the executive head of the organisation to ascertain whether the latter agrees that the act in question was indeed

---

[13] *Id.*, paras. 26-33.

[14] This, too, is discussed in the report referred to *supra* note 12, paras. 19-24 and 34-35.

[15] Article VII(1) of the Convention.

[16] See the final paragraph of section 5 below.

[17] See OPCW Policy on Confidentiality, Part IX.1(9).

[18] For the OPCW, see para. 5 of the individual Secrecy Agreement that members of the OPCW Secretariat are required to conclude (published in L. Tabassi (ed.), OPCW: The Legal Texts (1999)).

[19] See IAEA P&I Agreement, Section 21, and Part II(14) of the Verification Annex to the Chemical Weapons Convention.

[20] IAEA P&I Agreement, Section 18(a)(i); Verification Annex to the Chemical Weapons Convention, Part II(11), *chapeau*.

not performed in an official capacity. Should he or she hold that indeed the act was official and therefore a waiver is required — which the executive head then might grant or refuse depending on his or her evaluation of the interests of the organisation — then, of course, the organisation would also have to assume responsibility for the act of its official.[21]

Can an official prevent the organisation from waiving his or her immunity? In the OPCW it appears to be provided that the official can challenge a proposed waiver, and any resulting dispute would be resolved with binding effect by the Administrative Tribunal of the International Labour Organization (ILOAT).[22] There is no such provision in the IAEA, but presumably an official could challenge a waiver *post hoc* and here, too, the dispute would be resolved by ILOAT. However, as the challenge itself has no suspensory effect, should the official ultimately prevail (some years later) all he or she could insist on is that the Agency withdraw the waiver — with whatever legal effect that might have with respect to national legal proceedings that had, in the meantime, been initiated and perhaps even completed. The extent to which these arrangements would apply to a situation in which an organisation fails to assert immunity (on the ground that the acts complained of were not official) is nowhere explicitly regulated, but presumably those relating to explicit waivers might be applied by analogy.

5. Obligation of States to Allow Civil Suits and to Pursue Criminal Proceedings

It follows from the above that the only really effective way in which errant officials can be seriously punished, civilly or criminally, is through the cooperation of States in whose national courts the necessary decisions would be taken and whose prosecutors would pursue, at least, any criminal cases. This is so whether such a case is initiated by the employing IGO itself (section 3 above), or by a private plaintiff, whether domestic or foreign, or by a State, whether the one in which the official is located or some other.[23]

To allow a criminal proceeding to go forward, the act in question, i.e. the wilful (and perhaps even the grossly negligent) disclosure of confidential information in violation of the IGO's rules, would have to be characterised as a crime under national law. To allow extradition from another State, it might be necessary that that State should have similarly criminalised the conduct in question, and perhaps that the crime be included in a schedule in a mutual extradition treaty. For effective criminal prosecution, it might also be necessary to require States to cooperate in the taking of evidence, the provision of witnesses, etc. To allow the IGO to sue civilly, it might be necessary to provide in a civil code that a violation of the IGO's rules constitutes either a contractual or tortious violation. Similarly, in respect of other civil claimants (e.g., an enterprise damaged by the disclosure of an industrial secret) it might be necessary to provide a cause of action based on violation of the IGO's rules.

Nothing in the applicable IAEA legal instruments, i.e., its Statute, its Privileges and

---

[21] These issues were in part explored in the *Cumaraswamy* case in the International Court of Justice (*Difference Relating to Immunity from Legal Process of a Special Rapporteur of the Commission of Human Rights, Advisory Opinion*, 1999 ICJ Reports 62), in which the dispute concerned whether the Secretary-General was correct in asserting that certain statements, allegedly libelous, were made by a Special Rapporteur of the Human Rights Commission in his capacity as such, and therefore were immune from challenges in a national court.

[22] Part IX.1, para. 9.2 of the OPCW Policy on Confidentiality, read together with OPCW Staff Regulations 11.1 and 11.3.

[23] See also *supra* in this volume, F. Patel King, Possible Action in the Courts of the Netherlands for Serious Breaches of the OPCW's Confidentiality Regime.

Immunities Agreement, or the safeguards agreements concluded with the Agency, or even the NPT, provides any obligation for Member States to provide such cooperation.

The situation in OPCW is more complicated. Article VII(1) of the Chemical Weapons Convention does require States to criminalise certain conduct by individuals, and Article VII(2) requires other States to provide legal assistance in pursuing such crimes — but these do not seem to include violations of confidentiality provisions. Paragraph 21 of the Confidentiality Annex to the Convention requires States Parties, to the extent possible, to cooperate and support the Director-General's investigation of breaches of confidentiality and to take appropriate action if a breach has been established — but this falls short of requiring States to criminalise such conduct.[24] That this is so appears to be recognised by the OPCW Policy on Confidentiality, which foresees that the OPCW Conference of the States Parties might consider proposals for an arrangement that would ensure a consistent and comprehensive response by States to serious breaches of confidentiality by officials of the organisation.[25] The following section explores one such possible arrangement that would apply not only to the OPCW but also to other IGOs facing similar problems.

6. Proposed Multilateral Treaty Concerning Breaches of Confidentiality

The previous sections have established that: (a) concerns about confidentiality are an important consideration for States permitting IGOs to exercise intrusive controls and in defining the limits of such controls; (b) although the IGOs concerned are cognisant of this problem, their ultimate power to hold their officials accountable for breaches of confidentiality regimes are quite limited and arguably insufficient; (c) the only possibility of imposing appropriate punishments on errant international officials is through actions by States, and such actions may require inter-State cooperation; and (d) so far none of the existing control regimes provides an unambiguous obligation for States to take such actions and to provide such cooperation.

It is therefore proposed that consideration be given to the conclusion of a universal multilateral treaty that would provide for the criminalisation of defined breaches by international officials of the confidentiality regimes of their employing IGOs, and would also provide for the possibility of civil remedies against such officials by the IGOs as well as by States or individuals damaged by such breaches. Set out below are the provisions that such a treaty might have.

6.1 Scope of the Treaty

The treaty should apply to all regimes that call for intrusive control regimes carried out by IGOs in States. Although the regimes considered above are all related to arms control, similar problems might arise in control systems relating to environmental protection, to human rights and perhaps to other subjects.

There are various ways of specifying the regimes in respect of which the treaty would be applicable. One possibility is a mere generic description of the characteristics of these

[24] Parts. IX.1, para. 9.3 and IX.3, paras. 4.1 and 4.2 of the OPCW Policy on Confidentiality elaborate on this obligation by States, but these provisions do not constitute binding treaty obligations.

[25] Part IX.3, para. 4.2 of the OPCW Policy on Confidentiality.

regimes so that application would be automatic in respect of those that fit the description. Probably more satisfactory would be a listing, to be included in the first instance in the treaty itself, together with a procedure whereby additional regimes could be added later. Furthermore, it could even be provided that States Parties to the treaty would only be bound in respect of regimes in which they participate and/or that each could determine with respect to which regimes it is prepared to apply the provisions of the treaty.[26]

6.2 OBLIGATION TO CRIMINALISE

The treaty would specify what types of conduct would be considered criminal and require the States Parties to include appropriate provisions in their criminal codes.

In the first instance the conduct to be considered criminal would be deliberate wilful, and perhaps also grossly negligent, violations by an IGO official of its confidentiality regime resulting in the unauthorised disclosure of confidential information. Consideration might also be given to including such actions by other persons who wilfully cause such a disclosure, whether or not in collaboration with an official.

The treaty might also provide for the types of punishment to be imposed, such as fines and/or imprisonment, and perhaps specifying minimum and maximum terms.

6.3 CONSEQUENCE OF CRIMINALISATION

As provided in a number of recent treaties establishing various types of conduct as international crimes,[27] the consequences of criminalising the offences here under consideration should be:

(a) the obligation to pursue criminal proceedings against alleged offenders who are within a State's jurisdiction, especially if this is demanded by the IGO concerned; or

(b) to extradite such a person to any other State that has jurisdiction over the offence and that wishes to prosecute, for which purpose the treaty itself should be considered as an extradition agreement that may be required by national legislation in order to allow extradition — i.e. the *aut dedere aut judicare* principle.

(c) the obligation to cooperate with States that are conducting criminal proceedings by assisting in the collection of evidence, the interrogation of witnesses or their appearance before the competent court, etc.

---

26 This would be similar to the provisions under which States become parties to the Convention on the Privileges and Immunities of the Specialized Agencies, allowing them to specify from time to time the agencies in respect of which they will apply the Convention.

27 For example: 1989 International Convention against the Recruitment, Use, Financing and Training of Mercenaries; 1994 Convention on the Safety of United Nations and Associated Personnel; 1999 International Convention for the Suppression of the Financing of Terrorism; 2000 United Nations Convention against Transnational Organized Crime.

6.4 POSSIBLE SUBMISSION TO THE INTERNATIONAL CRIMINAL COURT

Although the initial jurisdiction of the eventual International Criminal Court (ICC)[28] is strictly limited to various types of serious offences arising out of war or similar situations,[29] there are provisions for adding other international crimes to the jurisdiction of the Court.[30] As provided in the ICC Statute, the Court can only take action in respect to individuals whom the States that would normally exercise jurisdiction are unable or unwilling to prosecute.[31] The proposed treaty might therefore provide for the eventual inclusion of the crimes it creates within the jurisdiction of the ICC — which would in no way detract from the possibility and obligation of States to prosecute.

6.5 PROVISION FOR CIVIL SUITS

The proposed treaty should also provide that officials, and perhaps others who violate an IGO's confidentiality regime, can be subject to civil penalties, especially for actual, and perhaps punitive, damages, in suits brought either by the IGO or by anyone, State, enterprise or individual, who is damaged by such violation.

6.6 ACTIONS AGAINST NON-COOPERATING STATES

If a State should refuse to comply with any aspect of its obligations under the treaty, appropriate action should, first of all, be taken within the affected IGO; if the violation is one that seriously compromises a regime of importance to peace and security, such as an arms control system, reference to the United Nations Security Council should be provided for.

IGO-operated control regimes, particularly arms control arrangements, are becoming more important features of international governance, and such regimes can only operate satisfactorily if the States concerned have confidence in them and in their adequate protection of confidential information. It is therefore necessary to reinforce the currently too weak sanctions that exist against individuals who would violate the rules designed to protect such information. The treaty proposed in this chapter would seem to be the simplest and most effective way of providing for such sanctions.

[28] 1998 Rome Statute of the International Criminal Court, entered into force 1 July 2002; UN doc. A/CONF.183/9*, as corrected by the procès-verbaux of 10 November 1998 and 12 July 1999. Corrected text available at http://www.un.org/law/icc.

[29] Rome Statute of the International Criminal Court, Art. 5(1).

[30] *Id.*, Articles 121 and 123(1).

[31] *Id.*, Article 17.

PART III

MODALITIES

SECTION III.1
Case Studies: Extradition and Special Challenges to Administrations in Transition

SECTION III.2
Gathering Evidence and Interviewing Witnesses in an International Context

SECTION III.3
The Police Component: International and National Perspectives

SECTION III.4
Customs Enforcement and Initiatives to Strengthen Regimes

SECTION III.5
Addressing Transboundary Criminal Activity through National Criminal Law Systems

SECTION III.1

CASE STUDIES: EXTRADITION AND SPECIAL CHALLENGES TO ADMINISTRATIONS IN TRANSITION

INTRODUCTION AND SUMMARY

The most commonly known (and even publicly visible when covered by the media) form of inter-State cooperation in criminal matters is extradition. This section brings together and discusses a number of aspects that arise in extradition procedure: the practical challenges in general terms, special problems faced by transitional States, and special considerations in respect of the Chemical Weapons Convention.

The purpose of extradition is to obtain the individual accused or convicted of a crime by transferring them from one jurisdiction to another so that prosecution and/or punishment can take place effectively. Notably, even the Belgian courts, well known in recent times for their invocation of the principle of universal jurisdiction, have concluded that trials on charges of international crimes *in absentia* do not constitute an effective means of dispensing international justice.

There are practical difficulties that are sometimes encountered in obtaining the individual from another country. Many States require that an international or bilateral agreement be in force with the requesting State before even contemplating extradition, and such an agreement must often be incorporated into domestic law before it can be applied. In addition, an administrative scheme needs to be in place to carry out the extradition request. Practical problems may arise in relation to the type of evidence that has to be provided to another State, the method of obtaining it and the form in which it must be presented in order to be admissible in the jurisdiction of the requesting State. The principle of dual criminality requires that the act be a crime in both States. The political offence exception may then come into play. This exception provoked much discussion at the 2001 OPCW Symposium, on the potential reach of the exception in the context of the production and transfer of chemical weapons. Other grounds for the refusal of a request include the military offence exception, the fact that many States will not extradite their nationals, the principle of double jeopardy, discrimination and lapse of time. Although extradition practice seems chaotic, it has actually improved in recent years.

In what can be called today's "global village," the emergence of new States and the relaxation of borders has increased opportunities both for law-abiding citizens and criminals. For some States this has caused a surge in organised and unorganised economic crime. Two authors in this section present the implications this has had for Ukraine and Georgia, respectively. In response to this threat, Ukraine started an active process of engagement with the international community. An impressive number of requests were received and sent abroad in 1999 and 2000. The Minsk Convention on Mutual Legal Assistance and Legal Relations in Civil and Commercial Matters was signed by twelve former Soviet republics in 1993, and many of these States subsequently became party to European and bilateral agreements on cooperation. However, a frequent complaint is that the European conventions are out of date. Decentralisation is the key to improving the system domestically so that requesting and responding agencies can contact each other directly. This view has been echoed by others who advocate direct contact between the authorities and emphasise that mutual trust, personal contacts, education, and language skills are needed in order for the process to function expeditiously. A simplified system has been set up under the Schengen Agreement which could be used as a model for other regions.

One author in this section criticises the decision in his country to designate the Ministry of Justice as the central authority for the purpose of implementing the European conventions on mutual legal assistance, and approves of the increased role given in that respect to the Office of the Prosecutor in recent legislative amendments. This approach has also been followed in the Czech Republic where the competence of the central authority is divided between the Ministry of Justice and the Supreme Prosecutor's Office. One suggestion at the Symposium called for a comprehensive international treaty on cooperation that would introduce the duties that are really necessary in today's practice. In the Czech Republic legal assistance can be provided even in the absence of an agreement.

The Chemical Weapons Convention is not specifically directed at criminal activity and States are, therefore, left to adopt domestic legislation criminalising the production, transfer or use of chemical weapons. Nearly half of the States Parties have adopted such legislation, although the scope varies. For example, the obligations under the Convention have been translated into detailed provisions in Georgia, including a crime of "ecocide," and carry quite heavy penalties. However, since the Convention does not contain an extradition clause, extradition in respect of acts falling within the ambit of the Convention is still governed by existing agreements. In this respect it has been proposed in section IV.2 of this volume that a new international treaty is needed: one which would define production, transfer or use of chemical weapons as international crimes entailing individual responsibility. The proposed treaty would cover extradition and would provide that the criminalised acts could not qualify as political offences. They would be subject to universal jurisdiction in accordance with the principle *aut dedere aut judicare* in order to ensure that national amnesties are ineffective. One question that arises in this context is the relationship between State responsibility and individual responsibility with respect to acts prohibited under the treaty. The proposed international treaty would be the ideal place to define this important relationship.

Nina Jørgensen

Rapporteur for Panel A.1 in the 2001 OPCW International Symposium; Research Fellow in International Criminal Law, Leiden University. The views expressed are not attributable to Leiden University or the OPCW.

EXTRADITION: THE PRACTICAL CHALLENGES

Kimberly Prost*

1. Introduction

Extradition, as the oldest form of international cooperation in criminal matters, is a critical component of an effective regime of enforcement in relation to any treaty or scheme involving individual criminal liability. Fundamentally, there is no prospect for the effective prosecution and punishment of individuals, without being able to obtain "the body".

However, by virtue of this fact — that it is a measure of cooperation that directly affects the liberty of individuals — extradition is perhaps the most challenging and complex form of cooperation, particularly as between States of a different legal tradition.

Achieving effective extradition is a challenge for all States but it is a particularly acute one for administrations in transition. The purpose of this chapter is to briefly explore some of the fundamental issues that States face in extradition practice

2. Basis for Cooperation

Extradition is the surrender by one State, at the request of another, of a person who is accused or has been convicted of a crime committed within the jurisdiction of the requesting State.[1]

In any particular case, the first issue will be whether there is a basis for extradition, given that many countries still require an international agreement of some form as a foundation for extradition. Unquestionably, this is changing, with the development of reciprocal schemes such as the Commonwealth Scheme for the Rendition of Fugitive Offenders (London Scheme)[2] and the growing acceptance of the concept of extradition based on comity and reciprocity. But the reality remains that there may well be an initial stumbling block to extradition because there is no underlying instrument upon which extradition to or from the country will be possible.

In relation to crimes that are the subject of international agreement, this issue is increasingly addressed through the inclusion of specific extradition clauses in the agreement.

*Head, Criminal Law Unit, Deputy Director, Legal and Constitutional Affairs Division, Commonwealth Secretariat. Note: any views expressed are those of the author and are not attributable to any government or organization.

[1] A.W. LaForest, Extradition to and from Canada, 1991.

[2] The London Scheme for the Rendition of Fugitive Offenders was adopted by Commonwealth Law Ministers in 1966. The scheme is not a treaty — it is a statement of agreed principles with each member country of the Commonwealth agreeing to enact legislation, which will allow surrender to another Commonwealth country in accordance with the scheme.

R. Yepes-Enríquez and L. Tabassi. (eds.), Treaty Enforcement and International Cooperation in Criminal Matters

For example, the Hijacking Convention,[3] the Hostage Taking Convention,[4] and the 1988 Drug Convention[5] all provide that where a State makes extradition conditional on the existence of a treaty, it may consider the convention to constitute such an agreement. In the case of the Chemical Weapons Convention,[6] as it is not primarily directed at individual criminal activity, no such clause has been included. Therefore, it would be unlikely[7] that it would constitute a sufficient agreement for these purposes and thus States would have to look for an alternative basis to found extradition in any given case.

3. Implementation of Obligations Under Domestic Law

Provided there is a basis for extradition, which for many countries will be found in a series of bilateral extradition treaties or an applicable regional multilateral instrument,[8] the next macro issue for States will be implementation of the obligations reflected in that agreement, by way of incorporation of treaty into law or the enactment of enabling legislation.

In the case of a country where treaties are self-implementing, this will not be an issue. The obligations and terms of the agreement will automatically form a part of domestic law and the relevant powers needed to make or execute a request will follow as a result.

For those States that require domestic laws to specifically implement international obligations, there will need to be either specific or general legislation for an extradition treaty to work in practice.

I think it can be said that, by and large, most States will have some domestic power in the area of extradition. However, many of the impediments to effective extradition flow from inadequacies in the provisions of the treaty itself or the domestic law used to implement it.

For example, many of the treaties in use today, in 2001, within the Commonwealth particularly but not exclusively, were actually drafted in the late 1800's. One can imagine the problems that arise in applying such antiquated instruments today. For example, in defining an extradition offence, the treaties employ the old technique of "listing" the relevant offences to which the treaty will apply. Thus, you will have the curious scenario where the offence of drug trafficking will not appear but the offence of piracy (which while still a problem in some areas of the world is very rarely the subject of prosecution) will. One can be certain that the offences created through the Chemical Weapons Convention will not be found in that list.

---

[3] The Convention for the Supression of Unlawful Seizure of Aircraft, signed at The Hague, December 1970; entered into force 14 October 1971.

[4] The International Convention against the taking of Hostages, concluded at New York, December 1979; in force 3 June 1983.

[5] The 1988 United Nations Convention against Illicit Traffic in Narcotic Drugs and Psychotropic Substances, in force 11 November 1990.

[6] 1993 Convention on the Prohibition of the Development, Production, Stockpiling and Use of Chemical Weapons and on Their Destruction, entered into force on 29 April 1997. Text, as corrected and changed, available at http://www.opcw.org.

[7] Whether the agreement would be sufficient in this regard would depend upon the requirements under domestic law.

[8] An example of a regional instrument would be the European Convention on Extradition, European T.S. no. 24 (12 December 1957); (First) Additional Protocol, European T.S. no. 86 (15 October 1975); Second Additional Protocol, European T.S. no. 98 (17 March 1978).

Similar problems exist with extradition legislation. By example, up until 1999, Canada had two pieces of extradition legislation dating from the late 1800's. One of them, the Fugitive Offenders Act, defined extraditable offence by reference to penalty, requiring that the offender face a penalty of a term of imprisonment for more then one year with hard labour. Needless to say it was a bit cumbersome to have to continually ask requesting countries to provide a description of their work programs in prisons in order to try and deal with a request for extradition.

This is but a limited example of the types of antiquated provisions that countries may find within their extradition treaties or legislation. Other problems include a lack of specificity of procedures, cumbersome provisions relating to jurisdiction and, in the case of common law States, prohibitive evidentiary requirements.

4. Administrative Regimes for Effective Implementation

One further "macro" problem requires mentioning. No matter how "state of the art" the underlying treaty or law is, an extradition system will fail in the absence of effective administrative regimes for implementation. In some legal systems, the administrative scheme and staff will have to be more extensive than others. For example, in a common law State it will be necessary to have general capacity and personnel to deal with the judicial hearing phase of extradition, which exists generally in all common law States. In other legal systems, extradition may be an entirely executive process, thus affecting the type of administration required.

But whatever the applicable system, there are certain fundamental requirements to make the extradition process workable. It begins with an identified office to receive and transmit requests which is known to other States. In most countries this will be the Ministry of Foreign Affairs, so this should not present any particular difficulties. At the same time, the Ministry of Foreign Affairs is unlikely to be the Ministry responsible for the execution of incoming requests or the preparation of outgoing requests, so there will be a need for a person, office or authority responsible to receive, review and arrange for the execution of incoming requests and, if possible, to review and vet outgoing requests.

Both offices will need to have fundamental equipment for communication, which in today's terms includes phone, fax, and computer.

There must also be access to, or personnel from, a police force who will be able to assist with the location and identification of suspects and, most importantly, to carry out their arrest. There must also be facilities for the detention of those suspects that are apprehended, pending surrender.

For those systems where there is a judicial hearing, the administrative structure will have to include personnel to bring the relevant applications and access to the court system within the relevant location in the country.

Finally, in addition to setting up the structure, there has to be some form of training for those that administer the system. What is noted over and over again is that one of the central problems in extradition practice is the lack of training and knowledge about the fundamental procedures and law in this field. While this issue is prominent in developing States or States in transition, it is not exclusive to such States. This problem is particularly acute in a system with a judicial hearing component, where often counsel and the judiciary are entirely unfamiliar with extradition.

5. The Practice of Extradition

5.1 Evidence

After concluding that there is a basic extradition relationship between the States, any authority seeking the extradition of an accused person for trial will face the fundamental question of what material must be provided to the foreign State in support of the request.

While a seemingly simplistic question, this issue has been and remains a critical problem in extradition, particularly extradition from a common law country.

For most civil law States, the issuance of an arrest warrant within a requesting State demonstrates that a judicial authority within that State has determined that there is sufficient evidence in the case. On that basis, the authorities in the requested State should be able to accept and rely on that determination and not look behind it to reassess the underlying basis of the decision.

In contrast, traditionally, common law States have required, in addition to the warrant, the submission of evidence by the foreign State, sufficient to meet a prescribed domestic standard. Many such States have also demanded that the evidence be adduced in a form consistent with the law of the requested State, before extradition will be granted.

Meeting those demands for evidence often proves to be one of the greatest challenges in the extradition process. The problem is simple; the solution is not. When evidence must be adduced to meet an unknown standard, in a completely foreign format, it can prove to be an insurmountable hurdle to extradition. To meet this burden the requesting authorities are forced to generate an entirely separate package of evidence — one that they would not normally produce — which cannot be used in any ultimate domestic trial process against the particular accused. For the investigating magistrate or prosecutor in a non-common law State, the requirement for evidence is unquestionably the major challenge in pursuing the extradition of a suspect.

An example may assist to illustrate the extent of the challenge. In many common law systems, the evidence submitted in an extradition case must be in the form of first person sworn statements that recount only what that person can attest to from his or her personal knowledge. Generally statements made to that person are not admissible for the purpose of proving the truth of those statements. The evidence adduced in this form must then be sufficient to meet the standard of a *prima facie* case, which means if this evidence stood alone at trial, a reasonable jury, properly directed, could accept it and find a verdict of guilty.

Thus, in every case, the foreign State has to compile sworn statements from those witnesses that are necessary to establish a case on this standard. And unless the requested State has general laws to facilitate the admission of documents and records, it may also be necessary to provide individual statements from the "maker" of any such document for it to be admissible. One can easily see what a cumbersome and onerous task this can be.

The problem is most pronounced when the offence in question is of a complex nature, as would be the case with offences under the Chemical Weapons Convention. If you think about the convention offences and then visualise having to demonstrate your case to a prescribed standard through individual first person witness statements, the magnitude of the problem becomes clearer.

Historically, the result has been that many fugitives have escaped justice or found safe haven because it was impossible for countries to generate the level of material required, in the form sought. Nor is the problem solely an irritant between systems with different legal traditions; it can also arise between countries with the same general traditions but differing rules of evidence and approaches to extradition.

5.2 DUAL CRIMINALITY

Dual criminality is a fundamental requirement in all extradition regimes. That is, the conduct for which extradition is sought must constitute an offence in both the requesting and requested State.

One would expect that when it comes to extradition relating to convention offences, such as the Chemical Weapons Convention, this requirement would not be difficult to establish. The very nature of the Convention is such that States are agreeing to certain obligations, which necessitate the creation of specified offences under domestic law.

Unfortunately, that may not always be the case under all conventions, for a combination of reasons. Some conventions are very specific as to the conduct to be criminalised, for example the 1988 Drug Convention details the types of offences in statutory language. However, other conventions leave much of the detail of offence provisions for elaboration under domestic law. Thus, it is possible that States will create quite distinct offences under domestic law in relation to the general convention obligations.

The dual criminality test in extradition has been considerably simplified in recent times. As the approach to defining extraditable offence has moved from listing the offences to a general test of punishment, so too has the analysis of dual criminality moved from a focus on the description of the offence to consideration of the underlying conduct. Many treaties now contain principles to that effect in relation to the dual criminality analysis. The United Nations 1990 Model Extradition Treaty,[9] for example, provides:

> Article 2, para. 2. In determining whether an offence is an offence punishable under the laws of both Parties, it shall not matter whether:
>
> (a) The laws of the Parties place the acts or omissions constituting the offence within the same category of offence or denominate the offence by the same terminology;
>
> (b) Under the laws of the Parties the constituent elements of the offence differ, it being understood that the totality of the acts or omissions as presented by the requesting State shall be taken into account.

To the extent that these principles are applied and the analysis is strictly focused on whether the conduct of the individual would be criminal in the requested State, then the different ways in which the convention offences are described in national law should not

[9] General Assembly resolution 45/116 (14 December 1990), UN GAOR, 45th Session., Supplement No. 49A (A/45/49).

prevent extradition. Unfortunately, in some jurisdictions this may not always be the case.

For example, some common law jurisdictions still apply a line of authority in extradition matters coming from a decision of the House of Lords in 1989, under which it was held that the ingredients or elements of the requesting State offence must correspond to the elements of the offence in the requested State. Thus, if in the requested State additional elements need to be proved for an offence to be established than required for the offence in the requesting State, dual criminality would not be established, even where the conduct disclosed on the evidence met all the elements of the offence in the requested State. In the case of *Government of Canada and Another v. Aronson*,[10] because the elements of the offence of fraud differed in this way as between Canada and the United Kingdom, a relevant offence for extradition purposes had not been established. The House of Lords specifically rejected the argument that regardless of the elements of the offence, the issue should be whether all of the conduct as disclosed by the evidence would have constituted an offence under the law of the United Kingdom, despite the fact that the "full conduct" test has been adopted in other jurisdictions. Ironically, the 1989 legislation in the United Kingdom has effectively "overruled" the *Aronson* decision there, but it remains good law in other jurisdictions.

In a jurisdiction which follows the *Aronson* decision therefore, establishing dual criminality will require proof not only of an offence on the basis of all of the conduct evidenced in the materials submitted but also similarity in terms of the requisite elements of the offence in both States. This could present significant problems in cases such as those that could arise under the Chemical Weapons Convention.

Even absent such legal hurdles, it is quite possible that differing interpretations of terminology or even of the nature of the obligations under a convention such as the Chemical Weapons Convention, will lead to an absence of dual criminality in particular cases.

For example, Article I, paragraph 1 of the Chemical Weapons Convention sets out some general agreed prohibitions including that the State Parties undertake "never under any circumstances... to assist, encourage or induce, in any way, anyone to engage in any activity prohibited to a State Party under this Convention".

It is quite possible that there will be different definitions accorded to terms such as "assist, encourage or induce", with the result that the conduct of the accused may constitute encouragement in one State but not in another.

Thankfully, one very thorny problem that we have seen arise in relation to other international convention offences — the requirement for both States to have similar extraterritorial jurisdiction — does not arise under the Chemical Weapons Convention because of the mandatory provision on jurisdiction on the basis of nationality of the accused. Thus, States Parties in compliance with the Convention should have the same basis for jurisdiction. Problems in this respect would then only arise if a State Party chose to extend jurisdiction on another basis under international law.

[10] 2 All E.R. 1025 (1989)

5.3 GROUNDS FOR REFUSAL

If the initial requirements for extradition are met (basis for extradition, extraditable offence, dual criminality, evidence if necessary) it is still possible that the request will be refused. Almost all extradition treaties or schemes and the related domestic law, incorporate some grounds for refusal — specified circumstances where extradition will be denied by the requested State. Some grounds for refusal are found in almost all instruments relating to extradition and are thus internationally recognised while others will vary in application depending on particular relationships and domestic law.

In certain instances an apparently simple extradition case can become exceedingly complex because the facts raise the possibility of refusal on the basis of an accepted or agreed ground.

While there are several accepted grounds for refusal in the context of extradition, a few require special mention here because of their potential application in relation to offences established under international conventions.

(a) *Political offence*

In ancient times and, in fact, up until the early 1800's, extradition was directed almost exclusively to the return of fugitives sought for political or religious offences. Extradition was viewed as a means to protect the political order of States.

In modern times, particularly the last hundred years, the focus of extradition has changed completely to common serious crimes, which in many ways has replaced political offences as a major challenge to the stability of nations. In fact, quite ironically, political offences, the original focus of extradition, are now generally excluded from extradition regimes.

The principle of excluding extradition for political offences has its roots in history, in that the exception began to be included in extradition regimes and practice at a time of revolution and struggle for democratic government. The rationale was that those who struggle against tyranny and in pursuit of a democratic government should not, if their efforts fail, face extradition but rather should receive asylum.

The definition of a political offence or an offence of a political character is an elusive one. The question has been considered extensively in several jurisdictions and is the subject of many decided cases.

Without attempting to define what escapes precise definition, in very general terms the purely political offence is conduct directed against the sovereign or its political subdivisions, constituting opposition to a political, religious or other ideology or to its supporting structures, which does not have any of the elements of a common crime. The best examples of such pure political offences would be treason, sedition and espionage.

The second category relates to offences that are of a political character. These will include an element of a common crime but with political sub-text. Because of the vagueness of the concept, much of the judicial analysis has focused on determining what constitutes an offence of political character and there are varying approaches to the matter amongst States. As an example, within the English common law there are some general criteria, developed through the years, which the courts will look for in determining whether the offence is one of a political character.

First, the offender must be politically motivated in committing the offence in question and the act must be committed for the purpose of promoting a political cause. This element is critically important, and the absence of it will preclude a finding that the exception is applicable.

Secondly, the act must be directed against the State, to force a change in the government or its policies. Historically, the courts took a very narrow view of this, requiring a connection between the offence and an insurrection, uprising or struggle for power. (See, for example, *In re Castioni*;[11] and *In re Meunier.*[12])

However in the benchmark decision of the *House of Lords, R. v. Governor of Brixton Prison, Ex Parte Schtraks*,[13] the Court took a more liberal view in interpreting what constitutes a political disturbance. The Lords were of the opinion that what was to be considered was whether the person was at odds with the State over an issue and the act was designed to bring about change related to that issue.

In considering this last criteria, the courts in different common law States may look at various considerations such as whether the act was within the context of a political disturbance, whether the person was the member of a political group, or whether the act is sufficiently direct in respect of the government or its institutions to be classified as being directed against the government.

There is also a third category of cases within this exception, which is essentially where the proceedings are taken to prosecute or punish the person for an offence of a political character. In these instances, while the offence for which extradition is requested is not of a political character, the prosecution is designed as punishment for political offences committed or the facts of the case give the offence a political character.

In relation to crimes established through international convention, often they are of such a nature that one can easily envisage arguments about the application of the political offence exception. For example, one can see how such arguments would be raised in relation to offences created by virtue of the conventions that address various aspects of terrorism, such as the Hijacking Convention or Hostage Taking Convention.

While clearly dependent on the facts of the case, one could see similar arguments being advanced with respect to offences created by virtue of the Chemical Weapons Convention.

It is, in fact, because of the strong possibility of these arguments being raised that some bilateral and multilateral treaties or schemes for extradition now specifically exclude the application of the political offence exception to crimes created by virtue of such conventions. For example, Annex 1 to the Commonwealth Scheme on the Rendition of Fugitive Offenders provides in part as follows:

1. It may be provided by a law in any part of the Commonwealth that certain acts shall not be held to be offences of a political character including ...
   (d) an act declared to constitute an offence under a multilateral international convention whose purpose is to prevent or repress a specific category of offences

[11] 1 QB 149 (1891)
[12] 2 QB 415 (1894)
[13] AC 556 (1964)

and which imposes on the parties thereto an obligation either to extradite or to prosecute the person sought.

Similarly, some recent multilateral conventions, for example Article 11 of the 1997 International Convention for the Suppression of Terrorist Bombings, specifically excludes the application of the political offence exception by providing that the offences under the Convention shall not be considered to be political offences.

As the Chemical Weapons Convention does not contain such an exclusion or an "extradite or prosecute" obligation, there remains the potential for the application of this exception to extradition cases relating to Convention offences. In some jurisdictions, a court determines the question of whether the offence should be classified as a political offence or an offence of a political character. If that is the case, given the very complex state of the law in this area, an extradition case where the fugitive raises the issue of political offence will be a complex and difficult matter.

(b) Military offence

Because of the nature of the offences under the Chemical Weapons Convention, it bears mentioning that military offences are generally excluded under all extradition regimes. However, that which is excluded is a pure military offence that is not also an offence under general law. Given that penal law will generally cover the offences under the Chemical Weapons Convention, it is unlikely that this issue will arise.

(c) Nationality

Many countries, by virtue of constitutional mandate, legislation, or policy will not extradite their nationals. In most instances however, States that do not extradite their nationals will have jurisdiction over offences by their nationals, wherever committed. As a result, most extradition treaties now provide for the requesting State to seek a prosecution in the requested State, when extradition has been refused for this reason. As previously noted, many of the multilateral instruments mandate such prosecution in lieu of extradition by application of the "extradite or prosecute" principle.

The Chemical Weapons Convention specifically mandates that State Parties establish extraterritorial jurisdiction for offences of nationals wherever committed. This clearly avoids any *lacunae* in terms of a legal basis for prosecution. Unfortunately, while prosecution *in lieu* goes some way to prevent safe haven for fugitives, it is not always effective in practice. There can be many problems surrounding a prosecution that relates to conduct that occurred in another State. Often such cases are not accorded high priority. There can be significant practical problems in obtaining and presenting the necessary evidence, which rests in another country. Thus, despite the extension of jurisdiction mandated under the convention, the non-extradition of nationals remains an issue in terms of the effectiveness of international cooperation of this form.

(d) *Other grounds for refusal*

There are as well other grounds for refusal which can arise in any given extradition case such as arguments relating to double jeopardy or *ne bis in idem*, discrimination, or lapse of time.

Increasingly, arguments are raised in opposition to extradition on the basis of the general conditions in the requested State. Extradition is opposed on the basis of matters such as human rights issues or questions with respect to the justice system and trial process. These can be exceedingly difficult matters to resolve in the context of an extradition case.

Finally, as we have seen in the Pinochet case in the United Kingdom, despite all legal requirements having been met, extradition may be refused on a humanitarian basis because of the health or other circumstances of the person sought.

6. Conclusion

Extradition is a central tool for cooperation in criminal matters. While the practice of extradition remains challenging, we have certainly seen a vast increase in the use of extradition in recent times, and this has generated many improvements to the effectiveness of the process throughout the world. As the attention of the world community continues to focus on the need for enhanced cooperation in combating all forms of crime, no doubt these improvements to this fundamental cooperation tool will continue.

EXTRADITION IN A TIME OF TRANSITION, WITH SPECIAL REFERENCE TO CRIMES INVOLVING CHEMICAL WEAPONS

John Dugard*

1. Introduction

Extradition provides for the rendition of an accused or convicted person to the State where the person is accused of a crime, or has been convicted of a crime, by the State on whose territory the person happens to be. In the present global village with easy travel and communication, transnational methods are required for the enforcement of criminal law. Gone are the days in which a State could rely on its own police force to enforce its criminal law. Today extradition, and police and judicial cooperation in the collection and production of evidence abroad, are essential features of criminal law enforcement.

International law has not, however, developed sufficiently to impose a general duty on States to extradite criminals or to engage in mutual legal assistance. States must still consent to extradition in extradition agreements, which, in seeking to strike a balance between the interests of individual liberty and law enforcement, place obstacles in the way of extradition. The most notable of these is the political offence exception.[1]

The question addressed in this chapter concerns the prospects of extradition for persons who commit crimes relating to the unlawful production and distribution of chemical weapons, with special reference to the case of societies in transition.

First, a word about the crime. The Chemical Weapons Convention[2] does not criminalise the production, transfer or use of chemical weapons. Instead it leaves it to States Parties to adopt domestic legislation for this purpose (Article VII). Nor does the Rome Statute of the International Criminal Court,[3] in its sweeping definition of war crimes, penalise the production and transfer of chemical weapons, though it does, in Article 8(2)(b)(xvii) and (xviii) criminalise the use of poisonous weapons and gases.

Many States have adopted domestic legislation to criminalise the production, transfer and use of chemical weapons,[4] but the extradition of offenders is governed by existing multilateral or bilateral agreements. These agreements, traditionally, contain a number of

* Professor of Public International Law, University of Leiden; Professor Emeritus, University of the Witwatersrand; Member of the International Law Commission; Judge, ad hoc International Court of Justice; Member of the Institute of International Law.

[1] See generally, C. van den Wijngaert, *The Political Offence Exception to Extradition* (1980).

[2] 1993 Convention on the Prohibition of the Development, Production, Stockpiling and Use of Chemical Weapons and on Their Destruction, entered into force on 29 April 1997. Text, as corrected and changed, available at http://www.opcw.org.

[3] 1998 Rome Statute of the International Criminal Court, entered into force 1 July 2002; UN doc. A/CONF.183/9*, as corrected by the procès-verbaux of 10 November 1998 and 12 July 1999. Corrected text available at http://www.un.org/law/icc.

[4] See Survey of National Implementing Legislation, OPCW doc. S/259/2001 (16 May 2001).

R. Yepes-Enríquez and L. Tabassi. (eds.), Treaty Enforcement and International Cooperation in Criminal Matters

exceptions to extradition. For the present purposes the most important is the political offence exception. The question must therefore be asked whether a person who unlawfully produces, transfers or uses chemical weapons may successfully argue that the crime falls within the scope of the political offence exception? In other words, may a person who has produced chemical weapons in order to serve a political purpose argue that the crime is political or politically motivated and is therefore not extraditable?

Take, for example, the case of Joe who in a State, called Arcadia, produces chemical weapons to assist in the overthrow of the government of Arcadia. If Joe flees to a third State, Utopia, Arcadia may request his extradition from Utopia. May Joe raise the political offence exception to an extradition request?

Or if Pete, in Arcadia, produces chemical weapons to be used against the political opposition of Arcadia, and the political opposition overthrows the government of Arcadia and later seeks to obtain the extradition of Pete from Utopia, may Pete claim that he qualifies for the political offence exception in extradition proceedings in Utopia?

In both cases the crime was *in fact* politically motivated. Was it *in law*?

This requires a brief overview of the confused law governing the political offence.

2. The Political Offence Exception

In the nineteenth century, as liberal democracies began to emerge from oppressive monarchies, there was considerable sympathy for the political offender, who was seen as a freedom fighter engaged in the struggle for liberation. Judicial decisions reflect this idealism. The political offence was interpreted broadly to ensure that opponents of oppressive regimes were not extradited to stand trial for crimes linked with the liberation struggle. Clearly treason was a political crime. But courts applied the political offence exception to "mixed crimes", that is, ordinary crimes like murder or robbery committed with a political motive.

In the early case of *In re Castioni* an English court[5] held that a Swiss national who shot and killed a member of the government of one of the cantons in a political uprising could not be extradited for murder; reasoning that his crime was incidental to a political disturbance related to the struggle of individuals to alter or abolish the existing government of their country. This political incidence test, followed in the United States, was generously applied in the United States, until recent times,[6] to allow members of the Irish Republican Army (IRA) to escape extradition to Britain for atrocities committed against civilians and the security forces in the United Kingdom.

During the Cold War English courts adopted another test to determine the scope of the political offence exception. In *Ex Parte Kolczynski*[7] the Court held that a crime committed in the course of escaping from an oppressive regime was, for reasons of humanity, to be labelled as a non-extraditable political offence. Later definitions have stressed that the political offender is one who commits a crime with the object of overthrowing or changing the government of a State or inducing it to change its policy.[8]

[5] [1891] 1QB 149.

[6] See *Quinn v Robinson* 783 F 2nd 776 (9th Cir 1986).

[7] *R v Governor of Brixton Prison ex parte Kolczynski* [1955] 1QB 540 at 551, [1955] 1 ALL ER31.

[8] *Cheng v Governor of Pentonville Prison* [1973] 2 All ER 204 (HL) at 209.

Sympathy for the political offender has waned in recent years as the image of the liberal freedom fighter has been replaced by that of the ruthless, automatic gun-waving terrorist determined to overthrow the government by acts of terror and hijacking. Courts have therefore refused to accept as political offences acts directed not at governmental institutions, but at civilian targets which have resulted in indiscriminate killings.[9]

Despite the present lack of sympathy for terrorists, international conventions dealing with hijacking and hostage-taking have not generally expressly excluded the political offence exception. The International Convention for the Suppression of Terrorist Bombings of 1998 has, however, expressly excluded the political offence exception as an obstacle to extradition. This course was followed by the 1996 European Union Extradition Agreement.

The political offence exception remains an elusive concept with no clear definition. Indeed, a distinguished English judge has hailed this lack of definition as an advantage as it permits courts to respond to new political situations.[10] In these circumstances it would be possible for Joe and Pete to argue that their crime — the production of chemical weapons to be used against political opponents — was political. Joe's crime was committed with the object of overthrowing the government, while Pete's, committed with the blessing of the government of the day, was designed to retain political power for that government.

Clearly this situation is unacceptable. What is needed is a clear affirmation, preferably by means of a treaty, that the production and transfer of chemical weapons for unauthorised purposes cannot, like terrorist bombings, qualify as a political offence. Alternatively, it is necessary to bring such conduct within the ambit of war crimes or crimes against humanity, as it is now accepted that such acts, although politically motivated, do not qualify as "political" for the purpose of extradition. This is a slow process, however, and can, in the absence of such a categorisation in the Rome Statute, probably only be achieved by judicial interpretation.

Two alternative proposals are made along these lines further in this volume. Professors Matthew Meselson and J. Perry Robinson have appealed for the adoption of a convention along the lines of the Terrorist Bombings Convention to criminalise the act of individuals who produce, transfer or use chemical weapons.[11] Lisa Tabassi has proposed an Optional Protocol to the Chemical Weapons Convention.[12] Both of these proposals would exclude such conduct from the political offence exception and ensure that the exception is not used as a protection for such offenders.

3. Amnesties

Switching now to another topical issue, assume that Pete, who produced chemical weapons in Arcadia to maintain the government in power, does not become a fugitive from justice when the political opposition overthrows that government. Instead, he is granted amnesty for his crime by the new government of Arcadia in pursuance of a policy of political reconciliation. In such circumstances Pete will be safe from prosecution in Arcadia. But if he

---

[9] *T v Secretary of State for the Home Department* [1996] 2 All ER 865 (HL).

[10] *Schtraks v Government of Israel* [1964] AC 556 (HL) at 589.

[11] See *infra* in this volume, M. Meselson and J.P. Robinson, A Draft Convention to Prohibit Biological and Chemical Weapons Under International Criminal Law.

[12] See *infra* in this volume, L. Tabassi, Legal Assistance under the Chemical Weapons Convention: an Optional Protocol to the Convention?

travels abroad to Utopia may he be prosecuted in Utopia? Or, if he visits Ruritania on holiday, may Utopia successfully request his extradition from Ruritania?

This raises the Pinochet precedent.[13] But there is an important difference. General Pinochet's crime was torture, which is outlawed both by treaty and customary international law. Thus he could have been extradited from Britain to Spain for crimes committed in Chile — had Britain not taken a generous view of his poor health. Moreover, no attempt was made to raise the amnesty he had been granted in Chile before the English Courts.

Pete would, I fear, be more kindly treated by the courts of Utopia and Ruritania. First, I suspect a foreign court would look favourably at the amnesty granted by Arcadia. It would reason, first, that Arcadia should be permitted to achieve political reconciliation in the way it thought best.

Second, unlike torture, genocide, war crimes or crimes against humanity, the production, transfer or use of chemical weapons *per se* is not an international crime for which national amnesty is to be ignored. (In the *Furundzija* case the International Criminal Tribunal for the former Yugoslavia indicated that national amnesties for torture should not be recognised.[14])

Third, it is likely that the courts of both Utopia and Ruritania would refuse to exercise jurisdiction over a crime committed within the territorial limits of Arcadia. They would not take the view that Pete's conduct constituted an international crime subject to universal jurisdiction, allowing Utopia or Ruritania to prosecute Pete as agents of the international communit, in the same way that Spain sought to prosecute Pinochet.

Again this illustrates the need for an international convention which designates the production, transfer, and use of chemical weapons as an international crime subject to universal jurisdiction obliging States to try or extradite offenders in accordance with the principle of *aut dedere aut judicare*.

4. Conclusion

International criminal law has come of age in the past decade. The creation of the International Criminal Tribunals for the former Yugoslavia and for Rwanda, and the permanent International Criminal Court, the decision of the House of Lords in *Pinochet* and the prosecution of General Pinochet in Chile, and the adoption of international conventions like the Terrorist Bombings Convention have created an awareness of the need to combat crime that threatens the safety and stability of the international community by new international means. The production, transfer and use of chemical and biological weapons at present occupy a strange place in the international legal order. There is an awareness that this conduct is of international concern, as evidenced by the conventions prohibiting the production and use of chemical and biological weapons. Yet the international community has largely left the enforcement of these conventions to the domestic law of their respective States Parties.

[13] On 16 October 1998 Augusto Pinochet Ugarte was arrested in the United Kingdom following an extradition request by Spain for the crimes of genocide, terrorism and torture committed on Chilean territory. General Pinochet, a Chilean Senator-for-life, was travelling on a Chilean diplomatic passport and was covered, in Chile, by an amnesty decree of 1978 approved by the then military government, in preparation for the return to democracy in Chile.

[14] Case No IT-95-17/1-7 (10 December 1998); (1999) 39 *ILM* at paras 151-157.

This is not to belittle the importance of domestic legislation. It is remarkable that so many States have enacted legislation to provide for the criminalisation of the production and transfer of chemical weapons. Yet few States have sought to extend the scope of the criminal law extraterritorially, except in respect of crimes committed *by* their own nationals abroad. The United States has gone further in conferring jurisdiction on US courts to prosecute such offences committed *against* US nationals outside the United States,[15] while Sweden has authorised a type of universal jurisdiction by conferring jurisdiction on a Swedish court "even if the crime is committed abroad and irrespective of the perpetrator's nationality."[16]

Surely the time has come for production, transfer, and use of chemical weapons to be converted into an international crime? One in respect of which there is no political exception for extradition and universal jurisdiction for prosecution?

In this brief chapter an attempt has been made to describe the consequences of the present situation for extradition and the recognition of foreign amnesties. Further in this volume, Professors Meselson and Robinson and Lisa Tabassi have presented broader appeals on this subject. One tangible way of measuring progress might be approval for the promotion of an international convention to criminalise, *under international law*, individuals who violate the conventions prohibiting the production and use of chemical and biological weapons.

[15] *Supra* note 4 at 86.
[16] *Supra* note 4 at 85.

INTERNATIONAL COOPERATION IN CRIMINAL JUSTICE: PROBLEMS, PERSPECTIVES AND HOW TO IMPROVE IT

Ihor Drizhchany*

1. INTRODUCTION: THE ROLE OF THE PUBLIC PROSECUTOR OF UKRAINE IN THE FIELD OF INTERNATIONAL COOPERATION

In Ukraine, as in other post-Soviet States following their attainment of independence, there has been an active process of engagement with the international community, including engagement in matters of legal assistance. Over the past decade Ukraine has become party to the European conventions and a whole range of bilateral treaties and other sources of international law concerning or involving legal assistance. The Office of the Public Prosecutor is defined in those instruments, or in the respective ratification acts, as the central authority for the purpose of providing legal assistance in criminal cases during pre-trial investigations. Thus, the Office of the Public Prosecutor operates in the interest of all the pre-trial investigative authorities in Ukraine, both for purely domestic cases as well as cases having international elements.

The following table presents a few figures reflecting the work of the Ukrainian Public Prosecutor in this area during 1999 and 2000. Over those two years almost 4,000 requests from the law enforcement agencies in Ukraine were sent abroad, including:

Table 1 Requests sent by Ukraine

Type of request	1999	2000
Procedural actions	1053	1207
Extradition	85	87
Transfer of criminal proceedings	829	681

Over the same period, the Office of the Public Prosecutor received and acted upon more than 4,500 requests from our foreign colleagues, including:

* Deputy Prosecutor General of Ukraine. The views expressed are solely those of the author and are not attributable to the Ukrainian Public Prosecutor.

R. Yepes-Enríquez and L. Tabassi. (eds.), Treaty Enforcement and International Cooperation in Criminal Matters

Table 2 Requests received from abroad

Type of request	1999	2000
Procedural actions	1774	1651
Extradition	251	198
Transfer of criminal proceedings	510	359

This illustrates the role played by the Office of the Public Prosecutor in Ukraine in the area of international cooperation for mutual legal assistance in criminal matters.

2. Problems and Perspectives for Improvement in International Cooperation in Criminal Cases

2.1 The Situation in Eastern Europe

Irrespective of certain differences in the level of political and economic development of some States, we are united by a common history and by our economic and social choices, as well as, unfortunately, the common experience of crime, which develops according to its own specific dynamics.

The end of the 1980s and the beginning of the 1990s were marked, for Europe, by the formation of a number of States that emerged from the former Soviet bloc and declared their democratic intentions. Due to their weight and number, the populations of these States began to have a considerable impact on economic and social relations in the European region.

At the same time, the new States became a source of criminally active elements for the countries that had long been democratic. The borders that had been closed while the socialist bloc existed had also acted as a barrier to crime. Once the new States emerged, the borders were opened not only for law-abiding citizens, but also for criminals. In the unregulated economic situation which now prevailed in these States, favourable conditions were created for the emergence and development of new forms of economic crime which relied on the establishment of international criminal connections, and which otherwise would not have existed within the framework of separate States. All these factors, taken together, formed the basis for the emergence of the so-called "Russian Mafia" phenomenon, which in West European countries and the United States is called organised crime. It occurs not only in the Russian Federation, but throughout Eastern Europe.

Unfortunately, the appearance of crime coming from the new States into the international arena, and the establishment of links between it and traditional organised crime, happened more quickly than the development of cooperation between the law enforcement agencies in the affected States. One consequence of the flourishing criminal activity, initially in the economic field, was the appearance of huge quantities of illegally acquired funds in bank accounts in Switzerland, Austria and other countries. This turn of events made it necessary for States to join in the existing machinery of legal cooperation in the fight against crime and for corresponding national mechanisms to be set up in those States.

Consequently, the 1993 Minsk Convention on Mutual Assistance and Legal Relations in Civil and Commercial Matters,[1] as well asa a range of bilateral agreements, were signed by 12 States that formerly were republics of the former Soviet Union. The Minsk Convention governs issues such as the execution of international requests, the handover of criminals between the parties, as well as a range of bilateral agreements.

Moreover, as these States joined the Council of Europe, they became party to the European conventions on legal assistance related to criminal prosecutions. Originally, these conventions came into force for Bulgaria, the Czech Republic, Hungary, Poland, Romania, and Slovakia, and also for the former Soviet republics of Estonia, Latvia and Lithuania. Later other States formerly belonging to the Soviet Union and the Federative Republic of Yugoslavia joined in: Georgia, Republic of Moldova, the Russian Federation, Ukraine, Croatia, Macedonia, and Slovenia.

The implementation of these international legal instruments was, in turn, regulated by the provisions of the internal law of each of these States. The application in practice of these international treaties is a sufficiently effective mechanism for combating traditional crime.

2.2 THE LAZARENKO CASE

In the process of collaborating with our colleagues from other States, we have also acquired some unique experience. Notably, there is the indictment by the Ukrainian Public Prosecutor of Pavel Lazarenko, the former Prime Minister of Ukraine, who caused the loss of State funds amounting to many millions through his illegal actions, embezzling State funds and laundering them through foreign banks and offshore companies. Lazarenko is now under arrest in the United States. The case against him has also been pursued in Switzerland, and a guilty verdict has already been reached.

Without going into the details, for that one criminal case alone the Ukrainian Public Prosecutor sent 298 requests for legal assistance to 56 countries. In response to most of our requests we have already received the assistance sought, and this has been vital in the successful prosecution of Larazenko and his fellow conspirators.

This example is a convincing one when we look at the significance of international cooperation among the law enforcement agencies. No single State would be able, on its own, to investigate illegal activity which relies on a complex web of international connections and modern technology in order to switch the destination of huge flows of money in a very few hours. In this case, the Public Prosecutor received legal assistance both in line with existing treaties and on a non-treaty basis, through what is called comity or "goodwill".

2.3 DECENTRALISATION AND DIRECT COMMUNICATION

Ukraine is now party to six European conventions in the field of criminal matters as well as the 1993 Minsk Convention. It is also party to 24 bilateral, interstate (intergovernmental) agreements on legal assistance, extradition and the transfer of criminal proceedings and convicted criminals. Thus, for the purpose of international cooperation between Ukraine

[1] Bulletin of Verkhovna Rada (Parliament) of Ukraine, no. 46 (1994).

and the majority of European States, as well as a number of States in other regions, there is a broad legal basis both in a geographical sense and as regards the subject. This web of cooperation agreements is also operating quite effectively.

At the same time, the need to observe the principles of due process and speedy trials and prosecutions, in respect of increasingly sophisticated types of crime with complex international linkages, requires that States react adequately, efficiently and in a practical manner to the crime by increasing the effectiveness of international cooperation among law enforcement agencies.

Unfortunately, this is not always possible without making changes to existing international agreements on legal assistance, in the broad sense of the term. The main European conventions, which are universal instruments of international law binding upon most European States, and specifically those on extradition and legal assistance, were prepared and signed over 40 years ago and do not take into full account the changes in the patterns of crime, the ways in which crime has gained strength internationally, and the current types of criminal activity.

The machinery that was effective in the 1950s and 1970s is already unable to meet the needs of fighting modern crime, which is becoming increasingly organised and mobile. In our view, the only adequate reaction to the international consolidation of crime may be to increase the effectiveness of mutual legal assistance by improving the mechanisms for providing it, and simplifying the interaction of law enforcement agencies in different countries.

The effectiveness of legal assistance depends directly on the mechanism for transferring requests for it to the competent authority for action. In our view, the only way to solve this problem is to decentralise, i.e., eliminate the current hierarchical system, and set up an arrangement for the requesting and responding agencies to contact each other directly. Unfortunately, most international agreements on extradition and mutual legal assistance, as almost everyone involved in their practical implementation knows only too well, suffer greatly from over-centralisation. This problem becomes especially acute when it is a matter of investigating crimes in border regions and it is necessary to question witnesses who live just a few kilometres away from the site of the investigation, but, alas, on the territory of another State.

A decentralised arrangement for communicating requests for legal assistance already is in operation between Armenia, Belarus, Kazakhstan, Tajikistan and Ukraine, for which the above-mentioned Minsk Convention is in force in the version of the 1997 Protocol.[2] The changes made by the Protocol enable law enforcement agencies, even those at the regional level, to communicate with one another directly in respect of requests for legal assistance

In dealings with Poland, this problem was solved bilaterally by the Public Prosecutors of Ukraine and Poland, who used special powers to set up direct contacts between the prosecutorial authorities. These powers were conferred by the provisions of a bilateral intergovernmental treaty on mutual legal assistance. In November 1998 an inter-agency agreement was signed which forms an integral part of the bilateral intergovernmental treaty. Under the provisions of this agreement, the two Offices of the Prosecutor of Ukraine and Poland were given the right to communicate directly with each other on matters of mutual legal assistance, and to transfer criminal cases for prosecution. This arrangement

[2] 1997 Protocol to the 1993 Minsk Convention, with the amendments to it, was published in the Bulletin of Verkhovna Rada (Parliament), no. 26 (1998).

has proved its worth. Instructions sent to Poland are now, as a rule, carried out in a period not exceeding two months, whereas previously they would have taken up to six months to be carried out. The experience of Ukraine and Poland in decentralising communications for the purpose of legal assistance may well serve as an example of increased effectiveness in international cooperation.

Similarly, following the conclusion of the Schengen Agreement,[3] the parties to it set up a highly simplified system for direct exchanges between law enforcement agencies. The necessary conditions for this step existed, including similar levels of economic and social development and similar crime situations among the parties. The establishment of the same sort of beneficial regime for exchanges among the competent authorities of States that are not party to the Schengen Agreement, but are obliged to combat increasingly sophisticated forms of crime, would be a relevant and necessary step for the community.

If law enforcement agencies cannot effectively fight crime on their own territory today, criminals from those countries will be carrying out their criminal activities in Western Europe tomorrow. With the situation as it stands at present, it is impossible to effectively fight crime with the resources of a single State alone.

2.4 CORRELATION OF DESIGNATION OF AUTHORITIES WITH NATIONAL POWERS

Inseparable from the issue of decentralising exchanges is the question of the relationships between the competent authorities at the various levels. We are convinced that the exclusive competence of the central authorities should be limited to determining the solution to problems concerning the application of the international treaties and the adoption of decisions on behalf of the State; in other words, the central authorities would be responsible for acts of a political nature or those which have a direct bearing on human rights. The central authorities certainly should not be involved in transferring requests for the handover of court documents, or for simple procedural acts which do not adversely impact on civil rights, and a number of other issues of this nature.

In the context of increasing the effectiveness of international cooperation and decentralising exchanges, we should also look at the question of deciding which authorities at the national level should be implementing the provisions of international treaties on legal assistance. The experience of Ukraine's ratification of the European conventions in the field of criminal law is instructive in this respect. Our State, when adhering to the European Conventions on Extradition,[4] on Mutual Assistance in Criminal Matters,[5] and on the Transfer of Proceedings in Criminal Matters,[6] designated the Ministry of Justice of Ukraine to be the sole central authority in the country responsible for their implementation. This designation was in blind imitation of the approach taken by the States of Western Europe in tackling these issues. We will not question the correctness of the approach to the situation found in States which ratified the conventions 20, 30, or more years ago.

[3] Convention of 19 June 1990, applying the Schengen Agreement of 14 June 1985, International Legal Materials, 84 (1991).

[4] European Convention on Extradition, Paris, 13 December 1957, European Treaty Series, no. 24.

[5] European Convention on Mutual Assistance in Criminal Matters, Strasbourg, 20 April 1959, European Treaty Series, no. 30.

[6] European Convention on the Transfer of Proceedings in Criminal Matters, Strasbourg, 15 May 1972, European Treaty Series, no. 73.

Ukraine's designation of the Ministry of Justice as its central authority for the purpose of implementing the European conventions, without taking account of national traditions, did not meet the needs of prompt justice, for a number of reasons:

- The Ministry of Justice does not have any involvement in the prosecution of criminal cases, and moreover has no procedural or supervisory powers at all in respect of Ukrainian legislation;
- In the preceding period before adhering to the European Conventions, matters of legal assistance in criminal cases were outside the purview and powers of the Ministry of Justice; and,
- The staff of the Ministry, as a rule, do not have any experience in the field of legal assistance, and are not even familiar with the duties of any procedural officer, be that investigator, prosecutor or judge.

This means that the Ministry of Justice of Ukraine is not capable, in an organisational, structural or staffing sense, to ensure timely and complete compliance with international requests. It has therefore proved itself to be unprepared to operate effectively as the central authority for the implementation of European conventions.

Practice has shown the decision to be ill considered. This arrangement has resulted in a situation where even requests which do not require complex organisational measures or serious monitoring have had to follow a circuitous route from the originator of the request to its executor and back again. From the *raion* level, the request travels to the *oblast* and from there to the capital, where it is transmitted from the law enforcement agencies to the Ministry of Justice, and then abroad, where once more it follows the same course down to the district level and back again. In this process, apart from the increase in postal costs, precious time vital to the investigation has been wasted. In cases where sometimes only one or two hours would be needed to carry out the requested steps in the investigation, instead months would elapse before the materials would be dispatched. This is so when the overwhelming majority of the issues requiring legal assistance arise at the very stage when the crime is being investigated.

Because of this, at the initiative of the Public Prosecutor, the Supreme Council of Ukraine has made certain relevant amendments to the legislation that defines the central authorities for the implementation of these conventions in our country. All requests originating from the investigating authorities mentioned in these conventions, and in the 1990 Convention on the Laundering, Search, Seizure, and Confiscation of the Proceeds of Crime,[7] are now directed through the Office of the Public Prosecutor of Ukraine. The latter convention is especially important, because it is aimed at removing the obstacles to depriving criminal groups of their sources of funding, obstacles caused by conflicts in national legislation.

Under the ratification acts of Ukraine for these conventions, the Office of the Public Prosecutor, together with the Ministry of Justice, is the central authority responsible for organising responses to requests received from investigating agencies for international legal assistance. The Ministry of Justice only organises compliance with requests from courts, which are not numerous. For requests concerning pre-trial investigations, the Office of the Prosecutor deals with all the issues. The role of the Public Prosecutor of Ukraine is defined

[7] Convention on the Laundering, Search, Seizure, and Confiscation of the Proceeds of Crime, Strasbourg, 8 November 1990, European Treaty Series, no. 141.

in a similar manner in the above-mentioned Minsk Convention. The Public Prosecutor is also responsible for organising legal assistance in criminal matters when it is being provided on the basis of any of Ukraine's bilateral treaties as well.

In our view it is in fact the Office of the Public Prosecutor who has the capacity and power to monitor compliance with the law by the agencies engaged in preliminary investigations since it holds all the necessary keys to providing effective and timely legal assistance when criminal cases are being investigated. This notion was stressed at the conference attended by European public prosecutors in May 2000 in Strasbourg, when the role of the public prosecutors in international cooperation was discussed as one of the most important items on the agenda. The Office of the Prosecutor is not only an authority which is professionally equipped, and has the necessary power and rights, to influence the timing, completeness and objectivity of the work of investigating agencies. Unlike the Ministry of Justice, the prosecutor has an interest (in the positive sense of the word) in the proper and expeditious carrying out of instructions, because the office is supervising the investigation and is motivated to comply with the time limits set for it.

As the central authority responsible for the fulfilment of obligations under international agreements on legal assistance, the Office of the Public Prosecutor has to formulate requests not only from its own suboffices, but also from investigators in all the law enforcement institutions of Ukraine. This means that the expansion of the framework of international cooperation is not merely of bureaucratic significance for the Office of the Prosecutor – in this area we act in the interests of all the law enforcement agencies.

This example clearly illustrates the need for adequate reflection, in international agreements and their respective ratification acts, of the so-called "national" powers of the competent institutions, and specifically those of the prosecutors' offices.

It is interesting that our Russian colleagues, possibly in the light of Ukraine's experience, have also acted to designate the Office of the Public Prosecutor in the Russian Federation as the central authority for the fulfilment of the 1957 and 1959 Conventions.

3. Conclusion

To sum up, I should like to reiterate the basic arguments for increasing the effectiveness of international legal assistance:

- Decentralisation of exchanges in legal assistance, giving the right to communicate directly, not only to individual law enforcement institutions, but also to their territorial authorities;
- Definition of the powers of the central authorities of States for international treaties in correlation with the internal functions of those offices nationally; and,
- Enhancement of the role of the Office of the Public Prosecutor in the field of international cooperation.

This chapter has been quite theoretical, and has only touched on a few aspects of cooperation among law enforcement agencies in fighting criminal activity that occurs on the territory of several different States. Ukraine continues to discuss and put into practice proposals for increasing the effectiveness of this cooperation, as long as they bring results. The experience gained in international cooperation has convinced us that we have excellent shared prospects.

IMPLEMENTATION OF LEGAL ASSISTANCE AGREEMENTS FROM THE PERSPECTIVE OF CZECH LAW

Jaroslava Novotná*

1. Introduction

The Czech Republic, particularly after 1989, became party to a large number of new international agreements in the criminal field. The effective implementation of these agreements encompasses a long and extensive process of evaluating the Czech legal system as a whole and, especially, the basic legal norms that regulate criminal proceedings (i.e., the Criminal Code and Criminal Procedure Code). In the Czech Republic many amendments to previous legislation and even the establishment of numerous new legal institutions has taken place and will continue to take place.

This process in the Czech Republic can be described as an ongoing and permanent effort by the State authorities. Moreover, it is a legal duty of the competent State authorities: within the framework of the legislative process in which a new law or an amendment to an already existing law is being prepared, the coordination of such law with the international obligations of the Czech Republic is prescribed by the Act of Government on Legislative Procedure. There is no doubt that the political, social and organisational, and especially appropriate legislative, measures are the basic preconditions for effective functioning of international agreements nationally and internationally.

In the criminal field one can speak primarily of the following obligations arising from international agreements:

- criminalisation of certain forms of human activity, i.e. changes in the substantive criminal law in the Criminal Code;
- legislative measures in criminal procedure law, i.e. establishment of the internal legal norms in the Criminal Procedure Code enabling effective international cooperation by the various competent authorities (judicial bodies, including public prosecutors, police and customs organs).

In my opinion, the development and the present situation in the Czech Republic in the field of implementation of international agreements can serve as an example of the developments that have taken place in a number of other States in transition. Therefore, the following overview of how issues have been addressed in the Czech Republic is illustrative.

* Director, International Legal Assistance Department, Supreme Prosecutor's Office of the Czech Republic. The views expressed are those of the author and are not attributable to the Czech government.

R. Yepes-Enríquez and L. Tabassi. (eds.), Treaty Enforcement and International Cooperation in Criminal Matters

2. Criminalisation of Certain Forms of Human Activity

The types of human activities that should be considered to be criminal acts (offences), and as such prosecuted and punished, is very much connected with the particular legal culture, society and mentality of a given region. However, it can be said that some similar or identical, generally accepted opinions exist concerning the criminalisation of certain acts. One can mention, for example, the killing of human beings: the offence of murder can, of course, be found in all existing legal systems worldwide.

As human society, in its great diversity, develops, opinions on the necessity to punish certain acts that have not, until now, been considered punishable are developing. There are also new forms of human activity that did not occur before. This development is traceable in individual States separately, but also in the international arena, where States undertake obligations pursuant to international agreements to, *inter alia*, prosecute and punish certain forms of a human behaviour. The following examples of this can be cited in respect of the Czech Republic.

2.1 The Chemical Weapons Convention

The Chemical Weapons Convention[1] has been in force for the Czech Republic since 29 April 1997. According to Article VII(1) of the Convention, the Czech Republic shall:

(a) Prohibit natural and legal persons anywhere on its territory or in any other place under its jurisdiction as recognised by international law from undertaking any activity prohibited to a State Party under this Convention, including enacting penal legislation with respect to such activity;

(b) Not permit in any place under its control any activity prohibited to a State Party under this Convention; and

(c) Extend its penal legislation enacted under subparagraph (a) to any activity prohibited to a State Party under this Convention undertaken anywhere by natural persons, possessing its nationality, in conformity with international law.

On 24 January 1997, Act No. 19 on measures connected with the prohibition of the chemical weapons was adopted. By this Act the Criminal Code was also amended to include the new criminal offence of "illegal self-arming": anyone designing, building or using premises for the production of chemical weapons will be punished by imprisonment up to three years. Organised forms of this criminal activity will be punished by higher penalties. The production, import, export, storage and procurement for another person of a highly dangerous substance (including chemicals) or a device for its production without a permit will be punished by imprisonment, from one year up to five years, prohibition of the activity, or a fine.

[1] 1993 Convention on the Prohibition of the Development, Production, Stockpiling and Use of Chemical Weapons and on Their Destruction, entered into force on 29 April 1997. Text, as corrected and changed, available at http://www.opcw.org.

In addition, the control of certain goods (substances) and technologies has been instituted. The illegal handling of such goods and technologies, or handling them without a permit, has been made punishable under new provisions of the Criminal Code. Weapons of mass destruction (such as nuclear, chemical and biological weapons) have been excluded from trade in military material, and violations have been made punishable under new provisions in the Criminal Code.

The Czech Criminal Code already contained the offence of using prohibited military means in war, which is punishable up to life imprisonment, depending on the actual circumstances.

2.2 OTHER AGREEMENTS

The Czech Republic is party to international agreements combating the following forms of criminal activity:

- illegal trafficking in drugs;
- traffic in human beings;
- money laundering;
- bribery of foreign public officials; and,
- organised crime as such.

It is also involved in international efforts concerning the confiscation of proceeds from crime, and the establishment and competence of international courts (such as the Hague tribunals).

All the above-mentioned and similar agreements created the necessity for legislative changes in the field of criminal law, especially the criminalisation of the specific forms of human behaviour. The necessary changes in the law of criminal and administrative procedure, as a precondition for effective international cooperation in combating transboundary criminal activity, are illustrated in the following section.

3. INTERNATIONAL COOPERATION FROM THE PERSPECTIVE OF CZECH LAW ON CRIMINAL PROCEDURE

As mentioned above, the Czech Republic is party to many international agreements. The following multilateral agreements are important for the procedure of international cooperation:

- European Convention on Extradition (Paris, 13 December 1957), party since 14 July 1992;

- Additional Protocol to the European Convention on Extradition (Strasbourg, 15 October 1975), party since 17 February 1997;

- Second Additional Protocol to the European Convention on Extradition (Strasbourg, 17 March 1978), party since 17 February 1997;
- European Convention on Mutual Assistance in Criminal Matters (Strasbourg, 20 April 1959), party since 14 July 1992;
- Additional Protocol to the European Convention on Mutual Assistance in Criminal Matters (Strasbourg, 17 March 1978), party since 17 February 1997;
- European Convention on the Transfer of Proceedings in Criminal Matters (Strasbourg, 15 May 1972), party since 15 July 1992;
- European Convention on the Suppression of Terrorism (Strasbourg, 27 January 1977), party since 15 July 1992;
- Convention on Transfer of Sentenced Persons (Strasbourg, 21 March 1983), party since 1 August 1992;
- Convention on Laundering, Search, Seizure and Confiscation of Proceeds from Crime (Strasbourg, 8 November 1990), party since 1 March 1997; and,
- Convention against Illicit Traffic in Narcotic Drugs and Psychotropic Substances (Vienna, 20 December 1988), party since 2 September 1991.

A large number of bilateral agreements, several of them treaties additional to the Strasbourg conventions, have been concluded between the Czech Republic and other States on mutual legal assistance in criminal matters. The cooperation with all States neighbouring the Czech Republic has been covered by bilateral treaties. Most recently, mutual legal assistance treaties were concluded with the United States and Canada and are now in force.

The relevant domestic provisions regulating judicial cooperation in criminal matters are Articles 375 to 384e of the Criminal Procedure Code (Chapter XXIV). These articles deal with different types of international assistance in criminal matters: extradition, transfer of criminal proceedings, and enforcement of foreign judgments. It should be pointed out that legal assistance can be provided when there is no international agreement in force between the Czech Republic and the requesting State. Only for requests for the enforcement of foreign judgments, including seizure, forfeiture and confiscation, or transfer of a sentenced person, must an agreement (treaty) be in force.

The following is an example of how specific issues concerning mutual legal assistance are dealt with by the Czech Criminal Procedure Code.

3.1 TAKING WITNESS TESTIMONY, SEARCHES, OBTAINING WRITTEN (DOCUMENTARY) EVIDENCE, SERVICE OF JUDICIAL DOCUMENTS

These are, besides extradition, the most frequently requested forms of mutual legal assistance. Judicial authorities can also order the police to search for a person or a thing. The requested measures are carried out according to Czech Criminal Procedure Code; however, the foreign procedural law can also be applied upon request if it does not contradict Czech public order. The presence of foreign defence counsel on behalf of the accused, as well as State officials (prosecutors, judges, police officers), can be permitted.

3.2 SEIZURE, FORFEITURE, CONFISCATION

A number of changes have been made to Czech laws in connection with the Council of Europe Money Laundering Convention. At the request of a foreign State, the Czech court may, upon a proposal by a prosecutor, order seizure or forfeiture of property, or a part thereof, in accordance with the terms and conditions of the relevant international agreement binding the Czech Republic. When the foreign State request is based on an international agreement under which the Czech Republic has the obligation to recognise and enforce a foreign judgment concerning the seizure of property, or its confiscation or forfeiture in a criminal proceeding, the procedure is as follows: The case shall be referred by the Ministry of Justice to the Supreme Court for its decision on the recognition of the foreign judgment in the Czech Republic. In the proceedings, the Supreme Prosecutor should be heard. If recognised, the enforcement of the foreign judgment falls within the competence of the local court and prosecutor. The property subject to seizure, confiscation or forfeiture shall belong to the Czech Republic, unless an asset sharing agreement is otherwise provided by the relevant international treaty.

3.3 TAPPING AND RECORDING OF TELECOMMUNICATIONS

This could also be provided as a measure of mutual legal assistance. The procedure and the conditions are determined by the Criminal Procedure Code. When the criminal proceeding is being conducted for an especially serious intentional offence, or for another intentional offence, the prosecution of which is obligatory pursuant to an international treaty in force, the presiding judge, in pre-trial proceedings upon the proposal of the prosecutor, can order tapping and recording of telecommunication, if it is justified that through the telecommunication important facts for the criminal proceeding will be transmitted.

3.4 EXTRADITION

Changes have also been made to Czech law in connection with the Council of Europe Additional Protocols to the Extradition Convention. Extradition of a person for the purpose of criminal prosecution, or for serving sentence in the requesting State, can also be granted in an expedited extradition proceeding if the person concerned declares that he/she agrees with his/her extradition. The general conditions are determined by international agreements and the Czech Criminal Procedure Code; the principle of double criminality and the principle of speciality apply, as well as the requirement that the time limit for prosecution not be expired. The Czech Republic does not extradite its own nationals, but, in such cases it is obliged to institute criminal proceedings.

3.5 SPECIFIC ITEMS IN JUDICIAL COOPERATION

The competence of the central authority is, in the sense of the above mentioned agreements on mutual legal assistance, divided between the Czech Ministry of Justice and the Supreme Prosecutor's Office. All requests for legal assistance in the pre-trial stage of the proceedings in the requesting State must be sent to the Supreme Prosecutor's Office. If the case in the requesting State has already been brought before the court, the central authority to which the request should be sent is the Ministry of Justice.

Competence for executing foreign requests for mutual legal assistance is also divided between the prosecutor's offices, police investigators, and the courts. The Supreme Prosecutor's Office forwards the request to the local competent prosecutor's office, while the Ministry of Justice hands over the requests to the local competent courts.

4. Conclusion

In summary, what are the most important elements affecting effective judicial cooperation?

- Treaty text creating for States Parties all obligations necessary for effective implementation.
- The effectiveness of the treaty must be under constant evaluation, in order to change it to respond to the rapid development of daily reality.
- Fulfilment of the obligations of the treaty by States Parties must also be monitored.
- Proliferation of international treaties can cause confusion between the cooperating officials.
- The formalism of relations between States has its limits.
- Prompt enactment or amendment of national legislation is a pre-condition.
- Establishment of direct contact between the competent lower judicial authorities, and creating networks of cooperating authorities and officials, for example, the European Judicial Network, the Schengen system, liaison officers, judges, and prosecutors.
- Changes in the role of the central authorities for mutual legal assistance (contact points, strategy, education, creating a registration centre, gathering knowledge and experience).
- Goodwill and mutual trust; a network of personal contacts.
- Language skills, cooperativeness and the ability to communicate.
- Police (operational) cooperation must support mutual legal assistance by providing the judicial authorities with special police investigative techniques.

GEORGIAN PENAL LEGISLATION IN THE CONTEXT OF ARTICLE VII OF THE CHEMICAL WEAPONS CONVENTION

David Bazerashvili*

1. INTRODUCTION

The geographical location of Georgia raises concerns about it becoming a transit channel for weapons, drugs and other contraband. This situation is exacerbated by the fact that the country has just obtained independence and has begun to build a State system of institutions, mechanisms and, of course, legislation. Notwithstanding the above, Georgia has become party to a number of instruments in order to defend its society, and the world in general, from the danger of weapons of mass destruction, drugs and other substances destructive to life. The new Georgian Criminal Code and Criminal Procedure Code, where the main principles and requirements of normative international conventions have been reflected, are a good example of this. However, national legislation cannot operate effectively without international cooperation. The aspiration for, and aims of, such cooperation are reflected in the bilateral and multilateral agreements concluded by Georgia.

2. RELEVANT PROVISIONS OF THE GEORGIAN CRIMINAL CODE AND CODE OF CRIMINAL PROCEDURE

How do the provisions of the Criminal Code and Criminal Procedure Code of Georgia operate in its jurisdiction with respect to transboundary criminal activity?

What obstacles are often met during the application of international agreements for mutual legal assistance on criminal matters?

As an example, let's briefly review the articles of the Criminal Code of Georgia that define the crimes related to activities prohibited by the Chemical Weapons Convention.[1]

Article 406 of the Criminal Code of Georgia, entitled "Production, Purchase or Sale of Weapons of Mass Destruction" forbids the production, purchase or sale of any chemical, biological or other weapon of mass destruction prohibited by international treaty to which Georgia is party. Violations carry legal consequences and penalties of imprisonment ranging from eight to fifteen years in length.

Article 409 of the Criminal Code of Georgia, entitled "Ecocide," meaning contamination of the atmosphere, land or water resources, mass destruction of flora and fauna or any

* Head, International Legal Relations Department, Ministry of Justice of Georgia. The views expressed are the author's own and are not attributable to the Ministry of Justice.

[1] 1993 Convention on the Prohibition of the Development, Production, Stockpiling and Use of Chemical Weapons and on Their Destruction, entered into force on 29 April 1997. Text, as corrected and changed, available at http://www.opcw.org.

R. Yepes-Enríquez and L. Tabassi. (eds.), Treaty Enforcement and International Cooperation in Criminal Matters

other action that could cause ecological disaster, shall be punishable by imprisonment ranging from eight to twenty years in length.

Article 288 of the Criminal Code of Georgia, entitled "Violation of Rules concerning environmentally hazardous substances or waste," deals with violations of rules on the handling of toxic, bacteriological, chemical or other environmentally hazardous substances or residue during production, transportation, disposal, storage, burying or use which, through negligence, caused substantial damage to human life or the environment or could have produced any other grave consequence. Violations shall be punishable by a fine or imprisonment of up to two years.

Aggravating circumstances of these offences will be considered to have occurred if the same negligent act has caused contamination of the environment, poisoning or ailment, or deterioration of human health, or has given rise to mass destruction of wildlife, as well as acts committed amidst ecological emergency or in an ecological disaster zone, if the negligent act has caused a person's death or mass illness of humans. In this case the punishment shall be increased by imprisonment of up to eight years.

Paragraph 2 of Article 237 of the Criminal Code, entitled "Illegal possession for misappropriation purposes or extortion of arms, ammunition, explosive material or an explosive device," reads as follows:

> Illegal possession, for misappropriation purposes or extortion, of nuclear, chemical, biological weapons or other mass destruction, or material or device for manufacturing such weapons, shall be punishable by prison sentence ranging from five to ten years in length.

3. Territorial and Extraterritorial Application

Article 4 of the Criminal Code defines the applicability of criminal law to crimes committed on the territory of Georgia. The crime shall be deemed to have been perpetrated on the territory of Georgia if it began, continued, or ended on the territory of Georgia. The Criminal Code also applies to crimes committed on the continental shelf of Georgia and in the Special Economic Zone (paragraph 2). Anyone who has perpetrated a crime on a vessel authorised to use the national flag or identification mark of Georgia, or against such a vessel, shall bear criminal liability under the Criminal Code of Georgia unless otherwise prescribed by international treaty to which Georgia is party (paragraph 3). If a diplomatic representative of a foreign country, or a person enjoying diplomatic immunity, has committed a crime on the territory of Georgia, the question of their criminal liability shall be settled in the manner and to the extent permitted by international law (paragraph 4).

In respect of applicability of the criminal law of Georgia to crimes committed abroad, the Criminal Code of Georgia, namely Article 5, entitled "Criminal Liability for Crime Perpetrated Abroad," states that any citizen of Georgia, as well as any person permanently resident in Georgia without having citizenship, who has committed an act proscribed by the Criminal Code of Georgia, and which is regarded as a crime under the legislation of the State in which it was committed, shall bear criminal liability under the Criminal Code of Georgia if the person has not been convicted in another State (paragraph 1).

Any citizen of Georgia, as well as any person permanently resident in Georgia without having Georgian citizenship, who has committed an act proscribed by the Criminal Code of Georgia which is not regarded as a crime under the legislation of the State in which it was committed, shall bear criminal liability under the Criminal Code of Georgia if it is a grave[2] or especially grave offence directed against the interests of Georgia, or if criminal liability for this offence is provided for by an international treaty to which Georgia is party (para. 2).

A citizen of a foreign State, as well as a person not permanently resident in Georgia and not holding Georgian citizenship, who has committed an act proscribed by the Criminal Code of Georgia shall bear criminal liability under the Criminal Code of Georgia if it is a grave or especially grave offence directed against the interests of Georgia, or if criminal liability for this offence is provided for by an international treaty to which Georgia is party, provided the person has not been convicted in another State (paragraph 2).

4. Extradition and Mutual Legal Assistance

Citizens of Georgia and stateless persons permanently resident in Georgia shall under no circumstances be extradited to another State for criminal prosecution, or for serving a sentence, unless otherwise determined by international treaty to which Georgia is party. A citizen of a foreign State, as well as a person not having Georgian citizenship and present on the territory of Georgia, who has committed a crime may be extradited to another State for criminal prosecution or for serving a sentence in the manner and to the extent determined by international treaties to which Georgia is party. Extradition should be refused for a person under asylum who has committed a crime and who is being persecuted for political beliefs. Extradition shall also be refused for any person who has committed an act not regarded as a crime under the legislation of Georgia, or a crime for which capital punishment is prescribed in the State requesting extradition. The question of criminal liability of such persons shall be settled in the manner and to the extent permitted by international law (Article 6 of the Criminal Code of Georgia).

The specific procedures for extradition are prescribed by the Criminal Procedure Code and in international agreements to which Georgia is party. Article 247, entitled "Forms of legal assistance," of the Criminal Procedure Code provides the following:

1. In conformity with international agreements on legal assistance to which Georgia is party, the court, prosecutor and investigator are entitled via the Ministry of Justice of Georgia or the Prosecutor General's Office of Georgia[3]:

---

[2] Article 12 of the Criminal Code of Georgia, concerning the maximum terms of imprisonment, provides for three categories of crime: (a) misdemeanor, (b) grave crime, and (c) especially grave crime.

'Misdemeanor' shall be the crime of aforethought or crime of negligence for practice whereof the sentence provided by the Code is not in excess of five years of imprisonment.

'Grave' shall be the crime of aforethought whereof the sentence provided by the Code is not in excess of ten years of imprisonment, also the crime of negligence for practice whereof the sentence provided by the Code exceeds five years of imprisonment.

'Especially grave' shall be the crime of aforethought whereof the sentence provided by the Code exceeds ten years of imprisonment or covers a full life term.

[3] The Ministry of Justice is responsible for requests relating to court procedures, and the Prosecutor General's Office is responsible for carrying out investigative procedures.

a) To request investigation and court procedures be carried out on the territory of Georgia; to perform such actions on the territory of Georgia on behalf of the competent authorities of the foreign state;

b) To request the extradition of a citizen of Georgia in order to bring him to trial and pass sentence upon him and to grant extradition of a foreign citizen to a foreign State for the same purpose;

c) To request extradition of Georgian citizens, sentenced in another State, so that execution of the sentence may be carried out in the homeland and to transfer a foreigner sentenced in Georgia for execution of the sentence in his home State.

2. In the absence of an agreement on legal assistance, for a specific case, the issue may be decided by agreement between the Minister of Justice of Georgia or the Prosecutor General of Georgia with the appropriate authorities of the foreign State. In this event legal assistance shall be performed in accordance with rules specified by Articles 248 to 260 of the Criminal Procedure Code.

In any event, it is clear that the Criminal Code, as well as Criminal Procedure Code, provides for exception being made by international agreements to which Georgia is party. In accordance with the "Law on International Treaties of Georgia," international agreements to which Georgia is party are an inseparable part of national legislation. In the hierarchy of normative acts of Georgia, international agreements, which must be compatible with the Constitution of Georgia, have superiority, followed by laws and other normative acts.

5. Effect

The international agreements on legal assistance on criminal matters that are currently in force in Georgia play a positive role in combating transboundary criminal activity. There are instances when such agreements have had decisive significance in the investigation, extradition or transfer of sentenced persons, and this must be so. However, frequently the particular international agreement does not provide for the specific procedures and mechanisms by which such legal assistance shall be carried out and, instead, makes reference to the national laws of the member States. At times these national laws contain significant differences in procedural matters, and this leads to the unreasonable protraction of the procedure. For example, when the terms for service of documents in one jurisdiction are different from the terms for service in another jurisdiction, the obstacles can be overcome, but it may cause significant delay. Of course, the elaboration and adoption of multilateral international agreements that will specify in detail the particular procedures appropriate for all member States is quite difficult to achieve, however; the existence of bilateral international agreements between neighbouring States, at least, is of the highest importance.

Currently, for mutual legal assistance, the multilateral international agreements within the framework of Commonwealth of Independent States (CIS), as well as the bilateral international agreement between Georgia and the Republic of Turkey, are in force. In addition to those, Georgia is party to the Convention on the Transfer of Sentenced Persons,[4]

[4] Strasbourg, 21 March 1983, European Treaty Series, no. 112.

the European Convention on Extradition,[5] and the European Convention on Mutual Legal Assistance on Criminal Matters,[6] which gives Georgia the opportunity to cooperate not only with neighbouring States but with the rest of Europe. Georgia will also ratify the Council of Europe Criminal Convention on Corruption, and United Nations Convention Against Transnational Organised Crime.[7]

[5] Paris, 13 December 1957, European Treaty Series, no. 24.
[6] Strasbourg, 20 April 1959, European Treaty Series, no. 30.
[7] United Nations Convention Against Transnational Organised Crime (doc A/55/383), Palermo, December 2000, not in force.

SECTION III.2

GATHERING EVIDENCE AND INTERVIEWING WITNESSES IN AN INTERNATIONAL CONTEXT

INTRODUCTION AND SUMMARY

As discussed in the general introduction to this volume and Section II.1 on Concurrent Jurisdiction, violations of the Chemical Weapons Convention may be prosecuted horizontally, in the State Party's jurisdiction and within its national system, or vertically, in an international court under relevant provisions of international criminal law, depending upon the gravity of the offence and the facts. Thus experience gained in preparing for and conducting trials in the international criminal tribunals for the former Yugoslavia (ICTY) and Rwanda (ICTR) is examined in this section, especially since it brings completely novel perspectives to the equation of States cooperating with judicial proceedings in other jurisdictions. New complexities arose in ensuring cooperation for court proceedings unconnected to a national judiciary, police force or executive administration, and in gathering evidence from localities and people that recently experienced large-scale armed conflict and human tragedy of unfathomable proportions.

Established by the Security Council under Chapter VII of the United Nations Charter, the ICTY is responsible for trying those individuals allegedly responsible for the serious violations of international humanitarian law committed in the region of the former Yugoslavia, with the goal of bringing them to justice, deterring future violations and restoring international peace and security. The Statute of the ICTY gives the prosecutor the special powers that she/he needs in order to ensure that the ICTY can identify and locate those individuals and carry out its mandate. These powers entitle the prosecutor, *inter alia*, to summon and interview witnesses, seek the assistance of any State and undertake emergency actions, such as arrest or seizure of property, when necessary. However, despite

R. Yepes-Enríquez and L. Tabassi. (eds.), Treaty Enforcement and International Cooperation in Criminal Matters

these special privileges, the unique circumstances of the ICTY and the crimes under investigation still pose a challenge for the prosecutor in gathering evidence. Some of the difficulties encountered have included gaining access to the crime scene and obtaining witness accounts soon after the crimes were committed. Despite these obstacles, it is essential for the attainment of the goals of the ICTY that these do not prevent the establishment of the facts.

The difficulties faced by both the prosecution and the defence in preparing cases for the international tribunals brought new perspectives to the principle of "fair trial." This principle is, of course, fundamental in both civil law and common law systems, although they each go about it in a different way. As for supranational judicial bodies, the statutes of the international tribunals contains elements of both civil law and common law systems and procedurally tend to follow the common law trial approach. The second author in this section, who acted as defence counsel in both the ICTY and ICTR, points out how the defence suffers in the hybrid system. While the prosecution has specific powers under the Statute, the defence does not, leaving the status of the defence with respect to the Tribunal at best unclear to States when the defence attorney is requesting cooperation to defend the client. The ICTY and ICTR statutes require States to cooperate with requests made by the tribunals. This obligation extends to requests made by the Office of the Prosecutor as an office within the Tribunal. In contrast, the defence attorney is usually a private individual hired by the defendant. This has important implications for the quality of the defence in the following ways. First, it immediately means that the defence will have limited financial resources with which to conduct an investigation. Second, because the defence lacks a statutory connection with the tribunal, the defence is left with little power in gathering potentially crucial evidence. It can ask that the court issue an order requiring the State to produce the evidence or it can ask the prosecution to obtain the evidence for the defence. Neither option is ideal to ensure that the defendant is able to receive the best defence possible and, consequently, the fairest trial. Although there are some variations depending on the individual circumstances, this problem is a very pressing one when considering the future of international criminal law. As in the common law system, the inherent weakness of the defence is balanced by the obligation of the prosecution to disclose any exculpatory evidence and by the prosecution bearing the burden of proof regarding the crimes in question. However, one could argue that in the international context the defence is even weaker than it would be in national context in a common law system. Although it is impossible to ensure an ideal trial, it is necessary to be aware of problems in the system in order to address them and strive for the best trial possible.

The last two authors in this section broaden the picture even further to bring consideration to witnesses and survivors. In the search for international justice through the establishment of international tribunals as in the case of the ICTY and ICTR, it is important to remember that the prosecution and defence are not the only players – witnesses and survivors are involved in the investigation and trial process. Arriving in the aftermath of tragic experiences, investigators from both the prosecution and defence must take steps to prevent further aggravation to them.

The successful conduct of proceedings before international tribunals, from initial evidence collection to in-court witness testimony, relies greatly on the cooperation of the victims, those most closely affected by those crimes under investigation. While the entire region is trying to come to terms with the unimaginable atrocities that were committed, these witnesses were touched personally, often by having seen the acts being committed or by losing a loved one. Although the primary purpose of the ad hoc Tribunals is to punish those responsible for the heinous acts of violence, a secondary purpose, and one intrinsic to re-establishing international peace and security, is healing of victims and the country as a whole. For many years, both the ICTY and the ICTR had poor track records on public relations, appearing all too often as an insensitive international organisation imposing its demands on the local people. If the international community wishes to protect its moral principles through the trial process at the international tribunals, it must combat this image. In recent years, programmes have been established to remedy the situation, but much work still needs to be done. The drafters of the Statute establishing the ICC took this issue into account by including numerous provisions to help victims. All too often, it is easy to forget the plight of the victims, but for the tribunals to truly fulfil their original purposes, they cannot afford to do so.

Clearly, the challenges faced in the collection of evidence in an international context are demanding. In addition to the usual obstacles faced in national courts, investigators in proceedings before international courts face a number of new complexities. They must depend upon cooperation and legal assistance by national authorities in a much broader domain. The number of parties affected is generally much greater and the crimes in question are usually much more egregious. The practical problems faced can seem beyond resolution, yet the trials in question are absolutely essential for the progressive development of moral principles in the future. By working to overcome the practical problems faced when gathering evidence, investigators for both the defence and prosecution are furthering the goals of international criminal law and the international community as a whole.

Pablo G. Kapusta

Précis-writer for Section III.2; Intern in the OPCW Technical Secretariat, Office of the Legal Adviser; Princeton University. The views expressed are not attributable to the OPCW or Princeton University.

PRACTICAL ASPECTS OF GATHERING EVIDENCE IN AN INTERNATIONAL ENVIRONMENT

Robert Reid*

1. INTRODUCTION

This chapter will discuss the practical aspects of gathering evidence and interviewing witnesses at the International Criminal Tribunal for the former Yugoslavia (ICTY). It is divided into three parts: the power to investigate and gather evidence; the mechanisms in place to enable investigators to gather evidence and the actual gathering of that evidence; and the interviewing of witnesses.

2. THE POWER TO INVESTIGATE AND GATHER EVIDENCE

The following Articles of the Statute of the ICTY and the Rules of Procedure and Evidence (the Rules) are relevant to the gathering of evidence (and interviewing witnesses).

2.1 THE STATUTE

Article 15 of the Statute requires the Judges of the Tribunal to adopt rules of procedure and evidence for the conduct of the pre-trial phase of proceedings, trials and appeals, the admission of evidence, the protection of victims and witnesses, and other appropriate matters.

Article 16(1) of the Statute specifies that "the Prosecutor shall be responsible for the investigations and prosecution of persons responsible...." Sub-paragraph 2 provides that, "The Prosecutor shall act independently as a separate organ of the International Tribunal. He or she must not seek or receive instructions from any Government or from any other source."

Article 18 of the Statute gives the Prosecutor the power to initiate investigations and prepare indictments. Article 18(2) allows the Prosecutor to question suspects, victims and witnesses; to collect evidence; and to conduct on-site investigations. In carrying out these tasks, the Prosecutor may, as appropriate, seek the assistance of the State authorities concerned.

Article 29 of the Statute is concerned with cooperation and judicial assistance. States must comply without undue delay with any request for assistance or an order issued by a Trial Chamber, which includes, but is not limited to: the identification and location of persons; the taking of testimony and the production of evidence; the service of documents;

* Deputy Chief of Investigations, International Criminal Tribunal for the former Yugoslavia (ICTY). Any views expressed are solely those of the author and are not attributable to the ICTY.

R. Yepes-Enríquez and L. Tabassi. (eds.), Treaty Enforcement and International Cooperation in Criminal Matters

the arrest or detention of persons; and the surrender or transfer of the accused to the International Tribunal.

2.2 THE RULES

Rule 39 gives the Prosecutor the power to:

i) summon and question suspects, victims and witnesses and record their statements, collect evidence and conduct on-site investigations;
ii) undertake such other matters as may appear necessary for completing the investigation and the preparation and conduct of the prosecution at the trial, including the taking of special measures to provide for the safety of potential witnesses and informants;
iii) seek, to that end, the assistance of any State authority concerned, as well as of any relevant international body including the International Criminal Police Organisation (INTERPOL); and,
iv) request such orders as may be necessary from a Trial Chamber or a Judge.

Rule 40 gives the Prosecutor, in the case of urgency, the power to request any State:

i) to arrest a suspect or an accused provisionally;
ii) to seize physical evidence; and,
iii) to take all necessary measures to prevent the escape of a suspect or an accused, injury to or intimidation of a victim or witness, or the destruction of evidence.

The State concerned shall comply forthwith, in accordance with Article 29 of the Statute. Rule 54 is a general rule which allows " . . .a Judge or Trial Chamber [to] issue [. . .] orders, summonses, subpoenas, warrants and transfer orders as may be necessary for the purposes of an investigation or for the preparation or conduct of the trial." Rule 90 *bis* allows for the transfer of a detained person whose personal appearance has been requested by the Tribunal.

3. GATHERING EVIDENCE

Some of the most important areas in the gathering of evidence are crime scene examinations, exhumations, search and seizure orders/warrants, subpoenas, expert evidence and witness interviews. The ICTY has carried out crime scene examinations, exhumations and executed search and seizure orders/warrants in a number of areas of the territory of the former Yugoslavia. In the Tribunal's infancy, it was extremely difficult to gain access to certain areas, particularly Republika Srpska.

In 1996, pursuant to an Order issued by a Judge under Rule 54, members of the Office of the Prosecutor (OTP) were able to enter Republika Srpska for the first time and commence to gather evidence. On that occasion the OTP went to the Prijedor municipality, where it carried out crime scene examinations of the three detention camps, Omarska, Keraterm and Trnopolje; worked throughout the entire municipality; and inspected towns and villages which had been shelled into virtual oblivion.

In 1997, again by virtue of a Rule 54 order, members of the OTP went to the Prijedor municipality in Republika Srpska and carried out a search and seizure mission. On that mission the team was able to enter a number of government buildings and seized documents relevant to on-going investigations. Since that time, search and seizure missions have been conducted in a number of other areas in the former Yugoslavia including the Federation of Bosnia and Herzegovina, Kosovo and the Republic of Croatia.

The OTP has carried out exhumations in Kosovo, the Republic of Croatia and the Federation of Bosnia and Herzegovina, including Republika Srpska. At present, the exhumations programme is manageable. In the Republic of Croatia it is a straightforward request from the Prosecutor to the Government. A similar mechanism is used in the Federation of Bosnia and Herzegovina and Kosovo. In Republika Srpska, a number of initial problems were overcome, initially with the assistance of IFOR, and then SFOR. The majority of the exhumations in Republika Srpska have been carried out in and around the area of Srebrenica, and the findings have been used in a number of the trials before the Tribunal. There have also been exhumations conducted recently in the Prijedor municipality.

The Prosecutor uses her authority under Rule 39 of the Rules to summon witnesses and suspects to appear for interview with respect to ongoing investigations and/or prosecutions. This investigative approach has largely been used in Republika Srpska with high-ranking military and political figures.

Expert witnesses assist the Trial Chamber by giving evidence, for example, about the historical/political nature of the conflict, or on military matters such as the proportionality of an attack. Scientific officers, such as anthropologists, archaeologists or scenes of crime officers, give expert opinions on their scenes of crime examinations, e.g. exhumations.

4. Interviewing Witnesses

The main duties of an investigator in the OTP is the interviewing of witnesses. Normally, a request is made to a State requesting permission to interview a witness. The witness may be an eyewitness to a crime, an expert witness or a witness who has gathered evidence shortly after a crime was committed, for example, a member of the European Community Monitoring Mission or a United Nations Monitoring Officer. In nearly every case the request has been complied with, and there have not been too many problems; each State has its own internal structures in place.

Whether the focus of the investigation is a head of State or the local camp guard, eyewitness testimony to crimes must be obtained. The crimes must be proven to have occurred beyond a reasonable doubt in either case. The presentation of the evidence before the Trial Chamber may be different for the head of State, but the crimes must nevertheless be proved.

Experience in national jurisdictions and at the Tribunal shows that evidence must be obtained as soon as possible after the commission of the crime or crimes. Two contrasting examples below highlight the difference between the ICTY using the work-product of non-governmental organisations (NGOs), and the ICTY working in cooperation with

NGOs so that both the Tribunal's and NGO's end products can be achieved.

The first example occurred in 1992, before the ICTY was established, when Bosnian Muslim and Bosnian Croat civilians were fleeing areas around Prijedor. When they reached the "free territories," as they put it, they were interviewed by NGOs, the media, government officials and/or Commissions of Experts. However, they were not interviewed with a criminal trial in mind. They were interviewed to assess their refugee status, to bring their plight to the attention of the outside world or a multitude of other reasons, but *not* for a criminal trial. These "prior statements," often taken by non-investigators and/or lawyers using non-certified interpreters, were then used in later proceedings. The Tribunal was non-existent and therefore was not in a position to work with these groups. However, information gathered by third parties and passed on to the Tribunal was analysed for leads.

The second example lies at the other end of the spectrum. In 1999, hundreds of thousand of Kosovars fled across the borders into Macedonia and Albania. The Tribunal was able to respond to this exodus and work with the NGO community and others both to obtain evidence of serious crimes, some of which had only occurred hours before, and to bring humanitarian assistance to these refugees. As a result of this cooperation, an indictment was issued fairly soon after the crimes occurred against those suspected of being the most responsible for committing them.

It should be noted that there are a number of potential pitfalls in the interviewing of witnesses that should be taken into account from the beginning of the interview. First, the ICTY does not have its own police force, so it needs the assistance of States in everything it does, including witness protection and victim and witness support. Second, language and cultural differences have to be taken into account.

5. Conclusion

This chapter presented a very brief overview of some of the main categories of evidence that the Tribunal has used in gathering evidence and then putting that evidence before a trial chamber for their determination.

There is nothing magical about it; in fact it consists of the traditional procedures for investigation and prosecution that are used almost daily in national jurisdictions. What complicates the issue is the international character of the investigation. For the investigation and the subsequent prosecution to be successful, the assistance of States is critical. Without this assistance, international investigations are doomed to failure before they even start.

COOPERATION ON CRIMINAL MATTERS: A DEFENCE LAWYER'S PERSPECTIVE

Michail Wladimiroff*

1. Introduction

In this chapter I will comment upon State cooperation in criminal matters[1] from a defence lawyer's perspective. Before touching upon State cooperation with supranational judicial bodies, I would first like to briefly review the European system for inter-State cooperation. The degree of cooperation exhibited in the network of instruments governing these activities is instructive when addressing comparable problems at the next level — State cooperation with international and supranational judicial bodies or even, in some cases, with international organisations. A number of issues arising in the context of bilateral cooperation between States similarly occur during State cooperation with international tribunals.

2. The Network of Inter-State Cooperation in Criminal Matters

2.1 Instruments

Within Europe there is a dense network of conventions and treaties initiated by the Council of Europe to regulate inter-State mutual assistance in criminal matters.[2] The best known example is the 1957 European Convention on Extradition and its Additional Protocols,[3] together with the resolutions and recommendations agreed upon to specify the details of their enforcement.[4] Other well-known examples are the 1959 European Convention on Mutual Assistance in Criminal Matters,[5] as well as the 1972 European Convention on the Transfer of Proceedings in Criminal Matters.[6] The conclusion and implementation of this latter convention depended upon States' willingness to accept the institution of proceedings,

* Senior Partner of Wladimiroff Waling Schreuders, advocates, The Hague, and former Professor of International Economic Criminal Law, University of Utrecht. The author gratefully acknowledges the assistance of Robert Delonis in the preparation of this chapter.

[1] See *infra* in this volume, H-J. Bartsch, Overcoming Obstacles in Achieving Wide Adherence to Multilateral Instruments: Some Comments from the European Perspective.

[2] Paris, 13 December 1957, European Treaty Series no. 24.

[3] (First) Additional Protocol to the European Convention on Extradition, Strasbourg, 15 October 1975, European Treaty Series, no. 86; and Second Additional Protocol to the European Convention on Extradition, Strasbourg, 18 March 1978, European Treaty Series, no. 98.

[4] Recommendation no. R (80) 7 of the Committee of Ministers to Member States Concerning the Practical Application of the European Convention on Extradition (1980), reprinted in E. Müller-Rappard and M.C. Bassiouni, (eds.), European Inter-State Co-operation in Criminal Matters: The Council of Europe's Legal Instruments 277 (1993); and Recommendation No. R (80) 9 of the Committee of Ministers to Member States Concerning Extradition to States not Party to the European Convention on Human Rights, reprinted in *Id.* at 278.

[5] Strasbourg, 20 April 1959, European Treaty Series, no. 30.

[6] Strasbourg, 15 May 1972, European Treaty Series, no. 73.

R. Yepes-Enríquez and L. Tabassi. (eds.), Treaty Enforcement and International Cooperation in Criminal Matters

over which they have jurisdiction, in other States, and to relinquish a certain degree of their sovereign power to prosecute by transferring such proceedings to other States.

There are other instruments that also merit examination in this context. Notable among them are the European Convention on Information on Foreign Law,[7] the 1970 Convention on the International Validity of Criminal Judgements,[8] the 1987 European Union Convention on Double Jeopardy,[9] and the 1983 European Convention on the Transfer of Sentenced Persons.[10] These instruments have created in Europe a coherent network of treaty law providing a basis for well-functioning mutual legal assistance among their member States.

In addition to the numerous bilateral treaties between States, there are some examples of treaties with a wider, global base, such as the North Atlantic Treaty[11] and the Single Agreement regarding the Status of NATO Forces in the Partnership for Peace.[12] The Status of Forces agreement is a useful reference when searching for legal tools on how to deal with that type of cooperation. For a specific territory within Europe, the Schengen Agreement[13] regulates the cooperation of States not only on judicial or prosecutorial matters, but also on the level of police enforcement. The Agreement serves as an important model of how police cooperation functions in practice when police authorities are conducting investigations in the territory of another State. Finally, the Europol Convention[14] governs similar matters, while at the same time deals with immunities and other issues that may arise in State cooperation with supranational or supranational judicial bodies.

2.2 THE IMPACT OF COMMON LAW VS. CIVIL LAW SYSTEMS ON COOPERATION

In practice, from a defence lawyer's perspective, this whole network of conventions and treaties must be viewed in conjunction with the two legal systems in Europe under which the instruments are enforced: the common law, and the continental European civil law. The position of defence lawyers dealing with a request under one of the conventions is totally different in these systems. In the common law "adversarial system," the defendant is a party in the trial, and the system tasks the prosecution and defence with fact development while the judge functions principally as an arbiter of the law. The continental civil law tradition, however, utilises the "inquisitorial system": the judge governs the trial as both an arbiter dealing with the law and an investigator fully developing the *dossier* of facts. The role of the prosecution is also accordingly different. Trials in common law jurisdictions can be characterised as "horizontal," with the two parties equally addressing the cause, while in a civil law "top down trial" the prosecution is actually very close to the bench and the defendant becomes the subject of the trial rather than a participant in it.

---

7 London, 7 June 1968, entered into force 17 December 1969; European Treaty Series, no. 62.

8 The Hague, 28 May 1970, European Treaty Series, no. 70.

9 Bulletin EU 5 (1987).

10 Strasbourg, 21 March 1983, European Treaty Series, no. 112.

11 Washington, D.C., 4 April 1949. Text available at http://www.nato.int

12 Agreement among the States Parties to the North Atlantic Treaty and the other States participating in the Partnership for Peace regarding the Status of their Forces, Brussels, 19 June 1995.

13 Schengen Agreement of 14 June 1985 between the Governments of the States of the Benelux Union, the Federal Republic of Germany and the French Republic on the Gradual Abolition of Checks at their Common Borders, Joint Ministerial Gazette 1986, p. 77ff.

14 Brussels, 26 July 1995, [EU] official Journal C 316/1.

An examination of the mechanisms established in the mutual assistance conventions reveals that requests for State cooperation operate in a manner fitting a continental European civil law orientation. These conventions give very little room for effective defence lawyer participation, through either making or complying with requests, because the defence has such a marginal role in the top down system. This problem comes into even sharper focus when defence lawyers need State cooperation in proceedings before an international tribunal. The special issues arising in these cases are illustrated below.

3. State Cooperation with International or Supranational Judicial Bodies

3.1 The Goal of a Fair Trial

Problems arise for a defence lawyer when State cooperation is requested in proceedings before a supranational judicial body such as the International Criminal Tribunal for the former Yugoslavia (ICTY) or the International Criminal Tribunal for Rwanda (ICTR). While the Tribunals' Statutes and Rules formulate State cooperation along lines similar to those governing general inter-State cooperation in criminal matters, the law and procedures that govern the Tribunals are more common law orientated. This means the role of the defence lawyer in proceedings before the ICTY and ICTR is much more active, since he or she has to put the case before the judges. The defence lawyer is in almost the same position as the prosecution, and that is where the problems start.

The assumption in all trials, wherever – nationally, in a common law or civil law system, or in supranational judicial bodies like the ICTY or ICTR – they are conducted, is that the standard should be always the same. All trials should be fair trials. But that begs a question: "What do you mean by 'fair trial'?" In my perception, the fairness of the trial is measured in the context of the system in which it is being conducted. What would be considered "fair" in a common law jurisdiction could, and should, be different than in a civil law jurisdiction. For example, the rights of the defence in a common law jurisdiction cannot function as a directly translated basis for evaluating the "proper" rights of the defence in a civil law jurisdiction because the rationale for the two systems' proceedings are not comparable.

Setting aside the question of the exact meaning of "fairness," let's agree in principle that a trial should be fair. Fairness can then serve as a criterion for examining the tools given to the defence by a legal system. Can a defence lawyer, utilising these tools, guarantee a fair trial by doing his or her job properly? If one looks at the legal instruments governing the two ad hoc tribunals and the International Criminal Court (ICC), and observes that the trials are being conducted on a basis similar to common law system trials, one notes that the drafters failed to provide the defence with tools comparable to those provided to the prosecution.

3.2 The Institutional Weakness of the Defence in the Ad Hoc Tribunals and ICC

Put simply, the system established in the ICC and the tribunals is one bench before which two parties present their case. To be able to meaningfully prepare a case in this common law-styled system, a defence lawyer must have adequate facilities to conduct an investigation, and adequate powers of investigation, including the power to compel the attendance of witnesses and the seizure of evidence, and the ability to conduct on-site investigations. Such powers are clearly granted to the prosecution,[15] but as discussed below, defence access to these powers is at best unclear. The Tribunals seem to allocate investigatory power with civil law procedural assumptions in mind, but their actual procedures were adopted from a common law system. This disconnect, and the power disparity it generates is, in my view, where one of the greatest dangers to fairness in the international administration of justice lurks.

This lack of defence power is magnified by the tribunals' necessary reliance on the cooperation of States, and by the differences in assumptions that arise between civil and common law jurisdictions. The Tribunal does not have its own arms and legs to perform the work normally conducted at the national level by the common body of government departments and services. This is doubly true for civil law jurisdictions, where the court carries more of the investigatory burden. There is no support network to compensate for loopholes because the Tribunal does not function within a broader legal system. Without enforcement agents of its own, an international tribunal must also rely upon the cooperation of States to exercise its powers *vis-à-vis* individuals *in situ* through their intervention. In short, a tribunal is a supranational judicial body, but it exercises its powers solely through the States.

In an effort to compensate for this lack of powers, Article 29 of the ICTY Statute,[16] and Article 28 of the ICTR Statute,[17] both oblige States to cooperate with the Tribunal and comply forthwith with any request of the trial chamber. This should apply to both the prosecution and the defence – but does it? In the case of the ICTY, the Office of the Prosecutor (OTP) is an official organ of the Tribunal[18] and, as such, doubtlessly falls under the aegis of Article 29. Defence lawyers, however, are not Tribunal organs; they are individuals, working on behalf of a defendant, and they are not a part of the Tribunal as such. This raises the question of whether they fall under either Tribunal's compliance articles.

The power to request and, ultimately, order the cooperation of States is a kind of secondary jurisdiction over states, separate from the primary jurisdiction of the Tribunal. This system, in which individuals are requested and ordered in their official state capacities to cooperate with the tribunal, may cause problems. For example, the *Blaskic* case[19] raised the issue of whether an order of the Tribunal is binding only upon a State, as a literal reading of the language of Article 29 would suggest, or upon individual State authorities as well. In *Blaskic*, the Appeals Chamber of the ICTY held that the OTP could issue binding orders to States under Article 29, but it could not issue binding orders upon

[15] For a discussion of the prosecutorial possession of these powers in the ICTY and ICTR Statutes and Rules, see *supra* in this volume, R. Reid, Practical Aspects of Gathering Evidence in an International Environment.

[16] The Statute of the International Tribunal, adopted 25 May 1993 by UN Security Council resolution S/RES/827 (1993), as amended by UN Security Council resolutions S/RES/1166 (1998), S/RES/1329 (2000) and S/RES/1411 (2002). Amended text available at http://www.un.org/icty.

[17] Statute of the International Tribunal for Rwanda, adopted 8 November 1994 by UN Security Council resolution S/RES/955 (1994), as amended by UN Security Council resolutions S/RES/1165 (1998), S/RES/1166 (1998), S/RES/1329 (2000) and S/RES/1411 (2002). Amended text available at http://www.ictr.org.

[18] See Article 16 of the Statute of the International Tribunal, *supra* note 15.

[19] *The Prosecutor v. Tihomir Blaskic*, Judgement, Case no. IT-95-14 (3 March 2000). See paras. 42-43 for a summary of the questions in the case relevant to the discussion here.

individual State government officers because the customary norms of international law do not grant the Tribunal power over them, nor do any specific provisions of the ICTY Statute.[20] This lack of authority could be a real issue if, for example, a defence lawyer wanted to interview an official of a State on matters that are highly relevant for the defence of the case. The same difficulty is encountered if a defence attorney sought to interview military personnel, organs of a State, or the authorities of the State, and again, the ability of defence attorneys to compel this cooperation is unclear.

The term "States" presents further interpretive problems in this context. It includes all States that are members of the United Nations,[21] but does it also cover non-UN member States or non-State entities? For example, in the ICTY's early days it needed to investigate in Republika Srpska. But what was Republika Srpska – a puppet State, a rebel State, or even a State at all? It may have been a State under the Montevideo criteria,[22] but arguments can be made both ways. And if it was not a State, did Article 29 apply to it? The answer is unclear, and that problem may cripple investigations or prosecutions. It will also certainly cripple the defence, which has no standing whatsoever because it not an organ of the Tribunal.

The defence was not addressed by the Dayton Agreement, in which all parties, including States and other factual entities within the Bosnian Federation, acknowledged the rights of the Tribunal to do on-site investigations. The defence was not discussed in the other principle document of international cooperation in these issues: Chapter VII of the Charter of the United Nations. The ICTY Rules[23] also provide little additional assistance on this issue. ICTY Rule 58, which stipulates that the obligations created in Article 29 of the Statute shall prevail over any legal impediment to surrender or transfer of the accused or a witness of the Tribunal, failed to mention the defence. Rule 56 reminds States of their obligations to act promptly with all jurisdictions to ensure proper and effective execution in accordance with Article 29, but is mute about the defence. And the other Rules are silent about supremacy, save Rule 7*bis*, which only warns States that failures to comply with obligations under Article 29 of the Statute shall be reported to the Security Council. On the whole, then, the defence is left in a vacuum; defence attorneys know neither their standing nor the tools with which they are equipped.

Against this background, imagine you are a defence attorney in a proceeding before the ICTY. You want to interview someone who is in the military, or is a policeman, and the State is not willing to cooperate with you because they say, "Who are you? You are an individual, not an organ of the Tribunal. We are not talking to you; any of your requests are totally irrelevant to us." Can you report that response to a trial chamber? What will the trial chamber do – will they order the State to cooperate with the defence?

It may, but now imagine what happens if you are looking for witnesses in the middle of an ongoing conflict. You have to come back to The Hague, ask for a court order, wait for it, get it, and then go back with the court order. And who is going to comply with the court order? The State? What if the State is not a UN member State, but a puppet or a rebel State?

[20] See Judgement on the Request of the Republic of Croatia for review of the Decision of Trial Chamber II of 18 July, 1997, Case no. IT-95-14-AR 108bis, paras. 25-31, 38-56 (29 October 1997).

[21] *Id.*

[22] 1933 Montevideo Convention on Rights and Duties of States, 165 LNTS 19, entered into force 26 December 1934.

[23] ICTY doc. IT/32/REV.22, dated 13 December 2001, as amended on 23 April 2002. Text available at http://www.un.org/icty.

Who is going to comply with the order if it is an individual lawyer who hands it over? Again, you are not an organ of the Tribunal. You are, politically speaking, no one. You are just an ordinary defence lawyer, acting on behalf of a defendant without any standing.

The obligation to cooperate with the Tribunal is only indicated in paragraph 1 of Article 29 and is without any specification to the defence. If the defence is to have any formal investigatory tools at all, one must interpret "tribunal" in Article 29 broadly to include all the elements functioning within it. The Article would then be seen as imposing an obligation on States to cooperate with the defence as well, since the defence falls under the "Tribunal" and thus has standing to make proper requests under the ICTY statute. Formal case law is required, however, so this point can be made utterly clear to States.

State cooperation with the tribunal may also be subject to national privileges recognised by international law, and the lack of clear defence standing in the ICTY statute compounds the difficulties these privileges can create. For example, the national security privilege can be an impediment to the defence in the context of Rules 66(c) and 70(b). These Rules state that the OTP may have access to state confidential materials, but they include no obligation of disclosure to the defence. If a defence attorney wishes to inspect such materials, however, his or her lack of standing means they would probably have no access to those documents; after all, a defence attorney cannot walk into a government building and demand documents, or raid a building and seize them. The State can refuse and invoke its national security privilege.

This limitation may be less of a problem in civil law jurisdictions, for in those jurisdictions the defence can request the prosecution or the investigative magistrate to do the job for it. Similar options are notably lacking in common law systems, however, where defence attorneys have to deal with court orders, which then have to be enforced by states, which can then again invoke their recognised privileges. And there is a further problem. If access to confidential documents were granted under the ICTY Statute and Rules, I believe that a proper understanding of the Statutes and Rules would oblige the defence to disclose that information to the OTP. But as noted above, the OTP is under no parallel obligation to the defence.

3.3 THE CHALLENGES PRESENTED BY NATIONAL LAW

Another issue I want to briefly explore is the fact that interstate cooperation on criminal matters is always envisioned with sole regard to the prosecution, and the resulting insufficient rules place the defence in a very limited position. It is essential, however, that the cooperation of States is regulated with a view to the fulfilment of the duties of all the parties in a trial: the judges, the prosecutors, and the defence. The current limitations of Article 29 of the ICTY Statute pose many potential problems to defence attorneys, though I think it safe to conclude that the development of ICTY case law can remedy these problems and avoid preventing the defence from doing their job properly.

These legal problems can also be viewed from a different perspective. If States do seek to comply with the Tribunals, and with the defence, what then? Then attorneys enter into a second area of problems, partially addressed in Europe by the conventions and treaties I alluded to above. For even if the State is fully willing to cooperate with the defence, there might be obstacles in their own national law.

For a very simple example, I was once arguing a case before the ICTY and wanted to locate possible witnesses who were among the refugees then located in Germany. I addressed the German authorities, asking them whether they would be able to assist the defence in locating these possible witnesses, and their answer was essentially: "No. Who are you?" Now it was their first case before the ICTY, and maybe these were beginner's problems. But once they were able to understand and identify my status, their answer was, "well, there is no provision under German law, so why should we answer your request?" My solution in those days was very simple: I asked the prosecution to do it. They got the right answers, and they passed the answers to me.

My solution is not, however, the normal common law routine; it's more or less a civil law orientated solution, and while it worked, it cannot be relied upon. Applying the ICTY system in a common law State renders the defence totally dependent on the prosecution, because defence attorneys can only get certain types of information through the prosecution. This system doesn't work. If I want documents in France, for example, and I want to inspect them because I have reason to believe that they are relevant to the defence, I cannot go to a French court and ask for an injunction ordering the French State to produce these documents for defence inspection. The prosecution may do so, but French national law gives no standing to defence lawyers in these matters. One faces the same problems under the European Conventions and treaties dealing with mutual assistance in criminal matters, because they are based on the civil law inquisitorial system.

In common law jurisdictions this is totally different. In the United States, for example, I have standing as a defence attorney working for the ICTY or ICTR to request an injunction in a US federal court. This difference underscores my central point. If a supranational institution is structured through a mixture of different legal systems, and its founders fail to thoroughly consider the implications of their theoretical and procedural differences (as arguably occurred in the ICTY, where the pre-trial proceedings are basically civil law in nature, while the trial is essentially a common law proceeding), the resulting institution faces many troubles because the melting pot merger of systems often leaves the defence in a procedural lurch. In order to properly argue the case of an accused person, defence counsel must be able conduct discovery in the areas containing the right information. The defence should, just like the prosecution, be able to locate, interview, bring forward, examine and challenge relevant witnesses. The same applies for documents and all other types of information.

4. Conclusion: Looking to the Future

I think my message is clear: the law needed to clearly meet the standards of a fair trial – one in which both parties are able to sufficiently present their case – is not present in current legal documents. This is an issue of international law, but it is also an issue of national law, because states comply with international obligations through domestic statutes. The practice of implementing these obligations in common law jurisdictions is totally different from the implementation in civil law jurisdictions, and legislators have overlooked the consequences of these differences on the powers and abilities of the defence.

I had hoped that, in drafting future legislation, the legislators would have seen this problem, but I participated in the drafting of the ICC Statute[24] and am sad to say that the same mistake has been made again. The drafters again forgot about the defence, the necessary wording is not in the documents, and the only immediately evident solution is to attribute powers to the ICC Registrar that may be mandated to the defence, thereby allowing the defence to act through the Registrar to meet its needs. There is, then, an important lesson to be learned from these experiences. When drafting treaties, protocols, conventions or statutes regarding state cooperation with international or supranational bodies, be they judicial bodies or not, the drafters must always remember that there are always at least two parties, and those parties should have, or at least be able to achieve, equal rights.

I believe that, under the European Conventions on assistance in criminal matters outlined above, the defence cannot always achieve what it ought to be able to achieve. But an important difference between this situation and a similar one under *supranational* law is that, under the latter, an attorney's greatest resource – the assistance of other attorneys – is replaced by a much less accessible and familiar institution: a state.

For example, in an interstate cooperation case between the Netherlands and France, I can ask a local French lawyer to deal with the issue on the basis of French law, and so long as he can act on behalf of an interested party he has standing to do so. In supranational institutions like the ICTY or ICTR, however, the addressee of my request is another State, and their compliance is complex because it often affects both their own nationals and people who are accidentally on their territory. The different and often novel law of supranational bodies further muddles the issue. In normal proceedings, when I retain my friend the French lawyer, he will be familiar with the mechanics of my request because he is familiar with international law on interstate cooperation. But were I to retain a lawyer in Banja Luka to address the local courts on an issue involving the ICTY, in the early days, and perhaps even today, he or she often had no clue what I was asking for. The remedy of retaining a national lawyer, then, functions within the European system of interstate cooperation, but does not yet do so on the supranational level.

As a final thought, one might wonder whether defence attorneys could just "play ball through the prosecution" and solve all these problems that way. Consider, however, the following example. You are a defence attorney looking for possible witnesses, but you're not sure whether you will call them once you have interviewed them because you don't know what they have to say. They may provide information that will be helpful to you, but they also might possess information that is not relevant to the case, or that is even incriminating to your client. If you have no access to *ex parte* proceedings, as is true in the tribunals, would you be willing to publicly inform the court, or worse yet the prosecution, whom you am looking for? Every time you did, you would be potentially directing the prosecutor to new witnesses who may support his or her case. As this example makes clear, defence attorneys cannot rely on prosecutorial help to conduct their investigations because reliance always runs the risk of doing more harm than good; this stifles thorough, risk-taking investigation. Defence attorneys must have access to independent investigatory tools

[24] 1998 Rome Statute of the International Criminal Court, entered into force 1 July 2002; UN doc. A/CONF.183/9*, as corrected by the procès-verbaux of 10 November 1998 and 12 July 1999. Corrected text available at http://www.un.org/law/icc.

and, at a bare minimum, access to a private or *ex parte* procedure to help fill the gaps in the current Tribunal statutes.

I do not seek procedures for guaranteeing the ideal trial; there are no ideal trials, for either the prosecution or the defence. But I do seek laws establishing a procedural standard that adequately fulfils the demands of fair trial in tribunal proceedings. And after a survey of the ICTY, the ICTR, the European conventions and treaties, and the Statute of the ICC, I am not yet satisfied.

THE QUEST FOR INTERNATIONAL CRIMINAL JUSTICE: CONSIDERING THE PERSPECTIVES OF WITNESSES, SURVIVORS, THE PROSECUTION AND THE DEFENCE

Harriet Solloway*

1. INTRODUCTION

In 1994, with the advent of the International Criminal Tribunal for the Former Yugoslavia (ICTY), the international community rekindled the quest for international criminal justice that had lain dormant since Nuremberg. The subsequent creation of the International Criminal Tribunal for Rwanda (ICTR) and the International Criminal Court (ICC) constitute an affirmation of the commitment of the international community to seek global justice for crimes that are the concern of all nations. If this approach is to be effective, the practical implications of universal criminal law will have to be considered.

Reconciling the concerns of a sufficient number of States into a single statute is no easy feat, yet it is only the beginning. A new statute may be likened to the creation of a new life form. All the elements may be present but the creature remains lifeless until it actually begins to breathe. Only once it acquires life can its character be observed, and the development of the creature will depend on the environment in which it lives.

The manifestation of any international statute is sure to be heavily influenced by the political and social contexts in which it is applied. Each word in any piece of international "legislation" is certain to carry significant implications for all actors in the quest for justice — including witnesses, victims, the prosecution and the defence. This chapter will highlight some practical factors that will influence the application of international statutes, and hence the development of international criminal law. These factors are likely to be common to every international effort that is intended to bring justice to a people, a region, and indeed, the nations of the world.

2. WITNESS PROTECTION

Measures required for the protection of potential witnesses and the relative effectiveness of these measures are heavily impacted by existing political and social structures. Rwanda, for example, is divided into provinces (formerly called prefectures) which are sub-divided into districts (formerly called communes) which are, in turn, sub-divided into neighbourhoods which are further divided into groups of ten families. Each of these entities has a political and functional head. Given the absence of communication infrastructure such as telephones,

* Former Senior Legal Adviser to the Organization for Security and Co-operation in Europe (OSCE) Mission in Kosovo; former Legal Advisor for Sex Crimes at the International Criminal Tribunal for Rwanda (ICTR). The opinions expressed herein are those of the author, and are not to be imputed to the OSCE, the United Nations, the ICTR or the Office of the Prosecutor.

R. Yepes-Enríquez and L. Tabassi. (eds.), Treaty Enforcement and International Cooperation in Criminal Matters

this social structure is vital for community support and information dissemination. So when one person is missing from their daily routine it is easy for all to know that something extraordinary is happening, thereby rendering it very difficult if not impossible to conduct interviews with potential witnesses without other people knowing about it. The difficulty in conducting discreet interviews in Rwanda is further compounded by the fact that the presence of foreigners is a novelty and attracts much attention, particularly those who arrive on the scene in big green 4x4 Nissan Patrols that are rare in rural Rwanda.

The international community and local communities must recognise structural limitations relating to witness protection and accept that perfect protection cannot be achieved. But the level of risk that a potential witness may be forced to assume as a consequence of cooperating with either the defence or the prosecution, and the need to cope with the devastating legacy that follows all conflict, must be considered by investigators and by the organisations on whose behalf investigations are being conducted.

3. The Plight of Victims

In conducting interviews, investigators for either the prosecution or the defence must understand the perspective of potential witnesses. When approaching witnesses, it is important to be cognisant of the fact that a victim population may not appreciate such international intervention. In the case of Rwanda, while international recognition of the suffering of the people was welcomed, a large segment of the population, if given the choice, would probably have chosen to have had the millions of dollars poured into international criminal justice poured into rehabilitation instead. It was not uncommon after interviewing a victim to have that person ask what could be done to get a roof put back on her house. Concerns over feeding several children, some belonging to the witness and others orphans for whom a victim had been caring since 1994, were the witness' understandable priority. It is difficult for a population in despair to care more about international legal principles than survival. Victims of devastation must be approached with the respect due to them, as persons who, in the wake of their personal tragedy, are serving the interests of the international community in its efforts to establish an international legal system for the benefit of all peoples. Investigators must be careful not to attempt to portray themselves as though they believe that they are knights in shining armour arriving to defend the rights of the downtrodden. For the victims it is too late to be saved. They have already suffered hardship of unimaginable proportion.

Failure to consider the impact of testimony on potential witnesses and a failure to consider the hardships faced by survivors, consequently diminishes or even destroys, at very least in the eyes of the victim population, the belief that the international community is capable of delivering justice.

4. Investigation

Most international investigations require the services of local interpreters. It would be unusual to find a pool of trained and certified interpreters adequate to meet the needs of an international investigation in any post-conflict zone. This will pose more or less of a challenge depending upon the location of an investigation. There are, for example, very few if any certified Kinyarwanda interpreters. So organisations and investigators in Rwanda, at least at the start of operations, had no choice but to rely upon untried and unproven interpreters with no capacity to evaluate, with any degree of certainty, their accuracy and effectiveness. Moreover, interpreting skills required in the field extend beyond classic training. Words are but a small part of communication and investigators rely on their interpreters to guide them through cultural nuances that greatly impact the significance, or even the true meaning of mere vocabulary. A small example is the meaning of the word "brother" in Kinyarwanda. It is frequently used to denote "cousin". The failure to understand this cultural application can result in inaccurate witness statements and could result in an eventual challenge to the credibility of a witness before a tribunal. The limitations on the ability of international investigators to obtain unequivocal witness statements must be recognised and accepted.

5. Equality of Arms

It has been advanced by some[1] that the current structure of international criminal statutes reflects an inequality of arms between the prosecution and the defence that results in inadequate protection for an accused. This perceived inequality seems to be largely associated with what is believed to be a heavy bias toward the common law approach in international statutes. These frustrations and concerns are not, strictly speaking, related to international tribunals. They are concerns common to the defence in domestic jurisdictions as well. But while the system created by current international statutes is far from perfect, there are counter-balancing factors. Further, it is not clear that a heavier bias in favour of a civil law system would offer greater protection for an accused.

5.1 Financial Resources

In common law domestic jurisdictions the defence must function within the confines of the resources at its disposal. For example, a defence attorney may have a client who claims to have an alibi — to have been in a different place at the time of the criminal act of which the client is accused. But if the client does not have the financial resources to hire private investigators, which is usual since most clients do not, then the defence must do what it can do in the circumstances. The system is imperfect domestically and, unfortunately, to the extent that the common law system is adapted to international jurisdictions, it is translated into imperfections in the international arena. It is, however, worthy of note that one particular imperfection has been addressed, at least to some extent, at the administrative level in both the ICTY and the ICTR by providing financial resources to the defence for hiring investigators.

5.2 Disclosure

The obligation on the prosecution to disclose evidence to the defence that could be exculpatory for the accused is one counter-balancing factor. That obligation rests on the

[1] See, *supra* in this volume, M. Wladimiroff, Cooperation on Criminal Matters: A Defence Lawyer's Perspective.

prosecution precisely in recognition of the fact that the prosecution does have more resources and is in a position to collect evidence. The additional obligation on the prosecution to disclose evidence that inculpates the accused allows the defence the possibility of preparing answers to the charges. In the common law system, there is no reciprocal obligation on the defence to disclose evidence to the prosecution (with the possible exception of an alibi defence), which in itself provides a counter-balancing advantage to the defendant.

5.3 BURDEN OF PROOF

Another way in which the common law system counterbalances the fact that the defence is at a disadvantage when it comes to the collection of evidence is through the standard of evidence required for conviction. Whereas in a civil law jurisdiction a judge must have an intimate conviction that the person is guilty in order to find the accused guilty, in a common law system there is a higher standard of proof, which is that of "beyond reasonable doubt". It is, however, difficult to say that there is a *quid pro quo.* In comparing systems to one another, there will be some disadvantages for the defence and there will be some disadvantages for the prosecution. There are counterbalances in the common law system, just as there are in the civil law system — it is simply that they are different.

5.4 STATE OBLIGATION TO COOPERATE

It has been advanced that inequality exists between the standing of prosecution investigators and that of defence investigators with respect to State cooperation.[2] This inequality of standing mirrors that which exists in common law domestic jurisdictions, when an investigation must be conducted outside the jurisdiction in which criminal charges have been laid. At the same time, the civil law system does not necessarily provide the answer. Relying upon investigating judges in the civil law system does not result in perfect balance. An investigating judge is also prosecution oriented and is more likely to seek out evidence that could convict a given suspect than he or she may be to seek out evidence that could exonerate the suspect. Consequently, it is difficult to conclude that international jurisdictions would be rendered more equitable through the adoption of more civil law approaches.

The defence in the international system, whether it is in the context of the ICTY or the ICTR, can appeal to the tribunal for subpoenas and for requests for State compliance with investigations. This may be viewed as a hindrance to the rhythm of investigation, but the fact that the prosecution must also follow protocol in order to obtain the cooperation of a State cannot be forgotten. On balance, there does not seem to be a real bias in this regard.

On occasion, in the international jurisdictions as well as in domestic jurisdictions, the defence may rely upon the assistance of the Office of the Prosecutor, to liase with a government in whose territory the defence wishes to conduct an investigation. There is no doubt that in doing so the defence may lose an element of advantage that it otherwise would have, particularly if the defence happens upon information that is prejudicial to the accused, in that the obligation of disclosure does not apply to the defence. In revealing the

[2] See, *supra* in this volume, M. Wladimiroff, *Id.*

purpose of the investigation to be conducted, the prosecution could be alerted to new sources of evidence that it could then exploit for the purpose of securing a conviction.

The conclusion that the need to follow protocol in obtaining the cooperation of States necessarily disfavours the accused is based upon the experiences of the past and present. In view of the clear commitment to international justice, formalities required to obtain State cooperation may very well favour suspects in the future. In the wake of conflicts, persons in positions of command and control believing that they may be subject to international scrutiny for criminal acts that they may have committed, may successfully exclude international investigators while defence investigators collect exculpatory evidence. It may be that in certain future contexts, a State would be more predisposed to assisting the defence than it would be to assisting the prosecution. In such a case it would be the prosecution which is disadvantaged.

6. Striking a Balance: the Search for the Perfect System

The evaluation of whether or not a justice system is "fair" may be highly subjective and will be significantly determined by the socio-cultural context in which it is applied. Moreover, the international community must bear in mind that justice can only be realised when international justice operates in tandem with local justice systems. Not all suspects can be, or should be, brought before an international tribunal. The obligation of the community of nations to assist a people emerging from terror and oppression, to develop or enhance a culture of human rights and rule of law that has been eroded to the point of near extinction, cannot be over-emphasised.

This obligation of the international community to restore or develop human rights and the rule of law has been recognised and efforts to that end have taken several forms. In Rwanda, the re-establishment of traditional law through the formalisation of the *gacaca* justice system is operating to provide justice to the thousands of detainees awaiting trial.[3] In East Timor the approach taken by the international community differs significantly from that of the ICTY and ICTR in that efforts are more coordinated and integrated with the local justice system.[4] And in Kosovo, while the ICTY continues its work, a regional organisation, the Organization for Security and Co-operation in Europe (OSCE), is working under the umbrella of the United Nations to support the rebirth of a justice system that will integrate internationally recognised standards of human rights and the rule of law. Such varied approaches demonstrate the capacity of the international community to consider different arrangements for different circumstances and to adapt accordingly.

The international community must unquestionably strive to preserve the rights of a defendant to a full and fair hearing. It must also take into consideration the necessarily present structural problems of conducting an investigation, be it for the defence or for the prosecution, toward the ultimate goal of achieving justice. The commitment to safeguard the rights of a defendant in international justice has been proven recently, with the refusal of the United Nations and funding States to enter into an agreement with the Cambodian government. A cooperative approach, similar to that in East Timor, was being sought for the prosecution of violations of international law by the Khmer Rouge. After more than

[3] See further *supra* in this volume, C. Mibenge, The Concurrent Application of International, National and African Laws in Rwanda.

[4] See further *supra* in this volume, M. Othman, Concurrent Jurisdiction: Legal and Policy Considerations.

four years of discussion, the United Nations withdrew from negotiations with Cambodia in February 2002, as the proposed Cambodian law that would have given rise to international-domestic cooperation failed to address the right of a defendant to be represented by counsel of his or her choice.

There is, however, unfairness in any criminal prosecution and defence system. No system can be perfect, whether it has its basis in civil law, common law, traditional law or a combination thereof. The best that the international community can do is to try to seek a balance. Perhaps in the International Criminal Court Statute that balance has been struck, perhaps it has not. But whether it might favour the prosecution or the defence will only be determined when life is breathed into the statute upon its application in a particular context. The ICC statute has been drafted based upon our experience with the past. The future remains to be seen.

THE ROLE OF VICTIMS AND WITNESSES IN INTERNATIONAL CRIMINAL TRIALS

Avril McDonald*

1. The Position of Victims within Criminal Justice Systems Generally

For most of the modern history of criminal justice, victims have served as cogs in the penal machine. Their principal role has been that of witnesses for the prosecution. Criminal justice systems have tended to be offender- rather than victim-oriented. The main goal has been to identify, prosecute and punish persons who commit crimes, rather than to offer support, recognition and remedies to victims.

Generally speaking, victims of serious national crimes cannot initiate criminal proceedings. In most cases, this is the prerogative of the public prosecutor or investigating magistrate.[1] Even in those national jurisdictions where victims can act as private prosecutors, once criminal proceedings have started, they must usually be taken over by a public prosecutor. If the prosecutor or magistrate decides not to proceed, victims have few avenues of redress besides civil proceedings.[2] They usually have no right to participate in criminal trials. Neither is the possibility of restitution envisaged within the predominant criminal justice model. Indeed, "[I]n many ways, victims have been the silent partners in the legal process (. . .)."[3]

* Managing Editor of the *Yearbook of International Humanitarian Law* and a research fellow at the TMC Asser Institute of International Law, The Hague.

[1] According to van Boven, "as a general rule the victim does not possess the right to pursue a criminal claim and to seek to bring the perpetrator(s) to justice. Such a right, which may even be a duty, falls within the domain of the competing prosecuting authorities." Th. van Boven, "The Perspective of the Victim," in E. Stamapotoulou, Y. Danieli and C.J. Dias (eds.), The Universal Declaration of Human Rights: Fifty Years and Beyond, (1998) at 21.

[2] Victims of IHL violations constituting crimes may be entitled to seek civil claims for compensation within their own and, sometimes, in other States. Regarding the latter, in recent years several civil suits have been successfully brought, for example, in the United States by non-US nationals under the Alien Tort Crimes Act (ATCA) in respect of IHL violations committed abroad. These cases involve, among others, the defendant Radovan Karadzic See, *inter alia, Kadic et al v. Karadzic*; *Jane Doe et al v. Karadzic*, Docket Nos. 94-9035, 94-9069, US Court of Appeals for the Second Circuit,. 70 F.3d232; 1995 US App. LEXIS 28826, 13 October 1995. See 1 Yearbook of International Humanitarian Law (1998) 522 525. For commentary, see J.J. Paust, *Suing Karadzic*, 10 Leiden Journal of International Law (1997) 91.

[3] R.S. Clark and D. Tolbert, *Towards an International Criminal Court*, in Stamapotoulou *et al*, *supra* note 1, 99 at 110.

R. Yepes-Enríquez and L. Tabassi. (eds.), Treaty Enforcement and International Cooperation in Criminal Matters

Generally speaking, continental criminal justice systems are perceived as being more victim-oriented than those of the common law. In some civil law jurisdictions victims can appear as *parties civiles*.[4]

The trend in recent years, in both civil and common law countries, *inter alia*, has been toward improvement of the position of crime victims by, for example, enhancing their procedural position and providing for the possibility for crime victims to obtain compensation. Despite the continued predominant emphasis on perpetrators, without doubt national criminal justice systems are more responsive to the needs and legal rights of crime victims today than ever before.[5]

The increased attention being paid to the needs and rights of victims at the national level is the result of the symbiosis of a top down and a bottom up approach to the issue. Standard-setting at the international level, for example, with the adoption by the General Assembly in 1985 of a Victims' Rights Declaration,[6] has had an impact at the national level as States implement the various provisions of the Declaration. Consensus-building around victims' rights at the international level, particularly in various UN fora,[7] encourages a more victim-oriented approach by States. For example, the implementation in European States of Recommendation (85) 11 of the Council of Europe on the Position of Victims in the Framework of Criminal Law and Procedure has done much, in Europe at least, to improve the position of victims.[8] At the same time, the grassroots work of the crime victims' lobby

[4] "[I]n many domestic legal systems the victim may become involved in the criminal procedure as *partie civile* to the criminal case and claim damages as a civil complainant. Such a course of action is commendable for various reasons. First, it makes the criminal offender more aware that not only was a wrong committed against public order and public welfare but, in addition, an injury was inflicted on one or more human beings. Second, it establishes a link between punitive measures and measures of reparation. Third, it tends to facilitate and expedite the process of obtaining civil damages." Th. van Boven, *id.* at note 1, at 21.

[5] Amongst common law countries, the United States, Australia and New Zealand have led the way in integrating victims into the criminal justice system and establishing compensation schemes. See for example, S.P. Green, *The Victim's Rights Movement Reaches Middle-Age: A Chronique of American Criminal Law (1996-1997)*, 68 Revue Internationale de Droit Pénal (1997), 433; R.P. Mosteller, *Victims' Rights and the United States Constitution: An Effort to Recast the Battle in Criminal Litigation*, 85 Geo. L.J. (1997), 1691; M.D. Kersh, *The Empowerment of the Crime Victim: A Comparative Study of Victim Compensation Schemes in the United States and Australia*, in 24 California Western International Law Journal (Spring 1994), 345.

[6] On 11 December 1985, the General Assembly of the United Nations adopted Resolution 40/34, annexed to which was the Declaration of Basic Principles of Justice for Victims of Crime and Abuse of Power. For commentary, see LeRoy L. Lamborn, "The United Nations Declaration on Victims: The Scope of Coverage," in M. Cherif Bassiouni (ed.), *International Protection of Victims*, 7 Nouvelles Etudes Penales (1988) 105; I. Melup, *The United Nations Declaration on Principles of Justice for Victims of Crime and Abuse of Power*, in Stamapotoulou, Danieli and Dias, *id.* at note 1, 53.

[7] In particular, by ECOSOC. See the reports of the Special Rapporteurs, Mr. Louis Joinet, Mr. Th. Van Boven and Mr. M. Cherif Bassiouni, UN docs. E/CN.4/Sub.2/1996/18, 29 June 1996, and E/CN.4/Sub.2/1997/20, 26 June 1997 (Joinet Reports); E/CN.4/Sub.2 1993/8 of 2 July 1993, Section IX (1993 van Boven principles), E/CN.4/Sub.2/1996/17 of 24 May 1996 (1996 van Boven principles), and E/CN.4/1997/104 of 16 January 1997 (1997 van Boven principles); E/CN.4/1999/65, 8 February 1999 (Bassiouni Report), Final report of the Special Rapporteur, Mr. M. Cherif Bassiouni, submitted in accordance with Commission resolution 1999/33. Commission on Human Rights, Fifty-sixth session, Item 11 (d) of the provisional agenda, E/CN.4/2000/62, 18 January 2000.

[8] For a comprehensive discussion, see M.E.I Brienen and E.H. Hoegen, Victims of Crime in 22 European Criminal Justice Systems: The Implementation of Recommendation (85) 11 of the Council of Europe on the Position of the Victim in the Framework of Criminal Law and Procedure (2000).

within States has helped to push the issue forward and create a climate in which complementary developments *vis-à-vis* international crimes could occur.

This chapter on the role of victims in international criminal trials looks first at the purpose of international criminal trials. The position of victims before the ad hoc International Criminal Tribunals, and the success of the Tribunals in achieving their stated aims *vis-à-vis* victims, are then assessed. Following this is a short consideration of the position of the victim before the International Criminal Court (ICC). A few conclusions round off the discussion. The analysis of the position and role of victims before international criminal courts is not meant to be comprehensive, but merely aims to draw attention to areas of particular interest and concern.

2. The Purpose of International Criminal Trials

While the primary purpose of an international criminal trial, like that of a national criminal trial, is to prosecute persons accused of serious crimes and to apportion blame where the accused is found guilty, international criminal trials have additional purposes beyond this punitive function. Like national systems of criminal justice, international criminal justice also has a didactic role. It is intended to restore and promote respect for the rule of law. Further, it is intended to emphasize the preemptory nature of the norms it seeks to uphold. International criminal trials not only provide a forum before which persons accused of the most serious crimes can be tried when the national judicial system is either unable or unwilling to act; they also give such proceedings a profile and an impartiality which they might otherwise lack. By subjecting an accused person to international criminal process, the seriousness of the offence and the interest of the whole community in repressing such crimes is proclaimed. Moreover, a restorative or reconciliatory role is often ascribed to international criminal justice, going beyond what is expected of national criminal justice. International criminal trials are expected to contribute to peace, security and reconciliation in the affected areas.[9]

International criminal trials might also be expected to have a further purpose, described by the ICTY's first President, Antonio Cassese, as giving a voice to the victims. Trials before international criminal courts, being generally public proceedings, reported in the media, should allow victims of international crimes the possibility to tell their story and for that story to enter into the transcript of the trial and, hence, into the legal and historical record. By virtue of its status as an internationally recognised judicial institution, an international criminal court is an authoritative finder of both fact and law and is thus able to establish an historical record which, while not beyond dispute, is widely accepted.[10]

[9] See V. Morris and M. Scharf, An Insider's Guide to the International Criminal Tribunal for the Former Yugoslavia, (1995), 332: "[T]he purpose of the International Tribunal is not only to punish the perpetrators but to restore peace." UN Security Council resolution 827 (1993) of 25 May 2993 establishing the ICTY expressed the Council's belief that the Tribunal would "contribute to the restoration and maintenance of peace." See also Report of the Secretary-General Pursuant to Paragraph 2 of Security Council Resolution 808 (UN doc. S/25704), Presented 3 May 1993.

[10] Madeleine Albright, Former US Ambassador to the UN, stated that a primary purpose of the ICTY was "to establish an historical record before the guilty can reinvent the truth." A. Kelly, *U.N. Convenes Yugoslavia War Crimes Tribunal, Amid Doubts*, Reuters European Community Report (17 November 1993).

Another of the ICTY's stated goals has been to render justice to the victims,[11] although one can argue about the meaning of justice from a victim's perspective. Different victims have different expectations, and justice means different things to different people. Yet the rendering of justice to the victims at the very least requires that victims feel vindicated and helped by their experience of participation or involvement in the criminal justice process, however extensive or limited this may be. Victims' sense of satisfaction with their position and role in international criminal trials, and with the work of international criminal courts, is crucial to ensuring these courts' legitimacy.

3. Victims and the ad hoc International Criminal Tribunals

From the point of view of victims, the work of the ad hoc International Criminal Tribunals for the Former Yugoslavia (ICTY) and Rwanda (ICTR) can be considered a disappointment in many respects. While admittedly hamstrung by the restricted role for victims provided for in their Statutes and Rules, the Tribunals have not worked hard enough to fulfil their mandated functions as being forces for reconciliation and providing a voice for victims. Efforts to reach out to the affected populations have been slow in coming and remain limited. For many victims, the Tribunals remain alien and alienating.

3.1 Provisions in the Tribunals' Statutes and Rules Relevant to Victims

The Statutes and Rules of the International Criminal Tribunal for the Former Yugoslavia (ICTY)[12] and Rwanda (ICTR)[13] restrict the role of victims in the proceedings to that of witnesses, and the protection and services available to them are limited to securing and performing their role as witnesses.

The ICTY and ICTR Statutes refer directly to victims in three provisions. Article 15 of the ICTY Statute and 14 of the ICTR Statute instruct the judges of the Tribunals to adopt Rules of Procedure and Evidence, *inter alia*, for the "protection of victims and witnesses." There is also a reference to victims in Article 20(1) of the ICTY Statute and Article 19(1) of the ICTR Statute, which provide that trials are to be conducted, "with full respect for the rights of the accused and due regard for the protection of victims and witnesses."

Direct reference to the victims of crimes is also found in Articles 22 and 21, respectively, of the Statutes of the ICTY and ICTR, providing for protective measures for victims and

---

[11] See, for example, the Speech by His Excellency, Mr. Claude Jorda, President of the International Criminal Tribunal for the Former Yugoslavia, to the UN Security Council, ICTY Press Release SB/P.I.S./512-E, 20 June 2000, where he stated, "To judge those responsible for ethnic cleansing, to render justice to the victims, to prevent recidivism and to work on ensuring that history is not rewritten by blind revisionism was, and is, the immense task entrusted in November 1993 to the eleven Judges from the five continents who were entrusted by the United Nations General Assembly." www.un.org/icty/latest/index.htm.

[12] Statute of the International Tribunal, adopted 25 May 1993 by UN Security Council resolution S/RES/827 (1993), as amended by UN Security Council resolutions S RES/1166 (1998), S/RES/1329 (2000) and S/RES/1411 (2002). Amended text available at http://www.un.org/icty.

[13] Statute of the International Tribunal for Rwanda, adopted 8 November 1994 by UN Security Council resolution S/RES/955 (1994), as amended by UN Security Council resolutions S/RES/1165 (1998), S/RES/1329 (2000) and S/RES/1411 (2002). Amended text available at http://www.ictr.org.

witnesses. These articles are supplemented by Rules 75 and 69 of the ICTY and ICTR Rules of Procedure and Evidence, establishing the substantive framework for providing protective measures for victims as witnesses, including, *inter alia*, non-disclosure of a witness' identity, closed court sessions, image or voice distortion and the assignment of a pseudonym.

While the Statutes of the ad hoc Tribunals did not provide for the establishment of a Victims and Witnesses Unit (VWU), Rule 34 makes such provision. Under this provision, for example, witnesses can be relocated.

Rule 96(i), which is the only provision that deals specifically with the issue of corroboration of testimony before the Tribunals, states that no corroboration shall be required in cases of testimony of victims of sexual assault.

There is no reference in the Statute or Rules to the question of victim compensation.[14] The only provision in the Statutes of the ICTY and ICTR that alludes to restitution is Articles 24(3) and 23(3), respectively, providing that the Tribunal may order, in addition to any sentence of imprisonment, the return of any property and proceeds acquired by criminal conduct to their rightful owners. Rule 105 of the (ICTY's) Rule of Procedure and Evidence[15] provides for the restitution of property in some cases, and Rule 106 (Compensation to Victims) provides for the communication to States by the Tribunal's Registrar of Judgements of the Court.

Under Rule 106, individuals must pursue their claims through their national courts, under their national legislation, although the judgment of the Tribunal is binding as to the criminal responsibility of the convicted person for any injury.[16] The problem with this approach is that it

> "assumes that domestic legal systems are equipped to provide victims of armed conflict with compensation. Most governments have no experience in this area. In addition, generally speaking, only sophisticated claimants of large sums will be in a position to pursue recovery through domestic channels. Many victims will be without the resources required to pursue recovery, and stateless persons are left without any recourse."[17]

[14] It seems that the question of victim compensation was not really considered by the Security Council, although a number of proposals for the Statute submitted by IGOs and NGOs had referred to victim compensation. Moreover, "[t]here was some question as to whether the International Tribunal would receive the necessary financial support to effectively perform its essential functions as a criminal tribunal. The proposal to have the International Tribunal also function as a claims commission could not be reconciled with existing financial constraints." V. Morris and M. Scharf, An Insider's Guide to the International Criminal Tribunal for the Former Yugoslavia, (1995), 286.

[15] ICTY doc. IT/32/REV.22, dated 13 December 2001, as amended on 23 April 2002. Text available at http://www.un.org/icty.

[16] Rule 106 provides: "(A) The Registrar shall transmit to the competent authorities of the States concerned the judgement finding the accused guilty of a crime which has caused injury to the victim. (B) Pursuant to the relevant national legislation, a victim or persons claiming through him may bring an action in a national court or other competent body to obtain compensation. (C) For the purposes of a claim made under Sub-rule (B) the judgement of the Tribunal shall be final and binding as to criminal responsibility of the convicted person for such injury.

[17] J.G. Gardam and M.J. Jarvis, Women, Armed Conflict and International Law (2001), 245.

It has been noted that "these rules fall well short of providing reparations or establishing a compensation scheme."[18] The UN Human Rights Commissioner's representative in New York, Bacre Waly Ndiaye, has expressed regret that the tribunals are not accompanied by compensation schemes for victims or their families.[19]

Neither the ICTY nor the ICTR have as yet evolved any jurisprudence dealing with the question of restitution. Furthermore, it does not seem that any action for compensation has yet been brought in a national court on the basis of a conviction by either Tribunal. There is no provision in the Statutes and Rules of the Tribunals allowing victims to participate in the proceedings, or for victims' voices to be heard other than in the capacity of witnesses.

If the statutory and regulatory framework is to be judged for what it is, rather than for what it is not, one can say that the provisions in the ad hoc Tribunals' Statutes and Rules concerning victims have proven a workable framework for the protection of witnesses, including the most vulnerable.[20] Applications for protective measures that have been made by both the prosecution and the defence are usually granted by the Trial Chambers. In the *Tadic* case, the Trial Chamber identified five types of protection that are available, though the list is not necessarily exhaustive: confidentiality, whereby the victim's and witness's identity is withheld from the public and the media; anonymity, whereby the witness's identity is withheld from the accused and his lawyers; protection from retraumatisation, by avoiding confrontation with the accused, for example, by testifying from behind a screen; miscellaneous measures for certain victims and witnesses, e.g., victims of sexual assault and children; and general measures available to all witnesses.[21]

For the most part, the application of the various protective measures available has been unproblematic. However, the granting of anonymity to a few witnesses has proven controversial.

The ICTY has upheld the use of anonymous witnesses, and the withholding of information about a witness's identity from the accused.[22] However, it has stated that this should be an exceptional measure, used only when certain clearly defined criteria are satisfied, including a real fear for the safety of the witness; the importance of the witness's testimony; the trustworthiness of the witness; and the availability of full cross-examination of witnesses on all issues other than identity.[23] The Trial Chamber in the *Blaskic* case added

[18] R.S. Clark and D. Tolbert, *Towards an International Criminal Court*, in Stamapotoulou *et al*, *supra* note 3, 99 at 106.

[19] Report is contained in UN doc. E/CN.4/1998/68.

[20] For a discussion of the position of witnesses pursuant to the ICTY Statute see A. Klip, *Witnesses before the International Criminal Tribunal for the Former Yugoslavia*, 67 Revue Internationale de Droit Penal (1996) 267.

[21] *Prosecutor* v. *Duško Tadic*, ICTY Case No. IT-94-I-T, Decision on the Prosecutor's Motion Requesting Protective Measures for Victims and Witnesses, 10 August 1995, para. 4.

[22] *Id.*, Judge Stephen dissenting. Confirmed and slightly qualified in *Prosecutor* v. *Tihomir Blaskic*, Decision on the application of the Prosecutor dated 17 October 1996 requesting protective measures for victims and witnesses, 5 November 1996.

[23] See *supra* note 21.

that the granting of anonymity should be subject to strict conditions, and that those conditions should be supported with relevant proof.[24]

The Trial Chamber in *Tadic* reached the conclusion that anonymity was permitted despite the fact that it is not specified in the Statute or Rules. Given that other forms of protection are specified, it would be odd if the drafters omitted to mention the most severe form of protection had it really been contemplated.[25] Judge Stephen, dissenting from the majority opinion in *Tadic*, held that anonymity was not foreseen by the Statute or the Rules, was not in line with the jurisprudence of the European Court of Human Rights, and was not compatible with a fair trial for the accused.

Some commentators argue that the use of anonymous witnesses unfairly benefits the witness/victim to the detriment of the accused.[26] One scholar has stated, probably correctly, that "international law has not yet accepted the position that the accused's right to a fair trial is subject to discount and "balancing" in order to provide anonymity to victims and witnesses".[27]

As a decision on a matter of procedure, the Decision of the majority in the *Tadic* case could not be appealed. This is unfortunate, given its fundamental impact on due process.[28] If the safety of witnesses is really a concern, then it can be addressed by means of witness relocation or a witness protection program.

3.2 APPLICATION OF RULE 92*BIS* IN THE *MILOSEVIC* CASE

While the participation of victims appearing before the ICTY may be restricted to the role of witnesses, they thought they at least could count on being able to tell their story in open court to a panel of judges and before the world media, at least insofar as it supported the prosecution case. However, in the *Milosevic* case, most of the so-called "crime-based" witnesses have been denied even that possibility.

The prosecution in *Milosevic* has called many of its crime-based witnesses pursuant to Rule 92*bis* (Proof of Facts other than by Oral Evidence), according to which the Trial Chamber may admit, in whole or in part, the evidence of a witness in the form of a witness statement in lieu of oral testimony.

Rather than being applied, as it was intended, as an exceptional measure, Rule 92*bis* has been widely resorted to in the *Milosevic* case as a time-saving device.[29] Because the Presiding Judge, Richard May, evidently more conscious of his duty to expedite the criminal process than its function as therapeutic tool, imposed an apparently arbitrary deadline on the prosecution case, the Prosecutor had to significantly scale back the number of witnesses it

---

[24] *Prosecutor* v. *Tihomir Blaskic*, *supra* note 22.

[25] See M. Leigh, *The Yugoslav Tribunal: Use of Unnamed Witnesses Against Accused*, 90 AJIL (1996), 235, at 236.

[26] Kittichaisaree, *International Criminal Law* (2001), 300.

[27] M. Leigh, *Witness Anonymity is Inconsistent with Due Process*, 91 AJIL (1997), 83 c.

[28] Leigh, *supra* note 25.

[29] H. Verrijn Stuart, *Tribunal Hands Milosevic Opportunity to Prolong Trial: Milosevic looks set to spin out his trial, despite a tribunal decision to cut down the length of the proceedings by admitting written statements*, Institute for War and Peace Reporting, Tribunal Update No. 261, April 8-13, 2002, http://www.iwpr.net index.pl?archive/tri/tri_261_7_eng.txt.

intended to call.[30] The original roster could not only have helped the prosecution to establish beyond doubt a pattern of criminality; it would have enabled the voices of the victims to be heard. Under pressure of time, the Prosecutor was reduced to calling only a handful of witnesses on each count of the Kosovo part of the indictment. Even many of these were denied the opportunity to be heard. One witness to a massacre, of which he was the only survivor, after being dismissed by Judge May, following a hostile if largely irrelevant cross-examination by Milosevic, exclaimed in astonishment: "But you didn't ask me how I survived."[31]

The resort to Rule 92*bis* as a routine rather than exceptional practice is unfortunate, although the Prosecution, with its back to the wall, cannot be blamed for desperate measures. While judicial economy is no doubt essential, it should not come at the expense of denying victims and witnesses a voice. In the case of the Milosevic trial, it can be argued that the Chamber has leaned too far in the wrong direction in its attempts to control the length of the trial. Counsel Milosevic has managed to secure for himself a much larger platform than he could ever have achieved merely as defendant Milosevic. The voice of the defence has, in this case, drowned out the voices of the victims.

The Chamber's over-indulgence of counsel Milosevic's pleas that his client is being denied a fair trial and, in particular, its permissive attitude to the irrelevant and hostile questioning of witnesses, is not only a question of poor courtroom management, it is also insensitive to witnesses and shows a lack of appreciation of their role in international criminal trials generally, and this one in particular. Even if one surmises the situation from a purely functional perspective, it is clear that most of the time wasting is by the defence.

Given the importance of crime-based witnesses to the prosecution case in the *Milosevic* trial, as well as every other trial before the ICTY, the Tribunal cannot afford to take the cooperation and sympathy of witnesses for granted. A number of crime-based prosecution witnesses purportedly withdrew after realising that they would be subjected to Milosevic's cross-examination.

Ironically, given the Chamber's permissive response to the counsel/defendant's sometimes contemptuous attitude, it was a prosecution witness that got a red card in the Milosevic case. Visibly frightened witness K12, when he refused to continue with his testimony — preferring to go to prison, where he would be safer, he said, than give

[30] M. Klarin, *Milosevic Prosecution "Emasculated": Move to abridge prosecution evidence may play into Milosevic's hands', Institute for War and Peace Reporting*, Tribunal Update No. 261, April 8-13, 2002. Available online at http://www.iwpr.net/index.pl?archive/tri/tri_262_1_eng.txt; M. Klarin, *Milosevic Prosecution Claims Court Unfair: The prosecution is to appeal against a trial chamber decision to conclude its case within a year*, Institute for War and Peace Reporting, Tribunal Update, No. 261, April 15-20, 2002. http://www.iwpr.net/index.pl?archive/tri tri_262_1_eng.txt.

[31] M. Klarin, *Kosovo Victims Gagged: Milosevic's alleged victims will in the future only be allowed to testify or speak in public about subjects he's interested in and which he deems relevant*, Institute for War and Peace Reporting, Tribunal Update, No. 263, April 22-27, 2002, http://www.iwpr.net/index.pl?archive/tri/tri_263_1_eng.txt.

evidence — was held in contempt of court. The Prosecution was directed to initiate contempt proceedings against the witness pursuant to Rule 77(C)(i).[32]

Holding terrified witnesses in contempt of court; denying crime-based witnesses the possibility of giving oral testimony; subjecting ill-prepared witnesses to the trauma of aggressive and largely irrelevant cross-examination by the defendant: the treatment of witnesses in the *Milosevic* case will do little to encourage other victims and witnesses to cooperate with the prosecution and agree to give evidence in this and future trials before the ICTY and other international criminal courts.

In a case of this magnitude, it was obvious that limits would have to be put on the participation of victims and witnesses, and on the length of the trial. Notwithstanding this, the virtual emasculation of the role of crime-based witnesses in the *Milosevic* case sets a dangerous precedent for future international criminal trials.

3.3 SPECIAL PROBLEMS AT THE ICTR

A similar sense of alienation from the work of the ICTR has been expressed by Rwandan victims. A report commissioned by the Centre for Constitutional Rights and the International Centre for Human Rights and Democratic Development, entitled "Witness Protection, Gender and the ICTR," reported that most Rwandan women's groups are "extremely critical of the ICTR's work and most have little to no contact with the ICTR. ... Lack of transparency has left women feeling bitter and suspicious. Survivors want to be informed of the work of the ICTR."[33]

The situation reached a crisis point in Spring 2002, when a number of victims' rights associations decided to withdraw all cooperation with the ICTR. The Association of Genocide Survivors in Rwanda (IBUKA), as well as the Association for Genocide Widows (AVEGA), announced that they were suspending cooperation with the ICTR because of their disillusionment with its functioning after it came to light that 41 genocide suspects were working as defence investigators at the Tribunal. The affect of such a decision on the Tribunal's work could be serious, as the President of IBUKA urged members not to give evidence to any Tribunal investigator.[34]

In its statement suspending cooperation with the Tribunal, AVEGA said that "while to date the survivor groups have tolerated the anomalies that are manifest if one observes [the] tribunal, ... [they] can no longer do so." The statement went on to criticise the security afforded by the ICTR to witnesses after they testify as "leaving a lot to be desired," and criticised the "persecution and harassment of witnesses, particularly the women." The survivor groups further decried what they termed the incrimination of IBUKA and other groups by defence investigators before the judges of the tribunal and the "non-representation of the victims in the process at the Arusha court while the right is recognised

[32] See the ICTY online Archive for the Milosevic case ("Kosovo, Croatia and Bosnia Herzegovina"), Update No. 223 - 7 June 2002. http://www.un.org/icty/latest/index.htm.

[33] NGO Coalition on Women's Human Rights in Conflict Situations. Letter to Justice Louise Arbor, Chief Prosecutor of the ICTY and ICTR, para. 25. Available online at http://www.ichrdd.ca/frame.iphtml?langue=0.

[34] M. Kimani, *Rwandan Genocide Survivor Group Suspend Co-operation with ICTR*, Internews (28 January 2002); S. Kaliisa, *Genocide Survivors' Association Reaffirms its Suspension of Co-operation with the ICTR*, Internews (28 February 2002).

for those presumed to be responsible for the genocide." IBUKA and AVEGA urged the Rwandan government to "study ways and means of suspending its cooperation with the tribunal until it rectifies all these mistakes and shows enough interest in the victims." "We believe that as long as all the above mistakes are not corrected, the court's decisions will only constitute stop-gap measures and a mockery of the genocide victims in the place of equitable justice," the statement declared.[35]

In March 2002, in response to allegations of mistreatment of witnesses, the ICTR and the government of Rwanda agreed to establish a four-member taskforce to investigate this issue, as well as claims that people involved in the genocide are working as defence investigators.[36] This investigation was later suspended.

Another major cause of grievance for victims before the ICTR is what they perceive as discrimination in the medical treatment available to accused persons and victims, particularly concerning the provision of HIV drugs. Many of the ICTR defendants, and even more of the victims, are HIV positive. Of AVEGA's 1,200 members, two-thirds are HIV-positive.[37] Victims are aggrieved that while defendants receive HIV medication, they do not. While the UN is bound to respect the rights of accused and convicted persons, and such persons are entitled to proper medical care, the double standard existing between accused persons and victims regarding access to medical care has fuelled perceptions of unfairness and a sense that the Tribunal is more concerned with the well being of accused persons rather than victims.

Countering these negative perceptions of the ICTR among its constituent population is essential. If the predominant view of the Tribunal among Rwandan people, and especially victims and their families, is that the Tribunal is corrupt, illegitimate or inefficient; that it is remote from the population and is not a Tribunal for the Rwandan people; and that victims are not being treated seriously or fairly, then the Tribunal will have failed in all but its most narrow of purposes — that of prosecuting the key offenders. In order to justify the great expense of establishing both the ICTR and the ICTY, they must also succeed in their supplementary roles, particularly as forces for reconciliation, as platforms for the voices of victims, and as providers of justice to the victims.

3.4 SENTENCING

When the ICTY handed down its first genocide conviction in the case of General Radomir Kristic,[38] the second most senior commander of the Bosnian Serb Army (VRS), the families of some of his victims, the so-called "women of Srebrenica", watching the sentencing hearing on television in Bosnia, reacted with shock, disappointment and a sense of betrayal as they heard the Trial Chamber sentence him to 46 years. For many of those watching, nothing less than a life sentence would match the gravity of his crimes. For others, even life would not be enough. A similar reaction was evinced by victims to the sentence rendered in another case concerning Srebrenica, widely believed to be the site of some of the worst

[35] *Id.*

[36] S. Chhatbar, *ICTR Sets Up Taskforce to Investigate Alleged Mistreatment of Witnesses*, Internews (5 March 2002).

[37] C. McGreal, *A Pearl in Rwanda's Genocide Horror*, The Guardian, (5 December 2001).

[38] *Prosecutor* v. *Radomir Kristic*, Judgement, ICTY Case No. IT-98-33-T, 2 August 2001.

crimes of the Bosnian war. Drazen Erdemovic was at the other end of the command structure and, unlike General Kristic, who was charged with command responsibility, had personally gunned down between 70 and 100 Bosnian Muslim civilian men and boys who had been herded into a field and lined up to be shot. Erdemovic, a Bosnian Croat who had served with the Bosnian Croat and Bosnian Government armies before joining the VRS, and who claimed to have been acting under duress, confessed and cooperated fully with the prosecutor. Following a rather convoluted sentencing process, he eventually received a sentence of five years. For the women of Srebrenica, many of whom still do not know the fate of their loved ones, such a sentence bore no relation to the gravity of the crime nor to the cold-blooded manner of its execution, even given Eredemovic's professions of remorse and cooperative behaviour. At the time the sentence was rendered, the Tribunal had not yet established an Outreach Program, and no attempt was made by it to explain to the victims in the region the basis for such a sentence. Far from promoting healing and reconciliation in the Balkans, these and other sentences of the ICTY have only served to alienate the victims from the Tribunal and reinforce a sense of injustice.[39]

Some of the ICTR's sentences have been greeted with similar surprise by victims in Rwanda. Victims have found it difficult to comprehend, for example, how the crime of genocide can earn life imprisonment in some cases,[40] and 12 years in another.[41]

Victims and witnesses cannot be blamed for failing to understand how crimes of such magnitude — crimes so heinous that they justified the establishment of the Tribunals in the first place — can attract what they perceive as inadequate sentences. Very little effort has been made by the Tribunals to explain their sentencing policy to victims and witnesses.

Both Tribunals have taken steps to address the problems regarding victims' negative perceptions of the Tribunals. While the Statutes or Rules of the ad hoc Tribunals do not stipulate that the effect or impact of a crime on the victim should be a matter to be weighed by the judges during sentencing, do not provide for the consideration of victim impact statements, and contain no provision for victims to be heard or represented in the sentencing process, clearly the Tribunals do not reach their decisions on sentencing without any consideration of the impact of the crimes on their victims. This is just done in a cursory way. In the Celebici decision, the Trial Chamber revealed that it had been considering victim effect statements submitted by the Prosecutor, in which the victims described the impact of the crimes committed against them. In addition, the Prosecutor submitted that the Trial

[39] J.E. Alvarez, *Seeking Legal Remedies for War Crimes: International versus National Trials*, 6 Journal of the International Institute, No. 1 (1997). Online at http://www.umich.edu/~iinet/journal/vol6no1/alvarez.html.

[40] Life imprisonment has been the standard sentence handed down by the ICTR for genocide. The former Rwandan Prime Minister at the time of the genocide, Jean Kambanda, received a life sentence notwithstanding his guilty plea. *The Prosecutor* v. *Jean Kambanda*, ICTR Case No. ICTR-97-23-S, 4 September 1998, upheld on appeal, Judgement, 19 October 2000.

[41] Georges Ruggiu was sentenced by the ICTR to 12-years imprisonment for direct and public incitement to commit genocide and crimes against humanity, following a guilty plea. *The Prosecutor* v. *Georges Ruggiu*, ICTR Case No. ICTR-97-32-I, Judgement and Sentence, 1 June 2000.

Chamber is able to consider the suffering of the victims in the context of the conditions of imprisonment as an aggravating factor.[42] In the Furundžjia case, the Chamber stated that apart from the usual aggravating and mitigating factors, "the Trial Chamber bears in mind the severe physical pain and great emotional trauma that Witness A had to suffer as a consequence of these depraved acts committed against her. It also notes the severe pain and suffering caused to witness D."[43]

In the same decision, the Trial Chamber reiterated the mandate and duty of the International Tribunal, in contributing to reconciliation, to deter such crimes and to combat impunity[44] — goals to which its sentencing policy should contribute.

3.5 OUTREACH

The best way to counteract negative perspectives and to clarify misunderstandings of the work of the Tribunals is clearly to improve communication between the Tribunals and their constituent populations. While the decisions to situate both Tribunals away from the territorial States (in The Hague, in the case of the ICTY, and Arusha, in the case of the ICTR) were taken for security reasons, the institutions' physical remoteness has had implications for their relevance to the lives of the local populations and effectiveness as forces for reconciliation.[45]

It seems remarkable that public relations and outreach were given so little consideration for so many years. Surely, given the Tribunals' mandates, they should have been a priority? The years when the Tribunals were failing to conduct outreach were years in which mis- and disinformation about the Tribunals spread. Belatedly, however, both Tribunals have begun to realise the importance of reaching out and communicating their work to the affected populations.

In October, 1999, the ICTY launched an Outreach Program. The fact that it took seven years to establish such a program, and was an initiative not of the institution as a whole but of a few dedicated individuals,[46] is testament to the low priority given to public relations by the Tribunal. Even still, it is not funded out of the regular Tribunal budget but operates by way of fundraising and donations. The Program's mandate is to break down the physical distance that separates the Tribunal from the region. Recognising that there has been a lot of misinformation and disinformation about the Tribunal, the Outreach program seeks to bridge the gap between the institution and its constituents, that is, the people of the region, and to act towards the restoration of peace. Education is one of the main ways in which this goal is accomplished. Its staff, based in The Hague and in the region, conduct training seminars, give lectures at universities and to Bar Associations and the public, and attend conferences in the region. Outreach also tries to match the needs of groups in the constituent countries of the region with the expertise available within the Tribunal, and experts in different fields are sent to the region to lecture to various groups. The program

[42] *Prosecutor v. Zejnil Delalic, Zdravko Mucic, Hazim Delic* and *Esad Landžo (Celebici)*, ICTY Case No. IT-96-21-T, 16 November 1998, para. 1256.

[43] *Prosecutor v. Furundžjia*, ICTY Case No. IT-95-17/1-T, Judgement, 10 December 1998, para. 287.

[44] *Id.*, para. 288.

[45] See N.J. Kritz, *Coming to Terms with Atrocities: A Review of Accountability Mechanisms for Mass Violations of Human Rights*, 59 Law & Contemporary Problems (1996), 127, 133.

[46] The Outreach Program was the brainchild of former President Judge Gabrielle Kirk McDonald.

also identifies and targets specific groups and finances their trips to The Hague, enabling them to learn more about the institution. Groups that have already benefited from this program include journalists and students from criminal law faculties.

One of the Outreach program's greatest challenges is to make available all Tribunal documents in Bosnian, Serbian and Croatian (BSC), and now, in cases concerning crimes committed in Kosovo, Albanian as well. Currently, and surprisingly in view of the Tribunal's educational mandate, it is not possible to obtain very many documents in BSC or Albanian. The idea is to find the resources to translate all documents into BSC and put them on the Internet. It is further planned to work with local partners to establish mini-archives for ICTY documentation in the capitals, and a video library in Zagreb. Outreach has also been responsible for other important initiatives, including the public broadcasts of trial proceedings via audio over the Internet, and supports relevant initiatives from outside the Tribunal which further its goals.[47]

The Outreach Program is still in its infancy, and much more needs to be done to educate the public of the former Yugoslavia about the work of the Tribunal. While efforts thus far have largely focused on targeting professional groups, victims' groups and the general public have been relatively overlooked. The ultimate success of the Outreach program will depend on how seriously it is taken by the Tribunal, whether it is brought within the Tribunal budget, and how successful it is at raising awareness and combating negative perceptions of the Tribunal within the region.

> "In the case of the Rwanda Tribunal, minimal outreach and public relations meant that, particularly for its first couple of years, most Rwandans — the people to whom it was most important that the ICTR communicate its message — received little if any information about what the tribunal was doing. It took far too long to arrange even brief radio transmissions from the trial proceedings in Arusha into Rwanda. This was further exacerbated by the inability to generate international press coverage of the tribunal."[48]

While even now the ICTR does not have an equivalent outreach program to the ICTY one, on 25 September 2000 the Rwanda Tribunal opened an Information and Documentation Centre in Kigali. Opening the Centre, the Tribunal's then-Registrar, Agwu U. Okali, told guests that while the principal work of the Tribunal is to try genocide suspects, it is important that the trials should make justice a reality to the Rwanda people and thus contribute to the process of national reconciliation within Rwanda itself. The Centre will be a focal point for the provision of information about the Tribunal to the Rwandan population. It will make available to the public materials such as Tribunal decisions and judgements in Kiryarwanda, video footage of trials and hearings, and computers with Internet access. It also offers a library with hundreds of books on international law, the Rwandan genocide, and related texts. Finally, the centre features a Victims Assistance Programme, which offers counselling to victims who are or may be witnesses before the ICTR. The latter program was launched in Taba commune, Rwanda on 26 September.[49]

---

[47] Interview with Liam McDowal, Coordinator of ICTY Outreach program, by the author, May 2000.
[48] N.J. Kritz, *supra* note 45, at 132.
[49] ICTR Information Centre Opens in Kigali, ICTR/INFO-9-2-241.EN., http://www.ictr.org.

"The Support Programme for Witnesses and Potential Witnesses will assist victims of genocide by providing facilities such as legal guidance, psychological counselling, physical rehabilitation and reintegration assistance."[50] The programme will also assist victims of sexual violence. The ICTR Support Program will be implemented by five Rwandan NGOs, selected because of their presence at the community level and their capability to extend the programme to various prefectures where the Tribunal has identified witnesses or potential witnesses.

3.6 EFFORTS TO INTRODUCE VICTIM COMPENSATION AND PARTICIPATION

The Chief Prosecutor of both Tribunals, Carla Del Ponte, and the Judges have lately expressed their serious concern at the failure of both Tribunals to address in any meaningful way the needs of victims, including to give substance to their legal right to reparations. The ICTY's Chief Prosecutor Carla Del Ponte stated that, "A system of criminal law that does not take into account the victims of crimes is fundamentally lacking, because the crime committed has enormous repercussions, whatever the crime."[51]

At the ICTY, the issue of victims was first raised by the ICTY Prosecutor and was discussed by the Judges during their plenary session in July 2000. During their 13 September 2000 plenary, they approved a report that concludes that "victims of crimes within the Tribunal's jurisdiction have a legal right to seek compensation for their injuries," and sets out some ideas for how that might be achieved. In October 2000, the report was forwarded to the UN Secretary-General for transmission to the Security Council,[52] which as of 1 July 2002 has not reacted on it. In an accompanying letter to the Secretary-General,[53] the President of the ICTY called for the introduction of procedures enabling enforcement of this right. It also called for victims' increased participation.

The report noted that while the Prosecutor, in her presentation to the ICTR plenary, had initially argued that the judges could adopt rules implementing a victim compensation scheme and providing for representation for victims, both she and the Judges now agreed that a statutory amendment would be necessary to implement the recommended changes. This, in turn, would necessitate the intervention of the UN Security Council.[54]

---

[50] ICTR Launches Victim Support Initiative in Rwanda, ICTR/INFO-9-2-242.EN, Arusha, 26 September 2000. http://www.ictr.org.

[51] Interview by Stéphanie Maupas with Carla del Ponte, chief prosecutor of the two international tribunals, 9 June 2000. Compensing Victims with Guilty Money, published online in Judicial Diplomacy. http://www.diplomatiejudiciaire.com/UK/Tpiruk/Prosecutor13.htm.

[52] *The Judges of the ICTY Acknowledge the Right of Victims of Crimes Committed in the Former Yugoslavia to Seek Compensation*, ICTY Press Release, The Hague, 14 September 2000, JL P.I.S./528-E. http://www.un.org/icty/latest/index.htm.

[53] Letter dated 12 October 2000 from the President of the International Criminal Tribunal for the Former Yugoslavia addressed to the Secretary-General. Annex to Letter dated 2 November 2000 from the Secretary-General addressed to the President of the Security Council, UN doc. S/2000/1063 (3 November 2000).

[54] "Victims' compensation and participation," Appendix to Letter dated 12 October 2000 from the President of the International Criminal Tribunal for the Former Yugoslavia addressed to the Secretary-General. Annex to Letter dated 2 November 2000 from the Secretary-General addressed to the President of the Security Council, UN doc. S/2000 1063 (3 November 2000), para. 25.

3.7 CONCLUSIONS DRAWN FROM THE EXPERIENCE IN THE TRIBUNALS

Analysis of the legal framework and work of the Tribunals reveals that the key problem areas concerning victims are the lack of access to the court and to participate in the proceedings; the impossibility of seeking reparations through the Tribunals; the limited possibility to tell their story and the sense of being used by prosecutors and the court; a sense of aggrievement by victims who perceive offenders as getting better treatment than them; and a sense of bewilderment with the sentencing regime and a lack of understanding of the incongruity between sentences. The Tribunals have not done enough to communicate understanding and appreciation of their work to the affected populations, although both Tribunals have begun to demonstrate their belated understanding of this problem.

Greater involvement of victims in the work of the Tribunals, and empathy of victims for the Tribunals, is not only essential to secure their legitimacy among the affected populations and their ability to foster a sense of reconciliation. Quite simply, without the cooperation and assistance of victims, the Tribunals cannot function. Unlike earlier international criminal courts, such as the Nuremberg and Tokyo Tribunals, those who wreaked havoc on the Balkans and Rwanda were careful not to leave a paper trail. The evidence of witnesses is therefore of fundamental importance for the Prosecution's building and proving a case. While this cooperation has been forthcoming for most of the existence of the Tribunals, the experience of late shows that it cannot be taken for granted. As much as cooperation of States, cooperation of victims and witnesses is a *sine qua non* for the ability of the Tribunals to function.

4. VICTIMS AND THE ICC

In contrast to the ICTY and ICTR, the position of victims was considered from the outset of the ICC process and victims fare well under the legal regime governing the ICC.[55]

> "The Rome Statute moves away from the exercise of purely retributive justice to incorporate a new dimension of participation of and restoration to victims. This new dimension is one of the most distinctive features of the Statute, which considerably differentiates the ICC both from the International Military Tribunals created after the Second World War and from the recent ad hoc Tribunals for the former Yugoslavia and Rwanda."[56]

---

[55] One commentator stated that "the Rome Statute for an International Criminal Court consistently underscores the fact that one of the ICC's primary purposes is to protect and vindicate the victims of the world's most heinous crimes." M. Bachrach, *The Protection and Rights of Victims under International Criminal Law,* 34 The International Lawyer (2000), 7.

[56] S.A. Fernández de Gurmendi and H. Friman, *The Rules of Procedure and Evidence of the International Criminal Court,* 3 Yearbook of International Humanitarian Law (2000) 289, 312.

It is clear that the ICC Statute[57] was strongly influenced by the work of the UN concerning victims, including the Victims' Declaration adopted by the General Assembly. "However, where the other documents were general in scope, the ICC Statute provides for the actual implementation of these principles."[58]

Provisions concerning victims fall into three main categories: those concerning victims' participation in the proceedings; those concerning protection of victims as witnesses; and those concerning reparations to victims.

4.1 VICTIMS' ROLE AS PARTICIPANTS BEFORE THE ICC

The ICC Statute contemplates a far greater role for victims than merely that of witnesses, by giving them greater access to the constituent organs of the ICC: the Registry, the Chambers, and the Office of the Prosecutor. The Statute and Rules provide the legal basis for full participation of victims as both witnesses and, more importantly, as victims, or individuals with a legal interest in the proceedings. As Ambos states: "[A]lthough the individual does not possess a status of a (accessory) party in the proceedings before the ICC, the individual victim can address the Court directly in various ways."[59] Another commentator notes that: "In the Rome Statute, ... those who have suffered have been elevated from a mere aid in the judicial process, with no interest of their own to protect but that of the criminal justice system, into full legitimate participants."[60] Under the Statute and Rules, victims have the right to participate in every stage of the proceedings, from the time the Prosecutor has submitted a request for authorisation to proceed with an investigation to the Pre-Trial Chamber, to the sentencing hearing. Victims may petition the court on everything from questions of jurisdiction and admissibility (Art. 19(3)), to any matter that concerns their personal interests.[61]

---

[57] 1998 Rome Statute of the International Criminal Court, entered into force 1 July 2002; UN doc. A/CONF.183/9*, as corrected by the procès-verbaux of 10 November 1998 and 12 July 1999. Corrected text available at http://www.un.org/law/icc.

[58] "Victims' compensation and participation," Appendix to Letter dated 12 October 2000 from the President of the International Criminal Tribunal for the Former Yugoslavia addressed to the Secretary-General. Annex to Letter dated 2 November 2000 from the Secretary-General addressed to the President of the Security Council, UN doc. S/2000/1063 (3 November 2000), para. 12. See also Clark and Tolbert, *supra* note 3, at 107.

[59] K. Ambos, *Judicial Accountability of Perpetrators of Human Rights Violations and the Role of Victims*, 6 International Peacekeeping (March-June 2000) 67, at 70.

[60] Shepard Forman, Director, Center on International Cooperation, Prologue to a report on The International Criminal Court Reparations to Victims of Crimes (Article 75 of the Rome Statute) and the Trust Fund (Article 79): Recommendations for the Court Rules of Procedure and Evidence. Prepared by Dinah L. Shelton and Thordis Ingadottir for the Centre on International Cooperation, New York University, for the 26 July – 13 August 1999 Meeting of the Preparatory Commission for the International Criminal Court.

[61] Article 68(3) of the ICC Statute provides that: "Where the personal interests of the victims are affected, the Court shall permit their views and concerns to be presented and considered at stages of the proceedings determined to be appropriate by the Court and in a manner which is not prejudicial to or inconsistent with the rights of the accused and a fair and impartial trial. Such views and concerns may be presented by the legal representatives of the victims where the Court considers it appropriate, in accordance with the Rules of Procedure and Evidence."

Rule 89 is particularly interesting and goes far beyond anything provided for in the ad hoc Tribunals' Rules. Victims and witnesses can apply in writing to the Registrar in order to present their views and concerns. The Registrar shall make copies of the application available to the Prosecutor and the defence, who can respond, within a time-frame stipulated by the chamber. What is especially interesting is that victims' participation can include making opening and closing statements. The Chamber can reject such application, either *proprio motu* or on application of the Prosecutor or defence, if it considers that the person is not a victim or that the criteria set forth in Article 68(3), are not otherwise fulfilled. A victim whose application has been rejected may file a new application later in the proceedings.

Rule 90 is also a totally new provision for victims, providing for their legal representation in the proceedings. It provides in paragraph 1 that a victim shall be free to choose a legal representative. Where there are a number of victims, under paragraph 2, the Chamber may, for the purposes of ensuring the effectiveness of the proceedings, request the victims or particular groups of victims, if necessary with the assistance of the Registry, to choose a common legal representative or representatives. In facilitating the coordination of victim representation, the Registry may provide assistance, *inter alia*, by referring the victims to a list of counsel, maintained by the Registry, or suggesting one or more common legal representatives.

Under paragraph 3, if the victims cannot select a common legal representative within the time limit stipulated by the Chamber, the Chamber may request the Registrar to choose one or more on their behalf. One can imagine that problems could arise when a single or a few legal representatives are chosen to represent a large group of victims. In particular, there could be conflicts of interest between victims, or between particular individuals and the group as a whole. According to paragraph 4, the Chamber and the Registry shall take all reasonable steps to ensure that, in the selection of common legal representatives, the distinct interests of the victims, particularly as provided in article 68, paragraph 1, are represented and that any conflict of interest is avoided. A victim or victims who cannot afford to pay for a common legal representative chosen by the Court "may receive assistance from the Registry, including, as appropriate, financial assistance, under paragraph 5." The qualifications of a legal representative for victims are the same as for defence counsel (Rules 22(1) and 90(6)).

Rule 91 regulates the participation of victims' legal representatives in the proceedings. Pursuant to paragraph 2, the latter are entitled to attend and participate in the proceedings in accordance with the terms of the ruling of the Chamber and any modification thereof given under rules 89 and 90. This shall include participation in hearings unless, in the circumstances of the case, the Chamber concerned is of the view that the representative's intervention should be confined to written observations or submissions. The Prosecutor and the defence shall be allowed to reply to any oral or written observation by the legal representative for victims.

Article 68(3) of the Statute makes it clear that where the personal interests of victims are affected, their views and concerns shall be heard and considered as and when the Chamber deems it appropriate, and in a manner which is not prejudicial to the rights of the accused.

As mentioned in the context of the ICTY, the satisfaction that a victim may gain by his or her assailant's prosecution and punishment may be outweighed or diminished by the strong sense of injustice caused by what the victim perceives as an inadequate or unfair sentence. It is thus very much to the victim's advantage, and in the interests of justice and reconciliation, that, under the Statute, he or she may have the opportunity to be heard during the sentencing phase of ICC proceedings.

During sentencing, under Article 76(2) of the Statute, the Trial Chamber may "on its own motion and shall, at the request of the Prosecutor or the accused, hold a further hearing to hear any additional evidence or submissions relevant to the sentence, in accordance with the Rules of Procedure and Evidence. During such hearings, any representations under article 75 shall be heard." While this provision does not explicitly provide for the views of victims to be considered during sentencing, it provides victims with the opportunity to express their views on this matter. The ICC may also decide to follow the practice of the ad hoc Tribunals in considering victim impact statements presented by the Prosecutor in reaching decisions on sentence.

4.2 PROVISIONS CONCERNING THE PROTECTION OF VICTIMS AND WITNESSES

Article 43(6) provides for the setting up of a Victims and Witnesses Unit (VWU) within the Registry, which "shall provide, in consultation with the Office of the Prosecutor, protective measures and security arrangements, counselling and other appropriate assistance for witnesses, victims who appear before the Court and others who are at risk on account of testimony given by such witnesses. The Unit shall include staff with expertise in trauma, including trauma related to crimes of sexual violence."

The Rules reiterate that responsibility for victims lies with the Registrar, who should assume an active role in assisting them during the proceedings. This includes providing notice to victims or their legal representatives, helping them to obtain legal advice and organising their legal representatives, whom they shall provide with adequate support, assistance and information, including, if necessary, direct assistance, such as the use of whatever facilities might be required. Rule 16(1)(d) enjoins the Registrar to take gender-sensitive measures to facilitate the participation of victims of sexual violence at all stages of the proceedings.

A single VWU is provided for in the ICC Statute and Rules, suggesting that it was originally envisaged that this unit would serve all victims and all witnesses. It would cater to both prosecution and defence witnesses, and it would also presumably protect and advance victims' interests when victims appear before the ICC not as witnesses but as parties in their own rights. Thus, it was envisaged that the VWU would fulfil two functions *vis-à-vis* victims: a protective one and a representational one. There has since been discussion, however, of creating a second unit, possibly called the Victims Participation and Reparation Unit, that would assist in services which the Statute requires for victims alone. These would include the actual payment of reparations and assistance to lawyers of victims.[62]

The ICC Statute attempts to preempt any potential imbalance between Article 68 of the ICC Statute and the rights of the accused and emphasises that the protective measures

[62] Draft Report on the Ninth Session of the Preparatory Commission, April 8-19, 2002. Coalition for the International Criminal Court, 23 April 2002. Prepared by Jennifer Schense.

adopted under the Statute in this regard shall not be prejudicial to or inconsistent with the rights of the accused and a fair and impartial trial.[63]

4.3 PROVISIONS RELATING TO REPARATIONS

Not only do victims have unprecedented access to an international criminal court, they have the possibility to claim reparations, either from the offender himself or from the Trust Fund for victims established under Article 79.

Article 75 of the Statute, empowering the Court to award reparations to victims, is one of the Statute's most far-reaching provisions. This article gives an international criminal court an unprecedented ability to become involved in what is, strictly speaking, a civil proceeding. Claims by individuals in respect of human rights or humanitarian law violations are normally pursued in separate civil litigation or through the method of diplomatic espousal. In this case, the ICC will be establishing principles relating to reparations, determining the scope of damages and making orders against convicted persons. Article 75 is supplemented by a number of rules.

Article 79 provides for the establishment of a Trust Fund. The beneficiaries of the Fund shall be the victims of crimes within the jurisdiction of the Court and their families (Art. 79(1)). "The Court may order money and other property collected through fine or forfeiture to be transferred, by order of the Court, to the Trust Fund" (Art. 79(2)). Criteria for managing the Trust Fund shall be determined by the Assembly of States Parties (Art. 79(3)). Rule 98 expands on Article 79.

5. CONCLUSIONS

It is obvious that, as compared with the ad hoc Tribunals, the position and role of victims will be greatly enhanced before the ICC. Whether or not victims actually have rights under the ICC Statute, as opposed to privileges, is an interesting question that cannot be tackled here. In any event, their status has been promoted from that of mere witnesses to full participants.

The importance of victims being able to participate in the criminal process, either directly or through their legal representatives, should not be underestimated. A common complaint of victims concerning criminal trials is their remoteness. By participating in the trial, and, even more importantly, by being recognised as persons with a legal and moral interest in the outcome, victims can experience a greater sense of empathy and ownership of the process.

Moreover, the ability of victims to claim reparations through the International Criminal Court and participate in reparations hearings bring the victims closer to the process and gives them a direct interest in the outcome.

The greater role for victims envisaged in the ICC's sentencing regime should help the court to avoid some of the misunderstandings engendered by the sentencing policies of the ad hoc Tribunals.

---

[63] K. Kittichaisaree, International Criminal Law (2001), 301.

Notwithstanding the far broader and more inclusive framework of the ICC regarding victims, the legitimacy of the ICC among the populations it will serve cannot be assumed. The ICC should take care to avoid the pitfalls of the ICTY and ICTR. Their experiences in dealing with victims, albeit only as witnesses, should serve as salutary lessons. Clearly, a top priority must be to establish an outreach program. This will be far more difficult in the context of the ICC than it has been in the case of the ICTY and ICTR. The ICC's constituent population is potentially the whole world; getting the message across will be a monumental task, and one that will probably have to be undertaken in cooperation with local organisations and institutions.

Responding to the legitimate concerns of local populations regarding perceived double standards in treatment of offenders and victims is part of the work of any outreach program. As the experience of the ICTR shows, dissatisfaction of local victims' groups with the court can stymie the work of the prosecutor.

Above all, the ICC must allow the voices of victims to be heard, in both theory and practice. As the example of the Milosevic case shows, prosecutors need adequate time to present their cases, and part of that case must consist of the voices of the victims. Victims need to be given the chance to give oral testimony in court. Silencing them, in order that prosecutors meet an artificial deadline, only discourages other witnesses from coming forward.

The position of victims under the ICC Statute means that the court can ensure justice for the victims of international crimes not only in an abstract and symbolic way but also in a very real and practical way. If the ICC fulfils its promise, victims shall no longer be silent partners in the legal process, but vocal and active participants.

SECTION III.3

THE POLICE COMPONENT: INTERNATIONAL AND NATIONAL PERSPECTIVES

INTRODUCTION AND SUMMARY

Enhanced, practical cooperation between the police in different jurisdictions for investigations and enforcement is obviously key to both the prevention of transnational crime and to prosecution once it has been committed. The mandate of Interpol is, first, to ensure and promote the widest possible mutual assistance between all criminal police authorities within the limits of the laws existing in the different countries and in respecting human rights, and second, to establish and develop all institutions likely to contribute effectively to the prevention and suppression of ordinary crimes. Interpol bureaux, called "National Central Bureaux," are a key element in the services provided by Interpol. These bureaux serve as a link between law enforcement agencies of one country and law enforcement agencies of the other member countries. In dealing with international crime, information exchange and multilateral cooperation among the different law enforcement agencies are indispensable. Exchange and cooperation are facilitated by modern telecommunications and data equipment. Interpol not only transmits information, but also keeps its own files on persons, stolen property and other cases. Interpol also provides an automated search facility. This allows police forces to have direct access to specific information.

No formal or informal relationship exists at present between Interpol and the OPCW, although one point raised at the OPCW International Symposium was the possibility that OPCW expert advice on chemical weapons issues or training might possibly be a resource

R. Yepes-Enríquez and L. Tabassi. (eds.), Treaty Enforcement and International Cooperation in Criminal Matters

Interpol may wish to request. In general terms, the following measures were recommended by the author on Interpol in this section in respect of crimes involving the use of chemicals:

- Technical training for police officers. A first response police officer dealing with crime should have a basic notion of what they are facing in order to protect themselves and the community;
- The availability of technical equipment to handle incidents;
- Cooperation among international organisations, such as the OPCW, WCO, the UN, and Interpol; and,
- Establishment of a response mechanism for cases involving chemical attacks.

The second author contrasts Europol with Interpol. Within Europol, the police, and if necessary, customs can cooperate for the purpose of preventing and combating crime in fields such as terrorism, drug trafficking and other serious forms of international crime, chiefly through the central exchange and analysis of information and intelligence. In comparing Europol with Interpol, one of the main differences is that Europol was exclusively set up to combat organised crime because the EU is vulnerable in this respect, due in part to the relaxation of some of its borders. Europol's activities are restricted to the territory of the European Union and it has no power to enact directly applicable legislation in the field of criminal law, except where such legislation aims at administrative control of criminal behaviour. Europol is not an FBI and is not intended to become a comparable EU instrument. All cooperation is based on intergovernmental cooperation and its role is limited to intelligence handling, support and coordination, between the EU members or by supporting joint teams. In contrast, Interpol has more general responsibilities: it is not only focused on organised crime, and its activities are nearly worldwide. One of the important forms of cooperation between Europol and Interpol in the near future will be data exchange.

In 1994-95, prior to entry into force of the Chemical Weapons Convention, Japan suffered the most flagrant case in history of chemical terrorism. These lethal nerve gas attacks by members of the Aum Shinrikyo cult. The transnational elements of that case consist of the membership outside Japan which provided funds and expertise, and the importation of chemical weapons production equipment. The forensic investigation described in this section gives an excellent picture of how the investigations of the attack were carried out. It is also not difficult to imagine the further steps that would have been necessary had the perpetrators fled abroad or if the chemical substances and equipment were illegally imported, in violation of the Chemical Weapons Convention (if it had been in force at that time) and implementing legislation, including import/export controls in Japan and the exporting State. For this reason, the case received considerable attention by the Preparatory Commission for the OPCW and its Member States at the time of the attacks. Further discussion of the terrorist activities of Aum Shinrikyo is covered, *infra* in this volume, in section IV.1.

The attacks in Matsumoto city in 1994 and in the Tokyo subway in 1995 killed 19 persons and injured many. Police were faced with a new type of organised crime: chemical mass terrorism by a terrorist cult. The National Research Institute of Police Science (NRIPS), in Japan, is engaged in research and development on police activity, identification and analyses of criminal evidence, and training for scientists in the local forensic science laboratories. Its chemistry section has been engaged in forensic investigation of chemical terrorism. In this case it was found that the special nature of nerve gas hindered police efforts for a rapid resolution of the sarin incidents. Nerve gases are highly toxic, lethal in trace amounts, and volatile, thus special caution is needed to handle samples. The gases are also difficult to detect because of rapid evaporation; they easily decompose in the body and in the environment, making it necessary to identify degradation products. In this case, GC/MS analysis of sarin hydrolysis products was effective for the confirmation of sarin exposure, use and production, and this provided concrete evidence in the criminal proceedings against Aum members. Early detection of sarin contributed greatly to the investigation.

The section concludes with a perspective from another region. Zimbabwe, an original State Party to the Chemical Weapons Convention, established the obligatory National Authority in the Ministry of Defence, to act as the national focal point for liaison with the OPCW and States Parties. The National Authority also coordinates liaison with and between all key institutions involved in the production, supply, use and control of chemicals in Zimbabwe. At this point in time, however, international cooperation in criminal matters among States in respect of the Chemical Weapons Convention is hampered by the following:

- Zimbabwe is still a new player in the regime. So far it did not receive a request for, or need, mutual legal assistance in the enforcement of the Convention;
- There is no regional contact point;
- Some countries in the region are not States Parties or even signatories; and,
- States Parties are at different levels of implementation. This can be a real hindrance for effective cooperation.

That last point is fundamental. One common thread through many of the issues being addressed by the OPCW within its mandate is the difference in the capacities of States Parties to fully implement the Convention. For example, although it is required by the Convention, less than half of States Parties have submitted information on their national implementing legislation. Depending upon the legal system and the scope of other legislation already in force, the Convention *may* be enforceable and the State Party *may* be able to cooperate in criminal matters with other States Parties in relation to it, but it is not certain or even likely. If violations of the Convention are to be prevented or punished, the police and judicial authorities need a proper legal framework to enable investigation, arrest, and prosecution. However, the fundamental requirement is, first and foremost, legislation criminalising the activity.

Brigitta Exterkate

Rapporteur for Panel B.2 in the 2001 OPCW International Symposium; Senior Legal Officer, OPCW Technical Secretariat, Office of the Legal Adviser. The views expressed are not attributable to the OPCW.

INTERPOL

Roberto Maroto*

1. Introduction

Interpol is quite well known by name but its activities and working methods, the work it carries out and how that work is carried out, is not commonly known. In the course of this chapter, the following points will be covered: Interpol tools to fight criminality; the structure within the Interpol General Secretariat; a few case studies involving chemicals and crime; and measures of possible cooperation.

2. Interpol's Tools to Fight Criminality

Interpol is an international organisation which provides a means for police forces of member countries to conduct criminal inquiries beyond their own borders. In the field of international crime prevention, Interpol's basic principles are, first, to ensure and promote the widest possible mutual assistance between all criminal police authorities within the limits of the laws existing in different countries, and in the spirit of the Universal Declaration of Human Rights. Second, Interpol aims to establish and develop all institutions likely to contribute effectively to the prevention and suppression of ordinary crimes. Interpol assists in this ultimate goal by providing police at the national level with some essential tools.

Interpol bureaux or "National Central Bureaux" (NCBs) are a key element in the services the organisation provides. NCBs are located in each Member State and serve as a link between the law enforcement agencies of one State and the law enforcement agencies of the other member countries. National Central Bureaux are a focal point for all Interpol investigative requests coming into and going out of a country. NCBs communicate amongst themselves, and with the Interpol General Secretariat, so that the latter can perform its task of maintaining a centralised repository of information related to international crimes and criminals.

In dealing with international crime, information exchange and multilateral cooperation among the different law enforcement agencies are indispensable. To enable this, the organisation possesses the most modern equipment available in terms of telecommunications and data processing. The General Secretariat of Interpol can offer direct, rapid and secure communications among each country's police service as well as a fully computerised international data base.

Interpol not only transmits information, it also keeps its own files on persons, stolen property and cases. Since 1989 Interpol has had one of the most advanced computer

* Crime Intelligence Officer, Public Safety and Terrorism Sub Directorate, Interpol General Secretariat Headquarters, Lyon. Any views expressed are solely those of the author and are not attributable to Interpol.

R. Yepes-Enríquez and L. Tabassi. (eds.), Treaty Enforcement and International Cooperation in Criminal Matters

systems in the world for filing and processing information. NCBs transmitting information via the central telecommunications station located at the Interpol General Secretariat can decide which items of their information should be entered in the computer databases and can decide which Member countries may have access to those items. It is even possible for information to be available to a single individual in the recipient country if he or she alone possesses the decrypting device. The system can also be used to transmit images of photographs and fingerprints, encrypted if necessary.

In order to extract and analyse data from the centralised database, a number of officials at the General Secretariat have been trained in crime analysis and now form the Crime Analysis Branch (CAB). Utilising modern analytical software, this unit has been designed to ensure that full advantage can be taken of the wealth of information that is stored in Interpol's criminal information system. For example, by establishing the links between crimes and offenders and disseminating that information for use by the member countries, Interpol provides law enforcement with *valuable* and *actionable* criminal intelligence.

Another valuable tool Interpol is able to provide is the automated search facility (ASF). This computerised system allows the police forces of Interpol's member countries to search, directly and in real time, a database of selected information. It contains photographs, fingerprints, and the particulars of over 128,300 international criminals. It is an excellent source of immediate information.

Interpol also uses a system of international notices to inform member countries of the movements of known international criminals either subject to arrest and extradition or suspected of criminal involvement. The colour-coded notices are printed and distributed by Interpol headquarters. Interpol is responsible for the publication and distribution of five types of international notices. The most important is the "red notice": an international notice based upon a national arrest warrant, seeking arrest where extradition will be requested. All notices are published at the request of member countries in the four official languages of Interpol, and each remains valid for five years (or until cancelled at the request of the originating country).

The "Operational Working Group" is another tool employed by Interpol, particularly in dealing with organised crime. Because the information contained in Interpol's database comes from many countries simultaneously and is constantly being collated and analysed, Interpol is able to identify relationships between individuals in various cross border criminal groups which are not readily apparent to police operating at the national level.

3. Structure Within the Interpol General Secretariat

Measures have been taken at all levels to fight illicit trafficking in nuclear, chemical or biological substances. International treaties have been concluded and international organisations have been mandated with this fight as a priority. Nevertheless, it is impossible to always prevent the misappropriation of these substances. Although such agreements are essential, they cannot prevent or abolish this kind of trafficking, and thus this type of crime falls into the jurisdiction of law enforcement.

Aware of this responsibility, the Interpol General Secretariat underwent a restructuring to address this issue. Until 1998 the group dealing with environmental crime under

Subdivision 2 was responsible for all incidents concerning nuclear or radioactive materials. In 1998, under Subdivision 1, the Anti-Terrorism Branch, or "TE Branch" as it was better known, was designated responsible to gather all possible information on what is sometimes referred to as "catastrophic terrorism" (the use of weapons of mass destruction in terrorist attacks). Thus proliferation and terrorist threats passed within the scope of competence of the TE Branch while the environmental aspects remained within Subdivision 2. In 2001, after 11 September, the Interpol General Secretariat restructured again, and the TE Branch became the Public Safety and Terrorism Sub Directorate, under the Specialised Crimes Directorate. Two new structures were specially created in order to help Interpol Member Countries exchange information and leads on the attacks: the Command Center and the Task Force.[1]

4. Sample Case Studies Involving Chemicals and Crime

In Interpol's databases there are several cases in which chemicals substances have been used to commit criminal acts. There are also examples of cases where individuals linked to commercial firms have tried to deal with countries subject to special restrictions under export controls or weapon control laws. The database also contains very detailed information regarding the terrorist attacks committed in Japan by the Aum Shinrikyo sect which is examined elsewhere in this book.[2]

One of these cases shows how an apparently inoffensive gas, if used in certain conditions, can be converted into a deadly weapon. In Lisbon, Portugal, on the night of 6 April 2000, approximately 800 people were present in the Luanda Disco. Two tear gas bombs were thrown in and, at the same moment, the lights were intentionally turned off. The gas containers had labels marked "grenade," possibly to deter anyone from daring to touch them. As a consequence of the panic that the tear gas and obscurity provoked, everyone rushed to try to leave the place at the same time. Seven people died and fifty more were injured. The case is still under investigation, but at this point it can be said that the motivation was a dispute between gangs for the control of the discotheque business. The Interpol channel was used for the exchange of information between the Portuguese authorities and the country where the gas spray was manufactured.

This is not the only case of the use of tear gas for more or less organised gangs of criminals. In the Nordic countries, some motorcycle gangs similar to the infamous Hell's Angels have declared a kind of war between gangs, causing major disruptions and armed attacks. In Finland, in the parking lot of a recreational centre, bikers were involved in a very serious fight among themselves. More than 30 of their members fought, resulting in some of them being injured. A series of confrontations followed and weapons were used. Besides the use of pistols, baseball bats and chains, tear gas was used as a weapon in several of these confrontations. Interpol has been used to exchange information between the countries involved and an analytical project on motorcycle gangs was created to study this particular crime area.

Another example of the use that member countries can make of Interpol channels is in the issuance of an internationally recognised arrest warrant against a person, the so-called

[1] See further, *infra* in this volume, R. Maroto, International Cooperation in Protection Against Terrorism through Interpol.

[2] See *infra* in this volume, Y. Seto, Forensic Investigation of the Sarin Gas Attacks in Japan.

"red notice." In this case, a European country charged a person for an offence against its war weapons control act and its foreign trade and payments law. The suspect, a European citizen, was the head of a subsidiary office located in a country subject to export restrictions. He had played an important role in the delivery of a waste gas washing plant in that country. The plant, allegedly set up for a legitimate purpose, turned out to have been intended for the production of chemical weapons. The suspect was involved in the planning and control of the establishment which knew the real purpose of this plant. The suspect had also coordinated the installation and testing of the plant by foreign engineers. The "red notice" or arrest warrant was issued in 1994 for those activities. He was finally arrested when trying to enter his own country.

In another case a person from a company was charged for the illegal export and diversion to a third country of the chemical substance thiodiglycol, which is a chemical precursor for mustard gas. An international arrest warrant was issued in this case, and the suspect was arrested in another country. The first judge rejected his extradition to the requesting country and released him. A further appeal to the supreme court cancelled the first tribunal decision and ordered his extradition. Other persons implicated in the transaction were also the subject of red notices.

At times, if the violation of the export law is not severe enough to charge the suspect and issue an arrest warrant, it is very important to reflect any additional laws the person may also have violated to commit the crime. If, for instance, the subject also committed accessory crimes, such as money laundering, conspiracy and giving false statements, these charges may also br brought, which may help to sustain the extradition request.

5. Measures for Cooperation

From the police perspective, and in order to fight against crimes involving weapons of mass destruction, the following preventive measures can be highlighted:

- Intelligence gathering is the most important preventive measure to be taken. Police services in the different countries should focus their attention on monitoring groups likely to use these weapons and share the information between each other.
- Technical training for police officers is of major importance. An investigator, as well as a first response police officer dealing with these crimes, should have a basic notion of what they are facing in order to protect themselves and the rest of the community.
- The availability of technical equipment is also fundamental for handling these incidents.
- Cooperation among international organisations such as the OPCW, the World Customs Organisation, the United Nations, Interpol, and other intergovernmental groups or institutions, is vital. Much has been done in this sense, and every day we advance a step further in this cooperation, with information exchange, participation in seminars, training courses, harmonisation of databases. However, there still remain many steps to be taken.

Even if all the above-mentioned preventive measures are taken, we cannot exclude the possibility of a chemical attack by a terrorist group. In case of such an attack, a response mechanism should be in place. A concerted, integrated and quick response should be set up, and a plan should be prepared in advance for any necessary response. The type of response depends on the particular circumstances of the case, but in general the areas covered by the plan should include:

1) who to notify, (law enforcement, emergency response units, hospitals);
2) the procedures to isolate the area and protect the population;
3) the protocol for evaluation of the possible remaining danger;
4) the procedure for gathering information concerning the circumstances of the attack;
5) the temporary storage arrangements for any chemicals that might be found;
6) the arrangements for transport to a final authorised storage or disposal facility;
7) the nomination of a laboratory where the substances should be sent for analysis; and,
8) the judicial procedures to be pursued for prosecution of the perpetrators.

EUROPOL

Willy Bruggeman*

1. Introduction

Any discussion of policing in Europe at this moment in time is both opportune and problematic. It is opportune in the sense that we appear to have entered a distinct period in which European governments see real benefits in striving toward enhanced practical police cooperation, both as a response to perceived threats to order and security and as a means of compensating for the removal of border controls. Problematic, since it can be argued at a European level that we are on shifting sands, with highly flexible strategic and tactical alliances and/or conflicts between supranational bodies, individual European Member States, police organisations, and their constituencies. Nevertheless, it was expected that international police cooperation in Western Europe would undergo a great deal of change.[1] Hence, the subject of my contribution concerns policing in Europe (and not policing Europe or the European Union (EU)), more particularly by studying the (future) role of Europol.

The police are the label, and policing the means, used by the State when asserting its exclusive title to the use or threat of force against dangers emanating from within its boundaries. This is one of the central questions underpinning the discussions on the forms of police cooperation appropriate to Europe in the nineties, namely, that of the nature of the relationships between "Europeanisation" initiatives within the police sector and forms of integration within the EU.

The police itself should be first analysed at the national level. It is mostly the case that police organisations (centralisation, decentralisation, unification, reorganisation), police legislation, penal law and criminal procedure differ from one country to another, and have often been recently reformed or reform is being discussed.

One of the key public rationales for intensified police cooperation as part of policing has been the prospect of the abolition of border controls between Member States of the European Union which, it is argued, will undermine the traditional filter functions of frontiers and remove a major impediment to cross-border criminality. Another identifiable factor is the emphasis that has been placed on the dangers of the growth in illegal immigration. It is obvious, given the concern as regards drug smugglers, immigrants, terrorists and securing internal order, that the objective of Euro-policing is a lively topic of discussion in most of the EU Member States, and different concepts are being discussed. The European policing field is criss-crossed by a multiplicity of initiatives and fora, and the

* Deputy Director, Europol. Any views expressed are solely those of the author and are not attributable to Europol.

[1] C.J.C.F. Fijnaut (ed.), The Internationalization of Police Cooperation in Western Europe, Arnhem (1993) SMP-Cahrer; 6 at 9.

R. Yepes-Enríquez and L. Tabassi. (eds.), Treaty Enforcement and International Cooperation in Criminal Matters

lack of empirical data rules out the assessment of relative performance. Until there is an appropriate supranational EU/EC police function, any evaluation of effectiveness will be confounded by the effect of interaction between cross-national and national (domestic) factors.[2] Therefore, it is useful to speculate on how effective alternative configurations of the European policing arrangements may be. While the Treaty on European Union has now assumed a kind of hegemony, there are still other contenders, which will be analysed later on in this chapter.

Before doing so, however, it is interesting to analyse the creation of Europol, having emerged as a new plant in the international law enforcement garden after a long and difficult germination period. With Schengen, this illustrates the intergovernmental approach, which is the most specific characteristic of current police cooperation.

I would therefore like to examine a number of historical, political and practical elements which, in combination with the growing number of tactical and strategic Europol activities in The Hague, should lead to an acceptable decision. And I close with a question: are Schengen, the Treaty on European Union in general, and the Europol Convention the start of a new wave?

2. Recent Developments in European Police Cooperation

Leaving aside the examples of bilateral cooperation between nation-states, this contribution is primarily concerned with recent forms of police cooperation in Europe in general, and in the EU in particular. From the perspective of the nineties, European police cooperation is an opaque and complex patchwork of institutions (official or otherwise), agreements and structures which aim to promote different forms of cooperation. Looking back across the 1970s and early 1980s, from the perspective of 1993 and the Treaty on European Union, police cooperation emerges as a series of ad hoc developments. The most significant structures for Europe are, without doubt, Interpol, the World Customs Organisation (WCO), Schengen and the European Union intergovernmental Trevi-derived network, this being the Third Pillar in general and Europol in particular. The Lord Scarman Centre for the Study of Public Order presents police cooperation as operating at three interrelated levels:[3]

- a macro-level, concerned with constitutional and international legal agreements and the harmonisation of national laws and regulations;
- a meso-level, concerned with police operational structures, practices, procedures and technology; and,
- a micro-level, concerned with the prevention and detection of specific offences and crime problems.

A general study shows that the complexity is a reflection of the organisational reality, best characterised as a 'crowded police space'.[4] European police cooperation can be viewed

---

[2] M. den Boer and N. Walker, *European Policing after 1992*, 31 Journal of Common Market Studies (1993) 3-28.
[3] J. Benyon, L. Turnbull, A. Willis, R. Woodward and A. Beck, Police Cooperation in Europe: An Investigation (1993) at 351.
[4] B. Hebenton and T. Thomas, Policing Europe: Co-operation, Conflict and Control (1995) at 40.

positively as such a space, with different countries and interest groups being responsible for placing the emphasis on particular areas of cooperation. In fact, almost all the European countries are member countries of Interpol, the WCO and the United Nations. Some of them are Benelux and Schengen countries, and 15 are EU Member States. With this in mind, Europe can be considered, in policing terms, as being made up of a series of concentric and overlapping circles. The 'map' shows overlapping institutional sources, territorial remits, functional specialisations and strategic emphasis.

This overlapping situation and the risk of duplication and redundancy is not just a matter of information storage, but mainly a problem of task differentiation and authority. Nowadays, the EU authorities are very much looking for an EU/Schengen framework for keeping police cooperation under full 'political' control. On a theoretical basis, various possibilities are contacts, liaison, coordination, joint action, parallel laws, the harmonisation of penal laws and/or criminal procedure, common law, and communautarisation (First Pillar).

It should be stressed that, also within the Interpol concept, a regional (European) approach became visible at the moment when new European Community developments were initiated. Schengen was created as a forerunner system for Europol, and the Schengen Convention should be read and analysed in this context. Unfortunately, not all the EC Member States joined the Schengen Convention. Thus the Maastricht logic became partly less ambitious than the Schengen approach, certainly as far as cross-border operational cooperation is concerned.

In the EU context, for many purposes, including policing, Member States continue to view the European level as a legitimate arena for action and decisions. However, while this function requirement is dated, I should also argue that the Member States are engaged in a process of bargaining within the framework of medium-term strategic goals, from which both the scope of cooperation and the institutional form of cooperation will emerge. Since November 1993, and the entry into force of the Maastricht Treaty, the EU Council of Justice and Home Affairs Ministers has coordinated a number of once distinct EC fora, including the Trevi forum. While at one level it can be argued that the Treaty presents a qualitative shift in at least the politics of police cooperation, with a general agreement on the need to pursue cooperation in the fields of Justice and Home Affairs, it may be a mistake to view the shift as non-problematic.

One of the problems is that it was never made clear, politically, what the specific role and added value of, for example, Europol and Interpol should be. The same can be said of various European Union institutions. The non-determining nature (civil enforcement) of current arrangements within the field of control and law enforcement, in comparison with the future role of Europol, illustrates this situation. This is particularly evident where the Community has developed its own 'policing capacity' against fraud through the establishment of OLAF (European Union Anti-Fraud Unit). In addition, the 1985 Schengen Convention presented a direct challenge, if not at its creation, then certainly by the end of 1992 when most of the EU countries had joined it.

Beyond the EU, the other highly significant institution has been, and remains, the Council of Europe, of which all EU States are members. Founded in 1940, and having undergone a certain amount of revitalisation since 1989, the question is now whether or not the EU may join the Council of Europe as a single member. Over the last 35 years, this

Council has been responsible for a number of measures, covering extradition, mutual legal assistance and, more recently, measures to encourage the suppression of terrorism and the confiscation of the proceeds of crime. This situation also illustrates the fact that most of those regulations are not recent decisions and are not always adapted to the specific EU political situation. The same can be said of three relevant international conventions on confiscation: the 1988 United Nations Convention against Illicit Traffic in Narcotic Drugs and Psychotropic Substances (the 1988 Drug Convention); the 1990 G-7 report of the Financial Action Task Force on money laundering; and the Council of Europe's own 1990 Convention on Laundering, Search, Seizure and Confiscation of the Proceeds of Crime.[5] While, for the most part, national laws have been — and sometimes still have to be — brought into line with these international agreements, it is not always clear as to how this would be put into practice effectively, particularly within the EU Member States.

3. The History of Europol in Terms of Treaty Law

Strictly speaking, the idea of a European drugs unit was first brought up in the Trevi meetings long before Maastricht. However, I would like to begin immediately with Article K.1(9) of the Maastricht Treaty. This article forms part of what is termed the Third Pillar, i.e. intergovernmental cooperation in the field of Justice and Home Affairs. The list of common matters of interest is obviously a response to the criticisms concerning the loose nature of Trevi, seeking to give it a more permanent form and link it more closely to the European institutions, however limited the input of these institutions may be. It also incorporates numerous elements from the Palma Document, resulting — oddly enough for the Schengen countries — in many instances in a two-track policy because internal border controls have yet to be abolished in these countries.

Putting the Third Pillar in place was proving to be a slow and painstaking task. There are a number of possible explanations for this, such as the principle of sovereignty, national (often different) penal laws and the fact that provisions for international cooperation originate mainly from the 1950s. Nevertheless, although it is still too early to form a proper opinion, it has had an undeniable effect on the dynamism of Europol, a subject which I shall return to later.

The approach also necessitates adequate democratic control over the decisions taken, and some way of enforcing compliance or imposing penalties if a Member State fails to cooperate, which, formally, is lacking at present. Public and political interest is currently most concentrated around the field of police and judicial cooperation, which is directed essentially at combating the growth in organised crime and dealing with the formidable and acute immigration problem. Decision-making in these areas tends to be based on conventions which, given the need for unanimity, is a long haul. Intergovernmental attitudes dominate the Community approach and hinder a more spontaneous form of harmonising criminal law and procedure. Many people believe that active Community responsibilities must be rooted in administrative law enforcement.

Some of the more extensive treaty provisions of the past (letters rogatory, legal assistance, the transfer of sentenced persons, extradition) have been substituted, initially by inter-police cooperation and now by intergovernmental police cooperation (Schengen, Maastricht,

[5] European Treaties Series, no. 141.

Amsterdam). As a direct consequence of this, a two-speed system has emerged, giving rise to feelings of surprise, frustration (e.g. when criminal proceedings are not instituted following police cooperation), legal uncertainty and powerlessness. What is more, there is no overall logic to intergovernmental law enforcement or to intergovernmental action by administrative law enforcement agencies. There are problems in the field of proactive police intelligence, due chiefly to differences between police regulations and police practices. The dangers of unlawful and inadmissible evidence are often all too close for comfort, particularly when two or more countries work together closely. These circumstances can only be beneficial to criminals.

Article K.1(9) of the Maastricht Treaty provided for the establishment of Europol. This is the first organisation to be created within the Third Pillar, in which the police, and, if necessary, customs can cooperate for the purposes of preventing and combating crime in fields such as terrorism, drugs trafficking and other serious forms of international crime. Such cooperation is chiefly achieved through the central exchange and analysis of information and intelligence. This certainly does not extend to executive powers, although the supplementary declaration appended to the Treaty refers to support, analysis of national prevention programmes, training and research and development. What this actually entails in practical terms is now defined by the Europol Convention (signed July, 1995 and entered into force October, 1998), which also defines in concrete terms the parameters of Europol's competencies.[6] Europol officials, analysts, and liaison officers from the various Member States will perform the tasks listed. Data will be stored centrally in the Europol data bank. It has been decided who should have access to what information, both 'hard' and 'soft', and which restrictions based on the 'need to know' and 'right to use' principles and/or other criteria have to be respected. The liaison officers will also provide cooperation support and coordinate activities (Article 5). Every country is obliged to set up a national intelligence service (the Europol National Unit). While this does not pose any problems for the United Kingdom and the Netherlands, which already have a National Criminal Intelligence Division, it may create difficulties for other EU Member States.

A great deal of thought was also given to defining Europol's mandate (now including terrorism), data protection, political accountability (to the ministers via the management board), democratic control, budgetary control and judicial control. The Cannes European Council (26 and 27 June 1995) reached agreement on the Convention establishing Europol. The Convention has been signed and ratified (October 1998), including a protocol which allows the Member States to opt in with respect to the jurisdiction of the European Court of Justice. Data protection arrangements, intelligence standards and regulations, and analytical regulations are now ready for implementation, and Europol took up its activities on 1 July 1999.

The provisions in the Treaty of Amsterdam reflect the increased attention in recent years on organised crime. Several Articles of the Treaty deal specifically with this phenomenon. Article 29 of the Treaty contains the provision that the objective of the Union shall be to provide citizens with a high level of safety within an area of freedom, security and justice by

---

[6] The text describes Europol's tasks as follows (Articles 3 and 5):

- the exchange of information;
- analysis;
- facilitating the coordination of ongoing investigations;
- increasing expertise; and,
- training.

developing common action among the Member States in the fields of police and judicial cooperation in criminal matters, and by preventing and combating racism and xenophobia. That objective shall be achieved by preventing and combating crime, organised or otherwise, in particular terrorism, trafficking in persons and offences against children; illicit drug trafficking and illicit arms trafficking; and corruption and fraud. The Article seems to not have been drafted by lawyers. The Third Pillar contains much more than topics on police and judicial cooperation *stricto sensu* and the examples chosen seem to be a choice of a political nature: one year it is fraud, and another year it is endangered species or illicit trafficking in nuclear materials which merits attention.

Two other new articles draw attention because they were drafted taking into account the fight against organised crime. Article 30 deals with Europol and enlarges the tasks of Europol in comparison with the Treaty of Maastricht. Europol may support investigative actions by the competent authorities of the Member States, including operational actions of joint teams comprising representatives of Europol in a support capacity. In other words, Europol gets the possibility to join operational actions of Member States, and the Member States are obliged to accept the participation of Europol. This probably needs some extra regulation, because it is unclear under which regime Europol personnel fall when performing this function, especially if this means they could support, for example, the searching for, and questioning of, suspects.

Europol may also ask the Member States to conduct and coordinate their investigations in specific cases. Member States are not obliged to comply with the request, which is logical because there is no political body to which Europol is responsible for questions relating to policy concerning the conduct of investigations in one field of crime or another, or in individual cases.

Article 31(e) provides for the adoption of measures by the Council to establish minimum rules relating to the constituent elements of criminal acts and to penalties in the fields of organised crime, terrorism and illicit drug trafficking. This concerns approximation/harmonisation of laws, which in practice also happened under the Treaty of Maastricht (for example, Convention and protocols on the protection of the financial interests of the EC).

The Council also recently decided[7] to implement the Amsterdam strategy, following a step by step approach. These initiatives are also subject to the so-called European strategy for the beginning of the new millennium,[8] mainly based on the conclusions of the Tampere Summit.

As far as Europol is concerned, the following initiatives are agreed upon:

Measures to be taken within two years:

- Improve Europol cooperation in the following areas:
  1. Examine the feasibility of setting up a database of pending investigations, within the framework of the provisions of the Europol Convention, allowing the avoidance of any overlap between investigations and the involvement of several European competent authorities in the same investigation, thus combining their knowledge and expertise.

[7] JAI 41
[8] CRIMORG 36

2. Direct Europol's documentary work towards operational activity. Wherever possible, its analyses should lead to operational conclusions.
3. Make the fight against illegal immigration networks one of the priorities of operational cooperation, particularly by using the national units as a network of national contact points responsible for dealing with them.
4. Combat terrorism: reinforce exchanges of information and the coordination of competent authorities of Member States in the fight against crimes committed or likely to be committed in the course of terrorist activities, using Europol in particular.
5. Extend the competencies of Europol to other activities, as necessary.

- Draw up an adequate legal instrument extending Europol's powers to the activities referred to in Article 30(2) TEU and focusing Europol's work on operational cooperation. An important subject is the place and the role of judicial authorities in their relations with Europol. One of the priorities stated by the Treaty is to determine the nature and scope of the operational powers of Europol, which will have to be able to "ask the competent authorities of the Member States to conduct and coordinate [their] investigations" and also to act within the framework of "operational actions of joint teams".
- Examine Europol access to Schengen Information System (SIS) or EIS investigation data.
- Develop the role for Europol concerning the exchange of information in order to implement the Pre-Accession Pact on organised crime.

Measures to be taken within five years:

- Promote liaison arrangements between prosecuting/investigating officials who are specialising in the fight against organised crime in close cooperation with Europol (Article 30(2)(c), TEU).
- Establish a research and documentation network on cross-border crime (Article 30(2)(d), TEU).
- Improve the statistics on cross-border crime (Article 30(2)(d), TEU).
- Set up a system for the exchange of information and analysis on money laundering.
- Examine whether and how Europol could have access to the Customs Information System.
- In cooperation with Europol, elaborate and implement an information strategy in order to make the work and powers of Europol known to the public.
- Study the possibility of setting up a system of exchanging fingerprints electronically between Member States.

The Tampere European Council noted that it was deeply committed to reinforcing the fight against serious organised and transnational crime.

The role of the First Pillar is becoming more and more important, especially when creating legal instruments to combat organised crime in connection with fiscal fraud (recommendation 4), the preparation of a comprehensive prevention strategy (recommendation 6), reviewing and improving legislation as well as control and regulatory policies at the national and the EU levels (recommendations 1 and 8), and developing measures to implement the principle of mutual recognition of judicial decisions to criminal cases (recommendation 22). Europol's role also has to be strengthened, and the Council has been requested to draw up and adopt, as soon as possible, a legal instrument concerning the establishment of Eurojust, specifying its structures, sphere of competencies, powers and responsibilities. Particular attention should be given to determining the general framework of the new body's relationship with national prosecuting authorities, Europol, Commission (OLAF) and the European Judicial Network.

Also worthy of mention is the Convention on Mutual Legal Assistance in Criminal Matters between the Member States of the European Union, which includes the creation of joint teams in Article 13. Unfortunately this convention could not be accepted at the last JHA Council, though agreement can be expected in the near future.

The role of prosecution will have to be defined in the framework of Eurojust.

Theoretically, one can distinguish seven models for future development at the international level (in addition to national initiatives):

- *status quo* (not to be considered as a new development);
- restructuring and qualitative improvement of the existing judicial framework, taking into account specific needs in order to facilitate an integrated and interactive police/prosecution department approach;
- liaison magistrates;
- national or contact magistrates, active within a European Union network;
- a formal European Union (Third Pillar) structure for improved cooperation between leading prosecution authorities in the Member States;
- integration of judicial authorities within the EU frameworks (OLAF, Europol);
- the creation of an EU prosecution department, as proposed by Mr De Angelis of the European Commission, making additional use of a network of specialised prosecution authorities in the Member States (Community fraud); and,
- a genuine European Union prosecution department.

The first five proposals appear particularly interesting and include ad hoc participation of the magistrate in international (for example, at Europol) initiatives for improved case-related coordination of investigations. The creation of any real European structures is premature at this stage, although in 1996-1997 a number of experts convened by the

European Commission[9] elaborated a proposal for a more effective system to fight EU fraud, that would also safeguard the human rights of the suspect. The proposal leaves the national court systems intact, but introduces a European Public Prosecutor whose jurisdiction would extend to the whole territory of the European Union.

The actual concrete plans are less ambitious, especially within the framework of the third pillar. Awaiting further clarification of the role of the European judicial network with Europol, one should first support the idea that all of the principles and implementing measures for international cooperation in criminal matters should undergo fundamental reconsideration.[10] Shorter and more direct lines of communication, including those leading from the public prosecution department via the national and liaison public prosecutors should be more firmly established in international agreements that determine whether and where pursuit is permitted, and by which authorities. Agreements containing well-defined conditions could serve to simplify a good number of the complex procedures resulting from such police actions (transfer, extradition, etc.). However, a real European public prosecution department could not be effective, or even necessary, until a legal system, and possibly a law enforcement agency with executive powers, is put into operation at the European level and European criminal law and criminal procedures are accepted.

As a final note we turn to the place and the role of judicial authorities in their relation with Europol, in step with the widening of its mandate and in view of its operative powers to work together with national authorities. As was already mentioned, under Article 30(2)(c) of the Treaty of Amsterdam, the Council of the EU would — within a period of five years after the date of entry into force of the revised Treaty — establish a "liaison arrangement between prosecuting/investigating officials, specialising in the fight against organised crime in close cooperation with Europol". The relation between the judicial network under establishment and Europol also has to be clarified within a period of three years. It remains open whether the relation is technical and/or operational. In this respect, it should be recalled that the High Level Group suggested that, if the experience of a network would prove to be positive, it could be examined whether, in the long run, the network should be transformed into a more permanent structure which could become an important interlocutor of Europol.[11]

4. History and Structure of Interpol

4.1 Introduction

As we will see, there is an overlap between the tasks of Europol and Interpol which will increase in the future when Europol extends its operational territory. Therefore, cooperation and coordination between these two organisations is essential to avoid duplication and a waste of human and financial resources and to combat organised crime effectively. In the next section, a short historical overview of Interpol will be given, followed by its structure and mandate. In section 5, a comparison between these two organisations will be made.

---

[9] The initiative came from DG CC (the Directorate General for financial control) and UCLAF.

[10] Algemeen Politieblad, no. 142 (1993) at 10-11.

[11] See Recommendation 21, Council of the European Union, 7421/97 JAI 14, 21 April 1997, 35.

4.2 INTERPOL'S ORIGIN

The official name today is the International Criminal Police Organisation Interpol (in short, Interpol). In September, 1923, police chiefs from 20 countries met in Vienna on the initiative of the Head of the State police force and Police Chief of Vienna, Mr Schober, and formed Interpol at a congress called the "Second International Criminal Police Congress" (ICPC).[12] Of the 138 delegates that attended the Vienna Congress, only 67 came from abroad and nearly all from Western Europe.[13] However, it was not clear whether the participants in 1923 were there as representatives of their country or their police force, or attended the congress in their personal capacity. Afterwards, this lack of clarity about the status of the participants caused problems in determining who were the members of Interpol: were they the States or the police forces the participants were representing?[14] In 1925, the participating States began establishing the National Central Bureaux. A permanent international bureau was created in Vienna. After the annexation of Austria by Germany in 1938, Interpol was taken over by the Nazis. In September 1946, a conference in Brussels took place to revive Interpol. It was determined in the statute of this conference that Interpol headquarters should be in France. Interpol was located first in Paris and, since 1989, in Lyon. From the beginning, the Europeans were a majority in Interpol. Fourteen out of seventeen participants at the Brussels meeting were European, with great influence from France.

4.3 STRUCTURE AND MANDATE OF INTERPOL

Interpol has a President and three Vice-Presidents. They are assisted by the Executive Committee to manage the organisation. The General Assembly and the Executive Committee meet periodically and have decision-making and supervisory powers. The General Assembly also elects the General Secretariat, which is responsible for implementing the decisions and recommendations adopted.[15] Interpol operates through the permanent administrative and technical body. As indicated above, there has been much confusion about the members of Interpol. Some say that the members of Interpol are not the States but the police forces of national states who are delegated by the country to be a member of Interpol, while others say that the States are the members. The latter view, which implies a broader and more practical interpretation of Article 4 of the Interpol Constitution, is the most accepted one.[16] In terms of juridical origins, the case of Interpol is extremely rare among international intergovernmental organisations. Neither Interpol nor its predecessor, the ICPC, was set up by an explicit agreement between States. Interpol's position as an international intergovernmental organisation has developed over time. International police cooperation has grown from a non-official meeting of representatives of police forces into an intergovernmental organisation recognised explicitly, for example, by the United Nations,

[12] M. Fooner, Interpol, Issues in World Crime and International Criminal Justice (1989) at 6-9.
[13] B. Fenton, Interpol (1992) at 17.
[14] Fooner, *supra* note 12, at 45-48.
[15] M. Anderson, Policing the world; Interpol and the Politics of International Police Co-operation (1989) at 2.
[16] The Constitution of Interpol, in force since 13 June 1956, see Fooner, *supra* note 12, at 185.

the Council of Europe, France, Thailand and the United States.[17] Interpol operates through National Central Bureaux (NCBs) which are established in many of its 177 Member States, manned by personnel from the local police force but each devoted solely to the organisation's work with its own connections to the headquarters in Lyon.[18] The NCBs, which are national bodies, are responsible for liaison between the Member States and with the General Secretariat of Interpol. The NCBs collect relevant documents and intelligence and transmit these to other NCBs and the General Secretariat. Whenever necessary, an NCB cooperates with another NCB, for instance, with regard to requests for information or the organisation of police actions. The NCBs communicate directly among themselves and keep the General Secretariat informed.[19] In 1985, it was decided to set up a European Liaison Bureau (ELB) to strengthen cooperation between European member countries. The main tasks of the ELB are to provide secretariat services for Interpol's European activities, to offer liaison facilities to European member countries in the context of complex cases requiring international cooperation, and to establish rapid contacts in urgent matters.[20] No Interpol official is empowered to make an arrest on foreign territory; only a policeman acting within his own territory can do that. Interpol is an international police force, the task of which is to assist police authorities of the Member States (now almost all the nations of the world), in collecting and sharing information on criminality. According to Article 2 of the Constitution of Interpol, the aims of this organisation are:

- To ensure and promote the widest possible mutual assistance between all criminal police authorities, within the limits of the laws existing in the different countries and in the spirit of the "Universal Declaration of Human Rights"; and,
- To establish and develop all institutions likely to contribute effectively to the prevention and suppression of ordinary law crimes.

The Interpol 1985 annual Progress Report states that "the fight against international crime is the Organisation's *raison d'être* and is the major concern of the NCBs and the General Secretariat."[21] Although not mentioned in the constitution, the combat of international crime is the spearhead of Interpol, although the content of the term international crime is not clear, and some legal theorists even doubt the existence of international crime.[22] Interpol's mandate is not limited to certain crimes, although terrorism was in the earlier days excluded from its activities because of political implications.[23]

In recent years, the attention of Interpol has concentrated mainly on organised crime, collateral criminal activities, and on developing different forms of technical assistance for those States more at risk of criminal infiltration, such as the Eastern European States.

---

[17] Anderson, *supra* note 15, at 57-58.
[18] Fenton, *supra* note 13, at 2.
[19] Articles 31 and 32 of the Constitution of Interpol of 13 June 1956.
[20] www.kenpubs.co.uk/interpol-pr/index2.htm.
[21] *Progress Report*, International Criminal Police Review, St.-Cloud, France (December 1985).
[22] SP Sinha, *Individual and Collective Responsibility in International Criminal Law*, in M. Cherif Bassiouni and P. Nanda (eds.), A Treatise on International Criminal Law (1973) volume I at 137.
[23] Fooner, *supra* note 12, at 9-11.

5. Europol and Interpol Compared

5.1 Restraints between Europol and Interpol

If we compare the two organisations, we come across some points of friction.

Interpol has more general responsibilities than Europol in all areas of crime. Its mandate is not necessarily focused on criminal organisations;[24] this in contrast to Europol, which is exclusively set up to suppress organised crime. Furthermore, the territory both organisations work on differs significantly. Europol is limited to the territory of the EU, while Interpol is active nearly everywhere in the world. However, Europol will expand its operational territory in the future.

The role of the Member States Liaison Officers is crucial for Europol. All communication with the Member States takes place via the Europol Liaison Officers (ELOs) and the National Units in the Member States. The success of Europol depends on the availability and dedication of the ELOs. They act as the representatives of their sending authorities. Especially as far as the quality and speed of the exchange of information and intelligence is concerned, their role is decisive. The ELOs are placed at Europol which means that they can be in direct communication with Europol. Interpol operates via the NCBs that are established in the Member States, which means that there is less direct communication. The European liaison officers at Interpol's ELB may have similar responsibilities in some areas, but they act as the liaison point at Interpol for all European countries and not as the representative of their sending country.[25] On the other hand, it is a big advantage that the NCBs have the opportunity to contact each other directly without the interference of Interpol. Furthermore, Interpol has a selected database directly accessible by the Member States' NCBs. Such a system will be operational within Europol in the future.

The Member States of Europol are the directors of Europol. Operational activities by Europol depend on the willingness and the prioritising of the Member States. They decide for what purpose data may be used transmitted by them. Confidentiality is highly prioritised within Europol. When, for example, during a meeting, the representatives of the Member States want a closed session to discuss operational issues, all other participants to the meeting can be excluded from this session, including representatives from Interpol.

With these differences in mind, it is not surprising that there is a sort of competition in the field where the mandates of both organisations overlap, for example, in the field of information exchange and organised crime. Furthermore, there is a great risk of duplication.

In a note of the Council of the EU on the relationship between EDU/Europol and Interpol, it is suggested that the identification of the complementary roles that Interpol and Europol play, as well as their respective differences in areas of specialisation, could serve to reinforce cooperation between the two.[26] The complementary role of the two organisations should be seen as a strategic objective to be pursued on a continuous and pragmatic basis. Some suggestions to achieve this object are included in this note as well. One of the suggestions (although not unanimously adopted) is that there should be cooperation

[24] Council of the European Union, Brussels, 28 April 1998, 7879/98, Limite Europol 53, Relationship between EDU/Europol and Interpol, section 2, Areas of Responsibility.

[25] *Id.*, Liaison Officers.

[26] *Id.*, section 3.1.

between the two organisations for the exchange of strategic information, data and experience. Some of the efforts toward establishing that cooperation should concentrate on developing the existing regular bilateral meetings between the Secretary General of Interpol and the Director of Europol in an unreserved spirit of reciprocity. Further development should focus on the common discussion and implementation of tasks and projects in the European region.

The complementary roles fulfilled by the two organisations can also be enhanced by avoiding simultaneous use of the communication channels of both organisations for the exchange of information.

(a) Data collection and data protection

Data exchange will be one of the important forms of cooperation between Europol and Interpol in the future. However, problems can occur when data exchange is concerned. In the first place, the provisions in the Europol Convention on data protection are more strict and may be an obstacle for the sharing of information with Interpol.[27] Neither the Constitution nor the General Regulations of the NCB policy of Interpol contain provisions on data protection. However, the data providers are the NCBs and as national law binds these departments, it seems obvious that data protection is subject to national law only.

The rules on data protection by Europol seem to be stricter than those used by Interpol because, besides the data protection on the national level, there is always a second check at the Europol level.[28] When the data exchange between Europol and Interpol was discussed, some Member States and Europol had their doubts about the level of data protection and confidentiality within Interpol. They thought it undesirable that the information provided to Interpol would be applicable for all the Members of Interpol. Although the differences on data protection are obvious, the Council of the EU, the Europol Management Board and the Joint Supervisory Body have judged the level of data protection within Interpol as sufficient, which means that further negotiations on the content of an agreement on cooperation between these two organisations can take place. However, there will be an additional provision in the agreement with Interpol, namely, that Interpol is not allowed to divert data made available by Europol to other countries or organisations. In the future, this provision may also be included in some agreements with Third States, but it is not yet part of the negotiations. One of the suggestions for cooperation by the Council of the EU in the note referred to earlier is to set up a cross-reference index, which means that both organisations have access to each other's data systems.

Another obstacle to the exchange of data may be that the Member States remain the owners of the information, and remain responsible for the information as well.[29] They can decide in what way, and for what purpose, their information will be used, and to whom this data may be transmitted. For example, Member States decide whether transmitting certain information to Third States and third organisations, like Interpol, is permitted. It is not always possible, therefore, to solve questions on data exchange between Europol and Interpol on a bilateral level.

---

[27] Especially Articles 14 to 22 of the Europol Convention.
[28] Articles 14 and 15 of the Europol Convention.
[29] See Articles 9(3) and 15 of the Europol Convention.

In relation to the drawing up of strategic reports, it happens quite frequently that the statistical output of the two organisations is substantially different on the same topics and in the same areas. There may be a duplication of effort in the collection and use of information at the national and international levels, but these situations should be avoided.

Intensified cooperation could be achieved to the organisation of conferences for, at the moment, conferences on a particular subject are often organised by both organisations, causing duplication and a waste of human and economic resources. A big difference in data collection between Interpol and Europol is that the first can only collect data in two instances: the establishment of a project for the purpose of analysis, and when trying to initiate operations on the national level. Within Europol, the Member States are obliged to provide Europol with information that may contribute to the combat of organised crime as far as an Analytical Work File is involved.[30]

Europol has made an agreement with its Member States that Europol is the appropriate organisation to cooperate with, and to submit information to, when only European countries are involved and the crime concerned falls within the mandate of Europol. This was agreed during one of the Heads of Europol National Units meetings at the end of 1999, which Interpol attended as an observer. This agreement causes some friction between Interpol and Europol, all the more so because Interpol is dependent on the European countries for 70 percent of its data. Interpol is afraid that Europol will take over part of its tasks. Therefore, intensive negotiations are going on between Interpol and Europol.

(b) Means of cooperation between Europol and Interpol

So far, three meetings have been organised to coordinate the activities of the two organisations. Cooperation is extremely important because most of Europol's Member States have urged Europol to avoid duplication and to cooperate with Interpol. If Europol ignores this request of the Member States, it is possible that the willingness of the Member States to submit information to Europol will decline.

There are three levels of cooperation between Europol and Interpol:

- *The management level.* On this level, the structures and forms of cooperation are created.

- *The level of experts.* There is substantive cooperation on this level. The issues both organisations are focusing on are coordinated on this level. Joint organisation of congresses and trainings can be discussed. Whether cooperation will be successful or not depends on the personal qualities and willingness of the experts on both sides. The future agreement between Europol and Interpol serve as a framework for further cooperation. This means that the content of the agreement will not be negotiated exhaustively during the negotiations. The coordination on content has to be done by the experts after the adoption of the agreement.

- *On the national level within the national units.* In many cases, the national units of Europol are combined with the NCBs of Interpol, which is preferable and will be

[30] Article 10(3) and (4) of the Europol Convention.

on three subway lines suffered toxic effects from an unknown gas. Some people escaped from the trains themselves and went to the hospital, but many victims were in need of immediate medical treatment. The patients complained of ocular pain and vomiting. So many patients rushed to nearby hospitals that the hospital staff panicked and could not adequately dispense medical care. Twelve passengers and station personnel were killed and approximately 5000 people were injured. Typical symptoms included darkened vision, ocular pain, nausea, miosis, hyperaemia, and nosebleeds. The autopsy findings were almost the same as those in the Matsumoto Sarin incident. In cooperation with the Metropolitan Fire Department, the Metropolitan Police Department (MPD) immediately started to carry out rescue operations, to conduct traffic control, and to investigate the incidents. Wearing protective suits and gas masks, police investigators proceeded to the dangerous crime scene. On-site evidence samples, such as containers, newspapers, and other remains, were collected and immediately transported to the FSL of the MPD. The liquid had been released from plastic bags, exposing passengers to the toxic gas. Sarin was released separately in five subway cars at 8 a.m. Early on, the first responses from the Metropolitan Fire Department mistakenly announced that acetonitrile had been detected. At 10 a.m. the Tokyo FSL, using laboratory gas chromatography/mass spectrometry (GC/MS), detected Sarin in a crime scene sample. This speedy result was possible because of the prior experience acquired during the Matsumoto Sarin incident. At 11 a.m., the Criminal Investigation Department announced the detection of Sarin to the press. The Defence Agency quickly responded to this incident, and helped the police to perform an on-site inspection and to carry out a decontamination of any poisoned sites.

For the previous ten years, the cult had started to construct facilities in a rural area of Yamanashi Prefecture near Mt. Fuji. In July 1994, just after the Matsumoto Sarin incident, inhabitants in the vicinity of a cult facility reported foul smells. A criminal investigation team assigned to the Matsumoto Sarin incident analysed the chemical process for the synthesis of Sarin and found that dummy companies operating on behalf of the cult had purchased large quantities of chemical raw materials. In addition, a Sarin hydrolysis product was detected and removed for forensic investigation from the soils taken near the site of the foul smell. The criminal investigators began to strongly suspect the cult. Police secretly searched cult facilities, but, before the search took place, the cult carried out the Tokyo subway Sarin gas attack. Two days after the Sarin incident, a simultaneous raid of Aum facilities was launched by 2500 members of the police in connection with the investigation of the death of a notary public manager who had died while being detained by the cult.

To help cope with the Sarin release, the Defence Agency provided the police investigators with anti-toxic gas suits and masks. The search uncovered a large amount of chemicals, including phosphorus trichloride as well as a chemical plant in the No. 7 Satyam building. Outside the building there were many pipes connected to the plants; inside the building, various types of equipment needed for manufacturing chemicals were found. The criminal investigation led the police to strongly suspect that Sarin was being produced. The police identification section gathered evidence samples from various reaction bottles. The NRIPS conducted a chemical examination of the on-site samples and was involved in all aspects of this case. Almost all the cult perpetrators were arrested within the next two months.

3. FORENSIC INVESTIGATION

The special nature of nerve gases slowed down police efforts in connection with the Sarin incidents. First, activities involving nerve gases are subject to the law on the Ban of Chemical Weapons and the Regulation of Specific Substances (in force since 1995). Second, nerve gases are highly toxic and are lethal in trace amounts, making them difficult to detect; they are also difficult to detect because they evaporate very rapidly. Third, they are volatile, and the handling of samples requires special caution. Fourth, nerve gases decompose easily in a body and in the environment. It is necessary to identify the degradation products. Sarin, soman, tabun and VX are representatives of organophosphorus types of chemical warfare agents. They invade the body through the skin and lungs and, because they strongly inhibit cholinesterases, are extremely toxic. The physico-chemical properties of nerve gases vary. Sarin is volatile and easily hydrolysed in water, whereas VX is not volatile and is rather resistant to hydrolysis. Because of their extremely lethal nature, it is sometimes impossible to detect nerve gases or their hydrolysis products in a victim's samples. Therefore, a decrease in blood cholinesterase activity is a good index of exposure to nerve gases.

Nerve gases can be analysed by GC/MS. Retention indices are useful indicators in identifying chemical warfare agents. Wiped samples and soils are extracted with both dichloromethane and water at neutral pH. Blood samples are deproteinised with perchloric acid, and the resulting supernatants are adjusted to neutrality, and extracted with dichloromethane. Nerve gases, synthetic intermediates and by-products are extracted into the organic solvent fraction, and after concentration under mild conditions, the residue is analysed by GC/MS using an apolar capillary column DB-5, and a multi-step temperature programme starting at 45°C. The hydrolysis products of nerve gases are extracted into the aqueous fraction, and after derivatisation, are analysed by GC/MS.

In water, nerve gases are easily hydrolysed and produce characteristic methyl phosphorus compounds that are metabolically stable and water-soluble. These alkyl methylphosphonates are specific for the original nerve gases. These are finally hydrolysed to methylphosphonate (MPA). Therefore, detecting the hydrolysis products gives indirect proof of the presence of a nerve gas. Tertiary-butyldimethylsilylation is adopted to convert the hydrolysis products to volatile derivatives, because its derivatisation efficiency is good, and the resulting derivatives are stable. The aqueous fraction is taken to dryness, and N-methyl-N(*tert*-butyldimethylsilyl)-trifluoroacetamide and acetonitrile are added, heated at 60°C for 1 hour, and injected into GC/MS. Two kinds of GC detection are used. Mass spectrometry using electron impact ionisation (EI) and isobutane chemical ionisation (CI) provide acceptable structural and chemical information. Atomic emission detection is selective in monitoring particular elements. Molecules in the cavity are degraded to their elements, and the atomic emissions are detected under selected wavelength. Their retention indices are distinctive; EI-mass spectra provide representative fragmentation patterns, and CI-mass spectra give clear quasi-molecular ions.

Using these established forensic toxicological techniques, NRIPS performed a forensic investigation on the evidence samples from the Sarin incidents. In the Matsumoto Sarin incident, Sarin gas was sprayed to murder the local court judges, but nearby residents also became exposed to toxic chemicals. The cholinesterase (ChE) activities of all of the fatal casualties were greatly decreased compared to the control blood levels. If Sarin were to be sprayed over a garden, the Sarin left on the leaves would undergo hydrolysis, producing hydrofluoric acid, and under these strong acidic conditions, the plant leaves would wither. We examined the levels of fluoride ions in aqueous extracts of the leaves by capillary electrophoresis. Background levels were detected after we analysed control leaves from a similar area. Extraordinarily high levels of fluoride and chloride were detected in the withered leaves. At that time, we were not able to prepare authentic Sarin. However, we could confirm the existence of Sarin by the four criteria of a retention index, an electron impact (EI) mass spectrum, a CI mass spectrum, and the presence of phosphorus.

From the organic solvent extract of the pond water, a Sarin peak was detected on an extracted ion chromatograph of m/z 99, with a very similar retention index to values mentioned in reference papers. The EI-mass spectrum was identical to that of Sarin (described in the literature and in reference papers). The CI-mass spectrum yielded quasimolecular ions of m/z of 141. An atomic emission monitoring with a phosphorus emission line, at the position of m/z 99 peak in the EI-MS resulted in the observation of a phosphorus peak. Sarin was also identified in the nasal mucosa of one victim. The Nagano FSL and PHI also identified Sarin from other on-site samples of water, soil, air, and from wiped samples from the scene. From the *tert*-butyldimethylsilyl (TBDMS) derivatised solution of various evidence samples, two peaks appeared on extracted ion chromatograms of m/z 153 and 267, with identical retention times, and with the mass spectra of the reference TBDMS isopropyl methylphosphonate (IMPA) and MPA. We have not presented quantification data for the levels of IMPA and MPA in the blood. However, the lowest detectable blood levels under GC/MS analytical conditions are 0.5 micro-g/ml for MPA and 1 micro-g/ml for IMPA. IMPA and MPA were detected from almost all the victims' blood, as well as from the blood taken from a dead dog. Diisopropyl methylphosphonate was also identified in the blood of nearly all the fatalities.

The perpetrators sprayed Sarin from evaporator-type spray containers in the car park, and the released fog-like gas moved and spread, causing many residents to be poisoned. The spraying device was made from refrigerator-car equipment, and had a heating-pot and a fan. The Sarin solution used in the Matsumoto Sarin incident was synthesised by the following procedure. Isopropyl alcohol was added to a mixture of methylphosphonyl difluoride and methylphosphonyl dichloride. But, because the choice of reaction conditions was poor, the synthetic yield was low, and reaction by-products were produced. After storing the solution for almost 3 months, they sprayed the crude solution by means of evaporation, which was brought about by ten minutes of forced heating. High levels of Sarin hydrolysis products were detected, even from the injured people. This fact suggests that the crude Sarin solution was composed not only of Sarin, but of other synthesis precursors and by-products as well.

In the Tokyo subway Sarin incident, the cult decided to use Sarin in trains on three subway lines, all of which stop at Kasumigaseki station near the MPD. Sarin was released in the locations. The blood samples taken at the autopsies were sent to the NRIPS laboratory. A scattered distribution pattern of blood plasma butyrylcholinesterase (BuChE) and red blood cell acetylcholinesterase (AChE) activities were observed in 11 of the fatalities. In only six victims were both ChE activities significantly decreased. They were admitted to the hospital in a state of cardiopulmonary arrest, and died immediately. Compared to the ChE activities in the Matsumoto Sarin incident, the degree of the decrease in activity was not significant and there were some victims whose blood activity levels were not decreased at all. Some victims were admitted to the hospital alive, but despite the fact that extensive medical procedures were performed, including the administration of the antidote PAM, they died from brain damage at an early stage. The rather high levels of ChE activities might have been due to the early discovery of patients, which then led to rapid medical treatment, and the blood ChE activity may have been restored by the reactivation mechanism. In the Tokyo subway Sarin gas attack, the perpetrators boarded the subway trains with plastic bags containing Sarin and released the gas by prodding the bags open with the metal tips of umbrellas.

At that time, NRIPS had no authentic Sarin. Therefore, we measured the Sarin content in the evidence samples by quantifying the hydrolysed Sarin product, IMPA, by means of capillary electrophoresis. From the analytical data of IMPA in the hydrolysed solution, the Sarin content was deduced to be about 30%. *n*-Hexane and *N, N*-diethylaniline (DEA) were also identified as major components. IMPA was detected from blood samples taken from only two of the victims. Considering the detection limit in TBDMS GC/MS analysis, blood levels of IMPA were below 1 ppm, except in the case of 2 victims. TNO Prins Maurits Laboratory in the Netherlands, using sophisticated retrospective analytical methods, detected Sarin-related compounds in the Japanese victims' blood samples. The Sarin solution used in the Tokyo subway gas attack was synthesised by the following procedure. Isopropyl alcohol was added to 1.4 kg of methylphosphonyl difluoride, using *n*-hexane as a solvent, and DEA as an acid neutraliser. The resulting solution, about 7 litres, was divided into 11 bags. Our analytical result, of about a 30% Sarin concentration, supports the testimony of the suspects who were arrested.

In investigating the suspicions as to how the Sarin was manufactured, our laboratory at the NRIPS and the FSL of the Tokyo MPD performed forensic investigations on hundreds of evidence samples taken from the crime scene of the suspected Sarin manufacturing location. When the police investigated the documents seized in the cult office, they discovered the synthetic route to the mass manufacture of Sarin. The process involved five steps. In the first step, phosphorus trichloride was reacted with methanol to produce trimethylphosphite. In the second step, trimethylphosphite was converted to dimethyl methylphosphonate (DMMP) through a rearrangement caused by the application of heat. In the third step, DMMP was reacted with phosphorus pentachloride by applying heat, to produce methylphosphonyl dichloride. In the fourth step, methylphosphonyl dichloride was reacted with sodium fluoride to produce methylphosphonyl difluoride. In the final step, methylphosphonyl difluoride and methylphosphonyl dichloride were mixed with isopropyl alcohol to produce Sarin.

Under the restricted conditions used by the cult members, a forensic investigation was carried out. From the wiped samples taken from the first-step equipment, trimethylphosphate, *n*-hexane and DEA were detected. From the second-step equipment, trimethylphosphate, DMMP, iodine and DEA were detected. From the third-step equipment, MPA, DEA, phosphorus oxychloride and sodium chloride were detected. From the fourth-step equipment, MPA, DEA, sodium chloride and sodium fluoride were detected. From the final-step equipment, IMPA, MPA, DEA, DMMP and sodium chloride were detected. From the chemical analysis of evidence samples taken from the manufacturing plant, only stable substances corresponding to the synthetic routes were identified, but these served to verify the synthesis of Sarin in the Aum plant facility.

4. Conclusion

The GC/MS analysis of Sarin hydrolysis products after TBDMS derivatisation was effective for confirming Sarin exposure, usage and production, and was used as definitive evidence in the court trial. The early detection of Sarin also contributed to the speedy criminal investigation. To save the lives of severely affected victims, early and fast aid, such as cardiopulmonary resuscitation, may be important. In Sarin poisoning, red blood cell AChE was inhibited more strongly than plasma BuChE. Measuring only serum BuChE is somewhat risky, in that it can lead to a misjudgement of poisoning. The accurate identification of causative toxic substances and the verification of poisoning should be anticipated as providing evidence for the court. In addition, we must be involved in managing the consequences when an act of chemical terrorism occurs. The rapid detection of causative toxic substances is necessary, both in forensic laboratories and sometimes, if possible, at the crime scene. As specialists, we must make our contribution to helping the police investigators and other first responders by providing scientific and technical information about chemical warfare.

THE POLICE COMPONENT: ZIMBABWE'S EXPERIENCE

Clemence Masango*

1. Introduction

Zimbabwe ratified, without reservation, the Chemical Weapons Convention[1] in 1997 and was an original State Party. This was followed by the enactment of Zimbabwe's implementing legislation: the Chemical Weapons (Prohibition) Act No. 9 of 1998, in accordance with Article VII, paragraph 1, of the Convention. Admittedly, Zimbabwe is still a very new player in this regard and still has a long way to travel towards full compliance with and implementation of the Convention.

2. National Implementation

Mindful of its obligations under Article VII of the Convention, Zimbabwe established a National Authority. In Zimbabwe's case, the functions of the National Authority are vested in the office of the Secretary for the Ministry of Defence. Over and above its functions as prescribed by Article VII, paragraph 4, of the Convention, the National Authority also coordinates liaison with and between all key institutions involved in the production, supply, use and control of chemicals in Zimbabwe.

These include:

- The security ministries (i.e., the Ministries of Defence, Home Affairs (under which the police fall) and State Security;
- Zimbabwe Defence Industries;
- The Departments of Customs and Excise and Research and Specialist Services;
- Agricultural Chemical Industries Association;
- Pharmaceutical Association of Zimbabwe;
- The Confederation of Zimbabwe Industries; and,
- Ministries of Industry and International Trade, Justice, Legal and Parliamentary Affairs and Foreign Affairs.

The Minister of Defence, to whom the administration of the Act is assigned and on whom the function to make regulations is delegated, is in the process of developing national implementation legislation which is intended, *inter alia*, to provide for:

* Legal Adviser to the Zimbabwe Commissioner of Police.

[1] 1993 Convention on the Prohibition of the Development, Production, Stockpiling and Use of Chemical Weapons and on Their Destruction, entered into force on 29 April 1997. Text, as corrected and changed, available at http://www.opcw.org.

R. Yepes-Enríquez and L. Tabassi. (eds.), Treaty Enforcement and International Cooperation in Criminal Matters

- the form and manner for maintaining records and submitting reports on the production, use, acquisition, production or possession of toxic chemicals; and,
- conditions under which certain toxic chemicals may be used, acquired or produced.

3. Challenges Facing the Nation and the Region in General

A number of factors confronting Zimbabwe and the region in general tend to militate against any strides for effective cooperation and assistance amongst States Parties:

- The Convention is a very recent and complex instrument. As a State Party, Zimbabwe is still a new player in this regard and still has a lot to learn;
- There have not yet been any requests for mutual legal assistance in the enforcement of the Convention. Thus the experience and challenges in this regard are yet to be seen;
- States Parties are at different levels of implementation. This can be a real hindrance to effective cooperation between them;
- There is no regional contact point. Contact and liaison is carried out only through the OPCW; and,
- Some countries within the region are not States Parties or even signatories to the Convention, while others just signed the Convention but have not yet ratified it.

The net effect of all these disparities in the status of countries vis-à-vis the Convention and compliance with, and implementation of, the Convention by those who are States Parties, presents a plethora of problems. The net effect frustrates the effective implementation of Article VII, paragraph 2, of the Convention.

Be that as it may, the development of a multilateral instrument would go a long way toward enabling States Parties to afford one another the necessary legal assistance. It is further suggested that steps be taken to encourage and, where necessary, assist those countries that have not yet signed and/or ratified the Convention to do so. Only when that is done, and hopefully every state has come aboard, will the idea of a single multilateral instrument possibly achieve the desired results of ensuring that the human race is protected against chemical weapons and other hazardous substances.

SECTION III.4

CUSTOMS ENFORCEMENT AND INITIATIVES TO STRENGTHEN REGIMES

INTRODUCTION AND SUMMARY

Together with the police, the other major arm in cooperation to prevent many types of crime is the national customs administration. The two organisations covered in this section deal with customs cooperation in a global context (World Customs Organisation (WCO)) and a regional one (the Common Market for Eastern and Southern Africa (COMESA)).

The World Customs Organisation (WCO) is an independent, intergovernmental body with worldwide membership. Its main objectives are to strengthen bilateral and multilateral cooperation, enhance the effectiveness and efficiency of customs administrations, and assist Member States in the areas of compliance with trade regulations, protection of society and revenue collection. Many international and regional organisations such as the OPCW, Interpol and the European Union share common concerns about chemical weapons proliferation and they initiated the move to harmonise the monitoring and control measures to be taken by Member States. Since 1994, the WCO has assisted Member States with the development of a comprehensive action plan to combat hazardous material smuggling and the chemical weapons issue has been included in this plan. The Secretariats of the OPCW and the WCO have negotiated a draft Memorandum of Understanding governing cooperation between the two organisations, which is pending approval. This initiative will certainly open a new opportunity for customs administrations and the OPCW National Authorities to

R. Yepes-Enríquez and L. Tabassi. (eds.), Treaty Enforcement and International Cooperation in Criminal Matters

strengthen national and international responses to illicit traffic in the toxic chemicals and precursors covered by the Chemical Weapons Convention.

COMESA is a regional organisation created by treaty. It became a free trade area in 2000 as the first step toward becoming a full customs union. Aimed at preventing customs offences, States Parties exchange lists of prohibited items, hold relevant consultations and maintain special surveillance. They also exchange information on operations and new techniques of smuggling, illicit trafficking and any other type of customs offences. They assist in investigations by providing information and evidence. Other areas of cooperation include harmonisation of customs documents and of procedures for valuation, re-export, and temporary admission of goods. States Parties to COMESA also have a duty to notify each other of actions and decisions related to customs offences. They institute national and joint institutional arrangements to implement the treaty, such as training programmes for customs officers. At the regional level, the treaty provides for sanctions for non-compliance. COMESA has identified the need for a regional Protocol establishing cooperation with international organisations.

A new challenge for the customs administrations of most States Parties to the Chemical Weapons Convention has been the necessary export/import controls. Since the entry into force of the Convention in 1997, the attention of National Authorities has focused upon the 43 chemicals and families of chemicals listed in the Convention's Schedules that, depending upon which of the three schedules they fall under, must be monitored to a greater or lesser extent. The focus by most States Parties so far has been on tracking those specific chemicals. However, it is essential that this trend does not undermine the general purpose criterion as set forth in the definition of "chemical weapons" in the Convention. Under the Convention, "chemical weapons" include all toxic chemicals and their precursors, except where intended for purposes not prohibited under this Convention, as long as the types and quantities are consistent with such purposes. Thus the definition of a chemical weapon is not based upon the properties of specific chemicals or limited to those listed in the schedules annexed to the Convention, but on the purposes to which chemicals are put.

The purpose-driven definition of chemical weapon in the Convention makes it a considerably broader concept than "chemical weapons" in common military parlance. The general purpose criterion has two primary functions: (a) it allows the Convention to keep up with technological developments; and, (b) it protects legitimate uses of dual-use chemicals. States Parties have undertaken under the Convention never to transfer, directly or indirectly, chemical weapons to anyone. In terms of the schedules, trade in Schedules 1 and 2 chemicals is banned with States not Party, and each export of Schedule 3 chemicals to a State not party requires an end-user certificate from the importing State.

National implementing legislation is very important to effectively monitor transfers of chemicals. A degree of harmonisation between States Parties is essential if the broad prohibitions contained in the Convention are to be properly implemented. The current situation with regard to national implementing legislation is worrisome. The OPCW Secretariat has developed model legislative acts to assist States Parties, but so far there has only been one initiative among States Parties to harmonise legislation. Cooperation between, and support for, National Authorities is particularly important, given the responsibilities upon them for monitoring trade in chemicals. Administrative cooperation between States Parties is also important to ensure accurate reporting of transfers among them and also as more free trade areas are established around the world. The implementation of the general purpose criterion is administratively difficult and therefore poses challenges to the enforcement of Convention export controls. One way to prevent these challenges from becoming insurmountable is to utilise the OPCW as a multilateral forum in which cooperation, assistance and information exchange can take place.

The challenges faced in implementing the Chemical Weapons Convention come at a point in time when customs administrations are under enormous pressure. The last author in this section points out that the technical expertise to produce and deploy a weapon of mass destruction, particularly chemical and biological weapons, is becoming increasingly accessible to terrorists, and the international agreements on export controls do not present a complete barrier to those intent on gathering the means to manufacture weapons of mass destruction. This poses a serious threat to the international non-proliferation regime. There is evidence that criminals are exploiting global transportation networks. Given the huge volume of international transfers, how confident can anyone be that a few pounds of a deadly biological or chemical agent destined for a terrorist could be successfully interdicted by their national border control agencies? How can the public and private sector be engaged to control weapons and dangerous substances? Policy makers, business leaders and port authorities, who are committed to customs and port modernisation, should welcome the ability to leverage the "security" argument as added justification for streamlining government procedures. Also, reforming obsolete labour practices, upgrading transportation facilities to improve road, rail, marine and aviation links, and curbing abuses by inept and sometimes corrupt officials are part of the solutions needed.

The work of the global organisation, the WCO, and regional customs arrangements, such as COMESA, serve to address the issues arising for customs administrations in the globalised movement of people and goods and new regulatory regimes. Effective implementation of the Chemical Weapons Convention requires a multi-agency approach and discipline to ensure harmonised interpretation and application and WCO efforts support that. Customs control of all toxic chemicals has been identified as a major challenge since the Convention covers all toxic chemicals not meeting the general purpose criterion, not just scheduled chemicals. Public and private sectors at a national and international level should work together to develop and implement a strategy to ensure the eradication of chemical weapons, maintain an effective control of the transfer of chemicals and, finally, to achieve universal implementation of the Convention.

Maria-Luisa Martinod-Jacome

Rapporteur for Panel C.1 in the 2001 OPCW International Symposium; Legal Officer, OPCW Technical Secretariat, Office of the Legal Adviser. The views expressed are not attributable to the OPCW.

THE ROLE OF CUSTOMS SERVICES AND THE WORLD CUSTOMS ORGANIZATION'S ENFORCEMENT PROGRAMME TO COMBAT THE ILLICIT MOVEMENT OF CHEMICALS

Ercan Saka*

1. INTRODUCTION

The effective implementation of the Chemical Weapons Convention[1] ("Convention") by States Parties, like many other international conventions, requires a multi-agency approach and discipline with a view to ensuring harmonised interpretation and application. This approach is particularly important when the international community wants to ensure the complete and effective prohibition of the development, production, acquisition, stockpiling, retention, transfer and use of chemical weapons, and their destruction. These prohibitions automatically bring national customs administrations to participate or assume a role in global national action plans as the national cross-border control agency. While the role of customs services has been broadened from revenue raising to the protection of society and the environment, customs administrations have found themselves in the situation where new strategies have become essential and required. This issue has already been taken to the World Customs Organization (WCO)'s board to assist Member States in effectively implementing the Chemical Weapons Convention.

2. WORLD CUSTOMS ORGANIZATION

The World Customs Organization (established as the Customs Co-operation Council[2] in 1952) is an independent, intergovernmental body with worldwide membership which has reached 161 customs services. The WCO's mission is to enhance the effectiveness and efficiency of customs administrations in the areas of compliance with trade regulations, protection of society, and revenue collection, thereby contributing to the economic and social well-being of nations. In order to fulfil this mission, the WCO:

* Senior Technical Officer, World Customs Organization (WCO) Compliance/Enforcement Sub-Directorate. Any views expressed are solely those of the author and are not attributable to the WCO.

[1] 1993 Convention on the Prohibition of the Development, Production, Stockpiling and Use of Chemical Weapons and on Their Destruction, entered into force on 29 April 1997. Text, as corrected and changed, available at http://www.opcw.org.

[2] In June 1994, the Council adopted the working name "World Customs Organization (WCO)" for the Customs Co-operation Council, to reflect more clearly the nature of the Organisation and its international functions. The Convention establishing the Organisation was not amended, thus the official name is still the "Customs Co-operation Council".

R. Yepes-Enríquez and L. Tabassi. (eds.), Treaty Enforcement and International Cooperation in Criminal Matters

- reinforces Members' efforts to secure compliance with their legislation, in particular by endeavouring to maximise the level and effectiveness of Members' cooperation with each other, and with international agencies, in order to combat customs and other transborder offences; and,
- assists Members in their efforts to meet the challenges of the modern business environment, and adapt to changing circumstances, by promoting communication and cooperation among Members and with other international organisations, and by fostering human resource development, improvements in the management and working methods of customs administrations, and the sharing of best practices.

3. International Concerns

There is no doubt that the use of chemical substances is in many ways essential to meeting countries' social, economic and medical goals. However, when they are not properly handled and managed, these substances present a considerable risk to people and the environment. As is well known, the health and environmental consequences of exposure to harmful chemicals have been a cause of concern for many years. The potential risk is immense when these substances are involved in any type of illicit trafficking or smuggling. Even relatively small amounts of certain chemical substances may cause serious damage to health if people remain in their vicinity or try to manipulate the substance without necessary safety and security measures.

Many international and regional organisations such as the International Atomic Energy Agency (IAEA), the Organisation for the Prohibition of Chemical Weapons (OPCW), the WCO, the International Criminal Police Organisation (ICPO/INTERPOL), the European Union, and some international summits have registered a heightened concern about chemical weapons proliferation, and have emphasised the importance of harmonised monitoring and control measures to be taken by States.

This concern at the international level has always included an invitation to Member States to review the existing preventive measures in place, and to reinforce them with a view to stopping illicit trafficking in chemical substances covered by the Chemical Weapons Convention. The invitation also encourages the relevant international organisations to enhance current ways and means for close cooperation.

In recent years, the international community has also become increasingly aware of the potential threat of chemical weapons proliferation. It seems that the threat of illicit traffic in toxic chemicals covered by the Convention will continue for the foreseeable future, posing special awareness problems for exporting, importing and transit States.

In sum, the international community, while trying to solve the existing issues related to the safety and security of other hazardous and radioactive materials, has added a new but very sensitive item to its agenda through the Chemical Weapons Convention. The international community has committed itself to dealing with this new phenomenon, and is in favour of stopping any illegal traffic in toxic chemicals covered by the Convention at national borders before the chemicals leave or enter the country. National borders are the frontline in this battle, so customs is expected to take an active part in the implementation of all preventive measures and plans drawn up by national institutions. This approach requires governments to pay attention to the legal, technical and administrative capabilities of customs and other law enforcement agencies taking part in controlling the international flow of people, vehicles and goods.

4. The Potential Threat to Customs Officers

Most chemical substances require special procedures and measures in every phase of their management, from mining to disposal. They are clearly different by nature from other goods. Consequently, they pose a hazard to people and property in proportion to the protective, distance and time conditions present. This hazard is greater under accident conditions involving package rupture. The same hazard occurs when a package is opened inadvertently or by inexperienced persons. The primary hazard is exposure through contamination by direct contact with the substance. This contact could be any form of skin contact, ingestion, inhalation or a combination thereof.

Even relatively small amounts of certain chemical substances can cause serious damage to health if people remain in short range or try to manipulate the substances without protective equipment and clothing.

However, customs officers are legally required and responsible for physically checking and monitoring the international flow of passengers, vehicles and goods. This means that customs officers are one of the groups of people who are at potential risk of contamination in the ordinary course of their work, due to the possibility of discovering unauthorised consignments and improperly packed or labelled prohibited chemicals in illicit traffic during the normal monitoring and checking process. It is clear that this risk will be higher for customs officers when there is insufficient awareness, knowledge, detection equipment, and safety and response measures for the discovery. Due to the nature of these substances, the WCO Secretariat always recommends its Members to cooperate closely with their national regulatory bodies when it is necessary to undertake a physical inspection, or if there is suspicion or detection of illicit traffic in toxic chemicals.

5. The Basic Role of Customs Services

The role of customs services throughout the world has been changed from time to time, and at times varies from country to country. However, these changes and differences have not altered their historical role as a revenue-generating agency through the collection of customs duties. Additionally, customs services have two additional tasks: the facilitation of international trade, and the protection of society and the environment. These additional tasks could be described as non-fiscal functions and require customs services to strike a balance between facilitation of trade and effective control. This is achieved through the application of risk assessment techniques.

Customs administrations, as governmental cross-border control agencies, have always played a key role in detecting and preventing the illicit transboundary movement of goods before they leave or enter a country. This role falls into the category of "protection of society and the environment" and it ranges from combating narcotics smuggling to prevention of illicit traffic in arms, including prohibited chemical weapons.

Customs services have also been one of the crucial agents in designing and implementing any national strategy for combating smuggling activities. The legal, administrative and technical capacities customs services bring to these strategies can be grouped into the following categories:

- the best physical location to stop the illicit transboundary movement of chemical weapons leaving or entering the national territory;
- the most appropriate national agency to monitor international trade through relevant documents, and to collect data on national foreign trade in terms of value, quantity, passengers, exporter, importer, means of transportation, goods and trends in foreign trade;
- the legal authority for the physical checking of goods, vehicles and passengers entering or leaving the country. Only physical checks and monitoring can result in the discovery of smuggled goods, including illicit traffic in toxic chemicals covered by the Chemical Weapons Convention;
- the legal authority for detecting and seizing illicit traffic in goods and conducting at least the preliminary investigation for smuggling or attempts to smuggle goods;
- its great experience in dealing with transboundary crime and criminals; and,
- its capacity for the worldwide exchange of information, intelligence and tools through the following means:

5.1 WCO GLOBAL REGIONAL INTELLIGENCE LIAISON OFFICES (RILO) NETWORK

The WCO Global Regional Intelligence Liaison Offices (RILO) Network connects more than 120 WCO Member States through ten regional offices. Each national customs intelligence unit collects seizure data relating to customs offences from all possible sources to identify new or unusual national and regional smuggling methods.

5.2 THE WCO CUSTOMS ENFORCEMENT NETWORK (CEN)

The WCO Customs Enforcement Network (CEN) is an information system for data exchange and communication between customs services, dedicated to enforcement needs. It is based on internet technology which allows for more reliable, sure and less expensive communication but also offers new opportunities to enhance and increase the exchange of information between customs administrations, and for the pooling of the data needed for strategic analysis of customs fraud like the trafficking of toxic chemicals.

5.3 MEMORANDA OF UNDERSTANDING (MOU) WITH TRADE ASSOCIATIONS AND INTERNATIONAL ORGANISATIONS

Customs administrations are encouraged by the WCO Secretariat to implement the Memorandum of Understanding (MOU) concept at the national level to create permanent communication and cooperation channels between the relevant national agencies or national trade representatives. The WCO Secretariat also has great experience with MOU initiatives, having concluding a significant number of MOUs with trade associations and relevant international organisations. These framework agreements serve as a model and reference for customs services entering into similar agreements.

5.4 WCO BILATERAL AND MULTILATERAL ADMINISTRATIVE AND LEGAL INSTRUMENTS

Customs administrations also have the opportunity to utilise other legal and administrative instruments created by the WCO, such as the Nairobi Convention, recommendations, and resolutions, to enhance or strengthen their cooperation and communication channels with other customs services.

5.5 WCO WEBSITES

The WCO public (http://www.wcoomd.org) and private websites have been created to enhance the customs community's information and communication capacity at national and international levels. Each customs service can easily link up with the websites of other Members and relevant international organisations in order to have the greater administrative, legal and technical background necessary for carrying out their work effectively.

5.6 AWARENESS AND TRAINING

Customs services are continuously being informed about the potential smuggling of toxic chemicals covered by the Chemical Weapons Convention and the risk posed to them, society and the environment. Within this in mind, most customs administrations are either holding their own awareness and training programmes and attending the relevant regional or national seminars, or they are participating in the meetings of the WCO and other relevant international organisations where these subjects are included and discussed.

5.7 EMPLOYMENT OF RISK ASSESSMENT TECHNIQUES

Customs services are advised and encouraged to use a targeting and selectivity approach through risk assessment techniques which enable them to assess the probability that goods being processed through customs control have not illegally entered or been falsely declared. These modern enforcement techniques help customs services to identify potential or suspected persons, vehicles or goods in advance to motivate further examination. This technique is not only facilitating the international flow of goods, but also enabling customs services to optimise their use of limited resources to detect any kind of fraud, including prohibited transfers of toxic chemicals covered by the Chemical Weapons Convention.

Risk assessment studies consider a broad range of factors present in the illicit traffic of toxic chemicals. Such factors include:

- the possibility of organised or transnational crime;
- the possibility of a link with other organised criminal activity, such as smuggling of narcotics, stolen vehicles, or firearms;

- false description or misclassification of goods;
- false origin of goods;
- falsified documentation (false licence, notification, invoice etc.);
- false packaging, labelling, markings;
- number of seizures made;
- legislative and current control measures;
- assessment of regional and international markets; and,
- identified routes and *modus operandi*.

6. The WCO Initiative on Action to Combat Chemical Weapons Smuggling

Since 1994, the WCO has invested significant time and energy to launching a special programme to assist its Members with the development of a comprehensive action plan to combat hazardous materials smuggling. Chemical weapons are covered by this initiative. The overall objective of the programme is to assist Member administrations to enhance their enforcement capabilities for preventing, detecting and responding to illicit traffic in hazardous materials, including toxic chemicals covered by the Chemical Weapons Convention. This programme is intended to provide the necessary awareness for initiatives to ensure that these chemicals are securely monitored and controlled, and that there are processes and procedures in place to detect and respond to any attempted illicit trafficking.

Current WCO activities in pursuit of this overall objective are summarised as follows:

6.1 Awareness Activities

The WCO awareness activities are as follows:

- the first Seminar on Dangerous and Toxic Products, held in Brussels on 14 and 15 March 1994;
- the first Working Group on the Identification of Nuclear Materials and Dangerous Goods, held in Brussels on 1 and 2 June 1995;
- adoption of a WCO Recommendation concerning Action Against Illicit Cross-Border Movement of Nuclear and Hazardous Material (including their waste), adopted by France (March 1998), Sweden (January 1998) and Finland (May 1998); and,
- attendance at the relevant international and regional seminars where customs input and experience are needed or shared.

6.2 TRAINING MATERIALS

At the request of its Members, the WCO has developed a very comprehensive customs enforcement training module on hazardous materials smuggling. This training module provides guidelines for customs trainers to develop their own national training programmes.

6.3 HARMONISED SYSTEM (HS)

To monitor and control the import and export of scheduled chemicals under the Chemical Weapons Convention, the Harmonised System (HS) is the most appropriate instrument, since 177 countries are using this system for their customs tariff and statistical nomenclatures. The most important toxic chemicals appearing in the Annex on Chemicals to the Chemical Weapons Convention have been identified in a Council Recommendation to promote their identification at the national level, and the WCO Secretariat is reviewing the HS classification of the other scheduled chemicals covered by the Convention.

6.4 EXCHANGE OF INFORMATION AND DEVELOPMENT OF A DATABASE

Timely, comprehensive and rapid exchange of information and intelligence is the principal element of effective global preventive efforts concerning the illicit transboundary movement of toxic chemicals covered by the Chemical Weapons Convention. For that purpose, the WCO Secretariat has developed a separate database and special seizure-reporting format for hazardous materials (including the toxic chemicals covered by the Convention). The basic aim of this database is to enable customs services to make their own information analysis and produce strategic, operational and tactical intelligence for their own needs, such as regional and international trends, *modus operandi* employed by smugglers, routes commonly used, etc. The specifications of this database can be summarised as follows:

- accessible to customs services through the WCO RILO and CEN systems;
- information gathered from Members and international organisations; and,
- protection with double passwords and encryption.

6.5 INTERNATIONAL COOPERATION

One of the pillars of the WCO enforcement programmes is to cooperate with the international organisations concerned to ensure the broadest communication channels for timely and accurate exchange of information, close cooperation, and harmonisation of actions to be taken at the international level in this arena. The IAEA, OPCW, ICPO/ Interpol, Europol, European Union, and the UN specialised bodies are covered in particular.

Within this concept, the WCO and the OPCW Secretariat have started to attend each others' technical meetings. This cooperation has brought the two Secretariats to the point of discussing the potential contents of an MOU relating to enforcement matters. The draft MOU is now being considered by their respective organs. The basic aim of this MOU is to enhance current cooperation by establishing an administrative basis for developing and implementing joint technical and training assistance projects for customs services and OPCW national authorities.

7. Results

It is widely recognised that customs services around the world have a role to play in preventing and detecting chemicals covered by the Chemical Weapons Convention in illicit trafficking, due to their presence at national borders as the governmental cross-border control agency. This role can be maximised through raising awareness, employment of risk assessment techniques, the deployment of detection equipment, and making customs an integral part of the national preventive strategy or action plan. The technical input and training assistance of the OPCW and its national authorities are also recognised as an essential and integral part of successful customs enforcement programmes. It is therefore very important to invite OPCW Member States to consider the further exploration and use of customs services to combat illicit traffic in toxic chemicals covered by the Chemical Weapons Convention.

The improved cooperation and MOU initiative between the WCO and the OPCW Secretariats will open a new avenue for customs and National Authorities to strengthen national and international responses to the illicit traffic in toxic chemicals covered by the Chemical Weapons Convention.

CUSTOMS ENFORCEMENT IN A REGIONAL INTEGRATION ARRANGEMENT: THE CASE OF COMESA

Stephen R. Karangizi*

I. Introduction

The Common Market for Eastern and Southern Africa (COMESA) is a regional integration grouping of 20 African States (Angola, Burundi, Comoros, Democratic Republic of Congo, Djibouti, Egypt, Eritrea, Ethiopia, Kenya, Madagascar, Malawi, Mauritius, Namibia, Rwanda, Seychelles, Sudan, Swaziland, Uganda, Zambia and Zimbabwe) which have agreed to promote regional integration through trade development and to develop their natural and human resources for the mutual benefit of all their peoples.

COMESA was established in 1994 to replace the Preferential Trade Area for Eastern and Southern Africa (PTA), which had been in existence since 1981 within the framework of the Organisation of African Unity's (OAU) Lagos Plan of Action and the Final Act of Lagos. The PTA was established to take advantage of a larger market size, to share the region's common heritage and destiny, and to allow greater social and economic cooperation, with the ultimate objective being to create an economic community.

The COMESA Treaty, which sets the agenda for COMESA, covers a large number of sectors and activities. However, the fulfilment of the complete COMESA mandate is regarded as a long-term objective and, for COMESA to become more effective as an institution, it has defined its priorities within its mandate over the short term as being the promotion of regional integration through trade and investment. The role of the COMESA Secretariat is to take the lead in assisting its Member States to make the adjustments necessary for them to become part of the global economy within the framework of World Trade Organisation (WTO) regulations and other international agreements. This is to be done by promoting "outward-orientated" regional integration. The aims and objectives of COMESA as defined in the Treaty and its protocols are, therefore, to facilitate the removal of the structural and institutional weaknesses of Member States so that they are able to attain collective and sustained development.

Among other things, COMESA Member States have agreed on the need to create and maintain:

(a) a full free trade area guaranteeing the free movement of goods and services produced within COMESA and the removal of all tariffs and non-tariff barriers;

(b) a customs union under which goods and services imported from non-COMESA countries will attract an agreed single tariff in all COMESA States;

* Director — Legal and Institutional Affairs, Common Market for Eastern and Southern Africa (COMESA) Secretariat. Any views expressed are solely those of the author and are not attributable to COMESA.

R. Yepes-Enríquez and L. Tabassi. (eds.), Treaty Enforcement and International Cooperation in Criminal Matters

(c) free movement of capital and investment supported by the adoption of a common investment area to create a more favourable investment climate for the COMESA region;

(d) a gradual establishment of a payment union based on the COMESA Clearing House and the eventual establishment of a common monetary union with a common currency; and,

(e) the adoption of common visa arrangements, including the right of establishment leading eventually to the free movement of *bona fide* persons.

2. Customs Management and Levels of Integration

The extent to which customs management and enforcement takes place in a regional integration group depends on the level of integration in that group. The higher the level of integration, the higher the requirements for customs management. The Member States within the grouping also make commitments at two different levels: regional and national.

The commitments made at regional level in a regional group like COMESA are on the basis of treaty provisions and protocols. As a specific undertaking, the COMESA Member States have agreed, under Article 4, paragraph 1 of the COMESA Treaty, as follows:

> In the field of trade liberalisation and customs cooperation:
>
> (a) establish a customs union, abolish all non-tariff barriers to trade among themselves; establish a common external tariff; cooperate in customs procedures and activities;
>
> (b) adopt a customs bond guarantee scheme;
>
> (c) simplify and harmonise their trade documents and procedures;
>
> (d) establish conditions regulating the re-export of goods from third countries within the Common Market; and,
>
> (e) establish rules of origin with respect to products originating in the Member States.

Further elaboration on the commitments the Member States have made under the COMESA Treaty is covered under Chapters Six (trade liberalisation and development; Seven (customs cooperation); Eight (re-exportation of goods); and Nine (simplification and harmonisation of trade documents and procedures). Article 63 of the COMESA Treaty provides that:

> The provisions of this Chapter [Six] shall apply to any activity being undertaken in cooperation among the member states in the field of customs management and the organisation of customs and shall include in particular:
>
> (a) matters concerning the application of Common Market tariff treatment for their exports and imports;
>
> (b) the simplification and harmonisation of trade documents, customs regulations and procedures with particular reference to such matters as the valuation of goods,

tariff classification, temporary admission, warehousing, re-exports, frontier trade and export drawback;

(c) the prevention, investigation and suppression of customs offences;

(d) national and institutional arrangements; and,

(e) training facilities and programmes for customs officials.

At a national level the Member States are under the obligation to take steps to secure the enactment and continuation of such legislation to give effect to the COMESA Treaty pursuant to Article 5. The Member States are also required to confer upon the regulations of the Council the force of law and the necessary legal effect within its territory.

3. COMESA FTA AND CUSTOMS UNION

3.1 COMESA FTA

The COMESA Free Trade Area (FTA) was launched on 31 October 2000. Nine countries are participating in the FTA: Djibouti, Egypt, Kenya, Madagascar, Malawi, Mauritius, Sudan, Zambia and Zimbabwe. Effective midnight on 31 October 2000, the nine countries started trading on duty-free terms for all goods originating from within their territories.

Goods that are eligible for duty-free treatment under the COMESA FTA are those that meet the COMESA Rules of Origin. Such goods are referred to as COMESA originating goods. The COMESA Rules of Origin are a set of criteria that distinguish between goods produced within the COMESA Member States which are entitled to duty-free or preferential treatment with respect to customs duty and/or other charges of equivalent effect, and goods considered to have been produced outside the region which require the payment of full national duties when traded.

COMESA Rules of Origin

The COMESA Rules of Origin as provided in the "Protocol on the Rules of Origin for Products to be Traded in Common Market for Eastern and Southern Africa" have five independent criteria. Goods qualify as originating in COMESA if they meet *any* one of the five criteria. The conditions and criteria to be met are as follows:

Direct consignment

The goods should be accepted as originating in a Member State if they are consigned directly from a Member State to a consignee in another Member State *and* meet any one of the following criteria:

Origin-conferring criteria

(i) The goods have been wholly produced or obtained in any one of the COMESA Member States (e.g. minerals mined in the Member State, agricultural crops grown in the Member State or fishery products caught in waters of a Member State, or animals bred and reared in the Member States); or,

(ii) They have been produced in the Member States wholly or partially from materials imported from outside the Member States but have undergone processing in the COMESA Member States such that the local content of the final good is not less than 40% of the total cost of the materials used in the production process; or,

(iii) the value-added resulting from the process of production accounts for at least 35 per cent of the ex-factory cost of the goods; or,

(iv) there is a change in tariff heading as a result of the process of production; or,

(v) they have been produced in the Member State and designated by the COMESA Council of Ministers to be goods of particular importance to the economic development of the Member States, *and* contain not less than 25 per cent of value added notwithstanding the provisions of criteria (iii) above.

The COMESA Rules of Origin also specify the form of documentary evidence and the imposition of penalties upon persons found to be engaged in fraudulent claims of COMESA tariff treatment. In practice, to prove origin an exporter or importer of each consignment of goods to be traded under the FTA and on preferential terms must produce an original Certificate of Origin to the customs authorities.

In order for the customs authorities of the Member States to better manage the regional regime, a *Manual of Guidelines on the issuance and Verification of the COMESA Rules of Origin* has been developed. Apart from all the other details on management of the trade regime, dispute settlement procedures are well spelt out in the *Manual*. The steps in the process are as follows:

(i) If customs officials doubt the authenticity of the Certificate:

Customs officials of the receiving Member State will send an enquiry on a prescribed form asking the exporting Member State to confirm that the certificate in question was issued by them.

The exporting Member State will confirm that it was issued by them *or* that it was not issued by them. If it was issued by them, the case is closed. If it was not issued by them, the case becomes one of cheating and the law in the receiving/importing Member State takes its course. Full duties become payable and other penalties prescribed by law may also be imposed.

(ii) If the customs officials doubt the origin of the goods:

Step 1: Customs officials of the receiving/importing Member State will request additional information from the exporting Member State regarding the origin status of the goods.

Step 2: If the customs officials of the receiving/importing Member State are not satisfied with the response of the exporting Member State, they may request an on-the-spot investigation to the company/factory/facility that is alleged to produce the goods in question.

Step 3: If even after the investigation customs officials of the receiving/importing Member State are not satisfied, the case may be referred to arbitration.

Step 4: If the recommendation of the arbitration panel is still not acceptable to either or both of the parties to the disputes, then the case is referred to the COMESA Court of Justice for a final and binding ruling.

3.2 COMESA CUSTOMS UNION

The establishment of a FTA in COMESA by the year 2000 is a prelude to the establishment of a Customs Union. The FTA is planned to operate for about four years during which time all administrative, legal, institutional and logistical preparations for the operation of the Customs Union are to be completed.

COMESA Member States have already committed themselves to the implementation of a Common External Tariff (CET) by the year 2004 of 0%, 5%, 15% and 30% on capital goods, raw materials, intermediate goods and final goods, respectively.

Significant work has been undertaken, or is in the process of being implemented, on the design and implementation of a CET, all with financial and technical support coming from the European Union. Notable among these are:

(a) The COMESA Customs Document (COMESA-CD)

The COMESA-CD was officially adopted by COMESA at the COMESA Council of Ministers meeting in April 1996. The Secretariat conducts training courses for customs officials in the COMESA countries on how to use the COMESA-CD as part of a programme to harmonise customs and trade statistics systems, including the Automated System for Customs Data and Management (ASYCUDA).

(b) Common Tariff Nomenclature

The COMESA Secretariat has developed a Common Tariff Nomenclature (CTN), adopted by the Council of Ministers in May 1999, which aims to:

(i) establish the number of product categories, if any, of each Member State vis-à-vis the four agreed COMESA categories: Capital Goods, Raw Materials, Intermediate Goods and Final Goods;
(ii) correlate the Member States' national categories to the agreed COMESA categories;
(iii) harmonise categories at the Customs Co-operation Council (World Customs Organization) Harmonised System (HS)[1] heading, subheading or product level; and,

[1] See also *supra* in this volume, E. Saka, The Role of Customs Services and the World Customs Organization's Enforcement Programme to Combat the Illicit Movement of Chemicals.

(iv) finalise a COMESA Common External Tariff (CET) based on the nomenclature and the four agreed product categories at the eight-digit level (except for subheadings currently not in use by any Member State, in which case the tariff may be at six digits).

The compilation, adoption and implementation of the CTN by the Member States is a prerequisite to the harmonisation and standardisation of the commodity coding system within the region, and Member States are being encouraged to adopt a common product description and commodity coding system such as the HS 1996. It should be noted that some COMESA members, including Kenya, Madagascar, Malawi, Mauritius, Namibia, Swaziland, Tanzania, Uganda, Zambia and Zimbabwe, have already adopted, and are using, the HS 1996 Code as their product description and coding system. Ethiopia, Sudan and Rwanda have acceded to the HS 1996 code but have yet to implement it.

3.3 ASYCUDA/EUROTRACE

The ASYCUDA/EUROTRACE programme is an important component of the overall regional integration programme of COMESA. ASYCUDA, designed as it is to make the customs process more efficient, promotes trade through reducing the time taken to clear goods (thus saving importers and exporters money), so reducing non-tariff barriers to trade. The ASYCUDA programme also has a strong positive effect on revenue generation by making the tariff collection procedure more efficient. This, in turn, allows national governments to streamline tariffs and reduce tariff rates without having an adverse effect on revenue collected.

Phase I of the ASYCUDA/EUROTRACE programme (which officially ended in December 1998) had some notable successes. ASYCUDA has been installed in thirteen COMESA countries. Nineteen countries, including seventeen COMESA Member States, have installed the EUROTRACE system, with two more in the process of installing the system.

The ASYCUDA system has a very valuable spin-off product: the trade statistics it collects which, when fed into the EUROTRACE system, is capable of producing very accurate and up-to-date trade statistics. In countries in which ASYCUDA is not being implemented, EUROTRACE has its own data collection system in place or can use data obtained from other computerised systems.

The two systems, working in harmony together, are therefore considered to be an extremely important component of COMESA's regional integration programme. Phase II of the ASYCUDA/EUROTRACE programme (titled "Regional Harmonisation of Customs and Trade Statistics Systems") became operational on 1 December 1999. Its focus is on harmonising and improving national customs practices; strengthening the capacity at the national and regional levels for producing high quality trade statistics; improving the links between customs departments and national statistical offices; and establishing a regional trade information system.

3.4 INSTITUTIONAL AND ADMINISTRATIVE FRAMEWORK OF A CUSTOMS UNION

The establishment of a Customs Union will necessarily entail institutional and administrative changes and transformations in the Member States. Such transformation will involve issues of sovereign authority with regard to the classification and categorisation of import products and the determination of tariff rates on such imports, and will involve issues of authority with regard to the collection and management of revenue from trade taxes.

The COMESA Secretariat completed a study on the administrative and legal aspects of the implementation of a Common External Tariff which recommends that, initially, revenues will be collected by individual member countries of the Customs Union at national boundaries and not shared among members. This has been accepted by COMESA Member States as being the initial stage.

Removal of non-tariff barriers

Steady progress has been made in elimination of non-tariff barriers (NTBs) such as the liberalisation of import licensing, removal of foreign exchange restrictions, removal of taxes on foreign exchange, removal of import and export quotas, removal of road blocks, easing of customs formalities, extending the time border posts are open, etc. There are, however, still a number of improvements required to make intra-regional trade easier, such as improving the transport and communications structures, easing visa requirements, improving information and access to information on trade opportunities, further reducing customs and bureaucratic procedures at border crossings, and so on. Many of these (such as improving the transport and communications infrastructure) will require significant investment and will only be achieved over a medium- to long-term timeframe and is an area in which donor support and foreign private sector investment will be needed for some time to come.

4. Areas of Specific Cooperation in Customs Management and Enforcement

There are three specific areas of customs cooperation that the Member States have agreed to under Article 66 of the COMESA Treaty. Those areas are in relation to prevention, investigation and suppression of customs offences.

To prevent customs offences, the Member States have agreed to carry out the following, *inter alia*:

(a) exchange lists of goods and publications, the importation of which is prohibited in their respective territories, and prohibit their exportation;

(b) exchange lists of goods subject to illicit traffic between their customs territories and maintain special surveillance over the movement of such goods;

(c) hold consultations on operations and establishment of border posts and customs offices;

(d) maintain surveillance over persons entering and exiting from their States who are suspected to be involved in activities contrary to the customs law of any State; and,

(e) maintain surveillance of the movement of particular goods suspected by any Member State to be the subject of illicit traffic towards the importing Member State.

The Member States have also agreed to exchange information relating to:

(a) operations which are suspected as customs offences in any Member State;
(b) persons, vehicles, ships, aircraft and other means of transport reasonably suspected of being involved in activities that may be in violation of the customs laws of any Member State;
(c) new techniques of committing customs offences; and,
(d) goods known to be the subject of illicit traffic.

At the request of a Member State, and as promptly as possible, Member States have to provide information:

(a) contained in customs documents relating to the exchange of goods between countries which are suspected of being in violation of the customs law of a requesting Member State;
(b) enabling false information to be detected, in particular with respect to dutiable value; and,
(c) concerning certificates of origin, invoices or other documents known to be, or suspected of being, false.

In addition, the Member States have agreed to assist each other in verifying the authenticity of customs documentation and to be responsible for carrying out investigations for each other. These obligations are intended to establish appropriate checks for suppressing customs offences.

5. Additional Enforcement Measures

The COMESA Treaty provides two additional measures that can be relied upon in the case of a State that is not complying with the Treaty provisions. These measures are in the form of sanctions that can be imposed under Article 171 on a State that defaults in performing an obligation under the Treaty or whose conduct is considered to be prejudicial to the existence or the attainment of the objectives of the Common Market.

Secondly, a COMESA Court of Justice has been established under the Treaty with wide jurisdictional powers to hear references (cases) from most stakeholders in the integration process. The Court is empowered to ensure the adherence to law in the interpretation and application of the Treaty. The Court has jurisdiction to hear references from the Member States, legal and natural persons and employees of the Common Market.

6. Conclusion

It is quite apparent that a regional grouping such as COMESA, which has advanced its integration process, is well placed to play an enhanced role in the control of trade in chemical weapons and toxic chemicals or their precursors. The existing organs of the institution can be relied upon to monitor the goods being traded across the borders of Member States. Through enhanced customs cooperation in the prevention, investigation and suppression of customs offences, Member States are better placed in a regional arrangement to assist in preventing the movement of illegal commodities.

Through a regional organisation such as COMESA, Member States are also better placed to collectively subscribe to important international conventions such as the Chemical Weapons Convention.

It is also important to note that the advancement of integration places a higher duty on the Member States to cooperate in customs control so as to ensure that the interests of Member States are safeguarded. Such coöperation comes in the form of the collective recognition of illicit goods and the adoption of measures to prevent their trafficking.

Table 1

Stages of Regional Integration Followed by COMESA

Stage	Description
Preferential Trade Area	Trade among countries is conducted on a preferential basis, in conformity with agreed rules of origin, with each country maintaining its own tariffs on goods imported from third countries.
Free Trade Area (FTA)	Tariffs and non-tariff barriers are eliminated between members of the FTA, in conformity with agreed rules of origin, with each country maintaining its own tariffs on goods imported from third countries.
Customs Union	Member countries operate a common external tariff and there is free movement of goods once they enter the customs union. Tariff revenues are either shared among Member countries or allocated according to the destination of the goods.
Common Market	There is free movement of goods, services, labour and capital, and the right of establishment and residency, between members of the common market .
Economic Community	In addition to the conditions of the common market, the economic community has a single currency issued by one monetary authority and common monetary and fiscal policies.

CHALLENGES IN THE IMPLEMENTATION OF EXPORT CONTROLS UNDER THE CHEMICAL WEAPONS CONVENTION

Daniel Feakes*

1. INTRODUCTION

The Chemical Weapons Convention[1] ("Convention") is a comprehensive multilateral instrument aimed at the verifiable elimination of chemical weapons and the preclusion of any chemical rearmament. It is a disarmament treaty, with extensive provisions for the verification of the demilitarisation of chemical weapons and related facilities. The prohibitions contained within the Convention are accordingly very broad, which has implications for another essential objective of the Convention, namely, preventing the proliferation of chemical weapons. To achieve this goal, the Convention also includes export control provisions.

Other regimes dealing with chemical non-proliferation, such as the Australia Group or the European Union's dual-use goods legislation, have a relatively narrow focus centred on lists of specific chemical precursors.[2] In contrast, the Convention's scope, including that of its export control provisions, is far broader, based as it is upon a so-called 'general purpose criterion' rather than lists of specific chemicals. Although the Convention does include three lists of chemicals, formally known as Schedules, they were included for a number of practical reasons related to the implementation of the Convention. The Convention states explicitly that they were not included to define the scope of the treaty.

Since the entry into force of the Convention in 1997, the attention of States Parties has inevitably focused upon those 43 chemicals and families of chemicals specifically listed in the Schedules. It is essential, however, that this trend does not become permanent and be allowed to undermine the general purpose criterion. One area in which such a danger exists is with regard to export controls. Although the implementation of the general purpose criterion presents problems for States Parties — even monitoring scheduled chemicals can

* Harvard Sussex Program on CBW Armament and Arms Limitation.

[1] Convention on the Prohibition of Development, Production, Stockpiling and Use of Chemical Weapons and on Their Destruction.

[2] Both regimes do also cover chemical production equipment. The Australia Group is an informal gathering which coordinates export controls on dual-use chemical and biological items and shares information and intelligence. Since October 2001, the Group consists of the following 33 countries, plus the European Commission: Argentina; Australia; Austria; Belgium; Bulgaria; Canada; Czech Republic; Cyprus; Denmark; Finland; France; Germany; Greece; Hungary; Iceland; Ireland; Italy; Japan; Luxembourg; Netherlands; New Zealand; Norway; Poland; Portugal; Romania; Slovakia; South Korea; Spain; Sweden; Switzerland; Turkey; United Kingdom; and the United States.

R. Yepes-Enríquez and L. Tabassi. (eds.), Treaty Enforcement and International Cooperation in Criminal Matters

cause difficulties — assistance and cooperation can be provided by States Parties and the Secretariat of the Organisation for the Prohibition of Chemical Weapons ("OPCW").

2. The Scope of the Chemical Weapons Convention and its Export Controls

2.1 THE GENERAL PURPOSE CRITERION

The general purpose criterion (which is a concept copied from the 1972 Biological Weapons Convention[3]) is defined in Article II. Three elements are listed which, together or separately, constitute a chemical weapon: toxic chemicals and their precursors (except when intended for non-prohibited purposes, as long as the types and quantities are consistent with such purposes), munitions and devices, and equipment specifically designed for use with such munitions and devices. The term "toxic chemical" is defined by Article II(2) as "[a]ny chemical which through its chemical action on life processes can cause death, temporary incapacitation or permanent harm to humans or animals." Thus, the definition of a chemical weapon is not based upon the properties of specific chemicals, but on the purposes to which chemicals are put.[4] As Robinson notes, a chemical weapon under the Convention is a "considerably broader concept than the chemical weapons of, say, common military parlance."[5] The general purpose criterion has two primary functions: it allows the Convention to keep up with technological progress, and it protects legitimate uses of dual-use chemicals.

It is sometimes assumed that the 43 chemicals and families of chemicals listed in the Schedules are the only chemicals to which the Convention applies.[6] Indeed, it would appear that some States Parties are keen to maintain this fiction in an attempt to restrict the verification regime of the Convention and the activities of its oversight body, the OPCW.[7] However, such an assumption is not in line with the text of the Convention or with the object and purpose of the Convention. There are a number of places in which the text of the Convention makes it clear that the scheduled chemicals are not to be seen as defining the scope of the Convention. In Article II it is pointed out that those toxic chemicals and precursors listed in the Schedules are simply those which have been "identified for the application of verification measures". During the Convention negotiations in Geneva, it was clear that intrusive verification measures could not be applied to all chemical warfare-

---

[3] Convention on the Prohibition of the Development, Production and Stockpiling of Bacteriological (Biological) and Toxin Weapons and on Their Destruction.

[4] For more on the general purpose criterion see: Julian Perry Robinson, *Practical National Implementation Measures for Entry into Force of the Chemical Weapons Convention*, in: Summary of Proceedings: OPCW Occasional Paper No. 3: Regional Seminar on National Authority and National Implementation Measures for the Chemical Weapons Convention, Warsaw, (7-8 December 1993), Graham Pearson, *The CWC general purpose criterion: How to implement?*, The CBW Conventions Bulletin, No. 49 (September 2000), 1-7;. Tom Inch, *The Chemical Weapons Convention: A Viewpoint from the Chairman of the Advisory Committee to the UK National Authority*, The CBW Conventions Bulletin, No. 50 (December 2000), 3-5.

[5] Julian Perry Robinson, *The CWC Verification Regime: Implications for the Biotechnological and Pharmaceutical Industry*, University of Bradford Briefing Paper No. 11 (July 1998) at 5, as posted at www.bradford.ac.uk/acad/sbtwc.

[6] There are actually many more than 43 scheduled chemicals, as many of those listed are actually families of chemicals. For example, the latest version of the OPCW Handbook on Chemicals issued by the OPCW Secretariat lists 932 scheduled chemicals and, in theory, there are millions more.

[7] For example, some States Parties have opposed the inclusion of information on unscheduled chemicals into OPCW analytical databases.

relevant chemicals as some were used on a large scale in the chemical industry, making verification impractical. Therefore, negotiators reached a compromise between political reality and risk assessment whereby some chemicals of most relevance were selected for the application of verification measures. In addition, the preambular paragraph to the Schedules underlines the point by reminding readers that "these Schedules do not constitute a definition of chemical weapons."

Paying due regard to the general purpose criterion is essential if the goals of the Convention are to be realised, since historically States have not always used scheduled chemicals in their chemical weapons programmes. For example, once restrictions were placed upon its acquisition of direct precursors in the mid-1980s, Iraq simply acquired what, under the Convention, are unscheduled chemicals (for example, 2-chloroethanol and sodium sulphide when access to the Schedule 2 mustard gas precursor thiodiglycol was restricted).[8] The validity of Convention export controls on unscheduled chemicals is accepted by many States Parties. For example, in 1996 the Islamic Republic of Iran, which is seen as an opponent of ad hoc regimes such as the Australia Group, proposed that end-use certificates under the Chemical Weapons Convention be required for exports of certain chemical equipment and those 20 chemicals[9] which appear on the Australia Group list but not in the Convention Schedules.[10] Some States Parties have argued that, given the precedent set by Iraq's chemical weapons programme, the Convention verification regime should actually be focused less on scheduled chemicals and more on unscheduled chemicals.[11] For these textual and practical reasons, the implementation of the Convention should not simply be restricted to scheduled chemicals.

While the scope of the Convention should be interpreted as broadly as possible, it is true that the international verification of compliance with the Convention does focus on scheduled chemicals. The verification regime overseen by the OPCW is based on the declaration and inspection of activities involving Schedules 1, 2 and 3 chemicals and those producing significant quantities of unscheduled 'discrete organic chemicals'. However, within many States Parties, it is likely that there are other activities involving toxic chemicals and their precursors which, while falling within the scope of the Convention according to the general purpose criterion, fall outside of its international monitoring mechanism because they are not declarable under the Convention. While such activities need monitoring to ensure that no violations of the Convention occur, it would be impractical to extend the scope of international oversight so far into the private industry of States Parties. Instead, responsibility for monitoring such activities rests with the individual States Parties and, in particular, with the National Authority which each State Party is required to establish or designate.[12] The Convention thus creates a division of labour between the National Authorities and the OPCW which means "that it is to the National Authorities, not to the

[8] Australia, National Export Licensing Measures, OPCW Preparatory Commission doc. PC-XIII/B/WP.9 (26 March 1996).

[9] Robert J. Mathews, A Comparison of the Australia Group List of Chemical Weapon Precursors and the CWC Schedules of Chemicals, Chemical Weapons Convention Bulletin, No. 21 (September 1993), 1-3.

[10] Iran, Implementation of Article XI in the Field of Chemical Trade, OPCW Preparatory Commission doc. PC-XV/B/WP.6 (5 November 1996).

[11] Australia, Non-paper: Chemical Weapons Convention (CWC) Industry Verification: Inspections of Schedule 3 and Discrete Organic Chemical (DOC) Facilities, OPCW doc. C-IV/NAT.7 (24 June 1999).

[12] Convention Article VII (4).

OPCW, that the CWC has assigned the task of overseeing implementation of a major provision of the treaty."[13] The task of the OPCW Secretariat is to validate the information which it receives from National Authorities by conducting on-site inspections, but such inspections focus primarily on scheduled chemicals. Given the importance of the general purpose criterion in upholding the scope of the Convention, it is essential that National Authorities and other relevant state agencies are properly empowered by effective national legislation to monitor and control transfers of all toxic chemicals, not just those in the Schedules.

2.2 PRIMARY EXPORT CONTROLS UNDER THE CHEMICAL WEAPONS CONVENTION

The primary export control provisions are found in Article I of the Convention. Article I(1)(a) requires States Parties to undertake never to "transfer, directly or indirectly, chemical weapons to anyone". Recalling the general purpose criterion, this reference to "chemical weapons" does not simply mean filled munitions or scheduled chemicals, but any toxic chemical or precursor intended for prohibited purposes, munitions, devices and equipment. In addition, Article I(1)(d) requires States Parties not "to assist, encourage or induce, in any way", anyone to engage in any prohibited activity. Cipolat argues that Article I(1)(d) "represents a kind of catch-all clause that expands the Convention's nonproliferation obligation from the core prohibition of activities with chemical weapons to any activity that is apt for and aimed at chemical proliferation."[14] Cipolat thus argues that Article I(1d) even prohibits the provision of equipment, financial resources, and intangible technology if they are to be used in connection with prohibited activities. The dangers posed by the transfer of intangible technology have recently been acknowledged by some States: "Intangible technology transfer is becoming an important proliferation concern in the export control community worldwide, and certainly within the multilateral nonproliferation regimes."[15] Although aware of the risk, States have found that intangible technology transfers are particularly difficult to monitor, and penalties can be hard to enforce. Many States have only recently introduced controls on such transfers.[16] Although Article I contains no explicit requirement for Convention States Parties to enact legislation or adopt regulations implementing the Article I prohibitions, it is at least implicit that provisions which are so central to the object and purpose of the Convention should be acted upon by all States Parties.

Further on in the Convention text, the *Molander chapeau* which opens Article VI(2) does explicitly require states parties to implement controls on one element of the "chemical weapon" definition. The *chapeau* states that "each State Party shall adopt the necessary measures to ensure that toxic chemicals and their precursors are only...transferred...for

[13] Robinson, The CWC Verification Regime, *supra* note 5, at 4.

[14] Urs Cipolat, The New Chemical Weapons Convention and Export Controls: Towards Greater Multilateralism?, 21 Mich. J. of Int'l Law 417, 418 (2000).

[15] Timothy Williams, US Controls on Technology Transfer by Intangible Means, 6 The Monitor: Nonproliferation, Demilitarization and Arms Control, 12-16, 12 (2000).

[16] See, for example, the recent EU dual-use goods regime, Council Regulation (EC) No 1334/2000 of 22 June 2000 setting up a Community regime for the control of exports of dual-use items and technology, Official Journal of the European Communities, L 159 (30 June 2000), 1-215; and the Export Control Bill implementing the EU regulation into UK law which was introduced into Parliament on 26 June 2001 and is posted on the internet at www.dti.gov.uk.

purposes not prohibited under this Convention". The key terms in this *chapeau* are 'necessary measures', and 'ensure'. Krutzsch and Trapp observe that there is an intimate relationship between Articles VI and VII (which deals with national implementation measures), and that the use of the term 'necessary measures' in both articles implies legislative and administrative measures, as well as the penal legislation which is explicitly required under Article VII(1)(a). The most effective way in which States Parties can 'ensure' that toxic chemicals and precursors are not transferred for prohibited purposes is by establishing a legally-based export control system which includes penal sanctions for violations.[17] Zedalis accordingly asserts that "no doubt exists that the CWC provides for controls over exports of toxic chemicals and their precursors."[18] The *chapeau* thus builds upon and reinforces States Parties' Article I non-proliferation obligations, at least for one element of the Convention definition of a chemical weapon. It also requires States Parties to acknowledge the general purpose criterion and implement it within their jurisdictions.

2.3 AUXILIARY EXPORT CONTROLS UNDER THE CHEMICAL WEAPONS CONVENTION

It is only later in the Convention that export controls on scheduled chemicals are specified. The Verification Annex includes a graduated regime prohibiting transfers of scheduled chemicals between States Parties and States not Party. The main features of this regime are as follows: Schedule 1 chemicals can only be transferred for particular purposes.[19] Transfers to and from States not Party are prohibited, and once transferred to another State Party, Schedule 1 chemicals cannot be re-transferred.[20]

Since 29 April 2000, Schedule 2 chemicals cannot be exported to, or imported from, States not Party.[21] Previously, States Parties had to ensure that chemicals exported to States not Party were not used for prohibited purposes or re-transferred by requesting that an end-use certificate be completed by the recipient State.[22]

End-use certificates are required for exports of Schedule 3 chemicals to States not Party. Beyond this obligation, Schedule 3 exports to, and imports from, States not Party are currently unrestricted.[23] In May 2001, the OPCW Conference of the States Parties considered the need to establish other measures regarding such exports, as required by the Convention.[24]

---

[17] Walter Krutzsch and Ralf Trapp, A Commentary on the Chemical Weapons Convention (1994) 98. See also, Cipolat, *supra* note 14, at 431.

[18] Rex Zedalis, New Export Controls for Chemicals on the Horizon?, 30 International Lawyer 148 (1996).

[19] Convention VA Part VI (2).

[20] Convention VA Part VI (3)and (4).

[21] Convention VA Part VII (31).

[22] Convention VA Part VII (32). In 1998, the OPCW decided that end-use certificates had to be issued by the "competent government authority" within the recipient state. OPCW doc. C-III/DEC.7 (17 November 1998).

[23] Convention VA Part VIII (26).

[24] Convention VA Part VIII (27). The OPCW Conference of the States Parties urged all States Parties to implement the provisions relating to end-use certificates and decided that such certificates would not be needed for products containing 30 per cent or less of a Schedule 3 chemical or for products identified as consumer goods. The OPCW Executive Council was requested to consider other measures and report back to the 2002 session of the Conference. Decision on the Provisions on Transfers of Schedule 3 Chemicals to States Not Party to the Convention, OPCW doc. C-VI/DEC.10 (17 May 2001).

Rather than being the only export controls required by the Convention, these specific restrictions should be seen as being auxiliary to those in Article I.[25] Almost until the end of the negotiations, Article I(1)(a) and (d) and the *Molander chapeau* were the only export control measures in the Convention, since they were considered "a sufficient basis for measures against Non-States-Parties."[26] While the Schedule 1 restrictions had been in the 'rolling text' from a fairly early stage,[27] the extension of the concept to Schedule 2 and 3 transfers was only introduced in 1991, and was only accepted in the final weeks of negotiations. The main reason for the inclusion was to provide a negative incentive for States to join the Convention; indeed, the initial proposal was entitled "measures to ensure universality" of the Convention.[28] This was recalled in a later Australian paper, which argued that the restrictions were included "primarily to ensure the Convention included an incentive, in the form of trade restrictions, for non-States Parties to join the treaty regime."[29] Since entry into force, the OPCW Secretariat has indeed used the trade restrictions on scheduled chemicals in its efforts to increase Convention universality, although the reasons for States deciding to join or not join the Convention are often more complex than access to particular chemicals. Therefore, while controls on the transfer of scheduled chemicals are an important element of Convention implementation, they are by no means the only measures with respect to toxic chemicals required by the Convention.

3. Convention Export Control Implementation Since 1997

3.1 National Implementing Legislation

Implementing the Convention is not simply a matter of ratifying or acceding to the treaty: "[t]he Chemical Weapons Convention is not self-executing. Each State Party's international obligations under the Convention must be given direct internal legal effect."[30] National implementation is therefore an absolutely essential foundation of the Convention. A note from the OPCW Director-General to the Executive Council states that "implementing legislation is the most fundamental aspect of enforcement of the ban on chemical weapons. Without the ability to apprehend and punish violators of the Convention, universality

[25] Cipolat, *supra* note 14, at 413. However, see also India, Chemical Trade and International Cooperation under the Chemical Weapons Convention, OPCW Preparatory Commission doc. PC-XIII/B/WP.7* (23 February 1996) at 2. Here, India argues that States Parties "will adopt, in full, the restrictions *specifically* provided for in the Convention without, in any way, going further than these restrictions. Any restrictions that would go further than the Convention would be incompatible with Convention obligations" [emphasis added].

[26] Ambassador Adolf Ritter von Wagner, Explanatory Note on the Draft Chemical Weapons Convention Contained in Document CD/CW/WP.400/Rev.1, Conference on Disarmament doc. CD/CW/WP.414 (26 June 1992) at 31.

[27] Specific language on Schedule 1 transfers first appeared in the Convention rolling text in 1987. See Conference on Disarmament doc. CD/734 (29 January 1987) at 37.

[28] USA, Measures to Ensure Universality, Conference on Disarmament doc.CD/CW/WP.357 (8 August 1991).

[29] Australia, *supra* note 8, Preparatory Commission for the OPCW, doc. PC-XIII/B/WP.9, at 1.

[30] Note by the Director-General: Compliance with Article VII: Legislation, Cooperation and Legal Assistance, OPCW doc. C-III/DG.1/Rev.1 (17 November 1998) at 1.

remains a hollow accomplishment."[31] Article VII requires States Parties to "adopt the necessary measures to implement its obligations under this Convention." However, national implementation is an area in which many States Parties have little or no experience. This is reflected in the fact that, as of 8 March 2001, only 53 states parties (38 percent) had notified the OPCW of their implementing legislation.[32] This total has not increased substantially since a 1998 survey of national implementing legislation; the total then was only 40, of which only 26 were judged by the Secretariat to be comprehensive enough for the State Party to be able to implement the Convention effectively in its jurisdiction.[33]

At the time of the survey, only 26 States Parties had notified the OPCW of their export control regulations. Of these 26, all but eight were Australia Group participants, who had probably had such regulations in place for a number of years.[34] Of the 26 which had notified the OPCW of their export control law, it is highly doubtful that all have recognised the general purpose criterion and extended controls to unscheduled as well as scheduled chemicals. In addition, these 26 States Parties only amount to just over half of the States Parties which have received Schedule 1, 2, 3 or DOC inspections since 1997.[35] This means that approximately half of the States Parties which are using scheduled and DOC chemicals above specific thresholds either have no export controls in place, or, more likely, have not notified the OPCW of their existence. Just as worrying, around two thirds of the 145 States Parties have not informed the OPCW of their implementing legislation at all. All participants in the Australia Group should have adopted controls over at least 20 toxic chemicals which are not listed in the Convention Schedules, and other countries have implemented 'catch-all' controls under which any transfers can be controlled if they are suspected of being diverted to a weapons of mass destruction (WMD) programme.

In June 2000, the OPCW Secretariat circulated a Legislation Questionnaire: Survey of National Measures to Regulate Scheduled Chemicals under the Chemical Weapons Convention. As its title implies, the survey inquired into regulations concerning scheduled chemicals, including therefore the auxiliary export controls described earlier, but not into regulations covering unscheduled toxic chemicals and precursors which are required by the *Molander chapeau*. Perhaps this limitation is realistic at this stage of Convention implementation, but it is to be hoped that it does not reflect an ignorance of the general purpose criterion. The preliminary analysis of the responses which the OPCW Secretariat circulated on 22 March 2001 contained some worrisome findings. Of the 52 States Parties which responded by 14 March 2001, 13 percent had not prohibited transfers of Schedule 1 chemicals or their precursors to or from States not Party, 36 percent had not prohibited transfers of Schedule 2 chemicals or their precursors to or from States not Party, only 65 per cent were enforcing the requirement for end-use certificates, and 10 percent had no penalties

[31] Report by the Director-General: National Implementation Measures, OPCW doc. EC-XXIV/DG.4 (22 March 2001).

[32] *Id.* This only includes States Parties which have notified the OPCW of their legislation, so it is possible that other States Parties have legislation but have failed to notify the OPCW.

[33] Survey of National Implementing Legislation, OPCW doc. S/85/98 (17 November 1998).

[34] Interestingly, this means that 12 Australia Group participants had not submitted information on their export control regulations to the OPCW, despite the fact that, as participants, they could be assumed to have some export control system in place.

[35] The OPCW Secretariat has carried out over 1,000 inspections in 49 States Parties. OPCW press release no. 15/2001, "The OPCW completes its 1000th inspection".

in force with which to punish violations of Convention requirements in respect of Schedules 1, 2 or 3 chemicals or their precursors.[36] One conclusion which the OPCW Director-General was able to draw from the preliminary results was that national implementing legislation drawn up by some States Parties "open up serious loopholes in the system established by the Convention for the tracking of scheduled chemicals. Such loopholes have prevented the Secretariat from being able to verify the non-diversion of scheduled chemicals."[37] These problems have been encountered in the implementation of the auxiliary Convention export controls, which are limited to scheduled chemicals. The fact remains that there are thousands of unscheduled chemicals which could be used for chemical warfare purposes, the transfer of which is very difficult to monitor without effective national legislation. Nor is legislation sufficient on its own; only in conjunction with enforcement can non-transfer be "ensured," as required by Article VI.

3.2 EXPERIENCE WITH TRANSFERS OF SCHEDULED CHEMICALS

The transfer of Schedule 1 chemicals to States not Party has been prohibited since the entry into force of the Convention. The international trade in such substances is tiny and already highly regulated. Despite this, it has not always been possible for the OPCW Secretariat to match notifications from the exporting and importing States Parties. Indeed, in 1999, 70-80 percent of Schedule 1 transfers could not be matched. Saxitoxin is the most transferred Schedule 1 chemical. This is primarily due to the fact that minute amounts are used in medical kits for diagnosing paralytic shellfish poisoning. However, this gave rise to a problem unforeseen when the Convention was negotiated. In September 1997, Canada (the main producer of diagnostic kits) informed the OPCW that it was encountering difficulties in meeting the 30 day advance notification requirement.[38] For this reason, and only for transfers of tiny amounts of saxitoxin, States Parties eventually agreed, over two years later, to change the Verification Annex, removing the requirement to give advance notification. Another problem regarding Schedule 1 transfers could not be resolved, however. The Convention prohibits re-transfers of Schedule 1 chemicals between States Parties. Prior to entry into force, a United Kingdom company had imported saxitoxin from North America, tritiated it and sold the tritiated product to other States Parties. Canada and the United Kingdom proposed another textual change to remedy this problem, but this proposal was later withdrawn.

States Parties are required to submit to the OPCW Secretariat annual declarations of aggregate amounts of Schedule 2 and 3 chemicals imported and exported. However, the OPCW Secretariat has been unable to reconcile the majority of these transfers for four main reasons: different States Parties use different calculating methods, customs-related problems, chemicals off-shore, and clerical errors. In fact, in 1999, out of 950 transfers of Schedule 2

[36] Legislation Questionnaire: Preliminary Analysis of Responses to the Survey of National Measures to Regulate Scheduled Chemicals Under the Chemical Weapons Convention, OPCW doc. S/249/2001 (22 March 2001).

[37] Report by the Director-General: National Implementation Measures, OPCW doc. EC-XXIV/DG.4 (22 March 2001).

[38] Worst affected were researchers working on paralytic shellfish poisoning. Debora MacKenzie, A Little Latitude Won't Kill Us, New Scientist (27 June 1998) 49; Megan Saunders, Shell Shock—Toxic War Erupts, The Australian (6 January 1999) 3.

and 3 chemicals involving 81 States Parties, 89 percent of the transfers could not be reconciled (meaning they were either declared by only one State Party, or the declared amounts differing by a significant amount).[39] One major cause of discrepancies has been the use by States Parties of different concentration levels for the declaration of Schedule 2 and 3 production and transfer. Concentration levels for transfers of Schedule 2 chemicals in mixtures were eventually agreed upon in May 2000, and Schedule 3 chemicals in mixtures in May 2001, but many other problems remain. In 1998, the OPCW Secretariat initiated a process of clarification with the States Parties involved, and encouraged bilateral or regional consultations. In January 2001, the OPCW Secretariat hosted a meeting of States Parties to discuss the discrepancies and consider possible solutions. The Director-General reported that the situation had improved somewhat since 1999, with 70-80 percent being irreconcilable.[40] As could be expected, the discrepancies are highest for those chemicals which are traded in the largest volumes, such as the Schedule 3 chemicals triethanolamine and methyldiethanolamine.

These are just a selection of the problems which have been encountered during the first four years of Convention implementation.[41] They are the difficulties which are of most relevance to a discussion on Convention export controls. It is important to note that these problems have arisen primarily during the course of the implementation of Convention controls on scheduled chemicals. Few States Parties, whether in the developed or developing world, have given much serious consideration to the implementation of the general purpose criterion. The best that can be said is that some "expressly recognised at least the guardianship of the General Purpose Criterion."[42] As Robinson notes, "the chief problem with the [general purpose] criterion is that, administratively, its is far less easy to implement than, for example, a list-based approach to what is and is not prohibited."[43] However, the disadvantages of such an approach have already been noted. There will soon come a time when it will be necessary to move beyond the current restricted implementation of the Convention, which concentrates mainly on scheduled chemicals, and address the general purpose criterion in pursuit of full and effective Convention implementation. The application of Convention export controls beyond scheduled chemicals will be an important part of this process. One possible opportunity to discuss these issues is presented by the first Convention review conference, which will convene in The Hague in 2003.[44] By this time, six years after entry into force, most States Parties should have enough experience of Convention implementation and the basic obligations of the Convention that they are ready to implement the full range of its prohibitions.

---

[39] Report of the Organisation on the Implementation of the Convention (1 January - 31 December 1999), OPCW doc. C-V/5 (17 May 2000) p. 19.

[40] José Bustani, Opening Statement by the Director-General to the Executive Council at its Twenty-second Session, paragraph 37 of EC-XXII/DG.12 (5 December 2000), as posted at www.opcw.org.

[41] For more detail on Convention implementation and the activities of the OPCW in particular, see the quarterly Progress in The Hague reports by Pamela Mills and Fiona Tregonning in Harvard Sussex Program on CBW Armament and Arms Limitation, The CBW Conventions Bulletin.

[42] Robinson, The CWC Verification Regime, *supra* note 5, at 4.

[43] Robinson, The CWC Verification Regime, *id.*, at 12.

[44] In September 2001, the OPCW Executive Council established an open-ended working group to begin preparations for the review conference, OPCW doc. EC-XXVI/DEC.4 (28 September 2001).

4. Possible Remedies

Article VII(2) requires that "each State Party shall cooperate with other States Parties and afford the appropriate form of legal assistance to facilitate the implementation of the obligations under paragraph 1." To date the implementation of this obligation by States Parties has been rather slow and ineffectual, although in 2000 the OPCW Conference of the States Parties did adopt a decision on national implementing measures which urged States Parties, the Executive Council and the Secretariat to assist States Parties in the fulfilment of Convention obligations.[45] Under this mandate, the OPCW Secretariat hosted an international legal symposium on the implementation of the Article VII(2) requirement in February 2001. The symposium looked at experiences from other international regimes and at ways forward for the OPCW.[46] As shown above, the obligations to which Article VII(2) refers include the implementation of the general purpose criterion in its broadest sense, and particularly the extension of Convention export controls to unscheduled toxic chemicals and precursors.

In contrast to the efforts at harmonisation practised within regional organisations such as the European Union or selective gatherings like the Australia Group, the OPCW provides a multilateral forum currently encompassing 145 States in which such issues can be discussed and through which cooperation can be focused. Some developments in this direction can already be seen, but much more is possible. The OPCW could facilitate discussions and information exchange among its members on the control of intangible technology transfers or the implementation of 'catch-all' export controls. For example, those States Parties with such controls could impart their experiences and offer assistance, in conjunction with the legal experts of the OPCW Secretariat. With the approach of the first Convention review conference, it is time that more attention is paid to such long-term issues, alongside the short-term concerns of ongoing Convention implementation. For each of the three areas discussed below, it would be useful if States Parties submitted reports on their programmes and activities to the OPCW Conference of the States Parties for the information of other States Parties.

4.1 Legislative Assistance

A degree of harmonisation between States Parties is essential if the broad prohibitions contained within the Convention are to be properly implemented in the real world. The current situation with regard to national implementing legislation, as outlined above, is worrisome, but there are measures which can be taken to rectify the situation. The OPCW Secretariat has already started down some of these roads. In 2000, it arranged two regional workshops on legislative issues, with the cooperation of the Spanish and Swaziland governments.[47] The OPCW Secretariat also continues to offer assistance to individual States

[45] Conference Decision: National Implementation Measures, OPCW doc. C-V/DEC.20 (19 May 2000).
[46] Report on the International Symposium on Cooperation and Legal Assistance for the Effective Implementation of International Agreements, The Hague, 7-9 February 2001, OPCW doc. S/251/2001 (22 March 2001).
[47] Report on the Workshop on Legislative Issues, Sevilla, OPCW doc. S/225/2000 (1 December 2000); Report on the Regional Workshop on Implementing Legislation and International Cooperation on Issues, Mbabane, Swaziland, 28-30 November 2000, OPCW doc. S/250/2001 (22 March 2001).

Parties in establishing the legislative and regulatory framework required to implement Convention export control provisions. An innovative approach has been the development by the Secretariats of the OPCW and the Organisation of Eastern Caribbean States of a model integrated legislative package linking the implementation of the Convention to the implementation of other regimes concerning the sound management of chemicals. The draft act combines Convention implementing legislation with legislation on pesticides, and incorporates provisions for controls on transfers of scheduled and unscheduled chemicals.[48] States Parties in the Latin America and Caribbean region have also established a Network of Legal Experts to assist and advise on the process of elaborating national legislation. The members of the network held their first meeting in February 2001.

More efforts could also be made bilaterally by States Parties. For example, the United States Department of Defense and Federal Bureau of Investigation (FBI) run a joint counterproliferation programme that "trains and equips the community of officials responsible for [nuclear, biological and chemical] interdiction in Eastern Europe, the Baltic States and the [former Soviet Union]." One element of the programme is assistance in developing appropriate legislation, laws, regulations and enforcement mechanisms.[49] Similarly, the United States Department of Commerce has a Nonproliferation and Export Control Cooperation Team which provides legal and regulatory assistance to the same regions. In addition, the government of the United Kingdom regularly conducts bilateral export control meetings to "address the practical issues surrounding export licensing and enforcement in detail."[50] Recognising that Article I requires States Parties to apply export regulations, at the Fourth Session of the OPCW Conference of the States Parties Sweden offered to provide assistance to other States Parties in the implementation of Convention legal obligations, in particular the legislative and administrative aspects of export controls.[51] Other States Parties are likely to have similar programmes or be willing to offer assistance. By submitting information to the OPCW Conference of the States Parties, States could increase awareness of such programmes. The enlargement of the European Union into central and eastern Europe could also serve as an opportunity to assist in the development of effective export controls in the applicant countries.

4.2 ADMINISTRATIVE COOPERATION

An essential component of the full and effective implementation of Convention export control provisions will be cooperation between States Parties. Legislation will need to be harmonised, as started to happen following the decisions in 2000 and 2001 on low concentration levels for transferring Schedules 2 and 3 chemicals in mixtures to States not Party. Administrative cooperation between States Parties will also be important, to ensure accurate reporting of transfers among States Parties and as more free trade areas are established

[48] An Integrated Approach to National Implementing Legislation: Model Act Developed by the Secretariat of the Organisation of Eastern Caribbean States, OPCW doc. S/190/2000 (23 May 2000).
[49] United States Department of Defense, Proliferation: Threat and Response (January 2001), 76-77, as posted on the internet at www.defenselink.mil.
[50] United Kingdom Department of Trade and Industry, Strategic Export Controls Annual Report 2000 (July 2001), 9-10, as posted on the internet at www.fco.gov.uk.
[51] Swedish Review Under the Chemical Weapons Convention Paragraph 2(e) of Article XI, OPCW doc. C-IV/NAT.1 (16 March 1999).

around the world. The OPCW Secretariat has encouraged those States Parties that have reported inconsistent export/import data to meet with their trading partners to try and remedy the situation. Possible solutions could include, for example, agreement on specific identification codes for each transaction.

One possible model is the dual-use goods regime established within the European Union.[52] Although the EU is an exceptionally highly developed regional organisation, there are elements of the regime which could be applied to other regions. In particular, its provisions for administrative cooperation between member States merit closer study. The regulation which created the dual-use goods regime states that EU member States "shall take all appropriate measures to establish direct cooperation and exchange of information between competent authorities."[53] The regime has thus created a network of export control officials from the 15 member States who consult regularly on individual exports and on policy issues. They also come together for regular meetings in Brussels.

Within the OPCW, the Secretariat has encouraged stronger cooperation between National Authorities, hosting an annual meeting in The Hague for all National Authorities and supporting regional meetings of National Authorities, such as those held annually in Latin America. At the annual meeting in The Hague in May 2000, one day of the event was devoted to enforcement issues, while the annual meeting in May 2001 included a one-day workshop on legislative issues. It is likely that other regions will also follow the example of Latin America and the Caribbean and, with support from the OPCW Secretariat, organise their own regional meetings. Such meetings are particularly useful given the amount of intra-regional trade which can go on, and given other factors often shared within a region, such as common languages and legal systems.

4.3 ENFORCEMENT ASSISTANCE

With respect to the enforcement of Convention export controls, further experience could be gained from the operation of the Australia Group and the interactions between its 34 participants. The practical experiences of Australia Group participants in controlling chemical precursors would be of direct relevance to Convention States Parties. Particularly interesting would be the mechanisms for cooperation between the law enforcement and customs authorities of Group participants. During the plenary meeting of the Australia Group in October 2000, a sub-group meeting of enforcement experts was held for the first time to increase the exchange of information on enforcement and licensing issues.[54] At the same meeting, the Australia Group also agreed on the importance of transparency in its operations, holding out the chance that the Group might come to play a more proactive role within the OPCW.

Again, individual States Parties also have a role to play. The United States Department of Defense and the United States Customs Service together operate an International Border Security Counterproliferation Program which is intended to train and equip customs officials and border guards in the former Soviet Union, Eastern Europe and the Baltic states. Under the programme, equipment and training have been provided to many countries, and advisers

---

[52] Council Regulation (EC) No 1334/2000.
[53] *Id.*, Chapter VI, Article 15, para 2, at 6.
[54] United Kingdom, Strategic Export Controls Annual Report 2000, *supra* note 50, at 9.

have even been provided to the International Atomic Energy Agency, perhaps offering a model for future programmes involving the OPCW.[55] The programme complements the aforementioned joint DoD/FBI counterproliferation programme, with both basing much of their training at the International Law Enforcement Academy.[56] On the subject of regulation and enforcement, a note from the OPCW Secretariat made the point that "the prevention of violations is one aspect of implementation, while the prosecution of violators is quite another."[57]

The OPCW and the World Customs Organization have recently drafted a memorandum of understanding to improve and increase future cooperation between the two organisations. The WCO maintains ten Regional Intelligence Liaison Offices around the world, linked by the Customs Enforcement Network, an internet based tool designed to pool information relating to seizures, methods of concealment and *modus operandi*.[58] By working with the WCO, the OPCW and its States Parties can enhance their efforts at improving the enforcement of the Convention.

5. Conclusion

In the years since entry into force the attention of States Parties, National Authorities and the OPCW have focused on the basic Convention obligations and, in particular, on scheduled chemicals. Were this trend to continue, the Convention would not keep pace with scientific, technological and industrial developments and would become less and less effective at its main goals of eliminating chemical weapons and preventing chemical warfare. The general purpose criterion was included in the Convention exactly to prevent such developments, and it therefore needs to be respected during Convention implementation. This applies as much to the implementation of Convention export controls as to any other aspect of Convention implementation. However, the implementation of the general purpose criterion is administratively difficult and therefore poses challenges to the enforcement of Convention export controls. One way to prevent these challenges from becoming insurmountable is to utilise the OPCW as a forum for cooperation and assistance. Cooperation between, and support for, National Authorities is particularly important, given the responsibilities upon them for the monitoring of unscheduled chemicals.

---

55 United States, Proliferation: Threat and Response, *supra* note 49, at 76.

56 The ILEA is based in Budapest and annually hosts around 250 students from law enforcement agencies in central and eastern Europe. The ILEA has a website at <www.usis.hu/ilea.htm>.

57 OPCW doc. S/249/2001 (22 March 2001).

58 The WCO is based in Brussels and has 159 member governments. The WCO has a website at www.wcoomd.org.

NEW APPROACHES TO STEMMING THE SPREAD OF WEAPONS WITHIN INTERNATIONAL TRANSPORTATION NETWORKS

Stephen E. Flynn*

1. INTRODUCTION

The international non-proliferation regime is unravelling. The explanation for this unhappy state of affairs is relatively straightforward. First, the technical expertise to produce and deploy a weapon of mass destruction (WMD), particularly chemical and biological weapons, are becoming increasingly accessible to radical states and terrorist organisations. Second, with a small modicum of ingenuity, the painfully constructed international agreements on export controls present no real barrier to those intent on gathering the means to manufacture weapons of mass destruction. Third, the United States appears increasingly inclined to shift emphasis away from multilateral efforts to prevent the spread of WMD and towards unilateral efforts to protect its national territory from an attack by them.

Given the information age in which we live, the technical-know-how genie cannot be put back in the bottle. Anyone with access to the internet can learn much about what it takes to construct extremely dangerous and destructive weapons. For the foreseeable future, the United States will face the twin realities that: (1) it will have adversaries intent on challenging its global reach and economic and cultural dominance, and (2) the conventional means of deterrence will not work against these adversaries. This leaves the cause of non-proliferation and global arms control only one remaining avenue to pursue: bolstering United States and international confidence that export controls can be effectively enforced so those with both the will and the know-how are denied access to the means to construct or obtain proscribed weapons.

2. THE PRICE OF TRADE

The post-Cold War movement toward more open societies and liberalised economies has not just facilitated the movement of products and workers — it has also expedited passage for terrorists, small arms, and sophisticated technologies. Despite this fact, governments have been increasingly reluctant to bolster regulatory, enforcement, and security operations at busy borders or ports of entry. This is because such endeavours place them on a collision course with easy trade, which is key to the sustained expansion and integration of the global economy. Most successful enterprises need to move workers and products quickly,

* The author is a senior fellow with the National Security Studies Program at the Council on Foreign Relations, New York. He is also a Commander in the United States Coast Guard and a member of the permanent commissioned teaching staff of the United States Coast Guard Academy. Any views expressed are those of the author and are not attributable to the CFR, the Coast Guard or its Academy.

R. Yepes-Enríquez and L. Tabassi. (eds.), Treaty Enforcement and International Cooperation in Criminal Matters

reliably, and affordably around the planet. Delays associated with intensified inspections along borders undermine the competitiveness of exports by raising transaction costs. Overseas buyers are likely to avoid ports of entry where there is a heightened risk that products will arrive damaged, spoiled, or late. And rapid, hassle-free immigration controls are essential to both global business and tourism.

The sheer volume of trade is overwhelming traditional border control agents. Five inspectors take, on average, three hours to conduct a thorough physical inspection of a loaded 40-foot container. Even with the assistance of new high-tech sensors, it has proven impractical to inspect all the cargo arriving in places like the Port of Long Beach, California, which received more than one million inbound containers in 1999 (more than double 1995 levels). Nor is it possible to check all the inbound vehicles at the world's busiest commercial land-border crossing — such as the Ambassador Bridge between Detroit, Michigan, and Windsor, Ontario, where a record-breaking 7,000 trucks entered the United States on a single day in February 2000. At these rates, United States Customs officials must clear one container every 20 seconds in southern California, and one truck every 12 seconds in Detroit.

Added to daunting resource demands of fielding more inspectors, there is the problem that there is little room for trucks or containers to wait for inspection. The explosion in international trade is pushing port, bridge, rail, and road infrastructures to their capacity and beyond. Congestion along the access routes, within port and airport terminals, and at border crossings is becoming more commonplace. For instance, the parking lot for secondary and tertiary inspections at Detroit's Ambassador Bridge can accommodate only 90 tractor-trailers at a time. Although it might be possible to double the number of inspectors doing primary inspections, there is no room for the labour-intensive and time-consuming follow-ups. Once the parking lot fills, trucks back up onto the bridge. The resulting pileup virtually closes the border, generating roadway chaos throughout metropolitan Windsor and Detroit.

All told, the United States Customs Service was responsible for monitoring 475 million people, 125 million vehicles, and 21.4 million import shipments that came into the United States in 1999. People and goods arrive daily at more than 3,700 terminals in 301 ports of entry. Intercepting the ripples of danger in this tidal wave of commerce must feel like trying to win a lottery. Still, despite these volumes, the United States Customs Service is mandated to monitor compliance with more than 400 laws and 34 international treaties, statutes, agreements, and conventions on behalf of 40 federal agencies.

Rising volumes are not the only consequence of economic globalisation making the lives of border control agents so difficult. In addition, agents must bear in mind that delayed shipment clearance raises costs for any business that engages in cross-border trade — and few companies can survive today without at least a minimum level of participation in other countries' markets. Media and scholarly discussions about the wonders of the modern global economy are ubiquitous, but most dwell on liberalised trade rules and the rapid spread of information-age technologies. Not enough attention goes to affordable and reliable transportation, the third leg of the global-market stool. Legal access to a distant client and instantaneous ordering will mean very little if the number of hours required, expense, and uncertainty of these transactions are high. Only efficient and rapid transportation can render large distances irrelevant; only when distance means little in economic terms does the construction of global assembly lines become possible.

More and more firms in a diverse array of industries are finding themselves (and their profit margins) dependent on international transportation. To retain their competitive edge, international companies must outsource production, have ready access to customers worldwide, and invest in new technologies to adapt the production process to its widening geographical breadth. The automotive giants' "just-in-time" delivery system, one such adaptation, means that the automakers do not need large inventory reserves to guarantee that the assembly line keeps running. Inventory guarantees that supply will be available to meet demand. But maintaining large stockpiles of goods consumes capital and may be wasteful if they sit around forever. According to one industry study based on United States Commerce Department sales and inventory reports for 1997, the total value of retail sales in the United States for that year was $2.6 trillion. To support these sales, retailers, merchant wholesalers, and manufacturers held $300 billion, $250 billion, and $450 billion in inventory, respectively — a total of $1 trillion. In order to help lower this cost, logistics and transportation providers are investing in faster and more efficient shipping, aviation, rail, and trucking fleets; constructing seamless chains; consolidating distribution networks; upgrading warehouse management systems; and incorporating state-of-the-art tracking, communications, and database technologies. This "value-chain inventory opportunity" is a powerful driver of the transportation and logistics revolutions.

Consider the example of the automotive industry. General Motors, Ford, and DaimlerChrysler buy some of the parts to build their cars and trucks from suppliers in the Canadian province of Ontario. The contract requires that within as little as six hours from receipt of an order, these Canadian suppliers must have made their deliveries to the assembly plants in the United States. Delivery trucks are loaded so that parts meant for specific vehicles can be unloaded and placed directly on the appropriate chassis as it moves down the assembly line. This "just-in-time" delivery system has given the Big Three automakers a more cost-effective and efficient production process. But the resulting savings could evaporate with a delay at the border. If trucks carrying the parts for a Ford Explorer are stuck in an inspection queue, assembly plants can quickly fall idle, with costs running as high as $1 million per hour.

After making such massive capital outlays in technology and infrastructure, companies now want the State to do its part to enhance the savings and efficiency resulting from these private-sector investments. Not surprisingly, customs, immigration, and other officials are finding themselves under mounting pressure to improve the "facilitation" of transborder flows. After all, a "just-in-time" delivery system works only if the goods actually do arrive just in time.

3. Clear and Present Danger

There is evidence that criminals are exploiting global transportation networks.[1] Conservative estimates are that in 1997 commercial air and maritime carriers delivered 129 to 172 metric tons of cocaine to the United States.[2] Smugglers have targeted commercial carriers apparently

---

[1] S.E. Flynn, *The Global Drug Trade vs. The Nation State: Why the Thugs Are Winning* in Mary Ann Cusimano (ed.), Beyond Sovereignty (1999).

[2] Statement of RADM Ernest R. Riutta on Coast Guard Drug Interdiction before the House of Representatives Subcommittee on Coast Guard and Maritime Transportation, 10 June 1998.

because the odds of successful interdiction are minuscule. By volume, only seven containers filled with cocaine would feed America's national habit for one year.[3] And it is not just illicit drugs that are finding existing border control measures to represent little in the way of a barrier. An estimated 5 to 10 million pounds of chloroflourocarbons (CFCs) are smuggled into the United States each year to supply the CFC black market.[4] Given that huge volume, how confident can anyone be that a few pounds of a deadly biological or chemical agent destined for a terrorist could be successfully interdicted by their border control agencies?

Hypothetically, Osama bin Laden could have a front company in Karachi, Pakistan, load a biological agent into a container ultimately destined for Newark, New Jersey, with virtually no risk that it would be intercepted. He could use a Pakistani exporter with an established record of trade in the United States. The container could then be sent via Singapore or Hong Kong to mingle with the half a million containers that are handled by each of these ports every month. It could arrive in the United States via Long Beach or Los Angeles and be loaded directly onto a railcar or truck for the transcontinental trip. Current regulations do not require an importer to file a cargo manifest with United States Customs until the cargo reaches its "entry" port—in this case, Newark, 2,800 miles of American territory away from where it first entered the country — and the importer is permitted 30 days' transit time to make the trip to the East Coast. The container could be diverted or the weapon activated anywhere en route, long before its contents were even identified as having entered the country.

This scenario may read like a plot for a Tom Clancy novel. Nonetheless, the fact remains that it is routine practice within our advanced global economy to allow air and maritime cargo to be hauled anywhere within the transportation network with little or no requirement to indicate its content, where it is from and where it is going, before it arrives at its final destination. Without changes that improve the capacity for the governments to monitor the rising tide of international trade and travel and which enhance their ability to filter the bad from the good, the international conventions designed to contain the spread of weapons of mass destruction will be effectively unenforceable.

4. Guarding the Global Achilles' Heel

A comprehensive approach to transportation security so as to bolster arms control conventions involves five initiatives:

- Bolster intelligence;
- Global cooperation;
- Increased transparency;
- Private-public partnerships; and,
- Marshalling resources and expertise.

---

[3] Based on an Office of National Drug Control Policy estimate of maximum annual cocaine availability at 376 metric tons (National Drug Control Strategy 1999) and the average size of a kilogram brick, 72 cubic inches. A 40-foot container could hold 55,753 kilo bricks.

[4] Environmental Protection Agency, Stratospheric Protection Division of Air and Radiation Report on the Supply and Demand of CFC-12 in the United States: 1999, Washington, D.C. (9 June 1999).

4.1 BOLSTER INTELLIGENCE

Building the means to collect and disseminate intelligence to support the targeting of high-risk movements of people and goods will be critical to supporting the best use of limited enforcement assets while facilitating the movement of legitimate trade and travel. Interpol and the World Customs Organization (WCO) should be resourced to produce intelligence products to support border control agencies globally. In addition, it is essential to engage and work with private security officials within the transportation community who are best positioned to know the security vulnerabilities and breaches within their industry.

4.2 THINK AND ACT GLOBALLY

Transportation security measures must be developed and harmonised globally. Unilateral efforts to tighten security within one nation's transportation infrastructure without commensurate efforts in neighbouring countries may lead carriers, shippers, and exporters to "port shop"; i.e., move business to entry points that clear goods quickly.

In addition, security improvements must apply throughout transportation and logistics networks. If limited to ports of entry, new security measures may produce a "balloon effect" pushing illicit activities to other points in the transportation and logistics systems where detection and interdiction are less certain. A layered defence approach is essential.

4.3 INCREASE TRANSPARENCY

New tagging, tracking, communications, and database technologies can promote transparency and facilitate private-public information sharing. Authorities can monitor transportation flows of goods and people and develop robust risk management practices. A transparent system ensures that free trade does not translate into excessive exposure to external threats.

Access to "near real time" data would enable the development of risk management models to focus limited enforcement resources on the highest risk targets. In addition, regulatory and enforcement agents gain "strategic depth" with the ability to act before a threat arrives. Advanced warning also would allow a controlled-delivery sting operation — delaying arrest and confiscation until the contraband reaches its destination. Enhanced capabilities like these also serve as deterrents.

Achieving the in-transit visibility of trade and passenger flows is not science fiction. The technologies and data management systems that are fuelling the supply-chain management revolution have provided the means for companies to maintain greater levels of oversight and control within international transportation networks. Delivering perishable goods to distant markets and running global assembly lines with minimally stocked shelves requires a degree of logistical choreography impossible a few years ago. The controls and databases represent a gold mine for national authorities monitoring the arrival of travellers and goods.

Major retailers like Wal-Mart are requiring wholesale suppliers to use trucks equipped with Global Positioning System (GPS) transponders. E-commerce providers like Onsale.com and Amazon.com provide customers with United Parcel Service and Federal

Express tracking numbers to monitor the movement of purchases from the warehouse to their front door. The Roadway Express website provides customers with live access to the company's database, allowing shippers and receivers to view account information for real-time shipment location and billing information.[5] For agencies policing transportation flows, such systems can allow "virtual" audits of inbound goods and people.

4.4 FORM PRIVATE-PUBLIC PARTNERSHIPS

Any strategy to improve transportation security requires a working relationship between the private and public sectors which is not easy to develop. Profit margins in the transportation and logistics industries are slim, and many shippers and carriers — particularly smaller firms — are likely to resist any security initiative that raises short-term overhead costs.

Moving away from traditional practices also is likely to meet resistance from some officials. Few government officials understand the global forces behind the changes in the transportation industry; many believe that the current challenges can be met by allocating more resources to their agencies. In locales in which corruption is common, transparency would undermine illicit supplements to officials' incomes. In short, many private sector and government groups are likely to have an interest in preserving the *status quo.*

But there are significant incentives for cooperation. Private companies active in transportation and logistics networks are vulnerable to asymmetrical attacks on critical infrastructure and are likely to be targets of organised crime. In South Florida, for example, drug trafficking organisations have been moving into cargo, particularly of high-tech goods. One leading technology company has reported a rise in cargo losses from $5,000 per theft in 1991 to $750,000 per theft in 1999.[6] Moreover, multinational corporations and others with ties to international commerce should be concerned that governments might impose draconian police measures at ports of entry and along frontiers.

The supply chain management revolution also is creating powerful incentives for the private sector to work with law enforcement and regulatory agencies. Logistics managers must decrease the risk of delay, and clearance within ports of entry represents the greatest and most unpredictable disruption in supply chains.

Governments, in turn, can leverage their regulatory and enforcement authority at ports of entry and elsewhere within the transportation system so that private sector companies contribute to safeguarding public interests. Manufacturers, freight forwarders, travel agents, carriers, importers, and retailers embracing approved security practices, maintaining tight control over logistics flows, and providing detailed and timely information to support investigations and other enforcement and regulatory activities could move through the trade equivalent of an "E-Z Lane." The benefit would be lower transportation costs and faster movement by reducing the risk of delay, spoilage, or wreckage at entry points. Regulators and enforcement officials would conduct spot checks to ensure compliance. Private sector firms unwilling or unable to strengthen security at the point of origin or to provide in-transit transparency would remain in the "slow lane" of traditional inspections and administrative hassles.

---

[5] B.M. Schwartz, *Information Integration*,in 40 Transportation & Distribution (Dec. 1999) at 46.

[6] Technology Asset Protection Association, Facts & Stats., available at www.tapa3.org/facts.htm.

Confident that the legitimate cargo and passengers on the transportation networks are low risk, authorities can concentrate limited enforcement resources on activities at high risk of compromise by criminals or terrorists. In this way, control measures are not at odds with the market but dovetail with it.

4.5 MARSHAL RESOURCES AND EXPERTISE

The first four requirements provide a foundation for an international effort to police the flows of cargo and passengers. The fifth requirement is to provide the resources and expertise to ensure that there is no national weak link in the transportation security system. The United States, Canada, the European Community, the World Bank, the regional development banks, and other appropriate organisations must provide for the resource needs of nations that are willing but unable to support a global transportation security agenda. The expertise can come from the World Customs Organization, the International Maritime Organization, private consultants, and leading airport and seaport police services.

The combination of (1) excessive delays from inefficient terminal operations, and (2) poorly executed inspection and enforcement activities within ports of entry create a high-risk security environment. Accordingly, policy makers, business leaders and port authorities who are committed to customs and port modernisation should welcome the ability to leverage the "security" argument as added justification for:

- streamlining government procedures;
- reforming obsolete labour practices;
- upgrading transportation facilities to improve road, rail, marine, and aviation links; and,
- curbing abuses by inept and sometimes corrupt officials

5. Ending the Neglect

The non-proliferation and arms control communities needs to cast their eye towards bolstering a capacity to monitor and detect threats within the transportation system if the international conventions are not to be routinely compromised by smuggling activities. Policy makers, public and private owners, and transportation system designers, engineers, and researchers must work together to develop and implement a strategy to ensure that vital transportation and information elements of this indispensable global network are both transparent and secure in the face of the increasingly complex proliferation threat of the 21st century.

SECTION III.5

ADDRESSING TRANSBOUNDARY CRIMINAL ACTIVITY THROUGH NATIONAL CRIMINAL LAW SYSTEMS

INTRODUCTION AND SUMMARY

The increase in transboundary criminal activity is one of the consequences of globalisation. The free flow of goods and people has facilitated the movement of criminals and criminal activities from time immemorial. As States find that they can no longer combat this problem alone, solutions for more effective police and judicial cooperation are being developed and institutionalised. Harmonisation of national legislation in various subject areas is a key component to streamline that effectiveness. The European Union (EU) is an important model for regional integration today. Both the concrete steps taken and the adaptation that will be necessary as its membership enlarges provide practical examples of cooperation and consensus building at the regional level. The role and actions of the EU in criminal matters, as well as that of its institutionalised police body, Europol, is presented in this section. The section closes with an exposé of the difficulties that arise when implementing legislation in the different States Parties is not harmonised. The implementation of the instruments of international humanitarian law, including the Chemical Weapons Convention ("the Convention"), which require implementation at the national level are used as reference points.

The EU's activities in transboundary criminal matters remain in the Third Pillar (Justice and Home Affairs), which works to reinforce intergovernmental cooperation. There were two reasons for substantially enhancing the provisions on transboundary police and judicial cooperation in criminal matters. First, "globalisation" is practised increasingly also by criminal gangs and can no longer be effectively combated by nation states acting individually. Second, the abolition of border controls among EU Member States needs to be compensated by enhanced cooperation among the police and judicial authorities. Common action is being taken in order to facilitate and accelerate cooperation among the judicial authorities regarding proceedings, enforcement of decisions and harmonisation in different areas of national penal law. The core provisions of the EU in respect of this are to be found in the Schengen Implementation Agreement which, however, is not applicable to all EU members. The Schengen provisions are to be complemented by conventions concluded in the framework of the Council of Europe. Adoption of future measures, notably in the area of mutual recognition of judicial decisions and judgments and the necessary approximation of legislation, are contemplated. Consideration should also be given to the establishment of accelerated extradition procedures and enhancing customs cooperation.

The European Police Office ("Europol") was established by the Member States of the European Union with a clear mandate: to improve the effectiveness and cooperation of the authorities in the Member States of the European Union tasked with preventing and combating serious forms of international organised crime. Since Europol took up its activities in July 1999, it has established a multitude of procedures for the various modalities of international law enforcement cooperation provided for by the Europol Convention. Due to the intergovernmental character of EU Third Pillar activities, Europol is not in a position to disregard the framework laid down by the national criminal law systems of its Member States. The modalities of law enforcement cooperation via Europol are: bilateral cooperation between States, cooperation between States and an international/regional organisation, and cooperation between international organisations.

Because of the growing international character of organised crime, efforts have been strengthened to encourage transboundary law enforcement cooperation in this area. In operational law enforcement exchanges, as one of Europol's core activities, "intelligence" should be understood as information which needs further investigation by law enforcement authorities. A harmonised concept of communication channels between judicial bodies and police authorities should be developed to increase the speed and effectiveness of communication. Two issues, influenced both by the Europol Convention as a regional legal instrument and by the legislation of Europol's Member States as the equivalent national mechanism, are confidentiality and data protection. The attempt to harmonise different confidentiality regimes in order to establish a common approach for the confidentiality regime of Europol, based upon different "packages" of security measures valid for the four confidentiality levels at Europol, led partly to over-classification of information. On the other hand, the Europol Convention provides for a well-accepted standard of data protection that corresponds to the standard resulting from the implementation of the principles established by the Council of Europe.

Concerning implementation of the Chemical Weapons Convention and the monitoring of relevant chemicals and precursors under it, there have been several changes in the Convention's institutional and legal framework on the EU side since its opening for signature in January 1993. Even though the EU has, under the Treaty of Amsterdam, still not been endowed with legal personality, it is possible for the Council of Ministers, acting on behalf of the Member States, to conclude, in the realm of the common foreign and security policy, agreements with States or international organisations. At the time the Convention was negotiated and signed, the European Community was considered to have no competency in matters of foreign and security policy. In view of the European Community's exclusive competence for trade measures, a dispute arose between Council and Commission on whether Convention's trade-related provisions required European Community's participation in the Convention. The European Court of Justice clarified the border between common commercial policy, on the one hand, and foreign and security policy. The Court ruled that all import and export restrictions fall under the common commercial policy, irrespective of the particular reasons for which they were adopted. A so-called "dual-use Regulation" was adopted in the meantime, which the EU implements, for goods which are not exclusively of a military character, the obligations under different non-proliferation regimes, including the trade restrictions imposed by the Convention.

The Chemical Weapons Convention cannot be fully implemented unless States Parties adopt extensive national implementing legislation with respect to a whole range of aspects required by the Convention. The full implementation of the Convention provisions depends on the completeness of the implementing measures enacted by each State Party. Formulating the measures is problematic because, in a number of matters, the Convention does not adequately specify the scope of some of the relevant provisions in adequate detail, and does not give procedural guidance on monitoring criminal activities and matters dealing with penal sanctions. Consequently, a number of questions arise, for example, what constitutes "complete" implementation legislation. Only political willingness on the part of Member States can remove some of the inconsistencies. Different approaches are suggested to minimise the impact of non-uniform domestic enforcement: the OPCW Conference of States Parties should further clarify terms that are not sufficiently clear; time-limits for implementation should be set for obligations that have no deadline; the mandate of the National Authorities and their enforcement powers in relation to transboundary activities should be further clarified; and domestic implementing legislation should be harmonised.

Mónica Martínez

Rapporteur for Panel B.3 in the 2001 OPCW International Symposium; Associate Legal Officer, Special Assistant to the Deputy Registrar, International Criminal Tribunal for the former Yugoslavia (ICTY). The views expressed are not attributable to the ICTY, the United Nations or the OPCW.

TRANSBOUNDARY CRIMINAL ACTIVITY: THE ROLE AND ACTION OF THE EUROPEAN UNION

Jörn Sack*

1. Introduction

The first part of this chapter addresses the competencies of the European Community with respect to the Chemical Weapons Convention[1] ("Convention") and analyses the consequences the existence of such competencies have for the implementation of the Convention by European Union Member States. The second, and major, part of this chapter points out how the European Union is preparing to combat transboundary criminal activity.

2. The Chemical Weapons Convention and the European Union

Shortly after the opening for signature of the Chemical Weapons Convention in January 1993, the institutional and legal framework changed considerably on the European side. With the entry into force a few months later of the Treaty of the European Union (TEU or "Maastricht Treaty,")[2] the European Union (EU) was founded and given the objective[3] to assert its identity on the international scene, in particular through the implementation of a common foreign and security policy (CFSP), including the eventual framing of a common defence policy which might in time lead to a common defence.

Although the EU has even under the Treaty of Amsterdam[4] still not been endowed with legal personality, Article 24 of the Treaty on European Union (TEU) makes it possible for the Council to now conclude, in the realm of the common foreign and security policy, agreements with States or international organisations. Although the TEU is not explicit on this point, it is supposed that the Council is acting in such case on behalf of the Member States and not the EU (for its lack of legal personality). If the Chemical Weapons Convention were to be negotiated today, Article 24 of the TEU could therefore be used for securing the

---

* Legal Adviser of the European Commission. All views expressed in this paper are purely personal.

[1] 1993 Convention on the Prohibition of the Development, Production, Stockpiling and Use of Chemical Weapons and on Their Destruction, entered into force on 29 April 1997. Text, as corrected and changed, available at http://www.opcw.org.

[2] Treaty of the European Union, Maastricht, 7 February 1992, entered into force 1 November 1993 ("TEU"), OJ no. C 191, 29 July 1992, 1.

[3] Formerly Articles J. - J.18, now Articles 11-28 TEU.

[4] Treaty of Amsterdam amending the Treaty of the European Union, the Treaties establishing the European Communities and certain related Acts, Amsterdam, 2 October 1997, entered into force 1 May 1999. OJ no. C 340, 10 November 1997.

R. Yepes-Enríquez and L. Tabassi. (eds.), Treaty Enforcement and International Cooperation in Criminal Matters

adhesion of EU Member States under the cover of signature and approval by the EU Council.

At the time the Chemical Weapons Convention was adopted and opened for signature, the European Community (EC) was considered to have no competency in matters of foreign and security policy. Since 1970, however, there has been exclusive EC competence for trade measures (the common commercial policy (CCP)) and the internal market objective was nearly fully achieved on 1 January 1993. It was therefore disputed between Council and Commission whether the trade-related provisions of the Chemical Weapons Convention (Articles VI and XI) required EC participation in the Convention. As by that time no clear Court ruling was available as to the precise boundary between the common commercial policy (and/or internal market rules) on the one hand, and foreign and security policy on the other hand, and since it was too late anyway to seriously consider EC participation in the Convention, such participation was rejected. The Member States simply made a declaration upon signature and ratification of the Convention stating that they would implement the provisions of the Convention in conformity with their obligations under the Treaties establishing the European Communities.[5]

That means in practice that in certain cases EC, not national, measures would be adopted in order to comply with the Member States' obligations under the Convention and that, as contracting parties to the Convention, the Member States would not apply in their relations to each other measures inconsistent with the achievements of the internal market, albeit formally required by the Convention. In practical terms this declaration permits a result close to EC participation in the Convention, i.e., the EC is acting as a unity, even in the framework of the Convention. Shortly after this internal struggle about competencies, the long-desired clarification was received from the European Court of Justice with respect to the boundary between common commercial policy and foreign and security policy. In its judgments of 17 October 1995 in the *Werner* and *Leifer* cases[6] the Court ruled indeed that all import and export restrictions are coming under the common commercial policy irrespective of the particular reasons (e.g. for reasons of foreign and security policy) for which they were adopted. The judgments came not only too late for the conclusion of the Chemical Weapons Convention, but also for the adoption of the so-called dual-use Regulation by which the EC implements (for goods which are not exclusively of military character) the Member States' commitments under the different non-proliferation regimes, including the trade restrictions imposed by the Chemical Weapons Convention.

For that reason the text of the former dual-use Regulation[7] was based on Article 113 (common commercial policy, now Article 133 of the Treaty Establishing the European Community (TEC)), whilst the lists of goods and the regime applicable to the different countries, to which the Regulation applied, were adopted under the "second pillar" (the common foreign and security policy, i.e. Article J.3, now Article 13 TEU).[8] In the new dual-

[5] The declarations are drafted in identical terms. For example, Austria's declaration reads: "As a Member State of the European Community, the Government of Austria will implement the provisions of the [Convention] in accordance with its obligations arising from the rules of the Treaties establishing the European Communities to the extent that such rules are applicable."

[6] Cases C-70/94 and C-83/94, ECR 1995, I-3189 and I-3231.

[7] Regulation (EC) no. 3381/94, OJ no. L 367, p.1.

[8] Decision 94/942/CFSP, OJ no. L 367, p.8.

use Regulation,[9] which is applicable as from 29 September 2000, the substantial provisions *and* the lists were adopted on the basis of Article 133 TEC, i.e. the common commercial policy, and integrated into the Regulation.[10]

It should also be noted that, in the meantime, the EC signed the Protocol on the Illicit Manufacturing of and Trafficking in Firearms, their Parts, Components and Ammunition to the 2000 United Nations Convention Against Transnational Organised Crime, on the basis of Articles 95, 133 and 300(2) TEC.[11]

3. The European Union's Action Against Transboundary Criminal Activity

After this cumbersome, but necessary, explanation of the relations between the Convention and the EU's activities under the "first" (EC) and "second" (CFSP) pillars, we come to the so-called "third pillar", i.e. the EU's activities in the area of Justice and Home Affairs (JHA).

The "third pillar" has indeed been much strengthened by the Treaty of Amsterdam, to such extent that some of its most important subject matters (in particular immigration policy and harmonisation of civil law) have to a great part been shifted to the "first pillar" and are coming under EC competence now (Articles 61-69 TEC).

The EU activities in the criminal law area remain, however, in the third pillar (which works more or less in the same way as the second one, i.e., not by supranational integration mechanisms, but according to principles of reinforced intergovernmental cooperation, the role of the Court being, however, in the third pillar more important than in the second one, from which it is merely excluded).

The third pillar provisions are regrouped in Title VI of the TEU (Articles 29-42). There were two reasons for substantially enhancing the provisions on police and judicial cooperation in criminal matters: first, "globalisation" is not restricted to peaceful, in particular commercial activities, but is practised increasingly also by criminal gangs and can no longer be effectively combated by nation States acting individually. The terrorist attacks of 11 September 2001 made the globalisation of crime more than evident. Second, in the particular case of the EU, the abolition of border controls among the Member States would have induced a lower level of security inside the EU had it not been compensated by enhanced cooperation among the police and judicial authorities.

It was therefore really unavoidable that the Member States accepted to act henceforth in common in an area which is traditionally considered to belong to the hard core of national sovereignty.

Although the case of the EU is certainly a special one, the way Member States cooperate in this area can, to some extent, serve as a model, or at least an inspiring example, in the framework of international agreements which require cooperation among police and judicial authorities. It must be admitted, however, that the progress made so far is relatively modest, given that the Treaty of Amsterdam has been in force for just over three years.

[9] Regulation (EC) no. 1334/2000, OJ no. L 159, p.1.

[10] Furthermore, Common Action no. 2000/401/CFSP concerning the control of technical assistance for military purposes has been adopted on the basis of Article 14 TEU because transborder services involving travel of persons do not fall under the common commercial policy (OJ no. L 159, p. 216). Assistance by telephone, fax and electronic messages is, however covered by the Regulation because these services fall under the CCP.

[11] OJ no. L 280, p. 5 (16October 2001).

As the specific perspectives of Europol are presented in detail elsewhere in this book,[12] the following focuses on judicial cooperation. The objectives and the legal framework for police and judicial cooperation among EU Member States are first examined.

The aim is a very ambitious one, i.e. to create an area of freedom, security and justice by developing common action among the Member States in the field of police and judicial cooperation on criminal matters, thereby providing a high level of safety to the citizen (Article 29 TEU). "That objective shall be achieved by preventing and combating crime, organised or otherwise, in particular terrorism, illicit arms trafficking ... through closer cooperation between police forces, customs authorities and other competent authorities, both directly or through Europol, . . . and between judicial and other competent authorities of the Member States" (Article 29).

To that end, common action shall be taken in order to facilitate and accelerate cooperation among the judicial authorities in relation to proceedings and enforcement of decisions, extradition, to secure compatibility of national rules and to prevent conflicts of jurisdiction, to adopt progressively minimum rules relating to the constituent elements of criminal acts and to penalties in the field of organised crime, terrorism and illicit drug trafficking (the last task means in clearer and simpler words: harmonise in the areas mentioned national penal law). (Article 31 TEU).

Very important is Article 32, which provides for the establishment of rules laying down the conditions and limitations under which national authorities may operate in the territory of another Member State. Such extraterritorial action is certainly the highest degree of cooperation. Equally important are the working contacts that are being established between the relevant departments of the administration and judiciary in order to avoid the terribly time-consuming passage through central authorities or contact points (Article 34(1)). The last two objectives are probably too ambitious for classical intergovernmental organisations.

The main instruments available for action under Title VI are common positions which define the approach of the EU to a particular matter and are, in particular, used to determine the EU position in international organisations; framework decisions for the approximation of national laws and regulations (conceived like EC directives); decisions for any purpose except approximation of laws; and finally, conventions which have to be adopted according to the constitutional rules of Member States and which contain detailed and complex rules of law for a broad subject matter (Articles 34 and 37 TEU).

As under the "second pillar" (CFSP), the Council can conclude agreements with States and international organisations on behalf of the Member States (Article 38 TEU).[13] Closer cooperation among certain Member States is allowed (Article 40 TEU). Decisions are taken, in principle, by unanimity.

[12] See *supra* in this volume, W. Bruggeman, Europol, and, *infra* in this volume, H. Felgenhauer, Institutionalised Law Enforcement Cooperation through Europol.

[13] Cf. *supra*, section 2.

3.1 SCHENGEN IMPLEMENTATION AGREEMENT

The achievements in the field of judicial cooperation on criminal matters are still scarce, but a lot of work has already been done and is actually being done to produce, on short notice, far-reaching results. The core provisions of EU law in this area are still a heritage from the past and are to be found in Chapters II to VII (Articles 48 to 91) of Title III of the Schengen Implementation Agreement.[14] The Chapters are "Mutual assistance in criminal matters" (Articles 48 to 53), "Application of the *non bis in idem* principle" (Articles 54 to 58), "Extradition" (Articles 59 to 66), "Transfer of the execution of criminal judgements" (Articles 67 to 69), "Narcotic drugs" (Articles 70 to 76), and "Firearms and ammunitions" (Articles 77 to 91).

The legal network created is actually rather complex and is difficult to oversee, even for the insider, because the Schengen provisions, although they have now in large part been transformed into Community law under Protocol no. 2 of the Treaty of Amsterdam, are totally or partly not applicable to Denmark, Ireland and the United Kingdom according to other Protocols attached to the Treaty. Moreover, the Schengen provisions refer to the Conventions on judicial cooperation and on extradition concluded, respectively, in 1959 and 1957 in the framework of the Council of Europe.[15] They complement these Conventions.

Nevertheless, some important progress has been made. Judicial cooperation in the EU is not only comprehensive (i.e. covers all kind of legal proceedings), but operates also when the act committed is only punishable under the law of one Member State, contrary to the rule in most classical mutual assistance agreements that the act must be punishable under both the legal orders. For seizures and interrogations of suspect persons, the conditions are set slightly higher (Article 51). Acts of procedure can be directly notified to persons living on the territory of another Member State. However, translations have to be joined in case the language of the notifying State is not understood. Furthermore, no injunction can be imposed on people if simplified notification is used (Article 52).

Still more important is the fact that the competent authorities can communicate directly with one another without passing through the Ministries of Justice (Article 53).

Article 54 establishes the principle of *non bis in idem* principle at EU level,[16] and Article 55 allows only a very restricted number of exceptions to it by way of expressing a reservation (mainly cases involving State security or national officials). But even in such a case, time spent in prison in another Member State has to be taken into account in case of new proceedings and judgement.

For extradition, Schengen refers in general to the 1957 Council of Europe Convention on Extradition,[17] with special provision being made for France in Article 61 since it is not party to the 1957 Convention. Article 63 extends extradition on a number of taxation

[14] Convention of 19 June 1990, applying the Schengen Agreement of 14 June 1985 between the Governments of the States of the Benelux Economic Union, the Federal Republic of Germany and the French Republic, on the Gradual Abolition of Checks at their Common Borders, 1991 ILM 84.

[15] See *infra* in this volume, H.-J. Bartsch, Overcoming Obstacles in Achieving Wide Adherence to Multilateral Instruments: Some Comments from the European Perspective.

[16] For the first time, this principle was established among EC Member States' jurisdictions by a specific Convention concluded on 25 May 1987. It appeared already in a Council of Europe Convention of 15 May 1972.

[17] European Convention on Extradition, Paris, 13 December 1957, European Treaty Series no. 24.

matters (those strongly harmonised by EC law which are not covered by the 1957 Council of Europe Convention). For extradition, involvement of Ministries of Justice is still mandatory (except in France, which has appointed the Ministry of Foreign Affairs) (Article 65).

For transmission of the execution of judgments, reference is also made to a Council of Europe 1983 Convention on the Transfer of Sentenced Persons. It covers mainly cases where a national of one Member State who has been sentenced in another Member State has evaded justice and is later found in his home State. In such cases, even though extradition of nationals is, in most Member States, still not possible, the sentence can be executed in the home State, even against the person's will. Furthermore, the Member States had adopted in 1991 a Convention on the execution of panel judgements. Unfortunately, it contains rather outdated, i.e. complicated, mechanisms.

In this context one should also mention, although it belongs more to police cooperation, the Schengen Information System (SIS), which lists, *inter alia*, persons whom one Member State is searching for.

3.2 ACTION IN PROGRESS AND FUTURE MEASURES IN THE AREA OF JUSTICE AND HOME AFFAIRS

The Schengen Implementation Agreement contains only basic provisions which have to be complemented or replaced by more detailed and advanced rules. To that end, the special European Council devoted exclusively to JHA matters, on 15 to16 October 1999 in Tampere, invited the Commission to submit a "scoreboard", i.e., a time table for the adoption of future measures in the area. Mutual recognition of judicial decisions and judgments and the necessary approximation of legislation was given priority. The principle of mutual recognition should also apply to pre-trial orders (to secure evidence and seize assets). Evidence lawfully gathered by one Member State's authorities should be admissible before the courts of other Member States.[18] The Commission was asked to adopt, by December 2000, a programme of measures to implement the principle of mutual recognition. In this programme, work should be launched on a European Enforcement Order.

In fact, already in July 2000, the Commission transmitted a paper to the Council and on that basis a work programme was established. It provides *inter alia* for review of the exceptions to the *non bis in idem* principle of the Schengen provisions (abandonment of the exception based on the ground that facts occurred partially on the Member State's own territory), the taking into account of previous convictions in other Member States when sentencing a person (this measure could require a central register of penal judgements), harmonisation of data protection, mutual recognition of court orders to block bank accounts, conserving testimony, arrests, avoidance of multiple proceedings for the same facts, execution of fines and measures of confiscation.

Furthermore, the European Council urged Member States to ratify the 1995 and 1996 EU conventions on extradition. In this context it considered that the formal extradition procedure should be abolished between the Member States regarding persons who are fleeing from justice after having been finally sentenced in a Member State. A simple transfer of such persons should take place. Consideration should also be given to fast-track extradition procedures.

[18] Nos. 33 to 37 of the Presidency's conclusions.

In March 2000 the Commission had submitted to the Council and the European Parliament the requested "Scoreboard"[19] which covers action in the entire area of justice and home affairs. It provides *inter alia* for the ratification of the extradition conventions by April 2001, and by the end of 2001 for the establishment of accelerated extradition procedures as well as the envisaged simple transfer of persons.

Full mutual recognition of decisions and judgements in criminal matters shall be achieved, but no final date was given. The Convention on Mutual Assistance in Criminal Matters shall, however, be ratified and applied by April 2001.[20] Enhanced customs cooperation, in particular the establishment of a computerised information system (SID), is already on the point of being achieved.

An important achievement in the aftermath of the terrorist attacks of 11 September 2001 was the political agreement at the Laeken European Council (December 2001) on the mutual recognition of arrest warrants established by national courts in a wide area of international crime (including drug trafficking, terrorism and corruption). This landmark political decision has now to be implemented.

It is impossible to present in detail all the proposals or draft conventions on the table. Some major projects shall however be highlighted. In the first place, I would like to mention three central organs of cooperation (apart from the still more important role Europol plays).

3.3 CENTRAL ORGANS OF COOPERATION

(a) *The European Judicial Network*

The European Judicial Network is a common action adopted by the Council in 1998[21] to combat organised crime related to drug trafficking, terrorism, corruption and criminal gangs. Member States are obliged to designate central contact points in their countries where each of the other Member States can rapidly obtain information about the applicable law, the competent authorities and the procedures pending with respect to the criminal activities mentioned. In regular meetings, experience related to the fight against organised crime is exchanged. In the meantime, a European Network for criminal prevention in general has been established[22] which uses similar working methods.

(b) *Eurojust*

Eurojust, although decided in principle by the Tampere Summit,[23] remained a project for quite long time. Germany finally launched an initiative (proposal) in order to take the necessary measures to establish it.[24] On that basis the Council shall, within short notice, now take a decision. It provides for the establishment of a central unit of judges, public

[19] Doc. COM (2000) 167 final.
[20] Status: , OJ no. C 251, p. 1, of 2 September 1999.
[21] OJ no. L 191, p.4.
[22] OJ no. L 153, p.1 of 28 May 2001.
[23] No. 46 of the Conclusions.
[24] OJ no. C 206 of 19 July 2000, p.1. A first, more modest exchange of judges and public prosecutors had been decided by common action 96/277/JHA, OJ no. L 105, p.1.

prosecutors and high ranking police officers ("liaison officers") who shall support investigations against serious internal organised crime affecting several Member States and requesting action in each of them. They shall work in close coordination with Europol and OLAF (the EC office against fraud in EC finances). Furthermore they shall deliver access to national crime registration offices and consider the establishment of such an office at the European level.

(c) FADO

FADO is a European Image Achieving System which allows the exchange, by computerised means and within short notice, of information which Member States possess concerning genuine and false documents (in particular, images of false and forged documents, genuine documents, and summary information on forgery and security techniques).[25] This kind of information system could be of interest for an organisation like the OPCW.

3.4 DRAFT CONVENTIONS ON EXTRADITION AND MUTUAL LEGAL ASSISTANCE

The draft Convention on Extradition among the Member States of the European Union[26] again complements the existing instruments of the Council of Europe and the Schengen Implementation Agreement.

Noteworthy in particular is Article 5, which largely reduces the possibility for Member States to refuse extradition on the basis of the political exception (although it is allowed under the basic Conventions). Reservations made by Member States to Article 13 of the Council of Europe Convention for the Suppression of Terrorism are explicitly excluded under this Convention. Furthermore, contrary to amnesty (Article 9), prescription in the requested State is not a valid ground for refusal of extradition (Article 8). Extradition of a Member State's own nationals can only be refused if a reservation has been made in that respect (applicable five years only, but can be renewed). There is the possibility to declare generally approval for all incoming extradition requests and procedural streamlining in comparison with existing rules (Articles 11 to 16). Unfortunately, ratification of such conventions is a terribly time consuming process even in the European Union (average five to six years), which is a rather discouraging factor for other international agreements and organisations.

A draft Convention on Mutual Assistance in Criminal matters between the Member States of the EU has been published in the Official Journal of the European Communities in 1999.[27] It was not possible to adopt the text formally before 29 May 2000,[28] in order to submit it to the Member States for ratification, because a number of outstanding issues were strongly disputed, among them the interception of telecommunications, data protection and joint investigation teams. Again, this Convention supplements existing Council of Europe instruments and the Schengen Implementation Agreement. The new draft Convention confirms and eases the two important achievements of Schengen, i.e. the direct transmission of procedural documents to persons living in another Member State

[25] See Common action 98/700/JHA, OJ no. L 333, p.4.

[26] OJ no. C 313 of 23 October 1996, p.11. See detailed commentary in OJ no. C 191 of 23 June 1997, p. 13.

[27] OJ no. C 251, p.1 of 2 September 1999.

[28] OJ no. C 197 of 12 July 2000, p.1.

and the direct communication between competent authorities (Articles 5 and 6). Much emphasis is also laid on the so-called spontaneous exchange of information (i.e. communications relating to criminal offences exchanged without prior request from an interested Member State) (Article 7). The principal merit of the draft Convention lies, however, certainly in the introduction of modern and, in some cases, entirely new, instruments of cooperation, such as:

- speedy restitution of property obtained by criminal means to the rightful owner in another Member State (Article 8);
- temporary transfer of persons held in custody for purposes of investigation (Article 9), or, as an alternative solution, the hearing of that person by videoconference, even as accused, or by telephone conference (witnesses and experts only) (Articles 10 and 11);
- controlled deliveries (Article 12);
- joint investigation teams, including covert investigations (Articles 13 and 14). The team carries out its investigations in accordance with the law of the Member State in which it operates; the leadership may be taken by a member of another Member State. Information lawfully obtained may be used, not only for the purposes the team has been set up for, but also, subject to the prior consent of the Member State where the information became available, for detecting, investigating and prosecuting other criminal offences; and,
- interception of telecommunications (Articles 17 to 20). To obtain such interception the requesting Member State has to give a short summary of facts when recording is requested. This does not apply in case of immediate transmission. An indication of the criminal conduct under investigation is sufficient. The interception can take only place on the territory of another Member State. Without its technical assistance, it is allowed to proceed with the interception while informing the State. The latter may impose certain conditions or completely stop the action if it is not permissible under its own law.

One can only hope that this useful and innovative Convention will be speedily ratified by the Member States. The European Union has, in the mean time, adopted a number of other detailed measures, for example concerning money laundering, forgery of documents, etc., which space does not allow to be presented here.

INSTITUTIONALISED LAW ENFORCEMENT COOPERATION THROUGH EUROPOL

Harald Felgenhauer*

1. Introduction

The European Police Office (Europol) was established by the Member States of the European Union (EU) with a clear mandate: Europol's objective is to improve the effectiveness and cooperation of the authorities in the Member States of the European Union competent for preventing and combating serious forms of international organised crime. Since July 1999, when Europol took up its activities, Europol and the authorities in the Member States had to establish a multitude of procedures for the various modalities of international law enforcement cooperation provided by the Europol Convention.[1] While Europol officials work in accordance with the Europol Convention, due to the specific character of the European Police Office, they may never disregard the framework laid down by the national criminal law systems of the 15 Member States of Europol.

2. A Few Facts

Europol was set up under the Treaty of the European Union with a view to assist its Member States in preventing and combating organised crime. The legal basis for Europol's activities is the Europol Convention. The 'convention' is a legal act foreseen by Title VI of the Treaty of the European Union. In accordance with the intergovernmental structure of the so-called 'Third Pillar' of the European Union, concerning intergovernmental cooperation in the field of Justice and Home Affairs, the Europol Convention needed to be ratified by all Member States of the European Union in accordance with their respective constitutional requirements. As a consequence, the Europol Convention forms part of the national criminal law systems of the Member States. It can therefore be concluded that through its sheer existence, the Europol Convention had an effect on the national law systems of the Member States.

The intergovernmental character of cooperation in the Third Pillar requires that all decisions regarding Europol have to be reached unanimously. It follows that every decision on Europol needs to be in accordance with the interests of all 15 Member States of the European Union.

For a correct understanding of the tasks and possibilities of Europol it is also crucial to bear in mind that Europol does not possess any executive powers. Again, following the

---

* Europol Legal Affairs Unit. The views expressed reflect the opinion of the author and are not attributable to Europol.

[1] OJEC C 316, 27. 11. 1995, p.1.

R. Yepes-Enríquez and L. Tabassi. (eds.), Treaty Enforcement and International Cooperation in Criminal Matters

guiding principle of intergovernmental cooperation, Europol was designed as a service provider for the national law enforcement authorities.

When looking at the main services that Europol can provide, it instantly becomes clear that Europol mainly provides *information* for national law enforcement agencies. Europol deals both with operational and strategic information, as well as specialised knowledge, in the area of preventing and combating organised crime. Furthermore, Europol assists its clients in areas such as training, best practices, etc.

From what was said so far it is apparent that the utilisation of Europol's products always takes place in the Member States. National law enforcement authorities combine information and intelligence from Europol with the products of their own investigations. Consequently, national authorities adopt concrete measures to prevent and combat organised crime. The effectiveness of Europol can therefore only be measured along the lines of national law and national procedures.

3. The Modalities of Law Enforcement Cooperation Via Europol

As the centralised body for law enforcement cooperation within the European Union, Europol offers the following modalities of cooperation.

3.1 Cooperation between States

Europol provides the legal basis, as well as practical support, for direct cooperation between the Member States of the European Union. Information exchange between the Member States is based on the national legislation of the States involved and, as regards procedural aspects, the Europol Convention.[2] The task of bilateral exchange of information is taken care of by Liaison Officers seconded to Europol from the 15 Member States. Liaison Officers are answerable to their superiors in the law enforcement authorities of the Member States only. It is important to add that all activities of the Liaison Officers are based on their respective national law. Even though bilateral information exchange forms the main part of the Liaison Officers' work, they are also involved in operational projects run by Europol as well as in the exchange of strategic knowledge.

3.2 Cooperation between States and an International or Regional Organisation

Cooperation between States and an international or regional organisation is the main area of activity for Europol. Upon request by Member States or at its own initiative, Europol identifies areas of criminality that need to be tackled in a coordinated manner. One example of such coordinated activity by Europol are the Europol analysis projects. In the Analysis Work Files Europol stores, modifies, and utilises data on criminal offences. The data are supplied by the Member States, which are at all times closely involved in the analysis process. The results of the analysis are disseminated to the Member States to be utilised by their authorities.

Other tasks of Europol include the development of specialist knowledge of investigative procedures; the provision of advice on investigations; the provision of strategic intelligence;

[2] Article 5 of the Europol Convention.

assistance with and promotion of the efficient and effective use of the resources available at the national level for operational activities; and preparation of general situation reports.[3]

Another form of cooperation between Europol and States is the exchange of information between Europol and non-European Union Member States. In March 2000, the Council of the European Union tasked Europol to negotiate agreements on the exchange of operational and/or strategic information with 23 States. The first agreements between Europol and non-EU Member States entered into force in 2001. Following a detailed procedure stipulated by the Europol Convention and the implementing rules thereof, Europol is currently in the process of preparing further agreements. The cooperation agreements are tailored to the needs of Europol and the individual cooperation partner. When negotiating these agreements, both partners take into account their operational interests together with possible restrictions based on the relevant legal situation in the individual State and at Europol.

3.3 Cooperation between International Organisations

Finally, the Europol Convention foresees direct cooperation between international organisations. Europol concludes agreements with international law enforcement organisations such as Interpol and the World Customs Organisation. In addition, the Convention foresees cooperation with European Union-related bodies such as the European Central Bank, and European Commission.

Considering the different modalities of cooperation that Europol can offer, it becomes apparent that Europol was established as an umbrella organisation for different methods of international police cooperation. Europol's role as service provider for its Member States shows that direct information exchange with the authorities of the Member States is the main task for Europol. After the start of cooperation with non-EU States and bodies, however, Europol is able to offer an additional service. For non-EU States and bodies, Europol will become the easiest way to approach the European Union in a specific request for law enforcement assistance. The European Union has, in the world of law enforcement, finally got a single number to call.

4. Different Interests at the National and the Regional Level?

It can be taken from the specific character of Europol as a service provider for its Member States that Europol has to closely follow the opportunities and possible restraints provided for by national criminal law systems. It goes without saying that, in essence, national criminal law systems aim at protecting the *interests of the State* against threats originating from criminal activity. In the past few years, the fight against *organised* crime has become an area of increased activity for national lawmakers. Even though experts are still trying to find a generally accepted definition of this very phenomenon that has become an issue of global concern, there is one element that is not questioned at all: the transboundary dimension of organised crime. Having this attribute in mind, one might have doubts whether national law systems, designed to protect the interests of one single State, can provide all the tools necessary to efficiently combat organised crime.

[3] Article 3 of the Europol Convention.

Unilateral attempts to provide a better basis for the fight against organised crime are necessarily limited in their efficacy to the boundaries of national law systems. This is because they are intended to protect national law and to safeguard public order in a territory with common values and standards, shared cultural and legal traditions, and a uniform administration. Conversely, the complexity of international criminal organisations is not always mirrored by rudiments of the national fight against organised crime. International cooperation provides essential benefits for national investigators, but, then again, does not always provide the tools that are, for legal or practical reasons, indispensable for combating organised crime. Since 1999, the European Union Member States have a third option. In addition to the opportunity for international cooperation and ongoing efforts at the national level, the Europol Convention provides additional possibilities to amplify organised crime investigations to the regional level. Within Europe, this is clearly a new experience in the field of law enforcement. The effects of the parallel existence of the Europol Convention beside 15 national criminal law systems still need to be examined in detail. A few examples for specific effects that national criminal law systems can have on the functioning of a regional institution like Europol and vice versa, however, can already be mentioned.

5. Impact of National Criminal Law Systems on the Coordinated Fight Against Transboundary Crime

5.1 Procedural Aspects

In considering briefly judicial follow-up to law enforcement cooperation, it is a well known fact that, at the European level, the speed and effectiveness of cooperation between judicial authorities does not always correspond to the needs of police investigators. It is now generally accepted that judicial cooperation within the European Union needs to be brought to the same level where police cooperation stands today. Various efforts have been taken within the European Union to overcome the present situation. I only want to mention a few of them: first, a European Judicial Network was established to facilitate mutual legal assistance between the Member States. This concept, which finally led to the installation of Eurojust, follows the idea that central units responsible for a speedy exchange of requests on legal assistance (and the answers to these requests) are of pivotal importance. A different approach was taken with the European Convention on Mutual Legal Assistance, where national provisions on legal assistance are being harmonised. It is expected that the Convention will significantly improve the current situation.

After that short comment on the field of judicial cooperation, I want to return to impediments that still exist in the field of law enforcement. In the day-to-day work of Europol, for instance, the exchange of *operational* law enforcement information is one of the core activities. In this field it was perceived that national systems are not always prepared for the different categories of police information that are nowadays exchanged at the international level. Europol as an 'intelligence' organisation provides processed information that basically consists of additional knowledge on licit or illicit activities and intentions of criminals often not yet known to law enforcement authorities. 'Intelligence', as Europol understands it, is therefore 'information designed for action'. 'Action' refers to further investigative activity by law enforcement authorities and does not, dissimilar to 'evidence', include the use of information in judicial procedures. Obviously, the fact that this information may not yet be forwarded to judicial authorities without prior approval of the provider does not mean that the collection, analysis and exchange of intelligence is not based on strict rules — the Europol Convention, with its detailed provisions on data processing and data protection, is a compelling example of a thorough legal framework for intelligence work for law enforcement purposes.

Still, the fact that the exchange of intelligence is adequately delineated by law does not remove the necessity to have specific procedures in place. Intelligence work requires methods other than working on evidence. The understanding that police data must be treated differently from information used in court procedures, however, is not always reflected in national criminal law systems. As a guiding principle, law enforcement officers should be able to correspond directly with law enforcement officers in other States, and members of the judicial branch should have direct communication lines to judges and public prosecutors. The variety of different systems in the 15 Member States makes it difficult to streamline communication channels between national authorities. This is partly due to a lack of understanding concerning the needs of European-wide exchange of information, and partly due to the predominant role of judicial authorities in the field of exchange of police information. From the author's point of view, it is desirable that a harmonised concept of communication channels between judicial bodies on the one side and police authorities on the other should come into existence.

There are various forms in which Europol undertakes to facilitate information exchange between the 16 partners involved (Europol and 15 Member States). Because Europol follows the so-called 'multi agency approach,'[4] there are always a number of different players at the national level to be taken into account. One of the main efforts in this respect is the promotion of 'Handling Codes'. These codes shall accompany every single item of information exchanged via Europol in order to make it possible for the provider to stipulate precisely in what way the data can be used and who can have access to it. This will allow Member States to protect their operational interests. It also ensures that possible legal restrictions are complied with, while still making information available to investigators all over the European Union. As a very useful side benefit, over the years Europol will be able to learn about the main operational and legal concerns of the national authorities. It is aimed to report these experiences to Member States in order to enable them to consider amending their national procedures accordingly.

5.2 SUBSTANTIVE ASPECTS

Without going too much into detail of substantive national law, I want to mention two issues that are influenced both by the Europol Convention as a regional legal instrument and the legislation of Europol's Member States as the equivalent national mechanism.

[4] Europol cooperates with all public bodies existing in the Member States which are responsible under national law for preventing and combating criminal offences (Article 2(4) of the Europol Convention).

(a) Confidentiality

From the very beginning, it turned out to be difficult to find a common approach for the confidentiality regime of Europol. The starting point was the existence of — at that time — 12 national confidentiality regimes, some of them drafted along the lines of international, mainly military, organisations. In some Member States, the confidentiality rules were applicable to all bodies of the executive branch; other States had different systems in place for law enforcement, for the military, for state police, etc. In the course of the negotiations of the Europol Convention, it turned out to be impossible to create an independent standard for the information exchanged via Europol that would autonomously be valid in the Member States. The solution accepted in the end was the establishment of different 'packages' of security measures valid for the four confidentiality levels at Europol. The incorporation of national classifications into the Europol system — and vice versa — follows a 'table of equivalence'[5] which lists the relevant national classifications next to the Europol levels. Even though this system turned out to be generally well accepted by the Member States, some topics have been identified as causing concerns among practitioners:

- The impossibility of harmonising national levels leads to a lack of confidence in the security level applied to information, disseminated via Europol. It will take some more time before most investigators at the national level will be sufficiently informed about the safeguards in international law enforcement cooperation.
- It was already mentioned that national protective measures for confidential police information were not always regarded to be sufficient for state secrets. Even though the Europol confidentiality levels provide a high level of protection, there is not a sufficient number of confidentiality levels offered by Europol that would adequately mirror the amount of different levels foreseen by national systems.
- There is some concern that minor differences in the confidentiality standards of the 16 partners (Europol and 15 Member States) might lead, if information is transmitted to several agencies, to a change in the confidentiality level required.
- Where information from different sources is collected, as a main principle it is stipulated that the confidentiality level applied shall be at least as high as that applicable to the information protected at the highest level. Also, a group of information can be given a higher protection level than that of each of its parts. Even though the operational flexibility required shall be considered when choosing a security level, over-classification based on lack of information continues to be an impediment to the exchange of operational information.
- Differing concepts of confidentiality in the Member States hamper a common understanding of the confidentiality measures required. An inconsistent understanding of confidentiality (restrictions in the use of data), the nature of the data (intelligence or evidence) and restrictions in the use of data can occasionally be noticed.

---

[5] Annexed to the Rules on the confidentiality of Europol information, OJEC 1999/C26/02.

In conclusion, inconsistent interpretation of Europol's confidentiality regime led partly to overly classified information. As a result, difficulties arose sporadically in the transmission, storage and, finally, use of this information. The countermeasures taken by Europol include ongoing awareness programs and a systematic use of pre-set codes for confidentiality, restrictions in the use of data and evaluations of the source of the information.

On a more general basis, one should keep in mind that trusting the confidentiality regime of an international cooperation partner is often the starting point for further collaboration. Without the relevant confidentiality measures in place, even the most advanced instruments for cooperation will not be utilised by law enforcement practitioners.

(b) Data protection

It is generally recognised that the Europol Convention provides for a well-accepted standard of data protection. The drafters of the Europol Convention stipulated that for any data exchange via Europol the standard of data protection shall be applied that corresponds to the standard resulting from the implementation of the principles established by the Council of Europe.[6] In addition, Title VI of the Europol Convention ('Common provisions on data processing') stipulates detailed provisions for the collection, analysis and exchange of data by Europol. Several data protection principles incorporated in the Europol *aquis*, however, are not always fully mirrored in the data protection legislation applicable to national law enforcement authorities.

Even though these differences do not cause practical problems in the exchange of information between Europol and the Member States, it will be interesting to see whether the new data protection *aquis* of Europol will, in the long run, influence national systems. It is also feasible that the Member States, which are at the same time Europol's customers and Europol's superiors, will decide to keep their national traditions in this respect.

6. Conclusion

Changes to the Europol *aquis* in the last 12 months demonstrate that the development of Europol is still ongoing. As of 1 January 2002, Europol was made competent for nearly all forms of international crime. Preparations for Europol's participation in Joint Investigation Teams with Member States' officials is underway. Europol was also designated as overall coordinator for the exchange of law enforcement information on counterfeiting of the Euro currency. And, as one would expect, the events of 11 September 2001 had a major impact on the day-to-day work of Europol. As an immediate effect of the 11 September events, an Operational Counter Terrorism Crisis Centre was opened. It operates seven days a week on a 24-hour basis to monitor ongoing developments and to produce daily briefing papers. Furthermore, following the conclusions of the European Council of 20 September, a Counter Terrorism Task Force was set up at Europol.

As demonstrated by these latest developments, the young age of the European Police Office does not allow for conclusive statements on the effect of the parallel existence of the

---

[6] Council of Europe Convention of 28 January 1981, and Recommendation no. R(87) 15 of the Committee of Ministers of the Council of Europe of 17 September 1987 concerning the use of personal data in the police sector (Article 14 of the Europol Convention).

Europol Convention and the 15 national criminal law systems in the European Union. Nevertheless, Europol as an example for law enforcement cooperation at the regional level gives an illustration of the various improvements that can be achieved when lifting collaboration among States to an institutionalised level. It also highlights some complications involved in this process. What should not be forgotten, however, is that it is sometimes less problematic to change the legal basis of law enforcement cooperation than to adapt national procedures to the new opportunities provided. It will remain a key concern to further create a common awareness of the different modalities for international collaboration in the field of law enforcement. The awareness and acceptance of these modalities, however, are indispensable for revealing the full potential of national, regional and international tools in law enforcement cooperation.

DIVERGENT NATIONAL IMPLEMENTING LEGISLATION AND NON-UNIFORM IMPLEMENTATION: THREAT TO THE OBJECT AND PURPOSE OF THE CHEMICAL WEAPONS CONVENTION?

Mtshana M. Ncube*

1. Introduction

The Chemical Weapons Convention ("Convention"),[1] like most international treaties, cannot be fully implemented unless States Parties adopt national implementing legislation with respect to a range of its obligations. According to paragraph 1 of Article VII of the Convention, each State Party is obliged to enact legislation that shall specifically:

(a) Prohibit natural and legal persons anywhere on its territory or in any other place under its jurisdiction as recognised by international law from undertaking any activity prohibited to a State Party under this Convention, including enacting penal legislation with respect to such activity;

(b) Not permit in any place under its control any activity prohibited to a State Party under this Convention; and,

(c) Extend its penal legislation enacted under subparagraph (a) to any activity prohibited to a State Party under this Convention undertaken anywhere by natural persons, possessing its nationality, in conformity with international law.

In paragraph 2, Article VII further provides that "[e]ach State Party shall cooperate with other States Parties and afford the appropriate form of legal assistance to facilitate the implementation of the obligations under paragraph 1. In addition, provisions to control transboundary movement of the chemicals listed in Schedules 1, 2 and 3 of the Annex on Chemicals to the Convention are required under Parts VI(1), VII(31) and VIII(26) of the Verification Annex to the Convention. While the use of chemical weapons, including their use by terrorists, is an offence under customary international law, the transportation of scheduled chemicals across State boundaries for prohibited purposes is not covered by

* Special Adviser for Legal Affairs, OPCW Secretariat; former Deputy Legal Adviser, former Special Assistant to the OPCW Director-General for Legal Adviser. The views expressed are the author's own and do not necessarily reflect those of the OPCW. Gratefully acknowledged is the assistance received from Ralf Trapp, Donald Clagett, and John Makhubalo, all on the staff of the Secretariat of the OPCW., in drawing up the Table contained in Annex 1 to this book. As will be seen from the Table, some of the terms have been clarified by the OPCW Executive Council or Conference of States Parties. While acknowledging the assistance received, the author takes full responsibility for any errors and omissions in the information provided or in the analysis in this chapter.

[1] 1993 Convention on the Prohibition of the Development, Production, Stockpiling and Use of Chemical Weapons and on Their Destruction, entered into force on 29 April 1997. Text, as corrected and changed, available at http://www.opcw.org.

R. Yepes-Enríquez and L. Tabassi. (eds.), Treaty Enforcement and International Cooperation in Criminal Matters

customary international law. States Parties will need to adopt measures to prevent the use of chemical weapons and illegal transboundary movement of scheduled chemicals, treating these two aspects as closely related activities. The penal sanctions should complement the measures in terms of the degree of seriousness with which the offences are regarded, if enforcement of the Convention is to be efficient and effective.

1.1 THE PROBLEM

The 2000 Annual Report of the OPCW noted with concern that the number of States Parties that had enacted implementing legislation "had barely increased since its previous session.... At the end of 2000, fifty-three, or 38%, of States Parties had fulfilled their obligation under paragraph 5 of Article VII of the Convention."[2] This failure by States Parties is particularly significant because the extent of domestic implementing legislation required to implement the Convention is greater than is commonly required in the majority of treaties, notwithstanding the fact that such extent differs from treaty to treaty. In some treaties only a few provisions of comparatively minor administrative and procedural significance are required beyond the usual legislation by which the treaty as a whole is made applicable to the territory of the State Party.[3] There is no question but that the full implementation of the Convention provisions depends on the completeness of the implementing measures enacted by each State Party. Formulating the measures is problematic because the Convention does not adequately define the parameters of the relevant provisions, nor does it provide procedural guidance on monitoring criminal activities and on the types of penal sanctions to be imposed with respect to those criminal activities. There is also the problem that the Convention is silent on whether the implementing legislation should be uniform in content across States Parties. Last but not least, the Convention gives no deadline by which the implementing legislation should be reported to the OPCW, in terms of paragraph 5 of Article VII. These facts are an important part of the problem why many States Parties to the Convention have not yet enacted their implementing legislation.

Consequently, a number of questions arise: what constitutes "complete" implementing legislation; is uniformity of provisions in all States Parties an essential ingredient in such completeness; and how is it to be measured and achieved? One of the conclusions in this chapter is that, while uniformity and consistency is important for non-discriminatory implementation, it will be difficult, if not impossible, to achieve these on account of the Convention's own lack of precision and prescriptive guidance on these issues. This lack of precision and prescriptive guidance creates conditions for non-uniform legislative measures in the different States Parties and non-uniform domestic enforcement, with the real possibility that down the road some States Parties may not comply and will escape responsibility.

---

[2] Annual Report 2000, at 40; Report of the OPCW on the implementation of the Chemical Weapons Convention in the year 2000, OPCW doc. C-VI/5 (17 May 2001) at 5.1- 5.2.

[3] The United Nations Charter, 24 October 1945, is the best example of a treaty in which actions required of UN Member States are not contingent upon prior domestic implementing legislation. See such Articles as 43 and 45 of the Charter. This is true also of the Vienna Convention on the Privileges and Immunities of the United Nations, 13 February 1946. Distinction should be drawn between such treaties and those that are not intended to have municipal effects, such as treaties of neutrality.

The completeness and correctness of implementing the measures adopted by States Parties will depend largely on how closely States Parties understand the provisions of Article VII.[4] To a lesser extent, they will also depend on how soon subsidiary bilateral treaties between each State Party and the Organisation,[5] and bilateral agreements between States Parties themselves,[6] are concluded. Although in practice, not many treaties require Member States to enact extensive domestic implementing legislation, the ones that do generally fall into three main categories.

The first category consists of those treaties that require complementary implementing legislation to allow monitoring and reporting, but with the legislation not extending to penal measures. Examples of this category are the Basel Convention on the Control of Transboundary Movements of Hazardous Wastes and Their Disposal (1992) and the Prior Informed Consent Procedure for Certain Hazardous Chemicals and Pesticides in International Trade (PIC).[7] Although these treaties require States Parties to enact municipal implementing legislation, it is significant that they do not specifically call for penal measures. Moreover, the measures are wholly focused internally with regard to violations, and make no positive requirement to criminalise any breaches, let alone require States Parties to exercise extraterritorial jurisdiction.[8] In this situation, divergences in municipal legislation of States Parties on how to translate verification terms into legislation, and what types of offences, penalties and procedures to include are of little consequence in the implementation process.

The Chemical Weapons Convention and the Comprehensive Nuclear-Test-Ban Treaty (CTBT) belong to the second category. Beyond monitoring and reporting, these treaties require that States Parties apprehend and punish offenders under domestic law, but do not define precisely what constitutes a crime and the penal sanctions thereof.[9] Although the CTBT does not specifically call on its States Parties to enact penal measures in their implementing legislation, such is implicit as a corollary to the prohibitions that the municipal legislation must implement.[10] The mandate to States Parties under the Convention to monitor, report or apprehend and punish, rests not in provisions of the Convention itself, but in measures States Parties themselves must adopt. The Convention does not give guidance on the content of the legislation, particularly as to the degree of comprehensiveness, the type of liability (criminal or civil), the modes of punishment, or

[4] The requirements of Article VII and paragraph 2(e) of Article XI of the Convention. The latter requires States Parties "...to review their existing national regulations in the field of trade in chemicals in order to render them consistent with the object and purpose of the Convention".

[5] Paragraphs 34 and 39 of Article VIII, and Section E of Article VIII and Section B of Part II of the Verification Annex, both parts dealing with the conclusion of privileges and immunities agreements between States Parties and the OPCW.

[6] These may be concluded between States Parties as foreseen in paragraphs 6 and 7 of Article X of the Convention.

[7] The Treaty on the Non-Proliferation of Nuclear Weapons (NPT) 1970, and the Customs Co-operation Council (CCC) 1952 (working name is World Customs Organization (WCO)) have passive provisions on how States Parties will manifest their adherence to the obligations. Forbearance not to carry out certain activities is adequate (NPT Articles I, II, and III), and a benign expectation not to breach certain other obligations is also considered adequate (NPT Articles IV, V, VI, and VII). Domestic implementing legislation raises, if at all, only minimal jurisdictional issues.

[8] See Articles 4 to 10 of the Basel Convention, and Article 11 of PIC. There is no reference to criminal sanctions in paragraph 9 of the Basel Convention on the illegal traffic of hazardous waste.

[9] See Article VII of the Convention.

[10] See Article III of the CTBT.

the extent of penalties. States Parties cannot therefore be expected to know precisely what measures to enact, and whether such measures should be uniform and consistent in all respects with those enacted by other States Parties.

In the final category are treaties that not only define the offences and penal sanctions, but also confer extraterritorial jurisdiction to apprehend and punish offenders. They are best exemplified by the United Nations Convention Against Transnational Organized Crime (UNCATOC) and its two Protocols,[11] and the Rome Statute of the International Criminal Court (ICC Statute).[12] The provisions in both these Conventions are instructive for purposes of the argument in this chapter. Unlike the provisions of the Convention, those of the UNCATOC and the ICC Statute are comprehensive enough on the type of liability, offences, penal sanctions, and procedures so that the additional municipal implementing legislation required of each State Party is unlikely to be divergent, at least not in the essential elements. For example, under the general obligations of States Parties to cooperate (Article 86 of the ICC Statute), the requests for cooperation made by the ICC to States Parties are governed by a set of stated principles and procedures (Article 87). Article 88 provides that all States Parties "shall ensure that there are procedures available under their national law for all of the forms of cooperation which are specified under this Part." In other words, the implementing legislation in this particular respect has to meet *set requirements* under the ICC Statute — the specified forms of cooperation. Under such guidance, there is little or no room for a lack of clarity, significant divergence, and absence of uniformity in the implementing legislation by States Parties.

1.2 THE PURPOSE OF THIS CHAPTER

This chapter aims to serve two purposes. The first is to assist in persuading States Parties to the Chemical Weapons Convention, OPCW policy-making organs and the OPCW Secretariat that clarification of certain unclear, problematic or disputed terms and concepts in the Convention, through the issuance of "understandings," will minimise the possibility of inconsistent legislation and non-uniform implementation and enforcement. The second objective of this chapter is to provide States Parties with reference points they may use in preparing implementing legislation in the absence of "understandings," "clarifications," "changes," or amendments to the Convention. The reference points take the form of explicit elements that each State Party should consider as an absolute minimum (offences, penalties and procedures) to be included in the implementing legislation.

2. Applying the Convention to the National Territory

The problem with most treaties is that, regardless of the legal system, ratification or accession alone is never sufficient to make a treaty fully operational. Nor is mere incorporation after

[11] The United Nations Convention Against Transnational Organized Crime, opened for signature on 12-15 December 2000 in Palermo, and its two Protocols: Protocol against the Smuggling of Migrants by Land, Sea and Air, and the Protocol to Prevent, Suppress and Punish Trafficking in Persons, Especially Women and Children.

[12] 1998 Rome Statute of the International Criminal Court, entered into force 1 July 2002; UN doc. A/CONF.183/9*, as corrected by the procès-verbaux of 10 November 1998 and 12 July 1999. Corrected text available at http://www.un.org/law/icc.

ratification or accession, even for States Parties whose treaties automatically become law upon ratification or accession. In that regard, Chief Justice Marshall said of the United States of America:

> Our constitution declares a treaty to be the law of the land. It is, consequently, to be regarded in the courts of justice as equivalent to an act of the legislature, *whenever it operates of itself, without the aid of any legislative provision*. But when the terms of the stipulation import a contract — when either of the parties engages to perform a particular act, the treaty addresses itself to the political, not judicial department; and the legislature must execute the contract before it can become a rule for the Court [emphasis added].[13]

In terms of the distinction in the foregoing quotation, the Convention is indeed like a "contract" in Chief Justice Marshall's sense above, because it is dependent on prior action (implementing legislation) by States Parties before it can fully take effect. And with respect to the subject of this chapter, it is safe to say that the differences in legal systems are not of much significance. Lord McNair observes that:

> Those treaties which do not require any legislation to make them operative are sometimes referred to as 'self-executing'. It seems that Congress has been so prompt to pass legislation for the implementation of treaties that there have been very few opportunities of judicial determination of the question which treaties actually require legislation, and which do not, and it does not follow that, because legislation was passed to implement a treaty, the legislation was essential."[14]

In the case of the Chemical Weapons Convention, legislation is indeed essential in order for States Parties to be able to implement fully the Convention because that treaty has, unwisely or not, specifically left that task to States Parties. With the treaty 'delegating' this task to a large number of independent authorities with differing legal systems and legislative approaches, one cannot expect adoption by States Parties of uniform legislation, applying with equal validity in their domestic spheres as well as extraterritorially, when the yardsticks are not provided. The resulting implementing provisions by the different States Parties cannot possibly be the same in scope, content and meaning for every State Party. The foundation of good legislation from a technical point of view is its ability to address all the essential issues; to provide the legislative support for the policy; and, where necessary, to put in place anticipatory measures for fulfilling the policy. As already pointed out, the Convention does not provide many of the necessary specifics indicating the essential elements of what should be the content of the implementing legislation under each obligation. The elements to be covered by the implementing legislation are not listed. The "set requirements" of Articles 86 to 88 of the ICC Statute are a good example of how the Convention ought to have framed its requirements in 'delegating' the task of enacting implementing legislation to States Parties. Such a list would have guaranteed concordance in the provisions of the implementing legislation among States Parties.

---

[13] *Foster v. Neilson* (1829), quoted in McNair, The Law of Treaties, 80 (1961).

[14] McNair, The Law of Treaties, 80 (1961).

Parenthetically, it should be noted that, even if the Convention provisions lack clarity as to the finer aspects of the content of the implementing legislation, such lack of clarity is not available as a defence to a State Party seeking to avoid its obligations under the Convention. Nor is it possible for a State Party to avoid its obligations on the ground of reservations. The Convention excludes reservations, except with respect to Annexes where reservations may be entered so long as they are not incompatible with the object and purpose of the Convention.[15] In any case, all States (including those in which "certain treaties automatically acquire municipal effect and, for that purpose, supersede existing laws and existing treaties"[16]) are bound by the principle of international law that "[i]t is the duty of a party to a treaty to see to it that its municipal law enables it to give effect to the treaty and that its organs — executive and judicial — are properly equipped with the powers required for that purpose...."[17] In the words of Lord McNair, "no State can plead a deficiency in its municipal law or organisation against a complaint of a breach of a treaty obligation or of a rule of customary international law."[18] However, in relation to the argument in this chapter, the fact that States Parties may not avoid their obligations does not remove performance difficulties, including failure to perform. The difficulty of performance, resulting from the lack of clarity and comprehensiveness in the Convention provisions, is a major hurdle in the efforts of States Parties to adopt implementing legislation that meets the criteria of good legislation addressing all the essential issues.

3. Lack of Clarity in Scope and Meaning of some Provisions in the Convention

The provisions of some articles of, and annexes to, the Convention are relevant to implementing legislation and lack sufficient clarity in either meaning or scope, or both, for States Parties to be able to enact exhaustive as well as uniform and concordant implementing legislation. There is a lack of clarity in Article VII terms specific to the process of adopting the requisite national implementing legislation. This absence of clarity of specific legislative requirements, at one level or another, falls into two categories: (a) terms whose meaning and scope are not clear because there is no adequate guidance as to the extent of the action required; and (b) the absence of provisions necessary to determine certain courses of action. Annex 1 to this volume provides the categories, as well as examples under each category, of the terms in question.[19] The Annex is divided into three sections, the first of which shows examples of verification related terms which lack clarity both with respect to declaration and production thresholds and the control of transfers of scheduled chemicals. The second section shows examples of concepts related specifically to legislation which are not provided, or of terms which are not precise. All of them have a bearing on what provisions should be put in the implementing legislation. The third section contains terms that the author believes should be referred to the OPCW Review Conference, to be convened in 2003.

---

[15] Article XXII of the Convention.

[16] McNair, *supra* note 14, at 79

[17] *Id.*, at 78.

[18] *Id.*

[19] The list is not exhaustive. However, it represents the majority of the terms. As the reader will see, the OPCW Conference of States Parties has clarified some of the terms and is expected to clarify others in the future. The problem is that the future is ahead of us. In the meantime, States Parties need guidance if they have to adopt consistent, non-discriminatory, implementing legislation.

When the lack of clarity in the provisions of Article VII, and others relevant to implementing legislation in the Convention, is coupled with the fact that there is a lack of clarity in some terms employed with respect to the verification process and confidentiality requirements, and which have a bearing on legislation, adopting the requisite national implementing legislation is proving for some States Parties to be a daunting task indeed. Clearly, mere incorporation of the Convention into national law is insufficient to give effect to all the prohibitions in the Convention because Article VII and other relevant provisions:

(a) do not give a timeline by which the implementing legislation should be in place;

(b) do not provide fully for the different considerations to be taken into account with respect to preparing and making declarations;

(c) do not define adequately the meanings of certain terms — whose meanings are crucial in defining the actions to be taken, including what sort of provisions should be put in the implementing legislation with regard to reporting activities relevant to the Convention;

(d) do not specify the quantity thresholds to adopt, particularly in relation to what shall be the low concentration levels for mixtures of certain scheduled chemicals when transferred;

(e) do not say which of the behaviour to be prohibited should be criminalised, and whether non-criminal breaches by "natural and legal persons" were contemplated, or whether any breaches by "natural and legal persons" could be dealt with in the same way as those by States Parties themselves under Article XII or some other civil proceedings;

(f) do not indicate what should be the basis for defining a crime with respect to the Convention;

(g) do not provide the rules and procedures to apply to arrests and extradition, collecting, processing and presenting evidence, the admissibility of evidence, the compellability of witnesses, the desirability or otherwise of adopting a statute of limitation for crimes; and,

(h) do not say whether uniformity with respect to types and levels of punishment across national boundaries and within domestic practice is an essential element in determining whether a State Party has met its obligations under Article II and related provisions.

3.1 THE ABSENCE OF A TIMELINE FOR ENACTMENT OF IMPLEMENTING LEGISLATION

Neither Article VII nor any other provision of the Convention requires States Parties to have implementing legislation by a set date. There is therefore a tendency among some States Parties to consider implementing legislation as less important than other activities that do have deadlines stipulated by the Convention. This may explain why, in the sixth year after entry into force of the Convention, only 60 States Parties (as of 31 May 2002) have informed the OPCW that they have adopted some form or other of implementing legislation. There is no specific sanction in the Convention for late adoption of implementing legislation. In the light of the limitations in the sanctions in paragraphs 2, 3 and 4 of Article XII, it would appear that those measures were not intended for this kind of non-compliance.[20]

The absence of a timeline for the enactment of implementing legislation negatively affects the verification regime, and does not do much for confidence-building among States Parties. The OPCW Conference of States Parties should adopt an "understanding," providing a timeline of one year from the date of the "understanding" for States Parties already on board, and one year after entry into force for States joining later.

3.2 LEGISLATIVE IMPLICATIONS FROM LACK OF CLARITY OF CERTAIN TERMS IN THE CONVENTION

Quite obviously, it is not sufficient for implementing legislation to merely list the prohibited activities specified in Articles I and Parts VI, VII and VIII of the Verification Annex and set penalties for violations thereof. 'Ranking' the prohibitions in terms of their seriousness, and specifying respective penalties for their violation, is essential. This has to be done in accordance with the interpretation of the specific provisions of the Convention, the spirit of the Convention, and the usual rules by which penalties are normally assigned for breaches of laws and regulations. However, the problem is that Article VII, on which this assessment is supposed to be based, is silent on too many legislative instructions, including the likely seriousness of each offence. There is also no guidance on how the necessary bodies referred to in the Convention may be set up, which also affects implementation, as will be seen in the subsequent section on the National Authority.

3.3 THE NATIONAL AUTHORITY

Article VII, paragraph 4, requires each State Party to designate or establish a National Authority to serve as the national focal point for effective liaison with the OPCW and other States Parties. In practice, these National Authorities serve as the mechanism through which compliance is achieved and demonstrated. Many of them have been tasked with the preparation of national implementing legislation. In any request for cooperation and legal assistance for the prevention or prosecution of a violation of the Convention, it is clear that the National Authority would need to work closely with the police, customs and/or the Ministry of Justice to fulfil that request.

Compliance with this obligation is, however, less than perfect. At an OPCW Workshop on legislative issues held in Swaziland, of the eight States Parties represented, only two had *formally* established National Authorities, inadequacies in the legislation notwithstanding. It emerged from the discussions at the workshop that the concept and functions of a National Authority among States Parties in the Southern African Development Community (SADC) region were not yet fully appreciated.[21] Many of the functions of the National Authority are currently carried out on an ad hoc basis by a ministry or a group of appointees. In some States Parties, some of the procedures relating to declarations were still to be put in place by the ad hoc National Authorities. The majority of the participating States Parties

[20] It is one more example of poor drafting that is evident in parts of the Convention.

[21] Report on the Regional Workshop on Implementing Legislation and International Cooperation Issues, Mbabane, Swaziland, 28 - 30 November 2000, OPCW doc. S/250/2001 (22 March 2001).

at the Swaziland workshop did not have declarations and reporting procedures for both State and industry related chemical activities. Several reasons were given for this situation. For some the task of preparing legislation is too time-consuming — taking away precious few resources from more urgent priorities. Others indicated that the process was too complex and they did not have the expertise to follow the Convention and its legislative requirements. Yet others were concerned that trying to meet the Convention legislative needs may conflict with legislation already in place with respect to activities related to chemicals or dangerous goods. Annex 1 lists declaration-related terms that were not clear, but which have since been clarified, and those that still remain to be clarified.[22]

Some of the reasons given by States Parties for not enacting the necessary legislation are that the States Parties are focusing on identifying declarable industry before addressing the practical aspects of controlling scheduled chemicals; the complexity of the legislation and competing legal demands internally; and the search for establishing mechanisms of control that do not interfere or conflict with other international conventions or existing national legislation.[23] In general, among all States Parties, the reasons for not enacting legislation timely are more or less the same as those given during the Swaziland Workshop. The complexity and lack of clarity of some terms in the Convention is one of them.

One OPCW Secretariat discussion paper documents the fact that the aggregate national data of imports and exports of Schedule 2 and Schedule 3 chemicals declared by States Parties during 1999, as required by respective paragraphs 1 of Parts VII and VIII of the Verification Annex, "do not match in 70 — 80% of the declared cases."[24] Even the basic requirement to submit an initial declaration not later than 30 days after the Convention enters into force for each State Party, poses difficulties for some States Parties. As of 27 June 2002, out of 145 States Parties, three had still to submit their initial declarations and 11 others had submitted incomplete initial declarations. These 14 are clearly in violation of the Convention. For still other States Parties, it was not clear, and may still not be clear, what exactly is to be declared under certain verification provisions. The OPCW Conference of States Parties has had to issue several "understandings" in order to provide, as far as possible, a common meaning for terms and processes referred to in the Convention and affecting declarations.[25] Furthermore, because the Convention does not harmonise the provisions regarding Schedule 2 and Schedule 3 chemicals in low concentrations, a "consistent and non-discriminatory and effective implementation of the Convention" was impossible. To this end, the Conference of the States Parties issued guidelines on low concentration

---

[22] See Annex 1, *infra*, paragraphs 1-39.

[23] OPCW doc. S/269/2001, 6-7 (16 August 2001).

[24] Discussion Paper: Declaration of Imports and Exports of Schedules 2/3 Chemicals, OPCW doc. EC-XXIII/S.1, 1 (12 January 2001).

[25] See paragraph 15 of the Table contained in Annex 1 *infra*. By decision C-I/DEC.39 (16 May 1997), the OPCW Conference of States Parties at its First Session agreed that the term "unscheduled discrete organic chemical" and the term "PSF-chemical" do not cover "oligomers and polymers, whether or not containing phosphorous, sulfur or fluorine"; "chemicals only containing carbon and metal." The decision also refers to essential elements in relation to declaration thresholds for each element. See also paragraph 21 of the Table contained in Annex 1 *infra*. In decision C-I/DEC.40 (16 May 1997), the Conference of States Parties defined the new term "mixed plants"(not in the Convention) as "plants which are individually covered under more than one Part of the Verification Annex related to Article VI. The term covers, for example, a multipurpose plant that manufactures, in the same process line but at different points in time or parallel in several process lines, Schedule 2 and Schedule 3 chemicals (and/or DOCs)."

limits for declarations for these chemicals, stating that "declarations are not required for mixtures of chemicals containing 30 percent or less of a Schedule 2B or a Schedule 3 chemical." The Conference attached to that "understanding" an instruction to States Parties "to take measures in accordance with Article VII, paragraph 1, to implement these guidelines by 1 January 2002."[26] Other understandings in this regard have been adopted by the Conference, for example, changes to annual declarations on anticipated activities required under paragraph 4(c) of Parts VII and VIII of the Verification Annex.[27] The same problem has arisen with respect to the low concentration declaration threshold for Schedule 2A* with the result that States Parties have different legislation on the issue. One State Party has enacted legislation setting the declaration threshold for Schedule 2A* at 1% while another has set it at 30%.[28] A threshold of 1% requires chemical industrial companies to constantly declare, while a 30% threshold relieves most companies from the obligation to report their activities. It is undoubtedly a discriminatory implementation of the Convention, and one that needs to be resolved quickly in order to achieve an even application of the Convention and an even burden on the chemical industry of States Parties.

3.4 INADEQUATELY DEFINED TERMS IN GENERAL

There are other areas, such as the regime of transfer of scheduled chemicals, which would benefit from intervention by the Conference of the States Parties. Clarity on what constitutes an acceptable low concentration limit with respect to Schedule 2 and Schedule 3 chemicals would result in non-discrimination among States Parties with respect to the transfer of those chemicals. On the basis of the "understandings" adopted, and the recommendations contained in Annex 1, States Parties are urged to revise, streamline, or adopt provisions in their legislation which do not conflict with those of other States Parties.

The Conference decision on "Guidelines Regarding Low Concentration Limits for Declarations of Schedule 2 and 3 Chemicals"[29] is, in reality, more than a matter of low concentration limits for declaration purposes: it is more an issue to do with uncertainties among States Parties about whether the adequacy of existing controls on Schedule 3 chemicals are adequate in relation to transfers. While the provision in paragraph 27 of Part VIII of the Verification Annex was meant to keep issues like the above open for review when five years implementation experience has been gained, that does not remove the problem of how to deal with the issue in the implementing legislation pending the review. In the meantime, the fears and suspicions generic in this field will continue, and tend to dampen enthusiasm among some States Parties for enacting implementing legislation. In some ways, the uncertainties act as a restraint on those that are less certain. The interesting fact to note is that in some draft legislation, Schedule 2 and Schedule 3 chemicals are treated as if they were not different with respect to their use and the potential threat each may pose to the object and purpose of the Convention.[30] The drafters of the Convention could have been clearer in the intended distinctions, and why.

---

[26] OPCW doc. C-V/DEC.19 (19 May 2000).
[27] OPCW doc. C-I/DEC.38 (16 May 1997).
[28] OPCW doc. S/269/2001, 12 (16 August 2001).
[29] OPCW doc. C-V/DEC.19 (19 May 2000).
[30] OPCW doc. S/269/2001, 8 (16 August 2001).

The sooner clarifications of these other terms are made, the easier the legislative process will be. There are two examples in this category: the transparency requirements of Article X, and the 'trade versus proliferation' issue of Article XI. The transparency requirements of Article X oblige States Parties to provide to the Secretariat annually information on their programmes for protective purposes. Paragraph 4 of Article X states:

> For the purposes of increasing the transparency of national programmes related to protective purposes, each State Party shall provide annually to the Technical Secretariat information on its programme, in accordance with procedures to be considered and approved by the Conference pursuant to Article VIII, paragraph 21(i).

The Conference has not decided on the procedure, nor indicated the required degree of disclosure. In the absence of an agreed 'level of disclosure,' it would seem from the language of paragraph 4 that States Parties should make full disclosure on the nature of the protective programme. At present, two opposing positions persist in the Organisation with respect to transparency in connection with national programmes for protective purposes. Proceeding with contradictory legislation from States Parties in accordance with their preferred declaration stance undermines the integrity of the implementation process and impacts confidence building among States Parties.

Another issue of similar importance is raised by paragraph 1(d) of Article I, which some States Parties interpret to mean that trade barriers ought to go up in order not "[t]o assist, encourage or induce, in any way, anyone to engage in any activity prohibited to a State Party..." — i.e. limiting trade will prevent proliferation — and Article XI, which encourages economic and technological development through trade among States Parties for peaceful uses of chemistry. The "anti-proliferation" States Parties argue that they need to first see the genuine implementation of the Convention on this issue before they will lift trade barriers. Such divergent positions cannot but lead to completely contradictory implementing legislation.

With regard to implementing legislation, the degree of seriousness of the above issues should be judged in the light of the fact that less than 50% of Member States have submitted their legislation, and that nearly 40% of that legislation has significant gaps. This means additional measures or complete redrafting, at the expense of the States Parties in terms of time, money and personnel resources if the competing positions have to be reconciled.

Furthermore, in the absence in Article VII of a stipulated list of elements to be covered and the absence of a stipulation that the legislation must be uniform, States Parties are having to second guess what standard the treaty drafters may have had in mind. The result is that, on matters of substance, there are as many versions of implementing legislation as there are States Parties that have submitted their legislation, with perhaps more variations expected from those that have still to enact legislation. Some important elements are left out. The inconsistencies can potentially create compliance problems.

3.5 LEGISLATION-RELATED TERMS/CONCEPTS NOT PROVIDED OR NOT PRECISE

There are additional terms that need explaining, elaboration, or qualification if implementing legislation is to approach uniformity of content and application. These terms relate specifically to Article VII of the Convention. There is one aspect relating to Section E of Article VIII on privileges and immunities. In this connection, there is still a question as to what protections or level of cooperation will be granted to police, customs or judicial officials who need to investigate suspected violations of the Convention in the territories of other States Parties. There are other issues relating to the meaning to be assigned to legislation-related terms or concepts that are either not precise, or are not provided:

(a) "in conformity with international law" in Article VII(1)(c);

(b) "afford the appropriate form of legal assistance..." in Article VII(2);

(c) "cooperate as appropriate with other States Parties..." in Article VII(3);

(d) "offence" under the Convention;

(e) whether there is any civil liability under the Convention, and for which wrongful acts;

(f) nature of liability and penalties for breach of policy on confidentiality (paragraph 10 Confidentiality Annex), and whether "penalties" referred to in paragraph 10 are distinct from the "appropriate punitive and disciplinary measures..." which the Director-General is authorised to take under paragraph 20 of the Confidentiality Annex to the Convention.[31] Also, should the same scale of punishment for OPCW staff members should apply to individuals in States Parties;

(g) how a violation of the Confidentiality Annex by industry is to be dealt with in regard to sanctions;

(h) "penal sanctions" in relation to the "offences" under the Convention;

(i) a scale of sanctions; and,

(j) procedures for investigations and arrest.

It is not the intention here to discuss each of the listed terms or phrases as to why they are not properly defined. Some key ones like "conformity with international law" are dealt with in some detail. Terms relating to offences and penal sanctions are discussed under the relevant sections.

The phrase "conformity with international law" is less illuminating than a cursory glance may suggest because no prior setting and context is given in the Convention for its application. The principles of international criminal law are not yet widely accepted. There is as yet no complete body of knowledge *on all aspects* universally acknowledged as international criminal law. It is only beginning to emerge. As United Nations Legal Counsel Hans Corell has noted: "The principle of the territoriality of penal law, namely that a State may, in principle, try only crimes committed in its own territory, has traditionally been among those most steadfastly held by States. The exceptions to this principle have always been very restrictive."[32] To what international law would States Parties be "conforming"? Do all States Parties accept the recent development in this nascent field of international criminal

[31] See *supra* in this volume, C. Sanhueza Bezanilla, The Chemical Weapons Convention Confidentiality Regime, and F. Patel King, Possible Action in the Courts of the Netherlands for Serious Breaches of the OPCW's Confidentiality Regime.

[32] "Evaluating the ICC Regime: The Likely Impact on States and International Law," Address by Hans Corell, Under-Secretary-General for Legal Affairs, The Legal Counsel of the United Nations at a training course, Peace Palace, The Hague, The Netherlands, 21 December 2000, p. 6.

law to allow them to make the leap from the exceptions and accept the emerging view, i.e. the principle of *aut dedere aut judicare*, an extension of the principle of universal jurisdiction? "The principle [of *aut dedere aut judicare*] not only grants the State in whose territory the alleged perpetrator of an international crime is to be found the power to try such person. It also creates for that State the legal duty either to try the alleged perpetrator before its own courts or to extradite the person to another State which, having jurisdiction on the case, requests the extradition."[33] The Convention fails to assist the reluctant States Parties to make the leap by defining what is meant by "conformity with international law" in its context. The principle would be most suitable as an underlying assumption in formulating offences and proper jurisdiction in the implementing legislation. It is recommended that, in adopting provisions relating to the criminal aspects of implementing legislation, States Parties should understand the term "in conformity with international law" as meaning substantive criminal law principles as they exist in customary international criminal law and procedures, together with those enshrined in the ICC Statute and UNCATOC.

The phrase "afford the appropriate form of legal assistance..." in paragraph 2 of Article VII is vague and could be interpreted subjectively. If each State Party applied its own standard of "appropriate," the result may be that what one State Party considers "appropriate" is no more than a minimalist approach unable to meet all the forms of legal assistance a particular situation may require. A list of actions required of a State Party in order to provide the legal assistance anticipated by the Convention would have removed the uncertainty, and potential subjective interpretations by States Parties, of what is required of them. Should lack of capacity by a State Party (as defined by itself) be judged adequate compliance under the Convention? Theoretically, a State Party could potentially hinder or delay the process of an investigation, arrest or extradition because it pleads incapacity. The "appropriate form of legal assistance" has been infrequently requested and scarcely offered! The author suggests an interpretation by the Legal Adviser to assist States Parties to grasp the parameters. States Parties are, of course, at liberty any time to request assistance from the Secretariat. It may also help to speed up the legislative process if States Parties sought legal assistance bilaterally. If offered, it goes without saying that the assistance should be relevant, and timely. The issue of cooperating "as appropriate with other States Parties" requires the same kind of clarification as the issue of "appropriate form of legal assistance."

3.6 Criminal Offences under the Convention

Over the centuries of criminal law development, the definition of criminal offences was once made up exclusively of common law criminal offences.[34] Now it includes a vast number of statutory and regulatory criminal offences. Statutory criminal offences are what a State makes into criminal offences, after weighing moral considerations, issues of harm, social conditions, and the state of international political and legal relations. There is no definition of a criminal offence in the Convention. There is also nothing to say that all activities in breach of the broad categories of prohibitions in the Convention should be taken as criminal offences. Herein lies the dilemma for the legislator who has to decide

---

[33] *Id.*, p. 7.

[34] These used to be murder, manslaughter, assault, rape, robbery, burglary, theft, besetting, and criminal damage, to name the most important.

which of these activities should be criminalised and by what criteria. It is suggested that the legislator should take two broad criteria as a guide: (a) the fact of the activity being prohibited; and (b) the degree of moral turpitude attaching to the consequences of carrying out the activity.

Understandably, the Convention reserves the issue of breaches by States Parties to a special mechanism under Article XII(3) and (4). In case of "serious damage to the object and purpose of [the] Convention" by a State Party, the procedure under that Article calls for "collective measures" by States Parties "in conformity with international law." The provision does not say what amounts to "serious damage to the object and purpose of [the] Convention." Presumably "collective measures" include suspension of rights or some political measures. These sanctions fall outside the sphere of criminal liability properly understood. For cases considered even more serious — "cases of particular gravity" — the breach is brought "to the attention of the United Nations General Assembly and the United Nations Security Council." Given the supremacy of the United Nations Charter in matters threatening international security, it would appear that the only other forms of punishing an errant Convention State Party would be the prerogative of the UN Security Council by way of military measures, economic sanctions, or ordering "reparations" of sorts. Once again, none of these come under international criminal law properly understood. In this regard, the question is whether it is open to States Parties to include in their implementing legislation measures that attribute criminal liability to a State. Naturally, criminal liability would not be based on the usual *actus reus* and *mens rea*, but on strict liability attributed by the legislator. The question of what the procedure for trial will be would arise. This appears far-fetched in the context of the usual practice in international relations.

A further question arises: is it intended that the legislatures of States Parties should translate the "collective measures" or the bringing of the breach to the Security Council (both of which are not criminal sanctions) of Article XII into a parallel process of civil sanctions against individual or corporate offenders? If so, what would be the basis for deciding to apply criminal or civil sanctions to particular activities? No criteria are given even for States Parties, except the words "serious damage to the object and purpose of the Convention" and "cases of particular gravity." It is reasonable to conclude that no such parallel concept was intended. Therefore, the Convention left it to States Parties to decide whether there would be "civil sanctions" (similar to those for States Parties under Article XII) in addition to the criminal ones for natural and legal persons. This very discussion underlines the problem of lack of clear definitions, and the difficulties for the national legislator trying to fashion comprehensive implementing measures. No one should be surprised if there are different approaches to this and other legislative questions under the Convention.

The only hint that some breaches of the Convention may amount to criminal offences is in paragraphs 1(a) and 1(c) of Article VII cited above. Paragraph 1(a) in effect says that all activities prohibited to a State Party shall be prohibited to "natural and legal persons" as well, as long as these persons are on the State Party's territory or under its jurisdiction. Significantly, the said paragraph goes on to say that the legislation to prohibit the activities will include penal legislation, but does not say for which activities. Paragraph 1(c) ensures that the legislation extends extraterritorially. Beyond this, the Convention gives no hint as to:

(a) where the line shall be drawn (and why) between civil wrongs and crimes (a distinction implicit in the formulation of paragraph 1(a) of Article VII);

(b) how a crime shall be defined;

(c) what activities are crimes? (is it that a developer should be treated less leniently than a producer, an acquirer, a stockpiler, or a transferor, or is it the other way round?);

(d) how non-criminal prohibited activities of "natural and legal persons" shall be dealt with as distinct from those of States Parties themselves;

(e) the sort of penalties that may be handed down for particular offences; and

(f) whether consistency and harmonisation of penalties is mandatory, desirable, or optional?

In effect, Article VII leaves it to each State Party to decide the answers to each of the questions posed under (a) to (f) above. What each State Party will find as the 'correct' answers, in terms of its understanding of the Convention, can safely be assumed to depend to a great extent on that States Party's legal system, policy and practice. An approach to penal legislation based on such criteria is not likely to produce consistent and uniform measures among all States Parties.

3.7 DEFINING A CRIME

At the Swaziland workshop referred to earlier, one observation was that States Parties had a difficult time determining what sort of offences should be ascribed to certain behaviour which breached the provisions of the Convention, and what penalties to assign to such offences. If the Convention is to be effective, and the mutual legal assistance to ensure the apprehension and punishment of individuals violating the Convention is to be forthcoming, it is essential that the crimes under the Convention be defined and understood in the same way by all States Parties. As already pointed out, the Convention has not provided such a definition, nor has it given a hint of what the definition might be. This gap is serious insofar as it provides no guidance to States Parties in drafting their implementing legislation. With a little more effort, it should have been possible to come up with a definition of a crime. A model definition of a crime is provided in UNCATOC and its two Protocols.

According to Articles 5, 6, 8 and 23 of UNCATOC, a criminal offence exists where a wrongful act is carried out with "knowledge, intent, aim, purpose or agreement." Each of these elements "may be inferred from objective factual circumstances."[35] The conduct scrutinised for crime under the UNCATOC consists in domestic or cross-border movements of proceeds, property, equipment or other "instrumentalities" and methods used for the transfer of the proceeds or other property; concealment or disguise of such proceeds; property, equipment or other instrumentalities, as well as methods and actions, to camouflage money laundering and transfer. In addition, conduct which amounts to conspiracy to

[35] See paragraphs 1 and 2 of Article 5 of UNCATOC.

engage in any of the acts described and to aid, abet, facilitate and counsel the carrying out of conduct that is wrongful may be a crime.[36]

There is a marked contrast between the comprehensive nature of the relevant provisions of the UNCATOC, upon which penal legislation by States Parties must be based, and those of the Chemical Weapons Convention. The Convention gives little or no guidance to national legislatures. The following is an indicative list of possible statutory criminal offences under the Convention: manufacturing chemical weapons (CW) by whatever method; procuring CW by whatever means; enticing others to manufacture CW; using CW; procuring or enticing others to use CW; engaging in military preparations to use CW; possession of CW in whatever form and for whatever purpose; selling CW for whatever purpose; purchasing CW for whatever purpose; constructing structures with the intent to produce or store CW; purchasing equipment capable of making CW and with an intent to produce CW; passing on to others the capability to make CW with intent that such capability shall be used to make CW; failure to declare any form of possession of CW; failure to declare any declarable activities; transferring toxic chemicals for purposes other than those not prohibited; unauthorised purchase or sale of scheduled chemicals; aiding and abetting illegal trade in scheduled chemicals; failure to report illegal activities in relation to CW and/or scheduled chemicals; any fraudulent dealings in CW and/or toxic chemicals; assisting others to commit any of the foregoing offences; failure to protect the environment in the course of implementing the Convention; failure to maintain proper records of all trade in or domestic consumption of scheduled chemicals; falsifying such records; deliberate suppression of information relevant to the commission or possible commission or a crime under the Convention; failure to disclose information about preparations to commit any of the above criminal offences; tampering with investigations relating to offences under the Convention to defeat the ends of justice; threatening witnesses or interfering with witnesses; interfering with customs procedures in order to commit a crime violating the Convention; and endangering the lives of the public in any way in relation to activities under the Convention.

If it is conceivable that the commission of the statutory offences listed above may indirectly result in the commission of ordinary crimes (murder, manslaughter, assault, rape, robbery, burglary, theft, besetting, criminal damage, etc.), it is advisable that States Parties include in the implementing legislation some reference to that possibility.

Without going into a detailed discussion of the procedural aspects to enable the prosecution of the above offences, suffice it to say that these tend to be standard in most jurisdictions. They should be scrupulously drafted to ensure that suspects are not let off on technicalities, and that the principles of justice and fair play are met. The UNCATOC and the ICC Statute are useful reference points in this regard for legislators drafting implementing legislation for the Convention. Articles 10 and 11 of UNCATOC, and Articles 53 to 61 of the ICC Statute, may be particularly useful guides. Careful crafting is necessary, particularly in respect of the requirement to provide for extraterritorial jurisdiction over activities of the State Party's nationals (natural person).

[36] See Articles 5, 6, 7, and 8 of UNCATOC.

3.8 PENALTIES

As to penalties, UNCATOC is equally precise. In the first place, Article 10 on the liability of legal persons states in paragraph 2 that: "Subject to the legal principles of the State Party, the liability of the legal persons may be criminal, civil or administrative." Under paragraph 3, "[s]uch liability shall be without prejudice to the criminal liability of the natural persons who have committed the offences." Under paragraph 4, States Parties under UNCATOC have an obligation to "ensure that legal persons held liable in accordance with this article are subject to effective, proportionate and dissuasive criminal or non-criminal sanctions, including monetary sanctions." As if to provide sentencing parameters, Article 2(b) defines "serious crime" as "conduct constituting an offence punishable by a maximum deprivation of liberty of at least four years or a more serious penalty." Except with respect to States Parties, the Chemical Weapons Convention makes no distinction between "criminal and non-criminal sanctions." Yet some Convention States Parties are making the distinction in their implementing legislation, as indeed they should.

The offences under UNCATOC cover the main ones that *can be* contemplated under the Chemical Weapons Convention. UNCATOC shows that it was possible for the Convention to be more exact in its definitions, and to provide concrete guidelines on offences contemplated under the Convention. Something in this order of categorisation in the Convention would have been very helpful to States Parties preparing their implementing legislation, and divergences would have been limited. Legislation adopted by States Parties shows such divergence that it is common to find, for the same serious offence, penalties ranging between six months to five years in some States Parties, and up to 25 years in others. One State Party has specifically set an upper limit of 10 years or life for what it calls "serious crimes," and four years for "illicit handling of chemical weapons." In another State Party, production and stocking of toxic chemicals there has a maximum penalty of two years in prison and, where death results, 10 years. Storage of toxic substances on the territory of that State Party may attract up to 10 years in prison. On offences relating to illegal transfers of scheduled chemicals, penalties range between six months and two years. These divergent scales of punishment are consistent with the absence of a clear indication from the drafters of the Convention on the need for consistency, uniformity, and concordance in the legislative measures and the penalties thereto. One result of this lack is that criminals may indeed relocate their 'operational bases' to States Parties that tend to take the offences lightly. It cannot be that the Convention permitted any form of punishment as adequate. Another result is that States Parties may be unable to provide mutual legal assistance when the penalties for the crime are widely divergent in the requesting and requested States Parties.

3.9 ENFORCEMENT

Enforcing the measures adopted by States Parties is a vital aspect of the implementation of the Convention provisions. One cannot talk about the detection of Convention-related crimes, or the apprehension of suspects and their prosecution, without at the same time addressing the importance of the police and customs cooperation internally and across State boundaries. The greatest assistance to police and customs officials is to present them with the clearest laws and the relevant regulations thereto. The more these officers face indecisive language in a statute, the more reluctant they are to act, or the actions of different officers may conflict in important respects, thereby exposing their organisations to a credibility gap. The importance of comprehensive and mutually concordant legislative measures from one State Party to another cannot be over-emphasised.

Since the Convention is silent on what constitutes crimes under its regime, it cannot be expected to provide clarity to police and customs officers charged with the task of enforcing the Convention's provisions. The implementing legislation needs specify what are the crimes under the Convention are, and it needs to be explicit on the powers and functions of the police and customs officials, particularly with respect to powers of search, arrest and seizure. Given the extraterritorial jurisdiction which Article VII of the Convention requires, corresponding measures ought to be put in place so that the police and customs officers are not hamstrung by inadequate laws. Transboundary and internal police and customs work is made more coherent and efficient when the police and customs officials of States Parties share a common knowledge base on the requirements of the implementing legislation, particularly with respect to export/import controls for scheduled chemicals; standard reference names for scheduled chemicals; jurisdiction; extent of collaboration with the police and customs officials of other States Parties; the ability to travel across State Party boundaries with minimum difficulties; adequate monitoring powers; and powers authorising examination of records in relation to Convention activities.

Transboundary police work has an established machinery in Interpol, Europol and other agencies. So do customs administrations through the Customs Co-operation Council (World Customs Organisation (WCO)). What is required to increase the efficiency of these organisations, and the domestic police forces, is a programme of information and continuous technical training on the changing nature of crime and crime methodologies. The programme of technical training is particularly relevant in regard to the complex nature of the subject matter of the Convention, and what aspects of chemical weapons and scheduled chemicals may attract criminal activity.

As pointed out above, there has to be a harmonised understanding in the implementing legislation and in related statutes, of what chemical weapons are, and how harmful they are to humans and animals. There should also be an understanding of the potentially dangerous uses to which toxic chemicals can be put. And perhaps more important, there is an urgent need for police and customs officials to know the likely methods of criminals engaged in smuggling chemical weapons or attempting to use them in terrorist attacks.

The WCO has several programmes. Its Global Intelligence Strategy will serve as "an overarching international information and intelligence plan. Such a strategy should identify the needs of Members and regions across all subjects and identify weaknesses in the current arrangements. Importantly, it should also identify areas where we can improve the quantity and quality of data collection and analysis and make better use of existing resources, particularly at regional and international level."[37] WCO also has a Draft Strategic Plan for the Regional Intelligence Liaison Office (RILO) Programme. The programme has several objectives that would be useful to guide customs and police authorities. Among the objectives are facilitating communication and exchange of intelligence on a multilateral or bilateral

[37] WCO Enforcement Committee, "Proposal for a WCO Global Intelligence Strategy," (EC0091E1), Brussels, 16 February 2001, p. 1.

level;[38] assisting Members "to effectively and efficiently react to new types of customs infractions, new illegal substances and new or unique concealment methods;" and "[r]e-enforce cooperation with other agencies and the private sector to strengthen customs controls and enforcement."[39] One of the goals of the plan is to "[b]ring a level of uniformity to the performance of the basic tasks of the programme.[40] Any implementing legislation that does not take these elements into account is likely not to provide adequate support to the police and customs officers in their implementation tasks.

Similarly, police and customs officers need to keep abreast of how criminals may inject themselves into the stream of legitimate transfers of toxic chemicals for purposes not prohibited in order to effect illegal transfers. A grasp of the changing criminal behaviour and practice will always help alert police and customs officers to the need to satisfy themselves that the transfers of toxic chemicals is done in accordance with the Convention and the implementing legislation by States Parties.

Specifically, technical training should cover the latest crime investigation techniques, including joint investigations,[41] prevention, detection, how to respond, and how to ensure the safety of the unsuspecting public and the officers themselves. Those States Parties with developed chemical industries should go out of their way to assist the police and customs officials of Member States with rudimentary or emerging chemical industries, so that the limited understanding in some States Parties of customs issues is not seized upon by criminals or terrorists to violate the Convention.

Apart from the technical training referred to above, one vital area to work on is assistance to enable police forces, across the spectrum of Member States, to be more efficient in their investigations, collection and storage of data, and processing it into crime dockets and other reports, so that it is readily available to other police or customs forces on a cooperative basis.

The effective prosecution of offences rests, once again, on clear definitions of crimes, and clearly stated rules of evidence and standard(s) of proof. Since they are not in the Convention, these should be included in the legislation. States Parties may look to the general body of international criminal law and, in particular, that of the UNCATOC, especially the latter's emphasis to its States Parties to ensure that the liability of legal persons "may be criminal, civil or administrative," even though natural persons committing the same crimes may be charged with criminal liability.[42] But it would be more effective for implementation purposes if the provisions are part of the national implementing legislation. States Parties of the Convention must remember that most of the crimes relating to chemical weapons and toxic chemicals are grave crimes. Indeed, the use of chemical weapons is already a crime under customary international law. In urging States in this direction, Article 11(2) of UNCATOC provides: "Each State Party shall endeavour to ensure that any discretionary legal powers under its domestic law relating to the prosecution of persons for offences covered by this Convention are exercised to maximise the effectiveness of law

[38] WCO Enforcement Committee, "Strategic Plan for the Regional Intelligence Liaison Office (RILO) Programme: Draft Document," (EC0091E2), Brussels, 16 February 2001, pp. 3.
[39] *Id.*, p. 5.
[40] *Id.*, p. 1.
[41] See Articles 19 and 20 of UNCATOC.
[42] Article 10 of UNCATOC.

enforcement measures in respect of those offences and with due regard to the need to deter the commission of such offences."

4. Conclusion

One main conclusion is that a proper, more efficient and effective implementation of the Chemical Weapons Convention calls for many more "understandings" on, or "clarifications" of, Convention terms and procedures than those already made. Clarifications already made serve both as evidence that there are terms that are not clear in the Convention, and that practical solutions can be found by the OPCW policy-making organs. Clarifications are making it easier incrementally for States Parties to prepare and adopt implementing legislation.

Lack of clarity in the meaning and scope of some key provisions has created difficulties for some States Parties in the drafting of legislation. The most concrete evidence of these difficulties so far is the delay in the adoption by many States Parties of implementing legislation. The other evidence of the difficulties is that some provisions in the legislation of States Parties are not in harmony in several aspects, such as what is to be declared in certain categories of the verification process and the identification of offences, penalties and procedures. There is no requirement to harmonise the provisions of the implementing legislation in order to ensure uniform implementation of the Convention by all States Parties, and this is an obstacle to the adoption of effective implementing legislation. Without such harmony, enforcement measures are made that much more difficult, with the possibility that non-uniform provisions, especially penalties, may be exploited by criminal organisations, groups and individuals.

Thus far, the forces for harmonisation of provisions are pitted against the majority of States Parties that would rather leave to individual Member States the adoption of whatever legislation that meets the minimum requirements of the Convention while not disrupting too much the existing domestic legislation and chemical industry procedures.

There is a significant divide on the implementation difficulties faced by States Parties between those with developed economies and those with developing ones. To date, the latter have less appreciation of the benefits of the Convention for them, and less comprehension of its terminology and requirements, with the consequence that they are behind in adopting implementing legislation. This is perhaps one of the most serious 'dislocations' in the implementation of the Convention, which, if left to ride, may be a threat to the implementation of the Convention and create safe havens for criminals.

The divergent and non-uniform implementing legislation coming out of States Parties, while not a threat as such to the object and purpose of the Convention, may seriously undermine the faithful implementation of the Convention.

It is still too early to be able to fully assess what the impact of non-uniform legislation will be on the police and customs organisations of Member States with respect to Convention related crime because to date there have been no reported Convention-related offences.

There is evidence that the campaign to have implementing legislation in place timely has not been going well, in spite of repeated pleas by the OPCW policy-making organs, the Director-General and the Secretariat. The failure, if one may call it that, of States Parties to comply with this obligation is due to the complexity of the Convention, the absence of clarity in many of its provisions, and the different interpretations by States Parties of what is required in the implementing legislation.

5. Recommendations

The campaign to have implementing legislation in force in all States Parties has achieved some limited results. There is clearly a need to try another tack. Adopting piecemeal "understandings" on individual terms that are not clear has its benefits because it meets the problem as it arises, but a systematic examination of the Convention as a whole may be more efficient. It is the author's belief that many of the additional clarifications (the need for which may be unrecognised so far) will actually help the Organisation remove some of the bottlenecks in its work, including persuading States Parties to adopt implementing legislation.

As this chapter has tried to show, there is a need for clarifications of terms in the Convention, its Verification Annex, and possibly the Confidentiality Annex. While Article VII is the main focus in this chapter, it is clear that a holistic approach to clarifications may yield better results. The author is also convinced that while there may be one or two issues that call for change or amendment procedures, the rest of the terms and provisions that need urgent attention, particularly those relating to implementing legislation, do not require change or amendment procedures. 'Rectification' should be carried out in any of the following ways:

(a) For issues not too complex to require consideration by the Review Conference mechanism coming up in 2003, presenting them to be dealt with as expeditiously as possible through interim guidelines by the OPCW Executive Council, and through adoption of "understandings" by the OPCW Conference of States Parties, or through change procedures as was done in the case of the Schedule 1 chemical, saxitoxin;[43]

(b) Making changes, where necessary (within the meaning of paragraph 4 of Article XV of the Convention);

(c) In order to use the Review Conference mechanism coming up in 2003,[44] beginning to compile data on those aspects of "the overall verification regime for the chemical industry..." over which experience shows a need to change the Organisation's practice. The focus should be on those aspects that have created the greatest difficulties. Amendments, changes, and understandings, should all be contemplated with the single aim of removing all inconsistencies and impractical demands, and improving hitherto inadequate provisions;

[43] See OPCW docs. EC-MII/DEC.1 (15 January 1999) and EC-XVII/DG.6 (10 November 1999).

[44] Paragraph 22 of Article VIII of the Convention, and also paragraph 26 of Part IX of the Verification Annex to the Convention.

(d) In the meantime, issuing more "understandings" by the Conference of States Parties to clarify all Convention provisions which States Parties consider unclear in relation to implementing legislation, and matters like the low concentration declaration threshold for Schedules 2 and 3 chemicals;

(e) Fixing a timeline for completing and submitting implementing legislation;

(f) Closer monitoring by the Secretariat of the adoption by States Parties of the necessary implementing legislation, with a view to encouraging the early completion of the process. In this regard, expanding legal assistance to States Parties, either bilaterally or from the Secretariat;

(g) Adopting guidelines on offences under the Convention, and what the Conference of States Parties considers appropriate penalties for each Convention related criminal offence. To include in such guidelines a readiness to review the situation with a view to creating new offences in order to ensure a strict enforcement regime for the Convention;

(h) Broadening, through a change procedure or an "understanding," the application of the Convention's privileges and immunities to specified categories of national law enforcement authorities to enable them to follow through with investigations of suspected criminal activities across State Party boundaries;

(i) Adopting, as a matter of urgency, a technical training programme for law enforcement agents either centrally or at regional level, with a particular focus on cross-border crime relating to chemical weapons and the transfer of toxic chemicals;

(j) Establishing an urgent programme to assist customs officials in States Parties to deal with the onerous task of identifying chemical substances at border posts;

(k) Recognition that harmonising the provisions of implementing legislation must be preceded by harmonising the differences of interpretation of issues raised in this chapter. The WCO HS System and the OPCW Handbook on Chemicals must also be harmonised;

(l) The OPCW Legal Adviser directly assisting States Parties with interpretations of certain legal terms relating to implementing legislation; and,

(m) Comprehensive implementing legislation, more or less in harmony in important respects with that of other States Parties, will assist the WCO in the delivery of assistance to States Parties.

NATIONAL ENFORCEMENT OF INTERNATIONAL HUMANITARIAN LAW

Maria Teresa Dutli*

1. Preliminary Considerations

International humanitarian law consists of detailed rules aimed at protecting the victims of armed conflict and restricting the means and methods of warfare. The development of this law — to expand the protection afforded to persons who are not, or no longer, taking part in fighting and to limit the means and methods of warfare — is a never-ending challenge. Developments in weapons technology, misuse of humanity's achievements, must be met with determination and imagination. There has been significant progress, such as the ban on blinding laser weapons agreed upon in the 1996 Protocol on Prohibitions or Restrictions on the Use of Mines, Booby-Traps and Other Devices as amended on 3 May 1996 (Protocol II to the 1980 Convention[1] as amended on 3 May 1996). In 1997, after a hard fought campaign, the Ottawa Convention banning landmines was concluded.[2] It has already been ratified by 124 States.

To develop the law is not sufficient. Law without action is merely a dead letter — a theoretical exercise. Implementation is undoubtedly the greatest challenge faced by international humanitarian law today. Those who have striven so hard to develop international humanitarian law have therefore also sought to develop mechanisms ensuring its respect. It is essential that all those affected by the law, civilians and members of the military, are aware of its provisions. The dissemination of international humanitarian law is both a clear obligation of governments and a major activity of the International Committee of the Red Cross (ICRC) and the National Red Cross and Red Crescent Societies. The ICRC also attaches the utmost importance to national action to prevent and punish violations of international humanitarian law. At the request of the international community, the ICRC has established an Advisory Service to assist and advise on a wide range of measures relating to the national implementation of international humanitarian law. In its first five years, the Advisory Service has been active around the world, encouraging the ratification of international humanitarian law treaties, promoting the establishment of national committees for the implementation of this law and advising on national

* Head of the International Committee of the Red Cross (ICRC) Advisory Service in International Humanitarian Law. Any views expressed are those of the author and are not attributal to the ICRC. See also Anna Segall (editor), "Punishing Violations of International Humanitarian Law at the National Level: A Guide for Common Law States", Advisory Service on International Humanitarian Law, International Committee of the Red Cross, Geneva, September 2001.

[1] Convention on Prohibitions or Restrictions on the Use of Certain Conventional Weapons which may be deemed to be Excessively Injurious or to have Indiscriminate Effects (1980 Conventional Weapons Convention).

[2] Convention on the Prohibition of the Use, Stockpiling, Production and Transfer of Anti-Personnel Mines and on their Destruction, 18 September 1997 (1997 Ottawa Convention), 2056 UNTS 211.

R. Yepes-Enríquez and L. Tabassi. (eds.), Treaty Enforcement and International Cooperation in Criminal Matters

implementing legislation.[3] This chapter presents an overview of the international humanitarian law and arms control treaties which may, or must, be enforced at the national level.

2. Implementing International Humanitarian Law

All States have a clear obligation to adopt and apply measures implementing international humanitarian law. These measures may need to be taken by one or more government ministries, the legislature, the courts, the armed forces, or other State organs.

International humanitarian law, in particular the 1949 Geneva Conventions and their 1977 Additional Protocols,[4] sets out a range of measures which must be adopted. The principal measures are:

- to prepare national translations of treaties;[5]
- to disseminate the texts of treaties as widely as possible — both within the armed forces and generally;[6]
- to suppress all violations of the law and, in particular, to adopt criminal legislation punishing war crimes;[7]
- to ensure that protected persons and places are properly identified, located and protected. In particular: civilians and persons *hors de combat* (wounded, sick, shipwrecked and prisoners of war), sanitary, religious and civil defence personnel, sanitary units, demilitarised or neutralised zones and non-defended localities, civilian and cultural property, according to the numerous related dispositions of the Geneva Conventions and their Additional Protocols;
- to adopt measures to prevent the misuse of protective emblems and signs;[8]

[3] Jacob Kellenberg (President of the ICRC), foreword, in Anna Segall, *supra* note 2.

[4] GCI: Convention (I) for the Amelioration of the Condition of the Wounded and Sick in Armed Forces in the Field, Geneva, 12 August 1949, 75 UNTS 31; GCII: Convention (II) for the Amelioration of the Condition of the Wounded, Sick and shipwrecked Members of Armed Forces at Sea, Geneva, 12 August 1949, 75 UNTS 85; GCIII: Convention (III) relative to the Treatment of Prisoners of War, Geneva, 12 August 1949, 75 UNTS 135; GCIV: Convention (IV) relative to the Protection of Civilian Persons in Time of War, Geneva, 12 August 1949, 75 UNTS 287; API: Protocol Additional to the Geneva Conventions of 1949 and relating to the Protection of Victims of International Armed Conflicts (Protocol I), 8 June 1977, 1125 UNTS, no. 17512; APII: Protocol Additional to the Geneva Conventions of 1949 relating to the Protection of Victims of Non-International Armed Conflicts (Protocol II), 8 June 1977, 1125 UNTS, no. 17513. Texts available on-line in the IHL database of the ICRC at http://www.icrc.org/ihl.

[5] Geneva Conventions I-IV, GCI Article 48/GCII 49/GCIII 128/GCIV 145; Additional Protocol I, Article 84.

[6] GCI Article 47/GCII 48/GCIII 127/GCIV 144; API Article 83, 87(2); APII Aricle. 19.

[7] GCI Article 49/GCII 50/GCIII 129/GCIV 146, API Article 85(1).

[8] GCI Article 44, 53-54; GCII Article 43-45; API Article 37-39, 56, 66, 85(3)f); APII Article 12.

- to ensure respect of fundamental and procedural guarantees;[9]
- to provide the appointment and training of qualified personnel, including legal advisers within the armed forces;[10] and,
- to ensure respect of humanitarian law in the location of military sites and in the development and adoption of weapons and military tactics.[11]

3. Punishment of Violations of International Humanitarian Law

International humanitarian law sets out detailed rules aimed at protecting victims of armed conflicts and restricting methods and means of warfare. It also establishes mechanisms to ensure that these rules are respected. The core treaties of international humanitarian law and related instruments all contain provisions concerning the punishment of violations. As far as punishment of violations of international humanitarian law is concerned, the Advisory Service initially focused its attention on the adoption of national legislation for the punishment of grave breaches of the Geneva Conventions for the protection of victims of war and their First Additional Protocol of 1977 applicable in international armed conflicts. It also encourages and assists States to adapt their criminal law to permit persons to be tried for:

- other violations of the Conventions and Protocols;
- violations of the 1954 Hague Cultural Property Convention and its Second Protocol (adopted on 26 March 1999);
- wilfully killing or causing serious injury to civilians through violations of Amended Protocol II (mines, booby-traps and other devices) to the 1980 Conventional Weapons Convention;
- violations of the 1997 Ottawa Convention (anti-personnel mines); and,
- crimes within the jurisdiction of the International Criminal Court.

4. Obligations to Punish Violations

States have an obligation to prevent and, where necessary, punish violations of international humanitarian law. This obligation may be found in the following humanitarian law and arms control instruments, which will be examined in chronological order. While crimes against humanity are not prohibited by a specific treaty, they will be briefly discussed.

---

[9] GCI Article 3,12; GCII Article 3, 12; GCIII Article 3, 13-17, 82-90, 95-108; GCIV Article 3, 27-35, 43, 64-78, 117-126; API Article 11, 44-45, 75-77; APII Article 4-6.
[10] API Article 6, 82.
[11] API Article 36, 56, 58.

4.1 THE 1948 GENOCIDE CONVENTION

States Parties to the Convention must enact legislation to provide effective penalties for persons guilty of genocide or criminal involvement in genocide. Persons charged with genocide shall be tried by a competent tribunal of the State in the territory of which the act was committed or by such international penal tribunal as may have jurisdiction in relation to the States which have accepted its jurisdiction.[12]

The Statute of the International Criminal Court, which entered into force on 1 July 2002, provides for the establishment of such a tribunal.[13]

Genocide is also a crime under customary international law. Under this law, any State may assert jurisdiction regardless of the place of the offence and the nationality of the alleged perpetrator.

4.2 THE 1949 GENEVA CONVENTIONS AND THEIR 1977 ADDITIONAL PROTOCOLS

(a) Grave breaches

States Parties are under an obligation to repress grave breaches of the Conventions and Protocol I in international armed conflicts on the basis of universal jurisdiction.[14]

These instruments impose a twofold obligation: to enact legislation to provide effective penal sanctions for persons committing, or ordering to be committed, grave breaches and to search for, and to try or extradite, such persons. Grave breaches are defined in these instruments.[15] The Geneva Conventions refer to grave breaches directed against the protected persons and Additional Protocol I extends the list by incorporating breaches to the law relevant to the conduct of hostilities.

(b) Other violations

States are also under obligation to suppress all violations of the Geneva Conventions and their 1977 Additional Protocols which are not considered to be grave breaches.[16] These violations are not defined in the treaties but must be considered as every conduct contrary to an obligation established by law.

---

[12] Convention on the Prevention and Punishment of the Crime of Genocide (Genocide Convention), Article 6, 78 UNTS 277.

[13] 1998 Rome Statute of the International Criminal Court, entered into force 1 July 2002; UN doc. A/CONF.183/9*, as corrected by the procès-verbaux of 10 November 1998 and 12 July 1999. Corrected text available at http://www.un.org/law/icc. Article 5-6.

[14] GCI Article 49/GCII 50/GCIII 129/GCIV 146; API Art.icle 85(1).

[15] GCI Art.icle 50/GCII 51/GCIII 130/GCIV 147; API Art.icle 11(4) and 85(2), (3), (4).

[16] GCI Article 49/GCII 50/GCIII 129/GCIV 146; API, Article 85(1).

4.3 THE 1954 HAGUE CONVENTION FOR THE PROTECTION OF CULTURAL PROPERTY AND THE SECOND PROTOCOL TO THE CONVENTION (ADOPTED ON 26 MARCH 1999)

(a) States which are party to the 1954 Hague Convention only

States Parties have an obligation to take all necessary steps, within the framework of their ordinary criminal jurisdiction, to prosecute and impose penal or disciplinary sanctions upon those persons, of whatever nationality, who commit or order to be committed a breach of the 1954 Hague Cultural Property Convention.[17]

This obligation applies in international and non-international armed conflict, although it is limited, in the case of the latter, to breaches of those provisions which relate to respect for cultural property in Art. 19(1) of the Hague Cultural Property Convention.

(b) States which are party to the Convention and its Second Protocol

States Parties to the Convention and its Second Protocol have an obligation, applying in international and non-international armed conflict,[18] to:

- establish as criminal offences under domestic law the following serious violations:
  1. making cultural property under enhanced protection the object of attack;
  2. using cultural property under enhanced protection or its immediate surroundings in support of military action;
  3. extensive destruction or appropriation of cultural property protected under the Convention and this Protocol;
  4. making protected cultural property the object of attack; and,
  5. theft, pillage or misappropriation of, or acts of vandalism against cultural property protected under the Convention.
- adopt such legislative, administrative, or disciplinary measures as may be necessary to suppress the following conducts:
  1. any use of cultural property in violation of the Convention or its Protocol; and,
  2. any illicit export, other removal or transfer of ownership of cultural property from occupied territory.[19]

When enacting legislation to criminalise offences, States must ensure that the legislation provides for jurisdiction:

- on the basis of territoriality and nationality; and,

---

[17] Second Protocol to the (1954 Hague) Convention for the Protection of Cultural Property in the Event of Armed Conflict (1954 Hague Cultural Property Convention), Article 28.
[18] Second Protocol to the 1954 Hague Cultural Property Convention, Article 22.
[19] *Id.*, Article 15 (1) and (2).

- for some specified offences, on the basis of the presence of the alleged offender on its territory.[20]

In relation to some of these offences, States Parties have an obligation, similar to that which applies to grave breaches of the Geneva Conventions and Protocol I, to try or extradite alleged offenders present in the territory.[21]

In addition to these rules, a State Party to the Second Protocol which occupies the whole or part of the territory of another State Party must prohibit and prevent, in relation to the occupied territory:

- any illicit export, other removal or transport of ownership of cultural property; and,
- any archaeological excavation, save where this is strictly required to safeguard, record or preserve cultural property.[22]

4.4 THE 1972 BIOLOGICAL WEAPONS CONVENTION

States Parties have an obligation to prevent and prohibit the development, production, stockpiling, acquisition or retention of biological weapons and delivery systems on the territory of the State or in any other place under its jurisdiction or control.[23] These prohibitions apply at all times.[24]

4.5 THE 1976 ENVIRONMENTAL MODIFICATION TECHNIQUES CONVENTION

States Parties have an obligation to take measures it considers necessary to prohibit and prevent violations of the Convention on territory under the State's jurisdiction or control.[25]

The Convention prohibits military or any other hostile use of environmental modification techniques having widespread, long-lasting or severe effects as the means of destruction damage or injury to any other State Party.[26]

4.6 AMENDED PROTOCOL II TO THE 1980 CONVENTIONAL WEAPONS CONVENTION

States Parties have an obligation to impose penal sanctions on persons who wilfully kill or cause serious injury to civilians through violations of the Protocol, whether committed in

[20] *Id.*, Article 21.
[21] *Id.*, Article 16.
[22] *Id.*, Article 17.
[22] Second Protocol to the 1954 Hague Cultural Property Convention, Article 9.
[23] Convention for the Prohibition of the Development, Production and Stockpiling of Bacteriological and Toxin Weapons and on Their Destruction (1972 Biological Weapons Convention), Article 3.
[24] 1972 Biological Weapons Convention, Article 1.
[25] Convention on the Prohibiton of Military or any other Hostile Use of Environmental Modifications Techniques (1976 Environmental Modification Techniques Convention), Article 4.
[26] 1976 Environmental Modification Techniques Convention, Article 1.

international or non-international armed conflict.[27] This obligation applies in relation to persons or territory under the State's jurisdiction or control.

In addition to this obligation to impose penal sanctions, there is an obligation to prevent and suppress all violations of the Protocol by persons or on territory under the State's jurisdiction or control.[28]

4.7 THE 1984 TORTURE CONVENTION

States Parties must ensure that all acts of torture are offences under their criminal law, punishable by appropriate penalties which take into account their grave nature.[29] States must establish jurisdiction over acts of torture committed in their territory, by their nationals and, when they consider it to be appropriate, when the victim is a national.[30] They must also establish jurisdiction in cases where the alleged offender is present in their territory if they do not extradite.[31]

4.8 THE 1993 CHEMICAL WEAPONS CONVENTION

States Parties have an obligation to enact penal legislation to punish violations of the Convention on the basis of territoriality or nationality, that is:

- on the territory of the State or in any other place under its jurisdiction or control; and,
- by its nationals regardless of the place where the offence was committed.[32]

The Convention's prohibitions on development, production, acquisition, stockpiling, retention or transfer, use, or engaging in military preparations to use, chemical weapons apply at all times.[33]

4.9 THE 1997 OTTAWA CONVENTION

States Parties have an obligation to prevent and suppress violations of the Convention by persons or on territory under the State's jurisdiction or control, including through the imposition of penal sanctions.[34] The Convention's prohibitions apply at all times.[35]

---

[27] Protocol (II) on Prohibitions or Restrictions on the Use of Mines, Booby-Traps and Other Devices, as amended on 3 May 1996 (Amended Protocol II to the 1980 Conventional Weapons Convention), Article 14.

[28] Amended Protocol II to the 1980 Conventional Weapons Convention, Article 14.

[29] Convention Against Torture and Other Cruel, Inhuman or Degrading Treatment or Punishment (Torture Convention), Article 4.

[30] Torture Convention, Article 5(1).

[31] Torture Convention, Article 5(2).

[32] Convention on the Prohibition of the Development, Production, Stockpiling and Use of Chemical Weapons and on Their Destruction (1993 Chemical Weapons Convention), Art. VII, para. 1.

[33] 1993 Chemical Weapons Convention, Article I, para. 1.

[34] Convention on the Prohibition of the Use, Stockpiling, Production and Transfer of Anti-Personnel Mines and on Their Destruction (1997 Ottawa Convention), Article 9.

[35] 1997 Ottawa Convention, Article 1, para. 1.

4.10 CRIMES AGAINST HUMANITY

Crimes against humanity are not prohibited by any specific treaty. It is nevertheless clear that crimes against humanity are crimes under customary international law. International and national tribunals have prosecuted crimes against humanity and the International Criminal Court established pursuant to the Rome Statute has jurisdiction over these crimes.[36] Because of the solely customary law status of these crimes, there is no treaty obligation on States to punish violations. States may, however, decide to assert jurisdiction and may do so on the basis of universal jurisdiction.

5. UNIVERSAL JURISDICTION

Universal jurisdiction refers to the assertion of jurisdiction over offences regardless of the place where they are committed or the nationality of the perpetrator. It is held to apply to a range of offences whose repression by all States is justified, or required, as a matter of international public policy. Certain offences are regarded as being subject to universal jurisdiction as a matter of customary international law. These include, for example, piracy, slavery, war crimes, genocide and crimes against humanity. Other offences are expressly made subject to universal jurisdiction in treaty law. These include grave breaches of the Geneva Conventions and Protocol I, torture, hijacking, attacks on aircraft and shipping, apartheid, attacks on United Nations and related personnel, and hostage-taking.

A key distinction must be made between those offences in relation to which States are obliged to assert universal jurisdiction (mandatory universal jurisdiction) and those offences in relation to which a State may, if it so chooses, assert universal jurisdiction (permissive universal jurisdiction). Where treaties provide for universal jurisdiction, they generally provide for mandatory universal jurisdiction — that is, they require States to assert jurisdiction. Conversely, where customary international law alone provides for the assertion of universal jurisdiction, this is generally permissive rather than mandatory.

6. RESPONSIBILITY FOR INTERNATIONAL CRIMES

International humanitarian law was one of the first areas of international law to make it clear that the individual, and not just the State, is responsible for his or her own actions.

6.1 PRINCIPLE OF INDIVIDUAL RESPONSIBILITY FOR WAR CRIMES

The system of grave breaches established by the Geneva Conventions and Additional Protocol I imposes criminal responsibility on those who have committed, or ordered to be committed, grave breaches and requires States Parties to enact legislation to punish such offences.[37] A State's criminal or military law must enable prosecution of grave breaches. In accordance with generally recognised principles of national and international law, the law should extend responsibility to persons other than those who directly commit, or order

[36] Rome Statute of the International Criminal Court, Articles 5 and 7.

[37] GCI Article 49/GCII 50/GCIII 129/GCIV 146, API Article 85(1).

the commission of, the act — for example, those who aid, abet or otherwise assist in its commission, who attempt to commit such an act, or who participate in a criminal conspiracy to commit such an act.

6.2 LIABILITY FOR OMISSIONS

The law also extends liability for grave breaches resulting from omission, that is, a failure to act when under a duty to do so, such as wilful killing by deprivation of food or care, unjustifiable delay in repatriation of prisoners of war or civilians.[38]

6.3 LIABILITY OF COMMANDERS AND SUPERIORS

The principle that commanders and superiors may be responsible for violations committed by their subordinates is well established in international humanitarian law. Additional Protocol I imposes an obligation on States Parties to require commanders:

- to ensure that members of the armed forces under their command are aware of their obligations under the Conventions and the Protocol;
- to prevent and, where necessary, suppress breaches by members of the armed forces under their command and other persons under their control;
- to report breaches to the competent authorities; and,
- where their subordinates or other persons under their control are going to commit, or have committed such breaches, to initiate disciplinary proceedings or penal action against violations.[39]

7. Defences and Immunities in International Law

Defences and immunities may be raised in proceedings for international crimes. In this area, some principles are recognised in the domestic criminal law of most States and endorsed, with some differences of formulation, in various international humanitarian law treaties. The main principles which may not relieve an accused of criminal responsibility are:

- ignorance of the law, unless it negates the mental element required for the crime;
- obedience of national law;
- sovereign immunity deriving from the official position or capacity;
- duress and necessity, unless the person acted necessarily and reasonably to avoid the threat and does not intend to cause a harm greater than the one sought to be avoided; and,
- superior orders, meaning the fact that the person acted pursuant to an order of a government or a superior (military or civilian) is not in itself a defence; it may however be taken into account in mitigation of punishment.

---

[38] API Article 86(1).

[39] API Article 87.

8. Conclusion

The experience of the International Committee of the Red Cross in implementing international humanitarian law and arms control treaties has largely focused on the ratification process and on the national implementation of the rules of international humanitarian law into the national legal systems. This process is open-ended since humanitarian law needs to be permanently adapted in order to introduce new rules which take into account technological developments.

In the five years since the establishment of the ICRC Advisory Service, great progress has been made. We can measure this progress in the growing number of treaty ratifications and in the increasing adoption of internal implementing measures — legislative or other — being taken by States in order to ensure compliance with their international obligations. Many States have or are in the process of modifying their criminal laws in order to introduce repression of violations of the major international law and arms control treaties. In this area, the importance of adopting a comprehensive approach which implements the whole range of prohibitions contained in all of the treaties should be underlined. It should also be noted that national jurisdictions have begun to play an important role in the repression of crimes under international humanitarian law. This tendency will certainly become increasingly significant when the International Criminal Court begins operating. It is clear that both national and international jurisdictions have the potential to play a crucial and complementary role in ensuring respect for, and in the enforcement of, international humanitarian law.

PART IV
CHALLENGES

SECTION IV.1

INTERNATIONAL COOPERATION IN PROTECTION AGAINST TERRORISM

INTRODUCTION AND SUMMARY

All terrorism analysts agree that international terrorism is a serious threat to international society. However, there is little other agreement beyond this fact. Few come to agreement as to the definition of terrorist violence, the likely motives and means for carrying out an act of terrorism, and, therefore, disagree about the methods for countering the international terrorist threat. Terrorism analysts in government, most non-governmental organisations, and the private sphere believe that the threat of weapons of mass destruction (WMD) terrorism deserves most of the counter-terrorism attention, as it is considered, theoretically at least, to be potentially the most devastating terrorist means.

Although terrorism analysts from governmental, private and non-governmental sectors have been calling for multilayered, multilateral cooperation for decades, increased funding for, and dedicated support of, the cross-jurisdictional counter-terrorism infrastructure has yet to be realised. Following the 11 September 2001 attacks on the World Trade Center and the Pentagon in the United States, several national governments and international organisations are rethinking/reorganising their counter-terrorist structures.

In this section, the infrastructure and strategy of Interpol's transnational counter-terrorism effort, which is supported by the national intelligence forces of 179 countries, is detailed. That infrastructure is, and will increasingly be, taxed by the alliances between terrorist groups and transnational organised crime groups. The background and organisation

R. Yepes-Enríquez and L. Tabassi. (eds.), Treaty Enforcement and International Cooperation in Criminal Matters

of one such group, Aum Shinrikyo, is discussed. Alliances being formed between terrorist and transnational organised crime groups, or the shift to crime in the terrorist group's focus, is identified as a trend. Even though they may have been ideologically founded, the need for funding drives terrorist groups into illegal narcotics and/or arms trade. The shift from ideological to material concerns can affect the ethics of the group and enables it to amass economic and political power, increasing its threat to society. What can be done? The OPCW Technical Secretariat in this section has outlined the possibilities for action to prevent chemical terrorism under the Chemical Weapons Convention. The final author stresses point again, which is the common thread running throughout this volume, that penal legislation should be in force to counter terrorism, and the legislation should enable law enforcement officers to work with their counterparts in other States.

The essence of the terrorism debate could be summarised as follows. Some believe that international law concerning terrorism should be based on "behaviour" rather than on "belief" for the criminal prosecution of terrorists; that is, if it can be established that a terrorist group had the means to, and attempted to, attack unarmed civilians (posing a credible threat), then they can be prosecuted for terrorist activity. Others believe that intent must be established, for example, the intent that the group is attempting to do harm to a group of unarmed civilians.

While a terrorist can act by means other than simply terroristic ones, such as sabotage, most terrorism analysts are still concerned with coming to agreement on a universal legal definition of terrorism. However, this may continue to prove an impossible task, as it has been over the decades, since one nation's terrorist threat is another nation's freedom fighter. Moreover, due to domestic politics, many nations may never condemn a terrorist group as terrorists regardless of the evidence, because it would have a domestic destabilising effect politically.

Others prefer to focus on supply-side counter-terrorist policy, such as tighter export controls, transhipment monitoring, etc. This is a pre-emptive strategy, one that has been utilised quite successfully over the years, in which international intelligence agencies work with local law enforcement to track terrorist group movements, and movements of their equipment, and stop them before reaching their attack destinations. As the evidence of the Aum Shinrikyo case showed, if there had been tighter export controls, if there had been any significant monitoring of shipments, Aum might not have had a chance to assemble its multimillion dollar chemical weapons production facility. Also, if international intelligence, as well as Japanese national intelligence, had worked daily with local law enforcement in Japan, Aum would likely have been stopped years before the devastating Tokyo Subway sarin gas attack of 1995.

All agree on increased intelligence monitoring of possible terrorist preparatory activities. However, some would like to see the international criminalisation of terrorists' attempts to gain WMD and/or their precursors, focusing on the acts of supply. Others believe the focus should be on the monitoring of the groups themselves: the profiling of terrorist group leaders and their organisational make-up, including gathering evidence of likely violent intent, and tracing their criminal connections, all of which would be in the pursuit of distinguishing a theoretical terrorist threat from a credible threat of catastrophic international terrorism, and therefore, would work toward building a prosecution case with a legal basis. Under that view, this is considered to be more efficient than a focus on the tonnes and tonnes of shipments of potentially lethal, but legal, precursors and/or dual-use technologies. Monitoring that category of dual use goods is an export control task that most national customs administrations find, quite simply, logistically impossible, and, in the end, one which provides very little evidence to help a counter-terrorist investigation into an international terrorist group, and ultimately bring about the arrest of its members. Even the United States Department of Commerce, with all the resources at its disposal, has indicated that it is unfeasible to monitor all vehicles entering the United States due to the sheer volume of transport; nor does there seem to be much of a technological fix in sight.

Since the legal issue of establishing intent or motive for the criminal prosecution of individuals engaged in planning terrorist acts is very difficult to do, the focus could, therefore, be on the criminalisation of the activities preparatory to those acts, such as the acquisition of WMD precursors by terrorist or criminal groups. To that it is argued that, although legally establishing intent or motive for the use or credible threat of use of WMD violence is difficult, it is nevertheless the only way to truly counter international terrorist organisations. Therefore, international legal and intelligence community cooperation against international terrorism should be focused on this profiling of terrorist groups (without treating innocent people as "terrorists") and their criminal and/or violent intent, since terrorist violence, regardless of a terrorist's use or threat of use of WMD or conventional weaponry, requires the same legal investigation. Safeguards must also be adhered to since, in the absence of an overt act of statement by the "terrorist", such intent can only be presumed and a wrong presumption can be oppressive. Any catastrophic terrorist act poses a major threat to international society, and catastrophic WMD terrorism, so far, has remained a theoretical, but very present, possibility.

Stephen Lustig

Rapporteur for Panel B.4 in the 2001 OPCW International Symposium; Center for Nonproliferation Studies, Monterey Institute of International Studies. The views expressed are not attributable to the Center, the Monterey Institute or the OPCW.

INTERNATIONAL COOPERATION IN PROTECTION AGAINST TERRORISM THROUGH INTERPOL

Roberto Maroto*

1. Introduction

At the Interpol General Secretariat, the Public Safety and Terrorism Sub Directorate, under the Specialised Crimes Directorate, is responsible for dealing with all matters concerning terrorism. The activities of this branch are primarily based on international cooperation against terrorism.

2. A Short Historical Background

At the Interpol 54th General Assembly in Washington in 1985, member countries authorised the creation of a specialised group at the General Secretariat to coordinate and enhance cooperation on international terrorism matters.[1] It also authorised the group to prepare a guide with the principles of cooperation in the subject of terrorism. At the succeeding 55th General Assembly in Belgrade in 1986, the guide was adopted by a resolution. In 1987, the Anti-Terrorism Branch was established at Interpol. In 2001, under a new structure at IPSG, the Anti-Terrorism Branch became the Public Safety and Terrorism Sub Directorate.

3. The Approach to International Counter-Terrorism

Over the past 10 years, the organisation has observed changes in the character of international terrorism which has now become increasingly institutional, brutal and global. The Interpol General Secretariat has concluded that, in every region of the globe, there continues to exist an ample number of disputes among groups, movements, etc. which could easily sustain a potentially devastating level of terrorism for decades to come.

International terrorist activities, which have attracted the attention of the public worldwide, have demonstrated the increasingly important role played by various extremist groups. It has been broadly accepted that terrorism is characteristically accompanied by universally recognised criminal acts of violence and/or threats which constitute ordinary crimes. The extremist groups attempt to achieve their objectives by perpetrating criminal activities and attempt to legitimatise these activities by offering "justification" based on their ideological goals and principles. Under the rule of law, there is simply no justification. Such criminal activities are the antithesis of civilised behaviour and are illegal.

* Crime Intelligence Officer, Public Safety and Terrorism Sub Directorate, Interpol General Secretariat Headquarters, Lyon. Any views expressed are solely those of the author and are not attributable to Interpol.

[1] Resolution AGN/54/RES/1.

R. Yepes-Enríquez and L. Tabassi. (eds.), Treaty Enforcement and International Cooperation in Criminal Matters

Traditionally, Interpol has the responsibility to protect people from this form of international criminal activity. Accordingly, the General Secretariat is prepared to fully extend its assistance in such matters, in keeping with the Interpol Constitution, applicable General Assembly resolutions and other pertinent rules and regulations of the organisation. Cooperation to the maximum extent possible among police worldwide is essential in order to effectively and efficiently address the terrorism challenges of the future.

In order to prevent and detect cases of terrorism, a systematic and carefully regulated approach to obtaining and processing information is necessary. To the maximum extent that national laws allow, and in conformity with Article 9 of the ICPO-Interpol Constitution, member countries should disseminate all relevant information concerning international terrorist crimes to the General Secretariat as well as to the member countries concerned.

The General Secretariat receives all information obtained as a result of investigations carried out in relation to crimes committed by terrorists. Member countries send all pertinent information relating to individuals, groups, instruments used to commit the crimes, evidence found at the crime scenes, and *modus operandi*.

It is presupposed that there exist sufficient, effective intra-country coordination efforts among the various components of each respective national administration. This is vital in order to collate all relevant information for dissemination to the Interpol member countries. The quality of the information contained in the Interpol database, and Interpol's ability to disseminate this information in a timely manner, determines, to a great extent, Interpol's success in the fight against international terrorist crimes.

4. Counter-Terrorism Strategy

The General Secretariat actively promotes a coordinated law enforcement strategy with respect to international terrorism. It is important to understand that this strategy is primarily intended for implementation at the National Central Bureau (NCB) level.[2] The criminal intelligence centres should rest individually within each respective NCB on a national basis. The strategy is twofold.

The first component of the strategy is prevention. The prevention phase includes information collection activity from a wide variety of available sources, through legal means, in order to acquire relevant criminal intelligence relating to groups and/or individuals who intend or are likely to carry out criminal acts for terrorist purposes. The information collected must be centrally, carefully analysed on a timely basis, and disseminated where appropriate with the ultimate view to prevent, pre-empt or deter a terrorist act and/or initiate an appropriate police response. Prevention through proactive legal law enforcement is Interpol's top priority.

Secondly, the response phase dictates that, should a terrorist incident occur, an active and immediate law enforcement response must follow. A thorough investigation and aggressive prosecution, along with extradition if necessary, must be immediately undertaken. The General Secretariat actively promotes the concept that swift, effective and efficient law enforcement investigation of terrorism incidents, culminating in arrests, convictions, incarcerations and extradition, serve as a powerful deterrent message to would-be terrorists. The Public Safety

[2] See *supra* in this volume, R. Maroto, Interpol.

and Terrorism Sub Directorate of the General Secretariat receives pertinent information which may be relevant to either the prevention of terrorist incidents, or to an appropriate law enforcement response. This is consistent with the aforementioned strategy. It is well known that terrorist incidents are most frequently planned and perpetrated by individuals within organisational structures or groups. Law enforcement, therefore has a legitimate investigative interest in such groups in order to address the criminal activities of individuals within the organisation(s).

5. Other Public Safety and Terrorism Sub Directorate Activities

5.1 Notices

While information management certainly accounts for the majority of the work being done by the Public Safety and Terrorism Sub Directorate, other duties are also very important to the international law enforcement community. The notice program has an important component that deals with terrorism and air traffic safety (an area traditionally handled by the Public Safety and Terrorism Sub Directorate).[3] There currently are approximately 500 outstanding notices for people wanted for crimes related to terrorism.

5.2 Symposia

Another important aspect of Public Safety and Terrorism Sub Directorate activity is the organisation of symposia and working groups. Working groups are organised to study a specific form of terrorism when the circumstances or the situation requires it. For example, in March 1998, the Public Safety and Terrorism Sub Directorate organised a working group in Algiers, in which approximately 15 countries participated, to discuss terrorism in North Africa and its international repercussions. Another working group was organised in March 2001 on the same issue.

Terrorism symposia are organised on an annual basis. In October 1998, the annual terrorism symposium was held in Spain with the theme "International Terrorism and Support Networks." It brought together close to 100 participants from 43 countries and six international organisations. In the Fall of 1999, the terrorism symposium was held in Sri Lanka with the theme "the Financing of Terrorism." In 2000 it was held in Lyon with the theme "Information Management in the Fight against Terrorism."

5.3 Warnings and Alerts

The Warnings and Alerts Programme allows NCBs the possibility to use the Interpol communication network to quickly disseminate any information on potential terrorist threats. It also allows the country receiving the information to take the necessary action to handle the threat.

In brief, the system allows any NCB to report a particular threat or event to the General Secretariat to a zone (that is, a limited number of countries, for example, in a geographical area), or to all member countries. The message will generally identify either the threat or an

[3] See further, *Id.*

event, together with the dates, people or countries concerned, and a request for any additional information. In the routine handling of these requests, the proper diffusion of the message to all countries which may have an interest is ensured first. Second, Interpol proceeds to check its databases for any useful information.

Requests that are received at the General Secretariat are varied. Threat alerts against people, airlines and, obviously, events are received. Notice of events range from the more routine visits of heads of State and other VIPs, such as the Pope or members of royal families, to cultural meetings or major sports events, such as the Olympic Games.

For the Sydney Olympic Games in 2000, due to its nature and the fact that a large number of threats were identified and exchanged between countries through the Interpol network, the Public Safety and Terrorism Sub Directorate initiated increased coverage so that all messages regarding the games could be reviewed and action taken 24 hours a day.

The Warnings and Alerts system rests on the principle that information should be shared to the maximum extent possible.

6. International Weapons and Explosives Tracking System (IWETS)

Another important system for international cooperation in combating terrorism, currently being developed and implemented, concerns the firearms and explosives needed by terrorists to commit their attacks. Interpol has established the system to combat international weapons trafficking.

IWETS is currently the only international analytical database designed to collate information on illegal firearms trafficking. IWETS provides current indexes of firearms manufacturers and other information that facilitates the identification of firearms. IWETS is also the only international system tracking stolen and/or recovered weapons.

While IWETS' primary subject is firearms and explosives, it could be also used in relation to chemical weapons. The history of the system is beyond the scope of this paper, but the major enhancement program for IWETS which is in progress at Interpol should be mentioned here. Plans include a vast improvement of the existing IWETS stolen and/or recovered firearms database. The initiation of a restricted access internet webpage for firearms is also planned for the existing Interpol website. This site will assist investigators by providing automated access to an improved database, identification reference tables, firearms tracing capability, electronic investigative information via a shared bulletin board, training programs, and another related firearms issues. The improved IWETS system will eventually facilitate firearms tracing by Interpol member countries and provide identification of firearms methods and patterns.

What Interpol is trying to accomplish is the full automation and decentralisation of the firearms and explosive system. In other words, if a police officer comes across a firearm in the city center of The Hague, for example, that officer should be able to query the national police database and find out if this weapon was stolen anywhere in the world, be it France, Japan, South Africa or wherever. The technology already exists to provide this information instantly. The vast majority of the 179 Interpol member countries are already connected through an Interpol communication network.

In the field of stolen vehicles, for example, national databases on stolen vehicles are linked with the Interpol databank which enables national queries to be made in any of several languages. To give an indication of the size of the database, there are currently over 1.5 million stolen vehicle reports on the system. Every month approximately 1000 stolen vehicles are recovered through the use of this system.

This is the kind of system that is being developed for firearms and explosives, and this is also the kind of system that could eventually be used to combat crime involving chemical weapons or other weapons of mass destruction.

7. Interpol's Response to 11 September

As a consequence of the tragic terrorist attacks on 11 September in the United States, Interpol immediately reorganised and reinforced its operational structure to better respond to the crisis. Two new structures were created in order to help Interpol Member Countries exchange information and leads on the attacks: the Command Center and the Task Force.

7.1 The Command Center

It was quickly recognized by the General Secretariat senior management that the 11 September attacks required the activation of a Command Center on a 24-hour basis. The Center would serve as the essential link between the General Secretariat and all Member States who were reporting information relevant to the 11 September attacks, and would coordinate and facilitate all responses and operational support.

7.2 The 11 September Task Force

The Task Force was established with the mission of providing strategic oversight and advice to IPGS Senior Executives and the Operational Command Center. This would ensure the most effective and efficient untilization of the General Secretariat's human, material and financial assets in direct support of the global law enforcement efforts to deal with crisis situations. After its creation, the Task Force met on a regular basis to address and resolve myriad personnel, material and financial issues regarding the General Secretariat's operational support of the investigation into the 11 September attacks.

As a result of the work done by these two structures, more than 1500 messages, containing information received from more than 70 countries, were exchanged. These exchanges led, in several cases, to the issuing of arrest warrants for some Al Qaeda members and, on other occasions, contributed substantially to investigations worldwide.

CHEMICAL TERRORISM: PRECEDENTS AND PROSPECTS

Alex P. Schmid*

1. INTRODUCTION

International cooperation between States, and the effective implementation of international agreements, are problems which loom large in the field of terrorism. A dozen international treaties and protocols, as well as seven regional conventions on terrorism, currently exist.[1] However, there is no internationally agreed definition as to what "terrorism" is, and the majority of actors in the field of terrorism are non-state actors. Effective implementation of international treaties implies that States have a monopoly on violence that many weak States, and States in transition, in reality do not possess. Even developed democracies find it hard to control transnational organised crime groups, militant anti-immigration parties, and religious cults on their territory.

* Officer-in-Charge of the Terrorism Prevention Branch, United Nations. The opinions expressed are entirely those of the author and have no official status or backing from the United Nations.

[1] *International Conventions and Protocols — updated status as of 28 March 2002*: 1963 Convention on Offences and Certain Other Acts Committed on Board Aircraft (Tokyo Convention; applies to acts affecting in-flight safety), parties: 173; 1970 Convention for the Suppression of Unlawful Seizure of Aircraft (Hague Convention; applies to hijackings), parties: 174; 1971 Convention for the Suppression of Unlawful Acts Against the Safety of Civil Aviation (Montreal Convention; applies to acts of aviation sabotage such as bombings aboard aircraft in flight), parties: 175; 1973 Convention on the Prevention and Punishment of Crimes Against Internationally Protected Persons, including Diplomatic Agents (protects senior government officials and diplomats), parties: 117; 1979 Convention on the Physical Protection of Nuclear Material (combats unlawful taking and use of nuclear material), parties: 64; 1979 International Convention Against the Taking of Hostages, parties: 106; 1988 Protocol for the Suppression of Unlawful Acts of Violence at Airports Serving International Civil Aviation (extends and supplements the Montreal Convention on air safety), parties: 113; 1988 Convention for the Suppression of Unlawful Acts Against the Safety of Maritime Navigation (applies to terrorist activities on ships), parties: 67; 1988 Protocol for the Suppression of Unlawful Acts Against the Safety of Fixed Platforms Located on the Continental Shelf (refers to terrorist attacks on fixed offshore platforms), parties: 60; 1991 Convention on the Marking of Plastic Explosives for the Purpose of Detection (chemical marking to facilitate identification of plastic explosives, e.g. to combat aircraft sabotage), parties: 77; 1997 International Convention for the Suppression of Terrorist Bombings (expands legal framework for international cooperation in the investigation, prosecution, and extradition of persons who engage in terrorist bombings), parties: 54 (EIF: 23 May 2002); 1999 International Convention for the Suppression of the Financing of Terrorism (tackles front organizations serving as financial conduits for terrorist organisations), parties: 24 (EIF: 10 April 2002). *Regional Conventions*: 1977 European Convention on the Suppression of Terrorism, parties: 37; 1971 Organisation of American States (OAS) Convention to Prevent and Punish The Acts of Terrorism Taking the Form of Crimes against Persons and Related Extortion that are of International Significance, parties: 14; 1987 South Asian Association for Regional Cooperation (SAARC) Regional Convention on Suppression of Terrorism, parties: 7; 1998 Arab Convention on the Suppression of Terrorism, parties: 12; 1999 Treaty on Cooperation among States Members of the Commonwealth of Independent States in Combating Terrorism, parties: 6; 1999 Convention of the Organization of the Islamic Conference on Combating International Terrorism, parties: 3; 1999 Organization of African Unity (OAU) Convention on the Prevention and Combating of Terrorism, parties: 3.

R. Yepes-Enríquez and L. Tabassi. (eds.), Treaty Enforcement and International Cooperation in Criminal Matters

Since the Aum Shinrikyo sarin attack on the Tokyo subway in March 1995, there has been rising apprehension about the existence of a new form of terrorism that does not shy away from using weapons of mass destruction (WMD). Half a decade later, these fears have not been realised — we have not seen nuclear, radiological or chemical attacks by non-State terrorists. However, we have witnessed in the aftermath of the 11 September 2001 terrorist attacks on New York and Washington, D.C., a biological attack in the form of letters containing Anthrax spores.

Most studies have so far concentrated on how vulnerable open urban societies are to the use of WMD by terrorist organisations, rather than on how to realistically assess the threat.[2] There is no denying that these types of weapons can cause huge catastrophes if they are used to their fullest potential. Theoretically, a teaspoonful of sarin can kill 5,000 persons. Yet, in practice, it would take something like 1,000 kilograms to kill 5,000 people outdoors. In theory, botulinum toxin (a biological agent, rather than a chemical one) is some 10,000 times deadlier than sarin, but in outdoor dissemination, it degrades in the environment, and so is no deadlier than sarin.[3]

There is a big gulf between the "theoretical possibility" and the "operational reality" of chemical and bacteriological terrorism.[4] The debate about terrorism and WMD has been one where exaggeration has been the order of the day. Milton Leitenberg has recently characterised the debate concerning terrorism and WMD in the past five years as the following: (a) spurious statistics (hoaxes counted as "biological" events); (b) unknowable predictions; (c) greatly exaggerated consequence estimates; (d) gross exaggeration of the feasibility of successfully producing biological agents by non-state actors; (e) the apparent continued absence of a thorough threat assessment; and (f) thoughtless, ill-considered, counterproductive and extravagant rhetoric.[5]

Rather than experiencing a catastrophic terrorist attack, all we have seen so far is mainly hoaxes, a few more serious threats, and very few actual uses. Most of the recorded uses were chemical incidents involving the use of "off-the-shelf", commercially-available industrial products which were used against individuals rather than against larger groups of people.[6] In this sense, the use of the term "weapons of mass destruction" is misleading, since what takes place with such chemical and biological agents has been mostly individual murder by poisoning, or a few killings with a substance that could also be a weapon of mass destruction if used to its full potential. Many such uses are criminal, and some are political, such as when some secret service agencies have used toxic agents to eliminate adversaries.[7] In addition, the use of chemical and biological substances we have seen so far might not even constitute terrorism — a point to which I shall return.

---

[2] J.B. Tucker (ed.), Toxic Terror: Assessing Terrorist Use of Chemical and Biological Weapons (2000) at 1.

[3] Gerald L. Epstein, *Chemical-Biological Terrorism: No Longer Hypothetical*, Washington, D.C., International Conference on Aviation Safety and Security in the 21st Century (13-15 January 1997) at 2, http://www.hfni.gsehd.gwu.edu/csm/aviation/track_ii/epstein.htm.

[4] The distinction is from Amy E. Smithson, Ataxia: The Chemical and Biological Terrorism Threat and the US Response (2001), as quoted in Vernon Loeb, *Making Chemical Weapons is No Easy Task*, Washington Post (5 February 2001), http://www.washingtonpost.com/wp-dyn/articles/A19900-2001Feb2.html.

[5] M. Leitenberg, *Terrorism and Weapons of Mass Destruction*, in A.P. Schmid and R. Grindley (eds.), Countering Terrorism Through International Cooperation, Milan, ISPAC (2001) at 50.

[6] *Id.* at 3.

[7] An example was the attempt by a Near Eastern country's secret service to spray a skin-penetrating nerve toxin behind the ear of Hamas leader Khaled Meshal in Jordan in 1997. Because of pressure by Jordan and the United States, the country suspected of being behind the assassination attempt had to release the antidote, which saved the victim's life. G. E. Schweitzer and C.C. Dorsch, Superterrorism: Assassins, Mobsters and Weapons of Mass Destruction (1998) at 92.

When we speak about terrorism and WMD, we have to differentiate. Of the different types of agents that can also be used as WMD, the radiological and chemical weapons are probably the easiest to acquire by terrorists. Chemical agents are often dual-use substances; that is, they and most of their precursors can be used for both commercial and military purposes.[8] This is not, however, the case with classic chemical warfare substances like tabun, sarin or VX.

2. Defining Chemical Terrorism

What is chemical terrorism? Clearly, not all offensive uses of chemical substances are terrorist in nature. Tear gas, for example is a non-lethal chemical agent. However, as outlawed instruments of warfare, chemical weapons, by their nature and the memories of their deployment in the First World War, inspire fear. The enhanced fear factor makes them terrifying. All WMD inspire terror — that is their purpose. But, not everything terrifying is also "terroristic". What is terroristic? There is still no agreed upon definition of "terrorism" in international law. The existing conventions outlaw specific acts — bombings, hijackings, hostage taking, etc. — but do not address the strategic goals and the political intent of the terrorists. Not everything a "terrorist" does is automatically "terroristic". Some activities of groups labelled "terrorist" might be legal, others might be non-violent, yet still others might constitute guerrilla warfare tactics. Only one element of their violent actions might be terroristic, in the sense that they are intended to intimidate a target group, to blackmail a government, or to serve the purpose of impressing a public.

The issue of assessing "intent" is a difficult one. Intent is hard to establish, since intent requires knowing the motivation. For example, the Chemical Weapons Convention defines chemical weapons as all toxic chemicals and their precursors, unless they are intended to be used for purposes not prohibited by the Convention.[9] This, too, raises the problem of assessing "intent". Intentions can change easily, especially if the chemical agents are already there. While there are many toxic chemical agents, those that have been weaponised are of special concern to us here; they are classified by their main effects on the human body. They include blister agents, pulmonary agents, blood agents, choking agents, tearing and incapacitating agents, nerve agents, and psychopharmacological agents. Each has the effect indicated by its name.

For terrorist use, weaponisation, however crude, of any of these agents is required. This includes the design, production or acquisition, stabilisation, and storage of the agent, and its transportation and delivery to the target population through mechanical, pneumatic, thermal or explosive means. The most effective, but also the most difficult, form of distribution is through aerosol generators. An aerosol disperses the toxic agent in tiny droplets that float above the ground, or they are blown through an air conditioning system until they come into contact with a target. For the purposes of this paper, chemical terrorism can be defined as the intimidation, blackmailing, or propagandisation of a target audience through the threat or use of weaponised toxic chemical agents against non-combatants.

---

[8] See F.R. Sidell, W.C. Patrick, T.R. Dashiell, Jane's Chem-Bio Handbook at 264-282 (1998), for a list of precursor materials and dual civil and military uses.

[9] 1993 Convention on the Prohibition of the Development, Production, Stockpiling and Use of Chemical Weapons and on Their Destruction, entered into force on 29 April 1997. Text, as corrected and changed, available at http://www.opcw.org. See Article II(1)(a) of the Convention.

3. Non-State Actors: the Present Situation

While there has been some use of chemical weapons by State actors in recent years, what is the situation with regard to non-State actors and, in particular, with regard to terrorists? One of the most extensive databases in the public domain, prepared by the Monterey Institute for International Studies' Center for Nonproliferation Studies, included 560 known cases of the attempted acquisition or use of chemical and biological weapons.[10] Since 1975, it has noted 154 fatalities from "chemical terrorism," but has also indicated that in 60 percent of incidents no one was killed or injured.[11] The database of the United Nations Terrorism Prevention Branch lists, for the period since 1945, about 100 events involving the use of chemical or biological agents. The following table gives some examples of the character of hoaxes, threats, acquisitions and uses of chemical weapons.

Table 1

Chemical Terrorism: Examples of Hoaxes, Threats, Aborted Attempts, and Use

Hoaxes	20 December 2000: The Airport Authority and the governor's office of the US territory of Guam received an e-mail warning that there would be a terrorist chemical attack on Guam on 24 December 2000, involving the use of nerve gas and targeting hotels, restaurants, and public places. The e-mail came from an unidentified group claiming to represent Osama bin Laden. It said that this attack was meant "to teach a lesson to the U.S. government not to harm the Afghan people and its allies".[12]
Threat	In 1978, the US city of Phoenix (Arizona) received a threat that its water supplies would be contaminated if extortion payments were not made; no payments were made. [13]
Considered Acquisition	Before 26 February 1993, when Ramzi Yousef carried out the World Trade Center bombing, he considered adding sodium cyanide to the explosive, but did not do so in the end because "it was going to be too expensive to implement". [14]
Attempt to Acquire	According to a 2000/2001 United States Central Intelligence Agency analysis, Al Qaeda (Osama Bin Laden's organisation) operated a dozen Afghan camps that trained as many as 5,000 militants, who in turn created cells in some 50 countries. Intelligence officials say the group was experimenting with chemical weapons, including nerve gas, and in one of its camps used sheep to test the agents.[15]

[10] Status at 1999. M.B. Maerli, *Relearning the ABCs: Terrorists and Weapons of Mass Destruction*, The Nonproliferation Review (Summer 2000) at 110.

[11] B. Hoffman, S. Carus, A. Sands and J. Pilat, *What Can the Past Tell Us About the Future?*, in The 'New Terrorism': Does it Exist? How Real Are the Risks of Mass Casualty Attacks?, Chemical and Biological Arms Control Institute and the Center for Global Security Research, Lawrence Livermore National Laboratories, Report of Conference Proceedings (April 29-30, 1999), http://www.cbaci.org/Newterrorism.htm, p. 4.

[12] Source: Emergency Response & Research Institute (ERRI) (22 December 2000), http://www.emergency.com/cntrter3.htm.

[13] R. Medd and F. Goldstein *International Terrorism on the Eve of a New Millennium*, Studies in Conflict and Terrorism, 284 (July-September 1997).

[14] J.V. Parachini, *The World Trade Center Bombers* (1993), in J.B. Tucker (ed.), see *supra* note 2.

[15] S. Engelberg, *One Man and a Global Web of Violence*, New York Times (14 January 2001), http://www.nytimes.com/2001/01/world/14JIHA.html.

Table 1 cont.

Attempt to Acquire	CIA Director George Tenet said in March 2000: "Although terrorists we've pre-empted still appear to be relying on conventional weapons, we know that a number of these groups are seeking chemical, biological, radiological, or nuclear agents. We are aware of several instances in which terrorists have contemplated using these materials. Among them is Bin Laden, who has shown a strong interest in chemical weapons. His operatives have allegedly been trained to conduct attacks with toxic chemicals or biological toxins".[16]
Acquisition	A US survivalist group, the Covenant, the Sword and the Arm of the Lord, in 1985 acquired 30 gallons of potassium cyanide, to be used to poison a municipal water supply, possibly in New York or Washington, D.C.[17]
Actual Use	The Japanese cult Aum Shinrikyo tried, but failed to develop nuclear and biological weapons, but succeeded in producing a small quantity of crude chemical weapons. The first major incident took place in June 1994 in Matsumoto; there were 7 deaths and some 260 injured; the second attack took place in March 1995 in the Tokyo subway; there were 12 deaths and forty seriously injured people. Some 1,000 people became "moderately ill" following that attack.

Since the last category is clearly the one that counts the most, let us have a closer look at the partly successful attempts of Aum Shinrikyo, a messianic religious group founded in 1987.

4. The Aum Shinrikyo Incidents

The apocalyptic Aum sect, founded in 1987, had some 40,000 members by 1995, most of them in Japan (10,000) and in Russia (30,000). It was, in many ways, a criminal organisation engaging in land fraud, kidnapping for ransom, drug dealing for profit, and multiple murders of defectors, critics, rivals, and opponents. Despite its track record of criminal activities, its cover as a religious organisation made the Japanese authorities very reluctant to prosecute Aum. The sect was in some ways comparable to a multinational corporation; it possessed a sheep ranch in Australia, a tea plantation in Sri Lanka, and a trading company in Taiwan. It had twenty facilities in Japan and headquarters at the base of Mount Fuji. Fourteen hundred of Aum's most devoted members in Japan lived in Aum facilities. The cult ran a chain of computer stores, trading companies, restaurants, training centres, a fitness club, and a medical clinic, with a total value of tens of millions of dollars. In its recruitment of members, the sect managed to attract young people who had studied medicine, biology, biochemistry, physics, and electrical engineering at top universities. There were about 20 scientists with graduate degrees at Aum; one of them apparently left university and joined Aum because its laboratories were better equipped.[18]

[16] G.J. Tenet, Statement by the Director of Central Intelligence Agency before the Senate Foreign Relations Committee (21 March 2000), cited by M. Leitenberg, *supra* note 5, at 10.

[17] Jessica Eve Stern, *The Covenant, the Sword, and the Arm of the Lord* (1985), in J.B. Tucker, *supra* note 2, at 150. Incidentally, the quantity of 30 gallons would have had no serious effects due to dilution.

[18] M. Sayle, *Nerve Gas and Four Noble Truths*, The New Yorker (1 April 1996), cited in M.B. Maerli, *supra* note 10, at 119. D.E. Kaplan, *Aum Shinrikyo* (1995), in J.B. Tucker (ed.), *supra* note 2, at 209-211, 223.

Within little more than one year, Aum Shinrikyo managed to produce more than 30 kilograms of Sarin, and used it as a crude weapon, killing 19 people in two incidents, and injuring more than 1,200. The following precursor substances were bought by Aum on the commercial market and intended for the production of chemical weapons;[19]

- 90 tonnes of methanol;
- 50 tonnes of diethylaniline;
- 180 tonnes of phosphorus trichloride;
- 54 tonnes of sodium fluoride;
- 51 tonnes of isopropyl alcohol;
- 0.95 tonnes of phosphorus pentachloride; and,
- 0.55 tonnes of iodine.

The goal of Aum was usually assassination, which is not the same thing as terrorism. The difference between an assassination and a terrorist killing is that in the former, a specific person is targeted and the victim is the target. In a terrorist killing, the victim is only a means to an end — e.g. to attract publicity for the terrorist organisation. Aum's use of chemical substances was in most cases not intended as terrorism, except perhaps for the last aborted incident in the Shinjuku subway station in May 1995.

Table 2

Chemical Agents Produced by Aum

March 1993	Aum member Hideo Murai (astrophysicist) instructs Aum member Masami Tsuchiya to carry out research and development for the mass production of chemical weapons.
May 1993	Tsuchiya repeatedly conducts basic experiments for mass Sarin production.
September 1993	Murai orders Takizawa to draw up plans for the construction of a Sarin production plant, for the manufacture of 70 tonnes.[20]
November 1993	20 grams of a standard sample of Sarin are manufactured; 600 grams of Sarin are manufactured.
February 1994	30 kilograms of impure Sarin are manufactured. Asahara assembles leaders engaged in the building of the Sarin plant, gives them instructions, and orders the quick completion of the plant.
July 1994	50 grams of Yperite (sulfur mustard) are manufactured; a remodelled refrigeration truck to heat and spray Sarin is completed. A Sarin attack in Matsumoto kills 7 and injures over 250.

[19] D.E. Kaplan, *Aum Shinrikyo* (1995) in J.B. Tucker, *supra* note 2, at 215.

[20] According to R.J. Lifton, the "seventy tonnes of sarin" were meant for an attack planned for November 1995, for which a large Russian helicopter had been purchased. R.J. Lifton, Destroying the World to Save It (1999) at 40.

Table 2 cont.

August 1994	Several litres of Phosgene and Prussic acid (hydrogen cyanide) are manufactured.
November 1994	100 grams of VX hydrochloride are allegedly manufactured.
December 1994	Tsuchiya allegedly manufactures around 50 grams of VX; 200 grams of Yperite (sulfur mustard) are also produced.
20 March 1995	Five Aum members puncture 11 nylon bags with sharpened umbrella tips in the Tokyo subway. Each bag contains 600 grams of Sarin, and a dozen people are killed and forty others are seriously injured.
5 May 1995	A planned hydrogen cyanide gas incident at the Shinjuku subway station is aborted by the alertness of a few station attendants. [21]

Within two years, some 20 Aum scientists managed to construct, with commercially available dual-use components, one or more chemical weapon agents, although they were not able to produce the 70 tonnes of sarin they had originally planned.

What were the motives behind the use of chemical agents? The general goal was to prepare and defend Aum members in an imagined coming war between the United States and Japan. The declared enemies of Aum were the United States, Jews, Freemasons, and in Japan, the imperial family, prominent politicians, and rival religious figures. The actual attacks had more narrow tactical goals.

The Aum Shinrikyo attack on the Tokyo subway was not primarily "terroristic", in the sense that it was intended to intimidate a large audience. This attack was *apparently* undertaken to preempt a planned police attack on Aum's premises the next day. It was only following the Tokyo subway incident that Shoko Asahara ordered Aum to resort to acts of terrorism in order to prevent his capture.[22] Table 3 identifies various uses, most of them non-terroristic in the narrow sense of the word.

---

[21] Source: L. Richards, Aum Shinri Kyo or 'Aleph': The Potential for Future Terrorist Activity, at 1-3, http://chembio.janes.com/subscribe/features/aum.html; *Prospects for the Future* in R.J. Lifton, *supra* note 20, at 179-181.

[22] The police raid came probably as a consequence of an attempt to assassinate Takaji Kunimatsu, head of the National Police Agency on 30 March 1995. On 5 May 1995, members of Aum placed plastic bags with cyanide gas in the crowded Shinjuku subway station, and on 16 May, the day Asahara was arrested, a parcel bomb meant for the governor, Yukio Aoshima, exploded in the city hall of Tokyo. R. J. Lifton, *supra* note 20 at 41.

Table 3

Motives Behind Aum Shinrikyo Use of WMD Agents

Recruitment	To self-fulfil prophecies of catastrophe, as in several unsuccessful biological agent releases meant to prove that Asahara's prediction of Armageddon were coming true, so as to attract new members to the group.
Experimental	As, in the spring of 1994, when they tested Sarin on a flock of Merino sheep in Australia.
Accidental	When mustard gas escaped in Aum's laboratory Satian No. 7 in June 1994, killing seven people and wounding 150-200.
Silencing Critics and Enemies	As in two failed Sarin attacks on rival religious sect leaders in late 1993.
Disruptive	As in the 27 June 1994 attempt to kill three judges in a land dispute matter against Aum Shinrikyo. The goal was to block a legal sentence against Aum. Over 200 people were injured and seven people died (but the three judges, though made ill, survived the attack in which 20 kilograms of sarin was used to "smoke out" the apartment building in which the judges lived).
Diversive	In order to prevent an imminent police raid. On 20 March 1995 five Aum members tried to kill Tokyo subway commuters on their way to government offices and the National Police headquarters. The goal was to forestall a police raid on the group which had been scheduled for the next day.[23]
Revengeful/ Terroristic	Attempt to cause havoc, as in the aborted attack on the Shinjuku subway station in May 1995.

5. Future Prospects

Was Aum Shinrikyo a harbinger of worse to come or an exception? In one sense, it was not a surprise that the first terrorist attack with potential WMD agents was a chemical, rather than a nuclear or biological, attack. What is worrying about chemical agents is their strong dual-use element, and the fact that there are so many professional chemical factories in the

[23] The attack in the city of Matsumoto (about 100 miles from Tokyo) interrupted the trial by three judges presiding over a land purchase fraud by Aum members and postponed the negative decision anticipated by Aum indefinitely Lifton, *supra* note 20, at 39. This "success" could have provided an incentive for repetition in the form of an attack on the Tokyo subway. According to R.J. Lifton, *supra* note 20, the Tokyo attack "was meant to be diversionary, to confuse the police and convince them that someone else was responsible and that Aum itself was being victimized". Lifton summarised the more general motivation as follows: "Sarin, then, was simultaneously a "defense" or "deterrent" against alleged evil and a trigger for Armageddon. The immediate evil being "defended" against was the authority of the state, and the Tokyo subway release was a desperate strategic effort, however absurd, to employ a limited amount of gas to divert the police and confuse the public." Lifton, *supra* note 20, at 40, 184.

world. In 1993, for instance, there were almost 20,000 chemical manufacturing plants in the United States alone, accounting for almost one-third of the world's total chemical production capacity. Such facilities are, if unprotected, sitting ducks for chemical terrorists. A recently disclosed study by the United States Army Surgeon General concluded that as many as 2.4 million people could be killed or injured in a terrorist attack against a United States toxic chemical plant in a densely populated area. While this represents a worst case scenario, even middle-range casualty estimates from an explosion of a toxic chemical manufacturing plant or a chemical weapons attack are as high as 903,400 people, according to this United States study. The study found that at least 123 United States plants each keep amounts of toxic chemicals that, if released, could form deadly vapour clouds that would endanger more than 1 million people. The study ranked the threat of attacks against chemical plants second only to the widespread use of biological weapons (such as smallpox) which could generate as many as 1.18 million casualties

Key ingredients for the production of nerve gas (such as ammonia, ethanol, isopropanol, sodium cyanide, yellow phosphorus, sulfur monochloride, hydrogen fluoride and sulfur) are industrial chemicals used in quantities of millions of tonnes in the commercial sector. It is therefore almost impossible to submit such chemicals to a watertight regime of control. For instance, one category of chemical agents, the blood agents, use cyanide as a basic ingredient. This substance is used for a wide variety of legitimate processes, e.g. in electroplating, mineral extraction, dyeing, printing, photography and agriculture, as well as in the production of paper, textiles, and plastics. The United States alone produces 300,000 tonnes a year for peaceful purposes.[24] Cyanide is commercially available as calcium-potassium or sodium salt. It is also used by governments for judicial executions.

There can be little doubt that many toxic chemical agents are relatively easy to obtain. Next to acquisition, motivation is the key factor when it comes to terrorism. How many sects and political and criminal organisations are likely and willing to use such weapons? Former United States Secretary of Defense William S. Cohen, in his January 1997 confirmation hearing, said he believed that "the proliferation of weapons of mass destruction presents the greatest threat that the world has ever known".[25] Before he left office in January 2001, he said:

> Our unrivalled supremacy in the conventional military arena is prompting adversaries to seek unconventional, asymmetric means to strike at what they perceive to be our Achilles heel. The race is on between our preparations and those of our adversaries. There is not a moment to lose.[26]

A recent report, *Global Trends 2015*, the result of a dialogue of the CIA with non governmental experts, came to the following conclusions:

> Between now and 2015 terrorist tactics will become increasingly sophisticated and designed to achieve mass casualties. We expect the trend toward greater lethality in

[24] F.R. Sidell, W.C. Patrick, T.R. Dashiell, *supra* note 8, at 14-15, 22.

[25] http://www.defenselink.mil/pubs/prolif97/index.html.

[26] M2 Press Wire. U.S. DOD: Department releases Proliferation report (11 January 2001); see http://defenselink.mil/pubs/ptr20010110.pdf for the third edition of the report, "Proliferation: Threat and Response," pages (i) and (ii) (or pages 4 and 5 of the Internet version).

> terrorist attacks to continue. Some potential adversaries will seek ways to threaten the U.S. homeland. Foreign governments and groups will seek to exploit such vulnerabilities using conventional munitions, information operations, and even WMD.... Chemical and biological threats to the United States will become more widespread; such capabilities are easier to develop, hide, and deploy than nuclear weapons.... Such weapons could be delivered through a variety of means, including missiles, unmanned aerial vehicles, or covertly via land, air, and sea.[27]

While Aum is proof that non-state actors can produce nerve gas, this came at a price. Some Aum members died in a laboratory accident. Even States pay a price for the production of such toxic substances. It has been reported that each year, one-third of the chemical workers in Iraq suffered occupational injuries while producing chemical weapons. Most amateur terrorists would presumably face even greater risks.[28]

Groups that have claimed to possess nuclear, biological or chemical (NBC) weapons, issue threats of NBC use, have attempted to acquire such weapons, or allegedly possess NBC weapons include Middle Eastern and North African groups, Caucasian rebels, ethnic separatists, and racist and survivalist groups. Yet there are other categories of actors who might pose a threat, such as lone-wolf scientists, disgruntled military specialists, or organised crime groups. White-collar criminals tampering with food production or with prepared food supplies of commercial competitors might become a source of concern. There is also the concern that fringe elements in the secret services, or some paranoid State actors, might decide to use the threat of NBC weapons, either in domestic power struggles, or as an act of revenge for defeats in interstate wars.

6. Conclusion

There is reason for concern about catastrophic acts of terrorism involving chemical, bacteriological, and nuclear weapons. In the light of the terrorist attack on the World Trade Center on 11 September 2001, a new sense of vulnerability has become apparent. The very instruments of modern science and technology can, with primitive means, be turned against society itself. There has been some speculation that the fourth aircraft which crashed in Pennsylvania was meant to hit a nuclear power plant in the vicinity. While the number of nuclear power reactors is so small — there are 110 in the United States — that upgrading security is relatively easy, the protection of some 20,000 chemical manufacturing plants is a huge task

At this moment chemical terrorism is, for most countries, still a low probability contingency. What is necessary is that early warning indicators are developed which can detect precursor events. Aum Shinrikyo spoke publicly about sarin before using it. Aum bought Israeli gas masks and precursor materials on the open market. It first tried to buy chemical weapons on the black market, but the "rogue state" with which Aum thought it was going to do business turned out to be a front organisation for the United States

[27] E. Pianin, *Study Assesses Risk of Attack on Chemical Plant*, Washington Post (12 March 2002) at A-8.

[28] Report of the Secretary-General on the Status of the Implementation of the Special Commission's Plan for the Ongoing Monitoring and Verification of Iraq's Compliance with Relevant Parts of Section C of Security Council Resolution 687 (1991), UN doc. S/95/864 at 16-19; see also G.E. Schweitzer with C.C. Dorsch, *supra* note 7, at 99.

Customs Service.[29] Intelligence agencies apparently failed to pick up such signals. Much can be done to prevent terrorism. Too little is done in a coordinated manner across international borders using synergies between anti-terrorist agencies, and using sound open and secret source research.

The role of anti-terrorist conventions in preventing chemical and bacteriological terrorism is important, but no panacea. There is no substitute for intelligence when it comes to prevention. A strong international legal regime, with a powerful monitoring and sanctioning capacity, will have a deterrent value, and will contribute to the creation of a climate where the taboo on the use of chemical weapons can be strengthened. Aum Shinrikyo has punctured that taboo, but seven years later — to use a Dutch metaphor — the dike has not ruptured.

[29] Smithson, as quoted by V. Loeb, *supra* note 4.

INTERNATIONAL TERRORISM: DEVASTATING CURRENT AND FUTURE TRENDS

Stephen Lustig*

The most recent Center for Security and International Studies[1] terrorism report, entitled, "To Prevail," states that, "the campaign against terrorism clearly will call for greater multilayered, multilateral cooperation than the United States has ever engaged in to date." This is entirely true, and although all terrorism analysts from governmental, private, and non-governmental sectors have been calling for such cooperation for decades, increased funding for, and dedicated support of, the cross-jurisdictional counter-terrorism infrastructure has yet to be realised. As Michael Dartnell writes, "Terrorism is an area in which the contradictions of the present global system (lack of enforcement and policy implementation) are obvious. An ideal international legal response would account for differences stemming from issues of jurisdiction, prosecution, extradition, and political asylum in order to facilitate a network of overlapping and intersecting jurisdictions."[2] Moreover, in the midst of this lack of effective and sustained international counter-terrorist cooperation, there is substantial evidence of some worrisome trends in international terrorism, which will only make successful international counter-terrorist operations more difficult than they are already. The following comments will serve to outline these trends.

1. Transnational Problems Require Transnational Responses

Nearly all of the terrorist groups that currently operate depend upon transnational networks for logistics, finance, and weapons procurement (including weapons of mass destruction (WMD) precursors). It is therefore logical that, in order to disrupt these activities before a devastating attack can take place, one needs a transnational network.[3] This transnational counter-terrorism effort already has an infrastructure, the one on which Interpol was founded, and it is supported by the national intelligence forces of 179 countries. However, criminologists have assessed that many of the national law enforcement and intelligence departments with cross-jurisdictional or interagency liaison tasks around the world are either underfunded, too hierarchical, or both. The problem of underfunding is obvious:

* Researcher, WMD Terrorism Project, Center for Nonproliferation Studies, Monterey Institute of International Studies. The opinions expressed herein are the author's own and do not necessarily reflect the opinions of the Center for Nonproliferation Studies.

[1] CSIS is a leading non-profit security policy research institute in Washington, DC.

[2] Dartnell, Research Associate at the York University Centre for International and Strategic Studies, Toronto, Canada, *A Legal Inter-Network for Terrorism: Issues of Globalization, Fragmentation and Legitimacy*, Terrorism and Political Violence (Winter 1999).

[3] See further, C. Dishman, *Terrorism,. Crime and Transformation*, Studies in Conflict and Terrorism (January 2001); P. Williams, *Transnational Crime Networks*, in Networks and Netwars: The Future of Terror, Crime and Military (RAND, 2001); and W. Laqueur, *Terrorism and Organized Crime*, in The New Terrorism (1999).

R. Yepes-Enríquez and L. Tabassi. (eds.), Treaty Enforcement and International Cooperation in Criminal Matters

there is simply not enough to support the long-term data collection and analysis needed for the long-term task of monitoring transnational illegal networks that support terrorists. Therefore, accurately predicting the movements of the increasingly sophisticated transnational criminal and terrorist networks in operation is impossible. The hierarchal structure of many counter-terrorism organisations further hampers them. This structure prevents the promotion of "team" structures needed for intelligence sharing and full cooperation with the relevant domestic and international counterparts. Both of these tasks are critical to responding rapidly to terrorist operations and disrupting or preventing attacks.

2. Current and Future Terrorist Trends: Illicit Transnational Networks

Terrorist groups' direct involvement in the international drug trade is well evidenced.[4] In fact, most terrorism experts agree that nearly all terrorist groups in operation today have shifted much of their focus to the illicit trade in arms, narcotics (mostly heroin), or both.[5] This shift in terrorist group focus was made possible by the creation of alliances with the existing transnational organised crime groups (TOCs). The net effect of this terrorist-TOC alliance has been the amassing of fortunes by terrorist groups, as well as making the terrorist groups more secure and powerful than ever before: such TOC networks are far more sophisticated, sturdy, and flexible than terrorist networks.[6] TOC networks standardly function by purchasing influence in (corrupting) regional and national government officials, who then serve the TOC and affiliated terrorist groups by shielding them from investigations and alerting them to counter-terrorist threats they might face.[7] Moreover, since TOC cells operate as a team, there is no single decision-making body. Operations can thus continue even if the members of one cell are arrested or killed. This small-cell structure makes it more difficult for counter-terrorists to detect and penetrate the cells, since each cell tends to have no more than eight to ten members.

Moreover, the trend seems to be that terrorist groups have learned from their affiliation with TOCs, and have re-engineered their own organisations to match the TOC structure. Also, since terrorists ultimately seek power, the economic power that they obtain from illicit trade is real and sustainable. Thus, a Terrorist-TOC hybrid has been born. As a result, contemporary terrorist organisations are generating real economic power, not just the perceived political power achieved by a terrorist attack.

An organisation that is economically and internally strong needs little or no support from the segments of society that lie outside the organisation. This will tend to permit the terrorist group to carry out catastrophic attacks without the need to worry about backlash from some outside constituency. Also, since organised crime is born of and prospers in

---

[4] W. Laqueur, *The New Terrorism: Fanaticism and the Arms of Mass Destruction*; F. Cilluffo, *The Threat Posed for the Convergence of Organized Crime, Drug Trafficking and Terrorism*; B.G. Thamm, *Die duestere Allianz: Buergerkrieg, organisiertes Verbrechen und Terrorismus*, Deutsche Polizei, 8/1999.

[5] M. Gheordunescu, *Terrorism and Organized Crime: The Romanian Perspective*, Terrorism and Political Violence (Winter 1999).

[6] P. Williams, *Transnational Criminal Networks*, in Networks and Netwars: The Future of Terror, Crime, and Militancy (RAND 2001).

[7] J. Albini, R.E. Rogers, J. Anderson, *The Evolution of Espionage Networks and the Crisis of International Terrorism and Global Organized Crime*, in E. Viano, ed., Global Organized Crime and International Security (1999).

societal chaos, such as the chaos that took over Albania in the early 1990s, catastrophic and violent terrorist attacks also benefit crime groups.

Furthermore, the shift of the terrorist group from political to economic (financial profit) concerns displays a shift from ideological (religious) to material concerns. This quite obviously affects the ethics of the terrorist group, permitting higher levels of violence, as there is no longer a need to justify such violence with political or ideological arguments. Terrorist-TOC groups may continue their political or religious rhetoric, but this no longer serves to motivate group members or improve group solidarity, as the economic power alone motivates.

3. Profiles of Three Terrorist-TOC Groups in Operation

The Islamic Movement of Uzbekistan (IMU) is perhaps the best example of a Terrorist-TOC. Founded in 1997 in the chaos spawned by several cross-border conflicts and the aftermath of the Tajik civil war, the group founders recruited members from the masses of unemployed in the region, promising them work and money, not spiritual salvation. As one Central Asian analyst described it, "the IMU is inherently both criminal and terrorist in nature. Primarily concerned with financial gain, the IMU has successfully used terrorism to destabilise Central Asia to maintain and secure narcotics transportation routes."[8] The IMU now controls one of the most important drug trafficking routes, a route worth billions of dollars annually. The IMU has maintained its Islamic rhetoric, however, since "by deterring public attention from the fact that its primary motivations are criminal in nature, the IMU has won popular support from sections of the Islamic communities within the region who believe that the IMU is fighting to free Muslims from government oppression."[9]

Even the originally religiously-motivated terrorist organization Hizbollah has made the transition to Terrorist-TOC.[10] Its involvement in narcotics trade is well established and expanding, with a network that extends from the Middle East to Europe. Also, Hizbollah is running protection rackets for organised criminals, and although Hizbollah claims to serve Shiite Muslims worldwide, Hizbollah cells were massively involved in the smuggling of Iraqi (anti-Shi'a) oil.[11] Azerbaijani authorities have reported that Hizbollah cells are operating in severely impoverished southern Azerbaijan, where 33% of the population has fled due to the severe unemployment and difficult living conditions (gas supplies have not been available since the early 1990s, and there is electricity only during certain times of day). Reports from the region support the view that Hizbollah is not there for spiritual guidance of the local population, but rather to recruit members for the expansion of their illicit trade operations. Hizbollah members were arrested in connection with the murder of the regional colleague of the Azerbaijani President, and two "suicides" occurred on the same day, one of which was the former regional director of the department for combating drug trafficking.[12]

The Kosovo Liberation Army (KLA) recruited most of its members in 1995, a time when official Albanian unemployment had reached 70%. The territory held by the KLA

---

[8] T. Makarenko, *Crime and Terrorism in Central Asia*, Jane's Intelligence Review (1 July 2000).

[9] *Id.*

[10] A. H. Schbley, *Torn Between God, Family, and Money: The Changing Profile of Lebanon's Religious Terrorists*, 23 Studies in Conflict & Terrorism (July-September, 2000).

[11] *Id.*

[12] *Azerbaijan: Economic Reasons Behind Spread of Wahhabism in South*, Baku Express (12 May 2001).

and affiliated criminal groups contain the route supplying 80% of the heroin to Europe, a route worth some $400 billion annually.[13] The KLA and supporting mafia groups have successfully erected money laundering networks, captured female war refugees for the international prostitution trade, and at one point in 1999 nearly managed to steal UNHCR humanitarian evacuation funds.[14] This is hardly the activity of a liberation movement seeking democratic involvement and self-determination for an ethnic minority. These are three examples, from approximately seven well-established Terrorist-TOC groups operating in territories stretching from the Middle East, Central Europe and even into Western Europe, that are well-documented as having amassed financial resources well beyond what any terrorist group would need to carry out its acts of terrorism.

4. Counter-Terrorism Strategy: Too Much Emphasis on Religious Motives and not Enough on Socio-Economic Motives

In view of the abovementioned success of terrorist organisations to recruit dedicated members and establish spheres of political and economic influence, it is quite obvious that nearly all terrorist organisations depended on the masses of impoverished, unemployed, and alienated segments of societies for recruitment. Early evidence has shown that the terrorists in Osama bin Laden's organisation and affiliate organisations were recruited from very similarly impoverished and alienated societal groups: recruited individuals are promised no need to work and financial fortunes if they train to fight and fight.[15] There needs to be less attention focused on the stated goals of the terrorist group leader and more analysis of the real goals and motives of the terrorists who are actually in the streets preparing for violence.

5. Terrorist-TOCs and Direct Access to Weapons of Mass Destruction (WMD) Precursors

Terrorist-TOC involvement in the international narcotics trade grants these groups direct access to the drug manufacturers, which permits access to chemical precursors and multi-million dollar laboratories that can either provide or easily obtain the resources necessary for crude but lethal chemical weapons production. Although this type of production would not yield military-grade agents and large quantities, such qualities and quantities are not necessary for terrorist strategies. Also, such drug laboratories and manufacturing facilities would possess sufficient equipment for the generation of biological agents. A laboratory need not be very sophisticated to permit the production of deadly pathogens for terrorist group purposes with crude weaponisation tactics.

Moreover, TOCs practice of purchasing influence in regional governments, particularly customs and border guards, has permitted, and will continue to permit, them the unimpeded shipment of illicit weapons and weapon precursors without detection. Moreover, criminal investigators have evidence that organised crime groups are highly proficient in the falsification

[13] Testimony of Frank Cilluffo before the US House Committee of the Judiciary-Subcommittee on Crime (December 13, 2000). Global Organized Crime Program, Center for Strategic and International Studies.

[14] B. G. Thamm, *Die duestere Allianz: Buergerkrieg, organisiertes Verbrechen und Terrorismus*, Deutsche Polizei, 8/1999.

[15] C. C. Malzahn, *Die Rekruten von Peschawar*, Der Spiegel 41/2001.

of export documents and end-user certificates, and many of the TOC networks include transport mafia elements, which makes the task of transhipment of weapons and weapons precursors to embargoed states and subnational groups easy and nearly undetectable.[16]

In the wake of the catastrophic attacks of 11 September 2001, national governments are rushing to reorganise their counter-terrorist structures now more than at any other time in history. Hopefully policy planners have realised that simple counter-terrorist strategies of increased border and immigration control are not sufficient for preventing international terrorist attacks, especially considering the aforementioned terrorist-TOC's efficient powers of transnational movement, including the procurement of false travel documentation. The only long-term successful counter-terrorism approach is one that will focus on increased cross-jurisdiction-based studies of terrorist organizational structures, their movements and real objectives. In short, the focus must be on what the terrorist group actually does, not simply on what it says it does. Moreover, individual character studies of terrorist group leadership also is not sufficient for countering terrorist groups: a successful terrorist organisation depends on the coordination between many transnational individuals, and often the leaders play very little role in the logistical planning and execution of terrorist attacks, as was the case in the attacks of September 11th.

If national governments do not organise in a way that ensures complete and long-term international cooperation for the analysis of terrorist and transnational organised crime networks, then the sophisticated international Terrorist-TOC entities will continue to amass further real economic and political power. Such power will enable them to control enough resources not only to ensure future successful catastrophic attacks, but also make these groups invincible, permanent, and daily threats to civil society internationally.

[16] V. Ruggiero, Organized and Corporate Crime in Europe (1996).

THE OPCW AND THE GLOBAL STRUGGLE AGAINST TERRORISM

OPCW Technical Secretariat*

1. Introduction

The approach followed in this chapter stems from two fundamental considerations. First, international multilateral organisations are part and parcel of the international community, and cannot shy away from the struggle against this new menace of terrorism, and should contribute to this struggle on the basis of their respective mandates and areas of expertise. Second, the threat of chemical terrorism must now be regarded as very real, and measures to address it must be assigned much higher priority than was the case before 11 September 2001.

This chapter analyses the provisions of the Chemical Weapons Convention[1] which apply to the danger of the terrorist use of chemical weapons (CW), with a view to identifying what role the implementation of the Convention has in the global struggle against terrorism.

The chapter starts from the realisation that the Convention aims to completely rule out the possibility of the use of chemical weapons. The Convention not only establishes legal norms for its States Parties, but also requires them to enact prohibitions for any of their individual citizens who, anywhere in the world, engage in activities prohibited to States Parties under the Convention. In fact, the Convention requires making the development, production, acquisition, stockpiling, transfer and use of chemical weapons a criminal offence in all States Parties, and for all citizens of all States Parties, irrespective of where the offence may have been committed. The same applies to assistance, encouragement or inducement to engage in such prohibited activities. There is, accordingly, no doubt that the Convention constitutes a solid legal basis for actions to prevent and prosecute chemical terrorism.

This chapter first analyses those provisions of the Convention that apply to all States Parties, and identifies the following areas in which action should be considered:

- the completion of the legislative and regulatory work required of all Member States under Article VII of the Convention, in order to ensure that terrorist activities involving chemical weapons can be effectively investigated and prosecuted;

* This chapter is an abridged version of the Note by the Director-General on the OPCW and the Global Struggle Against Terrorism, OPCW doc. EC-XXVII/DG.3 (9 November 2001), and Corr.1 (27 November 2001), together with the Note by the Secretariat on OPCW Capabilities Relevant to the Global Struggle Against Terrorism, OPCW doc. S/294/2002 (6 February 2002).

[1] 1993 Convention on the Prohibition of the Development, Production, Stockpiling and Use of Chemical Weapons and on Their Destruction, entered into force on 29 April 1997. Text, as corrected and changed, available at http://www.opcw.org.

R. Yepes-Enríquez and L. Tabassi. (eds.), Treaty Enforcement and International Cooperation in Criminal Matters

- the active promotion of universal adherence to the Convention, in order to broaden the geographical scope of such prohibitions;
- enhanced cooperation amongst Member States in the enforcement of the Convention's prohibitions;
- the full implementation of the provisions of Article VI, with the objective of increasing the level of difficulty and risk which will be confronted by terrorists trying to acquire the capability to employ toxic chemicals as a means of terrorist attack; and,
- the increased readiness to deliver, under Article X, effective and timely assistance to victims of chemical weapons use, in order to save human lives and to reduce human suffering, while striving to minimise the impact of terrorist chemical attacks.

The chapter, then, analyses the provisions that apply to States Parties in relation to chemical weapons, including old and abandoned chemical weapons, and chemical weapons production facilities, including provisions on their elimination. The following areas of possible action are identified:

- increasing physical security at locations containing chemical weapons, as well as for sensitive equipment, in order to prevent diversion or theft by terrorist organisations; and,
- full implementation of all requirements related to destruction operations, with a view to shortening the period of time during which chemical weapons and sensitive equipment remain potentially vulnerable to theft or attack.

Finally, the chapter looks at the competence which the Organisation as a whole — its Member States as well as its Secretariat — has acquired in the implementation process, and that could be brought to bear in the international struggle against terrorism.

2. Thoughts Following 11 September 2001

The terrorist attacks against the United States of America on 11 September 2001 have changed global priorities. The international community of nations finds itself in a new historical situation, in which not only States or national entities, but also organised terrorist groups, have the proven capacity to threaten international peace and security, to destabilise governments, and to foment regional, inter-regional, and global divisions, unrest, and instability.

The threat of the use of weapons of mass destruction by terrorists is real and continuing. Concerns have been raised at the highest level about the possibility of terrorists, *inter alia*, attempting to utilise chemical, biological, and nuclear materials. That terrorists will not be deterred from using chemical weapons was clearly demonstrated by the use of sarin in the Tokyo subway in 1995.

Terrorism is a menace to the whole of humanity. The struggle against this threat will require a multifaceted, well coordinated and integrated response by all relevant national and international authorities and agencies, on the basis of their respective competence and mandates. A range of national and international judicial, police, customs, financial, diplomatic, military, disarmament, non-proliferation and other measures need to be taken.

The Convention is founded on the premise that the States Parties are "determined for the sake of all mankind, to exclude completely the possibility of the use of chemical weapons, through the implementation of the provision of this Convention, thereby completing the obligations assumed under the Geneva Protocol of 1925...." From this, and from the requirements of Article VII of the Convention in relation to legislative action, including the enactment of penal legislation and the affording of international legal cooperation, it follows that the Convention does indeed contain provisions that are relevant to the struggle against terrorism. Global adherence to the Convention, and its comprehensive implementation, will facilitate more effective global action against chemical terrorism and will reduce risks associated with it.

While the OPCW's mandate has not changed since 11 September, the new level of threat posed by the possible use of chemical weapons by terrorists requires a re-evaluation of how the OPCW has been implementing its mandate. This re-evaluation must also encompass a consideration of whether Convention-related implementation practices, as well as the provisions of the Convention itself, respond adequately to this new level of threat. Accordingly, this chapter attempts to identify and analyse the relevant provisions of the Convention that have a direct bearing on the struggle against terrorism, in relation to actions by both the Member States and the Organisation at large. It has been prepared by the Secretariat to facilitate discussions on this issue, and to raise awareness about the possible contribution which the OPCW, within its mandate, can make to this cause.

3. General Obligations of All States Parties to the Chemical Weapons Convention, Definitions and Universal Adherence

Promoting universal adherence to the Convention contributes tangibly to the struggle against terrorism by enlarging the area of the world in which chemical weapons are banned, and in which measures against terrorist activities involving chemical weapons have a longer reach and much greater legal force than would be the case without the Convention. Universal adherence to the Convention has been an OPCW priority of overriding importance ever since the entry into force of the Convention.[2] The activities undertaken by the Member States, the Director-General, and the Secretariat to attract further ratifications and accessions were most recently detailed in the report by the Director General to the OPCW Conference of the States Parties ("Conference") at its Sixth Session.[3]

The Convention stipulates, *inter alia*, that each State Party shall undertake never under any circumstances to assist, encourage or induce, in any way, anyone to engage in any activity prohibited to a State Party under the Convention (Article I, subparagraph 1(d)). It also requires States Parties to prohibit natural and legal persons anywhere on their territory or in any other place under their jurisdiction as recognised by international law from undertaking

[2] See OPCW Conference of the States Parties decisions taken at the Second, Third, Fourth, Fifth and Sixth Sessions, OPCW docs. C-II/DEC.11 (5 December 1997), C-III/DEC.9 (20 November 1998), C-IV/DEC.22 (2 July 1999), C-V/DEC.21 (19 May 2000), and C-VI/DEC.11 (17 May 2001).

[3] Report by the Director General: Report on the Implementation of the Recommendation of the Conference of the States Parties at its Fifth Session on Ensuring the Universality of the Chemical Weapons Convention, OPCW doc. C-VI/DG.7 (15 May 2001).

any activity prohibited to a State Party, including enacting penal legislation with respect to such activity (subparagraph 1(a) of Article VII); not to permit, in any place under their control, any activity prohibited to a State Party by the Convention (Article VII, subparagraph 1(b)); to extend their penal legislation to any activity prohibited to a State Party undertaken anywhere by natural persons, possessing their nationality, in conformity with international law (subparagraph 1(c) of Article VII); and to afford the appropriate form of legal assistance to other States Parties, to facilitate the implementation of the obligations under paragraph 1 of Article VII (Article VII, paragraph 2). These general obligations, which are further amplified by the provisions of Article VI, clearly establish the responsibility of each Member State to actively prevent acts of terrorism involving chemical weapons, or preparations for them, and to cooperate with other Member States in the investigation and prosecution of crimes related to violations of the Convention.

The Convention defines chemical weapons in Article II, paragraph 1. From this provision, as well as from the provisions of paragraphs 2 and 3 of Article II, and from section B of the Annex on Chemicals, it is evident that the definition of "chemical weapons" is not limited to the chemicals listed in the Schedules of the Annex on Chemicals, but extends to all toxic chemicals and their precursors, except when they are intended for purposes not prohibited under the Convention, and as long as their types and quantities are consistent with such purposes. While most of the verification measures applied under the Convention relate to chemicals listed in the Schedules, the legislative, regulatory, administrative and law enforcement measures adopted by the Member States could be expected to extend to other relevant chemicals, and must be firmly based on the definition of the term "chemical weapon" contained in the Convention.

Many chemicals which are in circulation for legitimate applications would pose a considerable threat if they were used as chemical weapons by terrorists. It is prudent not to assume that terrorists will restrict themselves solely to the use of chemicals listed in the Convention's Annex on Chemicals. This is an important consideration to bear in mind when addressing the applicability of the Convention's provisions to the international struggle against chemical terrorism.

4. Provisions Affecting All Member States, in Relation to Articles VI and VII (Development and Enactment of Legislation)

Article VI, paragraph 2, requires each State Party to adopt the measures necessary to ensure that toxic chemicals and their precursors are only developed, produced, otherwise acquired, retained, transferred, or used within its territory or in any other place under its jurisdiction or control for purposes not prohibited under the Convention. Paragraphs 3-9 of Article VI stipulate the regime of declarations, verification through data monitoring and on-site inspections, and other measures applying to facilities and activities of States Parties in relation to activities not prohibited under the Convention. These provisions have to be seen in conjunction with the relevant provisions of Article VII on national implementation measures.

The full implementation of these already existing requirements by all Member States would contribute substantially to:

- denying terrorists access to chemicals that could be used as chemical weapons;
- deterring the potential supply to terrorists of knowledge, equipment and chemicals;
- ensuring that any involvement with chemical weapons could, and would, be effectively prosecuted; and,
- increasing the effectiveness of legal action against terrorists involved in activities prohibited to States Parties under the Convention, no matter where the terrorists are found, and irrespective of where the illegal activities have been conducted.

The following practical measures by Member States may be considered as having a direct bearing on the struggle against terrorism (with respect to terrorist activities involving chemical weapons):

(a) prohibitions, including the enactment of penal legislation, which would contain penalties sufficiently severe to deter a potential violator;

(b) extending prohibitions extraterritorially to natural persons possessing the State's nationality, for activities undertaken anywhere in the world;

(c) establishing the instruments or arrangements necessary to enable full and effective legal cooperation with all other Member States;

(d) the designation or establishment of National Authorities, to enable the Member States to fulfil their obligations under the Convention;

(e) regular reporting to the OPCW on progress in the development of national implementing legislation and related enforcement measures including, if required, seeking the OPCW's assistance (from both the Secretariat and Member States) in the preparation of such laws, regulations and measures;

(f) subjecting Schedule 1 chemicals to the prohibitions specified in Part VI of the Verification Annex, including those on production, acquisition, retention, transfer and use, except as provided for in paragraph 2 of Part VI of the Verification Annex, and the prohibitions on transfers and retransfers contained in section B of that Part;

(g) subjecting Schedule 1 facilities and chemicals to systematic verification and other measures in accordance with Part VI of the Verification Annex;

(h) considering measures to be adopted in relation to facilities that handle (store or consume) Schedule 1 chemicals, with a view to enhancing security and accountability;

(i) subjecting Schedule 2 and Schedule 3 chemicals and facilities to the measures stipulated in Parts VII and VIII, respectively, of the Verification Annex, amongst other things in relation to identifying declarable facilities and activities, and to the provisions on exports and imports vis-à-vis States not party to the Convention;

(j) considering which chemicals from Schedules 2 and 3, as well as other chemicals that are being manufactured, stored, transported or traded in their territory, may pose a particular danger if used by terrorists and may accordingly require additional measures to be taken including, as necessary, by the OPCW; and,

(k) reviewing the measures implemented to provide physical protection against terrorist attacks on chemical plants and storage facilities holding toxic chemicals, in order to minimise the probability of releases of toxic materials as a result of such attacks, and instituting such improvements as may be necessary.

In order to maximise the contribution that OPCW Member States can make to the struggle against terrorism, by fully exploiting the potential of the Convention in this regard, the policy-making organs, as appropriate, may wish to discuss recommendations concerning, *inter alia*:

(a) the conclusion, as soon as possible, with the assistance of the Secretariat, as necessary, of all legislative and regulatory work required of Member States by the Convention (including, for example, national implementing legislation incorporating penal legislation, export control regulations, and the establishment of National Authorities);

(b) measures to improve, where necessary, the framework and the arrangements necessary for appropriate legal cooperation between Member States (for example, to facilitate extradition or other mutual legal assistance in the investigation or prosecution of crimes involving chemical weapons when a suspect, an item of evidence, or a witness, are at a location under the jurisdiction of another Member State);

(c) increasing transparency and institutionalising the exchange of information, through the Secretariat, on relevant laws and regulations;

(d) measures to help Member States to accelerate the identification of solutions to outstanding industry declaration and verification issues, thus further harmonising the implementation of the Convention;

(e) encouraging Member States to review the effectiveness of their measures related to the development, production, acquisition, retention, transfer and use of chemicals listed in the Schedules, in order to identify and rectify any deficiencies. Such measures could, for example, include the following:

i. measures taken to prevent the theft or diversion of relevant chemicals, including Schedule 1 chemicals, during their production, storage, transportation and use;

ii. a reduction in the quantity of Schedule 1 chemicals stored at any given moment at Schedule 1 facilities (this may be particularly relevant to those single small-scale facilities that store larger amounts of Schedule 1 chemicals);

iii. measures related to the authorisation of the synthesis of Schedule 1 chemicals in quantities below 100 grams per year;

iv. measures to prevent transfers of Schedule 1 and Schedule 2 chemicals to States not party to the Convention (including cooperation between National Authorities in the identification, and, if necessary, interdiction of questionable transfers, and the reporting of any such acquisition attempts to the OPCW);

v. measures to ensure that the consumption of Schedule 1 chemicals is carried out only for purposes not prohibited under the Convention, and that such chemicals cannot be diverted during storage;

vi. the consideration and adoption of appropriate measures with regard to the recommendations of the Scientific Advisory Board on relevant issues, in particular in order to prevent unauthorised access to relevant chemicals through gaps in the regulatory framework;

vii. measures to ensure that end-use certificates are issued by the competent governmental authorities of States not party before exports of Schedule 3 chemicals are authorised to such countries, and also to ensure that the guarantees given in the certificates are in fact complied with (use only for purposes not prohibited, and no re-transfers);

viii. the consideration of possible measures to ensure the enforcement of the ban on transfers of Schedule 1 and Schedule 2 chemicals to States not party;

ix. measures to improve the accuracy of data reporting on exports and imports of chemicals listed in the Schedules (national implementation, data reconciliation and other forms of cooperation between National Authorities, as well as between National Authorities and the Secretariat);

x. the intensification of consultations on the need to establish other measures regarding transfers of Schedule 3 chemicals to States not party, as required under paragraph 27 of Part VIII of the Verification Annex, including the consideration of a ban on such transfers to States not party; and,

xi. making it a criminal offence to publish on the internet instructions for, or advice on, the synthesis of chemical agents for use as chemical weapons.

The preparation and enactment by each State Party of implementing legislation, including penal legislation, is required by the Convention under Article VII. So are legal cooperation and the affording of appropriate legal assistance between Member States. In relation to the struggle against terrorism, penal legislation will enable OPCW Member States to prosecute as criminal offences, not only the use of toxic chemicals by terrorists, but also any form of preparation for such use (including, *inter alia*, the development of chemical weapons or assistance therewith including financing, the acquisition or production of relevant chemicals, the construction of a CW production facility, CW testing, possession and storage, and environmental damage). Other forms of implementing legislation will enable Member States to exercise the necessary degree of monitoring in their respective jurisdiction the activities involving relevant chemicals, such as imports and exports. Legal cooperation and assistance between Member States will help to ensure that terrorist organisations attempting to use toxic chemicals cannot exploit loopholes in the net of prohibitions created by Member States, and also cannot escape the prosecution of criminal acts involving toxic chemicals.

The OPCW has experience in the development of legislation, including criminal law, related to both the toxic and precursor chemicals that could be used for CW purposes. This expertise could be used to provide support in the development and enactment of domestic legislation in countries currently lacking an adequate set of prohibitions and other necessary and enforceable laws related to both toxic chemicals and precursors. The OPCW has also been addressing issues related to legal cooperation between its Member States, including in relation to extradition. The Secretariat's capability includes, *inter alia*, the following:

(a) legislative support (international law, examples of existing national legislation, including the possible enactment of integrated fast-track legislation, and regulations in relation to the monitoring of chemical activities, including trade);

(b) relevant documentation (an OPCW legislation package including, *inter alia*, a legislator checklist, examples of legislation, and model texts for domestic implementing legislation);

(c) expertise related to a proposed "Draft Optional Protocol to the Convention on the Prohibition of the Development, Production, Stockpiling and Use of Chemical Weapons and on Their Destruction, relating to Article VII, paragraph 2, of the Convention";[4] and,

(d) capacity building in certain aspects of law enforcement, including advising other international organisations (such as the WCO) in relation to the inclusion of modules concerning toxic chemicals in their respective training programmes for officers from national law enforcement agencies.

In addition, the Secretariat has been working with legal experts from a number of Member States on such issues as the development of model legislation, including penal legislation, to implement and enforce the provisions of the Convention. These experts can be mobilised by the Secretariat as an additional resource of legal support. Furthermore, a network of legal experts from Member States in Latin America and the Caribbean has recently been created. The members of this network have been working with Convention related aspects of national legislation, and may be called upon to render legal support.

The Secretariat also stands ready to develop proposals on how it could further assist Member States in the development and implementation of their national measures to fully implement the provisions of the Convention. Such proposals could, for example, include:

(a) additional measures in relation to legal support provided by either the Secretariat or other Member States, or through regional networking;

(b) practical implementation support through information, training and other support for National Authorities and other relevant national agencies;

(c) the facilitation of exchanges between National Authorities;

(d) suggestions, based on inspection experience and the results of the implementation of the Convention's verification regime, for identifying and addressing areas which might be exploited by terrorists to obtain either toxic chemicals suitable for use in chemical attacks, or precursors suitable for the manufacture of such toxic chemicals; and,

(e) assistance in compiling lists of chemical production facilities under paragraph 1 of Part IX of the Verification Annex, as foreseen in paragraph 7 of Part IX of the Verification Annex, and other assistance in relation to identifying declarable facilities.

[4] See *infra* in this volume, L. Tabassi, Legal Assistance under the Chemical Weapons Convention: an Optional Protocol to the Convention?.

5. Provisions Affecting All Member States, in Relation to Article X of the Convention (Assistance and Protection Against Chemical Weapons)

Article X of the Convention reaffirms the right of States Parties to engage in activities necessary to protect themselves against chemical weapons (paragraph 2), and to participate in the fullest possible exchange of equipment, material and scientific and technological information concerning means of protection against chemical weapons (paragraph 3). It requires the Secretariat to establish and maintain, for the use of any requesting State Party, a data bank containing freely available information concerning various means of protection against chemical weapons, and to provide, upon request and within available resources, expert advice and assistance in identifying how programmes for the development and improvement of a protective capacity against chemical weapons could be implemented (paragraph 5). Paragraph 8 of Article X establishes the right of each State Party to request and receive assistance and protection against the use or threat of use of chemical weapons, subject to the procedures contained in paragraphs 9-11 of Article X. Paragraph 11 of Article X requires the Director-General, in the event that there is sufficient proof that there are victims of the use of chemical weapons, and that immediate action should be indispensable, to notify all States Parties and to take emergency measures of assistance, using the resources which the Conference has placed at his/her disposal for such contingencies.

The information available to the Secretariat in relation to the protective programmes of Member States, although clearly incomplete (only 23 States Parties have submitted to the OPCW information about their programmes for protective purposes, and three of these have indicated that they have no such programme) seems to indicate that many Member States lack adequate protective capabilities. This increases the risks associated with chemical terrorism. The lack of submission of such information by Member States, as required under paragraph 4 of Article X, makes it difficult for the Secretariat to develop its approach toward providing Member States with adequate expert advice on their protective capacity. It also restricts the pool of potential resources for the delivery of assistance — a mandatory requirement under paragraph 8 of Article X.

All the provisions of Article X have a direct bearing on the capacity of Member States to deter and withstand attacks against themselves with chemical weapons, and to deal with the aftermath of any such attacks. Their effective implementation can considerably reduce the impact of chemical weapons used by terrorists, and can thus save lives and minimise suffering. It should be recalled that the Convention defines assistance as "coordination and delivery to States Parties of protection against chemical weapons, including, *inter alia*, the following: detection equipment and alarm systems; protective equipment; decontamination equipment and decontaminants; medical antidotes and treatments; and advice on any of these protective measures" (paragraph 1 of Article X). An important aspect of the implementation of these provisions is the undertaking of the States Parties, under paragraph 7 of Article X, to provide assistance through the Organisation. This undertaking forms the basis of the OPCW's assistance delivery capability. Also important are the preparations undertaken by the Secretariat, together with the Member States, to establish and maintain a credible and cost effective operational capability for the delivery of such assistance.

In order to improve both the status of implementation of the provisions of Article X, and the Organisation's readiness to provide assistance, including in case of the use or threat of use of chemical weapons by terrorists, the policy-making organs, as appropriate, may wish to consider recommending to Member States measures such as the following:

(a) additional contributions to the Voluntary Fund for Assistance, which as of 30 June 2002 stands at only Euros 988,642. The latter amount will clearly not suffice to finance any significant and sustained delivery of assistance;

(b) the conclusion of bilateral agreements with the OPCW on the procurement, upon demand, of assistance, in order to increase the Organisation's capacity to plan assistance delivery operations in advance;

(c) a review of the pledges for assistance submitted under subparagraph 7(c) of Article X, with a view to providing additional detail on these pledges, and on the conditions under which the offered assistance would be made available;

(d) the submission of additional information and documents relevant to countermeasures against terrorist uses of chemical weapons, for inclusion in the data bank on protection;

(e) the nomination of experts who the Organisation can draw upon when it needs to act upon the use or threat of use of chemical weapons by terrorists. These experts could, for example, become members of the protection network. Relevant expertise may include such fields of expertise as medical countermeasures, risk assessment and management, emergency response planning involving protection against chemical weapons, and decontamination, or rescue operations involving toxic chemicals; and,

(f) a review of the resources placed at the Director-General's disposal for the adoption of the emergency assistance measures required of him, should there be victims of chemical weapons, and should immediate action be necessary.

Another important dimension of the implementation of Article X is the conduct of investigations of the alleged use of chemical weapons. The possibility of the terrorist use of chemical weapons adds an additional dimension and urgency to this issue, in particular in relation to situations in which it is not initially clear whether chemical weapons have been used, or whether biological, radiological or other kinds of weapons that can kill indiscriminately were involved in an incident.

6. The Provisions of Articles IV and V (Chemical Weapons and Production Facilities)

The Convention requires States Parties to take appropriate measures to secure their CW storage facilities and prevent any movement of their chemical weapons out of such facilities, except for their removal to CW destruction facilities (paragraph 4 of Article IV). This requirement includes physical security requirements during the storage, transportation and destruction of chemical weapons. The Convention requires States Parties to destroy their chemical weapons pursuant to the Verification Annex, and in accordance with the agreed rate and sequence of destruction (paragraph 6 of Article IV). States Parties are not precluded from destroying such chemical weapons at a faster rate (paragraph 6 of Article IV).

States Parties are required, during the transport, sampling, storage and destruction of chemical weapons, to assign the highest priority to the safety of people and to protecting the environment (paragraph 10 of Article IV). The Convention also prohibits the construction of any new CW production facilities or the modification of any existing facilities for any activity prohibited under the Convention (paragraph 5 of Article V). The Convention requires all CWPFs to be declared, closed and inactivated, subjected to systematic verification, and destroyed or converted for purposes not prohibited under the Convention (paragraphs 3, 4, and 6 — 10, and 13 — 18 of Article V, as well as the relevant provisions of the Verification Annex).

The full, effective and speedy implementation of these provisions will help to prevent terrorists from gaining access to chemical weapons and to equipment for their production. It would also shorten the time period during which chemical weapons and related production equipment remain potentially exposed to the danger of illegal activity.

7. Competence of the OPCW

Since the entry into force of the Convention, the OPCW has become an international centre of excellence in all matters pertaining to chemical weapons disarmament and non-proliferation, as well as to the delivery of assistance and international cooperation in this regard. The OPCW — its Member States and the Secretariat alike — has acquired technical competence in a number of areas that are relevant to dealing with threats of use, or actual use, of chemical weapons. The Secretariat's knowledge, understanding, and experience will be particularly valuable in relation to threats of terrorism involving chemical weapons, and includes the conduct of inspections at facilities containing chemical weapons, investigations of alleged use, advice on protection against chemical weapons, the provision of assistance, the implementation of regulations in relation to chemical industry inspections and other verification measures with regard to the chemical industry, as well as the legal support outlined under section 4 above.

The OPCW can provide, within its mandate and on the basis of the provisions of the Convention, a context for consultations, clarifications, assistance, exchanges of experiences, and international cooperation. This is available to address the threats posed by terrorists engaging in preparations for, and possibly the conduct of, acts involving chemical weapons as defined in Article II of the Convention, and to devise possible countermeasures.

The OPCW has the responsibility, as well as the capability, to significantly contribute to the strengthening of the ethical norms against chemical weapons. Well before 11 September 2001, the Secretariat had begun to address this dimension in its ethics project. This project aims at promoting the adoption of ethical norms against involvement in prohibited activities with chemical weapons by chemists, chemical engineers and other professionals, through channels including international and national scientific and engineering societies, as well as institutions teaching life sciences or chemical engineering. Other projects as well, for example the Associate Programme, can make a valuable contribution to the worldwide promotion of non-proliferation as a norm to which scientists and engineers from OPCW Member States subscribe. The Secretariat could be requested to review the effectiveness of these projects, with the aim of enhancing these efforts.

8. Conclusion

Various provisions of the Convention of special relevance to the combat of chemical terrorism have not yet been fully implemented by a very significant proportion of Member States. The policy-making organs, within their respective areas of competence, may wish to consider identifying high priority actions, in relation to the implementation of the Convention, that Member States could take in order to immediately enhance their capacity to effectively combat terrorism involving the possible use of chemical weapons.

Coordination with other international organisations would be a necessary precondition for effective work in this field, in order to avoid both the duplication of effort and possibly conflicting competencies. It is important in this context to recall that the United Nations Security Council, in resolution 1373 of 28 September 2001,[5] called upon all States to cooperate, particularly through bilateral and multilateral arrangements and agreements, to prevent and suppress terrorists attacks and take action against perpetrators. In the same resolution, the Security Council reaffirmed and again stressed the vital role of the United Nations in strengthening international cooperation in combating terrorism, and emphasised the importance of enhanced coordination among States, international and regional organisations. Cooperation between the OPCW and the United Nations in this context becomes indispensable. It should also be noted that Security Council resolution 1373 included references to a range of necessary actions that coincide with possible OPCW contributions identified in this chapter. Examples include the need for States to, *inter alia,* enact a range of prohibitions in their criminal codes including the establishment of terrorist acts as serious criminal offences in domestic laws and regulations, to eliminate the supply of weapons to terrorists, and to intensify and accelerate the exchange of operational information regarding traffic in arms, explosives or sensitive materials, as well as the threat posed by the possession of weapons of mass destruction. The resolution also noted with concern the close connection between international terrorism and transnational organised crime, illicit drugs, money laundering, illegal arms trafficking, and illegal movement of nuclear, chemical, biological and other potentially deadly materials, and emphasised the need to enhance the coordination of efforts at national, sub-regional, regional and international levels, in order to lay the foundation for a more powerful global response to this serious challenge and threat to international security.

It is the Secretariat's conclusion that the development of an action plan for the OPCW's contribution to the combat of terrorism, containing both immediate measures and long-term strategic tasks, is of paramount importance under these circumstances. Such a plan would naturally have to include an assessment of the cost implications of the measures proposed in it.[6]

---

[5] UN doc. S/RES/1373 (28 September 2001); reproduced in Annex III to this volume.

[6] Following discussion of the OPCW's contribution to global anti-terrorist efforts, the OPCW Executive Council identified five priority areas to focus on, and established a working group on terrorism. OPCW doc. EC-XXVII/Dec.5 (7 December 2001), reproduced in Annex IV to this volume.

COMBATING CHEMICAL TERRORISM WITH NATIONAL IMPLEMENTING LEGISLATION

Barry Kellman*

1. INTRODUCTION

The Chemical Weapons Convention[1] is humanity's most complete and important agreement to abolish an entire class of weapons. No State Party may use chemical weapons, for any reason. No State Party may possess chemical weapons nor take deliberate steps to acquire or develop them. Of course, all States Parties that have chemical weapons must destroy them. This is disarmament without parallel in human history.

But there is another challenge that must not be ignored, lest these accomplishments fail to provide security. This challenge is posed by non-State groups: "terrorists". If there is a lesson from 11 September 2001, it is that we ignore the threat of terrorism at our peril.

Imagine the horror if the planes that hit the World Trade Center had been filled with poison gas. The death toll, already enormous, would have multiplied. But a chemical attack need not be so elaborate. Aum Shinrikyo killed twelve people in the Tokyo subway in 1995; but for a tiny technical glitch, they could have killed thousands.

Chemical weapons are attractive weapons for terrorists. Relatively easy to make, they are devastating against unprotected civilians, especially in confined spaces: sports arenas, entertainment venues, transportation hubs. Most important from the terrorists' perspective, chemical weapons would cause widespread panic. If chemical weapons were used in one city, every other city in the world would tremble, knowing that they could be next.

It must be asked whether all that can be done to control this threat has been done. Having created the world's most important weapons abolition convention, has enough been done? The answer must be "No."

2. PENAL LEGISLATION

Article VII of the Chemical Weapons Convention provides that every State Party must enact penal legislation, applying the Convention's prohibitions to persons within its jurisdiction. Every State Party must also extend to each other legal assistance and cooperation in enforcing those penal prohibitions.

Many States have enacted implementing legislation that contains penalties for persons who engage in chemical terrorism. The problem here is that this legislation penalises "use" of chemical weapons, when it will be too late to prevent the loss of life. That is, penalties

* Director of the International Weapons Control Center, DePaul University, Chicago, USA.

[1] 1993 Convention on the Prohibition of the Development, Production, Stockpiling and Use of Chemical Weapons and on Their Destruction, entered into force on 29 April 1997. Text, as corrected and changed, available at http://www.opcw.org.

R. Yepes-Enríquez and L. Tabassi. (eds.), Treaty Enforcement and International Cooperation in Criminal Matters

for using chemical weapons are meaningful only *after* those weapons have been used. If we really want to prevent chemical terrorism, then we should give serious consideration to how to detect and interdict terrorists *before* they attack.

The point is this: every State Party to the Chemical Weapons Convention should enact legislation that enables their law enforcement authorities to detect or otherwise become aware of suspicious movements of chemicals, and to conduct investigations where appropriate. Most important, that legislation should enable those law enforcement officials to work with their counterparts in other States.

3. Elements of a Law Countering Chemical Terrorism

Consider the following elements of a comprehensive law to address threats of chemical terrorism.

First, in order to make clear that a chemical terrorist is an international criminal, anyone who uses chemicals as a weapon should be recognised as having committed a crime against humanity. Accordingly, principles of universal jurisdiction should apply. Anyone who uses chemicals as a weapon should have no place to hide, no refuge from the glare of law. Use of chemical weapons must be a crime everywhere.

The remaining measures address the problem of chemical terrorism in advance of the attack. Thus, the second measure should be a licensing system for Schedule 1 chemicals. The CWC limits the quantities and purposes of Schedule 1 chemicals that a State may have. But it is important to also know *who* has those chemicals. More important, only acknowledged, reputable enterprises, subject to government oversight, should have access to scheduled chemicals. Sale or transfer of those chemicals to a non-licensed entity should be a crime under national laws; possession of those chemicals without a license should also be a crime.

There is no reason to wait to prosecute until those chemicals actually kill people. Police should be authorised to treat unlicensed scheduled chemicals as contraband and to investigate accordingly. To make the system even more effective, it should be a crime to export scheduled chemicals unless the recipient is licensed; obviously, an unlicensed entity should be prosecuted for trying to import or export those chemicals.

While illegal possession or acquisition of scheduled chemicals need not be subject to universal jurisdiction, it is crucial that all States criminalise such behaviour within their national laws, if only to satisfy the dual criminality requirement to make extradition effective. National legislation should also specify that the "political offence" exception to criminality does *not* apply to chemical weapons offences. If necessary, that legislation should explicitly extend to corporations and other economic enterprises. Acts of aiding and conspiracy to commit these offences should be crimes as well. Penalties should, of course, be very strict.

Third, national legislation should address threats of illegal imports and exports of weapons-usable chemicals. Most States Parties that have enacted implementing legislation have established export restrictions in accord with the Chemical Weapons Convention's limits. These provisions regulate legal activity, but they do little to address illegal smuggling. To combat that threat, State Parties should enact measures to strengthen border and customs controls, and these measures should include strict penalties for persons who attempt to evade import/export laws.

Fourth, national legislation should ensure that there are capabilities to provide assistance and cooperation to other States that may be investigating chemical crimes. Too many States have enacted penal legislation that affects only illicit activity within their jurisdiction, and even among those States that have laws to address transnational criminality, too many have refrained from implementing capabilities to actually assist and cooperate.

4. Law Enforcement Cooperation

The problem here has to do with the segmentation of international criminal networks and the role that smuggling plays in these networks. It is likely that terrorists will obtain precursor chemicals in various States, minimising the chance of raising local law enforcement suspicions. Necessary materials and equipment to make those chemicals into weapons will likely be obtained in still other nations. Even the production process is likely to be segmented: taking place in discreet stages, and coming together into lethality only at the final stage. At every step, of course, smuggling routes otherwise used for drugs or guns will facilitate the terrorists' plans, even to the last step of getting the weapons to their target.

Their communications can be centered anywhere. A mastermind with a computer can manage the process from a cave in Afghanistan or a beach in Jamaica. The money to finance the operation can be laundered through banks a hemisphere away. Indeed, as the investigation of 11 September 2001 goes on, we will find that aspects of that crime were committed in many nations.

Terrorists cannot be allowed to take advantage of the international system with impunity while law abiding nations have to assemble new alliances every time an investigation is called for. If terrorists can cooperate across borders, then law enforcement officials must do so as well; if terrorists can gain the advantages and efficiencies of established networks for communication and transportation, then law enforcement officials must do so, too.

This requires a full commitment. National laws, in addition to criminalising unlicensed chemical activities, should criminalise any and all aspects of the weapons production process, including money laundering.

National laws should help forge networks of transnational legal cooperation. Information on suspicious activity should be shared, perhaps regionally, perhaps through a central institution such as the OPCW. Information will also have to be shared across agencies and disciplines. Criminal justice authorities and trade and commerce authorities will have to be able to exchange relevant data. Advanced computer systems are needed, able to integrate information on terrorist cells with information on chemical transfers and with information on money laundering.

Not just information integration is needed. Law enforcement officials should be able to conduct investigations as part of a network with each State's authorities contributing their part to a shared enterprise. If witnesses need to be questioned, property seized or arrests made, each State should be able to ask another State to do so and have that request carried out expeditiously, with minimum bureaucratic interference. The single warrant process that is currently being developed in the European Union is a good start in this direction.

5. Conclusion

There are three important points to make in conclusion. First, there is a special role here for the private sector. Even before there was a Chemical Weapons Convention, the international chemical industry demonstrated itself to be an ardent advocate of progress. Enlightened leaders of industry have shown that industry has no interest in seeing the products of its expertise used for mass murder. They did not merely allow the Chemical Weapons Convention to happen, they made a commitment to it, and that commitment has strengthened the Convention. Now, as attention turns to terrorism, industry's importance must be acknowledged. It is industry that will provide the sensors and detection systems that law enforcement will use. It is industry that will have the first indications of wrongful patterns as they monitor the movements of their products. Industry must be convinced that in the battle against terrorism, they are a cherished ally and not an object of suspicion.

The second issue has to do with resources. Even the best law is meaningless if there is no one to enforce it. A State can pledge itself to participate in a network of legal assistance and cooperation, but that pledge does not mean much unless there are agents in the field and computer banks of information. When State A requests assistance from State B, if State B has only one person in the Office of Chemical Terrorism and he is out to lunch, then law is just words on paper and not an effective force to defeat terrorism. Moreover, an army of people to carry out legal assistance functions is not particularly valuable if those people are not trained or are ill-equipped. It is not enough to want to join the fight against terrorism; there must be resources and planning and training.

This point should be taken to the wealthy nations who have been hit hard by terrorism or who are threatened by terrorism. These nations have asked the entire world community to join in the battle against terrorism. They have the right to make that request and are correct to do so. Every nation, no matter how small, no matter how isolated from terrorist attacks, should join this battle. Terrorism is a crime against humanity, and any State that would call itself part of humanity should respond. But that means resources and training and computers and tracking capabilities, and all of those things have to be paid for by the technologically-advanced, wealthy nations. There is an equation here that demands there be no benefits without responsibilities. Just as the smallest and poorest should not seek the benefits of international integration without accepting the responsibilities of stopping the use of their banks for money laundering, so the biggest and richest should not seek the benefits of cooperative counter-terrorism without accepting the responsibilities of providing resources to make that cooperation effective.

Third, this issue extends far beyond chemical weapons. Similar issues pertain to the on-going efforts to strengthen the Biological Weapons Convention. It will not be long before the international community will face analogous issues concerning the threat of nuclear terrorism. Only one organisation has taken the lead in highlighting the threats of terrorism involving weapons of mass destruction: the OPCW. That leadership deserves praise; more important, it signifies that the impact of its initiatives spread throughout humanity's quest for peace and security.

Osama bin Laden has thrown down a gauntlet for all humanity. Every petty tyrant who would seek to advance his distorted sense of his own self-importance could do the same tomorrow. We will rise to that challenge together, advancing the rule of law, or together we will be defeated by it.

SECTION IV.2

PROSECUTION OF INDIVIDUAL VIOLATORS OF THE CHEMICAL WEAPONS CONVENTION: POSSIBLE LEGAL FRAMEWORK FOR COMPLIANCE WITH ARTICLE VII(2)

INTRODUCTION AND SUMMARY

In carrying out a mandate to ensure the implementation of a treaty that requires inter-State cooperation and legal assistance by its States Parties, international organisations which act as treaty-implementing bodies, such as the OPCW, must also work to ensure that States Parties are in a position to prosecute individuals for violations of the treaty. Doing so will, in the case of the Chemical Weapons Convention, eliminate "safe havens" for those who manufacture and/or use chemical weapons, including terrorists. While most States Parties to the Chemical Weapons Convention treat chemical weapons offences seriously, a minority have enacted implementing legislation that has effect extraterritorially. Extension of legislation to nationals abroad is a requirement under the Convention. It is therefore in the greatest interest of the OPCW to work with its Member States and other international organisations with relevant mandates to encourage and assist States Parties in drafting and enacting proper implementing legislation, with extraterritorial application, which contributes to the cause of both eliminating existing chemical weapons and ensuring that they are never again produced or used. However, the real benefits of this "web" of legislation, designed to not only prosecute violations of the Convention but also deter those who might seek to attain or use chemical weapons, will not be realised without universality of the Convention.

The universal criminalisation of chemical and biological weapons (CBW) offences and the prosecution of individual violators is being addressed by the Harvard Sussex Program for CBW Armament and Arms Limitation in the form of a Draft Convention to Prohibit

R. Yepes-Enríquez and L. Tabassi. (eds.), Treaty Enforcement and International Cooperation in Criminal Matters

Biological and Chemical Weapons Under International Criminal Law, the text of which was drafted in coordination with a working group of legal experts. If adopted, this convention would provide universal jurisdiction over the crime of production or use of chemical or biological weapons. Other crimes for which universal jurisdiction applies include airline hijacking, airline sabotage, hostage taking, torture, and the harming of internationally protected individuals. With international jurisdiction, every State has the responsibility to either prosecute those who commit such acts, whether the crime occurs on their territory or not, or extradite the individual to another State for prosecution, as well as to cooperate in the course of the investigation. As such, the draft convention would serve as an extradition treaty. This subject, and the draft convention, itself takes on even greater importance when one considers the hostile purposes for which biotechnology will, inevitably, be used in the future. Biotechnology has the possibility to change the very nature of humanity, through processes like genetic manipulation, and therefore its use for criminal purposes must be prevented.

As an alternative to a broad, far-reaching international treaty criminalising and providing universal jurisdiction for those crimes under discussion, there is the possibility for the development of an optional protocol to the Chemical Weapons Convention that would address the deficiencies of Article VII(2) within the Convention regime. The optional protocol would specify the forms and procedures of legal assistance that must be undertaken under the terms of Article VII of the Chemical Weapons Convention. The draft optional protocol presented in this volume utilises the 1988 Narcotics Convention — which, with 167 States Parties (including nearly all States Parties to the Chemical Weapons Convention), enjoys the widest adherence of all multilateral regimes addressing one type of crime — as a guideline. The draft optional protocol obligates States Parties, both on an individual basis and through the OPCW, to assist in criminal investigations of individual violators of the Convention, including arrests, the gathering of evidence and extradition, if necessary.

The issue of State responsibility versus individual responsibility, and the danger of concentrating on one at the expense of the other, are concerns to keep in mind when addressing the topic of universal jurisdiction and individual prosecution. By providing for the prosecution of the individuals who engage in the production or use of chemical and/or biological weapons, is the State then released from any responsibility? This is especially relevant to the concept of State-sponsored terrorism. It must be further emphasised that the subject of universal jurisdiction is not "convention-dependent". The vigorous prosecution of individuals for crimes perpetrated in relation to chemical and biological weapons — by national governments, international organisations, or through cooperation between the two — is key to a future free of the threat posed by these and other weapons of mass destruction.

Pamela G. Mills

Rapporteur for Panel C.2 in the 2001 OPCW International Symposium; former Harvard Sussex Program Hague Researcher. The views expressed are not atrributable to the Harvard Sussex Program or the OPCW.

"NO SAFE HAVENS"

THE NEED TO STRENGTHEN INTERNATIONAL CONTROL REGIMES: IMPLICATIONS FOR NATIONAL IMPLEMENTATION

Keith Wilson*

1. INTRODUCTION

Assistance with legislative and regulatory measures has rapidly become a top priority in the efforts of the OPCW and its Member States to ensure the full and effective implementation of the Chemical Weapons Convention[1] ("Convention"). Are bans enforceable? Are States Parties to the Convention cooperating in the legal field? Can the non-proliferation objectives of the Convention be met in the absence of solutions involving all States Parties? How can the international community, acting together, address the critical issue of "safe havens", including for would-be terrorists?

In February 2001, the OPCW hosted the International Symposium on Cooperation and Legal Assistance for the Effective Implementation of International Agreements.[2] That significant event, from which the present volume grew, encouraged its participants to adopt an outward focus. It emphasised that all international crime has similar legal mechanisms for enforcement, irrespective of whether drugs, terrorism, or chemical weapons are involved. A recognition of cross-cutting issues holds the potential for political advances, more effective responses, and the increasingly efficient use of global resources. It is unlikely that these issues will be resolved satisfactorily, or that an adequate allocation of resources will be made, if they are approached individually, on a purely subject-matter basis.

In August 2001, the OPCW issued its Further Analysis of Responses to the Survey of National Measures to Implement the Chemical Weapons Convention.[3] That analysis of responses to a detailed legislation questionnaire issued by the Secretariat — together with submissions by States Parties under Article VII, paragraph 5, of the Convention, and the

* Political Affairs Officer, OPCW Secretariat. The views expressed are the author's own and do not necessarily reflect those of the OPCW Secretariat.

[1] 1993 Convention on the Prohibition of the Development, Production, Stockpiling and Use of Chemical Weapons and on Their Destruction, entered into force on 29 April 1997. Text, as corrected and changed, available at http://www.opcw.org.

[2] See *OPCW Synthesis*, Spring/April 2001; see also the report on the symposium, OPCW doc. S/251/2001 (23 March 2001).

[3] OPCW doc. S/269/2001 (16 August 2001).

R. Yepes-Enríquez and L. Tabassi. (eds.), Treaty Enforcement and International Cooperation in Criminal Matters

OPCW Surveys of National Implementing Legislation[4] — now provide a picture of the extent of the legislative implementation of the Convention in nearly half of the OPCW's Member States.[5]

The terrorist attacks in the United States in September 2001 gave a renewed, and focused, urgency to the task of ensuring the effective, and enforceable, implementation of international agreements such as the Chemical Weapons Convention. The key political and legal issue is, in short, the elimination of "safe havens" for the production of weapons of mass destruction, for their acquisition, for terrorist operations, and for illicit and unapprehended movements — of the weapons, precursors, and the terrorists themselves — to initiate and sustain such operations.

This much is clear: States now confront a set of transnational problems. We do ourselves an injustice if we reduce the effectiveness of our responses by setting national solutions against, or above, international solutions. The issue of the proliferation of the most destructive and insidious of weapons — amongst which chemical weapons and associated technologies are prominent — is high on the agenda for a coordinated transnational response. This demands full compliance with international obligations, while also requiring effective national controls and preparedness, and it involves a willingness to cooperate, and to assist by whatever means possible, to plug gaps in the applicable control mechanisms.

The Chemical Weapons Convention is, of course, not the only multilateral mechanism available to address these concerns. But the OPCW, and the unique features of the regime under its responsibility, has the clear potential to make a meaningful contribution.[6] The Convention itself contains the framework for international cooperation, as well as for legal assistance. However, it is recognised that the principles embodied in the Convention, including Article VII, paragraph 2, need to be given further content and operational significance.[7] This is where guidance, and political and legal acceptability, may be found by

---

[4] See OPCW Legislation Package, 15 November 2001, Annex OPCW doc. S/259/2001 (16 May 2001).

[5] The development of a global web of national legislation and enforceable sanctions to reinforce other disarmament regimes, and to detect non-compliance, is also incomplete. See *"International Criminal Law and Sanctions to Reinforce the BWC"*, The CBW Conventions Bulletin, Issue No. 54, December 2001, 1-2; see also T. Findlay and A. Woodward, *"State compliance with the Ottawa Convention: Self-reporting slow and loose"*, Trust and Verify, Issue Number 90, March 2000, 1-3, and www.domino.un.org/Ottawa.nsf.

[6] See the decision of the Executive Council on "The OPCW's Contribution to Global Anti-Terrorist Efforts", OPCW doc. EC-XXVII/DEC.5 (7 December 2001); also the Note by the Director-General, "The OPCW and the Global Struggle Against Terrorism", OPCW doc. EC-XXVII/DG.3 (9 November 2001); and the statement by the Chairman of the OPCW Executive Council "Consequences of Terrorist Attacks on 11 September 2001", OPCW doc. EC-XXVI/3 (28 September 2001). See also the Secretariat background paper on initial considerations regarding the OPCW's contribution to the global struggle against terrorism, OPCW doc. S/277/2001 (14 November 2001), the Note by the Director-General, "Possible Responses to Global Terrorist Threats", OPCW doc. S/292/2002 (29 January 2002), and the Note by the Secretariat on OPCW capabilities relevant to the global struggle against terrorism, OPCW doc. S/294/2002 (6 February 2002).

[7] See *infra* in the present volume, L. Tabassi, Legal Assistance under the Chemical Weapons Convention: Optional Protocol to the Convention?; also, a more ambitious draft treaty prepared by the Harvard Sussex Program, discussed and reproduced *infra* in this volume M. Meselson and J. Robinson, "A Draft Convention to Prohibit Biological and Chemical Weapons Under International Criminal Law."

looking to other existing control regimes (e.g. to those already in place to deal with narcotics, or terrorist bombings).[8]

This chapter offers a preliminary consideration of a number of these pressing issues, through: (1) a brief review of the responses received from States Parties to the OPCW legislation questionnaire; (2) the identification of potential areas with scope for common, or integrated approaches, and for strengthened relationships; and (3) providing additional impetus to the ever-present need for universal adherence to "core" regimes such as the Chemical Weapons Convention.

2. The OPCW Legislation Questionnaire

In June 2000, in order to assist States Parties with their efforts to undertake national implementation measures, the OPCW Secretariat, seeking to act upon the relevant decision of the Conference of the States Parties at its Fifth Session,[9] and responding to requests for assistance received from States Parties in the process of drafting legislation, issued its first "legislation questionnaire".[10] The methods for regulating scheduled chemicals and precursors were a major focus of the questionnaire, both in order to facilitate reporting under the Convention, and to improve the control of transfers of these chemicals in accordance with the Convention. Following a preliminary analysis of the responses to the questionnaire,[11] and in response to a request made during discussion of a draft intermediate analysis at the Third Annual Meeting of National Authorities, held at the OPCW headquarters from 11-13 May 2001, a further, more detailed analysis was carried out.

The responses received, as of 15 August 2001, from 57 States Parties to the Convention, were analysed,[12] together with clarifications submitted by many of these States Parties at the request of the Secretariat. The detailed analysis, which includes a number of tables providing a statistical breakdown of the responses, discussed the issues being faced, indicated the nature of possible solutions, and contained findings in relation to national legislation:

- the form and status of such legislation;
- its application, including its extraterritorial application;
- penalties;
- prohibitions on transfers of scheduled chemicals (Schedules 1 and 2);
- regulatory provisions for:
  - Schedule 1 chemicals, including salts, mixtures, transfers, and saxitoxin;

[8] L. Tabassi, *Id.*, and Annex V to this volume, Proposal for Draft Optional Protocol to the Convention, adapting language from existing regimes: e.g. the 1988 United Nations Convention against Illicit Traffic in Narcotic Drugs and Psychotropic Substances, entry into force 11 November 1990 (as of June 2002, it had 167 parties); and the 1998 International Convention for the Suppression of Terrorist Bombings, entry into force 23 May 2001 (as of June 2002, it had 64 parties).
[9] OPCW doc. C-V/DEC.20 (19 May 2000).
[10] See OPCW doc. S/194/2000 (8 June 2000).
[11] OPCW doc. S/249/2001 (22 March 2001).
[12] OPCW doc. S/269/2001 (16 August 2001).

  - Schedule 2 chemicals, including production, processing, and consumption, salts, mixtures, captive use, and transfers;
  - Schedule 3 chemicals, including production, salts, mixtures, transfers, and end-user certificates;
  - obtaining information on the production of discrete organic chemicals (DOCs); and,
- miscellaneous and additional issues.

The analysis indicated that States Parties are using a range of legal methods and regulatory instruments in relation to scheduled chemicals and DOCs. It noted that "although the extent to which the Convention's obligations are being implemented remains uneven, including amongst States Parties which have a significant chemical industry, the various measures being adopted serve the Convention's non-proliferation objectives, and the measures themselves are not an impediment to the effective implementation of the Convention". However, it saw value in better coordination and harmonisation, and in the provision of additional responses to the questionnaire. This is occurring gradually.

In summary, most respondents stated that they have legislation in place to implement the Convention, while others indicated that they were in the process of drafting legislation or had monist legal systems. Statistically, three-quarters or more of the respondents reported having legislation in place to regulate scheduled chemicals. This group of respondents included about three-quarters of States Parties with declared or inspectable facilities, but only about two-thirds of all States Parties involved in declared import/export activities for Schedule 1 chemicals, about one-half for Schedule 2 chemicals, and about one-third for Schedule 3 chemicals. About three-quarters of respondents regulated transfers of Schedule 1 (including re-transfers) and Schedule 2 chemicals, and two-thirds indicated that they are enforcing a requirement for end-user certificates for transfers of Schedule 3 chemicals. It was noted that the Convention requires all States Parties to put into place the measures necessary to regulate all relevant activities, including any eventual activities.

States Parties generally appear to regard the Convention as a serious counter-proliferation device. Most respondents report having a system of fairly severe criminal penalties or administrative fines in place. Moreover, the penalty regime in place in most States Parties does not distinguish between the scheduled chemicals (though a more lenient approach is generally taken in relation to unscheduled DOCs). This element — treating chemical weapons offences seriously at the national level — will be crucial to international cooperation and mutual assistance efforts, whether political, prosecutorial, or investigatorial. The potential for the imposition of a severe penalty — in terms of year(s) of imprisonment, is likely, in many cases, to be a prerequisite for action upon a request for any form of legal assistance.

A somewhat less encouraging sign was the finding that only about 20 States Parties were giving their Convention implementing legislation extraterritorial effect. Article VII, paragraph 1, of the Convention requires States Parties to extend their penal provisions for chemical weapons offences to their nationals abroad. Moreover, under paragraph 2 of Article VII, though additional content will provide greater clarity regarding the parameters and procedures,[13] States Parties have agreed that they *shall* cooperate with other States Parties by affording the appropriate form of legal assistance to enforce the Convention.

There is another advantage of a content-based, international instrument, protocol, or similarly agreed procedure pursuant to, or consistent with, the Convention: it will confirm and consolidate the norm that certain activities (chemical, biological, and other weapons offences, terrorist bombings, etc.) are *never, under any circumstances*, susceptible to obstacles, exceptions or excuses (for example, the traditional exceptions for political and fiscal offences) that could justify a refusal to assist.[14] Only a broadly-based mechanism for the provision of mutual legal assistance, to a State that can assert jurisdiction and prosecute an offender, will provide a solution to this problem and have any prospect of eliminating safe havens.

3. Relationships, Cooperation, and Integration

Strengthened relationships, between all relevant actors in the international community that are pursuing common goals, will be of the highest significance in future efforts to address issues of international concern, irrespective of whether the issue being tackled is poverty, environmental degradation, drug and health issues, illicit financial dealings, illegal arms trafficking, the proliferation of weapons of mass destruction, or terrorism. *Strengthened relationships are mandated*, and are required of all States, by applicable United Nations Security Council Resolutions, including under Chapter VII of the United Nations Charter, specifically recognising the "close connection" between many of these activities.[15] While work continues on the elaboration of an overarching draft convention on international terrorism, including its definition by a United Nations Working Group, Security Council resolution 1373 (2001) refers to international terrorism as a "serious challenge and threat to international security", and "*emphasises* the need to enhance coordination of efforts on national, subregional, regional, and international levels in order to strengthen a global response".[16]

In some cases, *integration* will be an appropriate element of the cooperation and coordination required, on the basis of a realistic but proactive approach. Integration may take the form of streamlined processes and "best practices" approaches,[17] "intensifying and accelerating the exchange of operational information",[18] the development of legislative models and guidelines, the consistent application of comparable issues occurring in the implementation of obligations under different international regimes, and appropriate common training. For an effective chemical weapons non-proliferation regime "there appears

[13] See L. Tabassi, *supra* note 7.

[14] *Id.*

[15] UN Security Council resolution 1373 (28 September 2001), paragraph 4, reprinted in Annex III to this volume.

[16] *Id.*, emphasis in the original.

[17] See Proceedings of the Thematic Workshop on Developing and Strengthening National Legislation and Policies for the Sound Management of Chemicals, Geneva, OPCW doc. S/127/1999 (1 July 1999): the "lessons learned" are discussed at subparagraph 3.7, indicating that several States Parties to the Convention already have structural integration in their National Authorities, for example to implement the Convention on the Prior Informed Consent (PIC) procedure for Certain Hazardous Chemical and Pesticides in International Trade, and the so-called "POPs" (Persistent Organic Pollutants) regime. Since it was opened for signature in Stockholm on 23 May 2001, more than 100 States Parties to the Chemical Weapons Convention have signed the International Legally Binding Instrument for Implementing International Action on Certain Persistent Organic Pollutants.

[18] Security Council resolution 1373, *supra* note 15, at subparagraph 3(a).

to be a continuing need to strengthen customs and other enforcement authorities which are central to implementing regulations relating to these matters, and to undertake practical activities in the area of international cooperation".[19]

Initially, integration can appear a daunting exercise. It will not always be possible, or necessary. But it is apparent that the question must be asked: is there scope for integration and, if so, what would be its benefits? In relation to the legislative implementation of the Chemical Weapons Convention, nearly half of the respondents to the OPCW Legislation Questionnaire reported adopting what is termed a "single act" approach, while one-quarter reported using an "integrated" approach. Respondents described the advantages of integrated legislation as including the following: more effective controls; better coordination; lighter administrative burdens for government and industry; laws which stood the test of time without amendment; the maintenance of transparency of existing export control legislation; and the coverage of all weapons of mass destruction, and of military equipment and dual-use products.[20]

The question of cost is also relevant, though the major part of the establishment costs — political as well as financial — will be addressed if there are already existing mechanisms in place in one or more of the areas that are candidates for integration. This potentially applies to responses to national, subregional and regional priorities, as well as to cooperative and integrated approaches between international organisations and other treaty-implementing bodies. In addition to specific assistance provided by the OPCW in relation to integrated legislative implementation of the Convention,[21] other relevant developments should be noted. First, the Relationship Agreement, signed and provisionally in force since 17 October 2000, provides for cooperation between the United Nations and the OPCW. It entered into force on 11 October 2001, following an exchange of written notifications. In addition, the OPCW Conference of the States Parties, at its Sixth Session, adopted a decision on cooperation with international organisations, whereby it gave its approval for the Executive Council to consider and conclude the negotiated texts of cooperation agreements between the OPCW and other international organisations, as may be required

[19] See Further Analysis of Responses to the Survey of National Measures to Implement the Chemical Weapons Convention, OPCW doc. S/269/2001 (16 August 2001), final subparagraph 8.20.

[20] *Id.*, subparagraph 2.5, responses to the question: *Has the integrated approach been beneficial? If so, for whom?* There are also early indications that more National Authorities are likely in future to be located in, or at least to work closely together with, ministries of the environment (e.g. in parts of Africa and the Pacific Islands), health, or agriculture (e.g. the Caribbean), where benefits may be derived from integrated approaches to legislative implementation. In other cases, a simpler model for declared non-possessor States Parties, for example for smaller island nations, may be preferred.

[21] A subregional legislation workshop was held in Saint Lucia in 2000, involving all the independent members of the Organisation of Eastern Caribbean States (OECS), and jointly sponsored by the Secretariats of the OPCW and the OECS. Model legislation was drafted, integrating implementation of the Chemical Weapons Convention and regulation of a subregional priority to address the issue of pesticides and other toxic chemicals. See OPCW doc. S/190/2000 (23 May 2000). Existing Pesticides Control Boards are intended to expand their responsibilities to include other toxic chemicals, and also to become the National Authorities for Convention implementation, with minimal additional cost and no additional regulatory infrastructure. Informal reports received during 2001 confirmed that legislation based on the draft model act was passed by the Parliament of Saint Lucia, and that associated regulations are being finalised.

for the effective implementation of the Convention.[22] Subsequently, in August 2001, a draft decision on a memorandum of understanding on cooperation between the OPCW and the World Customs Organisation was placed on the agenda of the Executive Council.

Finally, in terms of the enforceability of the Convention, the raw number of submissions made under Article VII, paragraph 5, cannot be considered to present a conclusive implementation picture.[23] As the responses to the OPCW Legislation Questionnaire demonstrate, it is the substance of the legislation, its operation within the national legal system of a specific State Party, and its compatibility with other national, regional and international legal efforts that is most significant. In this context, increasing demands may be expected regarding international cooperation programmes, and support provided in accordance with Article XI of the Convention, to work towards achieving the effective implementation of obligations under paragraphs 1, 2, 5, and 7 of Article VII.[24]

4. The Importance of Universality

All of the above developments have important ramifications for the aim of achieving universal adherence to the major international regimes. The Chemical Weapons Convention is one of the 25 "core" treaties identified by United Nations Secretary-General as reflecting the fundamental purposes of the United Nations. More recently, emphasis has also been placed on adherence to a list of twelve anti-terrorism conventions. The Convention is not a counter-terrorism treaty *per se*, but there is clear recognition of the contribution that the OPCW can make to the global struggle against terrorism, particularly in the field of chemical weapons.[25] Moreover, statements of the United Nations Secretary-General,[26] and resolutions of the General Assembly and of the Security Council, including under Chapter VII of the United Nations Charter, demand efforts to ensure the widest possible cooperation at all levels in this struggle.

[22] OPCW doc. C-VI/DEC.15 (17 May 2001).

[23] See Report by the Director-General on National Implementation Measures, OPCW doc. EC-28/DG.4 (28 February 2002).

[24] See, for example, the Statement of the Chairman of the Executive Council Chairman, *supra* note 6:

> "The Council appeals to all States Parties to redouble their efforts to ensure the universality of the Convention...and the taking of all necessary measures in accordance with Article VII of the Convention....
>
> The Council urges the development of further means and measures to provide legislative support and assistance to States Parties for the enactment at the national level of enforceable legal provisions for the effective implementation of the Convention."

In view of the useful results of the analyses of the first legislation questionnaire, the Secretariat has seen the utility of issuing a further, simplified questionnaire covering enforcement of the Convention as a whole. This simplified questionnaire focuses not on the form or the mechanisms, but on the fundamental question: can violators be prosecuted and punished in a given jurisdiction?

[25] *Id.*

[26] For example, the address of the UN Secretary-General on 1 October 2001 to the General Assembly's special debate on measures to eliminate international terrorism, emphasising the need to redouble efforts to ensure universality, verification and full implementation of key treaties; to promote cooperation among international organisations dealing with these weapons; and to tighten national legislation over exports of technologies needed to manufacture weapons of mass destruction and their means of delivery. See also J. Dhanapala, "Multilateral Approaches to WMD Threats After September 11", Address to Annual Luncheon of the Arms Control Association, Washington D.C., 22 January 2002.

The full and effective implementation of the Convention must continue to be the focus of the work of the OPCW over the coming period. But this ultimately cannot be achieved without universality. Lack of universality implies the potential for safe havens. Moreover, in an interdependent world, the effectiveness of one regime, organisation, State, or individual increasingly requires a willingness to cooperate with others — and to adopt an outward focus. Consideration of universal acceptance of one set of global norms cannot be dealt with in a vacuum, but must also take account of the degree of acceptance of other standards of behaviour.

The Chemical Weapons Convention now has 145 States Parties. When compared to the membership of other relevant international bodies, it may be noted that virtually the entire membership of the OPCW is also represented in organisations such as the United Nations and the World Health Organisation (WHO).[27] In addition, almost all (between 125 and 135) OPCW Member States are also involved in the activities of other bodies such the International Narcotics Control Board (INCB), the World Customs Organisation (WCO), and the Secretariat for the Basel Convention,[28] and more than 110 States Parties to the Chemical Weapons Convention are members of the World Trade Organisation (WTO), the Biological and Toxin Weapons Convention (BWC), and the International Atomic Energy Agency (IAEA).

5. Conclusion

These observations, and the figures quoted above, have more than legal and normative significance. There is a practical aspect: they make cooperation not only possible, but also potentially worthwhile. Given that, in each case, the level of common membership of the various regimes now includes a substantial majority of the international community, this has several advantages. First, the common membership of each regime is subject to common rules and rule-making procedures. Second, in terms of further advances toward universal adherence, usually only relatively small numbers of States are not bound either by the Chemical Weapons Convention or by the other regime(s) in question.[29] At a certain point in time, the respective treaty-implementing bodies could promote universal adherence

[27] For example, the OPCW, in relation to chemical weapons, and WHO are collaborating in compiling a final draft of international guidelines on responding to chemical and biological attacks by terrorists. See www.who.org.

[28] 1989 Basel Convention on the Control of Transboundary Movements of Hazardous Wastes and their Disposal, entry into force 5 May 1992. As of June 2002, it had 151 parties.

[29] For example, INCB-15 States; BWC-21; WTO-22; WCO-25; Basel-25; IAEA-27. Membership of the UN and the WHO is virtually universal and, in the case of other relevant treaties such as the Nuclear Non-Proliferation Treaty (NPT), is almost universal. In normative, if not practical, terms, there is often little more than a handful of States that have not at least *signed* one or both treaties. And, as reflected in the customary rule stated in the Vienna Convention on the Law of Treaties, Article 18, signature places these States under an obligation not to defeat the object and purpose of the relevant treaty or treaties. As a predictor, this is also of considerable relevance to more recent agreements closely associated with counter-terrorism efforts: again, more than 100 States Parties to the Chemical Weapons Convention have also signed the International Convention on the Suppression of the Financing of Terrorism, in force 10 April 2002 (as of July 2002 it had 41 parties), as well as the UN Convention Against Transnational Organised Crime, opened for signature on 12-15 December 2000 (not yet in force). In addition, more than half of the States not party to the Chemical Weapons Convention have already signed at least one, if not both, of these key conventions.

amongst their respective memberships, particularly when there is a common interest to cooperate for implementation purposes. In other cases, there may be scope for cooperation with other multilateral organisations, or regional bodies in under-represented regions, including through the regional activities of the United Nations in the areas of disarmament, development and other areas of priority and concern.[30] This may also prove relevant to the development of effective networks, non-confidential databases, and the harmonisation — or at least demystification — of varying regulatory measures adopted in different States, regions and legal systems.[31]

The implications for national implementation, and the need to strengthen international control regimes, are clear. On one hand, it should be accepted that few international instruments integrate all aspects of mutual assistance, and that few integrated instruments are universally adhered to.[32] On the other hand, the demand for international cooperation, in addressing global terrorism and many other urgent issues,is a call being made at the highest level in multilateral and regional bodies. Moreover, though international agreements and protocols may be negotiated in relation to specific subjects, this is far less likely to be the case at the level of implementation, where many authorities are involved, with responsibilities in different areas — all of which requires coordination.[33] Increased international cooperation will continue to be crucial, therefore, to the success of the Chemical Weapons Convention, to addressing chemical weapons proliferation, and to combatting the real risks presented by safe havens.[34]

---

[30] For example, representatives of the Caribbean Community (CARICOM) Secretariat's Regional Drugs Control Unit, and of the United Nations Regional Centre for Peace, Disarmament and Development in Latin America and the Caribbean, participated in the regional seminar, held in Jamaica in November 2001, to promote universal adherence to the Chemical Weapons Convention. See the report, *OPCW Synthesis*, Spring (March 2002), 32.

[31] For example, in the Latin America and the Caribbean Group (GRULAC), as well as Spain and Portugal, and possibly therefore in other lusophone countries in Africa and elsewhere, it appears that the Convention may be implemented through amendments to what are, in effect, the same range of laws, often even having the same titles. Such "pre-existing" integration may be particularly relevant to the work of the OPCW Network of Legal Experts in GRULAC. Moreover, in the case of agreements without any implementing body to date, such as the BWC — particularly given the similarities in subject matter — this also suggests that Chemical Weapons Convention mechanisms could, in practical and targeted ways, be utilised to achieve efficiencies and effectiveness in the implementation of the other regime, if States Parties so agree.

[32] See L. Tabassi, *supra* note 7.

[33] See OPCW doc. S/269/2001, *supra* note 4, at subparagraphs 8.6-8.8.

[34] For example, difficulties with customs reporting of imports and exports, identification of relevant chemicals, and the different thresholds and concentration limits applied in connection with declarable chemicals, are affecting implementation of the Convention. This is also relevant to future measures to strengthen the verification regime, with the Executive Council due to report to the Conference of the States Parties at its Seventh Session, in October 2002, in relation to transfers of Schedule 3 chemicals under paragraph 27 of Part VIII of the Verification Annex.

A DRAFT CONVENTION TO PROHIBIT BIOLOGICAL AND CHEMICAL WEAPONS UNDER INTERNATIONAL CRIMINAL LAW

Matthew Meselson and Julian Perry Robinson*

Any development, production, acquisition or use of biological or chemical weapons (CBW) is the result of decisions and actions of individual persons, whether they are government officials, commercial suppliers, weapons experts or terrorists. The international conventions that prohibit these weapons, the Biological Weapons Convention of 1972 (BWC)[1] and the Chemical Weapons Convention of 1993 (CWC),[2] however, are directed primarily to the actions of States, and address the matter of individual responsibility to only a limited degree.

Article IV of the BWC and Article VII of the CWC require each State Party to prohibit activities on its territory that are prohibited to a State Party. The CWC explicitly requires each State Party to enact penal legislation to this effect, applicable not only to activities on its territory but also to activities of its own nationals anywhere.

Nevertheless, the BWC and the CWC stop short of requiring a State Party to establish criminal jurisdiction applicable to foreign nationals on its territory who commit biological or chemical weapons offences elsewhere – and neither convention contains provisions dealing with extradition.

These deficiencies are not remedied by the provisions applicable to biological and chemical weapons in the Convention for the Suppression of Terrorist Bombings,[3] opened for signature in January 1998, or in the Statute of the International Criminal Court, signed in Rome in July 1998. The Terrorist Bombings Convention does not apply to the activities of military forces in the exercise of their official duties or to internal State acts, such as the use of CBW by a leader against a population within his own State. Nor does the scope of either of these agreements extend beyond the actual use of CBW weapons to include, as do the BWC and the CWC, their development, production, acquisition and stockpiling.

National criminal legislation, so far enacted by only a minority of States, is no substitute for international criminalisation. Purely national statutes present daunting problems of

*Co-directors of the Harvard Sussex Program on CBW Armament and Arms Limitation. Dr Matthew Meselson is Thomas Dudley Cabot Professor of the Natural Sciences in the Department of Molecular and Cellular Biology of Harvard University and Julian Perry Robinson is Professorial Fellow, SPRU - Science & Technology Policy Research, University of Sussex.

[1] Convention on the Prohibition of the Development, Production and Stockpiling of Bacteriological (Biological) and Toxin Weapons and on Their Destruction.

[2] 1993 Convention on the Prohibition of the Development, Production, Stockpiling and Use of Chemical Weapons and on Their Destruction, entered into force on 29 April 1997. Text, as corrected and changed, available at http://www.opcw.org.

[3] International Convention for the Suppression of Terrorist Bombings.

R. Yepes-Enríquez and L. Tabassi. (eds.), Treaty Enforcement and International Cooperation in Criminal Matters

harmonising their various provisions regarding the definition of crimes, rights of the accused, dispute resolution, judicial assistance, and other important matters. Neither do national criminal statutes convey the universal condemnation implicit in international criminal law. Moreover, purely national legislation would generally have no applicability in the case of a person present in State A who has, for example, ordered the production of biological weapons in State B, of which he or she is a national but which, for one reason or another, fails to take action.

What is needed is a new treaty, one that defines specific acts involving biological or chemical weapons as international crimes, obliging States to establish jurisdiction over offenders who are present on their territory, regardless of their nationality and of where the offence was committed. Treaties defining international crimes are based on the concept that certain crimes are dangerous or abhorrent to all and that all States, therefore, have the right and the responsibility to combat them. Certainly in this category, threatening to the community of nations and to present and future generations, are crimes involving the weaponisation of disease or poison and the hostile exploitation of biotechnology.

The Harvard Sussex Program on CBW Armament and Arms Limitation, with advice from an international group of legal authorities, has prepared a draft convention that would make it a crime under international law for any person to order, direct or knowingly to render substantial assistance in the development, production, acquisition, stockpiling, retention, transfer or use of biological or chemical weapons or in the construction, acquisition or retention of any facility intended for the production of such weapons or for any person to threaten to use biological or chemical weapons. Any person who commits any of the prohibited acts anywhere would face the risk of apprehension, prosecution and punishment or of extradition should that person be found on the territory of a State that supports the proposed convention.

The proposed convention would oblige each State Party: (i) to establish jurisdiction with respect to the specified crimes extending to all persons on its territory, regardless of the place where the offence is committed or the nationality of the alleged offender; (ii) to investigate, upon receiving information that a person alleged to have committed an offence may be present on its territory; and (iii) to prosecute or extradite any such alleged offender if satisfied that the facts so warrant.

The same obligations to establish jurisdiction and to extradite or adjudicate (*aut dedere aut judicare*) are included in international conventions now in force for the suppression and punishment of international crimes including aircraft hijacking and sabotage (1970 and 1971),[4] crimes against internationally protected persons (1973),[5] hostage taking (1979),[6] theft of nuclear materials (1980),[7] torture (1984)[8] and crimes against maritime navigation (1988).[9]

[4] Convention for the Suppression of Unlawful Seizure of Aircraft (1970) and Convention for the Suppression of Unlawful Acts Against the Safety of Civil Aviation (1971).

[5] Convention on the Prevention and Punishment of Crimes Against Internationally Protected Persons Including Diplomatic Agents (1973).

[6] International Convention Against the Taking of Hostages (1979).

[7] Convention on the Physical Protection of Nuclear Material (1980).

[8] Convention Against Torture and Other Cruel, Inhuman or Degreading Treatment or Punishment (1984)

[9] Convention for the Suppression of Unlawful Acts Against the Safety of Maritime Navigation (1988).

It was on the basis of the 1984 Torture Convention that Britain asserted jurisdiction in the case of Spain's request for extradition of former Chilean president Augusto Pinochet.

Biological and chemical weapons are defined in the proposed convention as they are defined in the BWC and the CWC, according to a general purpose criterion, and the definitions of prohibited acts are modelled closely on the definitions in these treaties. A prohibited act is defined as a crime only if committed "knowingly". It is an admissible defence that the accused person "reasonably believed" that the conduct in question was not prohibited. It is not a defence that a person acted in an official capacity or under orders of a superior.

The proposed convention includes provisions intended to guarantee due process and fair proceedings and requiring that any dispute between States concerning the interpretation or application of the convention be submitted, at the request of one of them, to arbitration or to the International Court of Justice in The Hague. There are also provisions requiring States Parties to cooperate in investigations and to provide legal assistance to one another in the adjudication of offences.

In conformity with the procedure by which other international criminalisation conventions have come into being, a group of sponsoring States might submit the proposed convention or a similar draft in the form of a resolution for consideration by the United Nations General Assembly, seeking its referral to the UNGA Sixth (Legal) Committee for negotiation and preparation of an agreed text. This might be completed in a year, in time for the following General Assembly. Following a resolution of commendation by the Assembly, the agreed convention would be opened for signature. After ratification by a specified number of States, it would enter into force. Alternatively, a regional or other grouping of States might convene a diplomatic conference with a view to producing an agreed text that could then be opened for signature and ratification by any State wishing to do so.

Adoption and widespread adherence to such a convention would create a new dimension of constraint against biological and chemical weapons by applying international criminal law to hold individual offenders responsible and punishable should they be found on the territory of any State that supports the convention. Such individuals would be regarded as *hostes humani generis*, enemies of all humanity. The norm against chemical and biological weapons would be strengthened, deterrence of potential offenders would be enhanced, and international cooperation in suppressing the prohibited activities would be facilitated.

Postscript. Three recent developments seem worth citing here. First, Switzerland, in its national statement to the Fifth BWC Review Conference on 20 November 2001, expressed support for the international criminalisation concept underlying the proposed convention. Second, the proposed convention was presented by the Netherlands to the Public International Law Working Group (COJUR) of the Council of the European Union at its meeting of 31 January 2002. COJUR agreed that delegations would submit the proposal to their governments for consideration, along with the positive comments made by a number of delegations during the meeting. Third, international criminalisation is included as one of eleven measures proposed for consideration in the UK government's consultative paper presented to Parliament on 29 April 2002 by the Secretary of State for Foreign and Commonwealth Affairs: "A New Convention on Criminalisation of CBW: there are already proposals, developed initially in the academic community, for a new Convention that introduces criminal responsibility for any individual indicted for violating the prohibitions of the Biological and Toxin Weapons Convention or the Chemical Weapons Convention. States would be obliged to prosecute or extradite indicted individuals."[10]

[10] Strengthening the Biological and Toxin Weapons Convention: Countering the Threat from Biological Weapons (CM 5484) (April 2002).

DRAFT CONVENTION ON THE PREVENTION AND PUNISHMENT OF THE CRIME OF DEVELOPING, PRODUCING, ACQUIRING, STOCKPILING, RETAINING, TRANSFERRING OR USING BIOLOGICAL OR CHEMICAL WEAPONS

PREAMBLE

The States Parties to this Convention,

RECALLING that States are prohibited by the Geneva Protocol of 1925, the Biological Weapons Convention of 1972 and the Chemical Weapons Convention of 1993, and other international agreements, from developing, producing, stockpiling, acquiring, retaining, transferring or using biological and chemical weapons, and that these prohibitions reflect a worldwide norm against these weapons;

RECOGNISING that any development, production, acquisition or use of biological or chemical weapons is the result of the decisions and actions of individual persons, including government officials, and that these activities are within the capability not only of States but also of other entities and of individuals;

AFFIRMING that all persons and entities should be prohibited from engaging in these activities, and should be subject to effective penal sanctions, thereby enhancing the effectiveness of the Geneva Protocol, the Biological Weapons Convention and the Chemical Weapons Convention;

REAFFIRMING that any use of disease or poison for hostile purposes is repugnant to the conscience of humankind;

CONSIDERING that biological and chemical weapons pose a threat to the well-being of all humanity and to future generations;

RESOLVING that knowledge and achievements in biology, chemistry and medicine should be used exclusively for the health and well-being of humanity;

DESIRING to encourage the peaceful and beneficial advance and application of these sciences by protecting them from adverse consequences that would result from their hostile exploitation;

DETERMINED, for the sake of human beings everywhere and of future generations, to eliminate the threat of biological and chemical weapons;

HAVE AGREED as follows:

ARTICLE I

1. Any person commits an offence who knowingly:
   (a) develops, produces, otherwise acquires, stockpiles or retains any biological or chemical weapon, or transfers, directly or indirectly, to anyone, any biological or chemical weapon;
   (b) uses any biological or chemical weapon;
   (c) engages in preparations to use any biological or chemical weapon;
   (d) constructs, acquires or retains any facility intended for the production of biological or chemical weapons;
   (e) assists, encourages or induces, in any way, anyone to engage in any of the above activities;
   (f) orders or directs anyone to engage in any of the above activities;
   (g) attempts to commit any of the above offences;
   (h) threatens to use biological or chemical weapons.

ARTICLE II

1. Nothing in this Convention shall be construed as prohibiting activities that are permitted under:
   (a) the Convention on the Prohibition of the Development, Production and Stockpiling of Bacteriological (Biological) and Toxin Weapons and on their Destruction, of 10 April 1972, or
   (b) the Convention on the Prohibition of the Development, Production, Stockpiling and Use of Chemical Weapons and on their Destruction, done at Paris on 13 January 1993, or that are directed toward the fulfilment of a State's obligations under either Convention and are conducted in accordance with its provisions.

2. In a prosecution for an offence set forth in Article I, it shall be a defence that the accused person reasonably believed that the conduct in question was not prohibited under this Convention.

3. It is not a defence that a person charged with an offence set forth in Article I acted in an official capacity, under the orders or instructions of a superior, or otherwise in accordance with internal law.

ARTICLE III

For the purposes of the present Convention:

1. "Biological weapons" means:
   (a) microbial or other biological agents, or toxins whatever their origin or method of production, of types and in quantities that have no justification for prophylactic, protective or other peaceful purposes;
   (b) weapons, equipment or means of delivery designed to use such agents or toxins for hostile purposes or in armed conflict.

2. "Chemical weapons" means the following, together or separately:
   (a) toxic chemicals and their precursors, except where intended for:
      (i) industrial, agricultural, research, medical, pharmaceutical or other peaceful purposes;
      (ii) protective purposes, namely those purposes directly related to protection against toxic chemicals and to protection against chemical weapons;
      (iii) military purposes not connected with the use of chemical weapons and not dependent on the use of the toxic properties of chemicals as a method of warfare;
      (iv) law enforcement including domestic riot control purposes. As long as the types and quantities are consistent with such purposes.
   (b) munitions and devices, specifically designed to cause death or other harm through the toxic properties of those toxic chemicals specified in subparagraph (a), which would be released as a result of the employment of such munitions and devices;
   (c) any equipment specifically designed for use directly in connection with the employment of munitions and devices specified in subparagraph (b).

3. "Toxic chemical" means any chemical which through its chemical action on life processes can cause death, temporary incapacitation or permanent harm to humans or animals. This includes all such chemicals, regardless of their origin or of their method of production, and regardless of whether they are produced in facilities, in munitions or elsewhere.

4. "Precursor" means any chemical reactant which takes part at any stage in the production by whatever method of a toxic chemical. This includes any key component of a binary or multicomponent chemical system, that is to say, the precursor which plays the most important role on determining the toxic properties of the final product and reacts rapidly with other chemicals in the binary or multicomponent system.

5. "Person" means any natural person or, to the extent consistent with internal law as to criminal responsibility, any legal entity.

ARTICLE IV

Each State Party shall adopt such measures as may be necessary:
   (a) to establish as criminal offences under its internal law the offences set forth in Article I;
   (b) to make those offences punishable by appropriate penalties which take into account their grave nature.

ARTICLE V

1. Each State Party to this Convention shall take such measures as may be necessary to establish its jurisdiction over the offences set forth in Article I in the following cases:
   (a) when the offence was committed in the territory of that State or in any other place under its jurisdiction as recognised by international law;
   (b) when the alleged offender is a national of that State;
   (c) when, if that State considers it appropriate, the alleged offender is a stateless person

whose habitual residence is in its territory;

(d) when the offence was committed with intent to harm that State or its nationals or to compel that State to do or abstain from doing any act;

(e) when the offence involved the intentional use of biological or chemical weapons and a victim of the offence was a national of that State;

(f) when the offence involved the intentional use of biological or chemical weapons against any persons, irrespective of their nationality.

2. Each State Party shall likewise take such measures as may be necessary to establish its jurisdiction over the offences set forth in Article I in cases where the alleged offender is present in its territory and it does not extradite such person pursuant to Articles VII and VIII.

3. This Convention does not exclude any criminal jurisdiction exercised in accordance with internal law, including any internal law giving effect to Article I.

4. Jurisdiction with respect to the offences set forth in Article I may also be exercised by any international criminal court that may have jurisdiction in the matter in accordance with its Statute.

ARTICLE VI

1. Upon receiving information that a person who has committed or who is alleged to have committed an offence as set forth in Article I may be present in its territory, a State Party shall take such measures as may be necessary under its internal law to investigate the facts contained in the information.

2. If it is satisfied that the circumstances so warrant, a State Party in the territory of which an alleged offender is present shall take that person into custody or shall take such other measures as are necessary to ensure the presence of that person for the purpose of prosecution or extradition.

3. Any person regarding whom the measures referred to in paragraph 2 are being taken shall be entitled to:

   (a) communicate without delay with the nearest appropriate representative of the State of which that person is a national or which is otherwise entitled to protect that person's rights or, if that person is a stateless person, the State in the territory of which that person habitually resides;

   (b) be visited by a representative of that State;

   (c) be informed of that person's rights under subparagraphs (a) and (b).

4. The rights referred to in paragraph 3 shall be exercised in conformity with the laws and regulations of the State in the territory of which the offender or alleged offender is present, provided that the said laws and regulations must enable full effect to be given to the purposes for which the rights accorded under paragraph 3 are intended.

5. When a State Party, pursuant to the present Article, has taken a person into custody, it shall promptly notify, directly or through the Secretary-General of the United Nations, the States Parties which have established jurisdiction in accordance with Article V, paragraph 1, subparagraphs (a) through (e), and, if it considers it advisable, any other interested States Parties, of the fact that such person is in custody and of the circumstances which warrant that person's detention. The State which makes the investigation contemplated in paragraph 1 of the present Article shall promptly inform those States Parties of its findings and shall indicate whether it intends to exercise jurisdiction.

ARTICLE VII

1. The offences set forth in Article I shall be deemed to be included as extraditable offences in any extradition treaty existing between States Parties. States Parties undertake to include those offences as extraditable offences in every extradition treaty subsequently concluded between them.

2. If a State Party which makes extradition conditional on the existence of a treaty receives a request for extradition from another State Party with which it has no extradition treaty, it may, if it decides to extradite, consider this Convention as the legal basis for extradition in respect of the offences set forth in Article I. Extradition shall be subject to the other conditions provided by the law of the requested State.

3. States Parties which do not make extradition conditional on the existence of a treaty shall recognise the offences set forth in Article I as extraditable offences as between themselves subject to the conditions provided by the law of the requested State.

4. The offences set forth under Article I shall be treated, for the purpose of extradition between States Parties, as if they had been committed not only in the place in which they occurred but also in the territories of the States required to establish their jurisdiction in accordance with paragraph 1, subparagraphs (a) through (e) of Article V.

5. The provisions of all extradition treaties and arrangements between States Parties with regard to offences set forth in Article I shall be deemed to be modified as between States Parties to the extent that they are incompatible with this Convention.

ARTICLE VIII

The State Party in the territory of which the alleged offender is found shall, if it does not extradite such person, be obliged, without exception whatsoever and whether or not the offence was committed in its territory, to submit the case without delay to competent authorities for the purpose of prosecution, through proceedings in accordance with the laws of that State. Those authorities shall take their decision in the same manner as in the case of any other offence of a grave nature under the law of that State.

ARTICLE IX

1. States Parties shall afford one another the greatest measure of assistance in connection with investigations or criminal or extradition proceedings brought in respect of the offences set forth in Article I, including assistance in obtaining evidence at their disposal which is necessary for the proceedings.

2. States Parties shall carry out their obligations under paragraph 1 in conformity with any treaties or other arrangements on mutual legal assistance that may exist between them. In the absence of such treaties or arrangements, States Parties shall afford one another assitance in accordance with their internal law.

3. States Parties may request technical assistance from competent international bodies in connection with investigations or criminal or extradition proceedings brought in respect of the offences set forth in Article I.

ARTICLE X

None of the offences set forth in Article I shall be regarded, for the purposes of extradition or mutual legal assistance, as a political offence or as an offence connected with a political offence or as an offence inspired by political motives. Accordingly, a request for extradition or for mutual legal assistance based on such an offence may not be refused on the sole ground that it concerns a political offence or an offence connected with a political offence or an offence inspired by political motives.

ARTICLE XI

Nothing in this Convention shall be interpreted as imposing an obligation to extradite or to afford mutual legal assistance, if the requested State Party has substantial grounds for believing that the request for extradition for offences set forth in Article I or for mutual legal assistance with respect to such offences has been made for the purpose of prosecuting or punishing a person on account of that person's race, religion, nationality, ethnic origin or political opinion or that compliance with the request would cause prejudice to that person's position for any of these reasons.

ARTICLE XII

States Parties shall cooperate in the prevention of the offences set forth in Article I, particularly by:

(a) taking all practicable measures to prevent preparations in their respective territories for the commission of those offences within or outside their territories;

(b) exchanging information and coordinating the taking of administrative and other measures as appropriate to prevent commission of those offences.

ARTICLE XIII

1. Each State Party shall inform the Secretary-General of the United Nations of the legislative and administrative measures taken to implement this Convention. In particular, each State Party shall notify the Secretary-General of the United Nations of the jurisdiction it has established under its internal law in accordance with paragraph 3 of Article V. Should any change take place, the State Party concerned shall immediately notify the Secretary-General.

2. Each State Party shall, in accordance with its national law, promptly provide to the Secretary-General of the United Nations any relevant information in its possession concerning:
   (a) the circumstances of any offence over which it has established its jurisdiction pursuant to paragraph 1 or paragraph 3 of Article V;
   (b) the measures taken in relation to the alleged offender, and, in particular, the results of any extradition proceedings or other legal proceedings.

3. The State Party where an alleged offender is prosecuted shall communicate the final outcome of the proceedings to the Secretary-General of the United Nations, who shall transmit the information to the other States Parties.

4. Each State Party shall designate a contact point within its government to which other States Parties may communicate in matters relevant to this Convention. Each State Party shall make such designation known to the Secretary-General.

ARTICLE XIV

Any dispute between States Parties concerning the interpretation or application of this Convention which is not settled by negotiation shall, at the request of one of them, be submitted to arbitration. If within six months from the date of the request for arbitration the parties are unable to agree on the organisation of the arbitration, any one of those parties may refer the dispute to the International Court of Justice.

ARTICLE XV

1. Ten years after the entry into force of this Convention, or earlier if it is requested by a majority of Parties to the Convention by submitting a proposal to this effect to the Secretary-General of the United Nations, a Conference of States Parties shall be held at [Geneva, Switzerland], to review the operation of the Convention with a view to assuring that the purposes of the preamble and the provisions of the Convention are being realised.

2. At intervals of seven years thereafter, unless otherwise decided upon, further sessions of the Conference may be convened with the same objective.

ARTICLE XVI

1. This Convention shall be open for signature by all States from [DATE] until [DATE] at United Nations Headquarters in New York.

2. This Convention is subject to ratification, acceptance or approval. The instruments of ratification, acceptance or approval shall be deposited with the Secretary-General of the United Nations.

3. This Convention shall be open to accession by any State. The instruments of accession shall be deposited with the Secretary-General of the United Nations.

ARTICLE XVII

1. This Convention shall enter into force on the thirtieth day following the date of the deposit of the [NUMBER] instrument of ratification, acceptance, approval or accession with the Secretary-General of the United Nations.

2. For each State ratifying, accepting, approving or acceding to the Convention after the deposit of the [NUMBER] instrument of ratification, acceptance, approval or accession, the Convention shall enter into force on the thirtieth day after deposit by such State of its instrument of ratification, acceptance, approval or accession.

ARTICLE XVIII

The Articles of this Convention shall not be subject to reservation.

ARTICLE XIX

The original of this Convention, of which the Arabic, Chinese, English, French, Russian and Spanish texts are equally authentic, shall be deposited with the Secretary-General of the United Nations, who shall send certified copies thereof to all States.

IN WITNESS WHEREOF, the undersigned, being duly authorised thereto by their respective Governments, have signed this Convention, opened for signature at United Nations Headquarters in New York on [DATE].

The preceeding draft of the proposed convention was prepared during 8-9 August 1998 by a working group consisting of James Crawford (Cambridge University), John Dugard (Leiden University), Philip Heymann (Harvard University), Matthew Meselson (Harvard University) and Julian Robinson (University of Sussex). It is based on an earlier Harvard Sussex draft and on discussions at a Harvard Sussex workshop on criminalising biological and chemical weapons held during 1-2 May 1998 at the Lauterpacht Research Centre for International Law at Cambridge University.

Workshop Participants, Lauterpacht Research Centre for International Law University of Cambridge, 1-2 May 1998

Dr Awn Al-Khasawneh, Member, International Law Commission. Amman, Jordan

Professor Igor Blichtchenko, Faculty of Law, Peoples' Friendship University of Russia. Moscow, Russia

Kathleen Corken, Senior Trial Attorney, Terrorism and Violent Crime Section, Justice Department. Washington, DC, USA

Professor James Crawford, Director, Lauterpacht Research Centre for International Law; Member, International Law Commission. Cambridge, UK

Mr Rajesh De, Harvard Law School, Cambridge, USA

Professor John Dugard, University of Witwatersrand; Member, International Law Commission. Johannesburg, South Africa

Ambassador Rolf Ekeus, Ambassador of Sweden to the US; Executive Chairman of the United Nations Special Commission for Iraq, 1991-1997. Washington, DC, USA

Professor Philip Heymann, Harvard Law School; Deputy Attorney General, Department of Justice, 1993-94. Cambridge, MA, USA

Dr Marie Jacobsson, Deputy Director, Division for International Law and Human Rights, Ministry for Foreign Affairs. Stockholm, Sweden

Mr Stuart Maslen, Legal Advisor to the Mines/Arms Unit, International Committee of the Red Cross. Geneva, Switzerland

Dame Anne McLaren, Wellcome/CRC Institute of Cancer and Developmental Biology. Cambridge, UK

Professor Matthew Meselson, Co-Director, Harvard Sussex Program; Department of Molecular & Cellular Biology, Harvard University. Cambridge, MA, USA

Mr Paul O'Sullivan, Minister and Deputy Chief of Mission, Embassy of Australia. Washington, DC, USA

Dr Graham Pearson, Director, Chemical & Biological Defense Establishment, Porton Down, 1984-95; HSP Advisory Board. Wiltshire, UK

Dr J.P. Pretorius, Deputy Attorney General, Ministry of Justice. Pretoria, South Africa

Professor Julian Robinson, Co-Director, Harvard Sussex Program; Professorial Fellow, Science Policy Research Unit, University of Sussex. Brighton, UK

Professor Valentin Romanov, Moscow Institute of International Relations; Advisor to the Foreign Ministry of Russia. Moscow, Russia

Professor Emma Rothschild, Director, Centre for History and Economics. King's College, Cambridge, UK

Dr Remi Russbach, Executive Director, The Geneva Foundation to Protect Health in War. Geneva, Switzerland

Mr Paul Schulte, Director, Proliferation and Arms Control Secretariat, Ministry of Defense. London, UK

Ms Noala Skinner, Research Associate, Common Security Forum. King's College, Cambridge, UK

Mr Justin Smith, US Courthouse. Washington, DC, USA

Dr John Walker, Principal Research Officer, Arms Control and Disarmament Research Unit, Foreign and Commonwealth Office. London, UK

(All of the above persons participated in their personal capacities only.)

LEGAL ASSISTANCE UNDER THE CHEMICAL WEAPONS CONVENTION: AN OPTIONAL PROTOCOL TO THE CONVENTION?

Lisa Tabassi*

1. Introduction

A crime by non-State actors involving chemical weapons use, or attempted use, would almost certainly have transnational elements: either the persons, the financing, or the substances involved would have crossed borders in the planning or the aftermath of the crime. The global response to the 11 September 2001 attacks on the World Trade Center and the Pentagon demonstrated the extent to which other States can become involved in the investigation of a crime, and in the prevention of further crimes. The immediate official international responses to those attacks fell to large extent into the category of inter-State cooperation in penal matters: requests to surrender suspected accomplices; arrests, searches, and seizures by police in more than ten countries;[1] the tracing of travel documentation and financial transactions; and the freezing of assets of suspected accomplices. The cooperating authorities in the various jurisdictions acting on such requests normally do so on the basis of bilateral or multilateral agreements covering one or more of these forms of mutual legal assistance. Exceptionally, in the case of the September 11 attacks, the legal basis for the cooperation may have been the United Nations Security Council Chapter VII resolutions aimed at countering terrorism and the financing of terrorist acts.

To rule out the possibility that criminals might evade the Chemical Weapons Convention[2] ("Convention") regime by moving their activities or their physical presence to the territory of another State, Article VII(1)(c) requires States Parties to extend their penal legislation covering the prohibitions to "any activity prohibited to a State Party under this Convention undertaken anywhere by natural persons, possessing its nationality, in conformity with international law." One State Party, Sweden, has gone beyond this obligation and, in its penal code, has provided that: "A crime against the Convention will be sentenced by Swedish law and at a Swedish court even if the crime is committed abroad and irrespective of the perpetrator's nationality."[3] The Convention's obligation to extend penal legislation

* Legal Officer, Office of the Legal Adviser, OPCW Secretariat. The views expressed are the author's own and are not attributable to the OPCW Secretariat. The author gratefully acknowledges the inspiration and mentoring of Walter Krutzsch.

[1] By one news account, "The US-led war on terrorism has resulted in the arrest of nearly 1000 Al-Qaeda operatives in more than 60 countries worldwide." J. Lumpkin, CIA Warns of Al-Qaeda Risk to Winter Olympics, Queensland Newspapers (8 February 2002).

[2] 1993 Convention on the Prohibition of the Development, Production, Stockpiling and Use of Chemical Weapons and on Their Destruction, entered into force on 29 April 1997. Text, as corrected and changed, available at http://www.opcw.org.

3 OPCW Survey of National Implementing Legislation, OPCW doc. S/259/2001 (16 May 2001), Annex, at 85.

R. Yepes-Enríquez and L. Tabassi. (eds.), Treaty Enforcement and International Cooperation in Criminal Matters

extraterritorially increases the probability that States Parties may be faced with the need for cooperation and legal assistance from another State for prosecuting a crime violating the Convention.

2. Article VII, Paragraph 2, of the Chemical Weapons Convention

The Convention specifically foresees the possible need for cooperation and legal assistance. In this respect, Article VII, paragraph 2, of the Convention provides that:

> Each State Party shall cooperate with other States Parties and afford the appropriate form of legal assistance to facilitate the implementation of the obligations under paragraph 1" [in summary, the prohibitions, enforcement, and the extraterritorial application of penal legislation].

The word "shall" indicates that States, as a Convention obligation, *must* respond positively to requests for legal assistance; however, the obligation is stated in only the most general terms. What is the possible scope of the obligation "to cooperate with other States Parties and afford the appropriate form of legal assistance," and how would that obligation be carried out in practice?

In prosecuting a crime involving a violation of the Convention or violation of national laws that stem from it, different States may be involved, and may need to make requests for cooperation and legal assistance from other States, depending upon the circumstances:

(a) the State on whose territory the offence has taken place;
(b) the State on whose territory the accused is residing or in custody;
(c) the State whose nationality is held by the accused; and,
(d) the State affected by the offence, or whose natural or legal persons suffered damages from the offence.

Cooperation and legal assistance could be requested for the following:

(a) in identifying the suspect;
(b) in locating and providing the addresses of those involved;
(c) in taking testimony or statements in the territory of the requested State(s);
(d) in producing or preserving judicial or other documents, records or pieces of evidence;
(e) in executing requests for searches and seizures;
(f) in serving judicial and administrative documents;
(g) in authenticating documents;
(h) in transferring proceedings; and,
(i) in extradition.

3. Obstacles to Cooperation and Legal Assistance Under Article VII, Paragraph 2

Even when two States Parties wish to cooperate and provide legal assistance under Article VII, paragraph 2, obstacles could arise, such as:

(1) inconsistent definitions of the crimes (generally the act must be defined as a crime in similar terms in both jurisdictions (dual criminality));
(2) inconsistent penalties (generally the crime must be a serious one subject to a penalty of at least one year's imprisonment);
(3) the extradition or mutual legal assistance agreement in force between the two States may provide for an exception which applies to the case; or,
(4) there is no agreement in force to provide a legal basis for the jurisdictions to cooperate with each other in the prosecution.

With respect to the first two obstacles, the greatest barrier of all to enforcement may be the slow pace of States Parties to enact the requisite national legislation to implement the Convention. Under the 1969 Vienna Convention on the Law of Treaties, failure to enact implementing legislation does not excuse the State from respecting its treaty obligations. Such failure will, however, impair the State's ability to prosecute individuals. The most recent *Survey of National Implementing Legislation,* published by the OPCW Secretariat in 2001,[4] shows that, at present, the legislation enacted by States Parties diverges widely in terms of prohibited activities and penalties.

With respect to the third obstacle, extradition or mutual legal assistance agreements typically contain two exceptions which would be inappropriate in the case of a crime related to violation of the Convention: the political offence exception and the fiscal offence exception. Any consideration of whether the political offence exception could be eliminated for chemical weapons offences should take note of the fact that, under the Convention, there would not exist any just cause justifying an act involving chemical weapons. The notion that certain acts are in *all* cases unjustifiable was incorporated in the 1998 United Nations International Convention for the Suppression of Terrorist Bombings, in which the political offence exception was ruled out. In addition, fiscal offences — those relating to public revenue, e.g. taxes, official fees, customs duties, exchange control — were traditionally not considered to be extraditable offences, the rationale being that fiscal offences in another country did not affect morality in the home jurisdiction. That concept is now changing. In the effort to combat organised crime and trafficking in drugs and weapons, it is now recognised that money laundering enables the funding of these and other criminal activities. In some cases, the financial trail will be the main one law enforcement can follow. Experts have indicated that illicit trafficking cannot be fought effectively if the economic benefits of crime are not also tackled in parallel.

With respect to the fourth obstacle, there is no customary practice in international cooperation and legal assistance in criminal matters: it is normally prescribed in bilateral treaties, and in a few multilateral instruments. If the legal system of a State Party (either requesting or receiving a request for legal assistance) makes cooperation conditional upon

[4] Annex to S/259/2001 (16 May 2001).

the existence of a treaty, the absence of one will, in practice nationally, act as an effective bar to providing the assistance needed, regardless of the State's international obligation under Article VII, paragraph 2, to provide such assistance. The principle of international cooperation has not yet been consolidated by the adoption of a universal multilateral treaty with uniform rules facilitating all forms of mutual legal assistance. While extradition treaties have long been concluded by States, agreements governing other forms of mutual legal assistance, even covering assistance needed at the pre-judicial stage, are very recent. The development of an approach integrating the various modes of inter-State penal cooperation is beginning at the national and regional levels, but the pace is slow. Existing bilateral and multilateral agreements are not comprehensive in scope and, in the case of multilateral agreements, reservations have been made to them. In any event, all modalities of inter-State cooperation in penal matters are almost never included together in an integrated instrument, and the few integrated instruments are not universally adhered to.

In preparing to implement Article VII, paragraph 2, States Parties to the Convention need to check whether their national law, and their various treaties concerning different forms of mutual legal assistance concluded with the other States Parties, will allow for cooperation. If two States Parties wishing to cooperate do encounter obstacles, only certain other non judicial coercive techniques may be available, based on comity or cooperation through organisations such as Interpol. Assistance can be granted on an ad hoc basis, on the basis of reciprocity, and can be requested through diplomatic channels. However, diplomatic channels may not meet the demand for expediency, which is especially important in criminal investigations or proceedings. Furthermore, the authorities using those channels will not be in a position to compel testimony or the production of evidence.

The wording of Article VII, paragraph 2, of the Convention itself does not provide any explicit mechanism that would allow the Convention itself to act as a mutual legal assistance instrument.

4. A Case for an Optional Protocol on Cooperation and Legal Assistance?

One option which could be considered by States Parties to the Convention is the elaboration of an optional protocol, binding upon the States party to it, enumerating the forms of cooperation in penal matters which a State Party will provide, and detailing the procedures for the provision of cooperation and legal assistance under the Convention. The primary utility of such a protocol would be that it would define the parameters of assistance, and in particular, that it would limit the possible excuses for refusing to give assistance.

A proposal for a draft Optional Protocol to the CWC was presented at the OPCW International Symposium on Cooperation and Legal Assistance in The Hague in February 2001. The text of the draft, contained in Annex V to the present volume, was drawn from language in other existing instruments. This approach could facilitate the acceptance of the text of the protocol by States: if they have agreed to specific language to fight crime in another subject area, for example, for drugs, it could be argued that the same language should also be acceptable to them when fighting an equally serious crime involving chemical weapons offences.[5]

[5] The status of adherence to the instruments used in preparing the Optional Protocol is contained in Annex VI to this volume.

Would States Parties be interested in this initiative? In 1998, the OPCW Secretariat distributed a document drawing attention for the first time to the potential difficulties which could arise in the actual implementation of Article VII, paragraph 2.[6] As a result, the Conference of the States Parties at its Third Session requested the Secretariat to convene a seminar on national implementation and legal cooperation, with a view to enhancing the possibilities for legal assistance amongst States Parties.[7] The Secretariat accordingly organised the International Symposium on Cooperation and Legal Assistance for the Effective Implementation of International Agreements.[8] After the 11 September 2001 attacks on the World Trade Center and the Pentagon, the OPCW Executive Council considered the consequences of those attacks within the context of the Convention, and its Chairman issued a statement:

> The Council appeals to all States Parties to redouble their efforts ... to comply fully with their obligations under the Convention, including ... the prevention of the diversion and illegal use of chemicals and chemical technologies, and the taking of all necessary measures in accordance with Article VII of the Convention. ...
>
> The Council urges the development of further means and measures to provide legislative support and assistance to States Parties for the enactment at the national level of enforceable legal provisions for the effective implementation of the Convention.[9]

Following the distribution of a background paper discussing the OPCW's possible contribution to the global struggle against terrorism,[10] the OPCW Executive Council identified the key areas to focus on, which included the item "full implementation of the legislative measures required by Article VII", and established an open-ended working group to advise the Council on specific measures to be taken in this regard.[11]

The terrorist attacks on the World Trade Center and the Pentagon brought into the limelight the need for international cooperation to combat this form of crime, and highlighted the need for streamlining the process. The United Nations Security Council, acting under Chapter VII, in its resolution 1373 (2001), noted with concern "the close connection between international terrorism and ... illegal arms-trafficking, and illegal movement of nuclear, chemical, biological and other potentially deadly materials and, in this regard *emphasises* the need to enhance coordination of efforts on national, subregional, regional and international levels in order to strengthen a global response to this serious challenge and threat to international security." It decided that all States shall "afford one another the greatest measure of assistance in connection with criminal investigations or

[6] Note by the Director-General on Compliance with Article VII: Legislation, Cooperation and Legal Assistance (OPCW doc. C-III/DG.1/Rev.1, dated 17 November 1998).

[7] Report of the Third Session of the Conference of the States Parties (subparagraph 19.3 of OPCW doc. C-III/4, dated 20 November 1998).

[8] Report on the International Symposium on Cooperation and Legal Assistance for the Effective Implementation of International Agreements, The Hague, 7-9 February 2001 (OPCW doc. S/251/2001, dated 22 March 2001).

[9] Statement by the Chairman of the OPCW Executive Council on the Consequences of Terrorist Attacks on 11 September 2001 (OPCW doc. EC-XXVI/3, dated 28 September 2001).

[10] The abridged version of the Secretariat's paper appears in Section IV.1 of this volume.

[11] OPCW Executive Council decision EC-XVII/DEC.5, dated 7 December 2001 (reproduced in Annex IV to this volume).

criminal proceedings relating to the financing or support of terrorist acts, including assistance in obtaining evidence in their possession necessary for the proceedings", and called upon all States to "find ways of intensifying and accelerating the exchange of operational information, especially regarding ... traffic in arms ... and the threat posed by the possession of weapons of mass destruction by terrorist groups".[12] The United Nations General Assembly urgently called for "international cooperation to bring to justice the perpetrators, organisers and sponsors of the outrages of 11 September 2001", and "to prevent and eradicate acts of terrorism."[13] Similar emphases on enhanced international cooperation for prevention and punishment of terrorist acts were contained in the Security Council and General Assembly resolutions adopted prior to 11 September.[14]

Finally, the draft Optional Protocol could also contribute to alleviating the practical effect which could possibly arise from the delay by many States Parties in extending their penal legislation extraterritorially. As mentioned above, Article VII, paragraph 1, of the Convention requires States Parties to extend their penal provisions for chemical weapons offences to their nationals abroad. OPCW surveys, however, show that as few as 15% of States Parties have done so. This may be because a number of States do not recognise the extraterritorial extension of legislation and thus are encountering a conflict with this treaty obligation under the Convention. Although this conflict does not excuse the State, at the international level, from meeting its treaty obligation,[15] in the meantime the objective (prosecution of violators of the Convention) can be achieved through the provision of legal assistance to a State that can assert jurisdiction on another basis.

5. Conclusion

In enforcing the Convention, States Parties have agreed in Article VII, paragraph 2, that they *shall* cooperate with other States Parties, and afford the appropriate form of legal assistance. Since the Convention does not contain the adequate mechanisms to implement that obligation, and an effective network of bilateral or multilateral penal cooperation agreements between all 145 States Parties to the Convention does not, and cannot, exist, States Parties may wish to consider a practical solution. The draft Optional Protocol on Cooperation and Legal Assistance is proposed as possibly constituting the simplest solution. Since the language used in the draft Optional Protocol is drawn mainly from texts adhered to in other instruments by almost all States Parties to the Convention, it should provide a starting point which should be acceptable to them from the outset. In view of the present concern by the international community to prevent and prosecute terrorist acts, the political climate is ripe for the acceptance of the draft Optional Protocol. And since it deals with only one very narrow subject — a very serious one which States Parties to the Convention have undertaken to criminalise and enforce — the Optional Protocol should not meet with the other barriers States may have encountered in adhering to regional or multilateral penal cooperation agreements concerning broader categories of criminal offences.

---

[12] UN Security Council resolution 1373 (28 September 2001), subparagraphs 2(f), 3(a) and 4. Emphasis in the original. Reproduced in Annex III to the present volume.

[13] UNGA resolution 56/1 (12 September 2001), paragraphs 3 and 4.

[14] For example, UNGA res. 54/110 and 55/158 and UNSC res. 1269 (1999).

[15] Article 27 of the 1969 Vienna Convention on the Law of Treaties.

SECTION IV.3

OVERCOMING OBSTACLES IN ACHIEVING WIDE ADHERENCE TO MULTILATERAL LEGAL ASSISTANCE INSTRUMENTS

INTRODUCTION AND SUMMARY

The primary barrier to implementation of States Parties' obligation to cooperate and render legal assistance under the Chemical Weapons Convention is the lack of a multilateral legal framework specifying in detail the scope and procedures for such cooperation and legal assistance, and the complementary national implementing measures to carry out the obligation nationally. Prevention and prosecution of crime is a vital interest of the international community. Ideally there should be a multilateral regime in force covering all forms of mutual legal assistance, universally adhered to and implemented nationally. What are the prospects of ever achieving that regime? This section examines the regional frameworks which have been developed so far and the obstacles in achieving wide adherence to them and application of them. Commentary from the perspective of four organisations is presented: the Commonwealth Secretariat, the Organisation of Eastern Caribbean States, the Council of Europe and the Organization of American States.

If one looks at the multilateral instruments in force and the significant number of bilateral agreements covering inter-State cooperation in penal matters, it would appear that there is wide international commitment to cooperation. However, the problem is not the need for new instruments necessarily, or adherence to international instruments, but their effective implementation. A large network of agreements exists, but application is either non-existent or ineffective.

R. Yepes-Enríquez and L. Tabassi. (eds.), Treaty Enforcement and International Cooperation in Criminal Matters

For example, there are 167 parties to the 1988 Narcotics Convention. It contains stand-alone articles on extradition and on mutual legal assistance. Typically, in implementing those provisions, three types of situations arise. First, there are States which adopt international instruments but do not, for various reasons, enact the requisite domestic legislation to implement them. Secondly, there are States which adopt domestic legislation but the legislation is incomplete or does not fully cover the field of cooperation. Finally, there are the States which have actually adopted complete implementing legislation. Even when there is comprehensive legislation in place to cover cooperation in a given situation, there is a good cooperation between States having similar legal systems, but not when the legal systems are very different. Legislation often lacks the flexibility needed to accommodate the system differences. There are a number of possible solutions. Lack of, or inadequate and inflexible programs and procedures for, effective implementation of mutual assistance must be resolved on a practical, case-by-case, level through practical interaction between Member States. Initiatives to increase awareness of solutions has been fruitful. It is also fundamental that a practical structure, such as a central authority, is established to handle the requests made or received under the international instruments for cooperation in criminal matters. In many States, such a central authority does not exist, is not identified or is not efficient. Next, and importantly, it is necessary to ensure that the persons administer the central authority are trained to be flexible and pragmatic when confronted with a different legal system.

As one regional example, judicial cooperation and assistance between the States of the Eastern Caribbean sub-region has been successful. At the root of this success is the establishment of a central legal and political arrangement for cooperation: the Organisation of Eastern Caribbean States (OECS). The OECS has successfully promoted joint action by the Member States in the legal and judicial fields (for example, by establishing unified services in police services, prison services, banking, customs and fisheries), or in the diplomatic field (for example, by formulating and adopting a common stance on many international issues). However, this success would have not been possible without two caveats. First, the Member States of the OECS were proactive in helping other institutions to fully implement the decisions taken by the OECS. Secondly, the resulting harmonisation and cooperation have allowed greater efficiency, and thus cost savings, which in turn has attracted donor funding. Occasionally, joint action has not been fully achieved, for example in the case of the Chemical Weapons Convention, which was signed by five of the six Member States of the OECS but ratified by only two of them. The OECS Secretariat provided assistance toward resolving that situation by drafting, with OPCW support, model implementing legislation. The Eastern Caribbean approach in overcoming obstacles in judicial cooperation and assistance appears to have been very successful. The OECS, however, is a smaller and far less complex organisation than the one that exists to achieve judicial cooperation in Europe.

In Europe, in the context of the Council of Europe, many difficulties were encountered in achieving judicial cooperation and assistance between 48 European States, 15 of which are associated under the umbrella of the European Union. It has been possible to determine three types of obstacles when implementing international treaties setting out judicial cooperation and legal assistance between Member States. First, a treaty may deal with complex or controversial issues such as the international validity of criminal judgments or the transfer of sentenced persons. Second, the European space is composed of multiple actors who are subject to various and sometimes overlapping treaties in the criminal field. Thirdly, international treaties are often ratified but States Parties enact either no domestic legislation.

Many of the difficulties in applying international treaties are also due to political obstacles. Criminal law and jurisdiction have traditionally been an expression of national sovereignty, and it is still difficult for some Members to relinquish some of their sovereignty in the criminal field. However, pragmatic solutions exist and have been used successfully. First, the application of a treaty can be guaranteed through judicial control. However, judicial control of a treaty is not always possible since the substance of the treaty itself must be clarified or the treaty must be reviewed so that an understanding, a recommendation or a protocol is adopted to allow an efficient application of the treaty. It is also crucial to organise seminars to inform practitioners, since they are the ones who ultimately apply international treaties and are confronted with the difficulties in their application.

In the Americas, the Organisation of American States (OAS) was set up to facilitate regional integration of its Member States and, in doing so, developed a number of treaties in the field of judicial cooperation and legal assistance between Member States and with other States. Of the total of adopted inter-American treaties, fifty per cent of them fall into the category of legal and judicial cooperation and rely on the appointment of a central authority to act as a contact point for cooperation and information exchange objectives. This shows that States Parties are aware that the effective implementation of these treaties cannot be conceived without efficient cooperation mechanisms. In this regard, a body for the setting up of "policies, programs, and action measures," the Inter-American Council for Integral Development, was established by the Protocol of Managua in 1993.

Now, more so than wide adherence, States are confronted with the problem of effective application of treaties nationally. This section shows that all regional approaches have a common yardstick: the need for pragmatism. The Eastern Caribbean approach clearly shows that judicial cooperation is made possible because of the proactive behaviour of States and continues because States have seen practical results from harmonising policies. On the other hand, the Council of Europe, marked by complexity factors, is looking for simplicity by creating a harmonised legal *corpus*, a unique court of justice, shorter and simpler versions of treaties, and by informing and training practitioners. The need for a central authority to deal with requests for assistance and cooperation is also crucial, and the American approach has chosen to overcome possible difficulties in implementing treaties by ensuring that such an entity is clearly established, defined and functional. In general, it can be said that effective implementation of treaties is subject to three requirements: flexibility, simplicity, and information.

Hafida Lahiouel

Rapporteur for Panel C.3 in the 2001 OPCW International Symposium; Legal Officer, Chambers Legal Support, International Criminal Tribunal for the former Yugoslavia. The views expressed are not attributable to the ICTY, the United Nations, or the OPCW.

TOWARD MEANINGFUL ADHERENCE TO MULTILATERAL INSTRUMENTS FOR INTERNATIONAL COOPERATION: THE CHALLENGES TO EFFECTIVE MUTUAL LEGAL ASSISTANCE

Kimberly Prost*

1. Introduction

With advances in technology and the ease of global travel, the world we live in has become, in many ways, as Canadian author Marshall McLuhan predicted, "a global village". This has had a dramatic impact on many aspects of life and society, and law enforcement is no exception.

The technological explosion, and the growth of transnational organised crime and the response of the international community to it, has created many new challenges, not the least of which is the impact on the jobs of law enforcement authorities. In a 1989 case, *United States of America v. Cotroni*, the Supreme Court of Canada made the following statement:

> The investigation, prosecution and suppression of crime for the protection of the citizen and the maintenance of peace and public order are an important goal of all organised societies. The pursuit of that goal cannot realistically be confined within national boundaries. That has long been the case, but it is increasingly evident today.[1]

Today States are increasingly faced with crime that spans borders. The result is that, more and more, international cooperation is an essential component of criminal investigations or prosecutions.

Of the instruments of cooperation, the tool that has seen the most advancement in the last several years is mutual legal assistance – the process by which States receive and provide assistance in gathering evidence for use in criminal investigations and prosecutions. The growth of mutual legal assistance is attributable to the reality that the effective detection, investigation and prosecution of crime today is not possible without cooperation between States with respect to evidence. As criminal activities span national borders, so too must those who seek to combat these crimes find ways and means to effectively gather the necessary evidence which is located outside their own borders.

* Head, Criminal Law Unit, Deputy Director, Legal and Constitutional Affairs Division, Commonwealth Secretariat. Any views expressed are those of the author and are not attributable to any government or organization.

[1] *United States of America v. Cotroni* (1989) 48 C.C.C. (3d) 193 at 215.

R. Yepes-Enríquez and L. Tabassi. (eds.), Treaty Enforcement and International Cooperation in Criminal Matters

It is clear that the international community has recognised the need for enhanced cooperation in evidence gathering. Much has been done to develop international instruments that can form the basis for the rendering of assistance in these matters. If one looks at the signature and ratification statistics for multilateral instruments that provide for cooperation, and the significant number of bilateral mutual assistance treaties that exist between States, it would appear that there is wide international commitment to cooperation in the gathering of evidence for investigations and prosecutions.

Unfortunately, in this case, appearances can be deceiving. While there is, in a technical sense, wide adherence to instruments for international cooperation, on a practical level there are still significant problems with the actual rendering of assistance between States. This paper considers the current problems with implementation of cooperation instruments and possible ways forward.

2. Overview of Mutual Legal Assistance Instruments

Mutual assistance in criminal matters is a mechanism of cooperation which allows, in a direct and efficient manner, for a wide range of assistance between States in the production of evidence. Generally rendered on the basis of bilateral treaty or agreement or multilateral convention,[2] mutual assistance provides a means for one State to obtain evidence from another State for use in a criminal investigation or prosecution.

One of the major advantages of this form of cooperation is that it covers a broad range of assistance including, *inter alia*, taking evidence or statements of persons, search and seizure, the provision of documents or evidentiary items, the service of documents, and the temporary transfer of persons to assist an investigation or appear as a witness. Assistance can also be rendered at any stage of a criminal process from investigation to appeal.

Importantly, the assistance is rendered on the basis of a request submitted pursuant to treaty, agreement, reciprocal legislation, or on the basis of the principle of comity. In most instances, the request can emanate from an authority in the requesting State who is responsible for the investigation or prosecution, and it need not be presented by a judicial authority.

Generally, mutual assistance can be rendered directly between central authorities, often Ministries of Justice, in the two States. This is one of the features of mutual assistance which makes it an effective and efficient mechanism of cooperation: the direct channelling of requests without necessity for use of diplomatic or other channels.

Over the last decade great strides have been made in the development of a framework of instruments for the rendering of assistance.

The first significant instrument for mutual assistance was the European Convention on Mutual Assistance in Criminal Matters, developed by the Council of Europe.[3] It was an important achievement of its time in its recognition of the necessity for specific instruments for cooperation in evidence gathering. However, like all new instruments, it had limitations. Perhaps the most notable, in this instance, was that the Convention was designed to operate amongst States of a similar legal tradition, the civil law States of Europe, and it

[2] In some countries, mutual assistance is provided for on the basis of domestic legislation, which is either applied generally to all States or to designated States on the basis of reciprocity. See, for example, the United Kingdom and Switzerland. Some States, like Canada, also provide for case by case assistance through administrative arrangement.

[3] Concluded on 20 April 1959; in force 12 June 1962. European Treaty Series, No. 30.

therefore did not address perhaps the most significant challenge to effective mutual assistance: bridging the differences between legal systems.

Similarly, within the Commonwealth, in 1986 Law Ministers in Harare, Zimbabwe,[4] adopted a scheme for mutual assistance. It is a non-treaty-based scheme which depends upon States enacting domestic legislation to permit the rendering of assistance in criminal matters. However, it also based on the commonality of systems.

Inbetween the creation of these two multilateral instruments of cooperation, individual States began to develop treaties, on a bilateral basis, to allow for the provision of assistance and, most notably, the provision of assistance between States of a different legal tradition. The oft-cited example of the first breakthrough instrument is the treaty between the United States and Switzerland that came in to force in January, 1977.[5] Since that time a network of bilateral instruments has developed between States of similar or diverse legal tradition. Those agreements are further supplemented by domestic legislation within some States which allows for assistance to be rendered on the basis of reciprocity, designation or administrative arrangement.

Similar to extradition, there has also been an increasing development of regional agreements for mutual assistance. Some recent examples include the Inter-American Convention on Mutual Legal Assistance in Criminal Matters,[6] and the Economic Community of West African States Convention on Mutual Assistance in Criminal Matters.[7]

Other significant advancements in the field of mutual assistance include the adoption by the General Assembly of the United Nations of the 1990 Model Treaty on Mutual Assistance in Criminal Matters[8] and the coming into force of the 1988 United Nations Convention Against Illicit Traffic in Narcotic Drugs and Psychotropic Substances (1988 Drug Convention) which contains a "stand alone" article on mutual legal assistance. Under this article States Parties to the Convention can seek and provide a broad range of assistance in evidence gathering.

A similar detailed article has been included in the recently concluded United Nations Convention against Transnational Organized Crime[9] (UNTOC Convention). Article 18, which was developed on the basis of the 1988 Drug Convention provisions on mutual assistance, contains 30 clauses providing for an elaborate and modern scheme for mutual assistance between State Parties.

The inclusion of "stand alone" provisions on mutual assistance within these Conventions, in addition to its practical effect, also constitutes recognition of the integral role mutual assistance plays in the fight against crime. While not of the same detailed nature, many other international conventions covering a broad range of subjects, including the various anti-terrorism conventions, contain general obligations to render legal assistance.

---

[4] Scheme Relating to Mutual Assistance in Criminal Matters within the Commonwealth, Commonwealth Secretariat, London, LMN (86) 13.

[5] Lionel Frei and Stefan Freschal, Origins and Application of the United States — Switzerland Treaty on Mutual Assistance in Criminal Matters, 31 Harvard International Law Journal (1990) at 77-79.

[6] Canada Gazette, Part I, p. 2483 (Vol. 130, No. 35).

[7] Signed July, 1992.

[8] General Assembly resolution 45/117, annex, 45 U.N. GAOR Supp. (No. 49A) at 215, U.N. Doc. A/45/49 (1990).

[9] UNGA, A/55/383 (2 November 2000).

The Chemical Weapons Convention[10] also makes reference to cooperation and legal assistance, albeit only in very brief terms. The framework of international instruments for the rendering of assistance, while still in need of expansion and improvement, is an impressive one.

However, no matter how complete the network of agreements may be, and regardless of how well-crafted the instruments of cooperation are, none of that is of much value if it is not possible to present a request for assistance and receive evidence in an acceptable form, and in an effective and timely fashion. Unfortunately, that very often remains the reality. In a great number of cases, despite the existence of an applicable instrument, evidence is not forthcoming; it arrives in such a form that it is not useful to requesting authorities; or it is provided so late as to be of little practical value. The problem is particularly acute in relation to requests for assistance in complex cases, where the types of assistance sought involve production of bank and company records and compelled evidence from very reluctant witnesses.

The critical problem is lack of, or inadequate and inflexible, programs and procedures for effective implementation of mutual assistance and the provision of evidence on a practical, case-by-case level. These problems arise in the context of the policy, legislative and administrative frameworks for mutual assistance, as well as day-to-day practice.

3. Policy, Legislative and Administrative Frameworks for the Rendering of Assistance

3.1 Policy

To be effective, mutual legal assistance has to be accorded broadly, with minimum restrictions on its application.

Unfortunately, the development of mutual assistance as a form of international cooperation was preceded by years and years of tradition and practice in the area of extradition. As a natural consequence, many States have imported concepts and principles appropriate to extradition into their process for mutual legal assistance, even where the principles may not be of similar value within the context of mutual legal assistance. For example, many States apply traditional extradition grounds for refusal, such as political offence, *autrefois convict*, or *acquit*, to mutual legal assistance. Extradition directly affects the liberty of individuals, while other forms of mutual legal assistance do not. It is questionable whether the principles relevant to extradition really are necessary when the requested State is not surrendering individuals for prosecution, but providing assistance by way of evidence.

In addition, many such instruments either require dual criminality or provide for a discretionary ground for refusal on that basis, generally or in relation to particular measures of assistance. The application of the dual criminality principles to mutual assistance can significantly delay or impede the rendering of assistance, and again, there is a fundamental issue as to whether it is a necessary requirement for cooperation in relation to evidence gathering.

[10] 1993 Convention on the Prohibition of the Development, Production, Stockpiling and Use of Chemical Weapons and on Their Destruction, entered into force on 29 April 1997. Text, as corrected and changed, available at http://www.opcw.org.

A more flexible approach adopted in some instruments is to include one general ground for refusal that protects fundamental State interests. It will allow for refusal where the requested State is of the opinion that execution of the request would prejudice its sovereignty, security, public order (*ordre public*) or other essential public interest. While at first glance this may appear to be an even broader restriction on the rendering of assistance, in practice that has not been the effect. As best can be determined, the provision is rarely invoked and simply serves as a protection in principle for States. And because it relates to fundamental State concerns, it is simply not applicable in relation to the vast majority of mutual assistance requests, unlike other traditional grounds such as dual criminality.

Admittedly, such a ground for refusal may be raised in the context of requests submitted under some of the multilateral conventions, such as the Chemical Weapons Convention. One can easily envisage situations where the evidence sought for prosecution of such offences could infringe national sovereignty or security. However, in reality, this problem is unavoidable given the very nature of the offences. In my view, it is preferable to address such concerns directly under this general ground of refusal than to include a detailed list of technical grounds for refusal that will have to be considered in every case. In addition, reducing the impact of such a ground for refusal within the context of these types of conventions, perhaps it would be possible to consider including a detailed procedure for consultations, and providing for the use of protective measures as an alternative to complete refusal of the request.[11]

Perhaps one way to improve the effectiveness of mutual assistance, therefore, is to challenge the application of traditional extradition rules to mutual assistance and to encourage countries to adopt an approach that is minimalist in terms of grounds for refusal and other barriers to the rendering of assistance.

3.2 LEGISLATION

There are several issues in mutual assistance that flow directly from the approaches taken in the implementation of mutual assistance obligations under domestic law.

Obviously, the most significant of those is where countries have failed to make the necessary changes under domestic law to meet the obligations set out in a relevant multilateral or bilateral instrument. For example, one of the major frustrations that States have faced in using the 1988 Drug Convention to obtain mutual assistance has been that many signatories lack the capacity to provide the requisite assistance. And such problems are not limited to multilateral instruments. There are instances where even the obligations undertaken in bilateral mutual assistance treaties cannot be met because of an absence of domestic legal power to provide the assistance. While the problem can be less acute in States where treaties are self-implementing, it can still be present if the treaty provisions are of a very general nature and there is no supplementary legislative base for the rendering of assistance.

The other prevalent problem in relation to legislative regimes is the inflexibility of the laws that have been developed and the inflexible application of treaty provisions under domestic law.

---

[11] For example, a provision could be included that allows for editing of materials, to protect the identity of witnesses or the sources of information.

Mutual assistance is only an effective tool if it allows the authorities of one State to obtain usable evidence from another State. This can be accomplished only where the laws, particularly in the requested State, are flexible enough to recognise and bridge the differences between legal systems. This is an acute problem within the context of different legal traditions, like civil law and common law systems.

There is a wide array of approaches to incorporating in domestic law the necessary powers to provide assistance to another State in evidence gathering. However, there is a very natural tendency to include powers for evidence gathering that reflect the process and procedures used in domestic law to gather that evidence. That creates a significant problem, because the goal of the legislation is not to produce evidence that is, in form and substance, admissible in proceedings in the requested State, but rather evidence which will be usable in the requesting State.

One illustration of the problem are the legislative approaches to taking compelled statements or evidence from witnesses. Almost uniformly, bilateral and multilateral mutual assistance treaties provide that a State may request the taking of evidence or statements of witnesses. Where those witnesses will not provide evidence or statements voluntarily, to fulfil its obligations, the requested State must have the capacity to compel the witness to attend at a location and provide the evidence or statement sought.

Many States meet this obligation by having a capacity for their courts, in these circumstances, to issue process compelling the witness to appear before domestic authorities who will record the evidence or statement of the witness for provision to the foreign State. The process is often considered to be a domestic one.

The evidence so recorded and transmitted, however, in many instances will be of little value to the requesting State. For some States it will be essential that officials from the requesting State be present when the evidence is taken. For other States, presence will not be sufficient and it will be critical that the witness is actually questioned by the relevant authorities of the requesting State, such as the prosecutor and the defence counsel for common law States or an investigating judge in a civil law context. For yet other States the form of recording the evidence may be essential — a *procès verbal* or a verbatim transcript. Unless the law of the requested State is sufficiently flexible, so that the various needs of States with respect to the taking of evidence or statements can be accommodated, the law simply does not achieve its central aim: the rendering of effective assistance.

Another interesting example is found in the domestic law relating to the objections that a witness, giving evidence in response to a mutual assistance request, can make. In some States, the law provides that a witness can object to answering questions on the basis of the law of the requested State, foreign privilege, or where answering the question would be a breach of the law of the foreign State.[12] But a query: if the evidence is to be used in a foreign proceeding, except perhaps with respect to matters such as privileges premised on important social policy considerations or the protection of confidential information, is there any reason why a witness should be able to object on the basis of the law of the requested State? Allowing such objections may significantly reduce the evidence that may be available to the foreign State without any real need for such a limitation.

[12] See The Mutual Legal Assistance in Criminal Matters Act, Revised Statutes of Canada, 1985 C-30; See also An Act to provide for the implementation of treaties for Mutual Legal Assistance in Criminal Matters, March 31, 1988 (Bahamas).

These examples are illustrative of the issue. The problem, which can arise in the context of all forms of assistance, is domestic law that is not flexible enough to allow evidence to be gathered in a manner different from that which would normally be done in a domestic proceeding.

Clearly, in implementing treaty obligations under domestic law, States will be confined by fundamental precepts of the relevant legal system, including constitutional provisions. However, within those limitations, unless domestic law is designed to accord maximum flexibility in the evidence gathering process, the effectiveness of the mutual assistance process will be severely hampered.

It is also significant to note that the requirement for flexibility in implementing laws is not restricted to the State called upon to provide the assistance. In many instances, the problem with obtaining useful evidence through the mutual assistance process can flow from the requirements of the law of the State seeking that evidence. Again, within fundamental limitations, States should consider whether it is possible to have relaxed rules applicable to evidence that is gathered outside of the country.

There is no easy solution to this problem of inflexible regimes for the delivery of mutual assistance. They stem from the differences between legal systems, and States remain entrenched in the view that assistance must be rendered in accordance with the normal procedures under domestic law. As long as that remains the view, we will not progress. Cases will continue to falter because critical evidence cannot be obtained in the necessary form.

Perhaps the only way to move forward is to continue to exchange information between States about applicable law and procedures. We certainly have seen progress over the past twenty years, as dialogue and practice have identified some of the impediments to effective assistance that arise from the distinct approaches to evidence gathering in various legal systems. This has led to more flexible approaches, for example law and practice allowing for the direct questioning of witnesses by officials of the requesting State. It is most likely that this trend toward the adoption of flexible legislation and policy will continue only if there is a better understanding, within all States, of the fundamental differences between legal systems and the need to overcome such distinctions in order to render and receive effective assistance.

In addition, we are starting to see improvements in the rendering of assistance as a result of the application of modern technology, and hopefully this will increase in the near future. For example, the use of live video or audio links to take evidence can significantly reduce the problems that arise from differences in laws of evidence and procedure.

3.3 ADMINISTRATIVE STRUCTURES

One of the key problems in mutual assistance practice is the absence of properly staffed and resourced "central authorities" responsible for coordinating requests and providing information and assistance to both domestic and foreign law enforcement, and prosecutorial authorities. While most treaties, bilateral and multilateral, require the designation of a so-called "central authority" for the transmission of requests, in some instances that obligation is not met, and in others the central authority may not be structured or resourced to provide both the coordination and advice function.

To have a "central authority" for mutual assistance is to have one central location through which all requests for mutual assistance will flow. The central authority will be responsible for coordinating and monitoring the progress of requests both made and received.

The critical role of a central authority in mutual assistance cannot be overstated. For authorities seeking assistance, having an effective central authority to deal with in the foreign State can make the difference between success and failure. Immediately, delay in transmission of a request will be significantly reduced, as the central authority will provide an identifiable direct entry point within that foreign State for the presentation of a request. Where the staff of the authority is specialised and, most critically, legally knowledgeable, they can provide by fax or phone or some other mode of communication critical information about relevant legislation and the execution process within that State. If the central authority is properly resourced, in terms of numbers and qualification of persons, and has the capacity to at least influence the executing authorities, the chances for timely processing of the request will be greatly enhanced.

Authorities within a country receiving a request for assistance similarly require that the request emanate from a State with a strong and effective central authority. The central authority within the requesting State will be able to review the outgoing requests to ensure that they are presented in a workable and usable form for the requested State, and that they contain sufficient information to allow for their execution in the foreign State. It can also provide a critical priorisation function, such that the most urgent and significant requests will be submitted in a timely and efficient manner.

The integral role of a central authority has been recognised in both mutual assistance instruments, bilateral and multilateral, and in the commentary and recommendations of international conferences and expert meetings on the subject of mutual assistance.[13] The United Nations Model Treaty on Mutual Assistance, the 1988 Drug Convention and the UNTOC Convention provide for a designated authority or authorities for the receipt and presentation of requests for assistance. At the 1994 Oxford Conference on Mutual Assistance,[14] there was a working group dedicated solely to the role of a central authority which made recommendations on that topic. The report of the Expert Working Group on Mutual Legal Assistance and Related International Confiscation, hosted by UNDCP in February 1993, highlights the important role of a central authority and makes specific recommendations for central authorities to help to solve or alleviate problems in mutual assistance practice. Most recently, the P8 Senior Expert Working Group[15] on combating transnational organized crime recommended the establishment of a central authority which could provide speedy coordination of mutual assistance requests.

It is critical to note that the establishment of a central authority for mutual assistance does not require the creation of an elaborate structure that is resource intensive. The models for successful central authorities are as varied as the number of States which have created

[13] See Naples Political Declaration and Global Action Plan adopted at the World Ministerial Conference on Organized Transnational Crime, November 1994; Report of the Oxford Conference on Mutual Legal Assistance, Commonwealth Secretariat, September 1994, Christ Church, Oxford; Recommendations of the P8 Senior Experts Working Group on combating Transnational Organized Crime.

[14] *Supra*, footnote 13.

[15] *Id.*

them. The possibilities range from a central authority created by statute, to a group of officials carrying out officially delegated functions within an established department, to a person who, by practice, is responsible to coordinate all such requests. There are, of course, advantages and disadvantages to each method. For example, legislated central authorities have the authority of statute, and can better control and influence the execution of requests. Legislation also provides an opportunity to clearly define the functions of the central authority.

On the other hand, legislation is costly and resource heavy, and provides only limited flexibility to an authority which may be required to change and adjust as the practice of mutual assistance develops. For smaller countries with limited resources, it may be more realistic to establish a central authority by practice, or as a delegated authority of a Minister or Ministry.

Despite the very real practical benefits and the repeated recommendations for the establishment of central authorities, there are persistent problems. Many countries have yet to establish such authorities or have such authorities but they are simply not functioning effectively.

3.4 IMPLEMENTATION IN PRACTICE

I suspect that every practitioner in the field of mutual assistance would strongly support the statement that effective implementation is not limited to legislation and administration. It runs far deeper than that. A country may have an excellent legislative and treaty scheme for mutual assistance, and an established administrative process, and it still may be virtually impossible to receive effective assistance. This is because the best designed system is only as good as the people who operate it on a practical level.

In many instances, success in mutual assistance is dependent almost entirely on the knowledge and, most critically, the flexibility of the authorities requesting and providing the assistance.

It is quite understandable that authorities raised within a particular legal tradition have a natural bias for the approach and practices of that legal tradition. In providing foreign States with access to compulsory process within a given State, there will be, whether by virtue of constitutional or legislative requirements, constraints on what measures are available and in what circumstances. This is obviously the case for judicial authorities, who are required to interpret and apply the relevant treaty and applicable legislation in accordance with the law of that State. However, that restriction does not mean there is no room for flexibility in the rendering of assistance.

Again, one of the most important goals of mutual assistance is the bridging of differences between legal systems. This goal can be realised only if the authorities entrusted with execution approach mutual assistance requests with a view to overcoming differences and not entrenching them.

The governing philosophy for mutual assistance must be to provide the widest scope of assistance possible under domestic law, and to provide that assistance in a usable form for the requesting State. For mutual assistance to succeed, the operative principle must be that requests will be executed in accordance with the law of the requested State and, to the extent not prohibited by that law, that assistance will be provided in the manner sought by the requesting State. In other words, while authorities in a requested State must always meet the standards prescribed by domestic law, unless the rendering of assistance in the form sought would constitute a violation of that law, it should be provided. If that principle does not govern at the operational level, mutual assistance will fail.

This is unquestionably the central challenge, and it is a very real challenge that practitioners face each day. The importance of this point is perhaps best illustrated by an example.

Generally, in common law legal systems, police and prosecutors are responsible for the questioning of witnesses. At the investigative stage, police or, in some systems, prosecutors will gather witness statements. During the trial process, it is the prosecutor and defence counsel who will conduct the examination and cross-examination of each witness. While a judge may occasionally ask a question during a trial, by the law of those States judges do not gather the evidence of witnesses nor conduct examinations before the court. In contrast, many civil law systems have investigating judges who will gather witness statements and include or summarise the same in the preparation of their files or "dossiers".

If an investigating judge seeks to interview a witness in a common law State, strictly speaking, it would be "inconsistent" with the law of the requested State for that judge to conduct the interview. It would not be, however, a "violation" of domestic law if the judge were allowed to conduct the interview. In this instance, success or failure depends entirely on whether the authorities in the requested State employ a flexible test and allow the evidence to be gathered in an appropriate form for the requesting State, even where it is inconsistent with the normal process employed in the requested State.

A similar example arises in the reverse scenario. In a civil law system, very often an investigating judge hearing a witness will prepare a summary or *procès verbal* of what the witness said.

In the common law, when a witness is examined and cross-examined before the court his or her evidence must be recorded verbatim. A summary or "procès verbal" is not admissible.

If a request is made by common law authorities to take the evidence of a witness on "commission" in the foreign State and to record the evidence verbatim, once again that process would be inconsistent with the law of the requested State. The foreign authorities would not, however, be violating the law by keeping the verbatim record. Again, it is a question of flexibility and the philosophy employed in the requested State.

Nor is the need for flexibility limited to authorities called upon to execute a request for assistance. Requesting authorities must strive to submit materials which will meet the requirements of the requested State and which will be workable and useful to authorities in a State of a different legal tradition. Submitting a request which meets all of the requirements of the domestic law of the requesting State, but none in the requested State, does little to facilitate the provision of assistance. This is, in fact, a major frustration for those who must present the requests before the court and those who must adjudicate upon them: the inability to extract sufficient information from the requesting State to meet the requirements of domestic law. Again, this is a particular problem when the two States involved have different legal traditions, procedures and requirements such that it is difficult for the authorities in the requesting State to understand what is required by the requested State.

The problem of lack of flexibility to accommodate system differences is perhaps the most significant challenge in mutual assistance practice.

4. Conclusion

Mutual assistance has "come a long way" in a very short period of time. The challenge for the future lies in the effective implementation of the instruments of cooperation that have been developed. The success or failure of mutual assistance rests not only with governments, but also with the competent authorities who seek and render the assistance on a practical level.

OVERCOMING OBSTACLES IN ACHIEVING WIDE ADHERENCE TO MULTILATERAL INSTRUMENTS: SOME COMMENTS FROM THE EUROPEAN PERSPECTIVE

Hans-Jürgen Bartsch*

1. Introduction

The Council of Europe was founded in 1949 as an international organisation for the purpose of achieving "greater unity between its members" (Article 1 of the Statute of the Council of Europe). With the accession of 19 central and eastern European countries in the last ten years, it has become a truly pan-European organisation. Following the admission of Armenia and Azerbaijan in 2001 and Bosnia-Herzegovina in 2002, the Council now has 44 members, including the fifteen European Union States.

Like the Organisation of American States and the Organisation for African Unity it is a regional international organisation, but from the beginning it has been defined ideologically rather than geographically; it was founded in deliberate opposition to the regimes imposed on Eastern Europe by the Soviet Union in the wake of World War II, on order to defend the common values of the then Western European community of States. These common values are reflected in the three basic conditions for membership: pluralist democracy, the Rule of Law, and the effective protection of human rights.

In conformity with this statutory aim, the Council has always been open to cooperation with like-minded States outside Europe. In particular, it has enjoyed their active participation in carrying out its legal cooperation programmes. In 1993, these relations have been institutionalised: any State willing to accept the principles of democracy, the Rule of Law, and the enjoyment of human rights, and wishing to cooperate with the Council, may be granted observer status with the Organisation. States enjoying this status may appoint a permanent observer and are entitled to send representatives to the Council's committees of experts. Observer status has been granted to Canada, the Holy See, Japan, Mexico, and the United States of America.

As regards legal cooperation, the Council's principal aim — to achieve greater unity between its members — is pursued in the form of two legal instruments: recommendations (until 1979 called "resolutions") and conventions. Whereas recommendations — adopted by the Committee of Ministers and addressed to Member States — constitute legal instruments of the Council of Europe, conventions do not; although initiated and elaborated in the Council's cooperation framework, they are, legally speaking, multilateral treaties which derive their legal force solely from the consent of those Member States wishing to be bound by them. For these reasons, the Committee of Ministers does not

* Head of the Department of Crime Problems, Council of Europe. Any views expressed are personal.

R. Yepes-Enríquez and L. Tabassi, (eds.), Treaty Enforcement and International Cooperation in Criminal Matters

adopt these conventions; it merely adopts the text and opens them for signature. They are multilateral treaties which are concluded *within* the Organisation, not *by* it. For that same reason, they are not called "Council of Europe Conventions"; their usual denomination is "European Conventions". As opposed to the European Communities, whose organs may adopt legal norms which, under certain conditions, are directly applicable in the member States, the Council of Europe is not a legislator. It is a lawmaker only in the sense that it promotes these European Conventions.

2. Cooperation in Criminal Matters

Crime control is no longer a task which can successfully be tackled within national boundaries only. Combating crime has become an international concern which requires a coordinated, transfrontier response.

The Council of Europe prides itself on having played, during the past 50 years, a pioneering role in the efforts to promote international cooperation in the fight against criminality. It has succeeded in establishing a comprehensive network of international treaties — European Conventions — providing for all conceivable forms of cooperation: extradition, mutual assistance, recognition and enforcement of foreign judgments (including those providing for the supervision of conditionally sentenced or released offenders) and transfer of criminal proceedings. It has successfully adapted these general conventions to the particular needs of modern crime control through amending protocols or through recommendations on the practical application of these treaties. Thus, to mention but a few examples, extradition and mutual assistance have been extended to fiscal offences, acts of terrorism have been "depoliticised" for the purpose of extradition, and the transfer of prisoners to their home countries has been facilitated.

The Council has also provided responses to modern forms of criminality such as computer-related crimes, environmental offences, trafficking in firearms, offences relating to cultural property, money laundering, corruption, and cyber-crime.

Today the "European Treaty Series" contains some 25 instruments — conventions, agreements, and additional protocols — in the penal field, and the Committee of Ministers has adopted more than 100 recommendations in this area, among them some 20 relating to the practical application of cooperation treaties. As these treaties require acceptance by Member States and implementation at the national level to become effective, an important part of the Council's efforts has been devoted to promoting and facilitating Member States' adherence to them. This is to say that the Council of Europe has, for several decades, been actively involved in solving the problems which are being discussed in this book.

3. Obstacles to Implementation of International Treaties

With the constant increase in treaty obligations arising from European Conventions, the need not only for facilitating their implementation, but also for ensuring their uniform application, has become a major concern. Problems may arise in respect of both the interpretation and the practical application of these treaties.

As there is no European jurisdiction with competence to monitor compliance by contracting States with their treaty obligations, most of the European Conventions provide for a procedure which is intended to help solve conflicts over interpretation: in the event of a dispute between two or several parties, the European Committee on Crime Problems — a steering committee with responsibility for overseeing the Council's activities in the penal field — "shall do whatever is necessary to facilitate a friendly settlement" of any difficulty which may arise out of the application of a treaty. This provision on the friendly settlement of disputes has become a standard feature of European Conventions in the penal field.

Apart from such specific disputes, which rarely arise, there is a general problem of ensuring the uniform application of European Conventions in contracting States. Even though these conventions are accompanied by explanatory reports designed to provide national law enforcement agencies with guidance as to their interpretation, difficulties may arise out of their practical application. To solve such difficulties, a permanent committee of experts was set up in 1981 to review the operation of all European Conventions in the penal field and propose measures for facilitating their application. The committee also examines obstacles to ratification which Member States may face, with a view to ensuring the widest possible acceptance of these treaties. It is this committee which prepared several additional protocols to European Conventions (on extradition, mutual assistance and transfer of sentenced persons), as well as recommendations on their practical application. This review procedure for developing cooperation treaties is to be recommended, particularly for international organisations lacking legislative powers and relying, like the Council of Europe, on the voluntary participation of its Member States.

What, then, are the obstacles found to impair adherence to the Council's international cooperation treaties and their effective implementation? Generally speaking, obstacles can be inherent in the treaty, or they can be due to factors outside the treaty.

Among inherent obstacles one could mention the complexity of the treaty and the ensuing impracticality in its application. The provisions governing the enforcement of sanctions involving deprivation of liberty provide a relevant example for this. The transfer of a foreign prisoner to his home country is possible under the European Convention on the International Validity of Criminal Judgments concluded within the Council of Europe in 1970. That convention, however, was found to have two major shortcomings: as it applies to *all* criminal sanctions — prison sentences, fines, confiscation orders — the procedure is complex, cumbersome, and not conducive to being applied in such a way as to ensure the rapid transfer of foreign prisoners. Secondly, only the sentencing State is entitled to request a transfer. To overcome these difficulties, a complementary treaty — the Convention on the Transfer of Sentenced Persons — was concluded in 1983. It is confined to prison sentences, the most frequent case involving recognition and enforcement of foreign sanctions, and it provides for a procedure which is both simpler and more expeditious. In comparison with the 1970 general convention, three features are worth noting: (i) a transfer may be requested not only by the State in which the sentence was imposed, but also by the State of which the sentenced person is a national, thus enabling the latter to seek the repatriation of its own nationals; (ii) the transfer is subject to the sentenced person's consent; and (iii) the Convention is confined to providing the procedural framework for transfers without imposing an obligation on the parties to comply with a request for transfer.

Obstacles may also be created by inadequate, or even incompatible, domestic legislation and practice. The smooth operation of cooperation treaties presupposes mutual trust in the judicial systems of the participating States. As all Council of Europe members are bound by the European Convention on Human Rights,[1] this trust generally exists, but difficulties may nevertheless arise where the requesting State's human rights standards for due process and the enforcement of sentences are found to fall short of certain requirements arising from the Human Rights Convention. Recently, the German Federal Constitutional Court had occasion to bar the extradition of an accused to the Russian Federation on the ground that the inhuman conditions of custody prevailing in Russian pre-trial detention centres did not conform with European human rights standards.

A serious obstacle exists in respect of jurisdictions that apply capital punishment. The Council of Europe is committed to creating a death-penalty-free-area in Europe, and ratification of the Sixth Protocol to the Human Rights Convention, providing for the abolition of capital punishment in peacetime, is now a condition for membership, with the result that extradition will invariably be refused where the person to be extradited risks being sentenced to death in the requesting State.

In this context, another problem needs mentioning: the European Convention on Extradition allows the parties to refuse the surrender of their own nationals, a provision which safeguards a principle which, in some countries, is enshrined in the constitution. Here again, the review committee has already discussed a possible solution; it is inspired by the legislation of the Netherlands: nationals may be extradited on condition that, after sentence, they are transferred back to their home country for the purpose of enforcing the sentence pronounced in the requesting State. This solution helps overcome the non-extradition obstacle by modifying the principle *aut dedere aut judicare* without, however, affecting the underlying aim of the provision, which is to enable convicted persons to serve their sentence "at home".

To illustrate the problem of conflicting, inadequate or badly adapted domestic legislation further, let me quote two other examples:

(a) In France, a defendant tried for a drug offence may not only be sentenced to imprisonment; he may also be liable to pay a customs fine which, although not a customs duty but a criminal sanction, is based solely on the value of the drugs found in his possession without regard to the person's assets, and his repatriation in application of the Convention on the Transfer of Sentenced Persons will not be considered before this fine is paid in full. The Convention is thus rendered inoperative for a large number of foreign prisoners otherwise eligible for transfer.

(b) A country which does not adopt legislation empowering its courts to order discovery or seizure of bank records, i.e. not to invoke bank secrecy, as required by the 1990 Convention on Laundering, Search, Seizure and Confiscation of the Proceeds from Crime, fails to implement an essential tool of that Convention.

Full implementation of international cooperation treaties at the national level may also be hampered by the absence of appropriate procedural rules. Member States, signatories to European Conventions, are therefore encouraged to follow the examples of countries such

[1] Convention for the Protection of Human Rights and Fundamental Freedoms (1950), as amended by Protocol no. 11 (1994; entry into force 1 November 1998).

as Austria, Germany or Switzerland which have enacted special laws on international cooperation in criminal matters that complement their codes of criminal procedure. To assist member States in preparing such legislation, the review committee is considering drafting a model law.

Finally, I need to mention a specific European problem: the co-existence of conventions concluded within the Council of Europe with those concluded by the member States of the European Union (outside the institutional Community framework), in the beginning within the European Political Cooperation and then within the so-called "third pillar" of the Maastricht Treaty, further developed by the Treaties of Amsterdam and Nice and now incorporating also the Schengen Agreements (except for Ireland and the United Kingdom, but including Iceland and Norway).[2] This proliferation of cooperation frameworks entails a serious potential risk of duplication, overlap, and possibly divergence and contradiction. I am told by a lawyer friend specialising in international criminal law that in a straightforward extradition case between two European countries, members of both the Council of Europe and the European Union, the practitioner has to consider eleven different instruments, both international (including reservations and declarations) and domestic. The situation will be aggravated once the European Union conventions on extradition and mutual assistance enter into force, not to mention the complications which may be caused by the parallel applicability of the Minsk Convention,[3] which binds twelve Eastern European States (several of them Council of Europe members), or the Nordic[4] or Benelux agreements.[5]

Better coordination, particularly between the "Europe of the 44" and the "Europe of the 15," is a matter which needs urgently to be addressed if international cooperation in criminal matters is not to suffer. The phenomenon of transboundary crime in Europe is not confined to the 15 members of the European Union. International instruments adopted for combating it should not, therefore, be confined to that area. The European Union has implicitly recognised this by declaring that the conventions concluded within the Council of Europe are part of the *acquis communautaire* which candidates for European Union membership are expected to implement. But the fundamental question remains: is it useful to create a parallel European Union network of international cooperation treaties applicable to fifteen European countries only? If crime control in Europe is to be effective, European "legislators" must avoid further division and fragmentation and create a truly pan-European network of international cooperation treaties.

---

2 See also, *supra* in this volume, J. Sack, Transboundary Criminal Activity: the Role and Action of the European Union.

3 1993 CIS Minsk Convention on Mutual Legal Assistance.

4 Nordic Agreements on Mutual Legal Assistance of 26 April 1974 (ratified on 1 May 1975).

5 Benelux Treaty on Extradition and Mutual Assistance in Criminal Matters of 27 June 1962, as amended by the Protocol of 11 May 1974; supplemented by Title III, chapter 2 of the Schengen Agreement.

THE ROLE OF REGIONAL ORGANISATIONS IN FACILITATING COOPERATION AND LEGAL ASSISTANCE: THE OECS EXPERIENCE

Victor Philip LaCorbiniere*

1. Introduction

The Member States of the Organisation of Eastern Caribbean States (OECS)[1] are committed under the 1981 Treaty of Basseterre[2] to coordinating and harmonising their policies in a number of areas.[3] This must be seen in the context of the purposes of the Organisation, which include assisting Member States in the realisation of their obligations and responsibilities to the international community, giving due regard to the role of international law as a standard of conduct in their relationships.[4]

The OECS is, therefore, the central legal and political arrangement for regional action and cooperation in the Eastern Caribbean. It is also instructive to note that the governments of the Eastern Caribbean are proactive in fostering such arrangements. In this regard, they have established additional regional entities such as the Eastern Caribbean Supreme Court, the Eastern Caribbean Central Bank and the Regional Security System.[5] Within the framework of the Organisation, a harmonised approach has also been adopted on a wide range of issues, including international trade, civil aviation, the procurement of pharmaceuticals, environmental regulation, judicial and legal reform, and telecommunications reform. This matrix of arrangements has enabled the adoption of homogeneous regional policies and has provided a unified developmental approach to critical issues. The adoption of common programmes, administered at the regional level, has generated cost savings which have been passed on to Member States. Efficiencies have also been realised in project implementation which, in turn, has provided a useful platform for attracting donor funding.[6]

---

* Legal Counsel, Organisation of Eastern Caribbean States (OECS). Any views expressed are those of the author and are not attributable to the OECS.

[1] The Member States comprise: Antigua and Barbuda, Commonwealth of Dominica, Grenada, St. Kitts and Nevis, Saint Lucia, St. Vincent and The Grenadines, Anguilla, The British Virgin Islands and Montserrat.

[2] The Organisation of Eastern Caribbean States (OECS) is a regional organisation with international personality, established by the 1981 Treaty of Basseterre.

[3] Article 3-2 of the OECS Treaty.

[4] Article 3-1 of the OECS Treaty.

[5] See the 1982 Eastern Caribbean Supreme Court Agreement; the 1983 Eastern Caribbean Central Bank Agreement; and the 1996 Treaty Establishing the Regional Security System.

[6] Recent donor funded projects include OECS/World Bank Telecommunications Reform Project, the OECS/World Bank Solid Waste Management Project and the OECS/CIDA Trade Reform Project.

R. Yepes-Enríquez and L. Tabassi. (eds.), Treaty Enforcement and International Cooperation in Criminal Matters

It is evident, therefore, that the framework for joint action and cooperation established by the 1981 Treaty of Basseterre forms an integral part of the international relations of Member States. This is tied to the implementation of a series of initiatives which have concrete inputs and benefits at the domestic level.

2. Cooperation in Legal and Judicial Matters

Within the overall framework already outlined, Member States are also pursuing a number of joint legal and judicial activities. Reference has already been made to the Eastern Caribbean Supreme Court, which is a Superior Court of Record and a Unified Court for the Contracting States.[7] The Agreement setting up the Eastern Caribbean Supreme Court[8] provides for the location of the Headquarters of the Supreme Court and the Judicial and Legal Services Commission.[9] The Governments of the Contracting States are required to take steps to secure the appointment of a Registrar of the High Court for the respective States, supported by relevant officers in the public service.[10] There are also obligations attendant to the financing and accommodation of the Court.

A noticeable obligation under the Agreement is the requirement for Contracting States to ensure conformity in their legislation regarding the Court and related matters. This is contained in Article 4 of the 1982 Eastern Carribean Supreme Court Agreement, which reads as follows;

> The Governments of the States shall take such steps as may be reasonably practicable, having regard to the circumstances of each State, to promote uniformity in the laws of the State conferring jurisdiction and powers on the Court of Appeal and the High Court and regulating the practice and procedure of those Courts, the execution and enforcement of the process of those Courts, the right of practising before those Courts and the representation of persons in any proceedings before those Courts.

This Agreement is complemented by appropriate domestic legislation and Rules of Court in the Contracting States.

In addition to the above, the Member States of the OECS have increasingly adopted a common approach to judicial and legal reforms in the Eastern Caribbean. In keeping with this approach, ongoing consideration is being given to the establishment of unified services in respect of the lower courts, the police service and the prison service. In the field of domestic legislation, Member States have agreed to adopt harmonised legislation in a wide range of areas.[11]

---

[7] The Supreme Court consists of a Court of Appeal and a High Court of Justice.

[8] *Supra* note 5.

[9] The Headquarters of the Court and the Judicial and Legal Services Commission are in Saint Lucia.

[10] Article 4, the 1982 Eastern Caribbean Supreme Court Agreement.

[11] For example, banking, customs, regulation of companies, misuse of drugs, fisheries, pesticides and toxic chemicals, Fifth Regulation of Solid Waste and telecommunications and integrity legislation.

3. Negotiating International Treaties

The OECS also promotes cooperation at the regional and international levels, with specific regard being paid to the Treaty establishing the Caribbean community and the Charter of the United Nations.[12] Member States have also undertaken to endeavour to coordinate, harmonise and pursue joint policies in their external relations, including overseas representation. This has been crystallised in the establishment of some common diplomatic representations. Against this backdrop, Member States have formulated and adopted a common stance on many international issues. This has been of particular importance in developing strategies to support the interests of these small States within the wider context of a liberalised political and economic environment.

The Member States of the OECS have tried, where practicable, to ensure a more unified approach to the negotiation and adoption of bilateral treaties. One of the ways in which they have achieved this has been through multilateral negotiations. Essentially, this means that bilateral treaties are negotiated by a group of Member States in a joint negotiating setting. In practical terms, it allows for harmonised bilateral arrangements in selected areas. This approach has been followed in negotiations on extradition and mutual legal assistance between the independent Member States of the OECS and the Governments of the United States and France, respectively.[13] The Secretariat of the OECS has played a pivotal role in coordinating and supporting some of these negotiations.

Overall, this arrangement allows Member States greater access to limited expertise. It is also cost effective. At the other end, non-Member States could find this a useful mechanism for fast-tracking bilateral negotiations and for ensuring homogeneity in their bilateral treaty arrangements with regional States.

4. The Chemical Weapons Convention and Related Model Legislation

The Chemical Weapons Convention[14] has been signed by five of the independent Member States of the OECS. However, only Dominica and Saint Lucia have ratified the Convention.[15] Notwithstanding only two ratifications at present, the Member States have taken their obligations under this Convention seriously.

The Chemical Weapons Convention provides that States Parties to the Convention prohibit natural and legal persons anywhere on their territory or in any other place under their jurisdiction from undertaking any activity prohibited to a State Party under the Convention. States Parties to the Convention are required to enact penal legislation to place sanctions upon such activities. Relevant legislation must also extend to cover prohibited activities undertaken by nationals abroad. All such legislation must be in keeping with

[12] Article 3 — 1(a) of the 1981 Treaty of Basseterre.

[13] The negotiations with France are ongoing.

[14] 1993 Convention on the Prohibition of the Development, Production, Stockpiling and Use of Chemical Weapons and on Their Destruction, entered into force on 29 April 1997. Text, as corrected and changed, available at http://www.opcw.org.

[15] Commonwealth of Dominica: signed 02-08-93, ratified 12-12-01; Grenada: signed 09-04-97; Saint Kitts and Nevis: signed 16-03-94; Saint Lucia: signed 29-03-93, ratified 09-04-97; and Saint Vincent and The Grenadines: signed 20-09-93.

relevant constitutional processes.[16] Each State Party is also required to cooperate with other States Parties and afford the appropriate form of legal assistance to facilitate implementation of the above obligations.[17]

Model harmonised legislation has been prepared by the Secretariat of the OECS, with the assistance and cooperation of the Secretariat of the OPCW.[18] This legislation has been structured to provide a comprehensive framework for the regulation of pesticides and other toxic chemicals. In addition, it seeks to implement key obligations under the Chemical Weapons Convention.[19]

Generally, the Model Act provides for the establishment of a Pesticides and Toxic Chemicals Control Board. The Board shall serve as a regulator of pesticides and toxic chemicals. It shall also serve as the National Authority for the Contracting States to the Chemical Weapons Convention. In accordance with the requirements of the Convention, the model legislation prohibits persons from importing, producing, storing and using certain scheduled substances and chemical weapons. An appropriate licensing and permit system has also been outlined. Stiff penalties have been incorporated in the Model Act. Appropriate subsidiary model regulations, entitled the Toxic Chemicals Control (Registration, Licensing and Permit Regulations), have been developed in tandem. The Model Pesticides and Toxic Chemicals Control Act and Regulations have been agreed to by Member States of the OECS and should soon be enacted in all the countries.[20]

Part 3 of the Model Act covers prohibitions which, under Article 4(1) of the Act, are extended to acts done, or omitted to be done, outside the State by a citizen or any person ordinarily resident in that State, or any person on board a ship or aircraft of that State.[21] Article 4(2) also provides that proceedings regarding a contravention of Part 3 of the Model Act anywhere outside of the State shall not, by virtue only of the provisions of the Model Act, be initiated in any court without the consent of the Attorney General. This must be supported with a certificate from the Attorney General indicating that it is expedient that the proceedings should be initiated.

In all, the model legislation has incorporated all relevant obligations outlined under the Chemical Weapons Convention. In particular, it provides for the regulation and prohibition of toxic chemicals, chemical weapons and other toxic substances. It also sets out a regime of criminal penalties for breaches of the Act.

5. Mutual Legal Assistance and Extradition

The Member States of the OECS are signatories to a few bilateral treaties on extradition and mutual legal assistance in criminal matters. Increasingly however, they have signalled

---

[16] Article VII(1), Chemical Weapons Convention.

[17] Article VII(2), Chemical Weapons Convention.

[18] The model harmonised legislation has been published in An Integrated Approach to National Implementing Legislation: Model Act Developed by the Secretariat of the Organisation of Eastern Caribbean States, OPCW doc. S/190/2000 (23 May 2000).

[19] The coverage, extended to both pesticides and toxic chemicals, is a useful approach.

[20] Assistance was given by the OPCW Secretariat to facilitate an OECS Seminar to review the Model Act and Regulations in its final drafting stages.

[21] Article 4(1) of the Model Act.

the need to harmonise these arrangements for the region. This is a positive development, and it offers opportunities for learning to other regional States.

It is also to be noted that the domestic legislation of OECS Member States provide a broad framework for dealing with extradition[22] and mutual legal assistance in criminal matters.[23] Generally, the legislation on extradition is varied, although in a number of countries similar United Kingdom legislation is applicable.[24] On the other hand, the legislation on mutual legal assistance is fairly well harmonised for the independent and non-independent Member States. It should also be stressed that, in respect of mutual legal assistance, the legislation of most of the Member States specifically provides that it does not derogate from executing forms and allows for the development of other forms of formal or informal cooperation.

6. Conclusion

The Member States of the OECS have, in accordance with the 1981 Treaty of Basseterre and other relevant treaty arrangements, developed a framework for ensuring unified policies and joint action, in a wide range of matters. Within this context of functional cooperation, harmonised programmes and measures have been implemented at the international and domestic levels.

It is therefore imperative that we work within this framework to realise cooperation and legal assistance for the effective implementation of existing international agreements. This would enable harmonised bilateral arrangements to evolve within the Eastern Caribbean. In addition, it would provide an efficient and cost effective mechanism for negotiating such bilateral treaties.

Finally, regional arrangements should always be harnessed in support of international action and treaty implementation. In this regard, such arrangements can present meaningful support, even where these initiatives are essentially bilateral in nature.

---

[22] See Antigua and Barbuda: Extradition Act, Number 12 of 1993; Commonwealth of Dominica: Extradition Act, Chap. 12:04; Grenada: Extradition Act, Chap. 99 (repealed with savings No. 22 of 1998); St Kitts and Nevis: Extradition Act, Chap 105. See also Extradition Act 1870 (UK); Saint Lucia: Extradition Act No: 12 of 1986; St Vincent and The Grenadines: Extradition Acts 1870-1935 (UK); Anguilla: Extradition Act, Chap. 105. Note that the Extradition Acts 1870: 1935 (UK) have been repealed with savings as to existing Orders); British Virgin Islands: Extradition Act, 1989 (UK); Montserrat: Extradition Act, Chap. 104. See also Extradition Acts 1870-1935 and 1989 (UK). There are repeals to some of the provisions of the UK Acts cited, but the Orders are generally preserved.

[23] See Antigua and Barbuda: Mutual Assistance In Criminal Matters Act, No. 2 of 1993; Commonwealth of Dominica: Mutual Assistance In Criminal Matters Act, No. 9 of 1990; Grenada: Mutual Assistance In Criminal Matters (Commonwealth Countries) Act, No. 5 of 1998; St. Kitts and Nevis: Mutual Assistance In Criminal Matters Act, No. 7 of 1993; Saint Lucia: Mutual Assistance In Criminal Matters Act, No. 10 of 1996; St. Vincent and The Grenadines: Mutual Assistance In Criminal Matters Act, No. 46 of 1993; Anguilla: Mutual Legal Assistance (USA) Ordinance, No. 12 of 1990; British Virgin Islands: Mutual Legal Assistance (USA) Act, No. 5 of 1990; and Montserrat: Mutual Legal Assistance In Criminal Matters (USA) Ordinance, No. 1 of 1991.

[24] *Supra* notes 22 and 23.

JUDICIAL ASSISTANCE AND COOPERATION AMONG MEMBER STATES OF THE OAS

Eduardo A. Bertoni*

1. Introduction

Judicial assistance and cooperation between States may be developed under the agreed provisions of treaties, either bilateral or multilateral. The Charter of the Organization of American States (OAS), as well as the "Declaration of Panama on the Inter-American Contribution to the Development and Codification of International Law"[1] indicate that the OAS-adopted treaties represent a valuable legacy that must be preserved, developed and broadly diffused.

This chapter is aimed at providing a brief description of the actual contents and status of the signature, ratification or enforcement of the OAS-adopted treaties related to legal and judicial assistance. The importance of these types of agreements is revealed by the fact that, without effective cooperation, many regulations on substantial aspects become impossible to implement in practice. Such treaties may be negotiated between two or more States, or unfold at a more general organisational level in which agreements develop under conditions of equality that allow expanded cooperation among a number of States.

It is worthwhile examining the reasons which led the international community in the past few decades to develop cooperation processes: possibly the end of the Cold War and the East-West confrontation or the democratisation processes in Latin America were contributing factors; or perhaps these historical circumstances increased commercial exchange among the countries of the region, thus giving rise to the need for increased cooperation. These globalisation processes generated a series of common objectives as an impetus towards regional integration. This integration cannot be envisaged without effective cooperation mechanisms among States, and legal or judicial cooperation and assistance is not far removed from these movements.

For example, among the common regional objectives one could denote the importance of preservation of the environment, sustainable population development, the joint efforts to combat drug trafficking, corruption, terrorism, arms trafficking, organised crime, etc. All these objectives, previously handled by States individually and today considered to be common targets, have generated an appropriate setting that requires greater coordination among States in order to achieve their goals. Moreover, this generates a demand for greater development in international law, especially regarding cooperation among States.

* Special Rapporteur for Freedom of Expression, Inter-American Commission on Human Rights, Organization of American States; Former Cabinet Adviser of the Minister of Justice of Argentina.

[1] Resolution AG/DEC.12 (XXVI-0/96).

R. Yepes-Enríquez and L. Tabassi. (eds.), Treaty Enforcement and International Cooperation in Criminal Matters

These concepts have been captured in the Protocol of Amendments to the Charter of the Organization of American States (Protocol of Washington), adopted in 1992. It reaffirmed that cooperation is one of the essential purposes of inter-Americanism. Likewise, the Protocol of Amendments to the Charter of the Organization of American States (Protocol of Managua), approved in 1993, established in the Organization the Inter-American Council for Integral Development (ICID) as a body destined to create "policies, programs, and courses of action in matters of cooperation for an integral development."

The following facts reveal the importance of cooperation among OAS countries: at the level of the Organization, 63 inter-American treaties have been negotiated and approved, on subjects such as human rights protection, arbitration, asylum, extradition, transport of goods, prevention of violence against women, and the fight against corruption. Of the total adopted treaties, 30 — almost 50% — discuss subjects connected to legal and judicial cooperation.

Nevertheless, some of these treaties are not enforced in the Americas, since ratification processes, following the internal legal system of each State, are yet to be completed. It is relevant to emphasise that organisations such as the OAS, or even the United Nations Latin American Institute for the Prevention of Crime and the Treatment of Offenders (ILANUD), in many cases provided States with the assistance needed in the internal process for adherence to the treaties, at any stage from signature through ratification.

2. Inter-American Regulation of Legal and Judicial Cooperation

The treaties adopted at the OAS level can be differentiated: first, there are conventions of which the main object and purpose are to establish judicial cooperation mechanisms. Second, there exist a significant number of conventions that, although not including true judicial cooperation mechanisms, do require them for their implementation.

Significant among the first category are, on criminal matters, the Inter-American Conventions on Extradition, on Mutual Assistance in Criminal Matters, and on Serving Criminal Sentences Abroad. On criminal procedure, one should note the Inter-American Conventions on the Taking of Evidence Abroad, on Letters Rogatory, on Jurisdiction in the International Sphere for Extraterritorial Validity for Foreign Judgements, on Proof of and Information on Foreign Law, and on Extraterritorial Validity of Foreign Judgements and Arbitral Awards.

Among the conventions that do not specifically focus on cooperation, but do require it for their application, one should mention the Inter-American Conventions on the International Return of Children, on Support Obligations, and on International Traffic in Minors. One can highlight as well the Convention to Prevent and Punish Acts of Terrorism Taking the Form of Crimes against Persons and Related Extortion that are of International Significance, the Inter-American Convention against Corruption, the Conventions on Diplomatic Asylum and on Territorial Asylum, and the Inter-American Convention against Illicit Manufacturing of and Trafficking in Firearms, Ammunitions, Explosives and other Related Materials.

3. Mechanisms Established under Specific Inter-American Conventions

The following is a brief description of the mechanisms established under some of the conventions referring to cooperation, either directly or indirectly.

3.1 Inter-American Convention on Extradition

This treaty was adopted at Caracas, Venezuela on 25 February 1981 at the Inter-American Specialized Conference on Extradition.

This Convention regulates extradition, adopting the internationally accepted criteria on this matter. In order to improve the transaction processes, the convention states that required documents being processed through diplomatic, consular or other direct government-to-government channels will not require legalisation. A detailed examination of the convention is beyond the scope of this chapter; nevertheless, it is pertinent to point out that every request for extradition obliges the State Party concerned to transfer to the other State Party the judicially demanded person(s) for prosecution, or alternatively, those already prosecuted, found guilty and sentenced.

Agreed exceptions permitting denial of a request for extradition, as well as the required elements of a request, are specified.

3.2 Inter-American Convention on Mutual Assistance in Criminal Matters

This treaty was adopted in Nassau, Bahamas, on 23 May 1992.

This Convention requires States Parties to provide mutual assistance in criminal matters. Assistance is based on requests for cooperation issued by the authorities responsible for investigating or prosecuting crime. Among the examples of assistance that may be requested are: notification of rulings and judgements; taking of testimony or statements from persons; immobilisation and sequestration of property, freezing of assets and assistance in procedure related to seizures; searches and seizures; service of judicial documents, transmittal of documents, reports, information and evidence; transfer of detained persons. The principle of "dual criminality" is not required for assistance, except in cases of coercive measures, such as immobilisation or sequestration of property, searches, and examinations of places. Requests for assistance are executed, under the Convention, in accordance with the domestic law of the requested State.

In order to improve transactions, the Convention requires that each State designate a "Central Authority" responsible for issuing and receiving requests for assistance. These authorities communicate directly among themselves.

3.3 Optional Protocol Related to the Inter-American Convention on Mutual Assistance in Criminal Matters

This Protocol was adopted in Managua, Nicaragua, on 11 June 1993.

Under this Protocol, States Parties agree that they will not exercise the right, provided for in the Article 9(f) of the Convention on Mutual Assistance, to refuse a request for assistance from another State Party to the Protocol solely on the ground that the request concerns a tax crime. A requested State will not decline a request for assistance concerning the execution of measures stated in Article 5 of the Convention (immobilisation and sequestration of property, searches, examinations and freezing of assets), if the act specified in the request corresponds to a similar tax crime under the legislation of the requested State.

3.4 INTER-AMERICAN CONVENTION ON SERVING CRIMINAL SENTENCES ABROAD

This Convention was adopted in Managua, Nicaragua, on 9 June 1993.

As its main object and purpose, this Convention allows sentenced persons to complete their sentence in the State of which they are a national and thus encourages a more extensive cooperation among States Parties regarding the transfer of sentenced persons. In order for the Convention to be applied, certain conditions must exist: the sentence must be final; the sentence to be served must not be the death sentence; time for completion of the sentence must be at least six months; the sentenced person must be a national of the receiving State and personally give his or her consent to be transferred; the act for which the person was sentenced must also constitute a crime in the receiving State; and the administration of the sentence must not be contrary to the domestic legislation of the receiving State.

The transfer of the sentenced person will take place in the location agreed by the Central Authorities designated to enforce the Convention. As soon as the person is received, the receiving State will be responsible for his or her custody and for all subsequent transportation charges.

3.5 INTER-AMERICAN CONVENTION ON THE EXECUTION OF PREVENTIVE MEASURES

This Convention was adopted at Montevideo, Uruguay, on 8 May 1979.

According to this Convention, the jurisdictional authorities of States Parties will enforce preventive measures that, decreed by judges or tribunals of another State Party, guarantee the security of persons, such as protective custody of minor children, preventive measures, such as the preventive attachment of immovable and movable property, immobilisation, preventive sequestration, or registration of the proceeding. Even though the preventive measure will be decided in accordance with the legislation, and by the judges, of the State where the procedure is taking place, its execution, as well as the pertinent objections, will be resolved by the judges of the State where its enforcement is requested. The Convention entitles third parties to intervene in order to protect their rights. It also allows the suspension of the principal proceedings for a period not to exceed sixty days.

Each State Party will inform the OAS General Secretariat of the Central Authority competent for receiving and issuing letters rogatory.

3.6 CONVENTION TO PREVENT AND PUNISH ACTS OF TERRORISM TAKING THE FORMS OF CRIMES AGAINST PERSONS, AND RELATED EXTORTION THAT ARE OF INTERNATIONAL SIGNIFICANCE

This Convention was adopted at Washington, D.C., on 2 February 1971.

The main object of this Convention is the adoption of general criteria for cooperation among States Parties in order to prevent and punish acts of terrorism, especially kidnapping, homicide, and other assaults against life and physical integrity of persons to whom the State Party concerned has the duty, according to international law, to give special protection, as well as the extortion related to those crimes.

In order to cooperate in the prevention and punishment of the aforementioned crimes, States Parties have agreed, *inter alia*, to the following obligations: to exchange information and to consider effective administrative measures for better fulfilment of the Convention, and to comply most expeditiously with requests for extradition.

3.7 INTER-AMERICAN CONVENTION AGAINST CORRUPTION

This treaty was adopted at Caracas, Venezuela, on 29 March 1996.

The Convention sets forth the objectives of promoting and strengthening the development, by each State Party, of the necessary mechanisms to prevent, detect, punish and eradicate corruption. It also has the objective of promoting, facilitating and regulating cooperation among States Parties in order to ensure the effectiveness of measures and actions to prevent, detect, punish and eradicate corruption in the performance of public functions, and acts of corruption specifically related with such performance.

3.8 INTER-AMERICAN CONVENTION AGAINST THE ILLICIT MANUFACTURING OF AND TRAFFICKING IN WEAPONS, AMMUNITION, EXPLOSIVES AND OTHER RELATED MATERIALS

This treaty was adopted at Washington, D.C., on 14 November 1997.

The object of this Convention is to prevent, combat and eradicate the illicit manufacture of, and traffic in, firearms, ammunition, explosives and other related materials. Furthermore, States Parties are under the obligation to exchange information and experiences in these areas. According to the Convention, States Parties shall afford one another the widest measure of mutual assistance, in accordance with their domestic law, setting forth those requests issued by the authorities that, according to their internal legislation, are competent to investigate, or prosecute, and execute other necessary acts in order to further procedures and actions related to their investigation or prosecution. States Parties must cooperate in tracing firearms, ammunition and other related material that could have been illegally trafficked. This cooperation shall include accurate and prompt responses to requests for tracing.

Under the Convention, States Parties must identify a national body or a single point of contact that will act as liaison between States Parties for the purpose of cooperation and information exchange.

4. Central Authorities: An Important Cooperation Mechanism

The designation of Central Authorities pursuant to the different treaties represents one of the most efficient and helpful means for providing mutual legal assistance and cooperation. The primary function of these Authorities is defined in each treaty, however, in general terms; these entities receive letters rogatory or requests from other Central Authorities, and later issue them to the particular national entities.

The Inter-American Specialised Conference on Private International Law first included this in two of the adopted treaties. The custom has been preserved throughout the Conferences held on the subject to date. The mechanism has also been applied in direct cooperation between States Parties when the Central Authority body represents an important element for implementation of a particular treaty.

In order to improve the establishment of and information on Central Authorities, the OAS, as Depositary of the Inter-American Conventions, receives information on the designation of the Central Authorities agreed upon for each instrument. The following table summarises the function of the Central Authorities under the Conventions referred to in this chapter as well as the entities which have been designated as such.

Table 1

Treaty	Central Authority Functions	Appointment
Inter-American Convention on the Taking of Evidence Abroad	-Receive and distribute letters rogatory for all purposes under the Convention	**El Salvador**: Supreme Court of Justice **Guatemala**: Supreme Court of Justice **Mexico**: Foreign Affairs Secretariat **Uruguay**: Ministry of Education and Culture, "Central Authority Advisor of International Juridical Cooperation" **Chile**: Ministry of Foreign Affairs, Juridical Affairs Direction **Ecuador**: Ministry of Foreign Affairs, Technical Juridical Advisor, General Legal Affairs Direction
Additional Protocol to the Inter-American Convention on the Taking of Evidence Abroad	-Receive letters rogatory from Central Authorities of States Parties and transfer them to the competent jurisdictional body for their handling, according to the applicable internal legislation. -Receive the letter rogatory, along with pertinent documents, from the competent jurisdictional bodies. -Certify the letter rogatory's execution to the Central Authority of the requesting State Party, or the grounds on which the letter rogatory was not executed. -Send corresponding documentation to the requesting Party, in order to be forwarded to the jurisdictional body that issued the request.	
Inter-American Convention on Mutual Assistance in Criminal Matters	-Send and receive requests for assistance. Mutually and directly exchange information for all purposes under the Convention. -Determine if the request includes all information required to justify the proposed measure. -Inform other Central Authorities of the existence in their territory of proceeds of crime. -Determine in advance if interested authorities or parties, or their representatives, from the requesting State will be present and participate in the execution of the request for assistance. -Register the person's willingness to appear in the requesting State and promptly inform the Central Authority of the requesting State of this decision. -Agree on the transfer of the person subject to criminal proceedings in the State from which he or she was sent. -Receive notification of the transit through the State where the person is subject to criminal proceedings. -If requested, specify conditions to preserve the confidentiality of information or evidence provided by the requested State. -Enter into negotiations when the requesting Party cannot meet the conditions of confidentiality.	**Venezuela**: Ministry of Justice
Inter-American Convention on the Serving of Criminal Sentences Abroad	-Execute functions determined by the Convention. Serve as intermediary for the request for transfer. -Agree on the location where the sentenced person will be transferred by the sentencing State to the receiving State. -Serve as intermediary between States Parties, enabling the sentencing State authorities to request reports on the status of serving the sentence by any sentenced person transferred to the receiving State under this Convention.	**Canada**: Correctional Service Administration and International Transfer of Canada **Costa Rica**: General Directory of Social Adaptation of the Justice and Grace Ministry **Mexico**: Government Secretariat **Venezuela**: Ministry of Justice
Inter-American Convention Against Corruption	-Issue and receive requests for assistance and cooperation referred to in this Convention. -Directly provide information under this Convention.	**Paraguay**: State Attorney General **Ecuador**: State Attorney General

5. Other Proposals for Cooperation

The OAS Department of Legal Cooperation and Information has proposed that, in addition to the traditional mechanisms of legal cooperation included in different treaties, other useful methods should be studied. Among them the following have been suggested:

- development of model legislation;
- prototype or model law development;
- horizontal cooperation and experience exchange;
- support to applied research programmes;
- support for training programmes; and,
- publications and legal information.

The scope of this chapter does not permit analysis of each alternative proposed. Nevertheless, they should be mentioned here, since their implementation would be of great importance to the improvement of cooperation among States, and it would be worthwhile to raise them for consideration in future discussions.

SECTION IV.4

PROTECTION OF NATIONAL SECURITY OR CONFIDENTIAL BUSINESS INFORMATION IN JUDICIAL PROCEEDINGS

Introduction and Summary

Article VIII, paragraph 1, of the Chemical Weapons Convention (CWC, or "Convention") states that the purpose of the OPCW is "to achieve the object and purpose of this Convention, to ensure the implementation of its provisions, including those for international verification of compliance with it...." The CWC regime is grounded in "informational transparency": State and industry compliance with the CWC is encouraged by the open exchange of information, demonstrating that other States and companies are also complying. This transparency, in combination with the design of the OPCW as a centralized supervisory agency, means that a large amount of sensitive national security and business information is in constant distribution through the OPCW's channels.

At the same time, however, States and firms will only be willing to permit OPCW Secretariat and State Party access to extremely sensitive information if they know that it will be kept within the confines of the CWC regime. The transparency critical to the CWC's success is tightly bound by equally essential confidentiality requirements. Breaches of that confidentiality must be deterred and prevented, their possible scope must be limited as much as possible, and should a breach occur, it must be dealt with swiftly and effectively. An effective confidentiality regime addresses all these challenges; applies to the full range of individual, corporate, State and organisational actors involved in every level of the CWC regime; has means of obtaining jurisdiction over all those actors; and covers the full spectrum of national security and confidential business information (CBI) that may be accessed during Convention-related activities.

R. Yepes-Enríquez and L. Tabassi. (eds.), Treaty Enforcement and International Cooperation in Criminal Matters

The need and methods for maintaining comprehensive confidentiality become problematic, however, when the setting shifts from administration to adjudication. In a trial setting, the need for confidentiality must be weighed against the rights and principles of a fair proceeding, including the right of the accused to have access to any and all potentially exonerating information, the right of the accused to challenge the validity of evidence presented during trial, and the principle of maintaining a structural balance of power between the prosecution and the defense.

Several different sets of tools have been implemented, at both the national and international levels, in an attempt to fairly balance these conflicting needs. On the national level, the U.S. legal system provides three interesting procedural models embodying a "managed access" system for information management. First, the Freedom of Information Act (FOIA) creates a system for compelling the public disclosure of sensitive documents, using a staggered scale to weigh the demand for disclosure against the need for secrecy (so extremely sensitive documents are often withheld despite requests for their release), and often releasing redacted documents. Second, and importantly, the United States' CWC national implementing legislation functions on a default of information non-disclosure and provides severe penalties, both criminal and civil, for unauthorized disclosures. The realm of acceptable disclosure is carefully and narrowly delineated in the statute.

The United States' "National Security Courts" provide a third example of a judicial system designed to maintain confidentiality. These courts are staffed, from judges and attorneys to clerks and receptionists, entirely of people sworn to confidentiality. Stiff penalties are levied for a breach of that commitment. The courts also conduct closed sessions, keep evidence under seal, and in cases of highly sensitive material, provide information access to the defense attorney, but not the accused. The United Kingdom has adopted some similar procedures, and the European Court of Human Rights has ruled that their application, in cases of strict necessity and with accompanying procedural safeguards and trial judge oversight, does not violate due process rights under the European Human Rights Convention. In short, these techniques are one way to strike the desired balance between confidentiality and fair judicial process.

These systems have proven cohesive and relatively effective, and they could be replicated in other States Parties – but not without difficulty. The FOIA and National Security Courts rely on a large, well-developed and expensive judicial bureaucracy that may not exist in all States, and they are rooted in a common law legal tradition and culture whose norms and standards of evidence and procedure may not translate well into civil, Islamic, or other justice systems. The reliance on managed access also comes with costs of its own, since its presumption of "non-disclosure, except..." may keep important information out of the realm of transparency, and its culture of secrecy and suspicion can inhibit institutional collegiality. In the end, these institutions are probably best seen as models to be adapted to fit each State's traditions, existing institutions and needs.

The same strengths and limitations apply equally to an international system of overlapping national institutions. Such an approach seems advisable, since it rests on a clear basis of national compliance, jurisdiction, and enforcement. But, if pursued, this tack demands a structured means of cooperation through a Convention protocol, multiple memoranda of understanding, or a common space for informal negotiation. Indeed, the experience of the International Criminal Tribunal for the Former Yugoslavia (ICTY) has been marked by many such informal negotiations as the Office of the Prosecutor (OTP) navigated its way through myriad different national systems of information security in its quest for evidence.

Were a new international system for confidentiality enforcement sought by the States Parties, the OPCW Confidentiality Commission, with its existing regime of rules and procedures, could act as a foundation. It possesses the significant benefits of standing within the OPCW confidentiality regime and avoiding the complexities of interlocking differing national secrecy systems. As it stands, however, the Commission is very evidently not an ideal judicial body. It possesses little legal expertise, its 20 person regional group-nominated membership would make for unwieldy and possibly politicized adjudication, it has no existing powers of enforcement, and the more gradual growth, to date, of the International Criminal Court (ICC) suggests that the willingness of all States Parties to submit their nationals to its "jurisdiction" would likely be lacking.

Change is possible, and there are a few institutions upon which an evolving OPCW-based body could model itself. The inchoate ICC could, down the road, be one such model. The ICTY is a current successful example, but its establishment was based on exceptional international political consensus and motivation, and it required careful disclosure rules, the development of a sophisticated evidence cataloguing and tracking system, and much informal consultation with the sources of its information. Pursuing a similar path within the OPCW would be costly, complex and politically challenging. At base, the ICTY also relies upon the good will of States, individuals and organizations to give it information; while it can technically "compel" information turnover, its only means of enforcing that compulsion, as would likely be the case with an OPCW-based entity, is to complain to the UN Security Council.

Such limitations and challenges do not mean that such an institution cannot be formed, but the process would be slow and difficult. In the meantime, States Parties would do well to develop and refine their national "confidential court" practices, and the OPCW would be wise to formalize its cooperation procedures to ensure that national practices interface smoothly and effectively.

Robert Delonis

Précis-writer for Section IV.4; Intern in the OPCW Technical Secretariat, Office of the Legal Adviser and the Media and Public Affairs Branch of the External Relations Division; New York University School of Law. The opinions expressed are not attributable to the OPCW or New York University.

PROTECTING NATIONAL SECURITY AND OTHER CONFIDENTIAL INFORMATION

Nancy L. Paterson*

1. INTRODUCTION

The field of international criminal law and procedure has evolved dramatically within the last decade. Starting with the creation of the International Criminal Tribunal for the former Yugoslavia (ICTY) in 1993, followed shortly thereafter by the International Criminal Tribunal for Rwanda (ICTR) in 1995, the actual practice of international criminal law was quickly forced to dust off many concepts previously discussed primarily in theoretical terms. Once established, the Tribunals were quickly confronted with the need to develop procedures to handle all variety of real-life scenarios not envisioned by the theoreticians. Their success in dealing with these challenges has been mixed.

Among the more challenging topics that demanded the immediate attention of the ad hoc Tribunals was the delicate and politically sensitive issue of protecting national security and other confidential information. While acknowledging the absolutely crucial need for the prosecutors to receive sensitive intelligence information and other forms of confidential information and evidence from States and other non-State entities, the two Tribunals had to deal with the issue of how to protect the legitimate security interests of the providers while balancing the equally compelling rights of the accused to access to both inculpatory and exculpatory evidence.

Although the ICTY has successfully navigated this difficult issue on several occasions, it has not been easy, nor has the success been achieved without confronting some particularly troublesome roadblocks along the way. While a number of provisions to deal with these issues are now included in the relevant Statutes and Rules of Procedure and Evidence (hereinafter "the Rules"), the fact that these safeguards were not in the original ICTY Statute illustrates the failure of the drafters to fully appreciate the significance and sensitivity of these complex issues.

2. COLLECTING, SECURING AND PROTECTING NATIONAL SECURITY AND OTHER CONFIDENTIAL INFORMATION FROM STATES AND ORGANISATIONS

In order to begin any criminal investigation, it is necessary to collect as much information as possible from a variety of sources, to review and analyse the information, and then to develop an investigative plan based on the leads provided by the information. The ICTY

* Investigator, Department of Institutional Integrity, The World Bank; Former Acting Senior Trial Attorney, International Criminal Tribunal for the Former Yugoslavia (ICTY). The opinions expressed are those of the author and do not represent the position or viewpoint of the World Bank or the United Nations.

R. Yepes-Enríquez and L. Tabassi. (eds.), Treaty Enforcement and International Cooperation in Criminal Matters

Statute and the Rules spell out a number of ways in which the Office of the Prosecutor (OTP) can obtain this information.

The power to collect the information derives from the ICTY Statute, Article 18, entitled Investigation and Preparation of Indictment:

1. The Prosecutor shall initiate investigations *ex-officio* or on the basis of information obtained from any source, particularly from Governments, United Nations organs, intergovernmental and non-governmental organisations. The Prosecutor shall assess the information received or obtained and decide whether there is sufficient basis to proceed.
2. The Prosecutor shall have the power to question suspects, victims and witnesses, to collect evidence and to conduct on-site investigations. In carrying out thes tasks, the Prosecutor may, as appropriate, seek the assistance of the State authorities concerned.

This provision is given additional "teeth" by Article 29, entitled Cooperation and Judicial Assistance which states unequivocally that all *States* shall cooperate with the Tribunal.[1] Significantly, however, Article 29 does not make reference to non-State entities or organisations, leaving its applicability in those situations open to question.

The means for obtaining the information is spelled out in several provisions in the Rules. Pursuant to Rule 8, entitled Request for Information, "the Prosecutor may request the State to forward all relevant information . . . and the State shall transmit such information to the Prosecutor forthwith in accordance with Article 29 of the Statute." Rule 39, entitled Conduct of Investigations, authorises the Prosecutor to record statements and collect evidence, to undertake other matters "as may be necessary for completing the investigation," to seek the assistance and cooperation of States and relevant international bodies, and to request orders from a Trial Chamber or a Judge. Of special significance is Rule 54 *bis*, entitled Orders Directed to States for the Production of Documents, which permits the OTP to seek an order from a Trial Chamber directing a "reluctant" State to produce documents that could contain important evidence. In addition, pursuant to Rule 98, entitled Power of Chambers to Order Production of Additional Evidence, a Trial Chamber itself has the power to "order either party to produce additional evidence."

Once the information is within its control, the OTP must comply with certain disclosure obligations. Rule 66, entitled Disclosure by the Prosecutor, sets out in some detail what information must be disclosed and when. It also provides for inspection of some evidence by the defence[2]. Significantly, however, Rule 66 also makes clear that certain information, after review *in camera* by a Trial Chamber, may not have to be disclosed if disclosure of the information "may prejudice further or ongoing investigations, or for any other reasons may be contrary to the public interest or affect the security interests of any State." Rules 68 and 70, which will be discussed in some detail below, address the disclosure of exculpatory evidence and explain what information is not subject to disclosure.

---

[1] See Annex VII for the full text of cited ICTY Articles and Rules.

[2] Rule 66(B).

3. Protecting National Security and Other Confidential Information in the Control of the ICTY

3.1 Collection and Storage of Information

When the ICTY commenced its work in the summer of 1994, it had the benefit of receiving a significant amount of information that had already been collected by other United Nations agencies as well as individual States and a variety of governmental and non-governmental organisations (NGOs). Although the OTP had a wealth of information, the office was lacking adequate means to store and protect the information, as well as any means to catalogue and classify the information according to its confidential nature and sensitivity.[3] As a result, one of the first major priorities addressed by the Office of the Prosecutor (OTP) was the development of a sophisticated evidence logging and tracking system complemented by a number of databases which allowed the investigators to sort through the huge volume of material and to separate out that information which demanded special security measures.[4]

Although a number of supportive States and organisations appreciated the need for such information, due to the lack of adequate safeguards for the confidentiality of the information, many of those countries were reluctant to provide the OTP with substantive confidential information until their security concerns were adequately addressed. Further complicating the situation was the fact that each country handled their intelligence information in different ways, and each country had different ideas as to how they wanted the OTP to handle and safeguard the information. While the Judges were confronting the issue of developing adequate statutory protections, the OTP took the initiative to establish a variety of procedures for the handling of sensitive information with several States and organisations. Over time, through an exchange of correspondence, several different "understandings" as to how the OTP would safeguard such information were concluded. With one or two exceptions, the procedures established were not based on formal Memoranda of Understanding (MOUs); rather, they evolved via less formal means.

3.2 Amendments to the Statute and Rules

Once it became apparent that additional safeguards were needed to protect the confidential information the OTP hoped to receive from States and other organisations, the Tribunal, through its plenary meetings, took steps to add provisions to the Rules to allay the concerns of the contributing States and organisations. The troublesome issues arose when consideration was given to how the OTP should handle this confidential information when it came to disclosure and use of the evidence at trial. With a quick look at the relevant rules related to disclosure, as they were originally drafted, it was glaringly apparent that neither Rule 66(C) of the ICTY Rules, entitled Disclosure by the Prosecutor, nor Rule 70, entitled Matters Not Subject to Disclosure, adequately addressed the issue of security and confidentiality concerns. In fact, there was no mention whatsoever of the issue. Once the

[3] See ICTY Rule 41, entitled Retention of Information.

[4] As of January 2001, the Tribunal had 2,350,000 pages of documentary evidence of which 164,000 pages is confidential information protected by Rule 70.

need for such provisions became apparent, the Fifth Plenary session of the ICTY, held on 30 January 1995, added the following sub-paragraph to Rule 66:

> (C) Where information is in the possession of the Prosecutor, the disclosure of which may prejudice further or on-going investigations, or for any other reasons may be contrary to the public interest or affect the security interests of any State, the Prosecution may apply to the Trial Chamber sitting *in camera* to be relieved from the obligation to disclose pursuant to Sub-rule (B). When making such application the Prosecutor shall provide the Trial Chamber (but only the Trial Chamber) with the information that is sought to be kept confidential.

Similarly, the following provision was added to Rule 70:

> (B) If the Prosecutor is in possession of information which has been provided to [him][5] on a confidential basis and which has been used solely for the purpose of generating new evidence, that initial information and its origins shall not be disclosed by the Prosecutor without the consent of the person or entity providing the initial information and shall in any event not be given in evidence without prior disclosure to the accused.

Not long thereafter, in October 1995, the Tribunal added four more subparagraphs that further elaborated the limitations on the use of so-called "Rule 70" evidence.

> (C) If, after obtaining the consent of the person or entity providing information under this Rule, the Prosecutor elects to present as evidence any testimony, document or other material so provided, the Trial Chamber, notwithstanding Rule 98, may not order either party to produce additional evidence received from the person or entity providing the initial information, nor may the Trial Chamber for the purpose of obtaining such additional evidence itself summon that person or a representative of that entity as a witness or order their attendance.[6]
>
> (D) If the Prosecutor calls a witness to introduce in evidence any information provided under this Rule, the Trial Chamber may not compel that witness to answer any question relating to the information or its origin, if the witness declines to answer on grounds of confidentiality.
>
> (E) The right of the accused to challenge the evidence presented by the Prosecution shall remain unaffected subject only to the limitations contained in Sub-rules (C) and (D).
>
> (F) Nothing in Sub-rule (C) or (D) above shall affect a Trial Chamber's power under Rule 89 (D) to exclude evidence if its probative value is substantially outweighed by the need to ensure a fair trial.[7]

---

[5] The phrase "to him" was changed to "the Prosecutor" on 12 November 1997.

[6] The sentence: "A Trial Chamber may not use its power to order the attendance of witnesses or to require production of documents in order to compel the production of such additional evidence" was added on 25 July 1997.

[7] This provision was re-numbered (became G) in July 1997 when a new sub-paragraph (F) was added.

Finally, in July 1997, the final sub-paragraph was added:

> (F) The Trial Chamber may order upon an application by the accused or defence counsel that, in the interests of justice, the provisions of this Rule shall apply *mutatis mutandis* to specific information in the possession of the accused.[8]

3.3 NON-DISCLOSURE OBLIGATIONS VERSUS EXCULPATORY INFORMATION — RULE 68 VERSUS RULE 70

While the safeguards added to Rules 66 and 70 have satisfied the concerns of the States and other organisations by providing a satisfactory means for protecting the confidentiality of sensitive intelligence information — information that sometimes rises to the level of national security concerns — these very safeguards also present the Tribunal with a difficult dilemma. In addition to the standard disclosure obligations set forth in Rule 66, the OTP also has a continuing duty, as set forth in Rule 68 of the Rules, to "as soon as practicable, disclose to the defence the existence of evidence known to the Prosecutor which in any way tends to suggest the innocence or mitigate the guilt of the accused or may affect the credibility of prosecution evidence."

If the OTP is obligated to keep certain information confidential, what is the OTP to do if that information is also arguably exculpatory? Do Rule 68 obligations to disclose exculpatory information supersede Rule 70 obligations to keep the information confidential, or do Rule 70 obligations override Rule 68 obligations?

According to Rule 70 (C), information provided to the OTP on a confidential basis "*shall not be disclosed* by the Prosecutor without the consent of the person or entity providing the initial information and shall in any event not be given in evidence without prior disclosure to the accused" (emphasis added). Assuming the State or organisation that provided the information gives its consent to disclosure, there is no problem. However, what if the exculpatory information is highly sensitive national security information and the provider is unwilling, perhaps even unable, to give consent for its release?

Unfortunately, neither Rule 68 nor Rule 70 addresses this conflict directly. Rule 68 says the OTP "shall" disclose exculpatory information, but Rule 70 says confidential information "shall not" be disclosed without the consent of the provider. The answer remains unresolved since the issue has not been addressed directly by any of the ICTY Trial Chambers in public decisions. However, one sentence in a decision issued by the Trial Chamber in the case of *Tihomir Blaskic* offers some limited guidance. In the Judgement, the Trial Chamber stated, "[t]he other paragraphs under Rule 70 [sub-paragraphs (B)-(F)] of the Rules deal *with the exception* to the disclosure obligation set down in Rules 66, 67 and 68 of the Rules."[9] This statement thus implies that Rule 70 must prevail over Rule 68 when they conflict and, if the provider does not consent to its release, the OTP cannot disclose the information provided under Rule 70 even if it falls within the purview of Rule 68 exculpatory information.

This interpretation of the rules receives additional support when one looks to ICC Article 72(3), the equivalent provision in the Rome Statute of the International Criminal

---

[8] When this provision was added, what had been sub-paragraph (F) was re-lettered sub-paragraph (G).

[9] *Prosecutor v. Tihomir Blaskic, Judgement,* Case No. IT-95-14-PT, Trial Chamber I, 3 March 2000, para. 31 (emphasis added).

Court (ICC).[10] Referring to article 54, paragraph 3(e) (the ICC equivalent of ICTY Rule 70(B)), the statute states:

> Nothing in this article shall prejudice the requirements of confidentiality applicable under article 54, paragraph 3 (e) and (f), or the application of article 73.

Furthermore, ICC Article 72(1) states unequivocally that the article, which specifically prohibits disclosure without consent of the provider, applies in "any case where the disclosure of the information or documents of a State would, *in the opinion of that State*, prejudice its national security interest. *Such cases include those falling within the scope of . . . article 67, paragraph 2 . . .*"(emphasis added).[11] Therefore, it seems clear that while it may be ethically challenging to most prosecutors, the practice of the ICTY and the Rules of the ICC imply that public policy concerns over maintaining confidentiality of national security and other highly confidential information, in some cases, outweighs the rights of the accused to disclosure of potentially exculpatory information.

While it is foreseeable that this difficult ethical dilemma will one day present itself, it is hoped that in most cases when exculpatory information falls within the purview of Rule 70 of the ICTY Rules (or its equivalents under the ICC Statute and Rules), the provider of the information will give consent to release of the information or, failing that, some kind of compromise will be fashioned that protects the needs of the provider and the rights of the accused. Most importantly, should the OTP come into possession of significant exculpatory information which casts serious doubt on the guilt of the accused, it is assumed that the OTP would exercise its prosecutorial discretion and choose not to pursue its case against that individual.

4. Power of the ICTY to Subpoena National Security and Other Confidential Information

Although Rule 54 *bis* allows the OTP to apply to a Trial Chamber for an Order directed to a State to produce certain documents, the application of this provision has been the subject of considerable debate. Despite the ruling in the case of *Prosecutor v. Tihomir Blaskic* that the ICTY can subpoena certain individuals and order them to produce documents,[12] the argument can be made that the actual impact of that ruling is highly questionable due to the limited enforcement power of the Tribunal.

During the course of the trial of Bosnian Croat General Tihomir Blaskic, the OTP sought an order directed to the Government of Croatia for production of certain documents believed to be of significant evidentiary value. Croatia challenged the authority of the Tribunal to issue such an order, which lead to the issuance of a benchmark ruling by the Appeals Chamber. In its decision, the Appeals Chamber addressed the issue of whether or not State officials, as opposed to private individuals, may be subpoenaed by the ICTY.

[10] See Annex VIII for other relevant ICC provisions.

[11] Article 67 (2) is the ICC equivalent to ICTY Rule 68 dealing with disclosure of exculpatory information. See full text of Article 67 in Annex VIII.

[12] *Prosecutor v. Tihomir Blaskic, Judgement on the Request of the Republic of Croatia for Review of the Decision of Trial Chamber II of 18 July 1997*, Case No. IT-95-14-AR 108 *bis*, Appeals Chamber, 29 Oct. 1997 ("Appeals Chamber Subpoena Judgement").

Discussing both the unique nature of the Tribunal and its special powers, the Appeals Chamber noted:

> [t]he International Tribunal is an international criminal court constituting a novelty in the world community. Normally, individuals subject to the sovereign authority of States may only be tried by national courts. If a national court intends to bring to trial an individual subject to the jurisdiction of another State, as a rule it relies on treaties of judicial cooperation or, if such treaties are not available, on voluntary interstate cooperation. Thus, the relation between national courts of different States is "horizontal" in nature. In 1993 the Security Council for the first time established an international criminal court endowed with jurisdiction over individuals living within sovereign States, be they States of the former Yugoslavia or third States, and, in addition, conferred on the International Tribunal primacy over national courts. By the same token, the Statute granted the International Tribunal the power to address to States binding orders concerning a broad variety of judicial matters.[13]

The Appeals Chamber then went on to discuss different scenarios in which this provision would apply:

> The spirit and purpose of the Statute, as well as the aforementioned provisions, confer on the International Tribunal an incidental or ancillary jurisdiction over individuals other than those whom the International Tribunal may prosecute and try. These are individuals who may be of assistance in the task of dispensing criminal justice entrusted to the International Tribunal. Furthermore, as stated above, Article 29 also imposes upon States an obligation to take action required by the International Tribunal vis-à-vis individuals subject to their jurisdiction.[14]
>
> ... The situation differs for a State official (e.g., a general) who acts as a member of an international peace-keeping or peace-enforcement force such as UNPROFOR, IFOR or SFOR. Even if he witnesses the commission or the planning of a crime in a monitoring capacity, while performing his official functions, he should be treated by the International Tribunal *qua* an individual. Such an officer is present in the former Yugoslavia as a member of an international armed force responsible for maintaining or enforcing peace and not *qua* a member of the military structure of his own country. His mandate stems from the same source as that of the International Tribunal, i.e., a resolution of the Security Council,[15] and therefore he must testify, subject to the appropriate requirements set out in the Rules (footnote omitted).[16]

While this decision makes clear that the Tribunal can order States to turn over documents and other information, including information that might impact on national security interests, there are nonetheless provisions in the Statute for protecting this confidential information from unnecessary disclosure. Rule 54 *bis* (F) and (G) specifically lay out several

[13] *Id.* at para. 47.
[14] *Id.* at para. 48.
[15] This would also apply to forces deployed under Article 53 of the United Nations Charter.
[16] *Prosecutor v. Tihomir Blaskic, Appeals Chamber Subpoena Judgement*, para. 50.

procedures and protective measures that allow the State and the Trial Chamber to address the issue of national security concerns. Among the protective measures available are *in camera* review of the documents by a single Judge, submission of redacted documents, conduct of the proceedings without production of a transcript, and use of only specially designated interpreters approved by the State.

Of course, the *Appeals Chamber Subpoena Judgement* loses much of its significance if there is no means to enforce the orders issued by the Tribunal. When a State fails to comply with its obligations under the Statute, Rule 7 *bis* allows both the Trial Chamber and the Prosecutor to advise the President of the Tribunal that the State is in non-compliance with its obligations and the President must then report the matter to the UN Security Council for action. The actual impact of this provision is significantly limited, however, since the imposition of meaningful sanctions lies only with the UN Security Council, a political body subject to political influence. The Security Council's willingness to impose sanctions with enough "bite" to force compliance can be diluted by the need to reach political compromise.

In reality, despite the provisions of Rule 7 *bis* (non-compliance with State obligations) and Article 29 (Cooperation and judicial assistance), the true enforcement power of the Tribunal is sadly lacking and leaves the *Appeals Chamber Subpoena Judgement* rather hollow.[17] President McDonald addressed the serious problem with lack of enforcement power in a letter to the President of the Security Council in November 1999:

> The Tribunal is at the mercy of the international community for enforcement of its orders. The Tribunal lacks coercive mechanisms and must rely on the international community to give effect to its arrest warrants and other orders. All too often, this assistance is lacking.[18]

Noting the fact that the Security Council itself had failed to respond to some reports by the ICTY President of non-compliance by States, President McDonald implored the Security Council "to take the effective measures necessary to bring these recalcitrant States . . . back into the fold of the community of law-abiding nations."[19]

5. National Security and Other Confidential Information in the Control of non-State Entities

While there are several provisions in the Statute and the Rules protecting the confidentiality of information within the control of the OTP, or within the control of a State, another scenario can arise in which the parties in a case before the ICTY want or need access to national security and other confidential information within the control of non-State entities. This particular scenario arose recently and presented the Court and the parties involved with yet more unique legal questions.

---

[17] In the *Blaskic* case, the Trial Chamber ordered Croatia to produce certain documents in July 1997; however, by the close of the trial two years later, in July 1999, there had still been no compliance with the order. In this instance, Croatia was not reported to the Security Council for non-compliance.

[18] Letter from President McDonald to the President of the Security Council Concerning Outstanding Issues of State Non-Compliance, 2 November 1999, UN doc. S/1999/1117.

[19] *Id.*

In September 1998, Stevan Todorovic, one of the accused in a publicly issued indictment, alleged that he was taken forcibly from the house where he was living in Serbia (having fled from Republika Srpska to avoid arrest), was transferred across the Drina River to Bosnia, and from there was taken into custody by American SFOR (NATO sponsored Stabilisation Force) troops who then turned him over to the ICTY. Defence counsel for Todorovic filed an often used pre-trial motion challenging the legality of the defendant's arrest and demanded that a number of records and other information related to the arrest of Stevan Todorovic be turned over to him by the OTP. The records and information he was seeking, however, were in the control of SFOR, not the OTP. SFOR said the documents contained information of a natural security nature and were otherwise highly confidential because they contained information about military operational matters that, if disclosed, could jeopardise future arrest missions and, more importantly, might endanger the safety and security of SFOR personnel and other persons co-operating with SFOR.

Since the records had never been turned over to the OTP, the material did not fall within the purview of Rules 66 or 70. In addition, since the OTP did not have access to the information, the prosecutors had no way of determining if there was any potentially exculpatory information in those records that fell within the purview of Rule 68. Although Rule 54 *bis* of the ICTY Rules provides a means for the Tribunal to issue binding orders to States, the rule is worded in such a way that it was not clear if a Trial Chamber can issue a binding order to non-State entities such as SFOR.

Although conceding that the Trial Chamber, pursuant to the ruling in the *Appeals Chamber Subpoena Decision*, does have the authority to issue a binding order to SFOR, the OTP argued that the court should use its discretionary power and not issue such an order in this case due to the unique and particularly sensitive nature of the information being sought.[20] In a controversial decision, the Trial Chamber rejected the arguments of both the OTP and SFOR,[21] and issued binding orders for the documents requested by the defence to the member States of NATO and other States who made up the SFOR contingent.[22] In its decision, the Trial Chamber relied on the *Appeals Chamber Subpoena Judgement*, but also argued that "in principle, there is no reason why Article 29 should not apply to collective enterprises undertaken by States" and applied what it called a "purposive construction" of Article 29.[23] This reasoning "suggested" that Article 29 should apply to organisations such as SFOR. Therefore, the Trial Chamber ruled that it had the authority to issue binding orders to SFOR.

[20] Prosecutor's Appeal against the Trial Chamber's Decision on Motion for Judicial Assistance to be Provided by SFOR and Others Dated 18 October 2000 or, alternatively, Application for Leave to Appeal Against that Decision and Request for a Stay of the Decision, *Prosecutor v. Simic*, Case No. IT-95-9-PT (25 October 2000).

[21] SFOR argued that Article 29 and Rule 54 *bis* should be read literally and only are applicable to States. Letter from Fred T. Pribble, Colonel, US Army, Legal Advisor for SFOR, to Judge Patrick L. Robinson, Presiding Judge, Trial Chamber, International Criminal Tribunal for the Former Yugoslavia (9 July 2000).

[22] *Prosecutor v. Simic, Decision On Motion for Judicial Assistance to be Provided by SFOR and Others*, Case No. IT-95-9-PT Trial Chamber III, (18 October 2000).

[23] *Id.* In addition, the Trial Chamber attempted to distinguish an earlier holding of its own that specifically stated that Article 29 does *not* apply to non-State organisations.

Furthermore, the Trial Chamber, using the same reasoning and relying on the holding in the *Trial Chamber Blaskic Subpoena Decision*,[24] also held that it had the authority to subpoena State officials serving in organisations such as SFOR since they "function as members of an international armed force responsible for maintaining or enforcing peace and not *qua* a member of the military structure of his own country."[25] The Trial Chamber, however, failed to distinguish that the scenarios envisioned by the Trial Chamber in the *Trial Chamber Blaskic Subpoena Decision* were significantly different from those presented in the *Todorovic* case.[26]

The OTP and several states subject to the Trial Chamber order challenged the ruling before the Appeals Chamber. However, before the appeal proceedings were concluded, Stevan Todorovic pleaded guilty and withdrew his requests for judicial assistance to secure documents relevant to the legality of his arrest. The appeals proceeding became moot, and the arrest issue was left unresolved.

6. National Security and Other Confidential Information in the Control of Other UN Agencies, the ICRC, NGOs, and Other Non-State Organisations

Another scenario that occasionally has to be addressed arises when groups such as NGOs, other UN agencies, and other non-State affiliated organisations control confidential information. The most interesting situation in this category arose when a former employee of the International Committee of the Red Cross (ICRC) approached the OTP and offered to testify at a trial. The ICRC objected, cited the confidential nature of the information and argued that subjecting ICRC employees to subpoenas and allowing them to testify at trial could endanger the view of the world community that the ICRC acted with strict impartiality in all conflicts.[27] Such a situation, they argued, could potentially endanger the lives and impair the work of other ICRC employees.[28]

Although the OTP respected the ICRC concerns, the Prosecutor argued that the ICRC could not unilaterally claim a special privilege against testifying as a matter of law; that only a Trial Chamber could decide if a privilege in law existed and, if so, under what circumstances the privilege should be exercised.[29] The primary concern of the OTP was the precedent that was being set should the ICRC be allowed to claim a special privilege.[30] If the ICRC could claim a privilege because of the unique nature of their work, what was to stop similar organisations such as Office of the United Nations High Commissioner for Refugees

---

[24] *Prosecutor v. Tihomir Blaskic, Decision on the Objection of the Republic of Croatia to the Issuance of Subpoena Duces Tecum*, Case No. IT-95-14-PT, Trial Chamber II (18 July 1997).

[25] Judgement on the Request of the Republic of Croatia for Review of the Decision of Trial Chamber II of 18 July 1997 (29 October 1997), para. 50.

[26] The scenario presented in *Blaskic* involved a member of SFOR who was an eyewitness to a war crime and clearly should testify before the Tribunal. In *Todorovic* the defence was asking to subpoena the commanding general of the United States SFOR troops who may have had knowledge of highly confidential SFOR operational matters related to the arrest, but clearly was not an eyewitness to anything.

[27] *Prosecutor v. Simic, Decision On The Prosecution Motion Under Rule 73 For A Ruling Concerning The Testimony Of A Witness*, Case No. IT-95-9-PT Trial Chamber III (27 July 1999), para. 9.

[28] *Id.* at para. 13.

[29] *Id.* at para. 24.

[30] *Id.* at para. 3.

(UNHCR) and other humanitarian NGOs from claiming a similar privilege? If all such organisations were to be exempt from the subpoena power of the Tribunal and they had the power to prevent their employees from testifying, the organisation would have no obligation to share any information with the Tribunal. Such a situation would significantly impair the ability of the OTP to conduct its investigations.

The OTP argued that witness privileges of the type envisioned by the ICRC exist in very limited fashion in national law, but are not generally recognised under customary international law.[31] In the alternative, the OTP contended that if the Tribunal were to recognise such a privilege, it should be applied very narrowly on a case-by-case basis, and evidence should be excluded only in extraordinary circumstances.[32] The ICRC, on the other hand, argued that to allow their staff to testify would violate principles of international humanitarian law concerning the role of the ICRC and its mandate under the Geneva Conventions.[33]

Of most concern to the ICRC was the impact such a ruling would have on its ability to discharge its mandate to investigate violations of the Geneva Conventions. It insisted that such a ruling was likely to deny or restrict ICRC access to prison and detention facilities if the warring parties believed that ICRC officials or employees might subsequently give evidence in relation to persons they met or events they witnessed.[34] In this case, the OTP cited the *Appeals Chamber Subpoena Judgement* as authority to subpoena non-State entities, but the ICRC argued that the scenarios were not analogous and that the ICRC had no connection whatsoever to any State.[35]

After receiving lengthy submissions from both sides, the Trial Chamber ruled in favour of the ICRC. Distinguishing the ICRC from other organisations, the Trial Chamber stated:

> It is widely acknowledged that the ICRC, an independent humanitarian organisation, enjoys a special status in international law, based on the mandate conferred upon it by the international community. The Trial Chamber notes that the functions and tasks of the ICRC are directly derived from international law, that is, the Geneva Conventions and Additional Protocols. Another task of the ICRC, under its Statute, is to promote the development, implementation, dissemination and application of international humanitarian law [footnotes omitted].[36]

In reaching its conclusion, the Trial Chamber held that "the Appeals Chamber Subpoena Decision [*Blaskic*] is not applicable to the instant case, which deals with the relationship between the ICRC and an international institution; that Decision deals with the relationship between the International Tribunal and States under Article 29 of the Statute, which provision

---

[31] *Id.* at para. 6.

[32] *Id.* at para. 5.

[33] *Id.* at para. 14. In fact, the actual language in the Geneva Conventions implies that the ICRC is *not* the only organisation to enjoy this special status. "An impartial humanitarian body, *such as* the International Committee of the Red Cross, may offer its services to the Parties to the Conflict." *Convention (I) for the Amelioration of the Condition of the Wounded and Sick in Armed Forces in the Field*, Geneva, 12 August 1949, Art. 3 (2) (emphasis added).

[34] *Prosecutor v. Simic*, *supra* note 27, at para. 13.

[35] *Id.* at para. 7.

[36] *Id.* at para. 46.

does not apply to international organisations."[37] Rejecting the argument of the OTP, the Trial Chamber noted that;

> [i]t is also generally accepted that most of their provisions are regarded as declaratory of customary international law. The Trial Chamber is of the view that, by accepting to be bound by the Geneva Conventions, the States party to them have agreed to the special role and mandate of the ICRC.[38]

This ruling by the Trial Chamber was later used as the basis for codifying the special privilege enjoyed by the ICRC in the ICC Statute.[39] Despite this statutory authority, there is, nonetheless, some irony in the fact that the very organisation entrusted to enforce international humanitarian law as promulgated in the Geneva Conventions is granted a unique privilege that may, in fact, make more difficult the prosecution of certain persons for serious violations of international humanitarian law. In addition, it remains to be seen how many other organisations may in the future argue that they, too, should be granted a similar privilege and, in so doing, keep significant amounts of vital evidence out of the hands of the Prosecutor.

7. Conclusion

Balancing the need to respect the legitimate interests of States to protect their confidential national security information with the need of international courts to use and disclose that information presents a difficult challenge to all parties involved. The rights of the accused must be protected and given full meaning, but what to do when protecting those rights comes into direct conflict with national security concerns presents a significant problem. Fortunately, the practical problems in this regard confronted by the International Criminal Tribunal for the former Yugoslavia have helped both to identify a variety of problem areas that must be addressed and to construct satisfactory statutory provisions to meet the conflicting demands of the parties. Many of the solutions fashioned by the ICTY have been adopted by the ICC and, no doubt, will also be copied by other international organisations confronted by similar problems. Nonetheless, there will always be a point at which a satisfactory balance cannot be achieved and the States and other entities will choose not to share their information, thereby frustrating the efforts of enforcement of international law. The serious challenges presented in this area must be respected, but efforts must continue to find new and creative solutions to the problem.

---

[37] Despite stating unequivocally that Article 29 did *not* apply to international organisations, the same Trial Chamber was later forced to distinguish this statement when it ruled to the contrary in the *Todorovic* IT-959/1.

[38] *Prosecutor v. Simic, supra* note 27, para. 48.

[39] ICC Rules of Procedure and Evidence, Rule 73 (4), entitled Privileged communications and information.

PROTECTION OF CONFIDENTIAL BUSINESS INFORMATION IN JUDICIAL PROCEEDINGS

Richard H. Burgess*

1. Introduction

In the United States' implementation of the Chemical Weapons Convention[1] ("Convention"), confidential business information is well protected. The first line of defence is the Convention itself, and the United States legislation provides that the United States Government will be liable if there is a taking or tortuous act resulting in loss of such information. If that happens, the United States then has a number of means to recoup any costs it has borne, including sanctions on individuals and countries. No instances are known for which such claims could be made. It is presumed that these protective measures will aid in legal cooperation rather than impede them.

The chemical industry participated very actively in the negotiation of the Convention, and especially in the development of its confidentiality provisions, primarily for three reasons. First, the industry sees substantial value in the Convention to humankind generally. Second, it sees value in the Convention to the chemical industry itself, because it minimises the likelihood of misuse of its products by others and maintains the confidence of the public in the industry. Third, the confidentiality provisions of the Convention, and of United States law, provide substantial protections to industry which, under the Convention, opens relevant facilities and plant sites to intrusive international inspections.

United States laws and regulations, enforced by administrative action and judicial proceedings, protect confidential business information ("CBI") from disclosure to the public, but permit disclosure under the Convention to the OPCW, States Parties, and to United States federal agencies for law enforcement purposes. This should not generally be a challenge to international legal cooperation under the Convention. Such cooperation should not normally require CBI to be made available to the public.

References to statutory provisions include many points that were written into the law to minimise the chance of an alleged perpetrator finding a loophole. Several are included below to show the depth and thoroughness of the legislation.

2. Confidentiality and Disclosure

Several documents embody United States law and practice relevant to cooperation and protection of CBI. We will focus here, in addition to the Convention itself, on three: the

* Consultant in trade and treaty compliance to DuPont Company and others, Newark, Delaware, USA.

[1] 1993 Convention on the Prohibition of the Development, Production, Stockpiling and Use of Chemical Weapons and on Their Destruction, entered into force on 29 April 1997. Text, as corrected and changed, available at http://www.opcw.org.

R. Yepes-Enríquez and L. Tabassi. (eds.), Treaty Enforcement and International Cooperation in Criminal Matters

Chemical Weapons Convention Implementation Act of 1998[2] ("CWCIA"), the Chemical Weapons Convention Regulations of the Department of Commerce[3] ("CWCR"), and the United States Senate's consent to ratification.[4]

Title II of the CWCIA — Penalties for Unlawful Activities Subject to the Jurisdiction of the United States — codified at 18 USC 11B, prohibits (section 229 — prohibited activities) many of the acts that the Convention prohibits to States Parties, including knowingly developing, acquiring, transferring, receiving, stockpiling, retaining, owning, possessing, and using or threatening to use any chemical weapon. There are substantial penalties (section 229A — penalties), including: fines up to US$100,000, forfeiture of property (section 229B — criminal forfeitures; destructions of weapons), revocation of export privileges (section 211), reimbursement of the government's expenses in enforcement, and even the death penalty or life imprisonment for causing the death of a person by violation of these parts of the CWCIA. Injunctions (section 229D — injunctions) are available against the prohibited acts or preparing for, or soliciting others to engage in such acts, and the United States Attorney General can ask for help of the military (section 229E — requests for military assistance to enforce prohibition in certain emergencies) in an emergency situation involving a chemical weapon.

Another part of the CWCIA, Title V(section 501) — Enforcement — provides both civil and criminal penalties for violations of record keeping, declaration and inspection-related violations, ranging from a maximum of US$5,000 on records-related violations to a maximum of US$25,000 per day for wilfully failing or refusing to permit entry or inspection, or disrupting, delaying or otherwise impeding an inspection. These violations generally require wilful action and/or are subject to Constitutional protections, such as requiring a warrant for an inspection. For a routine inspection, administrative warrants are required if consent is not given, but they should not be difficult for the government to obtain. However, for a challenge inspection, a criminal warrant must be obtained if consent is not given, based on an affidavit showing probable cause (which means that the agent seeking the warrant has reasonable basis to believe that a crime has been committed). Although the request for a challenge inspection may normally provide ample evidence of a crime, that may not necessarily be true in all cases.

Both Parts II and V of the CWCIA are subject to confidentiality provisions of Section 404 that prohibit disclosure of CBI, with certain exceptions and substantial penalties including fines, imprisonment up to five years and forfeiture of property, all of which apply to officers and employees of the United States and also to employees of the OPCW Secretariat. Inspectors have immunity from jurisdiction under the Convention, unless the Director-General waives it. That will be discussed further below.

The exceptions effectively include:

- disclosures required by the Freedom Of Information Act, 5 USC 552(a), (which does not extend to CBI disclosed to or acquired by the United States Government);
- information for the OPCW Secretariat or other States Parties in accordance with the Convention;

[2] Division I of Public Law No. 105-277 (1998), codified at title 22, chapter 75 Section 6701 to 6771.
[3] 15 Code of Federal Regulations Part 710 through 722, 30 December 1999.
[4] Senate Executive Resolution 75 of 24 April 1997, in the 105th Congress.

- information formally requested by Committees of Congress, which must still be kept confidential;
- information to be disclosed to United States Federal agencies for enforcement of the CWCIA or any other law, in a manner to preserve confidentiality to the extent practicable without impairing the proceeding; and,
- information disclosed in the national interest after notice to the owner of the CBI and a hearing in case of objections.

The CWCIA defines the CBI to be protected as being any trade secrets or commercial or financial information that is privileged and confidential, including:

- financial data;
- sales and marketing data (other than shipment data);
- pricing data;
- personnel data;
- research data;
- patent data;
- data maintained for compliance with environmental or occupational health and safety regulations;
- personnel and vehicles entering and personnel and personal passenger vehicles exiting the facility;
- any chemical structure;
- any plant design process, technology, or operating method;
- any operating requirement, input, or result that identifies any type or quantity of chemicals used, processed or produced; or,
- any commercial sale, shipment, or use of a chemical.

There is also a further limitation: the information must have been obtained from a United States person, through the United States Government, or through the conduct of an inspection on United States territory under the Convention.

The listing of all these categories as CBI, of course, does not mean they are exempt from disclosures required in declarations or in inspections, but it does identify what must be treated as confidential and not disclosed to the public or to others.

With the exemptions for disclosures to the OPCW and States Parties as required by the Convention and to Federal law enforcement agencies for the enforcement of any law with confidentiality needed only to the extent practicable without impairing the proceeding, there should be much room for legal cooperation. The statute itself does not give guidance on whether "any law" refers only to laws of or in the United States or includes laws of other countries, or perhaps just States Parties. It is not known whether this would slow down any legal cooperation under the Convention, but even with a most conservative interpretation, one can see much cooperation occurring.

In United States judicial proceedings, the court can decide to seal parts of the record to preserve CBI. In administrative hearings under the CWCR, the Administrative Law Judge in charge can also decide, on his or her own motion or at the request of a party, to create a restricted access portion of the record, with no public access.

3. Civil Liability of the United States and Recoupment

If someone's property, including CBI, is taken without just compensation, that person can bring a civil action against the United States in the Court of Federal Claims under Section 103 of the CWCIA — Civil Liability of the United States — or, if it is for less than US$10,000, in a U.S. District Court. One year's notice before filing the claim is required, during which time the United States will pursue diplomatic and other remedies. Then, once the plaintiff establishes a *prima facie* case that acts or omissions of an officer or employee of the OPCW, including an inspector, or of the United States Government, has taken or divulged proprietary information, the burden of proof shifts to the United States Government to disprove the claim.

Provision is also made in Section 103 for similar suits in the District Courts for tort liability. Sovereign immunity of the United States is waived. The United States can bring an action in the District Court for the District of Columbia against any foreign nation to provide indemnification for the actions of an inspector who is a national of that nation, or who acted at the direction or behest of that nation. The United States can also seek redress in actions in international tribunals, or in the courts of the nation of which the inspector is a national. Furthermore, individuals and businesses may sue in the District Courts any foreign national or business entity for an unauthorised or unlawful acquisition, receipt, transmission or use of property by or on behalf of such foreign national or business entity as a result of a tort under United States law, arising from acts or omissions of officers or employees of the United States or any member of an inspection team of the OPCW, taken pursuant to or under the colour of the Convention or the CWCIA.

It is the policy of the United States to recoup all funds paid for any such tort or taking. Sanctions are mandated against any foreign person, officer or employee of the OPCW for whose actions the United States has been held liable for a tort or taking pursuant to the CWCIA, or any foreign person or business entity which knowingly assisted, encouraged or induced in any way a foreign person to publish, divulge, disclose or make known United States CBI in any manner or to any extent not authorised by the Convention. Sanctions may be suspended upon full and complete payment of compensation by the sanctioned person, business entity or country to the United States Government, and the President of the United States can waive certain sanctions on a foreign government if he certifies to Congress that it is necessary to protect the national security interests of the United States.

Sanctions on individuals and business entities provide prohibitions for not less than ten years on many types of transactions, including:

- sale by the United States Government of any items on the United States Munitions List;
- export of any controlled goods or technology from the United States;
- international financial assistance;
- United States Export-Import Bank transactions; and,
- private bank transactions.

Assets will be blocked, for the purpose of recouping funds, in any transaction in any property subject to the jurisdiction of the United States in which the person has any interest whatsoever; and landing rights will be denied for any private aircraft or air carrier owned by such a person, except in safety emergencies.

Sanctions will be imposed for not less than five years on foreign governments which have knowingly assisted, encouraged or induced in any way a person to publish, divulge, disclose, or make known in any manner or to any extent not authorised by the Convention United States CBI. Sanctions include those correlating to the ones on individuals, plus termination of assistance from the United States to the country.

In addition, if an alien to the United States has committed any of the prohibited acts, resulting in financial losses or damages to a United States person for which United States has been found liable for a tort or a taking under the CWCIA, or traffics in United States CBI under similar circumstances, that person shall be excluded from the United States. This means no visas will be granted, existing ones will be revoked, and entry will be denied even if no visa would ordinarily be required. This applies not only to the individuals involved, but also to that person's spouse, minor children or agents. Furthermore, if an entity, such as a corporation, has been involved in an unauthorised disclosure of United States CBI, then all corporate officers, principals, shareholders with a controlling interest, and the spouse, minor children and agents of those persons, also shall be excluded.

If the above sounds severe, it is. The United States Congress decided to provide strong disincentives for anyone violating the confidentiality provisions of the Convention. Again, this need not impede legal cooperation in pursuing violators of the Convention and related legislation, and it may indeed be the basis of offences on which the United States could seek legal cooperation from other States Parties. It does, of course, set a standard for protection of CBI at all times, including during legal cooperation activities.

4. Waiver of Immunity

During the process of advising and consenting to the ratification of the Convention, the United States Senate included certain conditions in its Resolution of Advice and Consent (in contrast to being in traditional binding legislation, as are the other matters discussed above). These include Condition (16) on Protection of Confidential Information, which provides that if the President determines that an officer or employee of the OPCW has wilfully published, divulged, disclosed, or made known in any manner or to any extent not authorised by the Convention any United States CBI coming to him in the course of his employment or official duties, or by reason of any examination or investigation of any return, report or record made to or filed with the OPCW, resulting in financial loss or damages to a United States person, the President shall notify Congress within 30 days. Within 270 days after the notice to Congress, the President shall certify to Congress that the Director-General of the OPCW has waived the person's immunity from jurisdiction. If the President is unable to make that certification, then 50% of the United States annual contribution to the regular budget of the OPCW is to be withheld. This withholding is to last until the President makes that certification, or he certifies to Congress that the situation has been resolved in a manner satisfactory to the United States person who suffered the damages due to the disclosure of United States CBI.

5. Measures to Protect Sensitive Installations and Prevent Disclosure of Confidential Business Information

The Convention itself provides thorough and effective means to protect CBI. The most effective means are to not disclose what is not needed in the first place, either in declarations, during inspections, in legal cooperation or under other circumstances.

For instance, in Section C of the Confidentiality Annex to the Convention, paragraph 13 provides that the State Party may indicate to the inspection team the equipment, documentation or areas that it considers sensitive and not related to the purpose of the inspection. Paragraph 15 says that the inspection teams shall fully respect the procedures designed to protect sensitive installations and to prevent the disclosure of confidential data.

Part X of the Verification Annex to the Convention, on Challenge Inspections, is the location for other rules such as those on managed access[5] which can help greatly in avoiding unnecessary disclosures. Such rules also provide principles useful in doing legal cooperation without getting into CBI which could lead to difficulties with the United States rules on mishandling of CBI. If there is no need to know certain information, then it is safer not to obtain it in the first place. In Section C of Part X, paragraph 41 provides that the inspected State Party has the right under managed access to take such measures as are necessary to protect national security. It does go on to say that the provisions of this paragraph may not be invoked to conceal evasion of obligation not to engage in activities prohibited under the Convention.

These provisions are based on the Convention's Article IX, entitled Consultations, Cooperation and Fact-Finding. Under procedures for challenge inspections, sub-paragraph 11(c) of that Article provides that the inspected State Party has the right to take measures to protect sensitive installations, and to prevent disclosure of confidential information and data, not related to the Convention.

While these measures may have been, at least in part, negotiated into the Convention for protection of national security information and sensitive installations as well as CBI, both during legitimate routine and challenge inspections, and in case of an abusive challenge inspection, they provide a strong basis for avoiding disclosures beyond an inspector's need to know during an inspection. Again, these principles can lead to less exposure of information

[5] See also *infra* in this volume, J. Gilbert, Managed Access Principles Applied within a Judicial Framework.

during legal cooperation, less possibility to get entangled in United States measures to pursue those who act improperly with CBI, and a healthier atmosphere.

Under the provisions of the Confidentiality Annex to the Convention and the managed access parts of the Verification Annex, there are many practical measures an inspected site can take to protect its CBI. Rather than repeating the language of the Convention here, it can be summarised as providing the OPCW inspection team with what it needs to know related to the object and purpose of the Convention, and discretely using good judgement on other information at the plant site. If an atmosphere of cooperation is established, the inspectors are less likely to become suspicious, which could lead to them ask for information not related to the Convention. Alternative means of satisfying requests can avoid the disclosure of unrelated CBI.

6. Conclusion

Whether in declarations, inspections, or legal cooperation to pursue alleged perpetrators, one should seek only information that one needs to know. This can minimise the possibilities of coming into conflict with United States protective measures. Those who need to have United States confidential business information for their work in law enforcement need to be cautious with their handling of it.

United States chemical industry is generally satisfied with protection of its confidential business information available under principles of managed access with the protections available through the Convention and in the provisions of United States law. It is not expected that legal cooperation under the Convention needs to come into conflict with protection of confidential business information.

MANAGED ACCESS PRINCIPLES APPLIED WITHIN A JUDICIAL FRAMEWORK

John A. Gilbert*

1. Introduction

This chapter will address a concept called "managed access". This concept is currently used in some international arms control agreements and has been mentioned elsewhere in this volume.[1] It emerged from efforts undertaken over time to identify effective ways of meeting obligations in the implementation and application of international agreements of various types, while at the same time protecting the interests of the entities concerned and the integrity of the sensitive information. The chapter will first lay the ground work, describing more broadly what managed access is, what types of information it can protect, some ways to manage access, and then present some ideas on how managed access could apply during judicial proceedings.

2. Managed Access

First of all, managed access, despite its somewhat imprecise name, is actually a set of situation-specific methods, techniques, and procedures that can allow the use of important but sensitive information for a very specific purpose. National security information might be extremely critical to an international prosecution, but releasing all available information could jeopardise witnesses or informants or could compromise sensitive and/or unique information sources.[2] Managed access can protect the integrity and confidentiality of the most sensitive information, but will allow proceedings to be effectively conducted by releasing non-critical information. Some examples of what that might involve will be presented further on in this chapter.

Managed access has been widely used during international arms control inspections since at least 1988, when innovative procedures were first used during inspections conducted under the Intermediate-Range Nuclear Forces Treaty. Since then, both formally and in practice, managed access procedures have probably been used in virtually every one of the several thousand inspections conducted to date under the Chemical Weapons Convention and other multilateral and bilateral arms control agreements. Managed access is formally incorporated into the strengthened safeguards on nuclear material that are now entering into force. The Comprehensive Nuclear Test-Ban Treaty and a potential Biological Weapons Convention Verification Protocol both contain specific text relating to managed access use.

* Manager, Arms Control Compliance Division, Science Applications International Corporation (SAIC). Any views expressed are those of the author and are not attributable to SAIC.

[1] See *supra* in this volume, R. Burgess, Protection of Confidential Business Information in Judicial Proceedings.

[2] See *supra* in this volume, N. Paterson, Protecting National Security and Other Confidential Information.

R. Yepes-Enríquez and L. Tabassi. (eds.), Treaty Enforcement and International Cooperation in Criminal Matters

However, managed access methods that have been devised — and others that will be developed and refined in the future — have widespread applicability for purposes that go beyond their original intent. They could increasingly include use in criminal investigations and structured legal proceedings such as formal hearings or criminal trials.

It is not necessary to spend time discussing why it is important to protect sensitive information, but a key consideration is that confidential business information, as well as national security information, can be relevant to investigations and other international proceedings. Preventing the release of proliferation-sensitive information, such as in cases that might involve weapons of mass destruction, was also a major emphasis of some of the other chapters appearing in this volume.

3. Types of Information Requiring Protection

It is important to consider what types of information can be involved in managed access situations and decisions. Obviously, national security information or other sensitive information such as electronic intelligence data, informant statements, witness statements, or information gathered from other means beyond these can be sensitive, and the disclosure of such information requires careful management. Confidential business information can also require protection. For example, details of business transactions such as how much of what is sold at what price may not be relevant to judicial proceedings, but knowledge of what is sold to whom, and some conditions of a sale such as delivery date or location, could be extremely important but not as sensitive to business confidentiality. In this case, some relevant customer and delivery information could be appropriately reviewed, edited, and used. However, other information, such as industrial process parameters, research procedures or results, and patent and trademark data, may deserve protection in almost all cases. Proliferation-sensitive data of many types must also be carefully protected to ensure public safety.

4. Systems of Protection

There are several systems that have been applied successfully in the United States. I will discuss those with some specificity, and will also suggest some general principles that could apply internationally. In particular, attention is drawn to two procedures that are in use in the United States. One is the "Freedom of Information Act" (FOIA), and the other is a special set of "national security court" procedures originally instituted in the 1970's.

4.1 Freedom of Information Act (FOIA)

The FOIA applies to the public release of what is generally considered to be government information, i.e., information that the government has developed itself or that has been provided to the government. Some initial examples of this were environmental research reports and other publications whose disclosure supported the public's right to know about government public works proceedings or government approval of private commercial activities that could have environmental impacts. Over time, the FOIA has been found useful for many other purposes — including international criminal investigations. For example, government information included in documents held by the United States might be pertinent to investigations conducted in Europe.

Those documents that have relevant evidence may also contain sensitive information that cannot be publicly released without causing undue harm or risk. There are provisions in the FOIA, and in other model agreements, to withhold, that is to redact or conceal, certain types of information while releasing all other information that is pertinent to a request. Under the FOIA in the United States, there are criteria that specify how sensitive information is to be protected and describe the appeals process to request exceptional release of even sensitive information under conditions that will balance the competing imperatives of protection and adequate, but limited, disclosure. This is particularly important in cases where there is concern that exculpatory information may have been improperly withheld, but FOIA principles can protect sensitive information that is not essential to an investigation or prosecution and still allow release of remaining information for use in those proceedings.

4.2 NATIONAL SECURITY COURTS

Another managed access application involves a set of procedures that have been applied over time in what is called a "national security court" system in the United States. This was originally established to deal with the difficulty of prosecuting a criminal case — such as espionage — where evidence may largely be derived from sensitive sources such as electronic information.

A number of safeguards were put into place to allow prosecutions to go forward, but also to provide some degree of protection for the sources or the content of the information. Some of these procedures require all court personnel, including advocates for the accused, to respect confidentiality. For example, a defence attorney in this court system, before being allowed access to any of the evidence, agrees to respect its confidentiality and can face penalties for improper release of that information. Conducting occasional closed sessions is also a feature of this set of court procedures, as is keeping evidence under court seal — something which has been done in other types of cases and in other court systems. In this situation, sealed evidence will not become part of the public transcript or public record. It will instead be held under court custody and can be viewed only by those who have agreed to respect its confidentiality.

Another interesting feature of this court system is that there have been situations where information is provided only to the advocates for the accused, but the accused themselves are prohibited from seeing the information. This is particularly important where witness statements or other factors could identify an individual who might then be subject to intimidation or retaliation for having provided evidence or given testimony. This creates situations where defence attorneys have access to information that they cannot pass on to their client, but that they can act upon in constructing and carrying out a defence.

There have also been several innovative ways used to protect witness identities, even during live testimony. For example, a judge and the jury can be provided live video testimony by a witness whose appearance and even voice could be distorted or concealed, and the prosecutor and defence attorney will have an opportunity to question or cross-examine in real time through the video feed. In a case like this, the defendant may not be allowed even to know the identify of the witness, but the defence will still be able to challenge and evaluate the truthfulness and completeness of the testimony that is actually given.

It is particularly useful to examine how managed access can apply more generally during judicial proceedings, and it is fairly common knowledge that sensitive investigations are routinely conducted in many countries. Criminal investigations often proceed close to a conclusion before there is any public knowledge that the investigation is even occurring. In these cases, there probably is not much need for managed access procedures until a critical point has been reached.

4.3 TRANSNATIONAL PRECEDENTS

Transnational proceedings are much more difficult than those conducted entirely within a single national jurisdiction. The differing legal systems in different countries and in different regions are the root of complexity in providing mutual legal assistance internationally.[3] Even the differing traditions of English Common Law and the laws in place in other regions make the rules of evidence much more difficult to deal with on a consistent basis. One result of this may be a negotiated set of procedures to resolve differences that maintains and preserves the integrity of evidence while providing due process for the accused. The following are two examples of cases which had transnational elements and which attracted wide public interest.

First is the recent Lockerbie trial, which was conducted in a unique way. As is well known, the case concerned the bombing of Pan Am flight 103 on 21 December 1988 over Lockerbie, Scotland, killing 270 people. The case resulted in proceedings brought by Libya against the United Kingdom and the United States before the International Court of Justice; criminal proceedings against two Libyan nationals in a specially constituted Scottish court in the Netherlands;[4] and upcoming civil proceedings in New York. However, what is not widely known is that during the evidence collection and investigation process, a great deal of sensitive information came to light. Various countries, not just the United States and the United Kingdom, were able to develop very sensitive evidence that pointed in certain directions and that required even further investigation and ultimately justified the start of formal judicial proceedings. Because of differences in how that information was viewed and treated, there were negotiations at many stages of the investigation and, in essence, access to much of the investigating material itself was managed by the States involved even before being exchanged between investigators. This added length and complexity to the process, but the fact that there was a verdict in this case — after more than ten years — does speak for the fact that some of these procedures were, in fact, effective.

Another case that can be mentioned is directly related to chemical weapons production. In the early 1990's evidence came to light during United Nations Special Commission inspections in Iraq that indicated some material exported by a company in the United States had ultimately arrived in Iraq and was used as an ingredient in manufacturing chemical agent. However, there was no direct chain of evidence that led from the barrels of thiodyglycol

[3] See *supra* in this volume, K. Prost, Toward Meaningful Adherence to Multilateral Instruments for International Cooperation: The Challenges to Effective Mutual Legal Assistance.

[4] See further, A. Aust, *Lockerbie: the Other Case*, 49 International and Comparative Law Quarterly, Part 2 278-296 (2000).

found at an Iraqi chemical weapons production site back to the front door and the front office of the originating company in the United States. That discovery precipitated a fairly lengthy, complicated, and sensitive investigation which led through Europe. As evidence was developed, several sensitive sources came to light. There was, in fact, testimony from people who had knowledge of import/export transactions that could not be fully shared by all participants, and there was also confidential business information involving the European firms that took part in those transactions. Again, this was a fairly lengthy process, but it did result in prosecution and judicial resolution in the United States.

5. Conclusion

Obviously, managed access procedures could be applied during field investigations, interviews, preparation of evidence and the actual conduct of trials themselves, whether conducted nationally or internationally. I would like to suggest that managed access procedures can apply broadly to judicial proceedings if they are accepted by all participants. This is one of the keys — that managed access is, in essence, a negotiated way of sharing critical information and protecting sensitive information. Some procedures can be standardised. In doing so, it is important to realise that selecting proper precedents and cases where those precedents have worked, identifying factors common to a variety of situations, careful negotiation respecting the interests of all involved, and knowledgeable involvement of international organisations can ensure success.

In conclusion, I would like to note that managed access procedures and techniques have been applied in many ways — and probably for much longer than the last 13 years — to protect sensitive information. These procedures have allowed the use of critical information for inspections and investigations and the procedures have actually been used in trials. Wider application is possible in the future, particularly as international non-proliferation and arms control regimes advance. Successful implementation will require creativity, patience and commitment by the organisations, States and individual participants involved.

CONFIDENTIALITY AND JUDICIAL PROCEEDINGS: THE REGIME UNDER THE CHEMICAL WEAPONS CONVENTION AND THE CONFIDENTIALITY COMMISSION

Eric P.J. Myjer*

1. Introduction

One of the special features of the Chemical Weapons Convention[1] ("Convention") is its confidentiality regime. The fact that the Convention has a Confidentiality Annex especially devoted to the protection of confidential information underlines the special character of this treaty. This fact also points to one of the very sensitive areas encountered when negotiating the Convention, for the Convention concerns confidential business information as well as confidential military security information. Since verification of the chemical industry is essential to realising the purpose of the chemical weapons ban, heavy involvement of civilian chemical industries is necessary in the supervision process via declarations or inspections of chemical plants.

It is not surprising, then, that there was strong pressure from the chemical industry during negotiation of the Convention to include obligations to preserve the confidentiality of business information received by the OPCW in the course of verification activities. States Parties and their private industries had to be certain that there would be a sufficient deterrent to ensure that verifying inspectors, the Technical Secretariat and even States Parties who had received information would protect its confidentiality.[2] Therefore both grounds — the protection of military security and the protection of confidential business information — led to the adoption of a Confidentiality Annex to the Convention, the establishment of the Confidentiality Commission as a subsidiary organ of the Conference of States Parties, under paragraph 23 of that Annex, and more in general to the development of the Convention's special confidentiality regime with its deterrent effect.

These measures are some of the unique characteristics of the Convention, and they make it clear that the confidentiality of sensitive information will be maintained under all

*Associate Professor of Public International Law, Utrecht University; Member of the OPCW Confidentiality Commission since 1997.

[1] 1993 Convention on the Prohibition of the Development, Production, Stockpiling and Use of Chemical Weapons and on Their Destruction, entered into force on 29 April 1997. Text, as corrected and changed, available at http://www.opcw.org.

[2] In general, see E.P.J. Myjer, *The Organization for the Prohibition of Chemical Weapons: Moving Closer Towards an Iinternational Arms Control Organization ? A Quantum Leap in the Institutional Law of Arms Control* in E.P.J. Myjer (ed.), Issues of Arms Control Law and the Chemical Weapons Convention (2001) at 61-139, in particular, 100 *et seq.*

R. Yepes-Enríquez and L. Tabassi. (eds.), Treaty Enforcement and International Cooperation in Criminal Matters

circumstances. The Confidentiality Annex contains the general principles for the handling of confidential information. Those general principles were further detailed in an extensive document adopted by the Conference of the States Parties after entry into force of the Convention: the OPCW Policy on Confidentiality.[3]

An essential precondition of the deterrent effect of the confidentiality regime is the effectiveness of the response to cases of a breach of confidentiality. This may take place through either special procedures foreseen on the basis of, or under, the Convention, or through national procedures, but in both cases the protection of confidentiality is the crucial element. When these procedures involve individuals or private entities in judicial or semi-judicial proceedings, however, a dilemma arises: how does a state sustain confidentiality in these proceedings while still meeting the standards essential to a "democratic constitutional State," including (procedural) transparency,[4] participation, and accountability, which are reflected in fair proceedings?[5]

It is an accepted axiom that "justice needs to be seen to be done." Maintaining a high degree of transparency and openness is indeed an essential characteristic of judicial proceedings, for it ensures due process, as described in several human rights conven-tions,[6] even when breaches of confidentiality concerning national security or confidential business information are at issue. At the same time, however, the expectation that confidentiality will be maintained during the judicial proceedings is not surprising. A similar tension exists between the need for transparency under the duty to provide information, which is essential to the Convention's compliance control model, and the simultaneous need for protection of its confidentiality.[7]

Given these conflicting requirements — (informational) transparency versus confidentiality — the Convention introduces a special confidentiality regime in its Confidentiality Annex, establishing the Confidentiality Commission as a subsidiary organ of the Conference of the States Parties to settle disputes "related to confidentiality"[8] for breaches involving both a State Party and the OPCW. Against the background of the OPCW Policy of Confidentiality, specific Operating Procedures of the Confidentiality Commission were approved, and a special Registry Agreement was concluded between the

---

[3] OPCW doc. C-I/DEC.13 (16 May 1997).

[4] I make the distinction between procedural transparency and informational transparency. With the latter I refer to the demands of the supervisory mechanism of the Convention to provide the necessary information to demonstrate compliance with the commitments under the Convention.

[5] See C.H. Brants, P.A.M. Mevis, E. Prakken, *Legitieme Strafvordering*, Rechten van de mens als inspiraties in de 21ste eeuw (Legitimate Criminal Proceedings, Human Rights as Inspiration in the 21st Century) (2001) at 7.

[6] Compare Article 6 of the 1950 European Convention on the Protection of Human Rights and Fundamental Freedoms (the European Convention on Human Rights), or Article 14 of the International Covenant on Civil and Political Rights.

[7] Compare *supra* in this volume, T. Dunworth, Confidentiality Obligations of States Parties to the Chemical Weapons Convention and National Implementation: the New Zealand Experience. See also Myjer, *supra* note 2, at 130.

[8] Confidentiality Annex, paragraph 23.

OPCW and the Permanent Court of Arbitration to ensure fairness of procedure and enhance the protection of information[9] during any eventual proceedings.

The aim of this chapter is to examine whether and how the procedures foreseen in the context of the Convention's confidentiality regime respond to the criteria of a democratic constitutional State and to see if this examination leads us to some general conclusions. Specifically, these criteria include the dilemma outlined above: promoting procedural transparency and fairness, while at the same time maintaining confidentiality. This subject matter coincides, to a certain extent, with other contributions in this volume,[10] but my emphasis is on the procedures of response to a breach, either by national civil servants under the jurisdiction of States Parties or by international civil servants employed by the OPCW.

It is not surprising that States Parties' possible exercise of national jurisdiction (which could occur should the Director-General waive jurisdictional immunity in the case of a serious breach of confidentiality by a staff member) remains a central issue within the confidentiality regime, for it was one of the unresolved issues mentioned in the Final Report of the Preparatory Commission for the OPCW.[11] The possibility of concurrent jurisdiction between the Host Country and the State of the suspect's nationality, or the State where the breach took place, was also an issue.[12] These and other issues of confidentiality were topics that lead to heated debates, highlighting the crucial interest that States Parties attach to the issue of confidentiality and breaches thereof.

[9] In its decision of 5 December 1997, the Conference appointed the International Bureau of the Permanent Court of Arbitration in The Hague to serve as the Registry of the Confidentiality Commission. (OPCW doc. C-II/DEC.14, dated 5 December 1997) reprinted in L. Tabassi (ed.), OPCW: The Legal Texts at 512 (1999).

[10] See *supra* in this volume, Section II.3, Intrusive International Control Regimes and Breaches of Confidentiality: Aspects of the Exercise of National Jurisdiction, and Section IV.2, Prosecution of Individual Violators of the Chemical Weapons Convention: Scope and Possible Legal Framework for Compliance with Article VII(2). There, however, the emphasis is mainly on the improved regime in this respect of the IAEA (Laura Rockwood); possible actions in the courts of the host country (both criminal and civil) (Faiza Patel King); the New Zealand experience of national implementation arrangements with regard to assuring States Parties' obligation that information received will be accorded the necessary confidentiality protection (paragraph 4 of the Confidentiality Annex) (Treasa Dunworth); and how to discipline international officials effectively in case of breach of confidentiality (Paul Szasz).

[11] Compare the following unresolved issues listed in Section Four, Part 4, B. IV. Confidentiality, of the Final Report of the Preparatory Commission for the OPCW (PC-XVI/37, 15 April 1997), at 52:

> 115. The States Parties' possible exercise of national jurisdiction in the event that immunity from jurisdiction is waived by the Director-General in the case of a serious breach of confidentiality by a staff member of the Technical Secretariat, including the possibility of concurrent jurisdiction.
>
> 116. Any further proposals relating to the general issue of the application of national jurisdiction to natural or legal persons who have breached confidentiality.
>
> 117. Any further proposals that may be made concerning compensation for losses caused by breach of confidentiality.

[12] See Discussion Paper by the Executive Secretary on Breaches of Confidentiality: Liability for Damages and Prosecution through Penal Action (Preparatory Commission doc. PC-X/B/WP.3, 21 December 1994) and Note by the Executive Secretary on the Workshop on Legal Aspects of Breaches of Confidentiality (Preparatory Commission document PC-XIV/B/4, 12 June 1996).

Here the emphasis will be primarily on the protection of confidential information, be it related to national security or business, in judicial or semi-judicial proceedings. How, in other words, can the required level of confidentiality be maintained in potential judicial procedures concerning an actual breach? Given the sensitivity of the subject matter, this is a crucial topic. In the following paragraphs, therefore, I will address: a description of the confidentiality regime and the position of the Confidentiality Commission; confidentiality-related disputes and judicial proceedings; the tension between the principle of a fair trial in (semi-) judicial proceedings and the demands of maintaining confidentiality, including the view of the European Court of Human Rights in the cases of *Fitt v. UK* and *Jasper v. UK*; the protection of confidentiality and the procedural requirements of *Fitt v. UK* and *Jasper v. UK*; whether a more active role of the Confidentiality Commission in compliance control can be envisaged; and, in conclusion, some general observations.

2. Confidentiality and the Chemical Weapons Convention

2.1 The Confidentiality Regime of the Convention

The conclusion of a comprehensive arms control agreement on chemical weapons made a comprehensive compliance control system imperative. The Convention foresees the OPCW as a specialised international organisation whose sole purpose is the supervision of the commitments under this specific arms control treaty. Although this is not the appropriate place to expand on this model as an example of compliance management,[13] it is important to keep this design in mind. Characteristic of this model of management of Convention compliance commitments is the high degree of informational transparency resulting from the constant stream of information from national declarations, clarifications, or international inspections. In general, the information is highly sensitive, since it may involve information touching upon national security or confidential business information. For that reason, the Convention introduces a stringent confidentiality regime whereby both States Parties[14] and the OPCW[15] are under a duty to preserve the confidentiality of the information provided to them. The Confidentiality Annex to the Convention is central to this regime.

The Confidentiality Annex establishes the Confidentiality Commission as a subsidiary organ of the Conference of the States Parties whose function is to settle disputes "related to confidentiality."[16] The Conference subsequently adopted the detailed OPCW Policy on Confidentiality,[17] which deals, *inter alia*, with the OPCW Classification System for Confidential Information, General Principles for Handling and Protection of Confidential Information, and Breach Procedures. Breach investigation procedures are addressed in four steps (Part IX.1), followed by the Rules governing the Confidentiality Commission (Part IX.2) and the role of States Parties in relation to breach procedures (Part IX.3). Four possible scenarios are envisaged[18] in which a State Party's obligations concerning confidentiality could arise.

---

[13] See E.P.J. Myjer, *supra* note 2, at 127.
[14] See Article VII(6) of the Convention.
[15] See Article VIII(5) of the Convention.
[16] Confidentiality Annex, paragraph 23.
[17] OPCW Policy on Confidentiality (OPCW doc. C-I/DEC.13, 16 May 1997), reprinted in OPCW: The Legal Texts, *supra* note 9, at 209-251.
[18] Part IX.3, paragraph 2.

The two most important to the topic at hand are (1) a breach of confidentiality for which a State Party is directly responsible, or (2) a breach of confidentiality by a legal or natural person in the jurisdiction of a State Party. The other two scenarios are that of an OPCW investigation into a breach, or alleged breach, of confidentiality, or a waiver of immunity by the OPCW Director General in the event of a serious breach of confidentiality. The Confidentiality Commission may be involved, depending upon the particular breach.

2.2 THE CONFIDENTIALITY COMMISSION

It is clear that the Confidentiality Commission will only deal with cases involving a breach of confidentiality. This leaves aside potential breaches of other commitments under the Convention. Furthermore, it will, in principle, concern breaches involving both a State Party and the OPCW. The Operating Procedures of the Confidentiality Commission distinguish between three kinds of disputes:

- Disputes pursuant to paragraph 23 of the Confidentiality Annex, to be initiated by the Director-General on behalf of the OPCW or by one or more States Parties;[19]
- Disputes pursuant to paragraph 4 of Article XIV of the Convention, when the Conference entrusts the Confidentiality Commission with a dispute relating to Confidentiality other than the one mentioned above;[20] and,
- Disputes between two or more States Parties, or between one or more States Parties and the OPCW, relating to the interpretation or application of the Convention, where the Confidentiality Commission is chosen by them to consider a dispute concerning a matter of confidentiality as a means of resolving their dispute.[21]

The Commission is a body composed of 20 members, nominated by the five regional groups and appointed by the Conference, whose terms last two years and who are limited to three consecutive terms. Members serve in their personal capacity and have a background in one or more of the relevant fields of work of the Confidentiality Commission.[22] The Commission will primarily make use of mediation, fact finding and conciliation as its means of dispute settlement. When the parties so agree, arbitration is also possible.

Not only are the Operating Procedures of the Confidentiality Commission detailed, but they also stress the element of fair proceedings. With some minor amendments, the Operating Procedures provide for the use of the Permanent Court of Arbitration Optional Conciliation Rules, as well as the Permanent Court of Arbitration Optional Rules for Arbitration involving International Organisations and States, or, as appropriate, the

[19] Rule 12 of the Operating Procedures of the Confidentiality Commission (OPCW doc. C-III/DEC.10, 27 November 1998), reprinted in OPCW: The Legal Texts, *supra* note 9, at 502.
[20] *Id.*, Rule 13.
[21] *Id.*, Rule 14.
[22] "Nominees should be proposed by States Parties on the basis of individual competence, integrity and background in one or more fields relevant to the work of the Confidentiality Commission, such as dispute resolution of various types; the confidentiality and verification provisions of the Convention; the chemical industry; military security; data security; international law; and national legal systems" OPCW Policy on Confidentiality (OPCW doc. C-I/DEC.13, 16 May 1997, Part IX.2, para 1.3), reprinted in OPCW: The Legal Texts, *supra* note 9, at 245.

Permanent Court of Arbitration Optional Rules for Arbitrating Disputes between two States. The Operating Procedures are innovative because they provide for a separate Registry to receive the complaints addressed to the Confidentiality Commission. Since a dispute related to confidentiality will, in principle, involve the OPCW, it was thought that the OPCW would be at an inappropriate advantage if the Technical Secretariat acted as the Registry and complaints had to be sent to it. The Conference therefore appointed the International Bureau of the Permanent Court of Arbitration in The Hague to serve as the Registry of the Confidentiality Commission. A Registry Agreement between the OPCW and the Permanent Court of Arbitration was signed in December 1998.

Given the subject matter discussed, the proceedings are confidential and the final report with findings and conclusions will not contain confidential information. There may, however, be a confidential annex.[23] It can be held, then, that the Convention's confidentiality regime provides for a dispute settlement body that combines a high degree of fairness in its procedural rules with the preservation of confidentiality.

3. Confidentiality Related Disputes and Judicial Proceedings

What possible judicial proceedings can be envisaged involving confidential information related to national security or business information?

On the one hand, there is the possibility that, within a State, there is a breach of confidentiality regarding information the National Authority has received from either the OPCW or from the national chemical industry.

On the other hand, there may be a breach by a (former) OPCW staff member regarding information held by the OPCW. There also may be a breach regarding information that has come to the knowledge of a (former) OPCW staff member in the course of inspections, or otherwise, but which is not information that a particular State Party has declared to the OPCW.

In the first case there is, of course, the possibility of proceedings at the national level. Given that each State Party has agreed to "treat as confidential and afford special handling to information and data it receives from the Organization"[24] and to "cooperate and support the Director-General in investigating any breach or alleged breach of confidentiality and in taking appropriate action in case a breach has been established,"[25] a breach should, in principle, lead to a national judicial proceeding (criminal, administrative or even civil). More generally, it seems highly likely that in these instances there will be a breach of a State Party's national confidentiality system, which will be covered by national legislation. Furthermore, there may be national procedures concerning Article I obligations that may involve confidential information.

[23] "The final report shall not contain confidential information. The Confidentiality Commission may, however, include in a special annex to its final report such confidential details as it deems necessary for the implementation of conclusions contained in the report. The annex shall be classified and shall be made available only in accordance with the Confidentiality Policy." Rule 36(b) of the Operating Procedures of the Confidentiality Commission, reprinted in OPCW: The Legal Texts, *supra* note 9, at 508.

[24] Article VII, paragraph 6.

[25] Confidentiality Annex, paragraph 21.

In all of these procedures we may reencounter the conflict between the principles of procedural transparency and the demand for the preservation of confidentiality. This may cause problems, for even if there is non-disclosure of material, or a case is dealt with *in camera* (behind closed doors), such procedures may conflict with the right to a fair trial[26] since "[i]n the determination of his civil rights and obligations or of any criminal charge against him, everyone is entitled to a fair and public hearing...."[27] Most human rights instruments do permit the restriction that "the press and public may be excluded from all or part of the trial in the interest of morals, public order or national security." Such an exception to this basic right on grounds of national security may lead to a tension, for it will have to be weighed. And beyond all these concerns, it is still an open question whether a court session "behind closed doors" would preserve the confidentiality of the allegedly breached material, since the court proceeding would not only involve judges, prosecutors and lawyers, but also court personnel.

These cases possess an important international dimension as well, since the dispute may concern a breach of confidentiality regarding information belonging to another State Party or to the OPCW. The Director-General will first have to be asked to investigate the matter. If this investigation finds that a State Party appears responsible, a proceeding before the Confidentiality Commission seems appropriate.[28] The Confidentiality Commission may also be involved if, after the Director-General has made the proper investigation,[29] the OPCW appears to be implicated in either an inadvertent or intentional-breach.

There may, therefore, be two types of procedures, the first on the national level within the national jurisdiction, and the second on the international level within the context of the confidentiality regime. Which criteria need to be applied to each in order to satisfy the demands of both confidentiality and a fair trial?

4. Maintaining Confidentiality in (semi-) Judicial Proceedings and the Demands of a Fair Trial: the Cases of *Fitt v. the UK* and *Jasper v. the UK*

In judicial proceedings, be they of a private, administrative or criminal law character, the question may arise as to what extent certain information can be kept confidential while maintaining a procedure that meets the minimum standards for a fair proceeding. Take the example of a procedure whereby a chemical industry enterprise wants to obtain damages from an inspector for willingly passing on, to a competitor of that enterprise, confidential business information obtained during the course of an OPCW inspection. To what extent should all the relevant evidence be presented in a public session of the court for all to hear? Another case might be a criminal procedure under national penal legislation for violation

[26] See Article 6 European Convention on Human Rights; Article 14 International Covenant on Civil and Political Rights.

[27] Article 6 of the European Convention on Human Rights.

[28] "If an investigation finds that a State Party appears responsible for a breach, the Confidentiality Commission may be convened in case of disputes to consider the case in accordance with paragraph 23 of the Confidentiality Annex and the detailed procedures established for the Confidentiality Commission." Part IX, subparagraph 11.3 of the OPCW Policy on Confidentiality (OPCW doc. C-I/DEC.13, 16 May 1997), reprinted in OPCW: The Legal Texts, *supra* note 9, at 244.

[29] Confidentiality Annex, paragraph 19.

of an Article I obligation under the Convention. I leave aside the question of the extent to which judges, as organs of the State, might cause a violation of an international obligation by the State if they decide to allow information classified as confidential under the Convention's confidentiality regime to be presented in a public court session.

The more narrow issue at stake is how a fair trial can be ensured when not all evidence is being disclosed to both parties. With certain variations this may be the case in either common law or civil law procedures. Since the European Court on Human Rights has the duty to uphold, amongst other things, the fair trial principles embedded in the European Convention for the Protection of Human Rights and Fundamental Freedoms (the European Convention on Human Rights), in this context it is interesting to see what its views are on this matter. A recent case is *Fitt v. the United Kingdom.*[30] It concerns a case of attempted robbery in which the applicant was arrested on the basis of information the police had received. He was consequently convicted of conspiracy to rob, possession of a firearm and possession of a prohibited weapon and was sentenced to eleven years imprisonment.

In this case the prosecutor applied *ex parte* to the trial judge for an order that he should not be required to disclose certain material to the defence. The trial judge (Crown Court) was satisfied that there was a correct application by the prosecution, and he refused to order disclosure. The Court of Appeal upheld the judge's decision to not order disclosure. That decision was brought to the European Court of Human Rights on the grounds that the proceedings before the Crown Court and the Court of Appeal amounted to a violation of the European Convention on Human Rights, Article 6(1) in conjunction with Article 6(3)(b) and (d), since any failure to disclose relevant evidence undermined the applicant's right to a fair trial.

The applicant agreed that the right to full disclosure was not absolute and could "in pursuit of a legitimate aim such as the protection of *national security* or of vulnerable witnesses or sources of information, be subject to limitations,"[31] but argued that such restrictions should be strictly proportionate and counterbalanced by procedural safeguards adequate to compensate for the handicap imposed on the defence. The applicant also held that it was necessary for the purposes of Article 6 "to counterbalance the exclusion of the defence from the procedure by the introduction of an adversarial element, such as the appointment of an independent counsel."[32] Translated to the topic under discussion, it concerns the question of how to balance the fundamental requirement of disclosure, which allows for a proper adversarial procedure, with the requirement of the protection of confidentiality for reasons of national security.

The European Court on Human Rights held that there was no breach of Article 6(1) (right to a fair trial) in this case. The Court stressed that indeed "it is a fundamental aspect of the right to a fair trial that criminal proceedings, including the elements of such proceedings which relate to procedure, should be adversarial and that there should be equality of arms between the prosecution and defence." This means that both prosecution and defence must be given the opportunity "to have knowledge of and comment on the observations filed and evidence adduced by the other party..." "However, ... the entitlement to disclosure

[30] European Court of Human Rights, case of *Fitt v. the United Kingdom* (application no. 29777/96, 16 February 2000).
[31] Emphasis added.
[32] *Id.*, paragraph 39.

is not an absolute right" since "there may be competing interests, such as *national security considerations*.... However, only such measures restricting the rights of the defence which are *strictly necessary* are permissible under article 6 para. 1."[33] Such determination is for the national court to make. The role of the European Court is to scrutinise the national decision-making procedure "to ensure that, as far as possible, it complied with the requirements to provide adversarial proceedings and equality of arms and incorporated adequate safeguards to protect the interests of the accused." Although in a number of procedures the United Kingdom has introduced the possibility of a special council, for instance, in certain cases involving national security,[34] the Court did not hold that this was necessary in the present case where the defence was able to argue for disclosure. The Court also noted that the undisclosed material formed no part of the prosecution case and was never put to the jury.[35] Furthermore, the Court considered that, in this particular procedure, the need for disclosure was at all times under assessment by the trial judge, which provided a "further, important, safeguard in that it was his duty to monitor throughout the trial the fairness or otherwise of the evidence being withheld."[36] The Court was of the opinion that "... it can be assumed...that the judge applied the principles which had recently been clarified by the [UK, author] Court of Appeal...."[37] The Court then concludes that "the jurisprudence of the English Court of Appeal shows that the assessment which the trial judge must make fulfils the conditions which ... are essential for ensuring a fair trial in instances of non-disclosure of prosecution material." In other words, the applied standards were in conformity with the relevant principles of fair trial, which lead the Court to conclude "*..that, as far as possible, the decision-making procedure complied with the requirements of adversarial proceedings and equality of arms and incorporated adequate safeguards to protect the interests of the accused.*"[38]

On the same day the Court delivered an almost identical judgment in the case *Jasper v. UK*. This case involved an individual in the United Kingdom who was caught delivering approximately three tonnes of cannabis resin concealed in a consignment of frozen meat imported from Zeebrugge, and who was charged with fraudulent evasion of the prohibition on the importation of cannabis. The arrest of the suspect was based on information obtained by the police. In this case the prosecution made an *ex parte* application to the trial judge to withhold material on the grounds of public interest immunity. The defence was notified that such an application was to be made, but was not informed of the category of material which the prosecution sought to withhold. The defence, however, had the chance to outline their case to the trial judge and to request that the judge order disclosure of any evidence relating to these alleged facts. The trial judge examined the material in question and ruled that it should not be disclosed. The defence was not informed of the reasons for the judge's decision.[39] The defendant wanted to know "whether any potentially relevant

---

[33] Emphasis added. The Court continued: "Moreover, in order to ensure that the accused receives a fair trial, any difficulties caused to the defence by a limitation on its rights must be sufficiently counterbalanced by the procedures followed by the judicial authorities."

[34] See *Id.*, paragraph 30.

[35] *Id.*, paragraph 48.

[36] *Id.*, paragraph 49.

[37] "...for example that in weighing the public interest in concealment against the interest of the accused in disclosure, great weight should be attached to the interests of justice, and that the judge should continue to assess the need for disclosure throughout the progress of the trial." *Id.*, para. 49.

[38] *Id.*, paragraph 50. Emphasis added.

[39] European Court of Human Rights, *Jasper v. The United Kingdom* (16 February 2000), paragraph 9.

material, apart from the subject matter of the *ex parte* application, had not been disclosed." The Court issued an identical judgment on the same grounds as *Fitt v. UK*, with a minor exception regarding a possible telephone intercept.[40]

5. The Protection of Confidentiality and the Procedural Requirements of *Fitt v. UK* and *Jasper v. UK*

What lessons do *Fitt v. UK* and *Jasper v. UK* have for us regarding the need to maintain confidentiality and simultaneously assure a fair trial? To start with, both cases reaffirm the basic right to a fair trial and stress some of its conditions. The conditions include, as a rule, that procedures should be adversarial, that there should be equality of arms for both sides, the prosecution and the defence, and that this includes the right to disclosure. The Court, however, makes it clear that the right to disclosure is not absolute. The right may be limited in cases where there are competing interests, such as national security considerations, but that only those measures that are *strictly necessary* are permissible. This is, in the Court's view, for the national judge to decide. It is obvious that, in that respect, the European Court sees only a marginal role for itself. In other words, *national security considerations* are a strictly qualified exception, and do not amount to (an automatic) right to confidentiality.

The Court referred to the possibility of a special council in cases involving national security — as was a possibility in the United Kingdom in cases involving national security. It also referred to a situation where the defendant was able to argue for disclosure and the need for disclosure was under constant assessment by the trial judge. In other words, in order to respond to the criteria of a fair trial, the necessity for confidentiality had to be counterbalanced by either a special council or a judge who, to a certain extent, had assumed this role. Interestingly, this introduces an element of the civil law inquisitorial system where the judge has an active role. In both these instances, though the defendant may not be fully informed, someone is acting on his behalf, with his interests in mind.

Almost paradoxically, however, there does not seem much point in maintaining strict confidentiality via non-disclosure *vis-à-vis* the defendant in a procedure, given that he or she

[40] Another tension regarding the issue of disclosure is the case where non-disclosure is argued in order to facilitate the freedom of expression. Such a case is that of *Goodwin v. UK*. This case concerned a journalist who was provided with confidential information about a private corporation. The information had been derived from the corporation's confidential corporate plan. The High Court granted an application by the corporation for an *ex parte* interim injunction restraining the publishers from publishing any information derived from the corporate plan. The High Court ordered the journalist to disclose his notes. He appealed to the Court of Appeal and to the House of Lords, arguing that disclosure of his notes was not "necessary in the interest of justice". The appeal was dismissed, and the House of Lords upheld the Court of Appeal's decision. The journalist argued that the disclosure order "requiring him to reveal the identity of his source and the fine imposed upon him for refusing to do so constituted a violation of Article 10" (freedom of expression) (paragraph 27). The Court concluded that the disclosure order merely served to reinforce the injunction, and the additional restriction on freedom of expression which it entailed was not supported by sufficient reason for the purposesof Article 10(2) of the European Convention on Human Rights. The Court made it clear that the exceptions to this right under Article 10(2) "tip the balance of competing interests in favour of the interest of democratic society in securing a free press." The Court was therefore of the opinion that "both the order requiring the applicant to reveal his source and the fine imposed upon him for having refused to do so gave rise to a violation of his right to freedom of expression under Article 10" (paragraph 46).

will generally know the (secret) nature of the issue at stake. Take, for instance, a suspected breach by an OPCW inspector. The necessity for maintaining confidentiality is determined by the need not to let the information become (even more) public. Under such circumstances, for reasons of national security, the judge (court) may determine that, in order to maintain maximum confidentiality, there should be an exception to the rule of a public hearing and the court session should be held *in camera* instead. As discussed above, such a decision by the court or tribunal in question seems to be in line with the judgments of the European Court of Human Rights, for both aim to restrict information flow for reasons of national security. Here again there is a strict criterion, for the Court may decide to restrict only what is absolutely necessary.

Very interesting in this respect are the managed access procedures and techniques described elsewhere in this volume[41] whereby, via a set of methods, techniques and procedures, the use of important but sensitive information can be allowed for a very specific purpose. Of particular interest is the "national security court system" in the United States. Under this system some procedures apparently require all court personnel, including advocates for the accused, to respect confidentiality, and there are occasional closed sessions or evidence may be kept under court seal.[42]

Irrespective of whether a case concerns a State Party that is also party to the European Convention on Human Rights, some of the implications for both national and international procedures seem clear. The right to a fair trial is one of those basic human rights having a customary law character,[43] and the jurisprudence of the European Court of Human Rights can be regarded as an authoritative reading of the state of international human rights law in this respect.[44] In national proceedings, be they criminal or civil, a procedure can still be deemed to be fair if, for reasons of national security, the confidentiality of certain information needs to be maintained. This could be done via non-disclosure or, to a lesser extent, via a court session *in camera*. The lesser extent refers to the fact that, under those circumstances, a substantial number of people will still have knowledge of the confidential information.

6. A More Active Role for the Confidentiality Commission in Compliance Control?

When it is established at the international level, either by the OPCW Director-General during his investigation or by the Confidentiality Commission, that there has been a breach by a (former) staff member, or when that appears highly likely, what would be the most proper course of action? Several possible actions have been mentioned, administrative, criminal or civil in nature. This raises questions as to whether the most appropriate venue would be the country of nationality, the host country of the OPCW (the Netherlands), or the country where the crime has taken place. Whatever the outcome of that debate, it is

[41] See *supra* in this volume, J.A. Gilbert, Managed Access Principles Applied within a Judicial Framework.
[42] *Id.*
[43] This fundamental right to a fair trial is generally regarded as an expression of customary law, although there is still a difference of opinion on the exact contents of this right. See, for different formulations, Article 10 of the Universal Declaration of Human Rights; Article 4 of the International Convention on Civil and Political Rights; Article 6 of the European Convention on Human Rights; and Article 8 of the American Convention on Human Rights.
[44] A source in the sense of Article 38 of the Statute of the International Court of Justice.

highly likely that one will again be faced with the dilemma of balancing procedural transparency with the protection of confidential information. Given the special position of the Confidentiality Commission within the confidentiality regime of the Chemical Weapons Convention, it seems worthwhile to study the possibility of giving the Confidentiality Commission a role in following up the action(s) taken against a natural or legal person for breach of confidentiality, thereby enhancing its role in compliance control.

What kind of role could that be? Would it, for instance, not be possible to have the Confidentiality Commission decide on some form of pecuniary sanction against the natural person that has breached confidentiality, and even against natural or legal persons that have benefited from that breach? It could be decided, for instance, that in all cases in which it has been established, by either the Director-General or the Commission itself, that when there has been an instance of intentional breach by a (former) staff member, the Confidentiality Commission (first by a panel, followed by approval of the full Commission) decides on a form of pecuniary sanction as compensation for the injured party. For such a course there would have to be agreement amongst States Parties, and a formal, multilateral agreement would have to be created stipulating that such a pecuniary award shall be executed in the State Party of the nationality, or the State Party in which the natural person is resident or has attachable property.

The main advantage of involving the Confidentiality Commission is that one stays within the confidentiality regime of the Convention in the narrow sense.[45] This ensures a high degree of protection, as is clearly reflected, for instance, in Rule 19 of the Operating Procedures of the Confidentiality Commission, which deal extensively with the preservation of confidentiality. Furthermore, both the Operating Procedures of the Confidentiality Commission and the applicable Permanent Court of Arbitration rules foresee fairness in any proceeding, as is also exemplified by the separate Registry Agreement. The rules already provide for mediation, fact-finding, conciliation or arbitration. Admittedly, the criteria for appointment of the members are not comparable with those for a judicial office in different legal systems.[46] Nevertheless, if one would look upon it as an administrative sanction by a subsidiary organ of the OPCW, or alternatively as a decision by the Confidentiality Commission in special composition as an arbitral tribunal, this would not matter, provided that there is at least one qualified lawyer sitting on the panel dealing with the matter.

This is just one example of the possible involvement of the Confidentiality Commission. With these special characteristics of the Confidentiality Commission in mind, and given the conflicting requirements of transparency and confidentiality, it seems worthwhile to also consider other possibilities to better use the mechanisms which have already been provided for under the Convention. The Confidentiality Commission is best equipped to deal with different aspects of breaches of confidentiality within the confidentiality regime, and can thereby instil the necessary trust, which is also aimed for by the transparency rule in "regular" judicial proceedings.

---

[45] By the Confidentiality Regime in the *narrow sense*, I refer to the Confidentiality Regime as exclusively handled by the OPCW. For the Confidentiality Regime in the *broad sense*, see *infra*, note 47.

[46] Compare "The judges shall be chosen from among persons of high moral character, impartiality and integrity who possess the qualifications required in their respective States for appointment to the highest judicial offices." (Article 36, paragraph 3(a), of the Rome Statute of the International Criminal Court) (17 July 1998).

7. Concluding Observations

All national procedures regarding a Convention-related breach of confidentiality, whether of a criminal, civil or administrative nature, and irrespective of whether they concern national security information or confidential business information, should ultimately lead to a reaction at the international level since it involves the confidentiality regime of the Convention in the broad sense.[47] Under these circumstances, maximum use should be made of the existing subsidiary organ of the OPCW in the area of confidentiality, namely, the Confidentiality Commission, and the procedures specifically agreed upon by States Parties to facilitate the protection of information they have designated as confidential. It is clear that, for certain types of disputes concerning breaches of confidentiality, the best solution is to stay within the confidentiality regime of the Convention and utilise the Confidentiality Commission as a subsidiary organ of the Conference of the States Parties.

The Confidentiality Commission is best equipped to deal with different aspects of breaches of confidentiality within the confidentiality regime, and it ensures the necessary trust foreseen by the transparency present in "regular" judicial proceedings. Furthermore, the rules of procedure of the Confidentiality Commission (the Operating Procedures of the Confidentiality Commission[48]) are, to a large extent, based on the optional rules of the Permanent Court of Arbitration and provide that the parties can elect to make further use of Permanent Court of Arbitration rules for particular breach procedures. This should be interpreted as expanding even further the field of the Commission.

Having come to the conclusion of this contribution, it is necessary, however, to end on a rather alarming note on some recent developments in the OPCW. It should be observed that, at the time of writing, it appears that the main organs of the OPCW do not seem to hold the Confidentiality Commission to be as essential to the confidentiality regime of the Convention as the negotiators of the text of the Convention did when drafting it. The organs of the OPCW, apparently for budgetary reasons, have not ensured that the Confidentiality Commission, as a treaty-based subsidiary organ of the Conference,[49] could hold its regular annual meetings, which it is required to have in order for it to adopt and submit its annual report to the regular annual sessions of the Conference of the States Parties. In doing so, the organs also preclude the possibility for the Commission to submit

[47] By this I mean that all States Parties to the Convention by definition participate in the confidentiality regime in the *broad sense*, whereby even their particular national procedures play a role.
[48] See OPCW: The Legal Texts, *supra* note 9, at 498.
[49] See Confidentiality Annex to the Convention, paragraph 23.

"recommendations or proposals to the Conference as it sees fit."[50] Consequently, the rules adopted by the First Session of the Conference of the States Parties have been breached.

Since early 2001, when the budgetary problems arose, the Confidentiality Commission has not been able to hold its annual meeting as required by the OPCW Policy on Confidentiality. This also means that, *de facto*, the Confidentiality Commission is not operational, since there are no properly appointed chair or vice-chairs. There are, at present, only the 20 members (re-)elected at the Sixth Session of the Conference of States Parties in May 2001. Furthermore, no training of the members of the Confidentiality Commission is taking place. It is clear, however, that the Confidentiality Commission may meet on its own authority in the event that the Confidentiality Commission is being called upon to consider a dispute, and funding for that meeting would have to be found somewhere within the budget.

The apparent solution to the outlined problem appears simple: the Conference should realise the extreme importance that the existence of a properly functioning Confidentiality Commission holds for the confidentiality regime of the Convention. It should ensure that the annual budget provides for secure funding that cannot be transferred to solve larger structural budget problems within the OPCW. This would also ensure the independence of the Commission from the Secretariat.

If the confidentiality regime is eroded, the heart of the supervisory mechanism of the OPCW is diminished. The Convention foresees that an adequate verification regime, inspecting both military sites as well as private chemical industry, will be coupled with the maximum assurance that there are effective procedures in place to respond to a case of a breach of confidentiality. It is also quite clear that the issue of confidentiality will not disappear when all chemical weapons have been destroyed, since verification of chemical industry sites will continue. At that point, the issue of confidentiality with regard to confidential business information will simply become predominant. If States Parties can no longer be certain that all essential elements of the confidentiality regime are in place, they might lose the essential cooperation of their national chemical industries. This, in turn, might lead to the erosion of this exceptional arms control model.

---

[50] "At its initial and subsequent annual meetings, the Confidentiality Commission shall:

(a) choose by consensus a Chair to serve for the forthcoming year taking into account the principle of rotation among the regions designated in paragraph 23 of Article VIII of the Convention;

(b) consider and adopt a report to the Conference as to the outcome of disputes handled by theConfidentiality Commission during the previous year;

(c) consider and adopt a report to the Conference on the operation, effectiveness and efficiency of the Confidentiality Commission and consider any recommendations or proposals made by the Chair in this regard;

(e) issue such guidelines to or make such requests of the Chair as it sees fit; and,

(f) make such further recommendations or proposals to the Conference as it sees fit.

Part IX.2 of the OPCW Policy on Confidentiality (C-I/DEC.13 as amended by paragraph 3 of C-II/DEC.14), reprinted in OPCW: The Legal Texts, *supra* note 9, at 494-495.

ANNEXES

ANNEX I
National Implementation Legislation: Actions Taken or to be Taken to Clarify the CWC.

ANNEX II
ICC Statute, Part 9. International Cooperation and Judicial Assistance

ANNEX III
UN Security Council Resolution 1373 (2001)

ANNEX IV
OPCW Executive Council Decision EC-XXVII/DEC.5 (7 December 2001)

ANNEX V
Draft Optional Protocol to the Chemical Weapons Convention, related to the Implementation of Article VII, paragraph 2, of the Convention

ANNEX VI
Comparison of Parties to the Instruments Used in Compiling the Draft Optional Protocol to the Chemical Weapons Convention

ANNEX VII
Extracts from the ICTY Statute and Rules of Procedure and Evidence

ANNEX VIII
Extracts from the ICC Statute and Final Draft Rules of Procedure and Evidence

ANNEX I

NATIONAL IMPLEMENTATION LEGISLATION: ACTIONS TAKEN OR TO BE TAKEN TO CLARIFY THE CWC

Unclear CWC Provisions/Terms	Reference	Actions			
		Understandings/ Clarifications Adopted	Interim Action	Suggested Actions	
				Understandings/ Clarifications	Review Conference
Unclear Verification-related terms					
1. Applicable concentration limits for mixtures containing Schedule 2A and 2A* chemicals, in relation to declarations	Paragraph 5 Part VII Verification Annex (VA)	DG note EC-XXIV and separate draft decision	SAB[1] made its recommendation in SAB-IV/1 in response to, Para 2, C-V/DEC.19[2]	Decision byC-VI (Conference of States Parties)	
2. Declaration levels for Schedule 2 or a Schedule 3 chemical	Parts VII and VIII VA	Paras 1 and 2 of C-V/DEC.19 Paragraph 2 of C-IV/DEC.16[3] C-II/DEC.7[4]			
3. "Low concentration" level for Schedule 2B chemicals in mixtures in relation to declarations	Paris Resolution para 12(t), Paragraph 3 Part VII VA (see Legal Series PC-OPCW 1, 1994)	C-V/DEC.19, 30% for 2B and 3		See above C-V/DEC.19, 30% for 2B and 3	
4. Inspection of Schedule 2 Plants: Are *Schedule 2 plants operating below the verification* threshold declarable and inspectable at an otherwise declarable and inspectable Schedule 2 plant site?	Para 12,Part VII VA		Office of the Director of Verification is directing the	Understanding (Some argue that the text of the CWC is, in fact, clear; others hold	

[1] Scientific Advisory Body

[2] The Director-General was requested to task the SAB "to study all relevant aspects of the applicable concentration limits for mixtures of chemicals containing Schedule 2A and 2A* chemicals and report to EC. An ad hoc working group of the SAB studied the issue and concluded that it is regulatory, not scientific, in nature. See OPCW doc. SAB-IV/1 (6 February 2001).

[3] The confirmation reads, in part: "Declarations are required when the amount of a Schedule 2 or Schedule 3 chemical contained in a mixture exceeds the" applicable declaration threshold, and its concentration exceeds a concentration limit yet to be determined.

[4] The decision requests States Parties to provide concentration limits for Schedule 2 and 3 "applied in plant site declarations pursuant to Parts VII and VIII of theVerification Annex" and to supply the information to the Secretariat.

Unclear CWC Provisions/Terms	Reference	Actions			
		Understandings/ Clarifications Adopted	Interim Action	Suggested Actions: Understandings/ Clarifications	Suggested Actions: Review Conference
			preparation of an "understanding" paper	it is not)	
5. Inspection of Schedule 2 plants: Are imports/exports from plants which are below the delcaration threshold declarable and inspectable under para 8, Part VII of the VA. It should be noted that exports are not done but by the plant. Imports may be initiated by the plant or the State.			A paper on an "Understanding" was drafted by DG's office	Understanding	
6. Frequency of Schedule 2 inspections	Paras18 and 20, Part VII of the VA. As yet no agreement among States Parties		Consultations in the Industry Cluster have been tempoarily suspended pending submission of new ideas	Understanding States Parties need to arrive at an understanding in principle, execution could then be left to the Secretariat	
7. Selection of Schedule 3 plant sites for inspection	Para 14, Part VIII of the VA	EC-XVII/DEC.7. Decision to be reviewed "in the fourth year after the beginning of its implementation		A definitive understanding required because the same "information available to the Secretariat" could require clarification that it is not limited to declaration data. Not likely to be agreement.	
8. Selection of DOC/PSF plant sites for inspection	Para 11, Part IX of the VA	CSPs did not adopt a decision at its Third Session as required under para. 25 of Part IX of the VA	No decision reached in consultations in the industry cluster	Decision As Sched 3 plus an understanding on "proposals by States Parties"	Review Conference in terms of para. 26 of Part IX

Unclear CWC Provisions/Terms	Reference	Actions			
		Understandings/ Clarifications Adopted	Interim Action	Suggested Actions	
				Understandings/ Clarifications	Review Conference
9. Meaning of proposals by States Parties in para. 11(c) of Part IX of the VA	Para. 11(c) of Part IX of the VA	CSPs did not adopt a decision at its Third Session as required under para. 25 of Part IX of the VA	No decision reached in industry cluster	Understanding See item 9 above	
10. Specific types of equipment for specific types of inspections	Paris Resolution para 12 (f). The procedures or the inspection of equipment, were not developed by the Preparatory Commission.		Facilitiator continues consultations	Understanding	
11. Guidelines to assess the risk to the object and purpose of the Convention posed by the relevant chemicals produced, the characteristics of the facility and the nature of the activities carried out there, in accordance with Part VI, para 23 of the VA	Paris Resolution para 12(q). The guidelines for assessing the risk were not developed by the PrepCom.		For the time being, dropped from Industry Cluster.	Decision was almost adopted at the end of PrepCom. Proposals by Secretariat exist.	
12. Guidelines to assess the risk to the object and purpose of the Convention posed by the quantities of chemicals produced, the characteristics of the facility and the nature of the activities carried out there, in accordance with Part VI, para 30 of the VA	Paris Resolution para 12(s)		Dropped from Industry Cluster?	Decision was almost adopted at the end of PrepCom. Proposals by Secretariat exist.	

Unclear CWC Provisions/Terms	Reference	Actions			
		Understandings/ Clarifications Adopted	Interim Action	Suggested Actions	
				Understandings/ Clarifications	Review Conference
13. Additional measures in relation to transfer of Schedule 3 chemicals	Para 27,Part VIII of the VA	CSP decision C-VI/DEC.10 – a qualified decision setting percentage thresholds below which end-use certificates are not required for products containing Sched. 3 chemicals	EC proposed clarification during EC-XXIV A draft decision for CSP-VI exists, additional EC task required for CSP-7	Further decision by CSP is required on transfers of Sched. 3 chemicals five years after EIF (29-04-2002) (paras 26 and 27, Part VIII of the VA)	
14. Rounding up rules for Schedule 1 substances.	Part VI of the VA		No further discussions planned to be held in the Industry Cluster for the foreseeable future due to strong divergent views	"Understanding" by CSP	
15. Meaning of "Unscheduled discrete organic chemicals" in relation to declaration	Paragraph 7 Article VI, paragraph 2 Part IX of the VA	"Understanding" C-I/DEC.39[5]			
16. Meaning of "Production Synthesis" in relation to declarations, as to whether or not the term as used in Part IX VA "includes biochemical and biologically mediated processes"	Paragraph 1, Part IX of the VA and para. 7, Article VI	SAB-II made recommendation for inclusion, DG Note supported SAB-II view. Meeting of State Party experts recommended not decision now but to	Does or does not include biochemical and biological production of DOC/PSF, SAB recommendation exists but was not		Review Conference

[5] The "understanding" adopted defines the essential elements in the term in relation to declarations of amount of production for each element.

Unclear CWC Provisions/Terms	Reference	Actions			
		Understandings/ Clarifications Adopted	Interim Action	Suggested Actions	
				Understandings/ Clarifications	Review Conference
		keep following the situation	accepted by governmental experts, issue for Review Conference		
17. Meaning of "Production" in subparagraph 12(a) of Article II	Article II, subpara. 12(a)	"Understanding" C-II/DEC.6[6] Does not cover DOC/PSF	A further understanding on DOC/PSFs specifically	This does not address captive use or boundaries of production which are topics under consultation in the industry cluster	
18. Declaration requirements for chemical weapons buried by SP on its territory after 1976 or dumped at sea after 1984	Para. 1(a) Article III and Part IV(A) of the VA	"Understanding" C-I/DEC.30[7]	For sea-dumped CW: text appears to be clear but cannot be implemented; this may well be a practical matter		
19 Changes to annual declarations and declarations of additional activities in relation to Schedules 2 and 3	Parts VII and VIII and para. 4(c) Parts VII and VIII of the VA	"Understanding" C/I-DEC.38[8] Nil declarations are not required but encouraged	Perhaps decision on nil declarations should be taken by CSP finally, once and for all.		

[6] By decision of the Conference, " the term "production" as used in subparagraph 12(a) of Article II should be understood to include a scheduled chemical (i.e. a Schedule 1, Schedule 2 or Schedule 3 chemical) produced by a biochemical or biologically mediated reaction."

[7] Additional information required.

[8] Clarifies annual declaration requirements. Every time there are changes in a declaration, the changes should be reported to the Secretariat with the next declaration, and, "even where there is no change to the substance of a declaration compared to a previous one, the information required under that later declaration shall be provided in full." With regard to additional activities (Paragraph 4(c), Parts VII and VIII), the understanding specifies which change s need to be declared, and within what time-frames.

Unclear CWC Provisions/Terms	Reference	Actions			
		Understandings/ Clarifications Adopted	Interim Action	Suggested Actions	
				Understandings/ Clarifications	Review Conference
20. Verification of Mixed Plants Sites (Inspection of Mixed Plant Sites)	Para. 9 Article VI and Part VI of the VA; para 51 Part II, para. 25, Part VII, para. 20 Part VIII, para. 17 Part IX of the VA	"Understanding" C-I/DEC.34[9]			
21. Meaning of "Mixed Plants" in relation to declarations and inspections	Article VI, Section E of Part VI, paras. 23-39 Part VII, paras. 18-24 Part VIII or paras. 15-20 Part IX of the VA	"Understanding" C-I/DEC.40[10]			
22. Meaning of a "chemical weapon" in relation to Article II subparagraphs 1(b) and 1(c) in connection with Section D of the Draft Declaration Handbook	Article II.1(b) and 1(c)	"Understanding" C-III/DEC.13[11]			
23. Meaning of the term "incapacitation" in the definition of a chemical weapon in paragraph 1(a) Article II[12] Where would Adamsite be included? NOT	Definition of a CW – Article II, paragraph 1(a)		Interim measure urged to define "incapacitation"	"Understanding" by CSP. Two opposed views: If adamsite is	

[9] By way of clarification, the understanding gives the rules that will apply where access is made to plants liable for inspection under another Part of the Verification Annex related to Article VI.

[10] Defines "mixed Plants" as "plants which are individually covered under more than one Part of the Verification Annex related to Article VI. The term covers, for example, a multipurpose plant that manufactures, in the same process line but at different points in time or parallel in several process lines, Schedule 2 and Schedule 3 chemicals (and/or DOCs)." The understanding also says how the mixed plants will be declared and inspected.

[11] The Decision referred the issue to the Secretariat "to make an analysis of declarations submitted, and to compile a list of illustrative, non-exhaustive examples of chemical weapons meeting the definitions contained in subparagraphs 1(b) and 1(c) of Article II, and report to the results of the analysis to the Fourth Session of the Conference for a final decision."

[12] See Report of the Scientific Advisory Body SAB-III/1, 27 April 2000, on Adamsite, recommending that it should no longer be used as a riot control agent (RCA) because of its incapacitating properties which (depending on amounts used) can turn it into a chemical weapon.

Unclear CWC Provisions/Terms	Reference	Actions			
		Understandings/ Clarifications Adopted	Interim Action	Suggested Actions	
				Understandings/ Clarifications	Review Conference
in the Schedules because that would automatically preclude it as a RCA, and there are still some States Parties that have declared it as a RCA)			particularly with respect to Riot Control Agents (e.g. adamsite)	taken as an example, then on the basis of the analysis by the SAB, and in view of para. 2 of Article VI, recommendation is a Change action under paragraph 4 of Article XV by CSP in terms of paragraph 1 of Guidelines for Schedules of Chemicals – declare it a CW. Other view disagrees on the ground that the clarity that is required should not be attempted through a change in the Schedules. The implication would then be that an agent not listed in the Schedules is not a CW. What about the famous Novychock? What may need clarifying is that "incapacitation" is an undefined concept and relates to the temporary incapacitation of a person by whatever physiological effect	

Unclear CWC Provisions/Terms	Reference	Actions			
		Understandings/ Clarifications Adopted	Interim Action	Suggested Actions	
				Understandings/ Clarifications	Review Conference
				(there are some who think this relates only to psychedelic effects and that other so-called non-lethal agents may be legitimate.	
24. Clarification on what is Ricin, and what steps of its production and use need declaring, and which do not (the CSP decision on Ricin omitted this part because the Expert Group lost sight of the different results at each stage of production)	Schedule 1A chemical	Reporting recommendation SAB-II/1; Supported by DG Note and by a meeting of experts, C-V/DEC.17; declaration of saxitoxin transfers and change to Convention EC-M-II/1		One aspect of the SAB has not been dealt with: what actually constitutes Ricin (there are more than 100 different structural varieties). That can be done by an " understanding"	
25. How salts of Scheduled chemicals should be treated, and the function of CAS numbers in the Annex on Chemicals	Schedule of chemicals	Reporting recommendation SAB-II/1; Supported by DG Note, not supported by meeting of experts who recommend no changes, but to follow the situation		"Understanding" by CSP as part of Review Conference, this may actually lead to a Change (or a series of them) in the Schedules	Review Conference
26. Guidelines on usability of chemical weapons produced between 1925 and 1946.	Para. 5 Part IV(B) (subpara. B) of VA			"Understanding" by CSP	
27. Lack of consistency in submissions of aggregate national data (AND) on transfers of Schedule 2 and Schedule 3 chemicals. Needed agreement on what constitutes AND	Para. 1 of Parts VII and VIII of VA			"Understanding" on certain parameters by CSP desirable. Discussions continue in Industry Cluster	
28. How Free Trade Zones and Free Ports should	Not referred to in		This subject has	"Understanding" by	

Unclear CWC Provisions/Terms	Reference	Actions			
		Understandings/ Clarifications Adopted	Interim Action	Suggested Actions	
				Understandings/ Clarifications	Review Conference
be treated in relation to transfers of Scheduled chemicals and declarations	the CWC		been included in Industry Cluster discussion of AND	CSP	
Legislation Related Terms/concepts not provided or not precise					
29. The absence of a timeline in paragraph 1 of Article VII of the CWC in relation to adoption of implementing legislation by States Parties	Paragraph 1, Article VII			"Understanding" by CSP, adopting, *inter alia*, a time limit of one year after adoption of the understanding, or one year after EIF for new States Parties.	
30. Meaning of "in conformity with international law"	Paragraph 1(c) Article VII			Interpretation by the Legal Adviser	
31. Meaning of "afford the appropriate form of legal assistance..."	Paragraph 2 Article VII			"Understanding" by CSP	
32. Meaning of "cooperate as appropriate with other States Parties...	"Paragraph 3 Article VII			"Understanding" by CSP	
33. Definition of "offence" or "crime" as implied under Article VII, of the CWC	Article VII		In order to speed up adoption of legislation, SPs urged to use definition in UNCATOC, Articles 5, 6, 8 and 23, and any supplementary guidelines by the Legal Adviser.	Adoption by CSP of definition in UNCATOC	

Unclear CWC Provisions/Terms	Reference	Actions			
		Understandings/ Clarifications Adopted	Interim Action	Suggested Actions	
				Understandings/ Clarifications	Review Conference
34. Meaning of "penal sanctions in relation to the "offences" under the CWC, and a scale of sanctions			States Parties urged to use Articles 10, 11, 12, 13, and 14 of UNCATOC as reference points in drafting legislation. Should also seek additional guidelines from the Legal Adviser.		
35. Procedures for investigations and arrest			In addition to existing domestic legislation on these aspects SPs could use as reference for other ideas, UNCATOC's Article 2, and relevant elements of Articles 19 to 29, and guidelines from the Legal Adviser.		
36. Wrongful acts which may attract civil liability only under the CWC	Paragraph 1 Article VII		Initial working interpretation by the Legal Adviser	Recommendation of interpretation referred to CSP	
37. Nature of liability and penalties for breach of policy on confidentiality	Paragraph 10 Confidentiality Annex		Initial working interpretation by the Legal Adviser	Recommendation of interpretation referred to CSP	
38. How to deal with the violation of the			Initial working	Recommendation of	

Unclear CWC Provisions/Terms	Reference	Actions			
		Understandings/ Clarifications Adopted	Interim Action	Suggested Actions	
				Understandings/ Clarifications	Review Conference
Confidentiality Annex by Industry with regard to sanctions			interpretation by the Legal Adviser	interpretation referred to CSP	
Tentative List of Issues for the Review Conference					
39. Correcting paragraph 4(a) of Part VII by striking out the phrase "and, starting in the following calendar year;" at the end of paragraph 4(a)					Correction by Review Conference
40. The relationship between CWC and BTWC protocol in respect to overlapping areas of coverage (toxins)[13]					Review Conference
41. Clarification that the parenthetical text on the role of the Schedules does not imply that unscheduled toxic chemicals that meet the definition of chemical weapons as contained in para 1 of Article II are excluded from that term, and that instead such chemicals are to be treated as chemical weapons (and, depending on the circumstances, that they may be added to the Schedules by a Change procedure)	paragraphs 2 and 3 of Art II as well as in the chapeau of the Annex on Chemicals				Clarification should be sought from the Review Conference
42. The meaning of the term "primarily" in para 1(d) of Art III	Para. 1(d) of Article III			Understanding by CSP	

[13] Issue of jurisdiction between the CWC and the BTWC is extremely important for the smooth implementation of both regimes. The issue also affects planning and operations in both organisations

ANNEX II

ICC STATUTE,[1] PART 9. INTERNATIONAL COOPERATION AND JUDICIAL ASSISTANCE

ARTICLE 86
General Obligation to Cooperate

States Parties shall, in accordance with the provisions of this Statute, cooperate fully with the Court in its investigation and prosecution of crimes within the jurisdiction of the Court.

ARTICLE 87
Requests for Cooperation: General Provisions

1. (a) The Court shall have the authority to make requests to States Parties for cooperation. The requests shall be transmitted through the diplomatic channel or any other appropriate channel as may be designated by each State Party upon ratification, acceptance, approval or accession.

   Subsequent changes to the designation shall be made by each State Party in accordance with the Rules of Procedure and Evidence.

   (b) When appropriate, without prejudice to the provisions of subparagraph (a), requests may also be transmitted through the International Criminal Police Organization or any appropriate regional organization.

2. Requests for cooperation and any documents supporting the request shall either be in or be accompanied by a translation into an official language of the requested State or one of the working languages of the Court, in accordance with the choice made by that State upon ratification, acceptance, approval or accession.

   Subsequent changes to this choice shall be made in accordance with the Rules of Procedure and Evidence.

3. The requested State shall keep confidential a request for cooperation and any documents supporting the request, except to the extent that the disclosure is necessary for execution of the request.

4. In relation to any request for assistance presented under this Part, the Court may take such measures, including measures related to the protection of information, as may be necessary to ensure the safety or physical or psychological well-being of any victims, potential witnesses and their families. The Court may request that any information that is made available under this Part shall be provided and handled in a manner that protects the safety and physical or psychological well-being of any victims, potential witnesses and their families.

---

[1] 1998 Rome Statute of the International Criminal Court, entered into force 1 July 2002; UN doc. A/CONF.183/9*, as corrected by the procès-verbaux of 10 November 1998 and 12 July 1999. Corrected text available at http://www.un.org/law/icc.

5. (a) The Court may invite any State not party to this Statute to provide assistance under this Part on the basis of an ad hoc arrangement, an agreement with such State or any other appropriate basis.

   (b) Where a State not party to this Statute, which has entered into an ad hoc arrangement or an agreement with the Court, fails to cooperate with requests pursuant to any such arrangement or agreement, the Court may so inform the Assembly of States Parties or, where the Security Council referred the matter to the Court, the Security Council.

6. The Court may ask any intergovernmental organization to provide information or documents. The Court may also ask for other forms of cooperation and assistance which may be agreed upon with such an organization and which are in accordance with its competence or mandate.

7. Where a State Party fails to comply with a request to cooperate by the Court contrary to the provisions of this Statute, thereby preventing the Court from exercising its functions and powers under this Statute, the Court may make a finding to that effect and refer the matter to the Assembly of States Parties or, where the Security Council referred the matter to the Court, to the Security Council.

ARTICLE 88
Availability of Procedures under National Law

States Parties shall ensure that there are procedures available under their national law for all of the forms of cooperation which are specified under this Part.

ARTICLE 89
Surrender of Persons to the Court

1. The Court may transmit a request for the arrest and surrender of a person, together with the material supporting the request outlined in article 91, to any State on the territory of which that person may be found and shall request the cooperation of that State in the arrest and surrender of such a person. States Parties shall, in accordance with the provisions of this Part and the procedure under their national law, comply with requests for arrest and surrender.

2. Where the person sought for surrender brings a challenge before a national court on the basis of the principle of *ne bis in idem* as provided in article 20, the requested State shall immediately consult with the Court to determine if there has been a relevant ruling on admissibility. If the case is admissible, the requested State shall proceed with the execution of the request. If an admissibility ruling is pending, the requested State may postpone the execution of the request for surrender of the person until the Court makes a determination on admissibility.

3. (a) A State Party shall authorize, in accordance with its national procedural law, transportation through its territory of a person being surrendered to the Court by another State, except where transit through that State would impede or delay the surrender.

(b) A request by the Court for transit shall be transmitted in accordance with article 87. The request for transit shall contain:
   (i) A description of the person being transported;
   (ii) A brief statement of the facts of the case and their legal characterization; and,
   (iii) The warrant for arrest and surrender;

(c) A person being transported shall be detained in custody during the period of transit;

(d) No authorization is required if the person is transported by air and no landing is scheduled on the territory of the transit State;

(e) If an unscheduled landing occurs on the territory of the transit State, that State may require a request for transit from the Court as provided for in subparagraph (b). The transit State shall detain the person being transported until the request for transit is received and the transit is effected, provided that detention for purposes of this subparagraph may not be extended beyond 96 hours from the unscheduled landing unless the request is received within that time.

4. If the person sought is being proceeded against or is serving a sentence in the requested State for a crime different from that for which surrender to the Court is sought, the requested State, after making its decision to grant the request, shall consult with the Court.

ARTICLE 90
COMPETING REQUESTS

1. A State Party which receives a request from the Court for the surrender of a person under article 89 shall, if it also receives a request from any other State for the extradition of the same person for the same conduct which forms the basis of the crime for which the Court seeks the person's surrender, notify the Court and the requesting State of that fact.

2. Where the requesting State is a State Party, the requested State shall give priority to the request from the Court if:
   (a) The Court has, pursuant to article 18 or 19, made a determination that the case in respect of which surrender is sought is admissible and that determination takes into account the investigation or prosecution conducted by the requesting State in respect of its request for extradition; or,
   (b) The Court makes the determination described in subparagraph (a) pursuant to the requested State's notification under paragraph 1.

3. Where a determination under paragraph 2 (a) has not been made, the requested State may, at its discretion, pending the determination of the Court under paragraph 2 (b), proceed to deal with the request for extradition from the requesting State but shall not extradite the person until the Court has determined that the case is inadmissible. The Court's determination shall be made on an expedited basis.

4. If the requesting State is a State not Party to this Statute the requested State, if it is not under an international obligation to extradite the person to the requesting State, shall give priority to the request for surrender from the Court, if the Court has determined that the case is admissible.

5. Where a case under paragraph 4 has not been determined to be admissible by the Court, the requested State may, at its discretion, proceed to deal with the request for extradition from the requesting State.

6. In cases where paragraph 4 applies except that the requested State is under an existing international obligation to extradite the person to the requesting State not Party to this Statute, the requested State shall determine whether to surrender the person to the Court or extradite the person to the requesting State. In making its decision, the requested State shall consider all the relevant factors, including but not limited to:
   (a) The respective dates of the requests;
   (b) The interests of the requesting State including, where relevant, whether the crime was committed in its territory and the nationality of the victims and of the person sought; and,
   (c) The possibility of subsequent surrender between the Court and the requesting State.

7. Where a State Party which receives a request from the Court for the surrender of a person also receives a request from any State for the extradition of the same person for conduct other than that which constitutes the crime for which the Court seeks the person's surrender:
   (a) The requested State shall, if it is not under an existing international obligation to extradite the person to the requesting State, give priority to the request from the Court;
   (b) The requested State shall, if it is under an existing international obligation to extradite the person to the requesting State, determine whether to surrender the person to the Court or to extradite the person to the requesting State. In making its decision, the requested State shall consider all the relevant factors, including but not limited to those set out in paragraph 6, but shall give special consideration to the relative nature and gravity of the conduct in question.

8. Where pursuant to a notification under this article, the Court has determined a case to be inadmissible, and subsequently extradition to the requesting State is refused, the requested State shall notify the Court of this decision.

ARTICLE 91

Contents of Request for Arrest and Surrender

1. A request for arrest and surrender shall be made in writing. In urgent cases, a request may be made by any medium capable of delivering a written record, provided that the request shall be confirmed through the channel provided for in article 87, paragraph 1 (a).

2. In the case of a request for the arrest and surrender of a person for whom a warrant of arrest has been issued by the Pre-Trial Chamber under article 58, the request shall contain or be supported by:
   (a) Information describing the person sought, sufficient to identify the person, and information as to that person's probable location;
   (b) A copy of the warrant of arrest; and,

(c) Such documents, statements or information as may be necessary to meet the requirements for the surrender process in the requested State, except that those requirements should not be more burdensome than those applicable to requests for extradition pursuant to treaties or arrangements between the requested State and other States and should, if possible, be less burdensome, taking into account the distinct nature of the Court.

3. In the case of a request for the arrest and surrender of a person already convicted, the request shall contain or be supported by:

(a) A copy of any warrant of arrest for that person;

(b) A copy of the judgement of conviction;

(c) Information to demonstrate that the person sought is the one referred to in the judgement of conviction; and,

(d) If the person sought has been sentenced, a copy of the sentence imposed and, in the case of a sentence for imprisonment, a statement of any time already served and the time remaining to be served.

4. Upon the request of the Court, a State Party shall consult with the Court, either generally or with respect to a specific matter, regarding any requirements under its national law that may apply under paragraph 2 (c). During the consultations, the State Party shall advise the Court of the specific requirements of its national law.

ARTICLE 92
PROVISIONAL ARREST

1. In urgent cases, the Court may request the provisional arrest of the person sought, pending presentation of the request for surrender and the documents supporting the request as specified in article 91.

2. The request for provisional arrest shall be made by any medium capable of delivering a written record and shall contain:

(a) Information describing the person sought, sufficient to identify the person, and information as to that person's probable location;

(b) A concise statement of the crimes for which the person's arrest is sought and of the facts which are alleged to constitute those crimes, including, where possible, the date and location of the crime;

(c) A statement of the existence of a warrant of arrest or a judgement of conviction against the person sought; and,

(d) A statement that a request for surrender of the person sought will follow.

3. A person who is provisionally arrested may be released from custody if the requested State has not received the request for surrender and the documents supporting the request as specified in article 91 within the time limits specified in the Rules of Procedure and Evidence. However, the person may consent to surrender before the expiration of this period if permitted by the law of the requested State. In such a case, the requested State shall proceed to surrender the person to the Court as soon as possible.

4. The fact that the person sought has been released from custody pursuant to paragraph 3 shall not prejudice the subsequent arrest and surrender of that person if the request for surrender and the documents supporting the request are delivered at a later date.

ARTICLE 93
OTHER FORMS OF COOPERATION

1. States Parties shall, in accordance with the provisions of this Part and under procedures of national law, comply with requests by the Court to provide the following assistance in relation to investigations or prosecutions:
   (a) The identification and whereabouts of persons or the location of items;
   (b) The taking of evidence, including testimony under oath, and the production of evidence, including expert opinions and reports necessary to the Court;
   (c) The questioning of any person being investigated or prosecuted;
   (d) The service of documents, including judicial documents;
   (e) Facilitating the voluntary appearance of persons as witnesses or experts before the Court;
   (f) The temporary transfer of persons as provided in paragraph 7;
   (g) The examination of places or sites, including the exhumation and examination of grave sites;
   (h) The execution of searches and seizures;
   (i) The provision of records and documents, including official records and documents;
   (j) The protection of victims and witnesses and the preservation of evidence;
   (k) The identification, tracing and freezing or seizure of proceeds, property and assets and instrumentalities of crimes for the purpose of eventual forfeiture, without prejudice to the rights of *bona fide* third parties; and,
   (l) Any other type of assistance which is not prohibited by the law of the requested State, with a view to facilitating the investigation and prosecution of crimes within the jurisdiction of the Court.

2. The Court shall have the authority to provide an assurance to a witness or an expert appearing before the Court that he or she will not be prosecuted, detained or subjected to any restriction of personal freedom by the Court in respect of any act or omission that preceded the departure of that person from the requested State.

3. Where execution of a particular measure of assistance detailed in a request presented under paragraph 1, is prohibited in the requested State on the basis of an existing fundamental legal principle of general application, the requested State shall promptly consult with the Court to try to resolve the matter. In the consultations, consideration should be given to whether the assistance can be rendered in another manner or subject to conditions. If after consultations the matter cannot be resolved, the Court shall modify the request as necessary.

4. In accordance with article 72, a State Party may deny a request for assistance, in whole or in part, only if the request concerns the production of any documents or disclosure of evidence which relates to its national security.

5. Before denying a request for assistance under paragraph 1 (l), the requested State shall consider whether the assistance can be provided subject to specified conditions, or whether the assistance can be provided at a later date or in an alternative manner, provided that if the Court or the Prosecutor accepts the assistance subject to conditions, the Court or the Prosecutor shall abide by them.

6. If a request for assistance is denied, the requested State Party shall promptly inform the Court or the Prosecutor of the reasons for such denial.

7. (a) The Court may request the temporary transfer of a person in custody for purposes of identification or for obtaining testimony or other assistance. The person may be transferred if the following conditions are fulfilled:
   (i) The person freely gives his or her informed consent to the transfer; and,

   (ii) The requested State agrees to the transfer, subject to such conditions as that State and the Court may agree.

   (b) The person being transferred shall remain in custody. When the purposes of the transfer have been fulfilled, the Court shall return the person without delay to the requested State.

8. (a) The Court shall ensure the confidentiality of documents and information, except as required for the investigation and proceedings described in the request.

   (b) The requested State may, when necessary, transmit documents or information to the Prosecutor on a confidential basis. The Prosecutor may then use them solely for the purpose of generating new evidence.

   (c) The requested State may, on its own motion or at the request of the Prosecutor, subsequently consent to the disclosure of such documents or information. They may then be used as evidence pursuant to the provisions of Parts 5 and 6 and in accordance with the Rules of Procedure and Evidence.

9. (a) (i) In the event that a State Party receives competing requests, other than for surrender or extradition, from the Court and from another State pursuant to an international obligation, the State Party shall endeavour, in consultation with the Court and the other State, to meet both requests, if necessary by postponing or attaching conditions to one or the other request.
   (ii) Failing that, competing requests shall be resolved in accordance with the principles established in article 90.

   (b) Where, however, the request from the Court concerns information, property or persons which are subject to the control of a third State or an international organization by virtue of an international agreement, the requested States shall so inform the Court and the Court shall direct its request to the third State or international organization.

10. (a) The Court may, upon request, cooperate with and provide assistance to a State Party conducting an investigation into or trial in respect of conduct which constitutes a crime within the jurisdiction of the Court or which constitutes a serious crime under the national law of the requesting State.

(b)(i)The assistance provided under subparagraph (a) shall include, *inter alia*:

a. The transmission of statements, documents or other types of evidence obtained in the course of an investigation or a trial conducted by the Court; and,

b. The questioning of any person detained by order of the Court;

(ii) In the case of assistance under subparagraph (b) (i) a:

a. If the documents or other types of evidence have been obtained with the assistance of a State, such transmission shall require the consent of that State;

b. If the statements, documents or other types of evidence have been provided by a witness or expert, such transmission shall be subject to the provisions of article 68.

(c) The Court may, under the conditions set out in this paragraph, grant a request for assistance under this paragraph from a State which is not a Party to this Statute.

ARTICLE 94

Postponement of Execution of a Request in Respect of Ongoing Investigation or Prosecution

1. If the immediate execution of a request would interfere with an ongoing investigation or prosecution of a case different from that to which the request relates, the requested State may postpone the execution of the request for a period of time agreed upon with the Court. However, the postponement shall be no longer than is necessary to complete the relevant investigation or prosecution in the requested State. Before making a decision to postpone, the requested State should consider whether the assistance may be immediately provided subject to certain conditions.

2. If a decision to postpone is taken pursuant to paragraph 1, the Prosecutor may, however, seek measures to preserve evidence, pursuant to article 93, paragraph 1 (j).

ARTICLE 95

Postponement of Execution of a Request in Respect of an Admissibility Challenge

Where there is an admissibility challenge under consideration by the Court pursuant to article 18 or 19, the requested State may postpone the execution of a request under this Part pending a determination by the Court, unless the Court has specifically ordered that the Prosecutor may pursue the collection of such evidence pursuant to article 18 or 19.

ARTICLE 96

Contents of Request for Other Forms of Assistance under Article 93

1. A request for other forms of assistance referred to in article 93 shall be made in writing. In urgent cases, a request may be made by any medium capable of delivering a written record, provided that the request shall be confirmed through the channel provided for in article 87, paragraph 1 (a).

2. The request shall, as applicable, contain or be supported by the following:

(a) A concise statement of the purpose of the request and the assistance sought, including the legal basis and the grounds for the request;

(b) As much detailed information as possible about the location or identification of any person or place that must be found or identified in order for the assistance sought to be provided;

(c) A concise statement of the essential facts underlying the request;

(d) The reasons for and details of any procedure or requirement to be followed;

(e) Such information as may be required under the law of the requested State in order to execute the request; and,

(f) Any other information relevant in order for the assistance sought to be provided.

3. Upon the request of the Court, a State Party shall consult with the Court, either generally or with respect to a specific matter, regarding any requirements under its national law that may apply under paragraph 2 (e). During the consultations, the State Party shall advise the Court of the specific requirements of its national law.

4. The provisions of this article shall, where applicable, also apply in respect of a request for assistance made to the Court.

ARTICLE 97
CONSULTATIONS

Where a State Party receives a request under this Part in relation to which it identifies problems which may impede or prevent the execution of the request, that State shall consult with the Court without delay in order to resolve the matter. Such problems may include, *inter alia*:

(a) Insufficient information to execute the request;

(b) In the case of a request for surrender, the fact that despite best efforts, the person sought cannot be located or that the investigation conducted has determined that the person in the requested State is clearly not the person named in the warrant; or,

(c) The fact that execution of the request in its current form would require the requested State to breach a pre-existing treaty obligation undertaken with respect to another State.

ARTICLE 98
COOPERATION WITH RESPECT TO WAIVER OF IMMUNITY AND CONSENT TO SURRENDER

1. The Court may not proceed with a request for surrender or assistance which would require the requested State to act inconsistently with its obligations under international law with respect to the State or diplomatic immunity of a person or property of a third State, unless the Court can first obtain the cooperation of that third State for the waiver of the immunity.

2. The Court may not proceed with a request for surrender which would require the requested State to act inconsistently with its obligations under international agreements pursuant to which the consent of a sending State is required to surrender a person of that State to the Court, unless the Court can first obtain the cooperation of the sending State for the giving of consent for the surrender.

ARTICLE 99
Execution of Requests under Articles 93 and 96

1. Requests for assistance shall be executed in accordance with the relevant procedure under the law of the requested State and, unless prohibited by such law, in the manner specified in the request, including following any procedure outlined therein or permitting persons specified in the request to be present at and assist in the execution process.

2. In the case of an urgent request, the documents or evidence produced in response shall, at the request of the Court, be sent urgently.

3. Replies from the requested State shall be transmitted in their original language and form.

4. Without prejudice to other articles in this Part, where it is necessary for the successful execution of a request which can be executed without any compulsory measures, including specifically the interview of or taking evidence from a person on a voluntary basis, including doing so without the presence of the authorities of the requested State Party if it is essential for the request to be executed, and the examination without modification of a public site or other public place, the Prosecutor may execute such request directly on the territory of a State as follows:
   (a) When the State Party requested is a State on the territory of which the crime is alleged to have been committed, and there has been a determination of admissibility pursuant to article 18 or 19, the Prosecutor may directly execute such request following all possible consultations with the requested State Party;
   (b) In other cases, the Prosecutor may execute such request following consultations with the requested State Party and subject to any reasonable conditions or concerns raised by that State Party. Where the requested State Party identifies problems with the execution of a request pursuant to this subparagraph it shall, without delay, consult with the Court to resolve the matter.

5. Provisions allowing a person heard or examined by the Court under article 72 to invoke restrictions designed to prevent disclosure of confidential information connected with national security shall also apply to the execution of requests for assistance under this article.

ARTICLE 100
Costs

1. The ordinary costs for execution of requests in the territory of the requested State shall be borne by that State, except for the following, which shall be borne by the Court:
   (a) Costs associated with the travel and security of witnesses and experts or the transfer under article 93 of persons in custody;
   (b) Costs of translation, interpretation and transcription;
   (c) Travel and subsistence costs of the judges, the Prosecutor, the Deputy Prosecutors, the Registrar, the Deputy Registrar and staff of any organ of the Court;
   (d) Costs of any expert opinion or report requested by the Court;
   (e) Costs associated with the transport of a person being surrendered to the Court by a custodial State; and,

(f) Following consultations, any extraordinary costs that may result from the execution of a request.

2. The provisions of paragraph 1 shall, as appropriate, apply to requests from States Parties to the Court. In that case, the Court shall bear the ordinary costs of execution.

ARTICLE 101
RULE OF SPECIALITY

1. A person surrendered to the Court under this Statute shall not be proceeded against, punished or detained for any conduct committed prior to surrender, other than the conduct or course of conduct which forms the basis of the crimes for which that person has been surrendered.

2. The Court may request a waiver of the requirements of paragraph 1 from the State which surrendered the person to the Court and, if necessary, the Court shall provide additional information in accordance with article 91. States Parties shall have the authority to provide a waiver to the Court and should endeavour to do so.

ARTICLE 102
USE OF TERMS

For the purposes of this Statute:

(a) "surrender" means the delivering up of a person by a State to the Court, pursuant to this Statute.

(b) "extradition" means the delivering up of a person by one State to another as provided by treaty, convention or national legislation.

ANNEX III

UN SECURITY COUNCIL RESOLUTION 1373 (2001)

ADOPTED BY THE SECURITY COUNCIL AT ITS 4385TH MEETING, ON 28 SEPTEMBER 2001

The Security Council,

REAFFIRMING its resolutions 1269 (1999) of 19 October 1999 and 1368 (2001) of 12 September 2001,

REAFFIRMING also its unequivocal condemnation of the terrorist attacks which took place in New York, Washington, D.C. and Pennsylvania on 11 September 2001, and expressing its determination to prevent all such acts,

REAFFIRMING further that such acts, like any act of international terrorism, constitute a threat to international peace and security,

REAFFIRMING the inherent right of individual or collective self-defence as recognized by the Charter of the United Nations as reiterated in resolution 1368 (2001),

REAFFIRMING the need to combat by all means, in accordance with the Charter of the United Nations, threats to international peace and security caused by terrorist acts,

DEEPLY concerned by the increase, in various regions of the world, of acts of terrorism motivated by intolerance or extremism,

CALLING on States to work together urgently to prevent and suppress terrorist acts, including through increased cooperation and full implementation of the relevant international conventions relating to terrorism,

RECOGNIZING the need for States to complement international cooperation by taking additional measures to prevent and suppress, in their territories through all lawful means, the financing and preparation of any acts of terrorism,

REAFFIRMING the principle established by the General Assembly in its declaration of October 1970 (resolution 2625 (XXV)) and reiterated by the Security Council in its resolution 1189 (1998) of 13 August 1998, namely that every State has the duty to refrain from organizing, instigating, assisting or participating in terrorist acts in another State or acquiescing in organized activities within its territory directed towards the commission of such acts,

ACTING under Chapter VII of the Charter of the United Nations,

1. *Decides that* all States shall:

   (a) *Prevent* and suppress the financing of terrorist acts;

(b) *Criminalize* the wilful provision or collection, by any means, directly or indirectly, of funds by their nationals or in their territories with the intention that the funds should be used, or in the knowledge that they are to be used, in order to carry out terrorist acts;

(c) *Freeze* without delay funds and other financial assets or economic resources of persons who commit, or attempt to commit, terrorist acts or participate in or facilitate the commission of terrorist acts; of entities owned or controlled directly or indirectly by such persons; and of persons and entities acting on behalf of, or at the direction of such persons and entities, including funds derived or generated from property owned or controlled directly or indirectly by such persons and associated persons and entities;

(d) *Prohibit* their nationals or any persons and entities within their territories from making any funds, financial assets or economic resources or financial or other related services available, directly or indirectly, for the benefit of persons who commit or attempt to commit or facilitate or participate in the commission of terrorist acts, of entities owned or controlled, directly or indirectly, by such persons and of persons and entities acting on behalf of or at the direction of such persons;

2. *Decides also* that all States shall:

(a) *Refrain* from providing any form of support, active or passive, to entities or persons involved in terrorist acts, including by suppressing recruitment of members of terrorist groups and eliminating the supply of weapons to terrorists;

(b) *Take* the necessary steps to prevent the commission of terrorist acts, including by provision of early warning to other States by exchange of information;

(c) *Deny* safe haven to those who finance, plan, support, or commit terrorist acts, or provide safe havens;

(d) *Prevent* those who finance, plan, facilitate or commit terrorist acts from using their respective territories for those purposes against other States or their citizens;

(e) *Ensure* that any person who participates in the financing, planning, preparation or perpetration of terrorist acts or in supporting terrorist acts is brought to justice and ensure that, in addition to any other measures against them, such terrorist acts are established as serious criminal offences in domestic laws and regulations and that the punishment duly reflects the seriousness of such terrorist acts;

(f) *Afford* one another the greatest measure of assistance in connection with criminal investigations or criminal proceedings relating to the financing or support of terrorist acts, including assistance in obtaining evidence in their possession necessary for the proceedings;

(g) *Prevent* the movement of terrorists or terrorist groups by effective border controls and controls on issuance of identity papers and travel documents, and through measures for preventing counterfeiting, forgery or fraudulent use of identity papers and travel documents;

3. *Calls upon* all States to:

(a) *Find* ways of intensifying and accelerating the exchange of operational information, especially regarding actions or movements of terrorist persons or networks; forged or falsified travel documents; traffic in arms, explosives or sensitive materials; use of communications technologies by terrorist groups; and the threat posed by the possession of weapons of mass destruction by terrorist groups;

(b) *Exchange* information in accordance with international and domestic law and cooperate on administrative and judicial matters to prevent the commission of terrorist acts;

(c) *Cooperate*, particularly through bilateral and multilateral arrangements and agreements, to prevent and suppress terrorist attacks and take action against perpetrators of such acts;

(d) *Become* parties as soon as possible to the relevant international conventions and protocols relating to terrorism, including the international Convention for the Suppression of the Financing of Terrorism of 9 December 1999;

(e) *Increase* cooperation and fully implement the relevant international conventions and protocols relating to terrorism and Security Council resolutions 1269 (1999) and 1368 (2001);

(f) *Take* appropriate measures in conformity with the relevant provisions of national and international law, including international standards of human rights, before granting refugee status, for the purpose of ensuring that the asylum-seeker has not planned, facilitated or participated in the commission of terrorist acts;

(g) *Ensure*, in conformity with international law, that refugee status is not abused by the perpetrators, organizers or facilitators of terrorist acts, and that claims of political motivation are not recognized as grounds for refusing requests for the extradition of alleged terrorists;

4. *Notes* with concern the close connection between international terrorism and transnational organized crime, illicit drugs, money-laundering, illegal arms trafficking, and illegal movement of nuclear, chemical, biological and other potentially deadly materials, and in this regard *emphasizes* the need to enhance coordination of efforts on national, subregional, regional and international levels in order to strengthen a global response to this serious challenge and threat to international security;

5. *Declares* that acts, methods, and practices of terrorism are contrary to the purposes and principles of the United Nations and that knowingly financing, planning and inciting terrorist acts are also contrary to the purposes and principles of the United Nations;

6. *Declares* to establish, in accordance with rule 28 of its provisional rules of procedure, a Committee of the Security Council, consisting of all the members of the Council, to

monitor implementation of this resolution, with the assistance of appropriate expertise, and *calls upon* all States to report to the Committee, no later than 90 days from the date of adoption of this resolution and thereafter according to a timetable to be proposed by the Committee, on the steps they have taken to implement this resolution;

7. *Directs* the Committee to delineate its tasks, submit a work programme within 30 days of the adoption of this resolution, and to consider the support it requires, in consultation with the Secretary-General;

8. *Expresses* its determination to take all necessary steps in order to ensure the full implementation of this resolution, in accordance with its responsibilities under the Charter;

9. *Decides* to remain seized of this matter.

ANNEX IV

OPCW EXECUTIVE COUNCIL DECISION EC-XXVII/DEC.5 (7 DECEMBER 2001)

THE OPCW'S CONTRIBUTION TO GLOBAL ANTI-TERRORIST EFFORTS

The Executive Council,

RECALLING the determination of the States Parties to the Chemical Weapons Convention for the sake of all mankind, to exclude completely the possibility of the use of chemical weapons, through the implementation of the provisions of this Convention, thereby complementing the obligations assumed under the Geneva Protocol of 1925;

MINDFUL OF United Nations Security Council Resolutions 1373 (2001) and 1368 (2001) and United Nations General Assembly Resolution A/RES/56/1;

RECALLING the statement by its Chairman on the terrorist attack which had taken place in the United States of America on 11 September 2001 (EC-XXVI/3, dated 28 September 2001);

Hereby

1. Recognises that the full and effective implementation of all provisions of the Convention is in itself a contribution to global anti-terrorist efforts;

2. Stresses that, at this stage, the contribution to global anti-terrorist efforts in the context of the Chemical Weapons Convention should focus on the following main areas:
   (a) promotion of universal adherence to the Convention;
   (b) full implementation of the legislative measures required by Article VII;
   (c) full implementation of the provisions of Articles IV and V related to the destruction of chemical weapons;
   (d) full implementation of the provisions of Article VI related to activities not prohibited by the Convention; and
   (e) ability of the OPCW to respond to the assistance and protection provisions under Article X.

3. Decides to establish an open-ended working group, chaired by the Chairman of the Council, to examine further the OPCW's contribution to global anti-terrorist efforts, with a view to presenting a recommendation to its Twenty-Eighth Session, including specific measures, taking into account resource implications.

ANNEX V

DRAFT OPTIONAL PROTOCOL TO THE CONVENTION ON THE PROHIBITION OF THE DEVELOPMENT, PRODUCTION, STOCKPILING AND USE OF CHEMICAL WEAPONS AND ON THEIR DESTRUCTION, RELATED TO THE IMPLEMENTATION OF ARTICLE VII, PARAGRAPH 2, OF THE CONVENTION

The States Parties to the Convention on the Prohibition of the Development, Production, Stockpiling and Use of Chemical Weapons and on Their Destruction and to this Protocol,

HAVING REGARD to the undertakings contained in Article VII, paragraph 2, of the Chemical Weapons Convention relating to cooperation with other States Parties and legal assistance to facilitate the implementation of the obligations under Article VII, paragraph 1, of the Convention,

RECOGNISING the need to enhance international cooperation between States in devising and adopting effective and practical measures for the prevention of crimes related to violations of the Chemical Weapons Convention, and for the prosecution and punishment of their perpetrators, [1]

CONSIDERING that the occurrence of such crimes is a matter of grave concern to the international community as a whole, [2]

FURTHER RECOGNIZING that eradication of illicit traffic is a collective responsibility of all States and that, to that end, coordinated action within the framework of international cooperation is necessary,[3]

DETERMINED to improve international cooperation in the suppression of illicit traffic by sea,[4]

DESIROUS OF EXTENDING to each other the widest measure of cooperation under Article VII, paragraph 2, of the Chemical Weapons Convention,[5]

CONVINCED that the establishment of a multilateral arrangement for legal assistance will greatly contribute to the development of more effective international cooperation in the implementation of Article VII, paragraph 2, of the Chemical Weapons Convention,[6]

---

[1] Text taken, *mutatis mutandis*, from the 1998 United Nations International Convention for the Suppression of Terrorist Bombings ("1998 Terrorist Bombings Convention"), Preamble.
[2] Text taken, *mutatis mutandis*, from the 1998 Terrorist Bombings Convention, Preamble.
[3] Text taken, *mutatis mutandis*, from the 1988 United Nations Convention against Illicit Traffic in Narcotic Drugs and Psychotropic Substances (hereinafter "1988 Drug Convention"), Preamble.
[4] Text taken, *mutatis mutandis*, from the 1988 Drug Convention, Preamble.
[5] Text adapted from the United Nations 1990 Model Treaty on Mutual Assistance in Criminal Matters ("1990 Model Treaty on Mutual Assistance"), Preamble.
[6] Text adapted from the United Nations General Assembly resolution 45/117 (14 December 1990), adopting the 1990 Model Treaty on Mutual Assistance.

Have agreed as follows:

CHAPTER I: GENERAL PROVISIONS

1. **Definitions**. For the purposes of this Protocol:

1.1 "Chemical Weapons Convention" or "Convention" means the Convention on the Prohibition of the Development, Production, Stockpiling and Use of Chemical Weapons and on Their Destruction.

1.2 "Illicit traffic" means delivery on any terms whatever, dispatch, transport, importation or exportation of toxic chemicals and their precursors, constituting an offence covered by this Protocol;[7]

1.3 "Offence(s)" means criminal offence(s), established by the Parties under their domestic laws, falling within the scope of Article VII, paragraphs 1(a) and (c), of the Chemical Weapons Convention.

1.4 "OPCW" means the Organisation for the Prohibition of Chemical Weapons, established pursuant to Article VIII of the Chemical Weapons Convention.

1.5 "Precursor" has the same definition as that provided by Article II of the Chemical Weapons Convention.

1.6 "Proceeds" or "proceeds of crime" means any property derived from or obtained, directly or indirectly, through the commission of an offence covered by this Protocol;[8]

1.7 "Property" means assets of every kind, whether corporeal or incorporeal, movable or immovable, tangible or intangible, and legal documents or instruments evidencing title to, or interest in, such assets;[9]

1.8 "Toxic chemical" has the same definition as that provided by Article II of the Chemical Weapons Convention.

1.9 "Transit State" means a State through the territory of which toxic chemicals and their precursors are illicitly being moved, which is neither the place of origin nor the place of ultimate destination thereof.[10]

2. **Scope of the Protocol**. The purpose of this Protocol is to promote cooperation among the Parties so that they may address more effectively the various aspects of prevention, investigation and prosecution of offences having an international dimension. In carrying out their obligations under the Protocol, the Parties shall take

[7] Text inspired by the 1988 Drug Convention, Article 1(m) together with elements of Art. 3(1) and (2).
[8] Text taken, *mutatis mutandis*, from the 1988 Drug Convention, Article 1(p).
[9] Text taken, *mutatis mutandis*, from the 1988 Drug Convention, Article 1(q).
[10] Text taken, *mutatis mutandis*, from the 1988 Drug Convention, Article 1(u).

necessary measures, including legislative and administrative measures, in conformity with the fundamental provisions of their respective domestic legislative systems.[11]

3. The Parties shall carry out their obligations under this Protocol in a manner consistent with the principles of sovereign equality and territorial integrity of States and that of non-intervention in the domestic affairs of other States.[12]

4. A Party shall not undertake in the territory of another Party the exercise of jurisdiction and performance of functions which are exclusively reserved for the authorities of that other Party by its domestic law.[13]

5. **Offences and sanctions**.

5.1 This Protocol shall apply to offences as defined in Article 1.3 above.[14]

5.2 The Parties shall endeavour to ensure that any discretionary legal powers under their domestic law relating to the prosecution of persons for offences are exercised to maximise the effectiveness of law enforcement measures in respect of those offences and with due regard to the need to deter the commission of such offences.[15]

5.3 The Parties shall ensure that their courts or other competent authorities bear in mind the serious nature of the offences covered by this Protocol and the circumstances when considering the eventuality of early release or parole of persons convicted of such offences.[16]

5.4 Each Party shall, where appropriate, establish under its domestic law a long statute of limitations period in which to commence proceedings for any offence covered by this Protocol, and a longer period where the alleged offender has evaded the administration of justice.[17]

5.5 Each Party shall take appropriate measures, consistent with its legal system, to ensure that a person charged with or convicted of an offence covered by this Protocol, who is found within its territory, is present at the necessary criminal proceedings.[18]

5.6 Nothing contained in this Protocol shall affect the principle that the description of the offences to which it refers and of legal defences thereto is reserved to the domestic law of a Party and that such offences shall be prosecuted and punished in conformity with that law.[19]

---

[11] Text taken, *mutatis mutandis*, from the 1988 Drug Convention, Article 2(1) and the 2000 Protocol to Prevent, Suppress and Punish Trafficking in Persons, Especially Women and Children, supplementing the United Nations 2000 Convention Against Transnational Organised Crime, Article 4.
[12] Text taken, *mutatis mutandis*, from the 1988 Drug Convention, Article 2(2).
[13] Text taken, *mutatis mutandis*, from the 1988 Drug Convention, Article 2(3).
[14] Text taken, *mutatis mutandis*, from the 1988 Drug Convention, Article 6(1).
[15] Text taken, *mutatis mutandis*, from the 1988 Drug Convention, Article 3(6).
[16] Text taken, *mutatis mutandis*, from the 1988 Drug Convention, Article 3(7).
[17] Text taken, *mutatis mutandis*, from the 1988 Drug Convention, Article 3(8).
[18] Text taken, *mutatis mutandis*, from the 1988 Drug Convention, Article 3(9).
[19] Text taken, *mutatis mutandis*, from the 1988 Drug Convention, Article 3(11).

6. **Political offence not a bar.** None of the offences covered by this Protocol shall be regarded, for the purposes of extradition or mutual legal assistance, as a political offence or as an offence connected with a political offence or as an offence inspired by political motives. Accordingly, a request for extradition or for mutual legal assistance based on such an offence may not be refused on the sole ground that it concerns a political offence or an offence connected with a political offence or an offence inspired by political motives.[20]

6.1 Fiscal offence not a bar. None of the offences covered by this Protocol shall be regarded, for the purposes of extradition or mutual legal assistance, as a fiscal offence. Accordingly, States Parties may not refuse a request for extradition or for mutual legal assistance on the sole ground that it concerns a fiscal offence.[21]

6.2 States Parties may not refuse a request for mutual legal assistance on the ground of bank secrecy.[22]

6.3 Each State Party shall adopt such measures as may be necessary, including, where appropriate, domestic legislation, to ensure that offences covered by this Protocol are under no circumstances justifiable by considerations of a political, philosophical, ideological, racial, ethnic, religious or other similar nature.[23]

7. **Cooperation in prevention.** States Parties shall cooperate in the prevention of the offences covered by this Protocol, particularly:
   (a) By taking all practicable measures, including, if necessary, adapting their domestic legislation, to prevent and counter preparations in their respective territories for the commission of those offences within or outside their territories, including measures to prohibit in their territories illegal activities of persons, groups and organisations that encourage, instigate, organise, knowingly finance or engage in the perpetration of offences covered by this Protocol;
   (b) By exchanging accurate and verified information in accordance with their national law, and coordinating administrative and other measures taken as appropriate to prevent the commission of offences covered by this Protocol.

8. **Information to be furnished by the parties.** The Parties shall furnish to the OPCW information on the working of this Protocol in their territories and, in particular:
   (a) The text of laws and regulations promulgated in order to give effect to the Protocol;
   (b) Particulars of cases of illicit traffic within their jurisdiction which they consider important because of new trends disclosed, the quantities involved, the sources

[20] Text taken, *mutatis mutandis*, from the 1998 Terrorist Bombings Convention, Article 11.

[21] Text taken, *mutatis mutandis*, from the 1999 United Nations Convention for the Suppression of the Financing of Terrorism ("1999 Financing of Terrorism Convention"), Article 13.

[22] Text taken, *mutatis mutandis*, from the 1999 Financing of Terrorism Convention, Article 12(2).

[23] Text taken, *mutatis mutandis*, from the 1999 Financing of Terrorism Convention, Article 6.

from which the substances are obtained, or the methods employed by persons so engaged.[24]

8.1 The Parties shall furnish such information in such a manner and by such dates as the OPCW may request.[25]

CHAPTER II: EXTRADITION

9. **Scope of application of this Chapter.** This Chapter shall apply to offences as defined by Article 2 of this Protocol.[26]

10. **Obligation to extradite.** Each Party agrees to extradite to the other, upon request and subject to the provisions of the present Protocol, any person who is wanted in the requesting State for prosecution for an extraditable offence or for the imposition or enforcement of a sentence in respect of such an offence.[27]

11. **Extraditable offences.**

11.1 For the purposes of the present Chapter, extraditable offences are offences that are punishable under the laws of both Parties by imprisonment or other deprivation of liberty for a maximum period of at least one year, or by a more severe penalty. Where the request for extradition relates to a person who is wanted for the enforcement of a sentence of imprisonment or other deprivation of liberty imposed for such an offence, extradition shall be granted only if a period of at least four months of such sentence remains to be served.[28]

11.2 Each of the offences to which this Protocol applies shall be deemed to be included as an extraditable offence in any extradition treaty existing between Parties. The Parties undertake to include such offences as extraditable offences in every extradition treaty to be concluded between them.[29]

11.3 If a Party which makes extradition conditional on the existence of a treaty receives a request for extradition from another Party with which it has no extradition treaty, it may consider this Protocol as the legal basis for extradition in respect of any offence to which this article applies. The Parties which require detailed legislation in order to use this Protocol as a legal basis for extradition shall consider enacting such legislation as may be necessary.[30]

11.4 The Parties which do not make extradition conditional on the existence of a treaty shall recognise offences covered by this Protocol as extraditable offences between themselves.[31]

---

[24] Text taken, *mutatis mutandis*, from the 1988 Drug Convention, Article 20(1).
[25] Text taken, *mutatis mutandis*, from the 1988 Drug Convention, Article 20(2).
[26] Text inspired by the 1988 Drug Convention, Article 6(1).
[27] Text taken, *mutatis mutandis*, from the United Nations 1990 Model Treaty on Extradition, Article 1.
[28] Text taken, *mutatis mutandis*, from the 1990 Model Treaty on Extradition, Article 2(1).
[29] Text taken, *mutatis mutandis*, from the 1988 Drug Convention, Article 6(2).
[30] Text taken, *mutatis mutandis*, from the 1988 Drug Convention, Article 6(3).
[31] Text taken, *mutatis mutandis*, from the 1988 Drug Convention, Article 6(4).

11.5 Extradition shall be subject to the conditions provided for by the law of the requested Party or by applicable extradition treaties, including the grounds upon which the requested Party may refuse extradition.[32]

11.6 In considering requests received pursuant to this Protocol, the requested State may refuse to comply with such requests where there are substantial grounds leading its judicial or other competent authorities to believe that compliance would facilitate the prosecution or punishment of any person on account of that person's race, religion, nationality, ethnic origin, political opinions, sex or status, or would cause prejudice for any of those reasons to any person affected by the request.[33]

11.7 The Parties shall endeavour to expedite extradition procedures and to simplify evidentiary requirements relating thereto in respect of any offence covered by this Protocol.[34]

11.8 Subject to the provisions of its domestic law and its extradition treaties, the requested Party may, upon being satisfied that the circumstances so warrant and are urgent, and at the request of the requesting Party, take a person whose extradition is sought and who is present in its territory into custody or take other appropriate measures to ensure that person's presence at extradition proceedings.[35]

12. ***Aut dedere aut judicare.*** The State Party in the territory of which the alleged offender is present shall, if it does not extradite that person in respect of the offence and has established its jurisdiction in relation to that offence, be obliged, without exception whatsoever and whether or not the offence was committed in its territory, to submit the case without undue delay to its competent authorities for the purpose of prosecution, through proceedings in accordance with the laws of that State. Those authorities shall take their decision in the same manner as in the case of any other offence of a grave nature under the law of that State.[36]

13. Whenever a State Party is permitted under its domestic law to extradite or otherwise surrender one of its nationals only upon the condition that the person will be returned to that State to serve the sentence imposed as a result of the trial or proceeding for which the extradition or surrender of the person was sought, and this State and the State seeking the extradition of the person agree with this option and other terms they may deem appropriate, such a conditional extradition or surrender shall be sufficient to discharge the obligation set forth in paragraph 12.[37]

14. If extradition, sought for purposes of enforcing a sentence, is refused because the person sought is a national of the requested Party, the requested Party shall, if its law

[32] Text taken, *mutatis mutandis*, from the 1988 Drug Convention, Article 6(5).
[33] Text taken, *mutatis mutandis*, from the 1988 Drug Convention, Article 6(6), combined with the text of the 1990 Model Treaty on Extradition, Article 3(b).
[34] Text taken, *mutatis mutandis*, from the 1988 Drug Convention, Article 6(7).
[35] Text taken, *mutatis mutandis*, from the 1988 Drug Convention, Article 6(8).
[36] Text taken, *mutatis mutandis*, from the 1998 Terrorist Bombings Convention, Article 8(1).
[37] Text taken, *mutatis mutandis*, from the 1998 Terrorist Bombings Convention, Article 8(2).

so permits and in conformity with the requirements of such law, upon application of the requesting Party, consider the enforcement of the sentence which has been imposed under the law of the requesting Party, or the remainder thereof.[38]

15. The Parties shall seek to conclude bilateral and multilateral agreements to carry out or to enhance the effectiveness of extradition.[39]

16. The Parties may consider entering into bilateral or multilateral agreements, whether ad hoc or general, on the transfer to their country of persons sentenced to imprisonment and other forms of deprivation of liberty for offences covered by this Protocol, in order that they may complete their sentences there.[40]

17. In determining whether an offence is an offence punishable under the laws of both Parties, it shall not matter whether:
    (a) the laws of the Parties place the acts or omissions constituting the offence within the same category of offence or denominate the offence by the same terminology;
    (b) Under the laws of the Parties the constituent elements of the offence differ, it being understood that the totality of the acts or omissions as presented by the requesting State shall be taken into account.[41]

18. Where extradition of a person is sought for an offence against a law relating to taxation, customs duties, exchange control or other revenue matters, extradition may not be refused on the ground that the law of the requested State does not impose the same kind of tax or duty or does not contain a tax, customs duty or exchange regulation of the same kind as the law of the requesting State.[42]

19. If the request for extradition includes several separate offences each of which is punishable under the laws of both Parties, but some of which do not fulfil the other conditions set out in paragraph 1 of the present article, the requested Party may grant extradition for the latter offences provided that the person is to be extradited for at least one extraditable offence.[43]

20. **Channels of communication and required documents.**

20.1 A request for extradition shall be made in writing. The request, supporting documents and subsequent communications shall be transmitted through the diplomatic channel, directly between the ministries of justice or any other authorities designated by the Parties.[44]

[38] Text taken, *mutatis mutandis*, from the 1988 Drug Convention, Article 6(10).
[39] Text taken, *mutatis mutandis*, from the 1988 Drug Convention, Article 6(11).
[40] Text taken, *mutatis mutandis*, from the 1988 Drug Convention, Article 6(12).
[41] Text taken, *mutatis mutandis*, from the 1990 Model Treaty on Extradition, Article 2(2).
[42] Text taken, *mutatis mutandis*, from the 1990 Model Treaty on Extradition, Article 2(3).
[43] Text taken, *mutatis mutandis*, from the 1990 Model Treaty on Extradition, Article 2(4).
[44] Text taken, *mutatis mutandis*, from the 1990 Model Treaty on Extradition, Article 5(1).

20.2 A request for extradition shall be accompanied by the following:

(a) In all cases,

(i) As accurate a description as possible of the person sought, together with any other information that may help to establish that person's identity, nationality and location;

(ii) The text of the relevant provision of the law creating the offence or, where necessary, a statement of the law relevant to the offence and a statement of the penalty that can be imposed for the offence;

(b) If the person is accused of an offence, by a warrant issued by a court or other competent judicial authority for the arrest of the person or a certified copy of that warrant, a statement of the offence for which extradition is requested and a description of the acts or omissions constituting the alleged offence, including an indication of the time and place of its commission;

(c) If the person has been convicted of an offence, by a statement of the offence for which extradition is requested and a description of the acts or omissions constituting the offence and by the original or certified copy of the judgement or any other document setting out the conviction and the sentence imposed, the fact that the sentence is enforceable, and the extent to which the sentence remains to be served;

(d) If the person has been convicted of an offence in his or her absence, in addition to the documents set out in section 20.2(c), by a statement as to the legal means available to the person to prepare his or her defence or to have the case retried in his or her presence;

(e) If the person has been convicted of an offence but no sentence has been imposed, by a statement of the offence for which extradition is requested and a description of the acts or omissions constituting the offence and by a document setting out the conviction and a statement affirming that there is an intention to impose a sentence.[45]

20.3 The documents submitted in support of a request for extradition shall be accompanied by a translation into the language of the requested State or in another language acceptable to that State.[46]

21. **Simplified extradition procedure**. The requested State, if not precluded by its law, may grant extradition after receipt of a request for provisional arrest, provided that the person sought explicitly consents before a competent authority.[47]

22. **Certification and authentication**. Except as provided by the present Protocol, a request for extradition and the documents in support thereof, as well as documents or

[45] Text taken, *mutatis mutandis*, from the 1990 Model Treaty on Extradition, Article 5(2).
[46] Text taken, *mutatis mutandis*, from the 1990 Model Treaty on Extradition, Article 5(3).
[47] Text taken, *mutatis mutandis*, from the 1990 Model Treaty on Extradition, Article 6.

other material supplied in response to such a request, shall not require certification or authentication.[48]

23. **Additional information.** If the requested State considers that the information provided in support of a request for extradition is not sufficient, it may request that additional information be furnished within such reasonable time as it specifies.[49]

24. **Provisional arrest.**

24.1 In case of urgency the requesting State may apply for the provisional arrest of the person sought pending the presentation of the request for extradition. The application shall be transmitted by means of the facilities of the International Criminal Police Organization, by post or telegraph or by any other means affording a record in writing.[50]

24.2 The application shall contain a description of the person sought, a statement that extradition is to be requested, a statement of the existence of one of the documents mentioned in section 20.2 of the present Protocol, authorising the apprehension of the person, a statement of the punishment that can be or has been imposed for the offence, including the time left to be served and a concise statement of the facts of the case, and a statement of the location, where known, of the person.[51]

24.3 The requested State shall decide on the application in accordance with its law and communicate its decision to the requesting State without delay.[52]

24.4 The person arrested upon such an application shall be set at liberty upon the expiration of 40 days from the date of arrest if a request for extradition, supported by the relevant documents specified in section 20.2 of the present Protocol, has not been received. The present paragraph does not preclude the possibility of conditional release of the person prior to the expiration of the 40 days.[53]

24.5 The release of the person pursuant to section 24.4 shall not prevent rearrest and institution of proceedings with a view to extraditing the person sought if the request and supporting documents are subsequently received.[54]

25. **Decision on the request.**

25.1 The requested State shall deal with the request for extradition pursuant to procedures provided by its own law, and shall promptly communicate its decision to the requesting State.[55]

---

[48] Text taken, *mutatis mutandis*, from the 1990 Model Treaty on Extradition, Article 7.
[49] Text taken, *mutatis mutandis*, from the 1990 Model Treaty on Extradition, Article 8.
[50] Text taken, *mutatis mutandis*, from the 1990 Model Treaty on Extradition, Article 9(1).
[51] Text taken, *mutatis mutandis*, from the 1990 Model Treaty on Extradition, Article 9(2).
[52] Text taken, *mutatis mutandis*, from the 1990 Model Treaty on Extradition, Article 9(3).
[53] Text taken, *mutatis mutandis*, from the 1990 Model Treaty on Extradition, Article 9(4).
[54] Text taken, *mutatis mutandis*, from the 1990 Model Treaty on Extradition, Article 9(5).
[55] Text taken, *mutatis mutandis*, from the 1990 Model Treaty on Extradition, Article 10(1).

25.2 Reasons shall be given for any complete or partial refusal of the request.[56]

26. **Surrender of the person.**

26.1 Upon being informed that extradition has been granted, the Parties shall, without undue delay, arrange for the surrender of the person sought and the requested State shall inform the requesting State of the length of time for which the person sought was detained with a view to surrender.[57]

26.2 The person shall be removed from the territory of the requested State within such reasonable period as the requested State specifies and, if the person is not removed within that period, the requested State may release the person and may refuse to extradite that person for the same offence.[58]

26.3 If circumstances beyond its control prevent a Party from surrendering or removing the person to be extradited, it shall notify the other Party. The two Parties shall mutually decide upon a new date of surrender, and the provisions of paragraph 2 of the present article shall apply.[59]

27. **Postponed or conditional surrender.**

27.1 The requested State may, after making its decision on the request for extradition, postpone the surrender of a person sought, in order to proceed against that person, or, if that person has already been convicted, in order to enforce a sentence imposed for an offence other than that for which extradition is sought. In such a case the requested State shall advise the requesting State accordingly.[60]

27.2 The requested State may, instead of postponing surrender, temporarily surrender the person sought to the requesting State in accordance with conditions to be determined between the Parties.[61]

28. **Surrender of property.**

28.1 To the extent permitted under the law of the requested State and subject to the rights of third parties, which shall be duly respected, all property found in the requested State that has been acquired as a result of the offence or that may be required as evidence shall, if the requesting State so requests, be surrendered if extradition is granted.[62]

28.2 The said property may, if the requesting State so requests, be surrendered to the requesting State even if the extradition agreed to cannot be carried out.[63]

[56] Text taken, *mutatis mutandis*, from the 1990 Model Treaty on Extradition, Article 10(2).
[57] Text taken, *mutatis mutandis*, from the 1990 Model Treaty on Extradition, Article 11(1).
[58] Text taken, *mutatis mutandis*, from the 1990 Model Treaty on Extradition, Article 11(2).
[59] Text taken, *mutatis mutandis*, from the 1990 Model Treaty on Extradition, Article 11(3).
[60] Text taken, *mutatis mutandis*, from the 1990 Model Treaty on Extradition, Article 12(1).
[61] Text taken, *mutatis mutandis*, from the 1990 Model Treaty on Extradition, Article 12(2).
[62] Text taken, *mutatis mutandis*, from the 1990 Model Treaty on Extradition, Article 13(1).
[63] Text taken, *mutatis mutandis*, from the 1990 Model Treaty on Extradition, Article 13(2).

28.3 When the said property is liable to seizure or confiscation in the requested State, it may retain it or temporarily hand it over.[64]

28.4 Where the law of the requested State or the protection of the rights of third parties so require, any property so surrendered shall be returned to the requested State free of charge after the completion of the proceedings, if that State so requests.[65]

29. **Rule of speciality**.

29.1 A person extradited under the present Protocol shall not be proceeded against, sentenced, detained, re-extradited to a third State, or subjected to any other restriction of personal liberty in the territory of the requesting State for any offence committed before surrender other than:

(a) An offence for which extradition was granted;

(b) Any other offence in respect of which the requested State consents. Consent shall be given if the offence for which it is requested is itself subject to extradition in accordance with the present Protocol.[66]

29.2 A request for the consent of the requested State under the present section shall be accompanied by the documents mentioned in section 20.2(c) and a legal record of any statement made by the extradited person with respect to the offence.[67]

29.3 Section 29.1 shall not apply if the person has had an opportunity to leave the requesting State and has not done so within 45 days of final discharge in respect of the offence for which that person was extradited or if the person has voluntarily returned to the territory of the requesting State after leaving it.[68]

30. **Transit**.

30.1 Where a person is to be extradited to a Party from a third State through the territory of the other Party, the Party to which the person is to be extradited shall request the other Party to permit the transit of that person through its territory. This does not apply where air transport is used and no landing in the territory of the other Party is scheduled.[69]

30.2 Upon receipt of such a request, which shall contain relevant information, the requested State shall deal with this request pursuant to procedures provided by its own law. The requested State shall grant the request expeditiously unless its essential interests would be prejudiced thereby.[70]

---

[64] Text taken, ***mutatis mutandis***, from the 1990 Model Treaty on Extradition, Article 13(3).
[65] Text taken, ***mutatis mutandis***, from the 1990 Model Treaty on Extradition, Article 13(4).
[66] Text taken, ***mutatis mutandis***, from the 1990 Model Treaty on Extradition, Article 14(1).
[67] Text taken, ***mutatis mutandis***, from the 1990 Model Treaty on Extradition, Article 14(2).
[68] Text taken, ***mutatis mutandis***, from the 1990 Model Treaty on Extradition, Article 14(3).
[69] Text taken, ***mutatis mutandis***, from the 1990 Model Treaty on Extradition, Article 15(1).
[70] Text taken, ***mutatis mutandis***, from the 1990 Model Treaty on Extradition, Article 15(2).

30.3 The State of transit shall ensure that legal provisions exist that would enable detaining the person in custody during transit.[71]

30.4 In the event of an unscheduled landing, the Party to be requested to permit transit may, at the request of the escorting officer, hold the person in custody for 48 hours, pending receipt of the transit request to be made in accordance with paragraph 1 of the present article.[72]

31. **Concurrent requests.** If a Party receives requests for extradition for the same person from both the other Party and a third State it shall, at its discretion, determine to which of those States the person is to be extradited.[73]

32. **Costs.**

32.1 The requested State shall meet the cost of any proceedings in its jurisdiction arising out of a request for extradition.[74]

32.2 The requested State shall also bear the costs incurred in its territory in connection with the seizure and handing over of property, or the arrest and detention of the person whose extradition is sought.[75]

32.3 The requesting State shall bear the costs incurred in conveying the person from the territory of the requested State, including transit costs.[76]

CHAPTER III: MUTUAL LEGAL ASSISTANCE

33. **Scope of application.**

33.1 The Parties shall afford one another, pursuant to this article, the widest measure of mutual legal assistance in investigations, prosecutions and judicial proceedings in relation to offences covered by this Protocol.[77]

33.2 Mutual legal assistance to be afforded in accordance with this Chapter may be requested for any of the following purposes:[78]

(a) Taking evidence or statements from persons;[79]

(b) Assisting in the availability of detained persons or others to give evidence or assist in investigations;[80]

---

[71] Text taken, *mutatis mutandis*, from the 1990 Model Treaty on Extradition, Article 15(3).

[72] Text taken, *mutatis mutandis*, from the 1990 Model Treaty on Extradition, Article 15(4).

[73] Text taken, *mutatis mutandis*, from the 1990 Model Treaty on Extradition, Article 16.

[74] Text taken, *mutatis mutandis*, from the 1990 Model Treaty on Extradition, Article 17(1).

[75] Text taken, *mutatis mutandis*, from the 1990 Model Treaty on Extradition, Article 17(2).

[76] Text taken, *mutatis mutandis*, from the 1990 Model Treaty on Extradition, Article 17(3).

[77] Text taken, *mutatis mutandis*, from the 1988 Drug Convention, Article 7(1).

[78] Text taken, *mutatis mutandis*, from the 1988 Drug Convention, Article 7(2).

[79] Text taken, *mutatis mutandis*, from the 1988 Drug Convention, Article 7(2) and the 1990 Model Treaty on Mutual Assistance, Article 1(2).

[80] Text taken, *mutatis mutandis*, from the 1990 Model Treaty on Mutual Assistance, Article 1(2).

(c) Effecting service of judicial documents;[81]

(d) Executing searches and seizures;[82]

(e) Examining objects and sites;[83]

(f) Providing information and evidentiary items;[84]

(g) Providing originals or certified copies of relevant documents and records, including bank, financial, corporate or business records;[85]

(h) Identifying or tracing proceeds, property, instrumentalities or other things for evidentiary purposes.[86]

33.3 The Parties may afford one another any other forms of mutual legal assistance allowed by the domestic law of the requested Party.[87]

33.4 Upon request, the Parties shall facilitate or encourage, to the extent consistent with their domestic law and practice, the presence or availability of persons, including persons in custody, who consent to assist in investigations or participate in proceedings.[88]

33.5 Assistance shall not be refused solely on the ground of bank secrecy and similar financial institutions.[89]

33.6 The provisions of this article shall not affect the obligations under any other treaty, bilateral or multilateral, which governs or will govern, in whole or in part, mutual legal assistance in criminal matters.[90]

33.7 Sections 33.8 to 33.19 of this Chapter shall apply to requests made pursuant to this article if the Parties in question are not bound by a treaty of mutual legal assistance. If these Parties are bound by such a treaty, the corresponding provisions of that treaty shall apply unless the Parties agree to apply sections 33.8 to 33.19 of this Chapter in lieu thereof.[91]

33.8 Parties shall designate an authority, or when necessary authorities, which shall have the responsibility and power to execute requests for mutual legal assistance or to transmit them to the competent authorities for execution. The authority or the authorities designated for this purpose shall be notified to the Secretary-General. Transmission of requests for mutual legal assistance and any communication related thereto shall be effected between the authorities designated by the Parties; this

---

[81] *Id.*

[82] Text taken, *mutatis mutandis*, from the 1988 Drug Convention, Article 7(2) and the 1990 Model Treaty on Mutual Assistance, Article 1(2).

[83] *Id.*

[84] *Id.*

[85] *Id.*

[86] *Id.*

[87] Text taken, *mutatis mutandis*, from the 1988 Drug Convention, Article 7(3).

[88] Text taken, *mutatis mutandis*, from the 1988 Drug Convention, Article 7(4).

[89] Text taken, *mutatis mutandis*, from the 1988 Drug Convention, Article 7(5).

[90] Text taken, *mutatis mutandis*, from the 1988 Drug Convention, Article 7(6).

[91] Text taken, *mutatis mutandis*, from the 1988 Drug Convention, Article 7(7).

requirement shall be without prejudice to the right of a Party to require that such requests and communications be addressed to it through the diplomatic channel and, in urgent circumstances, where the Parties agree, through channels of the International Criminal Police Organization, if possible.[92]

33.9 Requests shall be made in writing in a language acceptable to the requested Party. The language or languages acceptable to each Party shall be notified to the Secretary-General of the United Nations. In urgent circumstances, and where agreed by the Parties, requests may be made orally, but shall be confirmed in writing forthwith.[93]

33.10 A request for mutual legal assistance shall contain:

(a) The identity of the authority making the request;[94]

(b) The subject matter and nature of the investigation, prosecution or proceeding to which the request relates, and the name and the functions of the authority conducting such investigation, prosecution or proceeding;[95]

(c) A summary of the relevant facts, except in respect of requests for the purpose of service of judicial documents;[96]

(d) A description of the assistance sought and details of any particular procedure the requesting Party wishes to be followed;[97]

(e) Where possible, the identity, location and nationality of any person concerned;[98]

(f) The purpose for which the evidence, information or action is sought;[99]

(g) Specification of any time-limit within which compliance with the request is desired;[100]

(h) Such other information as is necessary for the proper execution of the request.[101]

33.11 The requested Party may request additional information when it appears necessary for the execution of the request in accordance with its domestic law or when it can facilitate such execution.[102]

33.12 A request shall be executed in accordance with the domestic law of the requested Party and, to the extent not contrary to the domestic law of the requested Party and where possible, in accordance with the procedures specified in the request.[103]

---

92 Text taken, *mutatis mutandis*, from the 1988 Drug Convention, Article 7(8).
93 Text taken, *mutatis mutandis*, from the 1988 Drug Convention, Article 7(9).
94 Text taken, *mutatis mutandis*, from the 1988 Drug Convention, Article 7(10).
95 *Id.*
96 *Id.*
97 *Id.*
98 *Id.*
99 *Id.*
100 Text taken, *mutatis mutandis*, from the 1990 Model Treaty on Mutual Assistance, Article 5(1).
101 *Id.*
102 Text taken, *mutatis mutandis*, from the 1988 Drug Convention, Article 7(11).
103 Text taken, *mutatis mutandis*, from the 1988 Drug Convention, Article 7(12).

33.13 The requesting Party shall not transmit nor use information or evidence furnished by the requested Party for investigations, prosecutions or proceedings other than those stated in the request without the prior consent of the requested Party.[104]

33.14 Upon request:

(a) The requesting Party may require that the requested Party keep confidential the fact and substance of the request, except to the extent necessary to execute the request. If the requested Party cannot comply with the requirement of confidentiality, it shall promptly inform the requesting Party, which shall then determine whether the request should nevertheless be executed;[105] and,

(b) The requesting State shall keep confidential evidence and information provided by the requested State, except to the extent that the evidence and information is needed for the investigation and proceedings described in the request.[106]

33.15 Mutual legal assistance may be refused:

(a) If the request is not made in conformity with the provisions of this article;[107]

(b) If the requested Party considers that execution of the request is likely to prejudice its sovereignty, security, *ordre public* or other essential interests;[108]

(c) If the authorities of the requested Party would be prohibited by its domestic law from carrying out the action requested with regard to any similar offence, had it been subject to investigation, prosecution or proceedings under their own jurisdiction;[109]

(d) If it would be contrary to the legal system of the requested Party relating to mutual legal assistance for the request to be granted.[110]

(e) There are substantial grounds for believing that the request for assistance had been made for the purpose of prosecuting a person on account of that person's race, sex, religion, nationality, ethnic origin or political opinions or that that person's position may be prejudiced for any of those reasons;[111]

33.16 Reasons shall be given for any refusal or postponement of mutual legal assistance.[112]

33.17 Mutual legal assistance may be postponed by the requested Party on the ground that it interferes with an ongoing investigation, prosecution or proceeding. In such a case, the requested Party shall consult with the requesting Party to determine if the

---

[104] Text taken, *mutatis mutandis*, from the 1988 Drug Convention, Article 7(13).

[105] Text taken, *mutatis mutandis*, from the 1988 Drug Convention, Article 7(14) and the 1990 Model Treaty on Mutual Assistance, Article 9(a).

[106] Text taken, *mutatis mutandis*, from and the 1990 Model Treaty on Mutual Assistance, Article 9(b).

[107] Text taken, *mutatis mutandis*, from the 1988 Drug Convention, Article 7(15).

[108] *Id.*

[109] *Id.*

[110] *Id.*

[111] Text taken, *mutatis mutandis*, from the 1990 Model Treaty on Mutual Assistance, Article 4.

[112] Text taken, *mutatis mutandis*, from the 1988 Drug Convention, Article 7(16) and the 1990 Model Treaty on Mutual Assistance, Article 4(5).

assistance can still be given subject to such terms and conditions as the requested Party deems necessary.[113]

33.18 A witness, expert or other person who consents to give evidence in a proceeding or to assist in an investigation, prosecution or judicial proceeding in the territory of the requesting Party, shall not be prosecuted, detained, punished or subjected to any other restriction of his personal liberty in that territory in respect of acts, omissions or convictions prior to his/her departure from the territory of the requested Party. Such safe conduct shall cease when the witness, expert or other person having had, for a period of fifteen consecutive days, or for any period agreed upon by the Parties, from the date on which he has been officially informed that his/her presence is no longer required by the judicial authorities, an opportunity of leaving, has nevertheless remained voluntarily in the territory or, having left it, has returned of his/her own free will.[114]

33.19 A witness, expert or other person shall not, without his/her consent, be required to give evidence in any proceeding or to assist in any investigation other than the proceeding or investigation to which the request relates.[115]

33.20 A person who does not consent to a request under this Chapter shall not, by reason thereof, be liable to any penalty or be subjected to any coercive measure, notwithstanding any contrary statement in the request or summons.[116]

34. **Availability of other persons to give evidence or assist in investigations.**

34.1 The requesting State may request the assistance of the requested State in inviting a person:[117]

(a) To appear in proceedings in relation to a criminal matter in the requesting State unless that person is the person charged; or,

(b) To assist in the investigations in relation to a criminal matter in the requesting State.

34.2 The requested State shall invite the person to appear as a witness or expert in proceedings or to assist in the investigations. Where appropriate, the requested State shall satisfy itself that satisfactory arrangements have been made for the person's safety.[118]

34.3 The request or the summons shall indicate the approximate allowances and the travel and subsistence expenses payable by the requesting State.[119]

---

[113] Text taken, *mutatis mutandis*, from the 1988 Drug Convention, Article 7(17).
[114] Text taken, *mutatis mutandis*, from the 1988 Drug Convention, Article 7(18).
[115] Text taken, *mutatis mutandis*, from the 1990 Model Treaty on Mutual Assistance, Article 15(1).
[116] Text taken, *mutatis mutandis*, from the 1990 Model Treaty on Mutual Assistance, Article 15(3).
[117] Text taken, *mutatis mutandis*, from the 1990 Model Treaty on Mutual Assistance, Article 14(1).
[118] Text taken, *mutatis mutandis*, from the 1990 Model Treaty on Mutual Assistance, Article 14(2).
[119] Text taken, *mutatis mutandis*, from the 1990 Model Treaty on Mutual Assistance, Article 14(3).

34.4 Upon request, the requested State may grant the person an advance, which shall be refunded by the requesting State. [120]

35. **Service of documents.**

35.1 The requested State shall effect service of documents that are transmitted to it for this purpose by the requesting State. [121]

35.2 A request to effect service of summonses shall be made to a requested State not less than 60 days before the date on which the appearance of a person is required. In urgent cases, the requested State may waive the time requirement. [122]

36. **Obtaining of evidence.**

36.1 The requested State shall, in conformity with its law and upon request, take the sworn or affirmed testimony, or otherwise obtain statements of persons or require them to produce items of evidence for transmission to the requesting State. [123]

36.2 Upon the request of the requesting State, the parties to the relevant proceedings in the requesting State, their legal representatives and representatives of the requesting State may, subject to the laws and procedures of the requested State, be present at the proceedings. [124]

37. **Right or obligation to decline to give evidence.**

37.1 A person who is required to give evidence in the requested or requesting State may decline to give evidence where either:

(a) The law of the requested State permits or requires that person to decline to give evidence in similar circumstances in proceedings originating in the requested State; or,

(b) The law of the requesting State permits or requires that person to decline to give evidence in similar circumstances in proceedings originating in the requesting State. [125]

37.2 If a person claims that there is a right or obligation to decline to give evidence under the law of the other State, the State where that person is present shall, with respect thereto, rely on a certificate of the competent authority of the other State as evidence of the existence or non-existence of that right or obligation. [126]

[120] Text taken, *mutatis mutandis*, from the 1990 Model Treaty on Mutual Assistance, Article 14(4).
[121] Text taken, *mutatis mutandis*, from the 1990 Model Treaty on Mutual Assistance, Article 10(1).
[122] Text taken, *mutatis mutandis*, from the 1990 Model Treaty on Mutual Assistance, Article 10(2).
[123] Text taken, *mutatis mutandis*, from the 1990 Model Treaty on Mutual Assistance, Article 11(1).
[124] Text taken, *mutatis mutandis*, from the 1990 Model Treaty on Mutual Assistance, Article 11(2).
[125] Text taken, *mutatis mutandis*, from the 1990 Model Treaty on Mutual Assistance, Article 12(1).
[126] Text taken, *mutatis mutandis*, from the 1990 Model Treaty on Mutual Assistance, Article 12(2).

38. **Availability of persons in custody to give evidence or to assist in investigations.**

38.1 Upon the request of the requesting State, and if the requested State agrees and its law so permits, a person in custody in the latter State may, subject to his or her consent, be temporarily transferred to the requesting State to give evidence or to assist in the investigations.[127]

38.2 While the person transferred is required to be held in custody under the law of the requested State, the requesting State shall hold that person in custody and shall return that person in custody to the requested State at the conclusion of the matter in relation to which transfer was sought or at such earlier time as the person's presence is no longer required.[128]

38.3 Where the requested State advises the requesting State that the transferred person is no longer required to be held in custody, that person shall be set at liberty and be treated as a person referred to in section 31 of the present Chapter.[129]

39. **Provision of publicly available documents and other records.**

39.1 The requested State shall provide copies of documents and records in so far as they are open to public access as part of a public register or otherwise, or in so far as they are available for purchase or inspection by the public.[130]

39.2 The requested State may provide copies of any other document or record under the same conditions as such document or record may be provided to its own law enforcement and judicial authorities.[131]

40. **Search and seizure.** The requested State shall, in so far as its law permits, carry out requests for search and seizure and delivery of any material to the requesting State for evidentiary purposes, provided that the rights of *bona fide* third parties are protected.[132]

41. **Certification and authentication.** A request for assistance and the documents in support thereof, as well as documents or other material supplied in response to such a request, shall not require certification or authentication.[133]

42. The ordinary costs of executing a request shall be borne by the requested Party, unless otherwise agreed by the Parties concerned. If expenses of a substantial or extraordinary nature are or will be required to fulfil the request, the Parties shall consult to determine

[127] Text taken, *mutatis mutandis,* from the 1990 Model Treaty on Mutual Assistance, Article 13(1).
[128] Text taken, *mutatis mutandis,* from the 1990 Model Treaty on Mutual Assistance, Article 13(2).
[129] Text taken, *mutatis mutandis,* from the 1990 Model Treaty on Mutual Assistance, Article 13(3).
[130] Text taken, *mutatis mutandis,* from the 1990 Model Treaty on Mutual Assistance, Article 16(1).
[131] Text taken, *mutatis mutandis,* from the 1990 Model Treaty on Mutual Assistance, Article 16(2).
[132] Text taken, *mutatis mutandis,* from the 1990 Model Treaty on Mutual Assistance, Article 17.
[133] Text taken, *mutatis mutandis,* from the 1990 Model Treaty on Mutual Assistance, Article 18.

the terms and conditions under which the request will be executed as well as the manner in which the costs shall be borne.[134]

43. Any property, as well as original records or documents, handed over to the requesting State under the present Protocol shall be returned to the requested State as soon as possible unless the latter waives its right of return thereof.[135]

44. The Parties shall consider, as may be necessary, the possibility of concluding bilateral or multilateral agreements or arrangements that would serve the purposes of, give practical effect to, or enhance the provisions of this article.[136]

45. **Proceeds of crime.**

45.1 The requested State shall, upon request, endeavour to ascertain whether any proceeds of the alleged crime are located within its jurisdiction and shall notify the requesting State of the results of its inquiries. In making the request, the requesting State shall notify the requested State of the basis of its belief that such proceeds may be located within its jurisdiction.[137]

45.2 In pursuance of a request made under paragraph 2 of the present Article, the requested State shall endeavour to trace assets, investigate financial dealings, and obtain other information or evidence that may help to secure the recovery of proceeds of crime.[138]

45.3 Where, pursuant to paragraph 1 of the present Article, suspected proceeds of crime are found, the requested State shall upon request take such measures as are permitted by its law to prevent any dealing in, transfer or disposal of, those suspected proceeds of crime, pending a final determination in respect of those proceeds by a court of the requesting State.[139]

45.4 The requested State shall, to the extent permitted by its law, give effect to or permit enforcement of a final order forfeiting or confiscating the proceeds of crime made by a court of the requesting State or take other appropriate action to secure the proceeds following a request by the requesting State.[140]

---

[134] Text taken, *mutatis mutandis*, from the 1988 Drug Convention, Article 7(19) and the 1990 Model Treaty on Mutual Assistance, Article 19.

[135] Text taken, *mutatis mutandis*, from the 1990 Model Treaty on Mutual Assistance, Article 7.

[136] Text taken, *mutatis mutandis*, from the 1988 Drug Convention, Article 7(20).

[137] Text taken, *mutatis mutandis*, from the Optional Protocol to the 1990 Model Treaty on Mutual Assistance, Section 2.

[138] Text taken, *mutatis mutandis*, from the Optional Protocol to the 1990 Model Treaty on Mutual Assistance, Section 3.

[139] Text taken, *mutatis mutandis*, from the Optional Protocol to the 1990 Model Treaty on Mutual Assistance, Section 4.

[140] Text taken, *mutatis mutandis*, from the Optional Protocol to the 1990 Model Treaty on Mutual Assistance, Section 5.

45.5 The Parties shall ensure that the rights of bona fide third parties shall be respected in the application of the present Chapter.[141]

CHAPTER IV. TRANSFER OF PROCEEDINGS

46. **Scope of application.**

46.1 States Parties shall consider the possibility of transferring to one another proceedings for the prosecution of an offence covered by this Protocol in cases where such transfer is considered to be in the interests of the proper administration of justice, in particular in cases where several jurisdictions are involved, with a view to concentrating the prosecution.[142]

46.2 For the purpose of applying the present Chapter, the Parties shall take the necessary legislative measures to ensure that a request of the requesting State to take proceedings shall allow the requested State to exercise the necessary jurisdiction.[143]

47. The Parties shall give consideration to the possibility of transferring to one another proceedings for criminal prosecution of offences covered by this Protocol, in cases where such transfer is considered to be in the interests of a proper administration of justice.[144]

48. **Channels of communications.** A request to take proceedings shall be made in writing. The request, supporting documents and subsequent communication shall be transmitted through diplomatic channels, directly between the Ministries of Justice or any other authorities designated by the Parties.[145]

49. **Required documents.**

49.1 The request to take proceedings shall contain or be accompanied by the following information:

(a) The authority presenting the request;

(b) A description of the act for which transfer of proceedings is being requested, including the specific time and place of the offence;

(c) A statement on the results of investigations which substantiate the suspicion of an offence;

(d) The legal provisions of the requesting State on the basis of which the act is considered to be an offence;

---

[141] Text taken, *mutatis mutandis*, from the Optional Protocol to the 1990 Model Treaty on Mutual Assistance, Section 6.

[142] Text taken, *mutatis mutandis*, from the 2000 United Nations Convention Against Transnational Organised Crime (2000 Transnational Organised Crime Convention), Article 21

[143] Text taken, *mutatis mutandis*, from the United Nations 1990 Model Treaty on the Transfer of Proceedings in Criminal Matters ("1990 Model Treaty on Transfer of Proceedings"), Article 1(2).

[144] Text taken, *mutatis mutandis*, from the 1988 Drug Convention, Article 8.

[145] Text taken, *mutatis mutandis*, from the 1990 Model Treaty on Transfer of Proceedings, Article 2.

(e) A reasonably exact statement on the identity, nationality and residence of the suspected person.[146]

49.2 The documents submitted in support of a request to take proceedings shall be accompanied by a translation into the language of the requested State or into another language acceptable to that State.[147]

50. **Certification and authentication.** Subject to national law and unless the Parties decide otherwise, a request to take proceedings and the documents in support thereof, as well as the documents and other material supplied in response to such a request, shall not require certification or authentication.[148]

51. **Decision on the request.** The competent authorities of the requested State shall examine what action to take on the request to take proceedings in order to comply, as fully as possible, with the request under their own law, and shall promptly communicate their decision to the requesting State.[149]

52. **Dual criminality.** A request to take proceedings can be complied with only if the act on which the request is based would be an offence if committed in the territory of the requested State.[150]

53. **The position of the suspected person.**

53.1 The suspected person may express to either State his or her interest in the transfer of the proceedings. Similarly, such interest may be expressed by the legal representative or close relatives of the suspected person.[151]

53.2 Before a request for transfer of proceedings is made, the requesting State shall, if practicable, allow the suspected person to present his or her views on the alleged offence and the intended transfer, unless that person has absconded or otherwise obstructed the course of justice.[152]

54. **The rights of the victim.** The requesting and requested States shall ensure in the transfer of proceedings that the rights of the victim of the offence, in particular his or her right to restitution or compensation, shall not be affected as a result of the transfer. If a settlement of the claim of the victim has not been reached before the transfer, the requested State shall permit the representation of the claim in the transferred proceedings, if its law provides for such a possibility. In the event of the death of the victim, these provisions shall apply to his or her dependants accordingly.[153]

[146] Text taken, *mutatis mutandis*, from the 1990 Model Treaty on Transfer of Proceedings, Article 3(1).
[147] Text taken, *mutatis mutandis*, from the 1990 Model Treaty on Transfer of Proceedings, Article 3(2).
[148] Text taken, *mutatis mutandis*, from the 1990 Model Treaty on Transfer of Proceedings, Article 4.
[149] Text taken, *mutatis mutandis*, from the 1990 Model Treaty on Transfer of Proceedings, Article 5.
[150] Text taken, *mutatis mutandis*, from the 1990 Model Treaty on Transfer of Proceedings, Article 6.
[151] Text taken, *mutatis mutandis*, from the 1990 Model Treaty on Transfer of Proceedings, Article 8(1).
[152] Text taken, *mutatis mutandis*, from the 1990 Model Treaty on Transfer of Proceedings, Article 8(2).
[153] Text taken, *mutatis mutandis*, from the 1990 Model Treaty on Transfer of Proceedings, Article 9.

55. **Effects of the transfer of proceedings on the requesting State (*ne bis in idem*).** Upon acceptance by the requested State of the request to take proceedings against the suspected person, the requesting State shall provisionally discontinue prosecution, except necessary investigation, including judicial assistance to the requested State, until the requested State informs the requesting State that the case has been finally disposed of. From that date on, the requesting State shall definitely refrain from further prosecution of the same offence.[154]

56. **Effects of the transfer of proceedings on the requested State.**

56.1 The proceedings transferred upon agreement shall be governed by the law of the requested State. When charging the suspected person under its law, the requested State shall make the necessary adjustment with respect to particular elements in the legal description of the offence. Where the competence of the requested State is based on the provision set forth in section 43.2 of the present Chapter, the sanction pronounced in that State shall not be more severe than that provided by the law of the requesting State.[155]

56.2 As far as compatible with the law of the requested State, any act with a view to proceedings or procedural requirements performed in the requesting State in accordance with its law shall have the same validity in the requested State as if the act had been performed in or by the authorities of that State.[156]

56.3 The requested State shall inform the requesting State of the decision taken as a result of the proceedings. To this end a copy of any final decision shall be transmitted to the requesting State upon request.[157]

57. **Provisional measures.** When the requesting State announces its intention to transmit a request for transfer of proceedings, the requested State may, upon a specific request made for this purpose by the requesting State, apply all such provisional measures, including provisional detention and seizure, as could be applied under its own law if the offence in respect of which transfer of proceedings is requested had been committed in its territory.[158]

58. **The plurality of criminal proceedings.** When criminal proceedings are pending in two or more States against the same suspected person in respect of the same offence, the States concerned shall conduct consultations to decide which of them alone should continue the proceedings. An agreement reached thereupon shall have the consequences of a request for transfer of proceedings.[159]

---

[154] Text taken, *mutatis mutandis*, from the 1990 Model Treaty on Transfer of Proceedings, Article 10.
[155] Text taken, *mutatis mutandis*, from the 1990 Model Treaty on Transfer of Proceedings, Article 11(1).
[156] Text taken, *mutatis mutandis*, from the 1990 Model Treaty on Transfer of Proceedings, Article 11(2).
[157] Text taken, *mutatis mutandis*, from the 1990 Model Treaty on Transfer of Proceedings, Article 11(3).
[158] Text taken, *mutatis mutandis*, from the 1990 Model Treaty on Transfer of Proceedings, Article 12.
[159] Text taken, *mutatis mutandis*, from the 1990 Model Treaty on Transfer of Proceedings, Article 13.

59. **Costs**. Any costs incurred by a Contracting Party because of a transfer of proceedings shall not be refunded, unless otherwise agreed by both the requesting and requested States.[160]

CHAPTER V. OTHER FORMS OF COOPERATION AND TRAINING

60. The Parties shall cooperate closely with one another, consistent with their respective domestic legal and administrative systems, with a view to enhancing the effectiveness of law enforcement action to suppress the commission of offences covered by this Protocol. They shall, in particular, on the basis of bilateral or multilateral agreements or arrangements:

(a) Establish and maintain channels of communication between their competent agencies and services to facilitate the secure and rapid exchange of information concerning all aspects of offences covered by this Protocol, including, if the Parties concerned deem it appropriate, links with other criminal activities;

(b) Co-operate with one another in conducting enquiries, with respect to offences covered by this Protocol, having an international character, concerning:

(i) The identity, whereabouts and activities of persons suspected of being involved in offences covered by this Protocol;

(ii) The movement of proceeds or property derived from the commission of such offences;

(iii) The movement of toxic chemicals and their precursors listed in Schedules 1, 2 and 3 of the Annex on Chemicals to the Convention used or intended for use in the commission of such offences;

(c) In appropriate cases and if not contrary to domestic law, establish joint teams, taking into account the need to protect the security of persons and of operations, to carry out the provisions of this paragraph. Officials of any Party taking part in such teams shall act as authorised by the appropriate authorities of the Party in whose territory the operation is to take place; in all such cases, the Parties involved shall ensure that the sovereignty of the Party on whose territory the operation is to take place is fully respected;

(d) Provide, when appropriate, necessary quantities of substances for analytical or investigative purposes;

(e) Facilitate effective co-ordination between their competent agencies and services and promote the exchange of personnel and other experts.[161]

60.1 Each Party shall, to the extent necessary, initiate, develop or improve specific training programmes for its law enforcement and other personnel, including customs, charged with the suppression of offences covered by this Protocol. Such programmes shall deal, in particular, with the following:

---

160 Text taken, *mutatis mutandis*, from the 1990 Model Treaty on Transfer of Proceedings, Article 14.

161 Text taken, *mutatis mutandis*, from the 1988 Drug Convention, Article 9(1).

(a) Methods used in the detection and suppression of offences established in accordance with article 3, paragraph 1;

(b) Routes and techniques used by persons suspected of being involved in offences covered by this Protocol, particularly in transit States, and appropriate countermeasures;

(c) Monitoring of the import and export of toxic chemicals and their precursors listed in Schedules 1, 2 and 3 of the Annex on Chemicals to the Convention;

(d) Detection and monitoring of the movement of proceeds and property derived from, and toxic chemicals and their precursors listed in Schedules 1, 2 and 3 of the Annex on Chemicals to the Convention, used or intended for use in the commission of offences covered by this Protocol;

(e) Methods used for the transfer, concealment or disguise of such proceeds, property and instrumentalities;

(f) Collection of evidence;

(g) Control techniques in free trade zones and free ports;

(h) Modern law enforcement techniques.[162]

CHAPTER VI. COOPERATION IN COMBATING ILLICIT TRAFFIC

61. **International cooperation and assistance for transit states.**

61.1 The Parties shall cooperate, directly or through the OPCW or other competent international or regional organisations, to assist and support transit States and, in particular, developing countries in need of such assistance and support, to the extent possible, through programmes of technical co-operation on interdiction and other related activities.[163]

61.2 The Parties may undertake, directly or through the OPCW or other competent international or regional organisations, to provide financial assistance to such transit States for the purpose of augmenting and strengthening the infrastructure needed for effective control and prevention of illicit traffic.[164]

61.3 The Parties may conclude bilateral or multilateral agreements or arrangements to enhance the effectiveness of international co-operation pursuant to this Chapter and may take into consideration financial arrangements in this regard.[165]

62. **Illicit traffic by sea.**

62.1 The Parties shall co-operate to the fullest extent possible to suppress illicit traffic by sea, in conformity with the international law of the sea.[166]

---

[162] Text taken, *mutatis mutandis*, from the 1988 Drug Convention, Article 9(2).
[163] Text taken, *mutatis mutandis*, from the 1988 Drug Convention, Article 10(1).
[164] Text taken, *mutatis mutandis*, from the 1988 Drug Convention, Article 10(2).
[165] Text taken, *mutatis mutandis*, from the 1988 Drug Convention, Article 10(3).
[166] Text taken, *mutatis mutandis*, from the 1988 Drug Convention, Article 17(1).

62.2 A Party which has reasonable grounds to suspect that a vessel flying its flag or not displaying a flag or marks of registry is engaged in illicit traffic may request the assistance of other Parties in suppressing its use for that purpose. The Parties so requested shall render such assistance within the means available to them.[167]

62.3 A Party which has reasonable grounds to suspect that a vessel exercising freedom of navigation in accordance with international law and flying the flag or displaying marks of registry of another Party is engaged in illicit traffic may so notify the flag State, request confirmation of registry and, if confirmed, request authorisation from the flag State to take appropriate measures in regard to that vessel.[168]

62.4 In accordance with paragraph 3 or in accordance with treaties in force between them or in accordance with any agreement or arrangement otherwise reached between those Parties, the flag State may authorise the requesting State to, *inter alia*:

(a) Board the vessel;

(b) Search the vessel;

(c) If evidence of involvement in illicit traffic is found, take appropriate action with respect to the vessel, persons and cargo on board.[169]

62.5 Where action is taken pursuant to this article, the Parties concerned shall take due account of the need not to endanger the safety of life at sea, the security of the vessel and the cargo or to prejudice the commercial and legal interests of the flag State or any other interested State.[170]

62.6 The flag State may, consistent with its obligations in paragraph 1 of this article, subject its authorisation to conditions to be mutually agreed between it and the requesting Party, including conditions relating to responsibility.[171]

62.7 For the purposes of paragraphs 3 and 4 of this article, a Party shall respond expeditiously to a request from another Party to determine whether a vessel that is flying its flag is entitled to do so, and to requests for authorisation made pursuant to paragraph 3. At the time of becoming a Party to this Protocol, each Party shall designate an authority or, when necessary, authorities to receive and respond to such requests. Such designation shall be notified through the Director-General to all other Parties within one month of the designation.[172]

62.8 A Party which has taken any action in accordance with this article shall promptly inform the flag State concerned of the results of that action.[173]

---

[167] Text taken, *mutatis mutandis*, from the 1988 Drug Convention, Article 17(2).
[168] Text taken, *mutatis mutandis*, from the 1988 Drug Convention, Article 17(3).
[169] Text taken, *mutatis mutandis*, from the 1988 Drug Convention, Article 17(4).
[170] Text taken, *mutatis mutandis*, from the 1988 Drug Convention, Article 17(5).
[171] Text taken, *mutatis mutandis*, from the 1988 Drug Convention, Article 17(6).
[172] Text taken, *mutatis mutandis*, from the 1988 Drug Convention, Article 17(7).
[173] Text taken, *mutatis mutandis*, from the 1988 Drug Convention, Article 17(8).

62.9 The Parties shall consider entering into bilateral or regional agreements or arrangements to carry out, or to enhance the effectiveness of, the provisions of this article.[174]

62.10 Action pursuant to paragraph 4 of this article shall be carried out only by warships or military aircraft, or other ships or aircraft clearly marked and identifiable as being on government service and authorised to that effect.[175]

62.11 Any action taken in accordance with this article shall take due account of the need not to interfere with or affect the rights and obligations and the exercise of jurisdiction of coastal States in accordance with the international law of the sea.[176]

63. **Free trade zones and free ports.**

63.1 The Parties shall apply measures to suppress illicit traffic in toxic chemicals and their precursors in free trade zones and in free ports that are no less stringent than those applied in other parts of their territories.[177]

63.2 The Parties shall endeavour:

(a) To monitor the movement of goods and persons in free trade zones and free ports, and, to that end, shall empower the competent authorities to search cargoes and incoming and outgoing vessels, including pleasure craft and fishing vessels, as well as aircraft and vehicles and, when appropriate, to search crew members, passengers and their baggage;

(b) To establish and maintain a system to detect consignments suspected of representing illicit traffic in toxic chemicals and their precursors passing into or out of free trade zones and free ports;

(c) To establish and maintain surveillance systems in harbour and dock areas and at airports and border control points in free trade zones and free ports.[178]

64. **The use of the mails.**

64.1 In conformity with their obligations under the Protocols of the Universal Postal Union, and in accordance with the basic principles of their domestic legal systems, the Parties shall adopt measures to suppress the use of the mails for illicit traffic and shall co-operate with one another to that end.[179]

64.2 The measures referred to in paragraph 1 of this article shall include, in particular:

(a) Co-ordinated action for the prevention and repression of the use of the mails for illicit traffic;

---

174 Text taken, *mutatis mutandis*, from the 1988 Drug Convention, Article 17(9).
175 Text taken, *mutatis mutandis*, from the 1988 Drug Convention, Article 17(10).
176 Text taken, *mutatis mutandis*, from the 1988 Drug Convention, Article 17(11).
177 Text taken, *mutatis mutandis*, from the 1988 Drug Convention, Article 18(1).
178 Text taken, *mutatis mutandis*, from the 1988 Drug Convention, Article 18(2).
179 Text taken, *mutatis mutandis*, from the 1988 Drug Convention, Article 19(1).

(b) Introduction and maintenance by authorised law enforcement personnel of investigative and control techniques designed to detect illicit consignments of toxic chemicals and their precursors in the mails;

(c) Legislative measures to enable the use of appropriate means to secure evidence required for judicial proceedings.[180]

CHAPTER VII: ECONOMIC DEVELOPMENT AND TECHNICAL ASSISTANCE

65. States Parties shall take measures conducive to the optimal implementation of this Protocol to the extent possible, through international cooperation, taking into account the negative effects on society in general of illicit traffic and offences covered by this Protocol.[181]

66. States Parties shall make concrete efforts to the extent possible and in coordination with each other, as well as with international and regional organisations and the OPCW:

(a) To enhance their cooperation at various levels with developing countries, with a view to strengthening the capacity of the latter to prevent and combat illicit traffic and offences covered by this Protocol;

(b) To enhance financial and material assistance to support the efforts of developing countries to fight illicit traffic and offences covered by this Protocol and to help them implement this Protocol successfully;

(c) To provide technical assistance to developing countries and countries with economies in transition to assist them in meeting their needs for the implementation of this Protocol. To that end, States Parties shall endeavour to make adequate and regular voluntary contributions to an account specifically designated for that purpose in the OPCW. States Parties may also give special consideration, in accordance with their domestic law and the provisions of this Protocol, to contributing to the aforementioned account a percentage of the money or of the corresponding value of proceeds of crime or property confiscated in connection with the provisions of this Protocol.[182]

67. To the extent possible, these measures shall be without prejudice to existing foreign assistance commitments or to other financial cooperation arrangements at the bilateral, regional or international level.[183]

[180] Text taken, *mutatis mutandis*, from the 1988 Drug Convention, Article 19(2).
[181] Text taken, *mutatis mutandis*, from the 2000 Transnational Organised Crime Convention, Article 30(1).
[182] Text taken, *mutatis mutandis*, from the 2000 Transnational Organised Crime Convention, Article 30(2).
[183] Text taken, *mutatis mutandis*, from the 2000 Transnational Organised Crime Convention, Article 30(3).

CHAPTER VIII: FINAL PROVISIONS

68. **Relation with the Chemical Weapons Convention.**

68.1 In order to become a Party to this Protocol, a State must also be a Party to the Chemical Weapons Convention.[184]

68.2 A State Party to the Convention is not bound by this Protocol unless it becomes a Party to the Protocol in accordance with the provisions thereof.[185]

68.3 This Protocol shall be interpreted together with the Convention, taking into account the purpose of the Protocol.[186]

69. The original of this Protocol, of which the Arabic, Chinese, English, French, Russian and Spanish texts are equally authentic, shall be deposited with the Secretary-General of the United Nations, who shall send certified copies thereof to all States Parties to the Chemical Weapons Convention.[187]

70. Before its entry into force, this Protocol shall be open for signature for all States Parties to the Convention. This Protocol shall be subject to ratification by States Signatories according to their respective constitutional processes. Any State which does not sign this Protocol before its entry into force may accede to it at any time thereafter.[188]

70.1 Instruments of ratification or accession shall be deposited with the Secretary-General of the United Nations, as Depositary.[189]

70.2 This Protocol shall enter into force three months after the deposit of the tenth instrument of ratification or accession. For each State ratifying the present Protocol or acceding to it after its entry into force, the present Protocol shall enter into force one month after the date of the deposit of its own instrument of ratification or accession.[190]

71. The present Protocol shall apply to requests made after its entry into force, even if the relevant acts or omissions occurred prior to that date.[191]

72. Either Contracting Party may denounce the present Protocol by giving notice in writing to the Depositary. Such denunciation shall take effect six months following the date on which it is received by the Depositary.[192]

---

[184] Text taken, *mutatis mutandis*, from the 2000 Transnational Organised Crime Convention, Article 37.
[185] Text taken, *mutatis mutandis*, from the 2000 Transnational Organised Crime Convention, Article 37(3).
[186] Text taken, *mutatis mutandis*, from the 2000 Transnational Organised Crime Convention, Article 37(4).
[187] Text taken, *mutatis mutandis*, from the 1998 Terrorist Bombings Convention, Article 24.
[188] Text taken, *mutatis mutandis*, from the Chemical Weapons Convention, Articles XVIII, XIX and XX.
[189] Text taken, *mutatis mutandis*, from the Chemical Weapons Convention, Article XXIII.
[190] Text taken, *mutatis mutandis*, from the 2000 Optional Protocol to the Convention on the Rights of the Child on the involvement of children in armed conflict, Article 10.
[191] Text taken, *mutatis mutandis*, from the 1990 Model Treaty on Mutual Assistance, Article 21(3).
[192] Text taken, *mutatis mutandis*, from the 1990 Model Treaty on Mutual Assistance, Article 21(4).

In witness whereof, the undersigned, being duly authorised to that effect, have signed this Protocol.

Done at The Hague on the .... day of ...., two thousand and ....

ANNEX VI

COMPARISON OF PARTIES TO THE INSTRUMENTS USED IN COMPILING THE DRAFT OPTIONAL PROTOCOL TO THE CHEMICAL WEAPONS CONVENTION, RELATED TO THE IMPLEMENTATION OF ARTICLE VII, PARAGRAPH 2, OF THE CONVENTION

Status as of 18 July 2002

	State	1993 Chemical Weapons Convention[1] 145 Parties	1988 Narcotics Convention[2] 167 Parties	1997 Terrorist Bombings Convention[3] 64 Parties	1999 Convention for the Suppression of Financing of Terrorism[4] [41 Parties] (not in force)	2000 Convention against Transnational Organised Crime[5] [16 Parties] (not in force)
1.	Afghanistan	S	1992			S
2.	Albania	1997	2001	2002	2002	S
3.	Algeria	1997	1995	2001	2001	S
4.	Andorra		1999		S	S
5.	Angola					S
6.	Antigua and Barbuda		1993		2002	S
7.	Argentina	1997	1993	S	S	S
8.	Armenia	1997	1993		S	S
9.	Australia	1997	1992		S	S
10.	Austria	1997	1997	2000	2002	S

[1] 1993 Convention on the Prohibition of the Development, Production, Stockpiling and Use of Chemical Weapons and on Their Destruction, entered into force on 29 April 1997. Text, as corrected and changed, available at http://www.opcw.org

[2] United Nations Convention against Illicit Traffic in Narcotic Drugs and Psychotropic Substances, UN doc. E/CONF.82/15, Corr.1 and Corr.2 (English only), entered into force on 11 November 1990.

[3] International Convention for the Suppression of Terrorist Bombings, adopted by the UN General Assembly (A/RES/52/164), entered into force on 23 May 2001.

[4] International Convention for the Suppression of the Financing of Terrorism, adopted by the UN General Assembly (A/RES/54/109) on 9 December 1999, entered into force on 10 April 2002.

[5] United Nations Convention Against Transnational Organized Crime, adopted by the UN General Assembly (A/RES/55/25) on 15 November 2000. Opened for signature on 12-15 December 2000 in Palermo, Italy and thereafter at UN Headquarters until 12 December 2002. In terms of Article 31, 40 parties are necessary for entry into force.

	State	1993 Chemical Weapons Convention 145 Parties	1988 Narcotics Convention 167 Parties	1997 Terrorist Bombings Convention 63 Parties	1999 Convention for the Suppression of Financing of Terrorism [36 Parties] (not in force)	2000 Convention against Transnational Organised Crime [15 Parties] (not in force)
11.	Azerbaijan	2000	1993	2001	2001	S
12.	Bahamas	S	1989		S	S
13.	Bahrain	1997	1990		S	
14.	Bangladesh	1997	1990			
15.	Barbados		1992		S	S
16.	Belarus	1997	1990	2001	S	S
17.	Belgium	1997	1995	S	S	S
18.	Belize		1996	2001	S	
19.	Benin	1998	1997		S	S
20.	Bhutan	S	1990		S	
21.	Bolivia	1998	1990	2002	2002	S
22.	Bosnia and Herzegovina	1997	1993		S	2002
23.	Botswana	1998	1996	2000	2000	S
24.	Brazil	1997	1991	S	S	S
25.	Brunei Darussalam	1997	1993	2002		
26.	Bulgaria	1997	1992	2002	2002	2001
27.	Burkina Faso	1997	1992			2002
28.	Burundi	1998	1993	S	S	S
29.	Cambodia	S			S	S
30.	Cameroon	1997	1991			S
31.	Canada	1997	1990	2002	2002	2002
32.	Cape Verde	S	1995	2002	2002	S
33.	Central African Republic	S	2001		S	
34.	Chad	S	1995			
35.	Chile	1997	1990	2001	2001	S
36.	China	1997	1989	2001	S	S
37.	Colombia	2000	1994		S	S
38.	Comoros	S	2000	S	S	
39.	Congo	S			S	S
40.	Cook Islands	1997			S	

	State	1993 Chemical Weapons Convention 145 Parties	1988 Narcotics Convention 167 Parties	1997 Terrorist Bombings Convention 63 Parties	1999 Convention for the Suppression of Financing of Terrorism [36 Parties] (not in force)	2000 Convention against Transnational Organised Crime [15 Parties] (not in force)
41.	Costa Rica	1997	1991	2001	S	S
42.	Côte d' Ivoire	1997	1991	2002	2002	S
43.	Croatia	1997	1993		S	S
44.	Cuba	1997	1996	2001	2001	S
45.	Cyprus	1998	1990	2001	2001	S
46.	Czech Republic	1997	1993	2000	S	S
47.	Dem. People's Rep. Korea				S	
48.	Dem. Rep. of the Congo	S	S		S	
49.	Denmark	1997	1991	2001	S	S
50.	Djibouti	S	2001		S	
51.	Dominica	2001	1993			
52.	Dominican Republic	S	1993		S	S
53.	East Timor					
54.	Ecuador	1997	1990		S	S
55.	Egypt		1991	S	S	S
56.	El Salvador	1997	1993			S
57.	Equatorial Guinea	1997				S
58.	Eritrea	2000	2002			
59.	Estonia	1999	2000	2002	2002	S
60.	Ethiopia	1997	1994			S
61.	European Community		1990			S
62.	Fiji	1997	1993			
63.	Finland	1997	1994	2002	2002	S
64.	France	1997	1990	1999	2002	S
65.	Gabon	2000	S		S	
66.	Gambia	1998	1996			S
67.	Georgia	1997	1998		S	S
68.	Germany	1997	1993	S	S	S
69.	Ghana	1997	1990		S	
70.	Greece	1997	1992	S	S	S

	State	1993 Chemical Weapons Convention 145 Parties	1988 Narcotics Convention 167 Parties	1997 Terrorist Bombings Convention 63 Parties	1999 Convention for the Suppression of Financing of Terrorism [36 Parties] (not in force)	2000 Convention against Transnational Organised Crime [15 Parties] (not in force)
71.	Grenada	S	1990	2001	2001	
72.	Guatemala	S	1991	2002	2002	S
73.	Guinea	1997	1990	2000	S	
74.	Guinea-Bissau	S	1995		S	S
75.	Guyana	1997	1993			
76.	Haiti	S	1995			S
77.	Holy See	1999	S			
78.	Honduras	S	1991		S	S
79.	Hungary	1997	1996	2001	S	S
80.	Iceland	1997	1997	2002	2002	S
81.	India	1997	1990	1999	S	
82.	Indonesia	1998	1999		S	S
83.	Iran (Islamic Republic of)	1997	1992			S
84.	Iraq		1998			
85.	Ireland	1997	1996	S	S	S
86.	Israel	S	2002	S	S	S
87.	Italy	1997	1990	S	S	S
88.	Jamaica	2000	1995		S	S
89.	Japan	1997	1992	2001	2002	S
90.	Jordan	1997	1990		S	
91.	Kazakhstan	2000	1997			S
92.	Kenya	1997	1992	2001	S	
93.	Kiribati	2000				
94.	Kuwait	1997	2000			S
95.	Kyrgyzstan	S	1994	2001		S
96.	Lao People's Dem. Rep.	1997				
97.	Latvia	1997	1994		S	2001
98.	Lebanon		1996			S
99.	Lesotho	1997	1995	2001	2001	S
100.	Liberia	S				

	State	1993 Chemical Weapons Convention 145 Parties	1988 Narcotics Convention 167 Parties	1997 Terrorist Bombings Convention 63 Parties	1999 Convention for the Suppression of Financing of Terrorism [36 Parties] (not in force)	2000 Convention against Transnational Organised Crime [15 Parties] (not in force)
101.	Libyan Arab Jamahiriya		1996	2000	S	S
102.	Liechtenstein	1999			S	S
103.	Lithuania	1998	1998	S		2002
104.	Luxembourg	1997	1992	S	S	S
105.	Madagascar	S	1991	S	S	S
106.	Malawi	1998	1995			S
107.	Malaysia	2000	1993			
108.	Maldives	1997	2000	2000		
109.	Mali	1997	1995	2002	2002	2002
110.	Malta	1997	1996	2001	2001	S
111.	Marshall Islands	S				
112.	Mauritania	1998	1993			
113.	Mauritius	1997	2001		S	S
114.	Mexico	1997	1990		S	S
115.	Micronesia (Fed. States of)	1999			S	
116.	Monaco	1997	1991	2001	2001	2001
117.	Mongolia	1997		2000	S	
118.	Morocco	1997	1992		S	S
119.	Mozambique	2000	1998		S	S
120.	Myanmar	S	1991	2001	S	
121.	Namibia	1997			S	S
122.	Nauru	2001			S	S
123.	Nepal	1997	1991	S		
124.	Netherlands	1997	1993	2002	2002	S
125.	New Zealand	1997	1998		S	S
126.	Nicaragua	1999	1990		S	S
127.	Niger	1997	1992			S
128.	Nigeria	1999	1989		S	2001
129.	Niue					
130.	Norway	1997	1994	1999	S	S

	State	1993 Chemical Weapons Convention 145 Parties	1988 Narcotics Convention 167 Parties	1997 Terrorist Bombings Convention 63 Parties	1999 Convention for the Suppression of Financing of Terrorism [36 Parties] (not in force)	2000 Convention against Transnational Organised Crime [15 Parties] (not in force)
131.	Oman	1997	1991			
132.	Pakistan	1997	1991			S
133.	Palau			2001	2001	
134.	Panama	1998	1994	1999	2002	S
135.	Papua New Guinea	1997				
136.	Paraguay	1997	1990		S	S
137.	Peru	1997	1992	2001	2001	2002
138.	Philippines	1997	1996	S	S	2002
139.	Poland	1997	1994	S	S	2001
140.	Portugal	1997	1991	2001	S	S
141.	Qatar	1997	1990			
142.	Republic of Korea	1997	1998	S	S	S
143.	Republic of Moldova	1997	1995		S	S
144.	Romania	1997	1993	S	S	S
145.	Russian Federation	1997	1990	2001	S	S
146.	Rwanda	S	2002	2002	2002	S
147.	Saint Kitts and Nevis	S	1995	2001	2001	S
148.	Saint Lucia	1997	1995			S
149.	St. Vincent & Grenadines	S	1994		2002	
150.	Samoa	S			S	
151.	San Marino	1999	2000	2002	2002	S
152.	Sao Tome and Principe		1996			
153.	Saudi Arabia	1997	1992		S	S
154.	Senegal	1998	1989			S
155.	Seychelles	1997	1992		S	S
156.	Sierra Leone	S	1994		S	S
157.	Singapore	1997	1997		S	S
158.	Slovakia	1997	1993	2000	S	S
159.	Slovenia	1997	1992	S	S	S
160.	Solomon Islands					

	State	1993 Chemical Weapons Convention 145 Parties	1988 Narcotics Convention 167 Parties	1997 Terrorist Bombings Convention 63 Parties	1999 Convention for the Suppression of Financing of Terrorism [36 Parties] (not in force)	2000 Convention against Transnational Organised Crime [15 Parties] (not in force)
161.	Somalia				S	
162.	South Africa	1997	1998	S	S	S
163.	Spain	1997	1990	1999	2002	2002
164.	Sri Lanka	1997	1991	1999	2000	S
165.	Sudan	1999	1993	2000	S	S
166.	Suriname	1997	1992			
167.	Swaziland	1997	1995			S
168.	Sweden	1997	1991	2001	2002	S
169.	Switzerland	1997	S		S	S
170.	Syrian Arab Republic		1991			2002
171.	Tajikistan	1997	1996		S	S
172.	Thailand	S	2002		S	S
173.	The FYRO Macedonia	1997	1993	S	S	S
174.	Togo	1997	1990	S	S	S
175.	Tonga		1996			
176.	Trinidad and Tobago	1997	1995	2001		S
177.	Tunisia	1997	1990		S	S
178.	Turkey	1997	1996	2002	2002	S
179.	Turkmenistan	1997	1996	1999		
180.	Tuvalu					
181.	Uganda	2001	1990	S	S	S
182.	Ukraine	1998	1991	2002	S	S
183.	United Arab Emirates	2000	1990			
184.	United Kingdom	1997	1991	2001	2001	S
185.	United Rep. of Tanzania	1998	1996			S
186.	United States of America	1997	1990	2002	2002	S
187.	Uruguay	1997	1995	2001	S	S
188.	Uzbekistan	1997	1995	1998	2001	S
189.	Vanuatu					
190.	Venezuela	1997	1991	S	S	2002

	State	1993 Chemical Weapons Convention 145 Parties	1988 Narcotics Convention 167 Parties	1997 Terrorist Bombings Convention 63 Parties	1999 Convention for the Suppression of Financing of Terrorism [36 Parties] (not in force)	2000 Convention against Transnational Organised Crime [15 Parties] (not in force)
191.	Viet Nam	1998	1997			S
192.	Yemen	2000	1996	2001		S
193.	Yugoslavia	2000	2001		S	2001
194.	Zambia	2001	1993			
195.	Zimbabwe	1997	1993			S

ANNEX VII

EXTRACTS FROM THE ICTY STATUTE[1] AND RULES OF PROCEDURE AND EVIDENCE[2]

ARTICLE 18

INVESTIGATION AND PREPARATION OF INDICTMENT

1. The Prosecutor shall initiate investigations *ex-officio* or on the basis of information obtained from any source, particularly from Governments, United Nations organs, intergovernmental and non-governmental organizations. The Prosecutor shall assess the information received or obtained and decide whether there is sufficient basis to proceed.

2. The Prosecutor shall have the power to question suspects, victims and witnesses, to collect evidence and to conduct on-site investigations. In carrying out these tasks, the Prosecutor may, as appropriate, seek the assistance of the State authorities concerned.

3. If questioned, the suspect shall be entitled to be assisted by counsel of his own choice, including the right to have legal assistance assigned to him without payment by him in any such case if he does not have sufficient means to pay for it, as well as to necessary translation into and from a language he speaks and understands.

4. Upon a determination that a *prima facie* case exists, the Prosecutor shall prepare an indictment containing a concise statement of the facts and the crime or crimes with which the accused is charged under the Statute. The indictment shall be transmitted to a judge of the Trial Chamber.

ARTICLE 29

COOPERATION AND JUDICIAL ASSISTANCE

1. States shall cooperate with the International Tribunal in the investigation and prosecution of persons accused of committing serious violations of international humanitarian law.

2. States shall comply without undue delay with any request for assistance or an order issued by a Trial Chamber, including, but not limited to:
   (a) the identification and location of persons;
   (b) the taking of testimony and the production of evidence;
   (c) the service of documents;
   (d) the arrest or detention of persons;
   (e) the surrender or the transfer of the accused to the International Tribunal.

[1] Statute of the International Tribunal, adopted 25 May by Security Council resolution 827, as amended 13 May 1998 by resolution 1166 and 30 November 2000 by resolution 1329.
[2] Rules of Procedure and Evidence, adopted 11 February 1994, as amended 13 December 2001, ICTY doc. IT/32/Rev.22.

RULE 7 BIS
NON-COMPLIANCE WITH OBLIGATIONS

(A) In addition to cases to which Rule 11, Rule 13, Rule 59 or Rule 61 applies, where a Trial Chamber or a Judge is satisfied that a State has failed to comply with an obligation under Article 29 of the Statute which relates to any proceedings before that Chamber or Judge, the Chamber or Judge may advise the President, who shall report the matter to the Security Council.

(B) If the Prosecutor satisfies the President that a State has failed to comply with an obligation under Article 29 of the Statute in respect of a request by the Prosecutor under Rule 8, Rule 39 or Rule 40, the President shall notify the Security Council thereof.

RULE 8
REQUEST FOR INFORMATION

Where it appears to the Prosecutor that a crime within the jurisdiction of the Tribunal is or has been the subject of investigations or criminal proceedings instituted in the courts of any State, the Prosecutor may request the State to forward all relevant information in that respect, and the State shall transmit such information to the Prosecutor forthwith in accordance with Article 29 of the Statute.

RULE 39
CONDUCT OF INVESTIGATIONS

In the conduct of an investigation, the Prosecutor may:

(i) summon and question suspects, victims and witnesses and record their statements, collect evidence and conduct on-site investigations;

(ii) undertake such other matters as may appear necessary for completing the investigation and the preparation and conduct of the prosecution at the trial, including the taking of special measures to provide for the safety of potential witnesses and informants;

(iii) seek, to that end, the assistance of any State authority concerned, as well as of any relevant international body including the International Criminal Police Organization (INTERPOL); and,

(iv) request such orders as may be necessary from a Trial Chamber or a Judge.

RULE 41
RETENTION OF INFORMATION

Subject to Rule 81, the Prosecutor shall be responsible for the retention, storage and security of information and physical evidence obtained in the course of the Prosecutor's investigations until formally tendered into evidence.

RULE 54 BIS
ORDERS DIRECTED TO STATES FOR THE PRODUCTION OF DOCUMENTS

(A) A party requesting an order under Rule 54 that a State produce documents or information shall apply in writing to the relevant Judge or Trial Chamber and shall:

(i) identify as far as possible the documents or information to which the application relates;

(ii) indicate how they are relevant to any matter in issue before the Judge or Trial Chamber and necessary for a fair determination of that matter; and,

(iii) explain the steps that have been taken by the applicant to secure the State's assistance.

(B) The Judge or Trial Chamber may reject an application under Paragraph (A) *in limine* if satisfied that:

(i) the documents or information are not relevant to any matter in issue in the proceedings before them or are not necessary for a fair determination of any such matter; or,

(ii) no reasonable steps have been taken by the applicant to obtain the documents or information from the State.

(C) A decision by a Judge or a Trial Chamber under Sub-rule (B) or (E) shall be subject to appeal on the same grounds and conditions as set out in Rule 73(D) and (E).

(D) (i) Subject to any order of a Judge or a Chamber, the Registrar may transmit a certified copy of a warrant of arrest to the person or authorities to which it is addressed, including the national authorities of a State in whose territory or under whose jurisdiction the accused resides, or was last known to be, or is believed by the Registrar to be likely to be found.

(ii) Except in cases where the Judge or Trial Chamber determines otherwise, only the party making the application and the State concerned shall have the right to be heard.

(E) If, having regard to all circumstances, the Judge or Trial Chamber has good reasons for so doing, the Judge or Trial Chamber may make an order to which this Rule applies without giving the State concerned notice or the opportunity to be heard under Sub-rule (D), and the following provisions shall apply to such an order:

(i) the order shall be served on the State concerned;

(ii) subject to paragraph (iv), the order shall not have effect until fifteen days after such service;

(iii) a State may, within fifteen days of service of the order, apply by notice to the Judge or Trial Chamber to have the order set aside, on the grounds that disclosure would prejudice national security interests. Paragraph (F) shall apply to such a notice as it does to a notice of objection;

(iv) where notice is given under paragraph (iii), the order shall thereupon be stayed until the decision on the application;

(v) Paragraphs (F) and (G) shall apply to the determination of an application made pursuant to paragraph (iii) as they do to the determination of an application of which notice is given pursuant to Paragraph (D);

(vi) the State and the party who applied for the order shall, subject to any special measures made pursuant to a request under Paragraphs (F) or (G), have an opportunity to be heard at the hearing of an application made pursuant to paragraph (E)(iii) of this Rule.

(F) The State, if it raises an objection pursuant to Paragraph (D), on the grounds that disclosure would prejudice its national security interests, shall file a notice of objection not less than five days before the date fixed for the hearing, specifying the grounds of objection. In its notice of objection the State:

(i) shall identify, as far as possible, the basis upon which it claims that its national security interests will be prejudiced; and,

(ii) may request the Judge or Trial Chamber to direct that appropriate protective measures be made for the hearing of the objection, including in particular:

(a) hearing the objection *in camera* and *ex parte*;

(b) allowing documents to be submitted in redacted form, accompanied by an affidavit signed by a senior State official explaining the reasons for the redaction;

(c) ordering that no transcripts be made of the hearing and that documents not further required by the Tribunal be returned directly to the State without being filed with the Registry or otherwise retained.

(G) With regard to the procedure under Paragraph (F) above, the Judge or Trial Chamber may order the following protective measures for the hearing of the objection:

(i) the designation of a single Judge from a Chamber to examine the documents or hear submissions; and/or,

(ii) that the State be allowed to provide its own interpreters for the hearing and its own translations of sensitive documents.

(H) Rejection of an application made under this Rule shall not preclude a subsequent application by the requesting party in respect of the same documents or information if new circumstances arise.

(I) An order under this Rule may provide for the documents or information in question to be produced by the State under appropriate arrangements to protect its interests, which may include those arrangements specified in Paragraphs (F)(ii) or (G).

RULE 66

DISCLOSURE BY THE PROSECUTOR

(A) Subject to the provisions of Rules 53 and 69, the Prosecutor shall make available to the defence in a language which the accused understands

(i) within thirty days of the initial appearance of the accused, copies of the supporting material which accompanied the indictment when confirmation was sought as well as all prior statements obtained by the Prosecutor from the accused; and,

(ii) within the time-limit prescribed by the Trial Chamber or by the pre-trial Judge appointed pursuant to Rule 65 *ter*, copies of the statements of all witnesses whom the Prosecutor intends to call to testify at trial, and copies of all affidavits and formal statements referred to in Rule 94 *ter*; copies of the statements of additional prosecution witnesses shall be made available to the defence when a decision is made to call those witnesses.

(B) The Prosecutor shall, on request, permit the defence to inspect any books, documents, photographs and tangible objects in the Prosecutor's custody or control, which are material to the preparation of the defence, or are intended for use by the Prosecutor as evidence at trial or were obtained from or belonged to the accused.

(C) Where information is in the possession of the Prosecutor, the disclosure of which may prejudice further or ongoing investigations, or for any other reasons may be contrary to the public interest or affect the security interests of any State, the Prosecutor may apply to the Trial Chamber sitting in camera to be relieved from an obligation under the Rules to disclose that information. When making such application the Prosecutor shall provide the Trial Chamber (but only the Trial Chamber) with the information that is sought to be kept confidential.

RULE 68

Disclosure of Exculpatory Evidence

The Prosecutor shall, as soon as practicable, disclose to the defence the existence of evidence known to the Prosecutor which in any way tends to suggest the innocence or mitigate the guilt of the accused or may affect the credibility of prosecution evidence.

RULE 70

Matters not Subject to Disclosure

(A) Notwithstanding the provisions of Rules 66 and 67, reports, memoranda, or other internal documents prepared by a party, its assistants or representatives in connection with the investigation or preparation of the case, are not subject to disclosure or notification under those Rules.

(B) If the Prosecutor is in possession of information which has been provided to the Prosecutor on a confidential basis and which has been used solely for the purpose of generating new evidence, that initial information and its origin shall not be disclosed by the Prosecutor without the consent of the person or entity providing the initial information and shall in any event not be given in evidence without prior disclosure to the accused.

(C) If, after obtaining the consent of the person or entity providing information under this Rule, the Prosecutor elects to present as evidence any testimony, document or other material so provided, the Trial Chamber, notwithstanding Rule 98, may not order either party to produce additional evidence received from the person or entity providing the initial information, nor may the Trial Chamber for the purpose of obtaining such additional evidence itself summon that person or a representative of that entity as a witness or order their attendance. A Trial Chamber may not use its power to order the attendance of witnesses or to require production of documents in order to compel the production of such additional evidence.

(D) If the Prosecutor calls a witness to introduce in evidence any information provided under this Rule, the Trial Chamber may not compel that witness to answer any question relating to the information or its origin, if the witness declines to answer on grounds of confidentiality.

(E) The right of the accused to challenge the evidence presented by the Prosecution shall remain unaffected subject only to the limitations contained in Sub-rules (C) and (D).

(F) The Trial Chamber may order upon an application by the accused or defence counsel that, in the interests of justice, the provisions of this Rule shall apply *mutatis mutandis* to specific information in the possession of the accused.

(G) Nothing in Sub-rule (C) or (D) above shall affect a Trial Chamber's power under Rule 89 (D) to exclude evidence if its probative value is substantially outweighed by the need to ensure a fair trial.

RULE 98

POWER OF CHAMBERS TO ORDER PRODUCTION OF ADDITIONAL EVIDENCE

A Trial Chamber may order either party to produce additional evidence. It may *proprio motu* summon witnesses and order their attendance.

ANNEX VIII

EXTRACTS FROM THE ICC STATUTE[1] AND FINAL DRAFT RULES OF PROCEDURE AND EVIDENCE[2]

ARTICLE 54

DUTIES AND POWERS OF THE PROSECUTOR WITH RESPECT TO INVESTIGATIONS

1. The Prosecutor shall:

(a) In order to establish the truth, extend the investigation to cover all facts and evidence relevant to an assessment of whether there is criminal responsibility under this Statute, and, in doing so, investigate incriminating and exonerating circumstances equally;

(b) Take appropriate measures to ensure the effective investigation and prosecution of crimes within the jurisdiction of the Court, and in doing so, respect the interests and personal circumstances of victims and witnesses, including age, gender as defined in article 7, paragraph 3, and health, and take into account the nature of the crime, in particular where it involves sexual violence, gender violence or violence against children; and,

(c) Fully respect the rights of persons arising under this Statute.

2. The Prosecutor may conduct investigations on the territory of a State:

(a) In accordance with the provisions of Part 9; or,

(b) As authorised by the Pre-Trial Chamber under article 57, paragraph 3 (d).

3. The Prosecutor may:

(a) Collect and examine evidence;

(b) Request the presence of and question persons being investigated, victims and witnesses;

(c) Seek the cooperation of any State or intergovernmental organisation or arrangement in accordance with its respective competence and/or mandate;

(d) Enter into such arrangements or agreements, not inconsistent with this Statute, as may be necessary to facilitate the cooperation of a State, intergovernmental organisation or person;

(e) Agree not to disclose, at any stage of the proceedings, documents or information that the Prosecutor obtains on the condition of confidentiality and solely for the purpose of generating new evidence, unless the provider of the information consents; and,

---

[1] 1998 Rome Statute of the International Criminal Court, entered into force 1 July 2002; UN doc. A/CONF.183/9*, as corrected by the procès-verbaux of 10 November 1998 and 12 July 1999. Corrected text available at http://www.un.org/law/icc.

[2] Finalised draft text of the Rules of Procedure and Evidence, Addendum to the Report of the Preparatory Commission for the International Criminal Court, UN doc. PCNICC/2000/INF/3/Add.1 (12 July 2000). Initially issued as PCNICC/2000/1/Add.1 (adopted by the Preparatory Commission for the International Criminal Court at its 23rd meeting on 30 June 2000).

(f) Take necessary measures, or request that necessary measures be taken, to ensure the confidentiality of information, the protection of any person or the preservation of evidence.

ARTICLE 68

PROTECTION OF THE VICTIMS AND WITNESSES AND THEIR PARTICIPATION IN THE PROCEEDINGS

1. The Court shall take appropriate measures to protect the safety, physical and psychological well-being, dignity and privacy of victims and witnesses. In so doing, the Court shall have regard to all relevant factors, including age, gender as defined in article 7, paragraph 3, and health, and the nature of the crime, in particular, but not limited to, where the crime involves sexual or gender violence or violence against children. The Prosecutor shall take such measures particularly during the investigation and prosecution of such crimes. These measures shall not be prejudicial to or inconsistent with the rights of the accused and a fair and impartial trial.

2. As an exception to the principle of public hearings provided for in article 67, the Chambers of the Court may, to protect victims and witnesses or an accused, conduct any part of the proceedings *in camera* or allow the presentation of evidence by electronic or other special means. In particular, such measures shall be implemented in the case of a victim of sexual violence or a child who is a victim or a witness, unless otherwise ordered by the Court, having regard to all the circumstances, particularly the views of the victim or witness.

3. Where the personal interests of the victims are affected, the Court shall permit their views and concerns to be presented and considered at stages of the proceedings determined to be appropriate by the Court and in a manner which is not prejudicial to or inconsistent with the rights of the accused and a fair and impartial trial. Such views and concerns may be presented by the legal representatives of the victims where the Court considers it appropriate, in accordance with the Rules of Procedure and Evidence.

4. The Victims and Witnesses Unit may advise the Prosecutor and the Court on appropriate protective measures, security arrangements, counselling and assistance as referred to in article 43, paragraph 6.

5. Where the disclosure of evidence or information pursuant to this Statute may lead to the grave endangerment of the security of a witness or his or her family, the Prosecutor may, for the purposes of any proceedings conducted prior to the commencement of the trial, withhold such evidence or information and instead submit a summary thereof. Such measures shall be exercised in a manner which is not prejudicial to or inconsistent with the rights of the accused and a fair and impartial trial.

6. A State may make an application for necessary measures to be taken in respect of the protection of its servants or agents and the protection of confidential or sensitive information.

ARTICLE 72

PROTECTION OF NATIONAL SECURITY INFORMATION

1. This article applies in any case where the disclosure of the information or documents of

a State would, in the opinion of that State, prejudice its national security interests. Such cases include those falling within the scope of article 56, paragraphs 2 and 3, article 61, paragraph 3, article 64, paragraph 3, article 67, paragraph 2, article 68, paragraph 6, article 87, paragraph 6 and article 93, as well as cases arising at any other stage of the proceedings where such disclosure may be at issue.

2. This article shall also apply when a person who has been requested to give information or evidence has refused to do so or has referred the matter to the State on the ground that disclosure would prejudice the national security interests of a State and the State concerned confirms that it is of the opinion that disclosure would prejudice its national security interests.

3. Nothing in this article shall prejudice the requirements of confidentiality applicable under article 54, paragraph 3 (e) and (f), or the application of article 73.

4. If a State learns that information or documents of the State are being, or are likely to be, disclosed at any stage of the proceedings, and it is of the opinion that disclosure would prejudice its national security interests, that State shall have the right to intervene in order to obtain resolution of the issue in accordance with this article.

5. If, in the opinion of a State, disclosure of information would prejudice its national security interests, all reasonable steps will be taken by the State, acting in conjunction with the Prosecutor, the defence or the Pre-Trial Chamber or Trial Chamber, as the case may be, to seek to resolve the matter by cooperative means. Such steps may include:

(a) Modification or clarification of the request;

(b) A determination by the Court regarding the relevance of the information or evidence sought, or a determination as to whether the evidence, though relevant, could be or has been obtained from a source other than the requested State;

(c) Obtaining the information or evidence from a different source or in a different form; or,

(d) Agreement on conditions under which the assistance could be provided including, among other things, providing summaries or redactions, limitations on disclosure, use of *in camera* or *ex parte* proceedings, or other protective measures permissible under the Statute and the Rules of Procedure and Evidence.

6. Once all reasonable steps have been taken to resolve the matter through cooperative means, and if the State considers that there are no means or conditions under which the information or documents could be provided or disclosed without prejudice to its national security interests, it shall so notify the Prosecutor or the Court of the specific reasons for its decision, unless a specific description of the reasons would itself necessarily result in such prejudice to the State's national security interests.

7. Thereafter, if the Court determines that the evidence is relevant and necessary for the establishment of the guilt or innocence of the accused, the Court may undertake the following actions:

(a) Where disclosure of the information or document is sought pursuant to a request for cooperation under Part 9 or the circumstances described in paragraph 2, and the State has invoked the ground for refusal referred to in article 93, paragraph 4:

(i) The Court may, before making any conclusion referred to in subparagraph 7 (a)(ii), request further consultations for the purpose of considering the State's representations, which may include, as appropriate, hearings *in camera* and *ex parte;*

(ii) If the Court concludes that, by invoking the ground for refusal under article 93, paragraph 4, in the circumstances of the case, the requested State is not acting in accordance with its obligations under this Statute, the Court may refer the matter in accordance with article 87, paragraph 7, specifying the reasons for its conclusion; and,

(iii) The Court may make such inference in the trial of the accused as to the existence or non-existence of a fact, as may be appropriate in the circumstances; or

(b) In all other circumstances:

(i) Order disclosure; or,

(ii) To the extent it does not order disclosure, make such inference in the trial of the accused as to the existence or non-existence of a fact, as may be appropriate in the circumstances.

ARTICLE 73
THIRD-PARTY INFORMATION OR DOCUMENTS

If a State Party is requested by the Court to provide a document or information in its custody, possession or control, which was disclosed to it in confidence by a State, intergovernmental organisation or international organisation, it shall seek the consent of the originator to disclose that document or information. If the originator is a State Party, it shall either consent to disclosure of the information or document or undertake to resolve the issue of disclosure with the Court, subject to the provisions of article 72. If the originator is not a State Party and refuses to consent to disclosure, the requested State shall inform the Court that it is unable to provide the document or information because of a pre-existing obligation of confidentiality to the originator.

ARTICLE 93
OTHER FORMS OF COOPERATION

1. States Parties shall, in accordance with the provisions of this Part and under procedures of national law, comply with requests by the Court to provide the following assistance in relation to investigations or prosecutions:

(a) The identification and whereabouts of persons or the location of items;

(b) The taking of evidence, including testimony under oath, and the production of evidence, including expert opinions and reports necessary to the Court;

(c) The questioning of any person being investigated or prosecuted;

(d) The service of documents, including judicial documents;

(e) Facilitating the voluntary appearance of persons as witnesses or experts before the Court;

(f) The temporary transfer of persons as provided in paragraph 7;

(g) The examination of places or sites, including the exhumation and examination of grave sites;

(h) The execution of searches and seizures;

(i) The provision of records and documents, including official records and documents;

(j) The protection of victims and witnesses and the preservation of evidence;

(k) The identification, tracing and freezing or seizure of proceeds, property and assets and instrumentalities of crimes for the purpose of eventual forfeiture, without prejudice to the rights of *bona fide* third parties; and,

(l) Any other type of assistance which is not prohibited by the law of the requested State, with a view to facilitating the investigation and prosecution of crimes within the jurisdiction of the Court.

2. The Court shall have the authority to provide an assurance to a witness or an expert appearing before the Court that he or she will not be prosecuted, detained or subjected to any restriction of personal freedom by the Court in respect of any act or omission that preceded the departure of that person from the requested State.

3. Where execution of a particular measure of assistance detailed in a request presented under paragraph 1, is prohibited in the requested State on the basis of an existing fundamental legal principle of general application, the requested State shall promptly consult with the Court to try to resolve the matter. In the consultations, consideration should be given to whether the assistance can be rendered in another manner or subject to conditions. If after consultations the matter cannot be resolved, the Court shall modify the request as necessary.

4. In accordance with article 72, a State Party may deny a request for assistance, in whole or in part, only if the request concerns the production of any documents or disclosure of evidence which relates to its national security.

5. Before denying a request for assistance under paragraph 1 (l), the requested State shall consider whether the assistance can be provided subject to specified conditions, or whether the assistance can be provided at a later date or in an alternative manner, provided that if the Court or the Prosecutor accepts the assistance subject to conditions, the Court or the Prosecutor shall abide by them.

6. If a request for assistance is denied, the requested State Party shall promptly inform the Court or the Prosecutor of the reasons for such denial.

7. (a) The Court may request the temporary transfer of a person in custody for purposes of identification or for obtaining testimony or other assistance. The person may be transferred if the following conditions are fulfilled:

(i) The person freely gives his or her informed consent to the transfer; and

(ii) The requested State agrees to the transfer, subject to such conditions as that State and the Court may agree.

(b) The person being transferred shall remain in custody. When the purposes of the transfer have been fulfilled, the Court shall return the person without delay to the requested State.

8. (a) The Court shall ensure the confidentiality of documents and information, except as required for the investigation and proceedings described in the request.

(b) The requested State may, when necessary, transmit documents or information to the Prosecutor on a confidential basis. The Prosecutor may then use them solely for the purpose of generating new evidence.

(c) The requested State may, on its own motion or at the request of the Prosecutor, subsequently consent to the disclosure of such documents or information. They may then be used as evidence pursuant to the provisions of Parts 5 and 6 and in accordance with the Rules of Procedure and Evidence.

9. (a) (i) In the event that a State Party receives competing requests, other than for surrender or extradition, from the Court and from another State pursuant to an international obligation, the State Party shall endeavour, in consultation with the Court and the other State, to meet both requests, if necessary by postponing or attaching conditions to one or the other request.

(ii) Failing that, competing requests shall be resolved in accordance with the principles established in article 90.

(b) Where, however, the request from the Court concerns information, property or persons which are subject to the control of a third State or an international organisation by virtue of an international agreement, the requested States shall so inform the Court and the Court shall direct its request to the third State or international organisation.

10. (a) The Court may, upon request, cooperate with and provide assistance to a State Party conducting an investigation into or trial in respect of conduct which constitutes a crime within the jurisdiction of the Court or which constitutes a serious crime under the national law of the requesting State.

(b) (i) The assistance provided under subparagraph (a) shall include, *inter alia*:

a. The transmission of statements, documents or other types of evidence obtained in the course of an investigation or a trial conducted by the Court;

b. The questioning of any person detained by order of the Court;

(ii) In the case of assistance under subparagraph (b) (i) a:

a. If the documents or other types of evidence have been obtained with the assistance of a State, such transmission shall require the consent of that State;

b. If the statements, documents or other types of evidence have been provided by a witness or expert, such transmission shall be subject to the provisions of article 68.

(c) The Court may, under the conditions set out in this paragraph, grant a request for assistance under this paragraph from a State which is not a Party to this Statute.

ICC RULES OF PROCEDURE REGARDING DISCLOSURE

RULE 73

PRIVILEGED COMMUNICATIONS AND INFORMATION

1. Without prejudice to article 67, paragraph 1 (b), communications made in the context of the professional relationship between a person and his or her legal counsel shall be regarded as privileged, and consequently not subject to disclosure, unless:

(a) The person consents in writing to such disclosure; or,

(b) The person voluntarily disclosed the content of the communication to a third party, and that third party then gives evidence of that disclosure.

2. Having regard to rule 63, sub-rule 5, communications made in the context of a class of professional or other confidential relationships shall be regarded as privileged, and consequently not subject to disclosure, under the same terms as in sub-rules 1(a) and 1(b) if a Chamber decides in respect of that class that:

   (a) Communications occurring within that class of relationship are made in the course of a confidential relationship producing a reasonable expectation of privacy and non-disclosure;

   (b) Confidentiality is essential to the nature and type of relationship between the person and the confidant; and,

   (c) Recognition of the privilege would further the objectives of the Statute and the Rules.

3. In making a decision under sub-rule 2, the Court shall give particular regard to recognizing as privileged those communications made in the context of the professional relationship between a person and his or her medical doctor, psychiatrist, psychologist or counsellor, in particular those related to or involving victims, or between a person and a member of a religious clergy; and in the latter case, the Court shall recognise as privileged those communications made in the context of a sacred confession where it is an integral part of the practice of that religion.

4. The Court shall regard as privileged, and consequently not subject to disclosure, including by way of testimony of any present or past official or employee of the International Committee of the Red Cross (ICRC), any information, documents or other evidence which it came into the possession of in the course, or as a consequence of, the performance by ICRC of its functions under the Statutes of the International Red Cross and Red Crescent Movement, unless:

   (a) After consultations undertaken pursuant to sub-rule 6, ICRC does not object in writing to such disclosure, or otherwise has waived this privilege; or,

   (b) Such information, documents or other evidence is contained in public statements and documents of ICRC.

5. Nothing in sub-rule 4 shall affect the admissibility of the same evidence obtained from a source other than ICRC and its officials or employees when such evidence has also been acquired by this source independently of ICRC and its officials or employees.

6. If the Court determines that ICRC information, documents or other evidence are of great importance for a particular case, consultations shall be held between the Court and ICRC in order to seek to resolve the matter by cooperative means, bearing in mind the circumstances of the case, the relevance of the evidence sought, whether the evidence could be obtained from a source other than ICRC, the interests of justice and of victims, and the performance of the Court's and ICRC's functions.

RULE 81
Restrictions on Disclosure

1. Reports, memoranda or other internal documents prepared by a party, its assistants or representatives in connection with the investigation or preparation of the case are not subject to disclosure.

2. Where material or information is in the possession or control of the Prosecutor which must be disclosed in accordance with the Statute, but disclosure may prejudice further or ongoing investigations, the Prosecutor may apply to the Chamber dealing with the matter for a ruling as to whether the material or information must be disclosed to the defence. The matter shall be heard on an ex parte basis by the Chamber. However, the Prosecutor may not introduce such material or information into evidence during the confirmation hearing or the trial without adequate prior disclosure to the accused.

3. Where steps have been taken to ensure the confidentiality of information, in accordance with articles 54, 57, 64, 72 and 93, and, in accordance with article 68, to protect the safety of witnesses and victims and members of their families, such information shall not be disclosed, except in accordance with those articles. When the disclosure of such information may create a risk to the safety of the witness, the Court shall take measures to inform the witness in advance.

4. The Chamber dealing with the matter shall, on its own motion or at the request of the Prosecutor, the accused or any State, take the necessary steps to ensure the confidentiality of information, in accordance with articles 54, 72 and 93, and, in accordance with article 68, to protect the safety of witnesses and victims and members of their families, including by authorising the non-disclosure of their identity prior to the commencement of the trial.

5. Where material or information is in the possession or control of the Prosecutor which is withheld under article 68, paragraph 5, such material and information may not be subsequently introduced into evidence during the confirmation hearing or the trial without adequate prior disclosure to the accused.

6. Where material or information is in the possession or control of the defence which is subject to disclosure, it may be withheld in circumstances similar to those which would allow the Prosecutor to rely on article 68, paragraph 5, and a summary thereof submitted instead. Such material and information may not be subsequently introduced into evidence during the confirmation hearing or the trial without adequate prior disclosure to the Prosecutor.

RULE 82

Restrictions on Disclosure of Material and Information Protected under Article 54, Paragraph 3(e)

1. Where material or information is in the possession or control of the Prosecutor which is protected under article 54, paragraph 3 (e), the Prosecutor may not subsequently introduce such material or information into evidence without the prior consent of the provider of the material or information and adequate prior disclosure to the accused.

2. If the Prosecutor introduces material or information protected under article 54, paragraph 3(e), into evidence, a Chamber may not order the production of additional evidence received from the provider of the initial material or information, nor may a Chamber for the purpose of obtaining such additional evidence itself summon the provider or a representative of the provider as a witness or order their attendance.

3. If the Prosecutor calls a witness to introduce in evidence any material or information which has been protected under article 54, paragraph 3 (e), a Chamber may not compel

that witness to answer any question relating to the material or information or its origin, if the witness declines to answer on grounds of confidentiality.

4. The right of the accused to challenge evidence which has been protected under article 54, paragraph 3 (e), shall remain unaffected subject only to the limitations contained in sub-rules 2 and 3.
5. A Chamber dealing with the matter may order, upon application by the defence, that, in the interests of justice, material or information in the possession of the accused, which has been provided to the accused under the same conditions as set forth in article 54, paragraph 3 (e), and which is to be introduced into evidence, shall be subject *mutatis mutandis* to sub-rules 1, 2 and 3.

INDICES

Detailed Table of Contents

Index to Contributors

DETAILED TABLE OF CONTENTS

SECTION II.2. Case Studies: Cooperation with or between International Organisations

PART III. MODALITIES

SECTION III.1. Case Studies: Extradition and Special Challenges to Administrations in Transition

PART IV. CHALLENGES

SECTION IV.1. International Cooperation in Protection against Terrorism

Section IV.3. Overcoming Obstacles in Achieving Wide Adherence to Multilateral Legal Assistance Instruments

ANNEXES

INDICES

INDEX TO CONTRIBUTORS